Recommended Reading
600 Classics Reviewed

Recommended Reading
600 Classics Reviewed

from

The Editors of Salem Press

Publisher's Cataloging-In-Publication Data
(Prepared by The Donohue Group, Inc.)

Recommended reading : 600 classics reviewed / from the editors of Salem
  Press. -- New edition.
    pages ; cm
  Previously published as: Recommended reading : 500 classics reviewed. ©1995.
  ISBN: 978-1-61925-867-9 (hardcover)
  1. Best books--Reviews. 2. Literature--History and criticism. I. Salem Press. II. Title: 600 classics reviewed
Z1035 .R37 2015
028.1

PUBLISHER'S NOTE

Ten years ago, Salem Press published *Recommended Reading: 500 Classics*, which responded to "a need for quick access to information on works of literature that frequently appeared on high school and college reading lists." This new edition, *Recommended Reading: 600 Classics*, attempts to improve the value of the original list of 500, with 100 new reviews of literary masterpieces. Extra attention has been placed on young adult literature, a genre that has developed its own cultural influence on generations of readers.

In addition to the 100 entries, new to this edition are two indexes. The first, Literary Genre Index, lists all works by six major literary genres, and more than 100 sub genres, with many works falling into multiple categories. Readers will find that all 600 entries have revised and, in many cases, multiple genre classifications; main genres are bold and sub genres are not. The second new index, Publication Year Index, lists all works by publication date, from BCE to 2012. These two new indexes supplement the Author Index that appeared in the first edition, for a total of three indexes to make finding specific works quick and easy.

While the selection of the included works is based on those that continue to hold the interest of both general readers and literary specialists year after year, such a selection cannot hope to define a literary canon—and can give rise to dicussion of omitted works. We hope this compliation will lead readers to works of abiding literary value, and the subsequent controversy over selection will make them aware of many works not addressed within these covers. Our aim is to provide a place to start in any reader's quest to explore great literature.

Each review approaches one work of literature—fiction, nonfiction, poetry, or drama—and is introduced with brief ready reference data: title, author, date of first publication, type of work, and a brief abstract of the book's content or impact. The interested reader will gain, from the review that follows, both an impression of the work's content and an idea of the work's importance in the history of literature and ideas.

In the library, *Recommended Reading: 600 Classics* is an excellent tool to help readers find books that match their interests, refresh their memories about books read long ago, or gain an impression of how additional books by an author relate to a recently read or studied work. Reviews are arranged alphabetically by book title. Running heads guide readers to the first review found on an even numbered page, the last review on an odd numbered page.

TABLE OF CONTENTS

A

ABSALOM ABSALOM!
William Faulkner
1936
Novel
Southern Gothic, African American

Two young men in 1909 try to understand a murder which took place during the Civil War in Mississippi.

Quentin Compson—shortly before he goes to Harvard University where (according to *The Sound and the Fury*) he will commit suicide after his first year, learns from Rosa Coldfield and his father much of the story of Thomas Sutpen.

Sutpen appeared at Jefferson more than 20 years before the Civil War, quickly established a vast plantation, and married and fathered two children.

When his daughter, Judith, grew up, she was courted by Charles Bon, friend of her brother, Henry. Sutpen forbade them to marry and, as a result, Henry rejected his father. The boys soon joined the Confederate army. Near the end of the war, Henry and Charles appeared at the plantation, and Henry murdered Charles. Upon returning from the war, Sutpen attempted to reestablish his dynasty, including a proposal to Rosa, but he failed. He was killed by the father of a girl he had impregnated but whom he refused to marry when she bore a daughter.

At Harvard, Quentin and his Canadian roommate, Shreve, try to piece together this puzzle in order to explain several mysterious events, but the main one is why Henry killed his friend Charles at the gate of Sutpens plantation near the end of the war.

This explanation leads to a main theme of the novel, for it appears that the murder was racially motivated. Slavery and the racism it produces create barriers between people who ought to love each other, especially when, because of accident or irresponsible behavior, members of different races find themselves sharing family blood. Racism proves to be at the center of Sutpen's drive for power, and his failure to understand either racism or family love contributes to his fall.

ABSALOM AND ACHITOPHEL
John Dryden
1681
Poetry
Satire

An extended and freely adapted analogy employing the biblical account of Absaloms rebellion against King David serves as a satiric rejection of the Whig opposition to King Charles II.

The poem opens with a depiction of the Jews beset by fears and rumors of plots against King David by a discredited sect. Achitophel, leader of the king's opponents, inflames the crowd against their monarch with a view toward replacing the rightful heir with Absalom, the king's illegitimate son. Though reluctant to challenge David, who insists on the succession by established tradition, Absalom finds the attention and the prospect of power appealing and leaves the capital to gather support among the people.

After a lengthy discussion urging avoidance of extremes in government, the poem praises the king's allies. David himself brings the poem to a close with an oration strongly condemning factionalism and warning of punishment for those guilty.

The poem presents memorable satiric caricatures in heroic couplets, discrediting opponents of King David (Charles II): Achitophel (the Earl of Shaftesbury), Corah (Titus Oates), Zimri (the Duke of Buckingham), and others. Despite the biblical names, readers of the time easily recognized the objects of the satire, who are ridiculed by being portrayed as reckless, extravagant, and extreme. The heroic couplet, permitting easy antithesis, represents an effective metrical form for calling attention to contradictions inherent in human beings. Caricature and an analogy or parallel to biblical history represent two of Dryden's most effective satiric techniques.

In his memorable essay on government, Dryden identifies the norm with the status quo, but the poem is faithful to history in leaving the conflict unresolved at the end. Basically but not entirely a satire, it praises the king and his supporters and provides a defense of the English monarchy as it then existed.

ADAM BEDE
George Eliot
1859
Novel
Victorian

Set in rural England at the end of the 18th century, the novel explores the effects of a self-indulgent love affair on an almost idyllic pastoral community.

Although Adam Bede (a young carpenter who is a model of rectitude and diligence) is the titular hero of this novel, the principal actions that develop the plot of the novel are those of Arthur Donnithorne. He is the heir to a large country estate which is the source of income and employment for many of the characters in the novel. A handsome young man whose glamour is enhanced by his being a captain in the local militia, Arthur dreams of the time when he will inherit the estate and win the adoration of his tenants by his wise and generous policies. In spite of these lofty intentions, Arthur begins an affair with Hetty Sorrel, a dairy maid who is the niece of one of his principal tenants.

As infatuated by Arthur as he is by her, Hetty entertains naive fantasies of marrying across the social chasm that separates them and becoming a great lady. Adam, who also loves Hetty, discovers the affair and forces Arthur to break it off before he rejoins his regiment. By this time, however, Hetty is pregnant and desperately follows Arthur until she discovers that he has been sent to Ireland. When her baby is born, she abandons it and is subsequently tried for child murder.

Although Arthur—somewhat melodramatically—wins Hetty a reprieve from hanging, and Dinah Morris, a young Methodist preacher, moves her to repentance, the evil consequences of Arthur and Hetty's affair cannot be undone.

George Eliot's first full-length novel, *Adam Bede* has been admired for its rich descriptions and incisive characterization, especially of the often humorous minor figures. Her handling of the plot, however, seems less assured. Despite her psychological insight into Arthur and Hetty as they yield to infatuation, the final disposition of these characters is unsatisfying and the marriage of Adam and Dinah seems largely a concession to the Victorian taste for a happy ending.

ADONAIS
Percy Bysshe Shelley
1821
Poetry
Elegiac

This brilliant elegy on the death of John Keats begins with sorrow for the premature loss of a promising poet but concludes with a triumphant affirmation of immortality through art.

Adonais, like *Miltons Lycidas*, is a remarkably successful English adaptation of the classical elegy form perfected by the Greek poets Bion, Moschus, and Theocritus. Keats, whose early works Shelley had greatly admired, had died at Rome in 1821. The cause of death was tuberculosis, but Shelley believed that a hostile review of Keatss *Endymion* had crucially contributed to the poet's death. Thus the poems allusion to Adonis, a beautiful youth loved by Venus and killed by a savage boar, is aptly ironical as well as conventionally classical.

Shelley's poem, written in 55 Spenserian stanzas, closely follows the pattern of the pastoral elegy. The mournful beginning includes a reproachful invocation to the muse Urania, the natural worlds sympathetic participation in the bereaved poet's sorrow over Adonais, a procession of mourners (among them Shelley depicts himself and Lord Byron), and the obligatory attack on debased literary practitioners, the specific reference here being to Keats's harsh critic, John Wilson Croker of the *Quarterly Review.*

At stanza 38, the mood shifts from grief to comfort. Keats's spirit has become part of the Eternal, made one with nature and immortalized through his enduring works. Toward the end of the elegy, after the view of Keats's grave at Romes Protestant Cemetery, Shelley offers one of the finest English analogies for Plato's doctrine of the ideal: Life, like a dome of many-colored glass/ Stains the white radiance of Eternity/ Until death tramples it to fragments.

THE ADVENTURES OF AUGIE MARCH
Saul Bellow
1953
Novel
Picaresque

Augie March grows up poor, fatherless, but streetwise in the Chicago of the 1920s and 1930s and learns to reject middle-class respectability. He spends his life looking for something either more idealistic or more risky.

Like Mark Twain's *Huckleberry Finn,* Augie March is a picaresque hero, a restless wanderer who refuses to be civilized, a permanent outsider. He pursues innocence while renouncing possibilities for power, success, and commitment.

Augie's adventures take him throughout Chicago and its environs, to Mexico, to the North Atlantic during World War II, and to exile in Paris after the war. He works at an endless series of jobs, including doing research for an eccentric millionaire, who is writing a history of happiness. Drifting from one level of society to another, Augie has no idea where he should fit in. Several people try to take him in, but he always breaks away.

Augie is drawn to several father substitutes and eventually sees himself as a father figure, yet he has no one to whom he can be a father. He is equally unsuccessful in several love affairs.

Augie is, however, successful at minor criminal activity, finding crime attractive because it is a break from respectability. He understands the difference between right and wrong, but somehow good does not seem good enough. Augie therefore may be seen as alienated from his true self.

This plotless, deliberately formless novel has no obvious theme. Bellows point may be that because of modern mans restlessness, his life cannot have a theme imposed upon it; no such order exists. Augie March searches for something to give it all meaning, but such is unlikely to appear. The real value comes in the striving. The life worth living is one which embraces all of experience.

THE ADVENTURES OF HUCKLEBERRY FINN
Mark Twain
1884
Novel
Historical, Adventure

Probably the most influential novel ever written in America, and one of the greatest, this book follows the adventures of an outcast boy and a runaway slave, as they float down the Mississippi River on a raft.

Huck Finn, the young hero and narrator, is innately good, but his values have been formed by the deeply corrupt, slave-ridden society in which he lives. At the climax of the novel he refuses to betray his friend Jim, the runaway slave with whom he has been traveling, despite his belief that he has thereby condemned himself to Hell.

The story is set in the 1840s. Huck, the son of the town drunkard in St. Petersburg, Missouri, has been adopted by the Widow Douglas. To escape his father's bullying and the widow's misguided kindness, he runs away, and on Jacksons Island meets Jim, a slave who has also run away—to avoid being sold down the river. They set off together on a raft that they find, planning to float downstream to Cairo, Illinois, and there work their way up the Ohio River into the free territory. But they miss Cairo in a fog and end up at a small plantation near Pikesville, Arkansas. Jim has now been recaptured. Tom Sawyer arrives on the scene and masterminds a wildly romantic plot to set Jim free again, only to reveal at the end that Jim was freed when his owner died two months earlier.

Of central importance is the river, at once Twain's major structuring device and a source of spiritual freedom, which transcends freedom from institutional slavery. On the river the fugitives are happy and unfettered, even as they drift ever deeper into slave country. Frequently, however, they have encounters ashore—encounters which invariably involve violence or fraud, or both, and reveal the iniquity of a society which is itself enslaved.

Huck tells the story in his own words—a radical narrative technique at that time—and the gulf between what he sees and what he understands produces a richly ironic indictment of slavery in all of its forms.

THE ADVENTURES OF TOM SAWYER
Mark Twain
1876; illustrated
Novel
Historical, Adventure

Mark Twain used characters and events from his own boyhood in Hannibal, Missouri to create this children's classic.

Tom Sawyer is the American prototype of the good bad boy. Unlike his friend Huck Finn, a genuine outcast, he is always into mischief but never in real trouble. He is a member of society and shares its values—at the end of the novel, he will not let Huck be a member of his robber gang until Huck agrees to live a respectable life with the Widow Douglas. And despite the mean trick Tom plays on his Aunt Polly, (that is, pretending to be dead so he can attend his own funeral), his place in her family is never in doubt.

Tom Sawyer is episodic and open-ended, as much a series of loosely connected short stories as a novel. Tom plays hooky from school, and, condemned to spend Saturday whitewashing a fence as punishment, tricks his friends into doing it. He wins a prize at Sunday school, not by memorizing Scripture but by trading for the tickets issued to children who did memorize it. He plays pirates and robbers, then gets a taste of the real thing when he sees the outlaw Injun Joe committing a murder. Having fallen in love with Becky Thatcher, he accompanies her on a picnic that her parents give for the village children, and the two get lost in a cave. Finally—a touch without which no boys adventure book would be complete—Tom and Huck explore the cave again and find the treasure Injun Joe had hidden there.

*Tom Sawye*r is all innocent nostalgia, a rhapsodic memory piece. Told from an adults point of view, it is weakest where Twain intrudes and moralizes. At its best, it lacks the seriousness—the constant underlying awareness of the dark side of life—of *Huckleberry Finn*, its famous sequel. As an unpretentious boyhood idyll it is unsurpassed.

AENEID
Vergil
29-19 B.C.E.
Poetry
Epic, Mythology

Virgil's Aeneid *describes the Trojans search for a new city in the years following Troys fall. Their eventual settlement in Italy establishes the antiquity of Imperial Rome and the nobility of the Roman race, special concerns of the Emperor Augustus who commissioned the poem.*

The Aeneid emphasizes that warfare, suffering, and selfless piety established a new Troy at Lavinium, allowing Rome itself to eventually arise.

Fate prevents Aeneas from establishing a city anywhere except Italy, and the goddess Juno is determined to delay its founding. The storm which she inspires drives the Trojans to Carthage, where they are befriended by Dido, its widowed queen.

Venus, goddess-mother of Aeneas, rouses Dido's instant love for Aeneas, and the lonely queen offers Aeneas a home and equal power at Carthage. Destiny, however, requires an Italian bride for Aeneas, and Dido is left, forsaken and a suicide, as the Trojans depart.

The Trojans eventually land at Cumae near Naples. Apollo's priestess, the Sibyl, guides Aeneas through the Underworld to the ghost of his father, Anchises. Anchises reveals destiny for his son, a procession of as yet unborn notables (including Augustus) who will ensure Rome's greatness. Reassured of his mission, Aeneas continues northward on the Tiber, lands at Lavinium, but must fight a second Trojan War to obtain his fated Italian bride, Lavinia. This second war brings Trojan alliance with Evander, King of Pallantium, an Etruscan city on the site of Rome. It also allows Aeneas son Ascanius (Iulus) to distinguish himself in battle.

The Aeneid was written as a Latin odyssey-iliad, combining Homeric elements with Italian settings and imperial Roman emphasis. It implies that the Roman race is both ancient and blended from the best Trojan, Italian, and Etruscan stock, that endurance, piety, and selflessness produced the Imperial City. This was the vision Augustus had of Rome at the dawn of the Empire.

THE AGE OF INNOCENCE
Edith Wharton
1920
Novel
Victorian

This work presents a satirical but sympathetic view of old New York, the aristocratic society in which the author grew up in the 1870s and 1880s.

The central character, Newland Archer, is a well-to-do young lawyer who is connected with most of the city's leading families. Sensitive and intelligent, he prides himself on his ability to distance himself from the narrowness of his social circle. As the novel progresses, however, he realizes that this society he views so critically is a powerful force conspiring to confine him within its limits.

His conflict is embodied in the two women he loves. May Welland, who becomes his wife, is handsome, placid, and sheltered—the ideal bride of her class. Her cousin, Ellen Olenska, represents for Newland freedom and the life of the spirit. Although he initially disapproves of Ellen, who has returned from Europe to escape her dissolute husband, a Polish count, he soon falls in love with her. Ironically, their relationship begins after May's family asks him to help Ellen with her legal problems.

As Newland's love for Ellen develops, May and her family recognize the threat. Without a direct word or an overt act, the tribe, as Wharton calls it, closes ranks. Ellen is persuaded to return to Europe, though not to her husband, and Newland is absorbed back into the family as a prospective father.

Newland's story is not altogether a tragedy. In leaving, Ellen affirms the values of honor and duty that May represents and feels her sacrifice worthwhile. Many years later, Newland reflects that his quiet life of public service and family stability was not without rewards, though his deepest nature remained unfulfilled.

Although its main theme is serious, the novel provides devastatingly witty portraits of the pillars of society and pokes fun at the more absurd social rituals of the day. The books appeal rests both on its sympathetic characters and on its skillful portrayal of the flaws and virtues of a bygone world.

THE ALCHEMIST
Ben Jonson
1610
Drama
Comedy

When his master leaves London to avoid the plague, a butler invites an unscrupulous alchemist to use the house as headquarters to deceive gullible men who attempt to satisfy their avaricious pursuit of wealth.

A forerunner of the comedy of manners, the play comprises a succession of episodes in which Subtle (alchemist and confidence man) and Dol Common (his prostitute accomplice) cheat morally corrupt clients. The butler, Jeremy, is procurer and manager, finding customers, orchestrating visits, and extracting payments.

The first victim is Dapper, a lawyer's clerk who aspires to win at gambling. Then comes Drugger, a tobacconist who looks to necromancy for the secrets of success in business. The third client is Sir Epicure Mammon, who seeks through alchemy to become the richest man in the world. He is followed by Ananais the Anabaptist, who wants the property of his church transformed into gold.

The satiric intensity of the play increases with the procession, since each protagonist is more corrupt than his predecessor. Dapper's aspirations hurt nobody; but Ananais and his superior, Tribulation Wholesome, are religious hypocrites ready to cheat orphans in order to enrich themselves and their church.

The conspirators scheme seems endangered by a skeptical friend of Sir Epicure, Pertinax Surly, who had accompanied Mammon on his first visit and returns in disguise to expose the rascals, but the inevitable return of Lovewit, master of the house, proves to be their undoing. Subtle and Dol flee, leaving their booty to Jeremy, who confesses all to his understanding employer.

While the play treats alchemy and the occult as sophisticated confidence games, Jonson mainly uses them as means of satirizing people whose greed makes them gullible and easy prey for confidence men. Comedy, said Jonson, should show an image of the times and sport with human follies, not with crimes.

THE ALEXANDRIA QUARTET
Lawrence Durrell
1962
Novel
Tetralogy

This complex collection of novels examines the nature of love in the modern world through a concomitant exploration of the nature of time and of experience.

Darley, a writer, becomes involved with Justine, the wife of Nessim, a wealthy Egyptian Copt. Eventually, it is revealed that Nessim and Justine are engaged in smuggling armaments to Palestine and that Darley is a secret agent. Surrounding this basic plot and involved in it with greater or lesser degrees of awareness are Mountolive, the British Ambassador and former lover of Nessim's mother; Melissa and Clea, Darley's mistresses; Balthazar, a doctor who treats Justine; and various characters who flesh out the community of Alexandria.

The tetralogy's substance and appeal issue from its ever-changing points of view on the action. The first three novels cover the same events, but do so from different viewpoints. Darley is the narrator of *Justine* (1957) and of *Balthazar* (1958), which presents, however, the interlinear notes of its title character and corrects Darley's limited version of events. In *Mountolive* (1958), which is written in the objective third person, Darley becomes a character. *Clea* (1960) serves as a commentary on the whole and advances the narrative forward. Thus, each novel corrects the one before by providing more information from a different perspective.

The structure of the tetralogy, rather than its content, reflects Durrell's interest in the nature of reality and of knowing. This is reinforced further through the use of writers as characters and of journals, letters, diaries, and memoirs. The spirit of place, Alexandria, is also exploited by references to the poet Cavafy to suggest that perceptions of reality are affected not only by who we are but also by where we are.

ALICE'S ADVENTURES IN WONDERLAND
Lewis Carroll
1865
Novel
Children's, Fantasy

This childrens classic features an imaginative narration of Alices adventures and conversations in an eccentric world of mad hatters, talking mice, weeping turtles, and a diabolical Queen of Hearts.

Few authors have succeeded as well as Lewis Carroll has in writing a children's fantasy which is as entertaining for adults as it is for the younger readers. Alice's adventures begin on a drowsy day as she reclines near the bank of a river. Bored by her sister's company and her unillustrated book, she follows a white rabbit down a hole into an enchanted land of talking animals, uproarious conversation, and outrageous situations.

The plot of *Alice's Adventures in Wonderland* is difficult to paraphrase since it consists of loosely connected episodes which transport Alice from one hilarious encounter to another without much continuity. And while Alice does participate in a number of adventures, the central focus of the book really is upon the enchanting word play between Alice and such memorable characters as the Mad Hatter, the Dormouse, the Mock Turtle, and the Queen of Hearts. Along the way, Carroll, the pseudonym of Charles Dodgson, satirizes the conventions of children's books and succeeds in creating some of the most marvelous parodies of adult talk and typical adult behavior ever published. Alice often serves as a foil that exposes the absurdities of Victorian educational theory and the pretentiousness of literary analysis. All in all, these adventures are simply a delight to read aloud.

The real point of Alice's adventures is a celebration of childhood, a reminder of how innocent and literal the world of children is and, therefore, a rebuke to parents and others who want to take the world too seriously or to limit their children's imaginative life with an artificial realism.

ALL GOD'S CHILDREN NEED TRAVELING SHOES
Maya Angelou
1986
Nonfiction
Autobiography

Charting the experience of a well-known Afro-American performer in Ghana during the early years of independence, the fifth volume of Angelous autobiographical chronicle centers on the sometimes tense, but ultimately rewarding, relationship between members of the black expatriate community and their African hosts.

The fifth volume of the autobiographical chronicle begun in *I Knew Why the Caged Bird Sings* (1970) begins with the arrival of Maya Angelou in the West African nation of Ghana during the euphoria of the early years of independence. Already an established dancer and actress, Angelou journeyed to the capital of Accra in part to enroll her seventeen-year-old son, Guy, in the University of Ghana and in part to recover a sense of self-worth following the break up of the marriage described in *The Heart of a Woman* (1981).

One important, and familiar, motif concerns the development of her relationship with Guy, who suffers a near-fatal automobile accident shortly after their arrival. The story of Guy's successful recovery and his gradual assertion of individual selfhood—which Angelou experiences in part as a rejection of her maternal role—anchors the book in the frequently sentimental family-saga genre.

The real strength of the new installment—one of the most satisfying in the sequence—lies in its treatment of specifically Afro-American concerns. The exuberant self-confidence of the Ghanaian people under the leadership of Kwame Nkrumah contrasts, sometimes sharply, with the uncertainty of the Afro-American expatriates as they contemplate their own relationship with the struggle for civil rights in their native land. Of particular interest are Angelou's guarded comments concerning Martin Luther King and the March on Washington and her report on the visit of Malcolm X to Ghana.

Neither a celebration of African/ Afro-American kinship like Alex Haley's *Roots*, nor an ironic treatment like Richard Wright's *Black Power*, Angelous narrative of her search for a homeland is written in a familiar, colloquial style that should help maintain and broaden her readership.

ALL QUIET ON THE WESTERN FRONT
Erich Maria Remarque
1929
Novel
Historical, War

In a diary-like record, a young German soldier tells of the inhumanity of World War I. Translated into forty-five languages, this novel of blunt realism and quiet pathos has lost nothing of its compelling force for today's reader.

Barely out of school, the nineteen-year-old Paul Baumer finds himself in the trenches of the Western Front. After having his patriotic idealism crushed by the chicaneries of basic training, Paul increasingly hardens in his efforts to survive the endless shellings, the gas attacks, the nightly patrols, and the maddening fear of ever-present death. Only the bond of a cynical, though not insensitive, camaraderie among the common soldiers and a brief idyll with three French girls provide moments of human warmth in the general atmosphere of indiscriminate slaughter.

Baumer is forced to acknowledge how completely his life at the front has estranged him from the values of conventional society when he spends two weeks on home leave with his family. He must admit to himself that he will never be able to assume a normal existence in a postwar world and returns to the war, resigned to the fact that he has become a member of a lost generation for whom not even the prospect of peace holds any hope.

When guilt is assessed, Baumer and his comrades-in-arms place it with their parents and teachers, who had deceived them with sermons about love of fatherland and heroism. For the rest, this lost generation cannot even muster the strength to lash out against those who callously planned and executed its destruction.

Although written in the sparse style of an almost impassive objectivity, the novel was bound to arouse passionate reactions. In 1933, the Nazis publicly burned it and deprived Remarque of his German citizenship, actions, as it turned out, which only emphasized the novel's artistic and moral distinction.

ALL THE KING'S MEN
Robert Penn Warren
1946
Novel
Political, Historical

Suggested by the controversial political career of Huey Long, a governor of Louisiana who was shot while serving as the States United States senator, this consummate work of political fiction raises troubling questions about the role of principle and practice in public affairs and about the compromises and corruption inherent in the career of a power-seeking individual.

This novel has a double focus: first, on the narrator, Jack Burden, and his effort to understand his employer, Willie Stark, and second, on Stark himself, a protean figure who is sympathetically portrayed. Burden is a student of history, a Ph.D. candidate who abandons his notecards for the dissertation he never writes because he cannot make his sense of the past cohere. Stark is a man of the present, who believes that the means justify the end—that is, he operates in a world of graft, bribery, and coercion in order to build better highways, schools, hospitals, and the other things that contribute to the commonweal.

Each man, the intellectual and the activist, educates and supports the other, but neither is quite whole as a person or professional. By tracing the development of Stark's career—which constitutes the novels plot—Burden is simultaneously attempting to come to terms with his own inaction. Similarly, Stark uses Burden and others to rationalize the deals he has made to put his political program into practice.

Written with great compassion for human error, and in a profoundly philosophical style that occasionally is freighted with too much rhetoric, the novel manages to penetrate deeply into the human heart. Stark is very hurt by early disappointments which expose his naivete, and Burden is damaged by his unwillingness to accept that human beings have their limits, that they cannot always be loyal or faithful to their ideals or loves. In a sense, he fails to learn the lesson that Stark learns too well: that human beings are fallible.

The intricate plot—including a brilliant flashback to the story of Cass Mastern (Burdens 19th century ancestor)—reveals the catastrophic consequences of fanatical idealism and of a complete abandonment of principle. Jack Burden, in the end, must search for a language that balances the contrary positions of those human beings who would understand and shape history.

ALL'S WELL THAT ENDS WELL
William Shakespeare
c. 1602-1603
Drama
Comedy

Helena, the daughter of a distinguished physician, cures the King of France of an illness thought to be incurable, and, as a reward, the king offers her any husband she wishes. She chooses Bertram, the son of her ward, the Countess of Rousillon, much to the young man's displeasure.

Helena has been the companion and ward of the Countess of Rousillon since her father's death. The play opens when Bertram, the young son of the countess, and his friend Parolles leave for Paris to enter the service of the King of France. The countess discovers that Helena has fallen in love with Bertram and encourages her to follow Bertram to the French court.

By means of a rare prescription that her father left to her, Helena cures the King of a fistula and is given her choice of a husband. When she chooses Bertram, he rejects her because of her low rank. After their marriage, he sends her home to Rousillon. She receives a letter from him saying that he will never live with her until she obtains the ring from his finger and shows him a child begotten of his body.

By coincidence, Bertram's troops are entering Florence just as Helena returns from a pilgrimage. Bertram is trying to seduce Diana, the daughter of a widow who offers Helena lodging. Helena tells the two women who she is and asks for their assistance.

Diana begs the ring from Bertram and agrees to an assignation with him, but Helena takes her place. Believing Helena to be dead, the countess writes to Bertram, urging him to return. Before he leaves, he discovers the cowardice of his foppish companion Parolles.

Just as Bertram is about to be married to another woman, Diana and her mother appear and insist that he is already married. When Helena is finally led forth, she explains that she has met both the conditions imposed upon her. Bertram promises that if she can make me know this clearly/Ill love her dearly, ever dearly.

Shakespeare complicates the folktale motif of a repudiated wife who fulfills impossible tasks to win her husband by using the circumstances to explore the values of the characters. Ironically, it is the older generation who perceives Helena's worth despite her low birth. In the play, the nobility of a past society is juxtaposed with a present-day world in which fine clothes and rank are valued more than virtue.

THE AMBASSADORS
Henry James
1903
Novel
Psychological

A New Englander goes to Paris to bring home the son of his patroness and is converted to a richer, subtler sense of lifes possibilities.

Lambert Strether, a 55-year-old widower, edits a literary magazine sponsored by Mrs. Newsome, a wealthy widow, who sends him from Massachusetts to Paris to bring back her son Chad, who has overstayed his time and must return to take over the family business. If Strether succeeds, he will marry Mrs. Newsome, who fears that her son may be involved with a French mistress.

In Europe, Strether is taken in hand by Maria Gostrey, an American who escorts foreign visitors. She knows Chad, who is out of town, and his friends Mme de Vionnet, age 38, and her 18-year-old daughter, one of whom is probably Chad's mistress. When Chad returns, Strether finds him improved rather than corrupted by the relationship. The provincial has become a polished sophisticate. Strether is even more impressed by Mme de Vionnet, a charming person quite different from the domineering Mrs. Newsome. In Paris, he becomes aware that life can be far more intense than in a New England town and exclaims that a person must live all he can, while he can.

Chad is now willing to return home, but Strether persuades him to stay longer, and Mrs. Newsome sends her daughter on a second embassy to bring both men back. Eventually, Strether learns the identity of Chad's mistress, but knowing her to be a beautiful person of refined sensibilities, he cannot condemn her. He has moved from the puritan absolutism of New England to the pragmatic morality of William James, the author's brother. When Chad goes home, Strether remains, having found a fuller way of life in Europe.

One of his many international fictions, *The Ambassadors* was James's favorite and is the most critically esteemed of his novels. It has the complex style and characterizations of his major phase, making it difficult but rewarding in its rich ambiguities.

AN AMERICAN TRAGEDY
Theodore Dreiser
1925
Novel
Psychological

Based on an actual murder case, Dreiser's epic work is particularly effective because of his combination of documentary and mythic styles that explore the meaning of individuality in the United States.

Clyde Griffiths is a dreamer and social climber. His family is poor and fanatically religious. His narrow upbringing cannot, however, stifle the urge he has to make something of himself. One of his jobs (as a bellhop) fortuitously brings him in contact with a rich relative, who promises Clyde a job in the family-run factory.

Much of the novel centers on Clyde's deepening involvement with two women—Roberta, whom he meets in the Griffiths factory, and Sondra, a high-society girl he encounters at a family party. Having already committed himself to Roberta, a hazardous thing to have done considering that the Griffiths strictly forbid anyone in the family consorting with employees, he falls deeply in love with Sondra, for she represents that promise of everything he has dreamed of: wealth and recognition.

Clyde's predicament becomes intolerable when Roberta, now pregnant, forces the issue and demands that he marry her. Otherwise she will expose his double life to his rich relatives and ruin his glorious future. He procrastinates as long as possible and thereby backs himself into feelings he cannot control. In short, he plots Roberta's murder.

The denouement of the novel is particularly strong as Dreiser probes Clyde's confusion over exactly what he intended to do with Roberta. In what sense is Clyde an individual, and in what sense is he a victim of powerful forces that instill in him cravings for a prosperous, materialist culture?

His tragedy is not classical; he is no hero with a fatal flaw. Rather his tragedy is American precisely because he is in search of an identity he never finds. He is defeated, in the end, by the desire to be great, and he is typical of a nation that defines itself by how much it can consume.

ANDROMACHE
Euripides
426 B.C.E.
Drama
Classical, Mythology

Euripides' Andromache *takes place in Achilles district of Phthia in Thessaly. It focuses on Menelaus plot to kill Andromache and her son born to Neoptolemus. Anti-Spartan in tone, it likely was part of Athens propaganda campaign during the Peloponnesian War, a reaction to Spartas massacre of Plataean prisoners in 427 B.C.*

Action centers around Andromache's enslavement to Neoptolemus, murderer of her son by Hector. Andromache and Neoptolemus subsequently have a son whom Neoptolemus' barren Spartan wife, Hermione, threatens to kill. Menelaus, Hermione's father, lures Andromache from the altar of Thetis, where she has sought sanctuary, only to arrest and condemn her and her son to death. By implication, all Spartans practice sophistry and teachery.

Peleus, grandfather of Neoptolemus, enters to defend Neoptolemus' interests. Old and frail as he is, he frightens Spartan Menelaus away with harsh words and threats of violence. Spartans are also cowards.

Hermione threatens suicide when deserted by her father but is stayed by Orestes, who confides his plot to have Neoptolemus murdered while the young man is in Delphi at Apollo's sanctuary. This is sacrilege, though Neoptolemus himself is at Delphi to make amends for having cursed the god for allowing his father, Achilles, to die at Troy.

Peleus discovers the plot only after Neoptolemus' death, but Thetis, his goddess-wife, appears to console him. Thetis will see to it that Peleus himself will die soon. Then they both can journey to Elysium, paradise of heroes, and watch the ghost of their son Achilles at its warriors play.

Clearly this is not a tragedy, and critics have offered varied and sometimes farfetched interpretations of the play. Friction between northern and southern Greece, Spartan sophistry and duplicity, criticism of polygamy in Thessaly, failure of deities to defend any but their own interests are all possible, plausible, and noncontradictory explanations of Euripides' intentions.

ANDROMACHE
Jean Racine
1667
Drama
Tragedy

Trapped by the fatal implications of their passionate loves, four main characters, borrowed from antiquity, struggle to escape their destiny. This 17th century French classic tragedy remains a luminous example of the union of formal beauty with poignant theme.

Racine combines in this play a plot and characters drawn from the ancient tale of the Trojan war with his own strict rule of the three unities of tragedy. The play unfolds in a single day, in one room, and all the characters and action are settled on one problem, the reconciliation of four incompatible passions.

Orestes, son of Agamemnon, loves Hermione, daughter of Menelaus and betrothed of Pyrrhus, Achilles' son. Pyrrhus loves his captive, Andromache, but she is devoted only to her son and the memory of her dead husband, Hector. Orestes' arrival as the Grecian envoy, demanding the death of Hectors son, unleashes the conflict: Will Pyrrhus repudiate Hermione, daughter of Helen for whom Troy perished, in order to marry Hector's widow and befriend his son? Will proud Andromache marry the son of her husband's slayer, in order to save the last of Hector's family? What is the reaction of Hermione to Pyrrhus indecisions and rejections? How will the unstable Orestes choose between his sacred duty as an envoy and the demands of the slighted Hermione? Racine defines his characters in such a way as to leave no escape. The supple and elegant alexandrine verses which paint their uncontrollable passions hurry them along to destruction.

By curtain's fall, Andromache is acting as the widow of slaughtered Pyrrhus, Hermione is a suicide, Orestes runs mad and Fury-driven to future horrors. Racine has used the formal restraints of tragic verse and thematic restraints of classical myth to study human passion at its most intense.

ANECDOTE OF THE JAR
Wallace Stevens
1923
Poetry

One of Wallace Stevens' first published poems, included in his first volume of poetry titled Harmonium, *"Anecdote of the Jar" examines perspective, whether between objects—trees and a jar—or between a human observer and trees, and a jar. Many consider it a statement about how technological development affects nature.*

The poem opens with the narrator placing an empty jar "in Tennessee," on a hilltop. Thereafter, the "slovenly" forest—as contrasted with the solid, upright glass jar—seems changed, animated to "Surround that hill," as though the forest itself were moving, circling the tree. Following this simple act, the wilderness is no longer wild, a suggestion, perhaps, that technology has tamed nature, as the jar "took dominion everywhere." This small act changes a vast territory—a demonstration of what the scientist Edward Lorenz, pioneer in chaos theory, would later dub the "butterfly effect."

The poem is a short twelve lines. With an astounding economy of words, Stevens manages to quickly draw his reader from a broad view—Tennessee—panning to the hilltop where the jar rests, as though zooming in from above. Not only does the jar command the forest's attention, but it also alters the perceptions of a thoughtful reader.

Stevens expertly imbues the poem with a stateliness that belies his simple action. He "places" the jar, as if he has carefully thought out his plan. The jar itself is "tall and of a port in air"—a lofty way of describing the jar as tall and portly, full of air. The jar has dominion, an over-regal term for describing the power of an empty jar. On the other hand, he describes the wilderness as slovenly and sprawled. However, the jar is barren in contrast with the messy, alive wilderness.

Ultimately, Steven's "Anecdote of a Jar" is a testament to the power of language to alter human perceptions.

ANGELA'S ASHES
Frank McCourt
1996
Nonfiction
Autobiographical

With striking immediacy, compassion, and wit, Frank McCourt captures a childhood spent in grinding poverty, scarred by tragedy yet, at times, irresistibly redeemed by his father's Irish tales and songs. McCourt continued his memoirs in 'Tis *(1999) and* Teacher Man *(2005).*

Frank McCourt, born in August 1930, is the first child of Malachy and Angela Sheehan McCourt, who married in Brooklyn five months before his birth. Malachy, a former Irish Republican Army member, drinks away his wages leaving nothing for his growing family. His wife, Angela, finds herself trapped in a cycle of childbearing and extreme poverty. Frank is followed a year later by Malachy, then by twin boys, Oliver and Eugene. When a daughter, Margaret, is born, Malachy briefly seems transformed, but Margaret's death at seven weeks devastates the family. Angela is immobilized in despair. Angela's female cousins arrange for the family to return to Ireland. Seen through the eyes of the young Frank, these events reveal a heartbreaking yet profoundly comic gulf between the afflictions of the parents and the child's understanding.

The McCourts' fortunes only worsen. They are forced to go to Angela's family in Limerick. In the damp climate, living in decaying, unsanitary housing, and subsisting mostly on tea and bread, Angela miscarries; not long afterward, Oliver dies, followed six months later by Eugene. The family lives on the dole and donations from charitable societies; the children scavenge for fuel. Two more boys are born, Michael and Alphie. Malachy leaves for England to find work. Thereafter, Angela and the children must fend for themselves. Occasionally, Frank resorts to stealing restaurant leftovers, but is ashamed to see Angela begging. Angela survives pneumonia, and Frank, typhoid. At school, he and Malachy are scorned as Yanks and for their poverty. Discipline is harsh, but Frank's abilities are recognized. Nevertheless, he leaves school at thirteen, working various delivery jobs, hoping to save money to return to America.

Religion both oppresses and offers solace. Fourteen-year-old Frank believes he has damned the seventeen-year-old Theresa Carmody to hell when she dies of consumption following a sexual relationship between the two. In the book's climactic scene, sixteen-year-old Frank pours out all of his real and imagined sins to his patron saint, Francis of Assisi. He is absolved.

The death of the moneylender for whom he has been working unexpectedly provides Frank with the rest of the money he needs to emigrate, and he sails for America, promising to bring his family over after him. The book ends on a comic note with his bawdy reintroduction to America.

ANGLE OF REPOSE
Wallace Stegner
1971
Novel
Historical, Western

When the refined and genteel Susan Burling chooses to marry the taciturn mining engineer, Oliver Ward, she sets her path toward an extraordinarily unconventional and hardscrabble life, with challenges to her character, and to her marriage, she could hardly have anticipated. Not only does Angle of Repose document a family tragedy, it also examines the vast divide between a Victorian code of conduct and that of the late 1960s. The novel won Stegner a Pulitzer Prize in 1972.

Wallace Stegner chooses a crippled, wheelchair-bound, historian and scholar, Lyman Ward, to narrate the life story of the fictional character's extraordinary grandmother—a talented artist and writer from a genteel New York family, who ventures into a marriage just as challenging as the western mining camps and boomtowns where she tries to establish a life. Her husband, Oliver Ward, is a mining engineer with a passion for The West and the rugged kind of freedom he finds there. He is an adventurer at heart, with big notions about developing the western landscape. Though he is quite capable, he is also a dreamer whose principles about honesty and fair play impede his success, much to his wife's consternation.

Ward, the fictional biographer, uses correspondence between his grandmother and her best friend, Augusta Hudson, as his primary source, and gets narrowly close to portraying the life-long friends as lovers. At the very least, Susan Ward bases her own judgment about her life, and her husband in particular, on what Augusta thinks of her, and Augusta has never approved of Oliver.

Controversy erupted surrounding Stegner's treatment of his sources. Much of his characterization of Susan is based on the real life and letters of Mary Hallock Foote. Though he had permission to use Foote's letters, Stegner failed to acknowledge which parts of the novel were based on fact, and which were created for the sake of the story. Of particular import is the implication that Susan had an illicit relationship with another man.

ANIMAL FARM
George Orwell
1945
Novella
Dystopian

This novel, using a revolution by farm animals and its consequences as a symbolic treatment of modern history, is one of the most effective satires of the 20th century.

Major, an old pig, gathers the animals of the Manor Farm together to tell them that if it were not for the presence of man they could achieve a utopia. Soon afterward, the animals revolt against Mr. Jones, the owner, and take over the farm themselves, changing its name to Animal Farm.

For a time all goes well, but eventually the animals must yield much of the affairs of management to the pigs, the most intelligent of the animals. Among the pigs, Snowball and Napoleon continually vie for leadership, until Napoleon drives out his rival and declares him to be a traitor.

With the pigs responsible for all intellectual efforts, they soon become the master class and take on man's privileges, justifying everything through the propaganda of the pig Squealer. Napoleon establishes a personality cult around himself and becomes the leader, ordering all activities. The animals' lives move back into the pattern of the time before the revolution.

This novel can be seen simply as a satire on the Soviet Union and its betrayal of the ideals of socialism, but it is more than that. Orwell makes the animals revolt a symbol for any modern revolution. The rise of a ruling class of intellectual workers, the development of a leader figure, the use of scapegoats, and, above all, the rewriting of history and the misuse of language for party purposes, all figure in this satire.

The use of multiple historical references gives a universal quality to this work. Orwell appears to be saying that any revolutionary movement is self-defeating. This is a bleak picture, but the novel asks the reader to make his own decision.

ANNA CHRISTIE
Eugene O'Neill
1921
Drama
Tragedy

O'Neill's social drama recounts Chris Christopherson's reunion with his daughter, Anna, after a two-decade separation. Chris clings to a romantic notion of his daughter and her life but learns that she is a prostitute.

Chris Christopherson, once a seaman on globe-circling windjammers, is now captain of a coal barge, where he lives with an aging prostitute. Years before, Chris's wife moved with their daughter, Anna, from Sweden to Minnesota to live on a relative's farm.

Unexpectedly, Anna sends Chris a postcard announcing her first visit in 20 years. Chris, wanting to look respectable, allows his companion to leave. Anna arrives. Her dress and demeanor suggest that she is a prostitute, but Chris is blind to this.

Anna loves the barge and the sea. One night, she and Chris hear cries for help and rescue five sailors from a foundering boat. The rescued Mat Burke takes a fancy to Anna, and she falls in love with him, seeing in him her chance for a better life.

Chris is jealous; he hates Mat. They fight over Anna, who feels like a chattel, as she did in her past prostitution, which she now admits to Mat and Chris. Appalled, they leave the barge. Ultimately, Chris returns and decides to ship out to Capetown aboard the Londonderry and send money to Anna so that she can gain respectability. Ironically, Mat has also signed on the Londonderry. Finally, Chris and Mat reconcile, and Anna plans to marry Mat.

The ending suggests the pessimistic Nietzschean theme of eternal recurrence. Anna now faces the same lonely existence that ruined her mother's life and that caused her grandmother, wife and mother of sailors, to die of a broken heart.

ANNA KARENINA
Leo Tolstoy
1875-1877
Novel
Victorian

Leo Tolstoy sets his symphonic novel of manners in the Russia of the 1870s and distributes its narrative weight between two principal plots whose featured personages all belong to the upper class. One plot, involving a high-ranking official, his wife, and her lover, moves toward instability, despair, and death. The other, focusing on a couple whose relationship strongly resembles Tolstoy's courtship of Sonya Behrs and the early years of their marriage, contrastingly creates stability, hope, and continuity.

The novel begins with the charming but shallow Moscow bureaucrat, Stiva Oblonsky, discovered by his wife Dolly in one of a string of infidelities. Tolstoy thus immediately establishes the dominant concerns of his work: marriage, family life, and adultery. When Stiva's beautiful sister, Anna Karenina, visits the Oblonsky household to mend its broken tranquillity, she meets the dashing bachelor-officer, Count Vronsky, who is expected to propose marriage to Dolly Oblonsky's younger sister Kitty. Instead, Vronsky falls under Anna's spell, first at her arrival at the train station and then at an elegant ball where Madame Karenina, wife of a distinguished bureaucrat and loving mother of an eight-year-old son, is temporarily transcended by the other Anna: a glamorous, sexually magnetic woman with a frustrated hunger for passion. When Anna flees her barely awakened feelings by returning to her settled life in Saint Petersburg, Vronsky pursues her on the same train and confesses his love to her.

Anna struggles to deny her reciprocal ardor and forces herself to play the dutiful wife to her frigid and dull husband. Nevertheless, when Vronsky loses a brilliantly narrated steeplechase race, the watching Anna—and her observing husband—both know that she loves him. After some stormy scenes, she decides to live openly with Vronsky, and they leave Russia for an Italian honeymoon and then attempt to settle down on one country estate after another. Vronsky must, however, abandon his cavalry career and Anna her high position in society. While Tolstoy celebrates her grace, integrity, and courage in defying the dictates of a hypocritical community that sanctions affairs but forbids broken marriages, he also condemns her to deteriorations of mood and mind as her increased dependency on Vronsky makes her irrationally jealous and possessive. Eventually, the destructiveness of her passion and ostracism by respectable society drive Anna to suicide.

ANNE OF GREEN GABLES
L. M. Montgomery
1908
Novel
Children's, Historical

In Anne of Green Gables, the reader watches the young orphan, Anne Shirley, develop from a plucky, improper girl of eleven to a beautiful, brilliant schoolteacher. Her optimism and imagination compel both fellow characters and the reader to follow her many mishaps and adventures.

When elderly siblings Marilla and Matthew Cuthbert decide to adopt an orphan boy to help around the farm, everyone in the small town of Avonlea is surprised. But by accident (or providence) a girl has been sent for them instead: eleven-year-old orphan, Anne Shirley. Homely and skinny with bright red hair, she has had a difficult life, but remains joyous due to her "scope of imagination." Marilla wants to send her back, but Matthew, instantly charmed, convinces Marilla to keep her.

Anne is fun and smart, but knows nothing about what is proper. Her early years at Green Gables are filled with mishaps like screaming at a houseguest (the town gossip, Mrs. Rachel Lynde) for making fun of her hair, dressing inappropriately for church, and accidentally dyeing her red hair green, then having to cut it all off, among others. Yet, there are also many joys, such as adventures with her neighbor and "bosom friend" Diana, and her first tastes of ice cream and a concert in town.

Anne's time in school would be perfect if not for Gilbert Blythe, whose slate she smashes over his head when he makes fun of her red hair. This leads to an academic rivalry between them that extends to the end of the novel: both Gilbert and Anne pass their entrance exams to Queen's Academy, a sort of pre-college, with the two highest scores on Prince Edward Island. At the end of their year at the Academy, they receive the two highest honors again: Anne wins the Avery Scholarship to a four-year college to study English, and Gilbert wins the Gold Medal.

However, after Anne returns home from school, she finds out Marilla will soon go blind—and then, tragically, Matthew dies from the shock of a financial failure. Although Gilbert had gotten the job of teaching in Avonlea after

Queen's Academy graduation, he gives it to Anne so that she can remain at Green Gables with Marilla instead of going to college. This allows her friendship (and potential romance) with Gilbert to finally begin.

Throughout the novel, the reader watches Anne grow more beautiful and mature as the years pass, but always maintaining her childhood optimism and ambition. Additionally, her spirited ignorance of social norms makes her a harbinger of the outspoken young female protagonists featured in many wonderful novels of the twentieth century.

ANTIGONE
Sophocles
441 B.C.E.
Drama
Classical

Daughter of Oedipus, former king of Thebes, defies the orders of Creon, the present king, and buries the body of her fallen and dishonored brother, Polynices. Creon sentences her to death. Her death leads to the suicide both of Creons son and wife.

Oedipus' two sons, Polynices and Eteocles, each lead an army which clashes at the gate of Thebes. The two brothers kill each other. Their uncle, Creon, orders an honorable burial for Eteocles but orders that Polynices body be left to rot, vowing death to anyone who disobeys his command.

Antigone, Creon's niece and sister of the two fallen combatants, tries to persuade her sister Ismene to help her bury Polynices body. The fearful Ismene refuses. Antigone buries the body herself, contending that the laws of the gods supersede the laws of the state.

Discovering what Antigone has done, Creon sentences her to death, even though she is betrothed to his son, Haemon, who pleads for her life. Antigone is led to a cave where she is to be entombed and left to die. Tiresias, the seer, finally persuades Creon that his edict defies the will of the gods. Creon rushes to the cave but arrives too late. Antigone has already hanged herself.

Haemon discovers Antigone's corpse, rushes his father with a sword, spits on him, and then impales himself. Upon hearing that her son is dead, Creon's wife commits suicide. Creon's reign is over. He goes into exile outside the city-state.

The first written and performed play of the Oedipus trilogy, which also includes *Oedipus the King* (about 429 B.C.) and *Oedipus at Colonus* (about 407 B.C.), *Antigone* suggests that Oedipus whole line is doomed to ultimate disaster.

ANTONY AND CLEOPATRA
William Shakespeare
c. 1606-1607
Drama
Tragedy

This gripping tragedy explores the perennial conflict between the demands of passion and those of duty through depicting the love and political struggles of two historical figures who were world leaders.

Cleopatra is one of the most fascinating women in world history and literature, largely thanks to Shakespeare's multifaceted characterization of her. Volatile and passionate, impetuous and manipulative, trivial and dignified, she commands not only Mark Antony and Egypt but the audience as well.

The play revolves around their love, yet its focus is political, for its principals are rulers of the world and scenes take place all over the Roman Empire in the 4th century B.C. Cleopatra is the Queen of Egypt; Antony, Octavius Caesar (later Augustus), and Lepidus form the triumvirate ruling the Roman Empire. Caesar and Antony, however, are frequently at odds, especially because Antony spends more time amid the pleasures of Egypt than on the field of battle.

Caesar is a cool, calculating politician, while Antony is more the fiery soldier. Caesar tries to win Antony back from Cleopatra's spells by having him marry Octavia, his sister, but Cleopatra's appeal is too strong.

Unfortunately, Cleopatra's hold over Antony leads to his defeat. Yet their suicides signify a triumph over Caesar, for at least they shall not be his captives. In their deaths, they regain the valiant nobility absent from many of their prior acts.

The play's perennial conflicts—between reason and passion, politics and personal feelings—can never be resolved. Yet, however far from admirable these characters may sometimes appear, they have a grandeur of personality and magnificence of language that makes the reader or viewer perceive them almost as gods.

APPOINTMENT IN SAMARRA
John O'Hara
1934
Novel
Psychological

Taking its title from the tale of the Merchant of Baghdad who allegedly tried to outwit death, this chronicle of the days leading up to a supposedly inevitable suicide brought instant fame and recognition to its previously unknown, twenty-nine-year-old author.

Set during the Christmas holidays of 1930 in and around the fictitious town of Gibbsville—probably O'Hara's hometown of Pottsville—Pennsylvania (also the locus of many subsequent O'Hara fictions), the novel portrays the rapid decline and fall of thirty-year-old Julian English, a Cadillac dealer hitherto regarded as one of the rising bright lights in Gibbsville society. In less than a weeks time, Julian English discovers that his world has shrunk to such a degree that he can no longer live in it; as befits his occupation, he will leave the world from the drivers seat of his demonstrator Cadillac, sipping whiskey as the motor runs inside the closed garage.

Ostensibly, Julian's swift decline begins when, more than a little drunk and unable to restrain himself, he throws a drink in the face of Harry Reilly at a country-club party. Reilly is of Irish descent, and ethnic tensions are never far from the surface; still, the two men appear relatively free of prejudice with regard to each other, suggesting that the real reasons for Julian's downfall lie somewhat deeper.

With analytical skills that range freely between the social and the psychological, O'Hara flashes back and forth through Julian's brief life, concluding with the portrait of a man who has never seemed to know his place, whatever that may be. To be sure, Julian's own grandfather died a suicide, yet even that fact seems of minor importance as Julian rushes headlong into the creation of his own personal tragedy. Almost willfully, he proceeds from the Reilly incident into a fight with his wife Caroline, then to a brief tryst with a gangsters moll, and eventually to an improbable fistfight with a one-armed war hero who used to be one of his friends. At last, out of options and out of space, he retreats to the Cadillac and a death which is little understood by his survivors, least of all by Harry Reilly.

Deemed controversial in its time for its frank portrayal of sex (especially among married folk), the novel remains notable for its delineation of character and has since acquired validity as a period piece, recalling the last days of the Jazz Age and the beginnings of the Great Depression

THE ARABIAN NIGHT'S ENTERTAINMENTS
Unknown
Fifteenth century
Short Story
Collection, Historical

This collection of tales of adventure and romance, a favorite of both children and adults for centuries, is set in the colorful world of the Islamic cultures of the middle ages.

Little is known of the sources of the group of stories that has come to be known as *The Arabian Night's Entertainments, The Thousand and One Nights,* or simply *The Arabian Nights.* The identities of the many authors who contributed to it remain unknown, as do the dates of its composition. As is the case with any group of folktales whose origins are largely oral, many of its stories have been changed or fused over the centuries.

Though the collection remained unknown in the West until the 18th century, many of the stories were probably enjoyed by Arab and Persian audiences for a thousand years before they were ever translated into English. The most famous tales, apparently set in the 9th century reign of Haroun al-Raschid, Caliph of Baghdad, include the tale of Sinbad the Sailors adventures with the fearsome bird, Roc; the story of Ali Baba and the forty thieves; and the ever-popular story of Aladdin's lamp. The innumerable lesser-known tales range in genre from courtly romance to supernatural narrative.

Like Geoffrey Chaucer's *The Canterbury Tales* and Giovanni Boccaccio's *The Decameron, The Arabian Nights* is unified by a large story that gives rise to the others—in other words, a frame tale. In this case, the new wife of the Sultan Shahriar, Sheherezade, is only able to keep her husband from killing her by telling him a new story each night for 1001 nights.

Though the collection has been enjoyed by generations of children, it is in many ways a thoroughly adult work, full of tales of love and intrigue. It is also a valuable record of a Muslim civilization far more advanced artistically, philosophically, and scientifically than its Western counterparts during Europe's Dark Ages.

AREOPAGITICA
John Milton
1644
Nonfiction
Political

Issued as a pamphlet to combat government censorship of controversial printed matter, this essay stands as one of the most eloquent arguments for intellectual liberty ever written.

Milton, later to hold important office in Oliver Cromwell's government, composed the *Areopagitica* in the form of a classical oration in response to the English Parliament's resumption of a practice formerly exercised by royal decree: the licensing of printed matter. He had already defied authority in several of his own pamphlets on divorce, education, and church administration.

Milton based his defense not on "democratic" principles but, like the licensing law against which he directed it, on moral and religious grounds. Agreeing that books are strong influences for good or evil, he argues that knowledge is essential to oppose the latter. "I cannot praise a fugitive and cloistered virtue," he insists in a famous passage.

Like other English and American Puritans of his time, Milton saw human nature as weak and impure, but not for that reason should institutions shield and police it, for strenuous individual mental and moral exertion can strengthen and purify it.

Permitting the printing of books of the sort officials throughout history have sought to suppress as dangerous, Milton insists, gives potential virtue the test it needs by acquainting it with the evil that it must learn to overcome. Why should anyone truly concerned with the public good be afraid of any free and open encounter between truth and error?

The Areopagitica, then, is a vote of confidence for the intelligence and moral sense of a reading public provided notable for its delineation of character and has since acquired validity as a period piece, recalling the last days of the Jazz Age and the beginnings of the Great Depression

AROUND THE WORLD IN EIGHTY DAYS
Jules Verne
1873
Novel
Science Fiction

Verne's is the classic nineteenth-century adventure story. Its thirty-seven chapters first serialized in a French daily paper, the work pits an ironically unflappable English gentleman and his newly met French servant against tide and time, supposed "savages" of great variety, and bumbling mistaken-identity police work.

Phileas Fogg is a phlegmatic middle-aged Englishman of wealth and determination and extraordinarily regular habits, attended by a similarly iconic thirty-year-old Parisian servant named Passepartout, who after youthful turns as a singer, gymnast, and firefighter wishes to enjoy the settled life of domestic service.

However, when friends at Fogg's club doubt a newspaper estimate that the opening of a new railway in India will allow a traveler to circle the globe in eighty days, Fogg immediately wagers 20,000 pounds—half of his fortune—that he can do so. After calmly finishing his game of whist, he returns home to collect his astonished valet, and the pair, carrying only a single carpet bag with changes of shirts and socks—plus Fogg's remaining 20,000 pounds to finance the extraordinary undertaking—depart that very evening.

The book is a mixture of adventure and exotic travelogue, with journeys by steamship, railway, and even elephant-back and wind-powered sledge. Fogg's self-assured calm is contrasted with Passepartout's wide-eyed wonderment, and adding another amusing element is the detective Fix, who has mistaken Fogg for the gentleman-thief he must pursue.

As befits a serialized novel, Fogg's progress seesaws excitingly from missed connections and delays—including that of rescuing from forced suttee an Indian widow who at the end, of course, will become his wife—to resourceful catching-up. Characterization is by no means deep, and stereotypes are broad, but *Around the World in Eighty Days* still remains an enjoyable light Verne read.

ARROWSMITH
Sinclair Lewis
1925
Novel
Sociological
An idealistic doctor crusades for research to prevent and eliminate disease.

In the 1920's, Lewis was the leading American social critic, satirizing small-town provincialism in *Main Street,* right-wing anti-intellectualism in *Babbitt,* and religious fundamentalism in *Elmer Gantry.* In *Arrowsmith,* he challenged the medical establishment for being more concerned with prestige and profits than with combating disease. *Arrowsmith* is a fictional counterpart to *Microbe Hunter*s, whose author, Paul de Kruif, helped Lewis with research.

Martin Arrowsmith studies medicine under Professor Max Gottlieb, specializing in bacteriology. After getting his M.D. and marrying Leora Tozer, a young nurse, he spends some years as a country doctor. For a while he works for the Department of Public Health under Dr. Pickerbaugh, a medical Rotarian. But his real interest is in medical research, and after publishing papers on his own modest research, he gets a position in New York at the McGurk Institute of Biology, where he works on epidemiology.

When bubonic plague breaks out in the West Indies, Martin and the eminent Dr. Sondelius go there. Martin wants to conduct a controlled experiment with a serum that might be the antidote, giving it to only half the residents. Sondelius refuses to inject himself until Martin provides the serum for everyone. When Gottlieb and Leora both die of the plague, Martin damns his experiment and gives the serum universally. After Leora's death he marries socialite Joyce Lanyon, but realizing where his life's work should lie, he leaves her, gives up a remunerative career, and goes off with a fellow scientist to live a spartan life dedicated to medical research.

Despite its satiric elements, *Arrowsmith* is the most idealistic of Lewis's novels and was accordingly the most acclaimed, winning the Pulitzer Prize, which the author declined, and helping him become the first American Nobel Prize winner for literature. Though somewhat dated in style and content, *Arrowsmith* remains a compelling study of the scientific idealist.

AS I LAY DYING
William Faulkner
1930
Novel
Stream of Consciousness, Southern Gothic

A Mississippi poor white family endures anguish and disaster to carry the mother's body to the town where she wished to be buried.

Before Addie Bundren died, she made her shiftless husband promise to bury her with her family in Jefferson. She obtained this promise to gain revenge against Anse because he has never given her the deep, permanent love for which she longed and which she had experienced only temporarily, in pregnancy and in a brief, passionate affair with a local minister.

She probably never understood that Anse would be invulnerable to her revenge while the rest of her family would suffer badly. On the day of her death, rains flood the river between them and Jefferson, transforming the easy trip into an odyssey.

The family is delayed several days seeking a crossing and, again, after crossing, to replace the drowned mules and to set the broken leg of Cash, the eldest son. These physical barriers passed, they must then drive their wagon through a simmering landscape with the reeking corpse in a coffin on which Cash lays in pain, trailed by a cloud of vultures.

This journey is both ridiculous and tragic. While Anse talks about suffering without seeming to suffer, each of the children suffers intensely. Darl, the most sensitive brother, sees the promise as revenge and its consequence the destruction of the family. He opposes the trip whenever he can. Jewel, product of Addie's affair, seems an embodiment of her will, making every sacrifice to see the promise kept. Dewey Dell, the only daughter, wants to go to Jefferson to end her illegitimate pregnancy, but finds the price nearly unbearable. Vardaman, the youngest, is so involved in the family that its suffering is his suffering.

The story is told by means of the internal speeches of many characters in and out of the family. Though this technique makes the novel difficult reading, it also underlines one main theme, the inadequacy of language to express experience. One painful irony of this novel is that those who feel the deep communion that Addie desires and that cannot be expressed in words are the ones who can also suffer deeply, while those like Anse, who make language into a wall between themselves and experience, are almost immune to suffering. Everyone but Anse loses something precious; he returns with a new wife and several other new possessions.

AS YOU LIKE IT
William Shakespeare
c. 1599-1600
Drama
Comedy

In this spirited romantic comedy, a young couple, forced to flee envy and spite at home, find love and contentment in a pastoral setting, while their elders discover forgiveness and fellowship.

At court, young Orlando, though he attracts attention by beating the Duke's wrestler, has to flee the hatred of his eldest brother. His new love, Rosalind, is exiled by her uncle, the Duke, who has usurped her father's throne. Together with her faithful cousin Celia, Rosalind flees to the Forest of Arden dressed as a young boy; there the two settle as sheepkeepers.

Orlando meanwhile arrives and joins a band of merry outlaws headed by the exiled Duke (Rosaland's father). Rosalind in disguise undertakes to argue Orlando out of his passion for Rosalind; she feigns to scorn love and lovers. Eventually the usurping Duke repents and voluntarily restores his brother; Orlando weds Rosalind, Celia wins Orlando's brother, and all ends happily.

One of the most delightful of Shakespeare's romantic comedies, this play features various views of love: the head-over-heals passion of Rosalind, the scornful scoffing of her disguised male self, the sonnet writing of Orlando, the literary artificiality of the shepherd Silvius and the disdain of his beloved Phebe, the realistic lust of the clown Touchstone and his mate, the country wench Audrey.

There is discussion from several angles, too, of the relative virtues of urban and pastoral living, with the affectedly satiric Jacques providing a melancholy counterpoint to the joys of simple country life. His description of the seven ages of man is one of the most famous set speeches in Shakespeare's plays.

ASH WEDNESDAY
T. S. Eliot
1930
Poetry
Southern Gothic

Ash Wednesday is a poem of spiritual struggle in which Eliot records his attempts to escape the tyranny of self in order to come closer to God.

This is a poem of penitence, near despair, and hope. Its title derives from the first day of Lent, Ash Wednesday, during which a sign of the cross is made on the forehead of the penitent, a reminder of transitoriness and sinfulness.

Ash Wednesday, Eliot's first major poem written after his conversion to Christianity, focuses more on struggle and doubt than on belief. Eliot does not doubt God, rather his own ability to respond to Him.

The poem begins with a nearly despairing awareness of weakness and a very unmodern sense of personal sin. Consistent with his high church predilections, Eliot has his speaker appeal to an intermediary—a Beatrice-like woman—to plead his case before God. This intermediary is necessary not only because of the speakers spiritual weakness but also because this world is not a place conducive to spiritual renewal and growth.

Throughout his life and his poetry, Eliot wrestled with the tyranny of self and self-consciousness. He is keenly aware in this poem that he is a public figure who has made a very public and controversial conversion to religion. He confesses the painful difficulty of matching inner reality with outer pronouncements and wrestles with that false self who mocks the new Eliot with his old weakness.

By the end of the poem, Eliot is closer to his goal. He is still crying out, still struggling, but with the hope that after the dark night of the soul, the dawn is near.

Ash Wednesday represents a major transition in Eliot's poetry. Not only does it signal a move from emphasizing the despair of a wandering self in a decaying world to an exploration of the self seeking God, but it also demonstrates a shift in style from the dramatic and concrete to the lyric and symbolist.

Both of these movements are explored more fully in Eliot's religious masterpiece, *Four Quartets* (1943).

THE ASSISTANT
Bernard Malamud
1957
Novel
Psychological

In The Assistant *Malamud traces the miraculous transmission of goodness, reborn out of the squalor of urban poverty.*

Morris Bober is a sixty-year-old Jew who operates a small run-down grocery. Though he and his wife barely have enough to eat themselves, he does not have the heart to refuse credit to the poor families of the neighborhood. His failure is inseparable from his honesty and compassion.

His daughter, Helen, twenty-three, has had to abandon her dream of a college education so as to contribute to the family income.

Morris' bad luck is unremitting. A new, more modern store opens across the street and takes away his customers. Then he is held up and knocked unconscious.

Shortly afterward, a young Italian-American named Frank Alpine appears in the store, helping Morris out and gradually becoming his assistant. One of the holdup men, he has returned in order to atone for his crime. But his motives are mixed. He gives back the money he has stolen, but he continues to steal more. Obsessed with St. Francis of Assisi preaching to the birds, he is also fascinated by Helen Bober and watches through the window while she showers. The two fall in love.

Morris catches Frank stealing and sends him away. Before he can leave, he saves Helen from a rape attempt by Ward Minoghue, the other holdup man. But when Frank makes love to Helen, the act is not far from rape.

Meanwhile Morris' streak of bad luck continues. He has left the gas on at night; Frank saves him, but he is immediately hospitalized with pneumonia. The grocery is about to go under, but Morris cannot get another job. When Minoghue sets fire to another store and dies in the blaze, Morris finally gets a good offer for the store. He, however, dies while shoveling the sidewalk after a spring snowfall.

Frank, who has confessed everything both to Morris and to Helen, takes over the store, offering to use the money to send Helen to college. As the emblem of his inner transformation, he finally becomes a Jew.

ATLAS SHRUGGED
Ayn Rand
1957
Novel
Dystopian

Rand's 1957 philosophic, apocalyptic, dystopian novel dramatizes the failure of hybrid capitalism/socialism due to welfare spongers and corrupt bureaucratic looters who bankrupt society. The only remedy is for righteous, self-motivated titans of finance to seize control and usher in a new moral order based upon just individuals, guided by reason and personal sacrifice.

The novel employs the railroad industry as a prototypical "laboratory" example of a business corporation during a depression to explain how an industry thrives or dies. Dagny Taggert, Vice President of Taggert Transcontinental, faces twin evils of government regulation and worker unions. President James Taggert, her brother, continues to make unwise decisions, especially purchasing inferior steel from a legacy company that ritually delivers late when superior steel (from a secret manufacturing process) is available through Hank Reardon's company.

Discovering that her childhood friend and first bedmate appears to ruin his family's company for no discernable reason, Dagny becomes upset. She notes a developing pattern: all the important industry shakers and movers in society are disappearing; they just walk away in resignation before the tide of financial depression that sweeps the country.

Reardon proves the superiority of his steel to Dagny. They become lovers. In an abandoned factory they accidentally discover an unfinished Tesla-like machine that turns static electricity into kinetic electricity. They search for the inventor whom they eventually discover in a secret canyon, "Galt's Gulch," with all the other missing financial magnates. Their leader is inventor John Galt who has organized the massive strike of the Titans.

Dagny departs for New York City, and Galt follows her. In Manhattan, Galt hacks a prominent radio broadcast, delivering a long speech explaining social problems and ideal remedies for a better society. Galt's treasonous conspiracy succeeds and the federal government collapses. Nonetheless, Galt is arrested and jailed. Later, his followers rescue him. New York City is plunged into darkness as it loses electricity. Galt lectures his followers on how he will re-organize not only the United States, but also the whole world.

Like Plato's *Republic* which recommended state censorship along with banning drama and poetry, this controversial novel continues to have virulent detractors and ardent admirers. The book's title refers to the speculative situation of what Atlas, who bears the world on his shoulders, would do if more weight were added to his burden: the Titan would shrug—financial titans like Reardon and Galt resemble mythic gods.

ATONEMENT
Ian McEwan
2002
Novel

A subtle exploration of how the themes of mendacity, guilt, and art work themselves out in the lives of a privileged English family before, during, and after World War II.

In her seventies, main character Briony Tallis, now a literary celebrity, reworks the same material of her early novella, *Two Figures by a Fountain*, into a much more complicated book with a strong story line, one that, because it draws directly on actual incidents and people, cannot be published during her own lifetime. That novel, *Atonement* itself, reverts to the model of nineteenth century fiction, in which a narrative deity controls everything. The text of *Atonement* is an attempt to rewrite history. It is Briony's bid to repair a terrible wrong that she committed when she was thirteen.

The novel starts with thirteen-year-old Briony's actions during a hot summer day in 1935, during which she conscripts her three cousins, fifteen-year-old Lola Quincey and Lola's nine-year-old twin brothers, Pierrot and Jackson, to perform a silly play, *The Trials of Arabella*, that she herself has written. The cousins are not very cooperative, and the production is aborted. Robbie Turner, the son of the Tallis family's housekeeper, has recently graduated from Cambridge University and, despite the social chasm separating them, Robbie dares to love Cecilia, Briony's older sister, also a recent Cambridge graduate. Robbie asks her to deliver to Cecilia a lewd note that she opens and reads. Robbie had written another, less blunt letter of affection and does not realize that he has inadvertently given Briony the wrong note.

Latter in the evening, Lola reports that she was sexually molested, Briony concocts a story in which Robbie is the culprit. Lola does not contradict her, and Robbie is arrested, convicted, and imprisoned. In section 2 of the novel, Cecilia is furious and goes off on her own to work as a nurse in London. After three and a half years in prison, Robbie is mustered into the British Expeditionary Force as a private. In section 3, Briony suffers pangs of conscience for her false testimony and, rejecting the advantages of her social class, follows her estranged sister into nursing. In section 4, Briony is an aging literary luminary who is honored on her seventy-seventh birthday with a performance of *The Trials of Arabella*, the play she wrote at thirteen. Acutely aware of the disparity between her version of the sexual assault on Lola and what actually happened that evening, she has finally finished creating a richer, more reliable account. Though Briony cannot publish her revised account as long as Lola's influential and litigious rapist lives, she recognizes that, after writing it, "My fifty-nine-year assignment is over."

One of the most remarkable features of the book is how convincingly it represents the states of mind of not only of Briony but also of Robbie, Cecilia, and even her mother, Emily Tallis. Briony represents her own progress as a writer and a human being in her increasing ability to vary points of view. At thirteen, dreamy Briony suffers from a lack not of imagination but of imaginative sympathy, the ability to acknowledge the emotional autonomy of others. Fifty-nine years later, Briony demonstrates that she has grown far beyond the megalomaniacal fantasies of her early artistic efforts. Her mature writing is the product of research, not merely adolescent fancy. Like McEwan himself, she has spent many hours in the archives of the Imperial War Museum at Lambeth, and the result is successfully representing not only the genteel society in which Briony grew up but also the experiences of working-class nurses and military conscripts. Through her work, Briony transcends the narrow limits of her background and interests, and McEwan enters the mind of a woman born to privilege twenty-six years before he came into the world. The novel is a triumph of empathy if not atonement.

THE AWAKENING
Kate Chopin
1899
Novel
Feminist, Regionalist

This novel of the awakening of a young mother to her own identity reaches a candid and unsentimental conclusion that challenges the moral imagination of any reader interested in the aspirations of women.

The author skillfully evokes the atmosphere of New Orleans and of a fashionable island resort fifty miles south of the city in the late nineteenth century. As wife of a prosperous Creole businessman and mother of two sons, Edna Pontellier has been living the comfortable but idle life typical of her class.

A series of events—the circumspect attentions of a young bachelor named Robert Lebrun, her conversations with a physically ugly but talented woman musician, and her encounter with an enlightened and sympathetic doctor—draw Edna away from a conventional life to one that is radical, expressive, and, of course, deeply disturbing to her husband.

Discovering that the men who are attracted to her—even her sincere lover Lebrun—long to possess her, she realizes that she does not wish to be anybody's possession and succeeds in an ultimate and paradoxical assertion of her independence.

Woven throughout the novel in a manner reminiscent of Walt Whitman, whose poetry influenced Chopin's work markedly, are images of the sea, of birds, of music, and of art. Through the use of this imagery Chopin portrays a woman who awakens to the possibility of a sensual and creative life, and who realizes that, contrary to community opinion, she does not need to be a mother-woman to love her children and feel affection for her uncomprehending husband.

Upon publication of this novel, critics condemned it as sordid. It was ignored for decades, until, in the 1970's a new generation of critics begin to perceive it as a masterpiece.

B

BABBITT
Sinclair Lewis
1922
Novel
Satire

A 46-year-old Midwestern businessman looks for excitement and meaning in his life in this satire of middle-class American values.

Each chapter of the novel examines a different aspect of middle-class life, following George Babbitt's progression from discomfort with the mindless conformity of his society, to his rebellion and eventual return to conformity.

George Babbitt has a superficially perfect life as a happy husband, loving father, successful real-estate broker, and leading citizen of Zenith, yet he, like almost everyone he knows, is a hypocrite. He firmly believes in obeying all laws but speeds, supports Prohibition but drinks, is pledged to the sanctity of marriage but longs for an affair. He obtains an illegal loan to make an unethical investment but fires an employee for being dishonest.

When his best friend, Paul Riesling, shoots his nagging wife, Babbitt tries to seek new meaning for his life by associating with Tanis Judique and her friends, who consider themselves carefree Bohemians. He does this while his wife, Myra, is out of town. Inspired by a conversation with Seneca Doane, a socialist intellectual, Babbitt begins rejecting Zenith's conformist, conservative values. When his conservative friends begin to shun him, his business declines. After Myra returns and has an emergency appendectomy, Babbitt returns to his former way of life.

In attacking the materialism, anti-intellectualism, sentimentality, and smugness of his time, Lewis is not a superior cynic but an idealist disgusted with an America which has ignored or tarnished much of its idealism. The novel, generally considered Lewis' best, had an enormous impact in exposing a depth of conformity of which his society was not aware.

The novel is also notable for the language of Lewis's characters, who speak a more realistic dialect than those of any novelist since Mark Twain, as shown in the cliches and mixed metaphors in a public speech Babbitt gives. Lewis shows the connection between our words and our values.

THE BACCHAE
Euripides
c. 405 B.C.E.
Drama
Classical, Mythology

Euripides describes how Pentheus, King of Thebes, falls victim to Dionysus, Greek god of fertility, whose worship he has tried to suppress. The Bacchae *is Euripides' last play. It was written in exile in Macedonia and produced posthumously.*

The play emphasizes Pentheus' youth, his insecurity as heir to Cadmus, and his sexual insecurity. It parodies Dionysian ritual, for the maenads (frenzied female worshipers of Dionysus) turn the sparagmos (tearing to pieces) of the victim into human sacrifice. This establishes Euripides' intention: to show that if deities exist at all, they are essentially demonic enemies of humanity.

Cadmus has accepted his grandson Dionysus as a god, comically ironic considering Cadmus' age and Dionysus' association with fertility. By contrast Pentheus, Cadmus' very young grandson, is shocked at Greek worship of his effeminate first cousin, whose divinity he denies. Just as Pentheus is about to stop the orgia, his men appear with a priest of Dionysus, actually the god himself. Dionysus' strange appearance fascinates the virile Pentheus, and the young man agrees to go to Cithaeron dressed as a maenad to spy on their secret ritual.

The audience learns through a messenger that once at the revels, Dionysus sat the maenad Pentheus on a pine tree, then revealed him to the ecstatic women. Pentheus' mother Agave, his aunts Ino and Autonoe, as well as the other women, uproot the tree with superhuman strength and tear Pentheus apart. Agave appears on stage with her sons head in her hands. In Dionysian ecstasy, they had believed him to be a lion.

The Bacchae is a vivid, though distorted, portrait of Asiatic ritual in Greece. It reveals Euripides' own agnosticism, and stands as a psychological portrait of a young man who irrationally maintains supremacy of Apollonian order over Dionysian ecstasy.

THE BALLAD OF THE SAD CAFÉ
Carson McCullers
1943
Novel
Southern Gothic, Regionalist

This is the sardonically humorous but melancholy story of a hard-bitten, almost sexless woman from a tiny backwoods community, who is temporarily transformed by love.

Miss Amelia, dressed always in graceless men's clothing, runs the village store and sells corn liquor from her own secret still in the woods. She had once married the town bad boy but indignantly threw him out when he tried to gain sexual favors from her as well as work. The humiliated bridegroom, Macy, reverted to his delinquent ways and ended up in the penitentiary.

Enter the stranger—a bedraggled, hunchbacked dwarf who claims kinship to Miss Amelia. To the amazement of townsfolk, Miss Amelia takes in the penniless Cousin Lymon and he becomes a permanent fixture in her household. Moreover, because the self-centered cousin likes company, Miss Amelia converts her store into a restaurant which soon becomes the center of village social life.

All goes well until the vengeful Macy gets out of prison and returns to plague Miss Amelia. Such is the irony of fate that Cousin Lymon is irresistibly drawn to the vindictive Macy. The miserable Miss Amelia starts to work out with a punching bag. What follows is one of the most bizarre versions in literature of the barroom fist fight, when Miss Amelia and Macy square off for the attentions of the treacherous Cousin Lymon.

This brilliantly original variation on archetypal legend continues McCuller's meditations, begun in *The Heart Is a Lonely Hunter*, on the tragic and solitary nature of love. As Plato pointed out long ago, love exists in the mind of the lover, not in the beloved. The author suggests a more dismal observation, however, that if the beloved is incapable of returning the proffered affection, he tends to despise the lover.

BARABBAS
Pr Lagerkvist
1950
Novel
Historic

In this tale of Barabbas, chosen by the mob to be freed instead of Christ, Nobel Prize-winning novelist Lagerkvist deals with humanity's fear of death and search for God.

Drawn almost against his will to the Crucifixion, Barabbas tries to view it as an ordinary execution. When darkness descends, he concludes that his eyes have gone strange from prison. Afterward, he goes to a tavern run by a fat woman, who, like most of the characters, is never given a name, emphasizing Barabbas' isolation from others.

Barabbas' acquaintances expect him to be jubilant upon his release but find him moody and withdrawn. He lives briefly with the fat woman, while seeking the followers of the crucified rabbi. When they learn who he is, they shun him. Preoccupied with and afraid of death, Barabbas feels threatened when the rabbis followers tell him he died for their sins. Taken to a man raised from the dead, Barabbas is disconcerted by his corpselike appearance and manner.

Unable to maintain his leadership of the thieves, Barabbas disappears, becoming a slave in the mines, chained to Sahak, a Christian. In this subterranean hell, Barabbas wants desperately to believe and briefly converts. A new overseer, interested in Sahak's odd religion, arranges for them to work aboveground. Finding they are Christians, the master summons them. Barabbas denies being a Christian; Sahak affirms his faith and is crucified, with Barabbas watching unseen.

Taken to Rome, Barabbas seeks the Christians but becomes lost in the tomblike catacombs. Emerging to the light of fire and hearing that the Christians are burning the city, he zealously joins the arsonists. Imprisoned with Christians, he learns his mistake. Crucified, he commits his spirit to ambiguous darkness.

Comparable in tone to the films of his compatriot Ingmar Bergman rather than to Hollywood's biblical epics, Lagerkvist's is a brief, highly condensed novel. Told from Barabbas' limited perspective, the narrative is both a compelling story and an unusual and provocative view of the earliest Christians.

BARCHESTER TOWERS
Anthony Trollope
1857
Novel
This novel presents a shrewd yet largely sympathetic portrait of life in a 19th century English cathedral city.

Second and most famous of Trollope's chronicles of Barset, is a sequel to *The Warden* (1855). The story is set in the ancient cathedral city of Barchester (modeled on Salisbury), where the old bishop has died. The appointed successor is not, as some parties had hoped, the bishop's son, Archdeacon Grantly, but an outsider, Dr. Proudie. The uxorious Proudie, his haughty wife, and their chaplain, the oily Mr. Slope, bring with them Low Church practices unpleasing to the incumbent clergymen, especially the Archdeacon and his mild-mannered father-in-law, Mr. Harding.

Like Jane Austen, his favorite among novelists, Trollope is a discerning observer of human conduct. Under his gaze, the trivial details of daily life in Barchester become entertaining and instructive. Several interlocking rivalries animate the clerical world of *Barchester Towers*. The bishop must choose a warden for Hiram's Hospital, a charitable institution; and the candidates are the former warden Harding (supported by Grantly), Quiverful, (endorsed by Mrs. Proudie), and for a time Mr. Slope. Meanwhile Slope and his erstwhile patroness, Mrs. Proudie, vie for control of the impressionable bishop. Slope, though infatuated by the beautiful Signora Neroni, aspires to the hand and fortune of Harding's daughter Eleanor Bold, a prosperous widow also pursued by Bertie Stanhope, the feckless but charming brother of Signora Neroni.

Despite vigorous support from his son-in-law, Harding does not regain his old post as warden. The novel's remaining defeats fall to the hateful Slope, though. Mrs. Bold indignantly rejects his proposal. Signora Neroni merrily mocks his defeat in love. Mrs. Proudie, hating her former protege for presuming to cross swords with her, has him sent off to obscurity.

Before he vanishes in disgrace from the novel, Slope must endure the mortification of seeing a longtime enemy, Arabin, win both the woman and the clerical office he has coveted. Thanks to the interference of Signora Neroni, Mrs. Bold and Arabin recognize their love, which has been hidden by misunderstandings on both sides. Then, when Harding declines the deanship of Barchester, this post falls to Arabin; and the Grantly-Harding party, in eclipse as the novel began, prospers at the conclusion.

BARREN GROUND
Ellen Glasgow
1925
Novel
Historic, Psychological

This account of thirty years in the life of a rural Virginia woman reveals the author's deep mistrust of romanticism and her belief in the enduring power of the human spirit.

The heroine, Dorinda Oakley, is twenty when the book opens. Frustrated by the monotony of her life with her nervous Calvinist mother and her slow-witted but diligent father, she falls in love with a young doctor, Jason Greylock. Her dreams of joyful fulfillment are short-lived. Jason, by nature weak and unreliable, is forced into marriage with the daughter of a prosperous landowner. Dorinda, pregnant and disillusioned, flees to New York. She loses the baby in an accident but remains in the city for two years, trying to come to terms with life.

Her father's illness calls her back to Virginia and to the land that will restore her self-esteem. With intelligent use of new farming techniques and unrelenting labor, Dorinda turns her parents worn-out acreage into a prosperous dairy farm.

As her fortunes rise, Jason's fall. He drinks himself into oblivion and his wife, now mad, commits suicide. After many years, Dorinda achieves bittersweet revenge, first buying his bankrupt farm, then caring for him in his dying weeks. Yet she can never restore the joy he stole when he jilted her. Her marriage in middle age to a homely but kind widower is a relationship of companionship and shared labor, devoid of romance.

Glasgow's theme is embodied in natural images throughout the book. Dorinda's initial disillusionment is symbolized by broomsedge, the prolific weed that overruns potentially fertile farmland. The pine tree that her father watches from his deathbed comes to represent Dorindas endurance and her conviction that the land itself is the only source of fulfillment.

Glasgow's world is a bleak but not a hopeless one. Though life destroys the weak-willed Jasons, those who, like Dorinda, grow beyond the romantic illusions of youth can find strength and integrity.

BARTHOLOMEW FAIR
Ben Jonson
1614
Drama
Satire

In this hectic Elizabethan comedy, a representative group of Londoners on holiday look for fun or profit at Bartholomew Fair and encounter unexpected adventures.

At Smithfield, horse dealers and cloth manufacturers hold an annual fair—complete with games, sideshows, and entertainments—on St. Bartholomew's Day. Jonson uses the fair as a microcosm of society. Here men and women pursue pleasures, connive to get ahead, and try to escape life's limitations. Hardly any of them find what they expect.

Justice Overdo, disguising himself in order to detect criminals, unwittingly befriends a pickpocket and finds himself accused of stealing. By the days end he has been beaten, arrested, and locked in the pillory.

Bartholomew Cokes, a self-assured man of means, accompanies his fiancee Grace Wellborn to show off his sophisticated tastes and worldly wisdom. Within hours he is broke: defrauded by a toy-maker, cheated by a gingerbread woman, and robbed twice by pickpockets. Grace decides on a more sensible beau and chooses the gamester Winwife who knows how to keep his money and to get more.

Zeal-of-the-Land Busy, a Puritan who condemns the fair's pleasures, is positive he can resist temptation and lead others away from them. His visit teaches him otherwise: He cannot resist the pork pies, and his penchant for preaching leads him to argue with a puppet. His female counterpart Win-the-Fight gullibly believes a bawd's promise that the path to wealth is the body.

These characters and many others come together to witness a fifth-act play-within-a-play. Puppets perform a de-based version of an idealistic story about love and friendship. The puppet play reminds the fair-goers that human behavior inevitably falls short of expectation and self-image.

BARTLEBY THE SCRIVENER
Herman Melville
1853
Novella
Philosophical

His story of the mysterious Bartleby, a man who prefers not to, reflects a major theme within Melville's canon: Man's tendency to compromise his virtue for worldly gain.

On his third day as scrivener for a lawyer on Wall Street, Bartleby tells his employer that he prefers not to copy any more legal documents. This enigmatic response becomes the scrivener's constant reply to further requests for copy work.

While Bartleby's passive resistance toward work angers the lawyer, it also arouses his pity. The scrivener is given six days to leave his job, but he prefers not to leave. Distraught with emotion for this wreck in the mid Atlantic, the lawyer asks Bartleby to move in with him. This request does not meet the scrivener's preference.

The lawyer finally decides to rid himself of Bartleby. He moves his business to an address unknown to the scrivener. The lawyer later learns that Bartleby, refusing to leave his previous home, has been declared a vagrant and sent to prison. Here, Bartleby is further surrounded by walls. He responds by choosing not to eat his rations.

Bartleby represents Melville's concept of man's existence. Placed in a world with societal expectations, the man who prefers not to conform may retreat into his own Walden Pond. However, Bartleby, the former dead-letter office clerk, chooses not to protect himself from those who label him a threat to their materially oriented world.

Similar to Thoreau, who does not escape the tax collector at Walden, Bartleby pays a dear price for his individual preference.

THE BEAN TREES
Barbara Kingslover
1988
Novel

Escaping Kentucky for Tucson, a tough and warmhearted woman acquires a child, a community, and a connection to important issues

Opening mid-anecdote, with the direct voice and assured eye for humorously specific details that have become a hallmark of the new generation of local color writers, *The Bean Trees* makes an immediate impact. One slows down to savor the rich invention and pointed observations and to appreciate the narrator's spunky, down-to-earth self-aware-ness. Better yet, before long one comes to appreciate that this first novel by Barbara Kingsolver has a project more am-bitious—and ultimately more compelling—than simply to create bits of life that would fit neatly into semiconnected short stories. The characters grow, change, and are worth caring about. The themes—introduced without preaching—are both important and resonant. By book's end, one is full of admiration for the careful construction which brings together assorted threads and leads the plot to a breathtaking and touching conclusion.

The first-person narrator, Marietta Greer, buys an old Volkswagen and heads west, with plans to take a new name wherever the gas tank runs dry, and to stop and settle when the car itself gives out. She becomes Taylor Greer as she coasts into Taylorville where, outside a roadside café, an Indian woman thrusts a child into Taylor's car and disappears. Taylor called the abused girl, who is silent and slow, Turtle.

Alternating chapters in introduce another Kentucky woman, Lou Ann Ruiz, and the story passes permanently to Taylor's first-person narration and to working out a plot of discovery, strength, and tenderness. Taylor and Lou Ann are two ordinary working women with small children, scraping by through the practical sharing of space and responsibilities and working out ways to get along with each other.

The most refreshing quality of Kingsolver's characters is their genius for taking the right actions instead of examining their feelings or conducting intellectual arguments. The novel is grounded in an awareness of the range of issues that are women's issues and demonstrates the profoundly woman-centered nature of much working-class life. Kingsolver's apparently effortless style sets up a background that is virtually unnoticed until suddenly convergences and revelations occur. Turtle's fascination with planting seeds in the garden extends also to toy trucks and dollies—and each time the action reappears it accumulates resonance and extends meaning.

The plot, like the characters, engages specific individual actions that speak to larger issues. Despite the poverty of her childhood, Taylor's strength and self-confidence have protected her from recognizing the extent to which people can be helpless and victimized. She is jolted by finding evidence of the abuse that Turtle suffered and numbed when she learns about the political realities of Central America—and the complicity of the United States government that supports repressive regimes and refuses asylum to endangered refugees.

Kingsolver does not preach; there are no embedded lectures or passages of political rhetoric. Yet she has created a novel full of old-fashioned meaning. Taylor Greer encounters political realities by seeing what has happened to real people, and she does what is required for both practical and moral survival. The threads of the plot are resolved convincingly with a breathtaking climax that is—all at the same time—comical, surprising, moving, and ultimately gratifying.

THE BEGGAR'S OPERA
John Gay
1728
Drama
Opera, Comedy

A handsome highwayman tries to escape several women demanding marriage and fellow thieves plotting to betray him.

Gay's opera ingeniously blends comedy and satire. It has clever stage business. It spoofs the affectations of Italian opera and the sentimentalism of popular plays. It draws a stinging analogy between thieves and politicians. It attacks society's worship of power and money.

The audience first meets the Beggar, the opera's author, who hopes for success by catering to contemporary theatrical taste. The opera then begins, showing the plot of Peachum (ringleader and fence) to betray Macheath. Though a skilled robber, Macheath is expendable: Peachum must sacrifice some criminal to the authorities, and Peachum resents Macheath's wooing of his daughter Polly.

Peachum imprisons Macheath, but Lucy, jailer Lockit's daughter, has also been promised marriage by Macheath; moreover, she is pregnant. Hoping a free man will prove a good husband, Lucy helps Macheath to escape.

Lockit arranges another betrayal of Macheath, who is immediately sentenced to execution. He laments his fate until four more wives appear; preferring death to marital confusion, Macheath willingly heads for the gallows. The Beggar now intervenes. Since audiences like happy endings, the Beggar changes the denouement and spares his hero.

The plot is less important than the satiric dialogues and soliloquies. Peachum and Lockit compare their professions to that of the politician. Polly and Lucy lament the infidelity of lovers and of the world in general. Macheath possesses the veneer of a dramatic hero, but at heart he is a deceiver.

Nonetheless Gay makes his satiric points with great humor. A crowd of clownish thieves and comic prostitutes populate the underworld, and the play resounds with ironic songs set to traditional English ballad tunes which express the singers' knavery in sweet, lyrical melody.

THE BELL JAR
Sylvia Plath
1963
Novel
Psychological

A young woman descends into madness in this powerful portrait of the void at the center of contemporary life.

Esther Greenwood sees society as artificial and hypocritical but, at the same time, wants to belong to it. Her story is one of several popular examinations of insanity from the 1960's and 1970's.

Esther, a college student with literary aspirations, is repelled by the conventional, boring lives American women were expected to lead in the 1950's. Her mother leads such a life. Esther feels suffocated by her mother and has not felt happy since her father died when she was nine.

Esther is confused about and afraid of sex. She wants to lose the burden of her virginity but distrusts men, who always let her down. Smug Buddy Willard wants to marry her but is a phony. He tries to teach her how to ski without knowing how himself and has been having an affair with a waitress. Esther is upset by the double standard of sexual conduct.

She would like to emulate other women but always sees their weaknesses. No one is complete. No one is what he wants to be or thinks he is.

After a suicide attempt, Esther is exposed to the horrors of modern psychiatry. Mental institutions are not places for making people well but for forcing them to be what society considers to be normal. Esther becomes friends with another patient, Joan, who is her psychological double. As Esther's mental condition improves, Joan's worsens.

This autobiographical novel, originally published under a pseudonym, romanticizes insanity but is an insightful exploration of the superficial, materialistic values of middle-class America and is a haunting portrayal of the individual's quest for a distinctive identity. It has also helped pave the way for the feminist fiction of the 1960's and 1970's.

BEOWULF
Unknown
c. 1000
Poetry
Epic, Mythology

This 3182-line, Anglo-Saxon poem details the heroic exploits of Beowulf, son of Egtheow and nephew of Hygelac, King of the Geats.

Beowulf and 14 retainers sail to Denmark to help Hrothgar, the king, purge his hall of the monster, Grendel, which for 12 years has been ravaging Heorot. After much feasting, Beowulf and his men are left alone in the hall.

Before long, Grendel creeps into Heorot and kills one of Beowulf's men. Beowulf, unarmed, struggles with the monster and pulls its arm off. Grendel flees, leaving a trail of blood. The next day, Beowulf follows Grendel's bloody path to a far-off lake.

The next night, Hrothgar and his followers sleep at Heorot, which is invaded by Grendel's mother. She kills another of Hrothgar's men, dragging off his corpse. Beowulf, now armed with a sword and wearing protective clothing, plunges into the lake to which Grendel's bloody trail has led him. In the water, he fights with Grendel's mother, killing her.

Then Beowulf finds the mortally wounded Grendel in the lake, decapitates him and presents the monster's head to Hrothgar, who rewards him lavishly. He returns home a hero, there to be rewarded handsomely by Hygelac, who is king. When Hygelac dies, his son Heardred replaces him. On Heardred's death, Beowulf becomes king and reigns for 50 prosperous years. Ultimately a monster invades his kingdom. The aged Beowulf slays this dragon and receives a fatal wound in doing so.

Beowulf represents more than one-tenth of the approximately 30,000 lines of Old English poetry presently extant. It is a significant poem in the epic Germanic tradition and has often been compared with Virgil's *Aeneid*.

THE BERLIN STORIES
Christopher Isherwood
1935 and 1939
Sacred Text
Christian

The vividness of the two novellas comprising this book stems from the fact that they were based on Isherwood's own experiences in Berlin during the chaotic and often grim period of Hitler's rise to power.

William Bradshaw, the young British observer of Berlin life in *The Last of Mr. Norris*—the first of the two novellas—is a thinly disguised self-portrait of Isherwood. A would-be writer with an eye for unusual people and experiences, he is fascinated when he meets Mr. Norris on a train. The bewigged Arthur Norris soon reveals to William a bizarre world of prostitutes, decadent German statesmen, Communists, and millionaires.

A man who survives by his wits alone, Norris eventually comes to the end of his powers to deceive and double-deal. His enemies force him to leave the country. William realizes that he also has been used by Norris, and—somewhat wiser, but still fascinated—he sees Norris off at the station.

Isherwood, himself, replaces William as the observer in the second novella, *Goodbye to Berlin*. Here, the pages are crowded with a gallery of portraits from the streets and alleys of Berlin. Many of them pass through the doors of Fraulein Shroeder's lodgings, where Isherwood lives.

Isherwood's most famous character, Sally Bowles, dominates this book. Apparently the runaway daughter of a respectable British family, she sings in a low-class nightclub and makes a habit of doing what she pleases. Her mixture of sophistication and naïveté astonishes Isherwood and fascinates the readers of the book. Pretending to be 25, she actually is a rather worn 19 and more vulnerable than she likes to admit. She, too, shamelessly uses people—including Isherwood.

The vivid characters who wander through Isherwood's pages never obscure the menace and horror of the Berlin of the early 1930's. The lurid games played by the desperate people of Berlin, the rising racial hatred and political opportunism, all color these sketches. By the end of the book, it is clear that there is no hope for these people, and perhaps not for the world. Although the book is witty and colorful, it remains an indictment of that period of Western history. And Isherwood, the character, realizes that one cannot remain the passive observer forever.

THE BIBLE
Various
1500 B.C.E.-100 C.E.
Nonfiction
Sacred Text

The Bible comprises the sacred scriptures which undergird the faith of both Jews and Christians throughout the globe and represents the world's most widely translated and best-selling volume. It is available in a number of modern and contemporary English translations from the original Hebrew and Greek.

The Bible consists of two distinct testaments, the Old and the New, the former consisting of 39 separate books, and the latter consisting of 27. (There are also twelve Apocryphal or disputed books which are sometimes included in the Old Testament canon; these twelve volumes are accepted as authentic by Catholic theologians but not by Jewish or Protestant theologians.)

The Old Testament may be segmented into three divisions: the Law (Torah), which includes the writings of Moses; the Prophets, which contains both history and prophecy; and the Writings, which contain the wisdom and literature of ancient Israel, including the Psalms, the Book of Job, and the Proverbs of Solomon.

The Old Testament is essentially the story of God's mighty acts in history and his holy character, particularly: the creation of the world (Genesis); his covenant with a special people, the children of Israel (Exodus) who are called to be his witnesses; his passion for justice and righteousness in the earth (the Prophets); and his desire for love and mercy in the nation of Israel and in the world at large (the Proverbs and the Psalms).

The New Testament, revered by Christians—who read it as a fulfillment of and companion volume to the Old Testament—consists of 27 separate books, including four gospels (narratives about the life of Jesus Christ), one historical treatise (the Acts of the Apostles), letters written by early Christian leaders to their converts in various locations in Europe and Asia.

The New Testament is essentially the story of the life, death and resurrection of Jesus Christ, whom Christians regard as the unique Son of God and the fulfillment of Jewish prophecies about a coming Messiah. The New Testament also tells the story of the early Christian church and its battle for survival in a hostile environment.

The Bible has represented a reservoir of hope, courage, and inspiration for many centuries of readers, religious and nonreligious, and continues to be a source of light to many seeking a sense of purpose, meaning, and value in their lives.

BILLY BUDD FORETOPMAN
Herman Melville
1924
Novella
Adventure

Set aboard a British navy ship at the end of the 18th century, Melville's final work, left unpublished at his death in 1891, is a moral drama in which an overriding concern with the struggle between good and evil permeates the action.

Billy Budd, called the Handsome Sailor, displays near physical perfection and possesses a purity of innocence alien to the world he inhabits; but a single flaw leads to his destruction as this symbolic tale unfolds in its leisurely paced, digressive, yet powerful manner.

A British navy ship, short of hand, borrows Billy from a homeward bound merchant vessel. Unfazed by his impressment, Billy boards the *Indomitable* and soon earns the crew's admiration for his good nature. Even the strong-willed Captain Vere takes special note of him.

Like an Adam aboard a floating Garden of Eden, Billy has no grasp of wrongdoing. So when the master-at-arms, John Claggart, makes his hatred and envy known, Billy fails to guard against the evil that Claggart manifests. Eventually Billy's flaw—his stutter—causes him to murder Claggart. The circumstances surrounding Billy's punishment provide a dramatic and significant climax to this sad account of the Handsome Sailor.

The novel gives yet another version of the Fall of Man, so apparent are the symbolic roles of the major characters: Billy as Adam; Claggart as Satan; Captain Vere as the Almighty Judge. It takes up, as well, the eternal opposites embedded in love and hate. For the innocent Billy, love is spontaneous and natural; yet such love is his undoing. For the depraved Claggart, hatred becomes the twisted response to a love so pure. And for Captain Vere, whose name means truth, love must be tempered and tested with intellect.

This dark vision of man's spiritual state offers neither set answers nor a solution to the riddle of existence. Rather it shows how perilous and contradictory is man's place in the universe.

BIOGRAPHIA LITERARIA
Samuel Taylor Coleridge
1817
Nonfiction
Autobiography

An important poet and critic of the English Romantic period sets out to state his views on poetry and the poet, and to settle a controversy about the nature of poetic diction. Before he is finished he has also expressed his views on politics, religion, and philosophy as they affect the principles of poetry and literary criticism.

The book's 24 chapters constitute a narrative of Coleridge's literary life spanning approximately two decades—from the publication of his first book of poems at age 24 through his mid-forties. But the narrative, as Coleridge admits, serves only to give continuity to a statement of his views on a variety of subjects.

Central to his critical thought is his theory of imagination. Drawing on the German philosopher Kant's distinction between understanding and reason, Coleridge distinguishes between fancy and imagination. Fancy is a mechanical human faculty, the ability to manipulate sensory data, to categorize and generalize about the natural world. Imagination is organic, a synthetic and magical power which can predetermine and transfigure sensory data, and give us knowledge of ultimate truths.

Of greatest interest and continuing importance are four chapters. Chapter 4 discusses Coleridge's relationship with Wordsworth and their publication of the *Lyrical Ballads*, which initiated the Romantic movement in England. The chapter concludes with a distinction between fancy and imagination, which is further developed in chapter 13. Chapter 14 returns to the *Lyrical Ballads* and ends with philosophical definitions of a poem and of poetry, and chapter 18 explains the difference between poetry and prose.

Coleridge's distinction between scientific and poetic discourse, his view of the organic unity of a work of art, and especially his theory of imagination (the living Power and prime Agent of all human Perception, chapter 13) have been influential in 20th century literary criticism.

THE BIRDS
Aristophanes
414 B.C.E.
Drama
Comedy

The most whimsical of Aristophanes' comedies, The Birds won second place at the Great Dionysia of Athens in 414 B.C.E. Its extravagant costuming, constant action, and lively dialogue have made it popular with modern audiences as well.

Tired of the strife and complexity of modern urban life, Pisthetairos and Euelpides leave Athens to find Tereus, a king who was changed into a bird. Because Tereus has flown extensively, they hope that he can tell them where to find a peaceful place.

After learning how pleasantly the birds live, though, they determine to create a bird empire in the sky that will overthrow the gods. The birds at first object but at length are persuaded to construct an airy Cloud-Cuckoo-Land that will blockade Olympus into submission. Starving, the gods yield. Pisthetairos marries the divine Basileia and is transformed into a bird-god.

In the desire of Pisthetairos and Euelpides for peace one senses the war-weariness of the Athenians after decades of conflict with Sparta, but this topic is in the background. The chief object of the satire is instead the inability of Athenians, perhaps of Man, to accept a quiet life. Pisthetairos and Euelpides are not content with the uncluttered existence that the birds enjoy; they reject the Athenian empire only to found another.

The play also warns against the dangers of ambition. Fired by dreams of divinity, the birds make Pisthetairos their ruler. Yet at the end of the play, he celebrates his wedding and apotheosis with a dinner of roasted birds. Aristophanes thus warns his audience against demagogues.

Despite these serious concerns, the play remains lighthearted. Throughout, Aristophanes shows a love of nature and her bounty, and in Pisthetairos' transformation, he presents the ultimate fusion of man and nature. The Athenians cannot escape from their basic impulses, but in Cloud-Cuckoo-Land audiences can find relief from, as well as insights into, their daily lives.

BLACK BOY
Richard Wright
1945
Nonfiction
Autobiography

This recollection of a black American writer's childhood and adolescence stunned whites and blacks alike with its revelation of the physical and intellectual deprivation typical of blacks of Wright's generation and its defiantly indi-

vidualistic stance with respect to the Southern black traditions of family, religion, and subservience as a method of survival against racism.

Much like a work of fiction, this autobiography moves by the creation of vivid scenes and characters and the repetition of several motifs. Fire, physical violence, hunger, and the power of language to transform reality are the strongest of these.

Born in 1908, Wright begins his story at age 4 when, with his grandmother ill, he amused himself and his younger brother by feeding broomstraws to the fire until, possessed by curiosity, he set the billowy white curtains ablaze and burned down half the house while he hid beneath it terrified. He received a brutal beating which caused a life-threatening fever. Surrounded by ice packs, he recovered but carried the memory of his mother's wrath throughout his life; that she had nearly beaten him to death and was later to become an invalid herself became emblematic of the suffering blacks were made to bear and the suffering they inflicted on one another for the sake of conformity. Wright takes his epigraph from the Old Testament Book of Job, and the theme of his book might be Job's question: Why must the righteous suffer?

The abiding ingredient in Wright's life is hunger. Physical hunger precedes a deep emotional and intellectual hunger, as Wright is forced into a life of daily deception, caught between the pressures of the white and black communities. Gradually he learns to manage the tensions of working for whites while stealing for his exodus, but the price is the onset of emotional death. He discovers early that stories can make him feel again, can in fact alter reality for the better, and once the spark of language is kindled in him, his life is rife with a new hunger, a hunger for words that will sustain him on his passage North, where his hopes of becoming a writer and a freer man are lodged.

BLEAK HOUSE
Charles Dickens
1852-1853
Novel
Victorian

Bleak House is the story of a mother and daughter separated and then reunited by the injustices of Victorian society. It is both one of Dickens' finest entertainments and a novel of social protest unrivalled in its visionary sophistication.

Among the many orphans of a society that refuses to take paternal care of its weak and helpless, Richard Carstone and Ada Clare could be called the novel's protagonists. But their tragic love pales in significance beside the fate of the beautiful and haughty Lady Dedlock, whose mysterious secret threatens to shake the aristocracy out of its irresponsible stupor.

Along with almost everyone else in the novel, Lady Dedlock is caught up in Jarndyce and Jarndyce, a infamously protracted case in the Court of Chancery which provokes some of Dickens most brilliant satire. But he is doing more than urging the reform of legal institutions. Chancery symbolizes an entire social system. Linking the novel's extraordinary array of comic and grotesque characters, it also links Lady Dedlock to her illegitimate daughter, Esther Summerson, the housekeeper of an eccentric philanthropist named Jarndyce. When the villainous lawyer, who tries to blackmail Lady Dedlock, is murdered, the truth comes out, despite the efforts of Inspector Bucket, the English novel's first detective hero.

Experimental in form, the novel is narrated from two alternating and very different points of view. One narrator is an anonymous observer, while the other is Esther, so humbly virtuous that she cannot understand the impersonal forces that are destroying her friends and are nearly fatal to her. The central symbol of those forces is the London fog, emanating from the Court of Chancery and carrying the misery and disease of the slums into the homes of the rich. In *Bleak House* Dickens for the first time identifies his real enemy not as individual evil but as what he calls "the system"

BLOOD MERIDIAN
Cormac McCarthy
1985
Novel
Southern Gothic, Horror

Cormac McCarthy's fifth novel is a horrific, violent story of a band of scalp hunters who roam the West in the mid-1800's. A difficult and often gruesome novel, it is nevertheless a brilliantly written study of man's capacity for evil and need for grace.

The main character of the novel is known only as the Kid. At the age of fourteen, he leaves his birthplace in the mountains of Tennessee and travels west. In New Orleans, he is shot and almost killed. When he recovers, he continues his journey, no longer a child though retaining a kind of odd innocence that stays with him throughout all the atrocities he commits and experiences.

Moving away from the last vestiges of civilization, the Kid joins forces with a group of scalp hunters, led by the mad Captain John Glanton and a self-proclaimed judge named Holden (both men are based on historical figures). Glanton has dedicated himself to killing every Apache he encounters. Holden, a huge, completely hairless monstrosity, is given to moments of philosophical eloquence and to acts of gentleness, but he is capable of awful perversity and depravity.

McCarthy recounts the Kid's adventures in a dispassionate, understated manner that often heightens the horror of the deeds. Each chapter is prefaced by an outline of the events which occur in that section, a dry recitation of outrages. Acts of violence are repeated with numbing regularity, to the point that the reader becomes almost immune to the cruelty. Yet McCarthy's purpose is ultimately a moral one. Although the Kid participates in the bloodletting, he tries to resist the enticement of Holden, for whom evil is a path to knowledge. The book ends ambiguously. McCarthy's world is dark and foreboding but not totally without hope. Nevertheless, *Blood Meridian* will prove a demanding and harrowing experience for the reader.

THE BLUE HOTEL
Stephen Crane
1898
Short Story

This bizarre murder story is, along with the author's "The Bride Comes to Yellow Sky," one of the best serious fictional treatments of the Old West in American literature.

In a small Nebraska town named Fort Romper, events unfold against a howling blizzard one winter evening in the late 1880's. Three characters—a Swede, an Easterner, and a cowboy—are guests at the hotel run by Scully, who is noted for his hospitality.

From outward appearances it seems that the men are secure. They are gathered around a hot potbellied stove, and they are constantly reassured by their host that all is well. Then, a discordant note is struck. The Swede suddenly becomes alarmed and wildly asserts that he will be murdered in the hotel that night.

The Swede's peculiar behavior is a puzzle to everyone except the Easterner. He understands that the poor foreigner's view of the West has been distorted by dime novels. The Swede refuses to believe that he is in a respectable hotel, and Scully's attempt to calm his nerves with a drink of whiskey results in his getting drunk and becoming even more belligerent.

Subsequently, a fierce fist fight breaks out between the Swede and Scully's teenaged son, Johnny, who is thrashed by the older man. The Swede's earlier assertion that he will be killed that night proves prophetic.

Full of bravado and confidence after whipping Scully's son, the Swede goes to a saloon and picks a fight with another man, who kills him suddenly with a knife in the ribs.

The whole story is told in a detached style that is full of scrupulous, symbolic details. Underneath the parody of the Old West, Crane is working out a deeply skeptical, naturalistic theme: man's inability to perceive the world clearly. The whole tragic web of misunderstanding is caused by each character's distortion of reality. In an atmosphere that should have provided security from the wild external forces of nature, there was something internal, in the heart of man, that was, ironically, an even more lethal threat to survival than the raging storm outside. The blue color of the hotel serves as a chromatic symbol of the sad human situation.

THE BONFIRE OF THE VANITIES
Tom Wolfe
1987
Novel
Psychological, Satire

A popular sociological and satirical novel that skewers the pretenses of New Yorkers and paints a comic portrait of Wall Street, news reporting, and the Bronx criminal court system.

Sherman McCoy, a vacillating fool, possesses great wealth, but lacks conscience and substantive culture. As in Fitzgerald's *The Great Gatsby*, McCoy becomes involved in a hit-and-run car accident. Maria, his bubbled-headed mistress, persuades him to not report the accident. From this incident a catalogue of folly and an ensemble of fools evolve both in high society and low society.

An alcoholic English reporter, Peter Fallow, works for a gutter tabloid. He publishes a series of stories about the young black youth injured in the auto incident. A Harlem minister, the Reverend Bacon, attempts to exploit and capitalize on the situation. The muckraking of Fallow's articles pushes Abe Weiss, a media-conscious District Attorney up for re-election, to demand McCoy's arrest. Yale-educated McCoy is arrested, loses his remunerative job; everyone he knows deserts him; his wife takes the children away. McCoy returns to his Park Avenue apartment to find street protests outside his building.

Fallow hears a rumor that McCoy's mistress was behind the wheel at the time of the accident. He travels abroad to locate her husband, Arthur, who then dies of a heart attack during the interview. An Assistant District Attorney offers Maria the choice to wear a wire to entrap McCoy, (in return for immunity). Maria wears the wire, but when McCoy's lawyer, Tommy Killian, comes up with evidence that contradicts Maria's grand jury testimony, the judge dismisses the case.

A satiric epilogue affirms that the saga was even more tainted. Further lawsuits offer an endless circus without resolution, except that nothing looks good for the now impoverished McCoy.

New York City is depicted as a viper's nest of greed, ambition, and immoral conspiracy. What enhances the depth of the novel is that Wolfe limns the human drama in its full tragic dimension, while directing his satiric barbs at the hypocrisy of his characters.

THE BOOK THIEF
Markus Zusak
2005
Novel
Historical, War

After moving in with her foster parents, Liesel Meminger, a German girl, begins stealing books from Nazi book burnings, as her own small rebellion. The Book Thief *features emotionally complex characters in an unstable world, from the unique perspective of Death, an aloof narrator that becomes fascinated with, and eventually respectful toward, the little girl he feels drawn to.*

Focusing on the life of a nine-year-old German girl named Liesel Meminger during World War II, the narrator, Death, reads about the war years from Liesel's journal. After her brother's unexpected death, Liesel arrives to her foster parents, Hans and Rosa Hubermann, distressed with nightmares and bedwetting. Hans, a soft-spoken man, starts staying up with Liesel, teaching her to read using the few books the Hubermanns can afford.

Liesel's best friend, Rudy Steiner, a gifted athlete, is the epitome of an Aryan boy with his blonde hair, blue eyes and athletic build. He is in love with Liesel from the day the two meet. He resists the Nazi youth propaganda, and stands up to the bullies that taunt Liesel.

During this time, Max, the son of a Jewish friend, shows up seeking protection. Soon he is moved into the house basement where he and Liesel bond over their kindred passion for the power of writing and art. In an effort to show gratitude towards Liesel, Max begins creating books for her about his life and Hitler's impact on his life.

As the war progresses, German quality of life deteriorates further, and the country falls deeper into deprivation and poverty. Liesel begins "borrowing" books from Ilsa Herman, the mayor's wife, who allows Liesel to come into her library to read books. Eventually, the two become friends. Max decides to leave the Hubermanns, thinking he has become too dangerous for the household. After his departure, Liesel starts to write her story, the story of a book thief. One night, while she is writing in the basement, an enemy air raid demolishes the town. Many perish, but Liesel is protected because she was in the basement. Years after the war, Liesel and Max are reunited. Death finally meets her when she is an old woman who has lived a full life.

THE BOSTONIANS
Henry James
1886
Novel
Manners

James's account of a struggle of wills between a feminist and a Southern gentleman for the destiny of her young protege is one of his most enjoyable and accessible works.

Basil Ransome, unemployed lawyer and aspiring writer, comes from Mississippi to seek his fortune. In Boston, he visits his wealthy cousin Olive Chancellor who, though younger than he, already seems to be a settled spinster. She challenges Ransome to accompany her to a feminist meeting where he is unimpressed by feminist ideas but fascinated with the speaker, lovely young Verena Tarrant.

Verena's inspired speeches are set in motion by the mystical mediation of her father, an unscrupulous itinerant preacher and lecturer. Disliking Tarrant and wanting to mold Verena's career herself, Olive offers him a yearly stipend for his daughter's services, on condition that the parents do not interfere. Olive in turn is approached by a reporter, Matthias Pardon, who proposes to help the feminist cause by exploiting Verena's talents commercially.

Ransome soon has a rival in Henry Burrage, wealthy and socially prominent, who is willing to support Verena's career if they marry. Ransome is not. Olive insists that Verena forswear marriage for the feminist cause. The novel builds to a surprising climax as Verena becomes increasingly successful and assured but perplexed by the decisions she must make.

Most daring for the 1880's is James's treatment of the relationship between Olive and Verena, which has a number of lesbian overtones, though critics disagree as to both the characters' and James's awareness. Through sensitive and perceptive yet unsparing characterizations, James examines from all sides the worthy and unworthy motive in the public advocacy of a cause, the exploitation of talent, the inevitable corruptions inherent in a public career, and feminist issues, notably marriage versus a career.

James's conclusion is a dramatic but not facile solution to the questions he raises. For its relatively straightforward style and subtly ironic humor, the novel is a good choice for the reader who would like to become acquainted with James's works.

BOSWELL'S LONDON JOURNAL: 1762 1763
James Boswell
1950
Nonfiction
Diary/Journal

The London Journal *provides a fascinating account of Boswell's second visit to London, beginning with his departure from Scotland on November 15, 1762, and ending on August 4, 1763, as he prepares to leave the city for Utrecht.*

Boswell had come to London ostensibly to petition the Duke of Queensberry and the Countess of Northumberland for a commission in the Footguards. In fact, he came to enjoy the city. He admitted as much in his brief preface to the diary: "I shall regularly record the business or rather the pleasure of every day." For Boswell pleasure meant eating, drinking, conversing, and making love, and these are the subjects that fill the pages of his journal.

In recording these events Boswell used a number of literary devices to render his account more interesting. For though the record was personal, it was intended for his close friend, John Johnston of Grange. Boswell had a good ear and a long memory for dialogue, and the diary is full of conversations that place the reader in the midst of a scene. Because he did not in fact write out events daily as they occurred, he was able to select what was important and to tie matters together through suspense and ironic reversals. Certain episodes thus become virtual short stories.

Boswell accompanies his record with analysis, probing his own reasons for acting as he does. The journal is therefore a record of his thoughts as well as of his actions.

Despite the pleasures of London, the trip was an apparent failure, since Boswell did not secure his commission. Unknown to him, though, he had in fact found his life's work. Under May 16, 1763, in the most famous passage of his journal, he recorded his meeting with Samuel Johnson, whose life he would write more than twenty-five years later. That biography, and the journals that provided much of its content began with the abortive yet fertile expedition recorded in the pages of the *London Journal*.

BRAVE NEW WORLD
Aldous Huxley
1932
Novel
Dystopian

Two misfits, a "savage" and an intellectual, unsuccessfully challenge the premises and authority of a society that worships Henry Ford and that applies the principles of mass production and consumption to every aspect of life.

The story begins with the Director of Hatcheries and Conditioning giving a guided tour of his baby factory to a group of students. He explains how four levels of humans are artificially created in bottles, each predestined for a specific role.

Bernard Marx is a discontented intellectual, vaguely bothered by the values of his culture, which emphasize promiscuous sex, conspicuous consumption, and thought control. He and Lenina take a holiday in New Mexico, inhabited by "savages" who live in families, worship Christ, suffer pain, and often die of old age.

There they find John, the son of the Director. John has learned English from his mother and a volume of Shakespeare's plays. Bernard brings the savage to England where John becomes an instant celebrity. The savage, however, cannot reconcile his traditional Christian morality and Shakespearean humanism with the life he sees in England, where everyone is happy but no one is free.

After a clash with authorities over the practice of giving Soma (a hallucinatory but nonaddictive drug) to workers, John is permitted to live as a hermit in an isolated lighthouse.

However, his whereabouts are discovered, and he is hounded to suicide by a public that will not leave him alone.

Brave New World is often contrasted with George Orwell's *Nineteen Eighty-Four* as each represents aspects of present society taken to their extreme. In Huxley's dystopia, citizens are controlled less by force than by excess pleasure.

Sleep teaching and controlled mass media ensure complete obedience to the state. In a celebrated passage, John the savage debates with the Controller, Mustapha Mond, arguing for man's right to be unhappy in his own way.

Though often criticized as contrived and loosely written, *Brave New World* commands the attention of ordinary readers and serious thinkers for its clear depiction of the basic conflicts in modern society, particularly those involving science and technology as agents of social control and manipulation.

THE BRIDE COMES TO YELLOW SKY
Stephen Crane
1898
Short Story
Comedy

This comic story concerns the clash of cultures, myths, and stereotypes at a decisive moment in American history, the late 19th century, when the rapid expansion of the railroads made possible, indeed inevitable, the sudden juxtaposition of old and new, of East and West, of frontier and city.

The "bride" of Crane's title plays a rather minor role in this story, in which her arrival in the jerkwater town of Yellow Sky is treated in a decidedly ironic manner. An extraordinarily plain woman from San Antonio, she has recently married the town's sheriff, Potter, a man as ignorant of Pullman car etiquette as he is of the marital state and, more especially, of how Yellow Sky, which has pretensions to Eastern respectability, will respond to the fact of his marriage, about which the townspeople have not been forewarned.

Crane compounds the general ignorance and its attendant uncertainty in the next two of the story's four parts, in which he introduces a drummer (traveling salesman) from the East, who knows nothing of the wild West, and Scratchy Wilson, the drunken desperado who is in fact an old man dressed as a kid dressed as an outlaw. The actual confrontation between Wilson, hurling challenges at Potter's empty house, and Potter, slinking along the streets, hoping no one will see him and his bride, is funnier still.

The sheriff does indeed vanquish the desperado, not with his sixgun but with his bride. Wilson, no longer having Potter to play with anymore, shuffles off into the distance of history and obscurity. Potter, however, is vanquished too, by Crane's deadly irony and by his own delusions about his bride, whom he mistakenly associates with the ersatz grandeur of his one Pullman-car experience.

Because it concerns the sudden juxtaposition of ideas, myths, and regions, it is appropriate that the story have a fragmented narrative structure and focus on no one single character, for Crane's subject is not Potter or Wilson or the bride but, instead, the question of point of view, one which has cultural as well as aesthetic implications. Crane is concerned with the ways in which man perceives—or more often misperceives—his world and himself. He presents each character's perceptions only to undercut them by presenting or implying a more realistic frame of reference. Crane clearly understood that there was a reality, but he also recognized that man's understanding of that reality was often based upon a kind of optical illusion, as he suggests in the story's opening sentence: "The great Pullman was whirling onward with such dignity of motion that a glance from the wit window seemed simply to prove that the plains of Texas were pouring eastward."

BRIDESHEAD REVISITED
Evelyn Waugh
1945
Novel
Historical

A first-person narrative in the form of a fictional memoir, the novel has romance and faith as its dominant and conflicted themes. Set primarily in England between the two World Wars, it incorporates elements of the bildungsroman, the academic novel, and the aesthetic novel and should appeal to a wide range of readers.

In 1943, Captain Charles Ryder, a successful architectural painter turned soldier, finds his company stationed at Brideshead, the country estate of Lord Marchmain. As overpowering memories of the previous 20 years arise, he begins an account of the family. The memoir is highly selective, omitting the 10 years between the decline of his friendship with Sebastian Flyte, son of Marchmain, and the beginning of his romance with Julia, Sebastian's sister. Charles accounts for the emphasis and imbalance by explaining that with the Marchmains he had felt most alive and inspired.

When Charles had gone to Oxford 20 years earlier, after an unhappy, lonely childhood and adolescence, he gravitated toward the group of English Catholics surrounding Sebastian, a group known for their eccentricities, hedonism, and aestheticism. Surprised by their warmth and kindness, the agnostic Charles found their way of life novel and appealing.

When he became close to Sebastian's family, he observed that as members of a small Catholic aristocratic minority they were alienated, socially and psychologically, from the mainstream. For Charles they became a kind of substitute family, and they helped launch him into a successful career in art. Yet he drifted away from them after his friend Sebastian sank hopelessly and inexplicably into alcoholism.

Years later, returning by sea from a tour of Latin America, Charles encounters Julia Mottram, Sebastian's sister, and they begin a romance. Having recognized his mediocrity as an artist, Charles views marriage to Julia as his best chance for happiness. Although she wishes to marry him, her religion prevents it in a way he finds difficult to understand.

The novel, tinged with sentimentality, portrays the Catholic aristocracy in England between the two World Wars. Much more than a class novel, it probes the psychological effects of religious affiliation upon adherents. Written in an ornate and poetic style, it depicts in a compelling way the vulnerability of human beings.

A BRIEF HISTORY OF TIME
Stephen W. Hawking
1988
Nonfiction
Scientific

One of the leading figures in modern theoretical physics presents his view of the struggle to develop a unified theory of the universe and what success in this endeavor would mean to the human race

A Brief History of Time: From the Big Bang to Black Holes is a challenging, qualitative examination of historical and contemporary views on the nature of time and the universe by one of the major figures in theoretical physics in the 1970's and 1980's. Stephen W. Hawking, Professor of Mathematics at Cambridge University and victim of amyotrophic lateral sclerosis (Lou Gehrig's disease), he has been slowly losing control over his physical faculties, but his mental abilities have remained unimpaired. In this, his first effort at writing for a nontechnical audience, Hawking provides brief excursions into a number of areas of modern physics, but his real concern is cosmology. Using but one equation, he traces the changing concepts of the size, structure, history, and nature of the universe from the work of ancient Greeks, through that of Galileo, Newton, and Einstein, to his own work. He presents clear but sophisticated and demanding descriptions of such phenomena as black holes and the arrow of time.

Hawking begins with a review of the many cosmologies that have appeared in Western civilization. The second chapter examines the changing views of space and time, culminating in Einstein's theory of general relativity. Then comes a discussion of the concept of an expanding universe. The next two chapters, on the uncertainty principle and the fundamental particles and forces, complete the background discussion. Two chapters on black holes are followed by one presenting Hawking's views on the origin and future of the universe. The penultimate chapter discusses arrows of time, devices which distinguish the past from the future, providing a direction for the passage of time. In the final chapter, Hawking considers what a unified theory might look like. Included in the book are biographical sketches of Einstein, Galileo, and Newton, as well as a glossary of scientific terms.

Hawking did not make this book easy to read. Although he discarded his usual mathematical manipulations, he has made few other concessions. The concepts about which he is writing are not easy to understand, but he refuses to risk oversimplification. His analogies are relatively infrequent, and he relies on graphs or graphic drawings to make his points.

This is also a very personal and particular explanation of cosmology. Integrated into Hawking's exposition of scientific theories and experiments are personal asides, autobiographical details, and commentaries. *A Brief History of Time* serves as Hawking's intellectual memoir. Historians of science and some of his colleagues will object to the way in which he distributes credit for scientific discoveries. They will also find the account highly subjective. The history of physics, as opposed to the history of the universe, presented in these pages reflects Hawking's personal reading of the significance of particular scientific theories and experiments. It does not always match up with the scholarly consensus. His habit of carefully identifying those scientists who disagreed with his views and were later obliged to change their own opinions comes across as egotistical intellectual strutting. This book should not be approached as an objective record of the efforts of scientists to understand nature, but as one scientist's account of his struggle.

And Hawking goes beyond what many readers might think to be the legitimate boundaries of science, asking questions not frequently found in science books. He wants to know why events occur in the way they do. Interwoven in his popular scientific exposition is a philosophical tract raising fundamental metaphysical and theological questions. Hawking asks, without providing any final answers, Why does the universe exist? Is there a creator of the universe? If so, who created the creator? Is there a master plan for the universe, and if so, what is it? What he is doing is examining the place and nature of God in the universe. He sees science as a search for understanding God's will and in raising such, in some minds, unscientific questions, Hawking reveals his discomfort with the boundaries that divide contemporary realms of knowledge.

A Brief History of Time is not especially significant as a nontechnical exposition of science. The presentation will probably prove too terse and difficult for its intended audience. As an illumination of Hawking's mind, however, it is invaluable. Its greatest reward will be for those readers concerned with the conflict between science and religion, the gulf between the humanists and the scientists, and the segmentation of human knowledge. Hawking has issued a plea for the restoration of the unity of knowledge in the guise of a description of the search for a unified field theory. It is a plea worthy of thoughtful consideration.

THE BRIEF WONDEROUS LIFE OF OSCAR WAO
Junot Díaz
2007
Novel
Political

This novel presents the story of Oscar de Leon (nicknamed Oscar Wao) for most of the novel a lonely, overweight kid from the Dominican Republic growing up in Paterson, New Jersey. He is obsessed with science fiction, writing novels, and girls who do not like him back. The reader learns about his and his family's misfortunes through the lens of the fukú, a curse cast on those who disobeyed dictator Rafael Trujillo (ruled 1930-1961).

The novel opens with Oscar as a seven-year-old who has two girlfriends, the only time he has any luck with girls. Like most chapters, this one is narrated in the all-knowing Dominican slang of Yunior—English peppered with Spanish.

Lola, Oscar's older sister, narrates Chapter 2, describing her wild punk adolescence and her hatred of her mother, who sends her back to the Dominican Republic (DR) to stay with her grandmother, La Inca.

Then comes Beli's (Hypatía Belicia Cabral), Oscar's mother's, teenage years in the DR. At first a miserable adolescent, she becomes beautiful after puberty. Because of her sexual relations with an older gangster, government police nearly beat her to death in a cane field, and when she is about to die, she sees a Golden Mongoose—a symbol of survival. To escape Trujillo, La Inca, her adoptive aunt, sends her to New York.

Part II is narrated most directly by Yunior, Lola's college boyfriend. He volunteers to be Oscar's roommate to keep an eye on him for her. Yunior and Oscar develop an odd friendship. Oscar attempts suicide by jumping off the New Brunswick Bridge; as with his mother, when he is near death, the Golden Mongoose appears.

The next chapter describes Beli's father, Abelard, a respected doctor whose life, and his family's lives, are destroyed by his disobedience to Trujillo. Each person dies under conspiratorial circumstances. As a baby, Beli is shuffled from one terrible home to another, until father's cousin, La Inca, adopts her.

Chapter 6 returns to the 1990s. Oscar moves home and is a substitute teacher. Oscar decides to accompany his family to the DR that summer. He falls for a middle-aged prostitute named Ybón. Their relationship is dangerous because her boyfriend is a police captain. After the police beat Oscar, he is sent back to New Jersey.

In Part III, Oscar returns to the DR, knowing he will be killed. History repeats itself when the police murder him in a cane field; the Mongoose appears. Oscar has sent his journals and manuscripts to Yunior in the case of his death. Though Yunior and Lola break up, they share their grief for Oscar.

BRIGHTON ROCK
Graham Greene
1938
Novel
Psychological

This 1938 prequel to the author's first novel, A Gun for Sale (1936), portrays gang racketeering and the tragic corruption of youth aside religious paradoxes, yet morality and conscience appear to be sociological phenomenon, products of class and upbringing, that develop separately from religion.

Set in Brighton, England, a summer tourist resort of carnival rides and petty gambling, impoverished seventeen-year-old Pinkie Brown aspires to be a kingpin thug. The novel's title refers to rock candy sold at this seaside resort on whose piers vendors pay for protection.

Pinkie attempts to lead his own gang to rival the larger established Colleoni gang. He murders Fred Hale, a journalist, because of an article Hale had published which exposed a slot machine scam his gang ran. Pinkie marries Rose, a naive sixteen-year-old Roman Catholic waitress, to prevent her from testifying against him. Rose does not know she can destroy Pinkie's alibi. Although the murder has been ruled a natural death, the investigation is not closed. Pinkie remains nervous that the false evidence Spicer, one of his men, had planted at the restaurant could be exposed.

Ida Arnold, suspicious because Hale had told her his life was in danger due to his article, takes a matronly interest in young Rose, seeking to protect her from being exploited. Disturbed by Rose's sudden marriage, Ida investigates. She unexpectedly wins a large sum of money from a horse race, and uses the miraculous windfall to bribe gang members and the gang's lawyer.

Pinkie doesn't trust Spicer, so he makes a deal with Colleoni to have Spicer murdered, but the gang attempts to murder both of them. They survive the assault, yet Pinkie murders wounded Spicer by hurling him down a flight of tenement steps.

Pinkie fears Rose will break down under interrogation, so he bullies her into a double suicide pact. Pinkie's man, Dallow, disapproves of this ruse and tells Ida. She persuades Dallow to inform the police. The police appear on the scene to stop Rose's suicide. Pinkie, who fears a life in jail, commits suicide by throwing himself off a cliff.

The heroine Ida, a non-believer, saved Rose's body but not her soul; she muses whether she should resume her affair with Tom in London. A priest tries to console bewildered Rose, but having committed the sin of despair, she now appears to be insane, sunk in a living hell.

THE BROTHERS K
David James Duncan
1992
Novel
Psychological, Western

Duncan's epic novel on sibling rivalry weaves themes of ambition, baseball, the Vietnam War, and true religion (as opposed to fundamentalism) into a coherent tapestry of Americana.

The story of the four Chance brothers in Washington state is narrated by the youngest, Kincaid. Father and sons are obsessed with baseball, while their Seventh-day Adventist mother dotes on popular misconceptions about the Bible. Former minor-league pitcher and Korean War veteran, Hugh Chance, crushes his thumb in a paper mill accident. To reignite his farm-team pitching career, a surgeon transplants Hugh's big toe to his hand. Papa Toe becomes coach and relief pitcher. Wise-guy humor of the fifties energizes the struggling family's mirth. Duncan's polished knack for period nostalgia continues to entertain throughout the novel.

Everett, Irwin, Peter, and Kincaid illustrate four types of sociological response to turmoil during 1960s and 1970s as they outgrow the secular religion of baseball, which offers many homely analogies of common sense wisdom. Long-haired Everett becomes an atheist campus radical, fleeing to Canada to avoid the draft. Yale-educated Peter goes on a mystical Buddhist pilgrimage to India. Irwin, a conscientious objector who accepts the piety of his mother, believes God will protect him and is sent to Vietnam. Kincaid escapes the draft due to an eye injury. Two twin sisters enjoy amateur science experiments.

Irwin returns home from war with Post-Traumatic Stress Disorder. Veteran's Affairs doctors attempt to cure Irwin with torture: shock treatment and mind-altering drugs. The family rallies around Irwin to comfort and cure the man destroyed by the State.

As a spiritual quest novel, Duncan synthesizes all evil (war, hunger, poverty, and even villains) into the inevitable transcendental woof toward goodness, as espoused by the philosopher Pierre Teilhard de Chardin who became popular in the 1970s. The myth of progress functions as the novel's turbine—it hallows the belief that a divine non-denominational spiritual presence hovers over history and individual lives. Kincaid's defective eye and occasionally slanted reporting becomes the artistic camera eye that marvelously records and preserves the family album.

The book's title highlights parallels and stark contrasts to Dostoevsky's *The Brothers Karamazov*, as well as referencing the "K" symbol, short-handing a baseball strike-out. While the family experiences many individual failures, they are, at the end of their diverse trials, a successful team, wherein lies the saga's sentimental achievement.

THE BROTHERS KARAMAZOV
Fyodor Dostoevski
1880
Novel
Psychological

A selfish, sensual old man, Fyodor Pavlovitch Karamazov, is murdered by one of his four sons, each of whom has reason to hate him. In the process of revealing the murderer, Dostoevski explores the roots of human guilt and the strengths and failings of persons of radically different temperament.

Each brother is a vivid, individual personality. Yet, as a group, they represent the classically recognized spectrum of human traits. Ivan Karamazov, one of the famous characters in modern literature, is the tortured intellectual who questions the justice of both man and God, the forerunner of modern philosophical nihilists who see no evidence of moral purpose in the world.

Dmitri, the man of passion, actually threatened to kill his father, for they both vie for the favors of the young courtesan Grushenka. If intent of the heart establishes guilt, then Dmitri must be guilty and is, in fact, arrested for the crime.

Young Alexey, called Alyosha, represents spirituality and purity, a contrast to the violence and sensuality of Dmitri and the rationality of Ivan. Yet he secretly recognizes his own tendency toward sensuality and his resentment of their irresponsible father. His mentor is Father Zossima, whose teaching on behalf of spiritual brotherhood provides a counterweight to the ambivalent, passionate nature of the Karamazovs.

The fourth son, Smerdyakov, is a servant in the household and does not bear the family name. He was born to an idiot woman raped by Fyodor Pavlovitch. He is understandably vulnerable to Ivan's skepticism about human and divine justice.

Although this complex family tragedy promotes the vision of Christian redemption, its exploration of intellectual doubt and metaphysical rebellion seems, to some readers, more convincing. Ivan's famous "Legend of the Grand Inquisitor" often appears in anthologies dealing with existentialist literature.

BURY MY HEART AT WOUNDED KNEE
Dee Brown
1970
Nonfiction
Historical, Western

This 1970 international best seller chronicles the history of Native Americans in the second half of the nineteenth century. Brown writes from the perspective of native tribes who have recorded treaty betrayal, gross misconduct, and atrocities by the U. S. Federal government.

The book's first chapter begins in 1492 with Columbus and rapidly moves to 1860 when increased immigration and settler expansion pushed westward. Federal policies of native removal and resettlement are highlighted.

Subsequent chapters are written from the point of view of individual native tribes and their tragic experiences with the U. S. Federal government. Principal tribes covered in the narrative are: the Navajo Nation, Sioux tribes (Santee Dakota, Hunkpapa Lakota, Oglala Lakota, and Miniconjou Lakota), Cheyenne, and Apache people. Minor consideration treats the Arapaho, Modoc, Kiowa, Comanche, Nez Perce, Ponca, Ute, and Miniconjou Lakota tribes.

Specific events concerning these tribes are put through an historical microscope.

Native Americans who surrendered with a guarantee of safety were often executed. Treaties were violated in blatant or obscure ways. Natives were frequently arrested on bogus charges. When there were court trials, they were propaganda events in which the accused could not defend themselves. Aspects of native culture like the Ghost Dance were criminalized.

Conflicts surrounding the 1858 Pike's Peak Gold Rush in Colorado reduced the Cheyenne population by 90%. Deteriorating relations with the Apaches begins with events surrounding Cochise, the principal chief of the Chokonen band of the Chiricahua Apache, culminating in the revolt of Geronimo.

Brown vividly covers the Sioux story of Chief Red Cloud and Sitting Bull, which began with the Black Hills Gold Rush of 1874. The battle of Wounded Knee began over a single native who refused to surrender his gun. The resulting battle claimed the lives of about three hundred Native Americans and about thirty federal soldiers. Surviving Lakota natives returned the next day to bury their dead at Wounded Knee.

The book's title comes from the final line in Stephen Benet's 1927 poem "American Names." Wounded Knee marks the last great battle between Native Americans and the federal government.

C

THE CALL OF THE WILD
Jack London
1903
Novella
Adventure

Buck, a large crossbreed dog, is kidnaped from a life of ease on a California ranch and sold into servitude as a sled dog in the harsh Alaskan wastes, where he triumphs over the environment's primordial savagery.

This is a novel of "devolution" which traces the process of releasing Buck's savage, atavistic nature beneath its civilized veneer. Through the brutality of various human masters and the cunning of the other dogs he meets, Buck learns not only to adapt and survive his ordeal but also to prevail over the hostile wilderness; by the novel's end Buck is leading a pack of wolves in the Yukon. At only one point in the story does Buck experience gentle treatment and that is when he is nursed back to health by John Thornton, but when Thornton is killed by hostile Indians, Buck is forever free of men and their civilization.

This story may be read on several levels. As an adventure tale it is a rollicking good yarn about life in Alaska. As a historical romance it can be read as a somewhat faithful depiction of the perils of seeking gold in the Yukon during the Klondike gold rush, in the 1890's. Finally the novel can also be read as a philosophical work reflecting London's interest in social Darwinism and notions of racial survival.

In spite of the obvious absurdities of Buck's reflections on his Nietzschean racial fulfillment as a super being, the novel is surprisingly successful as a work of early twentieth century symbolism. Certainly London's most famous, and perhaps best, work of fiction, it incorporates the graphic world of violent action which captures the vitality and metaphysical vision that he discovered in the "white silence" of the uncompromising environment of the North and which came to represent the indifferent triumph of the amoral universe over man's fate.

CANDIDA
George Bernard Shaw
1897
Drama
Satire

This carefully constructed and popular play, a witty domestic comedy set in a middle-class clergyman's household, reverberates with Shaw's customary irreverence toward traditional virtues.

The plot of *Candida* is a simple one: A woman must make a choice between two men in her life. This may be one reason for the popularity of the play during the 80 years since it was first produced in London. But, as always, Shaw turns the situation upside down. The Reverend James Morell—a highly regarded and popular public speaker and an imposing figure of a man—actually cannot function without his wife. Candida, his vivacious wife, dominates the household with subtlety and cleverness.

The young, idealistic poet Eugene Marchbanks is the catalyst who moves into this situation and sets the wheels of the plot spinning. The sensitive, ranting, dreamy youth worships Candida and is convinced that he is the only man worthy of her. But sensible Candida realizes that this is not the issue. She decides to bestow herself and her many virtues on the man who needs her the most.

The three major characters in the play learn something in the course of the drama. Marchbanks learns that he is stronger than he believed and leaves with a more powerful conviction of his own grandiose destiny. Morell becomes more humble, respects his wife, and realizes that he is but a man who, like any other man, needs a woman to take care of him. And Candida discovers that service is more important than contentment, triumphing in the fact that she is needed.

This brilliantly constructed drama, with its sparkling dialogue and clever situations, challenges the conventions of society as effectively as Shaw's more openly revolutionary plays. However, he is more insidious here, ridiculing conventionality more subtly and praising the unconventional with less fury then usual. In the end, Shaw leaves no doubt that his money is on the poet, Marchbanks, who will produce great works of art. Candida and Morell will continue together, the one serving both his ego and his congregation, the other serving the needs of her husband.

CANDIDE
Voltaire
1759
Novella
Philosophical

Voltaire's vivid satire of philosophical optimism, the belief that everything necessarily works out for the best in this "best of all possible worlds," takes its title character through an extravagant series of devastating disasters.

After Candide is evicted from idyllic Westphalia for embracing Cunegonde, the Baron's daughter, the constitutionally naive young man is beset by one misfortune after another. Conscripted by the Bulgars to fight the Abares, he escapes and arrives in Lisbon, in time for the catastrophic earthquake and to be flogged and hanged by the Inquisition. Rescued by Cunegonde, who had been raped and stabbed by the Bulgars, he kills the Inquisitor and the Jew who have been keeping her on alternate days.

Candide and Cunegonde flee to South America, where she is immediately appropriated by the governor of Buenos Aires. Candide escapes inland, where the native Biglugs almost devour him before discovering that he is not a Jesuit. After leaving them, he finds himself in the remote and happy land of Eldorado. Yet Candide soon becomes bored in this Utopia and returns to the world of catastrophes and villainy.

Cheated of a fortune during his voyage back to Europe and imprisoned in France, Candide eventually makes his way to Venice, to be reunited with his beloved Cunegonde. Now a slave to a Turk, she has been rendered hideously ugly by disease. Candide is reunited with her and with his odd tutor, the fatuously complacent Pangloss, and they settle on a small farm near Constantinople.

Through the wild implausibility of its events and the overt artifice of its structure, the book mocks the pretensions of rational control. Voltaire cynically depicts human beings as both obtuse and vile, perversely pursuing actions that are counter to their own best interests.

Voltaire is more interested in examining general questions about happiness and human nature than in providing rounded, individualized characterizations. He rejects intolerance and fanaticism, holding blind allegiance to abstract systems responsible for most of the troubles that beset the world. The book's famous closing line, "We must cultivate our garden," urges that we accept our imperfections and labor with what we have.

THE CANTERBURY TALES
Geoffrey Chaucer
1387-1400
Poetry
Narrative

Although The Canterbury Tales *is a poem, Chaucer ranks not only as poet but also as keen social observer, humorist, and master storyteller. This work brings 14th century England to life and creates characters who remain recognizable in the 20th century.*

It is April. Thirty pilgrims have gathered at the Tabard Inn just south of London prior to departure for the shrine of St. Thomas a Becket, martyred in his cathedral at Canterbury two centuries earlier.

Socially they range from the Franklin, a wealthy landowner, to the Plowman; morally from the Parson, who has taught Christ's word ("but first he followed it himself") to the Pardoner, a rascally confidence man. The proprietor of the Tabard offers to accompany them as Host and suggests that they entertain themselves on the way by telling stories in turn; the teller of the most entertaining and morally instructive tales will later receive a free meal.

The tales also vary, illustrating popular medieval genres: romance, fable, saint's life, fabliau (a coarse, comic tale), exemplum (a story designed to illustrate the theme of a sermon). Chaucer the pilgrim burlesques a type of popular romance, but his satirical purpose goes unrecognized and the Host will not allow him to finish. The Wife of Bath, on the lookout for a sixth husband, tells a tale cunningly contrived to prove that the main ingredient of domestic happiness is rule by the wife.

The Miller, somehow drunk early on the first day, tells of a carpenter deceived and made the laughing stock of his neighborhood by his wife and her lover. The hot-tempered Reeve, a carpenter by profession, responds in kind. The Wife of Bath baits the Monk, who has interrupted her. The Knight averts a brawl between the Host and the Pardoner.

The Canterbury Tales is fragmentary and unfinished, but Chaucer carefully concludes with the tale (actually sermon) of the good Parson, who reminds them all that they are on a pilgrimage not merely to Canterbury but to heaven.

Several modern translations of the poem are available, but to master Chaucer's Middle English repays the effort. Many editions and introductions summarize handily his spelling, pronunciation, and grammar.

CANTOS
Ezra Pound
1917-1969
Poetry
Epic

This most infamous of poems is a modernist epic of legendary difficulty. In it Pound seeks moments and places throughout history that are hospitable to the creation of art, because only when the arts thrive, according to Pound, can society be healthy.

The above summary somewhat begs the central question regarding the Cantos because many ask whether it has any central message or overarching form at all. This is partly due to its serial creation over 50 years of Pound's life, and partly because it is the epitome of the modernist poetic style of allusion (often arcane or private), juxtaposition, fragmentation, and the like.

Whatever else it is, *The Cantos* is a poem that centers on history—the history of Europe, of the East, of America, and, mixed in throughout, Pound's own personal history. One interpretation sees the poem as a voyage to various times and places in history in search of enlightenment. Various cantos focus, for instance, on Confucian Chinese emperors, or Renaissance Italian princes, or Jeffersonian America.

The enlightenment Pound seeks concerns, among other things, how to govern, the role of money in society, and the best conditions for the creation of art. He peoples *The Cantos,* as Dante does *The Divine Comedy,* with heroes and villains. Pound's heroes are versatile people of action who are creative, honest, and sincere. The chief of his villains is usury, the manipulation of money to produce more money with no concern for the health of society.

Even Pound conceded that he was not able to make the whole cohere. Only an unusually sympathetic and hardworking reader will persevere through its genuine difficulties. The poem remains, nonetheless, one of the great creative efforts of the 20th century.

CAPTAINS COURAGEOUS
Rudyard Kipling
1897
Novel
Adventure, Coming of Age

After fainting on the deck of an ocean liner, a wealthy American boy awoke to find himself aboard a New England fishing schooner. His story provides a vivid record of seafaring and of life in late 19th century America.

The brisk narrative focuses on the maturing of 15-year-old Harvey Cheyne, the only son of an American business tycoon. Through Harvey's encounter with raw nature, hard work, and ordinary men, the once pampered youth learns the meaning of the American dream and prepares himself to pursue it.

Rescued from the sea by New England fishermen, Harvey at first finds life difficult aboard the schooner called *We're Here*. The captain refuses to believe Harvey's stories of wealth, so he puts the uninvited guest to work to earn his keep. For a time Harvey resists, but soon he discovers the joy of physical labor, the outdoors, masculine companionship, and even hardship. During the next few months, every misfortune imaginable at sea strikes the crew aboard the *We're Here*.

Yet they survive and land safely at their home port in Gloucester where Harvey's true identity is revealed. Here Harvey faces new trials as he attempts to reconcile his former life with the knowledge he has gained through the forced passage into manhood while aboard the schooner.

Although on one level a sea adventure with a happy ending, the novel also reflects lasting American values. Through his adventures, Harvey learns to respect hard work, forthrightness, and social equality. And he gains self-reliance, pride in a job well done, and a spirit of adventure. He has thus prepared himself to take his place in the unfolding American drama.

As the title suggests, there are two "captains courageous": the captain of the *We're Here* and Harvey's father. The first captain is an ordinary sort who makes an honest living through physical labor. The second captain is an entrepreneur whose vision takes in all of America's potential. As Harvey learns, a successful man incorporates the diverse qualities of the two captains who have molded him.

THE CASK OF AMONTILLADO
Edgar Allan Poe
1846
Short Story
Gothic

One of Poe's tightest and most sardonic tales, this story involves the reader in the first-person confession of a vengeful murderer. Although simple on the surface, it is filled with complex ironies.

Furious because of unspecified insults by Fortunato, the nobleman Montresor seeks revenge. By appealing to his enemy's pride, Montresor lures Fortunato into his family vaults to sample some wine to determine if it is true Amontillado. Once there, Montresor bricks the drunken man into a niche in the wall to die. Montresor tells the story of his crime fifty years later to an unnamed someone who knows well the nature of his soul.

The clues to the basically ironic nature of the story can be seen in many separate details which suggest that the truth is just the opposite of the surface appearance. The central irony lies in Montresor's coat of arms—which depicts a large human foot crushing a serpent whose fangs are embedded in the heel—and his family motto: No one harms me with impunity. There is irony also in Montresor's criteria for a successful revenge: that a wrong is unredressed when retribution overtakes its redresser or when the avenger does not make clear that he is acting out of revenge.

At the end of the story, although Montresor does indeed murder Fortunato, he never really makes clear to him why he is doing it. Moreover, the fact that fifty years later he confesses his crime, perhaps to a priest, might mean that he has been punished by guilt all this time. The question left in the reader's mind is: If Montresor is represented by the foot crushing out the life of the serpent Fortunato, then are the fangs of Fortunato still embedded in Montresor's heel? If so, it might be said that Fortunato fulfills Montresor's criteria for revenge more perfectly than Montresor himself does.

THE CASTLE
Franz Kafka
1926
Novel
Dystopian, Fantasy

K., allegedly a land surveyor, attempts in vain to gain access to the inscrutable realm of the castle authorities. Replete with irony and tragicomic scenes, Kafka's most mature novel is a masterpiece of modern narrative.

Late one evening K. stumbles into the snowbound village at the foot of a group of ramshackle buildings known as the castle. Despite a rude welcome in the village inn and a rebuffed telephone call to the castle, K. insists that he has come to work in the village at the castle's request and that his assistants will arrive the next day.

Although the reader may readily sympathize with K.'s plight at the hands of the elusive castle officials, as the story unfolds one gradually senses K.'s dishonesty about his true identity and motives and his folly in trying to confront the authorities. When the castle sends two good-natured assistants to help K. in his "work," K. maligns them and their attempts to divert him from his grim insistence on meeting Klamm, the functionary who becomes the focus of K.'s futile efforts.

While K. works himself deeper and deeper into the trap of his own duplicitous tales, not even the love of Frieda, Klamm's former girlfriend, can save him from his relentless pursuit of stories about the activities of the castle authorities. Shunning Frieda and the playful help of the assistants, K. grows increasingly isolated, yet he refuses to leave the castle village.

The narrator follows K.'s every move with a deftly veiled irony and counters K.'s deadly seriousness with a comic perspective that takes the reader outside the narrow frame of K.'s hopeless wanderings. Written in 1922, shortly after the end of centuries of Austrian rule in Kafka's native Bohemia, the novel is less a satirical critique of bureaucratic chicanery than a self-ironic coming to terms with Kafka's own need for recognition by and access to the patriarchal society of Prague's Jewish community.

CAT ON A HOT TIN ROOF
Tennessee Williams
1955
Drama
Sociological, Southern Gothic

This searing drama portrays the results of lying to oneself through the story of one man's internalized homophobia, which has hurt several lives besides his own.

In course of a single evening characters assemble for emotional fireworks and the explosion of the lies by which they all are living.

It is Big Daddy's 65th birthday, but he does not realize it will be his last. His two sons and their wives, however, know he is dying of cancer and want him to determine which of them will inherit his huge plantation. Brick has the edge, being his parents' favorite, yet Gooper and Mae keep pointing to his drinking and his childless wife and then to their own five offspring.

The major force in the play is Brick's wife, Maggie, whose vitality has survived Brick's persisting sexual rejection of her. Deeply in love with Brick, she wants to produce a grandchild for Big Daddy. Both she and Big Daddy try to make Brick face the facts of his drinking and his sexual abstention.

Brick started drinking and stopped making love with Maggie when his best friend and fellow football star, Skipper, died. He refuses to acknowledge any sexual element in their closeness, having been so indoctrinated by his society with the idea that a sexual relationship between two men is dirty.

The resolution of the play remains ambiguous, but the well-drawn characters and Williams' splendidly rhetorical Southern dialogue create high-powered drama, with some superb comedy as well. Maggie ("the Cat") and Big Daddy remain two of American drama's most vital and fascinating characters.

CATCH-22
Joseph Heller
1961
Novel
Dark Comedy

A black comedy about an American bomber squadron based in Italy during the last days of World War II, Catch-22 was completed sixteen years after Germany's surrender. It has less to do with the war, in fact, than the society that came out of it.

Yossarian, the protagonist, opens the novel in the hospital, where he is happily feigning illness in order to avoid combat. The outcome of the war is no longer in doubt, and his goal is survival. Indeed, the goal of the army itself seems to be anything but winning the war. The commanders who keep raising the number of missions the men must fly are concerned with their own careers; the bureaucrats who interrupt meals with loyalty oaths are pushing their own departments. Entrepreneurs such as Milo Minderbinder are only interested in making a profit. Heller's army is a metaphor for the McCarthyism, big business, and big bureaucracy of the Eisenhower 1950's: a total system with no way out.

The novel's tricks with chronology give an impression of chaos, but it is carefully structured. Its hysterically humorous skits circle obsessively around the nightmare scene in which Yossarian tries to comfort the dying Snowden. Giving him first aid for a wound in his thigh (the entrepreneurial Milo has sold the morphine), Yossarian learns too late that, hidden inside the flak jacket, Snowden's guts have been blown out.

Structure is also provided by the steady rise of exemplary figures such as Milo, who makes a tidy profit by renting planes to the Germans to bomb his own men, and the aptly named Scheisskopf, whose mindless devotion to parades leads him from lieutenant to general.

What hope does the novel hold out? At the end, Yossarian is offered the chance to assure his own safety by selling out. Instead, he sets off for neutral Sweden in a rowboat. The humor and the protest, bound together, give *Catch-22* a good claim to the status of our greatest postwar novel.

THE CATCHER IN THE RYE
J. D. Salinger
1951
Novel
Coming of Age, Bildungsroman

Holden Caulfield, a neurotic, insecure middle-class teenager, feels he is surrounded by phonies. He must decide between fantasizing about escape and trying to live in the real world.

Expelled from the latest in a long line of preparatory schools, Holden journeys home to Manhattan wishing he were safe in the uncomplex world of childhood, but a series of mishaps begins his initiation into adulthood.

Holden is uncomfortable around his conceited, sex-obsessed classmates and even more ill at ease around adults; they are condescending and incapable of understanding him, so he always tells them what they want to hear. He has never been able to communicate with anyone but his late, saintly brother, Allie, and his ten-year-old sister, Phoebe. He can be himself only in the world of precocious innocence.

After disastrous encounters with three spinster tourists, a young prostitute and her pimp, a girl he thinks he likes, a former classmate, and a former teacher, Holden visits Phoebe, avoiding their parents. He says he is heading west to live alone, and Phoebe, realizing he can never look after himself, insists upon going too. These adventures force Holden to recognize, but not completely understand, certain truths about himself and his world.

Holden longs to protect children, including himself, from the fall away from the innocence of childhood into the decadence of adulthood. He is a romantic, unrealistic idealist on a quest for his identity.

Salinger's world is divided into those who compromise their ideals to fulfill what they consider their objectives and those who refuse to compromise. Yet Holden must compromise to survive.

Salinger asks if it is possible to separate the authentic from the phony, if it is possible to create value and meaning, and what beliefs are essential for survival. That he poses these questions with originality, insight, humor, and pathos has made his book one of the most popular American novels.

CAT'S CRADLE
Kurt Vonnegut
1963
Novel
Satire

This novel, filled with a variety of bizarre but all-too-human characters, focuses primarily on the ironic legacy of modern science, which, according to Vonnegut, promises mankind progress but only hastens the cataclysmic end of the world.

As John, the narrator, researches the background for his book on the atomic bomb, he becomes fascinated by Dr. Felix Hoenikker. Hoenikker is the archetypal scientist, isolated from human contact, dedicated to his work, and completely without moral awareness. Like the child's game cat's cradle, which is meant to amuse but only terrifies his son, Hoenikker's scientific games are anything but harmless.

Ironically the atomic bomb is not even Hoenikker's most devastating creation. Working on the rather innocuous problem of how to get soldiers out of the mud, he synthesizes "ice-nine," which is both better and worse than expected: It would freeze the water so soldiers stuck in the mud could lift themselves out, but this freezing action would continue until every bit of water on earth was turned into solid ice-nine.

At his death Hoenikker's secret substance is entrusted to his children, who are predictably irresponsible and use the power of ice-nine only for their personal advantage. Vonnegut shows sympathy for Newton, Angela, and Frank Hoenikker, frail human beings who are simply incapable of the moral strength and wisdom demanded of them, but this makes the satire even more powerful: Mankind continually refuses to acknowledge what may be called its terminal stupidity and therefore perpetually threatens its own existence.

There are a few positive forces in the novel, but each is undermined. Love, for example, is presented as a worthy but impossible, even comical ideal, symbolized by Mona Monzano and her insatiable habit of making love only by rubbing bare feet with another. Bokononism, a religious philosophy expounded throughout the volume, usefully focuses on man as sacred but is of limited comfort and no help in saving the world. *Cat's Cradle* is not a dreary book, since it is constantly enlivened by Vonnegut's wild humor and inventive style, but it is far from optimistic about man's fate. Vonnegut's vision of mankind's unintentional self-destruction, for all its exaggeration, may well be prophetic.

THE CELEBRATED JUMPING FROG OF CALAVERAS COUNTY
Mark Twain
1865
Short Story
Comedy

Mark Twain's story depends for its humor not so much on the plot as on the manner of its telling. Crucial in appreciating the humor is the knowledge that Simon Wheeler, who tells the tale to the narrator, is really perpetrating a hoax. Wheeler knows that the narrator is incredulous and flustered, but the trick in telling such an absurd tale is in not letting on, of telling it not as if it were a joke but as gospel fact.

Wheeler's story is slight. Jim Smiley, who would bet on almost anything, once trained a frog to jump so well that Smiley wagered his frog would beat any other. A stranger takes Jim's bet, though he confesses to having no frog of his own and forcing Jim back to the marsh to catch one for him. In Smiley's absence, the stranger takes hold of Smiley's frog, pries open its mouth and pours a bellyful of buckshot down its throat. When Smiley returns and pits his frog against the new one of the stranger's, Smiley's frog is virtually stuck to the ground. Unable to jump, the frog loses the contest, and Smiley loses his wager.

What makes the story so effective is Twain's handling of the obvious tall tale. While telling the story to the narrator in dialect, Wheeler prolongs the events of the tale by bringing in extraneous material, red herrings that circle and swim about but bear little relevance to the main action. Yet the reader is aware that Wheeler knows what he is doing. His straight-faced delivery is part of the hoax, part of the trickery played on the narrator whose style of literary formality contrasts humorously with Wheeler's colloquial freedom.

The successful mixture of dialect, delay, deadpan tone, and absurd detail makes this story a fine example of the tall-tale tradition in American literature.

THE CELESTIAL OMNIBUS
E. M. Forster
1911
Short Story
Fantasy

Perhaps E. M. Forster's most widely read short story, "The Celestial Omnibus" concerns a boy who travels via a mysterious omnibus to a heaven of literary figures and characters and who must later contend with his skeptical elders, one of whom unfortunately follows him on a return trip.

The story opens in a stuffy middle-class neighborhood in suburban London, where a small boy is puzzled by a sign pointing up a blank alley and carrying the inscription "To Heaven." A patronizing, name-dropping neighbor, Mr. Bons ("snob" spelled backward) reveals that the sign was the joke of a person named Shelley. Asked if he knows who Shelley was, the boy admits that he does not and hangs his head in shame because he considers Mr. Bons "probably the wisest person alive."

That evening, the boy returns to the alley and discovers a mysterious notice announcing the daily operation of an omnibus service, which he resolves to explore the next day. At first he is skeptical and embarrassed to have been taken in by an obvious joke. Then, as if out of nowhere, the omnibus appears in the alley with steaming horses and great white lamps.

The driver, Sir Thomas Browne, ushers the boy aboard. They ascend for two hours through the fog, during which time the boy discovers that Sir Thomas Browne had been a doctor but gave it up to be a "healer of the spirit." He worries privately that his parents will miss him for lunch, but when Browne asks whether he is afraid, the boy answers that he is not.

The omnibus descends through thunder and lightning on a rainbow and arrives at last at a fantastic landscape situated between a precipice and a river, from which maidens surface, singing and playing with a golden ring. In his exuberance, the boy calls to them, and they answer back.

On returning, the boy is punished for lying: He must memorize poetry. Mr. Bons is present for a dinner party, and the boy is summoned to recite what he has learned. Both the boy's father and Mr. Bons exchange condescending remarks, but it is Mr. Bons who, pretending to take the boy's side, listens to his recitation of a Keats sonnet. The familiarity of the images is such that the boy cannot help insisting on their reality—an insistence that Mr. Bons finds silly.

Mr. Bons agrees to accompany him the following day "to settle the matter." When the omnibus appears, Mr. Bons is startled out of his complacency, all the more so when the sunken-eyed driver turns out to be Dante.

As the journey nears its end, the boy sticks his head out the window and announces his arrival, which is greeted with joy. But when he announces that he has brought Mr. Bons, he is met with silence. As the omnibus lands, the boy springs out onto the shield of Achilles, who holds him lovingly aloft, whereas Mr. Bons begins to plummet, as if through a cloud, to his death.

The driver, Dante, sums up the story's theme: "For poetry is a spirit; and they that would worship it must worship in spirit and in truth." The boy, then, is accepted as he accepts, while Mr. Bons, the consummate phony for whom culture is merely status, is dealt an unexpected lesson in "poetic justice."

THE CENTAUR
John Updike
1963
Novel
Psychological, Thriller

This novel relies on the disjunction between its classical, heroic allusions and its literal realism to fashion a work of literary richness and intellectual complexity.

Peter Caldwell, a second-rate painter living in Greenwich Village, remembers three days during his adolescence in 1947 and infuses the experience with mythological significance. Updike uses a mixture of realistic narration and mythological figures, Peter as Prometheus, his father, George, as the centaur Chiron, to structure a novel which opens with a invocation of the father's godlike presence and concludes with the son's perception of his father's human mortality, his loss of deification. Peter's artistic vision collapses in the face of his father's spiritual resignation to the demands of everyday life.

George Caldwell, a high school science teacher, sacrifices himself for the good of his son and the community in which he lives. Like Chiron, who relinquished his life to exonerate Prometheus (the fire-bringer and legendary creator) George literally sacrifices his own ambitions and desires for the good of his artistically talented son. During the three days of the novel's duration, George and Peter experience a series of events, some of mythic significance, some mundane, as they struggle through a winter snowstorm to the comfort of their home in the country.

Part of the novel's fascination, and confusion, lies in the fact that the chapters of mythology are interspersed among the chapters of reality without stylistic separation, thereby creating a disjunctive intellectual shift in the reader's perception. Although widely criticized at the time of its publication, *The Centaur* is now regarded as one of Updike's finest and most demanding works, the one which firmly established him as a major novelist. Placing an interesting perspective on adult nostalgia for lost childhood, the story suggests the need for an adult mythic vision fashioned from our adolescent fantasies about our parents and the past amid a growing awareness of their fallibility and our misplaced veneration.

CHARLOTTE'S WEB
E. B. White
1952
Novel
Children's

"Suppose you were only allowed five words to save the life of your friend. What would they be?" So begins the special Afterward created for the 50th anniversary, retrospective edition of Charlotte's Web, a classic children's tale about a society of barnyard animals who work together to save the life of Wilbur the pig, who was destined for slaughter—until one little girl, Fern Arable, stepped in, and one little spider, Charlotte, learned to spin words into her web.

Charlotte's Web begins with the birth of a litter of pigs, and the little girl, Fern, asking, "Where's papa going with that axe?" Once she learns that he means to kill the extra runt of the litter, Fern runs to rescue Wilber (as she later names him) from the chopping block. After a short stint in the house, under Fern's care, Wilbur is taken to Uncle Zuckerman's barn, where barn animals set about educating the young pig, about life on a farm, and about what happens to pigs once they've matured and grown fat.

Charlotte—a barn spider whose full name, Charlotte A. Cavatica, is based on her scientific classification—takes a special interest in Wilbur, and she devises a plan to keep Wilbur from the inevitable. She weaves the words, "some pig" into her web, where Lurvy, the farm hand, takes notice. Soon, Wilbur has become a special phenomenon, bringing international attention to the Zuckerman farm, and the brilliant pig living there. Charlotte sends the curmudgeonly rat, Templeton, to rummage through the garbage to find more words for her to spin. She spells "terrific," "radiant," and finally "humble," ultimately winning Wilbur special recognition at the fair. She is rewarded with the certainty that Wilbur will never be butchered.

Charlotte is an ideal mother, patiently answering Wilbur's many questions, even sending him to bed when it is time. She is wise and thoughtful, and not only does she save Wilbur's life, she lays 514 eggs that she eventually entrusts to Wilbur's care, once she is gone.

The book's ending garnered some criticism originally, from those who thought death was an inappropriate theme for young children. While friendship and community are important themes, death is the central reality in the story. It begins with Wilbur's life being threatened, and the continued attempts to keep him alive, but it ends with Charlotte's death and Wilbur's personal mission to continue her legacy of care.

THE CHARTERHOUSE OF PARMA
Stendhal
1839
Novel
Manners

In Parma, a small, early nineteenth century autocratic principality in northern Italy, everyone jockeys for position, envies, gossips, intrigues, and conspires: The favor of the prince may be won and lost in the same hour.

The book opens with the entry of Napoleon's victorious troops into Milan in 1796. One of them, a handsome lieutenant, wins the heart of the married Marchesa del Longo. Fabrizio is the offspring from their brief affair and becomes the romantic leading man of the novel. At seventeen he runs off to France and manages to be blurredly present at the Battle of Waterloo.

Fabrizio soon returns to Parma and the fond protection of his brilliant aunt, the spectacularly operatic Duchess Gina Sanseverina. Through much of the novel Fabrizio is little more than a chivalrous, dazzlingly attractive juvenile, living the customary aristocratic life of gallantry and sexual dalliance, playing the roles of young man-about-court and fashionable cleric. Maturation arrives for him when, through complex twists in the state's affairs, he finds himself imprisoned in its great tower only to fall in love with the jailer's daughter, Clelia.

Stendhal laces the novel with ironies: Not only is Fabrizio happiest when captive, but his aunt, hopelessly in love with him, insists on plotting his escape and scorning her devoted companion, Mosca, who has repeatedly endangered not only his career but also his life in her and Fabrizio's behalf. Discovering that Fabrizio has sighs only for Clelia, Gina nonetheless rescues him from a second imprisonment, buying his freedom in a wretched sexual bargain with the despot Ranuccio-Ernesto V. She then accepts the permanent frustration of her grand passion, relinquishes Fabrizio to Clelia, resigns herself to marriage with Mosca, but lives only "a very short time" after Fabrizio's early death.

THE CHERRY ORCHARD
Anton Chekhov
1904
Drama
Tragicomedy

This play depicts the last visit to her home and family of an aristocrat before their estate is to be forcibly sold. The play's complex structure and fascinating characterizations yield a remarkable portrait of Russia around 1900.

Madame Lubov Ranevskaya returns from a disastrous love affair in Paris to her family and her ancestral home, with its famous cherry orchard, ostensibly to try to save it from the auctioneer's block. But she is unable to accept the idea of breaking up the property to use it commercially, thus condemning it by her inaction.

During the months she is home, the play's six major and six minor characters gather around, sometimes offering conflicting views and advice. They flirt, do magic tricks, picnic, dance, and gossip. The young teacher and Lubov's daughter, who are in love, look ahead eagerly, while the heroine and her brother can only mourn the passing of their home and its beautiful orchard, symbolic of the old order. Thus the play portrays many views on this changing society and world.

The play's fame, however, rests on its tone and style as well as its rich characterizations, its musical structure, so lifelike in its apparent casualness, its astonishing gamut of emotions from pathos to farce.

Its compassionate and sympathetic portrayal of so many different character types results in its being subject to many conflicting readings. The author called it a comedy, and the characters' foibles and weaknesses do render them comic from a dispassionate perspective. Nevertheless, the play's basic situation is tragic. Thus, without seeming to be planned or forced, the play reveals the subtlest interactions of human society seen in this microcosm of a world in transition.

CHILDE HAROLD'S PILGRIMAGE
Lord Byron
1812-1818
Poetry
Narrative

Childe Harold's Pilgrimage is a poetical diary of two trips. The opening cantos present Byron's excursion in 1809-1811 through Portugal and Spain (Canto I), Greece and Albania (Canto II); Cantos III and IV deal with his travels through Belgium, Germany, Switzerland, and Italy after he permanently left England in 1816.

Byron was already an established writer by 1812, but with this work he replaced Sir Walter Scott as England's most popular poet. His audience was eager for material dealing with the Near East, and this he supplied. Of particular interest were his vivid descriptions of Albania, which Byron was one of the first Englishmen to visit.

The poem also created the popular Byronic hero—proud, brilliant, and attractive, but also bored, gloomy, lonely, disillusioned, and isolated from the rest of humanity. This figure, who narrates the poem, provides much of whatever unity the wide-ranging poem possesses.

This hero offers moral and personal reflections as he travels, thus combining the poetry of landscape and travel with the confessional and the meditative. He contrasts the power and permanence of nature with the insignificance and transience of man. Waterloo will fade from the memory; Venice will crumble into the sea. The tone of the poem is therefore somber: Byron's tour passes through a fallen and decayed world.

Yet it is a world capable of redemption. If Waterloo and Venice will not endure, Marathon, Shylock, and Othello will. Through noble deeds and great art, mankind can achieve immortality.

CHILDHOOD'S END
Arthur C. Clarke
1953
Novel
Science Fiction

When enormous, eerily quiet spaceships take position over the earth's greatest cities, humanity can't know the role these alien beings will play in the end of the human species, nor can they imagine the means of humanity's demise. Commonly referred to as "overlords," this alien species acts as midwife to a new life form, utterly alien to the humans from whom it arises.

At the height of the Cold War, alien spaceships hover over the greatest cities of the Earth. Their mysterious inhabitants have no stated purpose, and refuse to show themselves lest humans strike out in prejudice and fear at the sight of them. The UN secretary-general, Stormgren, has established a close relationship with "supervisor" overlord, Karellan, when the rebellious "freedom league" kidnaps Stormgren, leading to the overlords' agreement to appear before humanity in fifty years' time.

Following the fifty-year wait, the overlords are fixtures in human society, which has reached its utopian zenith—beyond war, hunger, and poverty—yet life is also facile, with its parlor games and gadgets. The profoundly intelligent overlords reveal their interest in "the paranormal," as they search Rupert Boyce's unique library. When a Ouija Board session provides the exact location of the overlord's home planet, the overlord, Rashaverik, realizes that a new era in human development is about to emerge. The astronomer Jan Rodricks makes plans to get to the overlords' home, regardless of the their ban on space exploration. He will learn that the overlords' species is barren and utterly subservient to the awesome and terrifying "overmind."

Finally, disappointed with the meaninglessness of life, George and Jean Greggson join an isolated, island society called New Athens, where inhabitants live according to a bygone era, growing their own food, and leaving their over-mechanized existence. But the children begin behaving strangely, as though living on a higher or extraterrestrial plain, to the extent that their consciousness becomes entirely internal, and they exhibit little or no outward interaction with each other or their parent generations. It becomes clear that the overlords are facilitators in human evolution. The all-powerful "overmind," seeks to absorb humanity into itself.

Upon returning to earth, Jan Rodricks realizes he's the last human being and helps chronicle the final moments of humanity and its planet, Earth.

Childhood's End examines superstitions and stereotypes; the highly intelligent overlords are interested in paranormal phenomena—something often dismissed by modern science as ignorant superstition. Clarke forces his readers to examine their own prejudice when the overlords (who look like evil demons) are patient and even, at times, compassionate. When humans try to outsmart him, Karellan is remarkably non-reactive. The scene where Karellan reveals himself for the first time, and asks for the children to come to him, is strikingly similar to the common Christian image of Christ, surrounded by children.

THE CHOSEN
Chaim Potok
1967
Novel
Historical

A line drive from Danny Saunders' bat to the pitcher's mound, and into Reuven Malter's eye, brings two rivals together in a special bond of friendship. This coming-of-age story is as much about the contradictions in American Jewry as it is about the lives of these two Jewish boys, both sons of prominent rabbis.

When Danny and Reuven first meet on the baseball field, they each carry prejudice and suspicion about their opponents, but when Reuven is severely injured and hospitalized after Danny's ball hits him, they realize they have much more in common than they imagined. Both are gifted students and athletes, devoted to studying their religion, and they are each the sons of highly regarded rabbis. However, as their friendship deepens, they begin to learn about the profound differences in their relationships with their fathers that reflect a fundamental difference at the heart of their religious beliefs.

Danny's father is the spiritual Rebbe in his Hassidic community, which places him on a divine pedestal. He is a messianic Jew, who aims to help usher in the long-awaited messiah. He is a stern man who constantly tests his son's (and Reuven's) knowledge of Talmud (Jewish law). His position as Rebbe is an inherited one going back many generations, and Danny is his presumed successor. He has not spoken directly with his son in years, except in Talmudic argumentation, causing Danny great pain. Danny also dreams of becoming a psychotherapist like Freud, but is afraid to tell his father. It would mean the unthinkable: breaking that inherited rabbinic chain.

Reuven, on the other hand, is extremely close to his father, a well-known rabbi who is involved in the Jewish reform and Zionist movements. His father is deeply affectionate and loving. By coincidence, before Reuven was injured, Rabbi Malter had been gently guiding Danny in reading secular books out of Danny's hunger for secular knowledge. Though he knew Rabbi Saunders would not approve, he took it upon himself to guide Danny thinking some guidance was better than none.

When the world learns of the Nazi atrocities, a great divide rises between the two boys and their fathers. Reuven's father speaks out for the necessity of a secular Jewish state. Rebbe Saunders is outraged, considering it blasphemous that the non-religious should build a Jewish homeland. A rift opens up between the boys who, at the behest of Rabbi Saunders, endure complete silence for several years. Though they eventually renew their friendship, it will never be the same. In the end, both boys are shocked to learn that the great Rebbe Saunders knew all along that his son would not succeed him.

A CHRISTMAS CAROL
Charles Dickens
1843
Novella
Victorian

Perhaps the most familiar of all works of Victorian fiction, this short narrative tells how the visits of four ghosts convert Ebenezer Scrooge to a believer in the joy of celebrating Christmas.

This story opens on Christmas Eve in the office of Scrooge, a miserly Victorian businessman. Opposed to Christmas as pointless frivolity, Scrooge refuses to make a contribution to Christmas charities, begrudges his employee Bob Cratchit a holiday on Christmas day, and rejects his nephew's Christmas greeting with the now-famous phrase "Bah! Humbug!"

Returning to his lonely and desolate dwelling, Scrooge is confronted by the ghost of Jacob Marley, his former partner, who promises that he will be visited by three spirits. The first of these, the Ghost of Christmas Past, shows Scrooge scenes from his lonely boyhood at boarding school; from the lively and festive Christmas celebration of Mr. Fezziwig, the man to whom Scrooge had been apprenticed; and of his final encounter with his fiancee, who releases him from their engagement because she realizes that he already loves money more than he loves her.

The next spirit, the Ghost of Christmas Present, shows him a number of celebrations of Christmas, most memorably that of the Cratchit family, who are jovial and happy in spite of their meager income and the threat that their youngest child, Tiny Tim, will die of a disease that has already crippled him. Finally, the Ghost of Christmas Yet to Come shows Scrooge scenes of his own death, lamented by no one—his servants have even stolen his bedclothes before his burial—and of the Cratchit family mourning the death of Tiny Tim. Moved by these visions, Scrooge awakens on Christmas morning a new person and engages in a whirlwind of generosity and good fellowship.

A Christmas Carol is the most notable example of the Victorian "Christmas book," a type of short, attractively printed book designed to be given as a Christmas gift and usually embodying the themes of generosity and joy associated with the season. The degree to which this story and its characters have remained popular indicates how well Dickens succeeded in this genre.

THE CHRONICLES OF NARNIA
C. S. Lewis
1950-1956
Novel
Children's, Series

As a children's fantasy epic spanning seven books, considered to be Lewis' life's work and literary masterpiece, The Chronicles of Narnia *have become a cultural staple for many early readers, and those inspired by fantasy. Consisting mostly of allegorical tales of good versus evil,* The Chronicles *feature themes heavily influenced by classic biblical tales.*

In book 1, *The Lion, the Witch and the Wardrobe*, the Pevensie siblings, Peter, Susan, Edmund and Lucy find themselves in the mystical land of Narnia. With the help of the Lion, Aslan, the children are able to defeat the evil White Witch, who had been ruling over Narnia, in a state of perpetual winter, for over a century.

In book 2, *Prince Caspian: The Return to Narnia*, the Pevensies return to Narnia in order to aid Prince Caspian in becoming King.

Book 3, *The Voyage of the Dawn Treader*, focuses on the now King Caspian, in his quest to find seven lords who had been banished by his evil uncle, Miraz.

In Book 4, *The Silver Chair*, the Pevensies' cousin, Eustace, and his friend, Jill, are given the task of finding King Caspian's son, Rilian, who had been missing for the past ten years.

Book 5, *The Horse and His Boy*, tells the story of a talking horse named Bree and a young boy named Shasta as they make their return home to the land of Narnia.

Book 6, *The Magician's Nephew,* is a prologue to the rest of the saga, and answers many questions regarding the true nature of Narnia and its creation.

Finally, in book 7, *The Last Battle*, the Chronicles end with the untimely destruction of the realm of Narnia, as the god-like creature Aslan leads his faithful followers into the true Narnia, ushering in a golden age that would last eternity.

THE CID
Pierre Corneille
1637
Drama
Baroque
An idealistic young hero must choose between family honor and his true love; this greatest example of French baroque drama paints towering emotions in poetry which has stood the test of the ages.

A tale of 11th century Spain furnishes the main characters and plot of this drama, although a 17th century French psychology dominates it. Three main elements influence the course of events: romantic love, family honor, and feudal duty.

A pair of young lovers, Rodrigue and Chimène are at the point of betrothal when their fathers quarrel over a royal honor; Chimène's father insults and slaps Rodrigue's father in a fit of wounded pride. Only Rodrigue can avenge this affront. Doing so, he kills Chimène's father in a duel. Now Chimène in her turn must uphold family honor by seeking justice for her dead father. What power can mediate this seemingly irreconcilable conflict?

The answer lies in the hands of Don Fernand, the incarnation of kingly wisdom and dignity. He can judge Chimène's father in his failings of arrogance and insubordination while regretting his courage and military skill. He alone can offer her a new filial allegiance to the crown. When a sudden attack by the Moors places the kingdom in danger, Don Fernand can offer Rodrigue a chance at redemption as replacement for the dead count in battle.

Rodrigue rides out with a small force, seeking death in the king's service and returns covered with glory to claim the new name of "le Cid." Chimène's assumption of hatred comes with ill grace against such a hero. She is able to admit her love when she mistakenly believes Rodrigue dead in a trial by combat; this admission allows the king to reconcile the lovers. As the curtain falls, love can once again hope for fulfillment; the king sends Rodrigue on a year's quest for glory, with Chimène his promised reward.

CIVIL DISOBEDIENCE
Henry David Thoreau
1849
Nonfiction
Political
This influential essay advocates breaking an unjust law rather than debasing one's conscience by obeying it.

Thoreau went to jail in July, 1846, for refusing to pay his poll tax. He objected not to the uses to which it was put but to the fact that paying it supported his state, Massachusetts, which supported such federal policies as slavery and the Mexican War, a dispute over territory and treaties in which the United States was not clearly the wronged party.

Thoreau expressed his ideas on the individual's relation to government first in a speech in 1848, which was originally published under the title "Resistance to Civil Government." While he looked forward to a day when government should be unnecessary, he did not object to his government on general principles. He was happy to pay taxes for what will benefit the public good. He did not, however, wish to support a government whose actions he disapproved of.

Most people, he observed, simply go along with their government's actions, even while disagreeing, simply because it is easier. Such people relinquish what makes them human.

When unjust laws exist, people have the choice of obeying them, obeying them while trying to change them, or refusing to obey them. For Thoreau, the choice is clear: only the third way keeps one's conscience clear.

It is not enough to wait until enough people agree to change a law by voting. One must simply break the law. Even if one lands in jail, one is morally free, for, as Thoreau says, when anyone is imprisoned unjustly, the only place for a just person is in prison. Even a single individual, if right, can constitute a majority of one.

Thoreau's moral challenge and courageous ideas inspired such twentieth century social-political leaders as Mahatma Gandhi, in India's quest for freedom from British rule, and Martin Luther King, Jr., in the struggle against American racism. The civil disobedience Thoreau advocated remains a powerful method for political change.

CLARISSA
Samuel Richardson
1747-1748
Novel
Epistolary, Tragedy
In a series of letters the tragedy of Clarissa Harlowe and Robert Lovelace unfolds.

Facing a mercenary marriage about to be imposed upon her by her family, Clarissa flees to the protection of another suitor, Lovelace, despite her reservations about him. Her fears prove justified as Lovelace repeatedly attempts to seduce her and, finally, drugs and rapes her. Clarissa dies, and Lovelace is killed by Clarissa's cousin, Colonel Morden, in a duel.

While the novel contains sex and violence, these elements are secondary to Richardson's psychological probing of his characters. Through their letters they reveal their innermost thoughts and mercilessly explore their motives.

In the process they call into question traditional views and values. Richardson's preface and postscript offer conventional, moralistic observations on codes of behavior and the proper relationships among family members, but the world he depicts in the novel itself belies these pious platitudes. In one sense Clarissa is the pure, Christian heroine betrayed by her money-hungry relatives and a diabolical Restoration rake, but her letters reveal her attraction to Lovelace even as she recognizes how dangerous he is. Nor does Lovelace torment only Clarissa, for he suffers even more than she from his actions, and his death is as much a suicide as hers.

Beneath the glittering, seemingly rational world of eighteenth century bourgeois society so minutely depicted, *Clarissa* reveals a nightmarish world of sadism and masochism aptly summed up by Lovelace: "There is more of the savage in human nature than we are commonly aware of." *Clarissa* is a pessimistic novel not only because Clarissa and Lovelace die, but also because, long before Freud, it exposes the heart of darkness lurking within its characters—and its readers.

A CLEAN, WELL-LIGHTED PLACE
Ernest Hemingway
1933
Short Story
Existential
Virtually plotless, this highly abbreviated and cryptic story depicts a man's discovery of the meaninglessness of life and the only solace that remains once this discovery is made.

The basic situation is that of two waiters—one older, one younger—sitting in a bar late at night, waiting for their last customer, a deaf old man, to leave. Most of the action consists of the dialogue between the two waiters in which the older waiter is sympathetic with the old man, while the younger one is impatient to get home to his wife.

The subject of the dialogue revolves around the knowledge one of the waiters has that the old man tried to commit suicide the previous week.

When the old man finally leaves, the older waiter, identifying with the old man, engages in a conversation with himself. He knows that the old man wanted to stay in the bar because it was clean and well-lighted, and that what the old man feared was not anything particular but rather a nothing. The old waiter emphasizes his own nihilism by reciting the Lord's Prayer, in which for certain words he substitutes the Spanish word for nothing—nada: "Our *nada* who art in *nada, nada* be thy name...."

The story is difficult, not only because the dialogue is confusing and the plot minimal, but also because the philosophic idea that underlies the story is a complex existential one. The old waiter knows that nothingness—the sense that there is no God or external value in the world—is the only ultimate reality. The clean, well-lighted cafe is a little island of order in the midst of the nothingness of reality; such concrete actualities constitute the only meaning that remains.

A CLOCKWORK ORANGE
Anthony Burgess
1962
Novella
Science Fiction

In a dystopic, socialistic England of the near future as imagined from the early 1960s, remorseless teens rule the night with robbery, mayhem, rape, and "ultra-violence." When at last the State develops the ultimate "cure," however, which is the worse inhumanity?

A Clockwork Orange presents a world of shocking violence and utter societal failure. Somewhere far above are lunar colonies and worldwide television-relay satellites, but crime runs unchecked, and the brutal prisons need to be cleared of criminals to make way for more political prisoners.

Alex, the novel's fifteen-year-old narrator, who is adept at hoodwinking reform schools, social workers, and parents alike, speaks in a sometimes-alienating but flavorful mixture of cockney rhyming slang, schoolboy reduplications, and pervasive Russian borrowings. His main joys are his gang's nightly rampages, in which the inevitable blood that flows is a welcome old friend, along with his expensive stereo and its discs of Bach and Mozart.

Alex eventually is convicted of murder, and two years into a fifteen-year stretch he volunteers for a special new two-week program that will culminate in release. Rather than merely put him back out on the streets for more "ultra-violence," however, the Ludovico Technique conditions him so strongly that, still unrepentant, he is debilitated even to imagine violence.

Released for State propaganda, he ends up beaten by police officers who just two years earlier had been fellow criminals. The opposition party, after worsening his injuries, then uses his case to topple the ruling government. The American edition of the novel published before 1986 ends with the brainwashing reversed, and a gleeful Alex ready for more savagery; the original—and restored—version ends with Alex maturing into true humanity.

Whatever the version, Burgess asks the most fundamental questions of free will, and right and wrong.

THE COLOR PURPLE
Alice Walker
1982
Novel
Sociological, African American

The life story of a poor, black woman in rural Georgia in the first half of this century brings alive issues which concern us today. This best-seller offers a rich literary experience. Highly recommended. Winner of 1982 Pulitzer Prize and American Book Award for Fiction.

At the center of this triumphant story is Celie, who gradually overcomes her disadvantages and achieves a sense of self-worth. Ranging from the early 1900's to the 1940's, the novel consists almost entirely of letters, many written in Celie's limited but highly expressive dialect.

The first letters, those of the young Celie, are addressed to God: she does not know where else to turn. Raped repeatedly by her stepfather (she believes him to be her natural father), Celie is delivered of three children by him: the first is taken out and killed; the second and third, a boy and a girl, are given to a local couple. Celie's stepfather forces her to marry Albert, who beats her and badly mistreats her.

Strangely, Albert's mistress, a blues singer named Shug Avery, frees Celie from Albert's bondage, first by loving her, then by helping her to start a custom sewing business. From Shug, Celie learns that Albert has been hiding letters written to her from Africa by her sister Nettie, a missionary. These letters, full of educated, firsthand observation of African life, form a moving counterpoint to Celie's life. They reveal that in Africa, just as in America, women are persistently oppressed by men.

Not a feminist tract, this novel nevertheless shows how black women are the victims of black men, themselves locked into destructive cultural myths concerning the nature of masculinity. In Celie's relationship with the stubbornly independent Shug Avery, "sisterhood" becomes more than a cliche.

From Shug, Celie gains not only self-respect but also a pantheistic faith in a God that is in everything and everyone. This faith is Alice Walker's as well, and it gives her unflinching portrait of racial and sexual oppression a transcending hopefulness.

THE COMEDY OF ERRORS
William Shakespeare
1592
Drama
Comedy

When a shipwreck separates twin brothers in their infancy, one comes to be reared in Syracuse, the other in Ephesus. Eighteen years later, Antipholus of Syracuse goes looking for his lost brother. After searching for seven years, he finally arrives in Ephesus and confusion ensues.

The *Comedy of Errors* opens with the threat of death. Aegeon, an elderly merchant from Syracuse, is condemned to death by the Duke of Ephesus because of enmity between the two cities. He wins the duke's sympathy by telling the story of how he was separated from his wife and one of his twin sons in a shipwreck many years before. Shakespeare intensifies an already complex plot, one that he borrowed from Plautus' Menaechmi, by adding two twin slaves, each serving a master who is himself a twin.

In the first of many coincidences, the son whom Aegeon reared, Antipholus of Syracuse, arrives in Ephesus with his slave Dromio. He is astonished when he encounters merchants and tradesmen who hand him gold chains or bills. After a woman he has never met insists upon taking him to her house for dinner and treating him like her husband, he concludes that the inhabitants of Ephesus are mad or possessed by witches.

In the last act, Antipholus of Syracuse takes refuge in a priory. When disaster seems imminent, the confusion is resolved, and Aegeon discovers that the Lady Abbess is his wife. Antipholus of Syracuse also has begun to court Luciana, the unmarried sister of his brother's wife, Adriana. Even though the play ends happily, there is a suffering as well as humor in the problems which arise from the confused identities. By making the potential for violence and unhappiness quite vivid, Shakespeare makes the audience rejoice in the happy ending.

THE COMPLETE STORIES OF SHERLOCK HOLMES
Arthur Conan Doyle
1927
Novel
Detective, Collection

The Scots physician, Arthur Ignatius Conan Doyle, invented a pipe-smoking detective by the name of Sherlock Holmes in an 1886 short story called "A Study in Scarlet" where, for the first time in fiction, a magnifying glass appears. Holmes was partially based upon Doyle's former Edinburgh Medical School professor, James Bell. Doyle began writing stories because he had few clients. In all, he wrote four novels and fifty-six short stories about Holmes.

Crime fiction and detective stories, a notable creation of English literature, were invented in early 18th century London newspapers by journalists attempting to publicize and solve crimes. Detective fiction was somewhat codified by the novels of the philosopher William Godwin, whose daughter, Mary Shelley, invented the science fiction novel.

Doyle quickly became weary of repeating his Holmes character and serial format, yet the substantial increase of revenue kept him churning out stories about Holmes and his sidekick, Dr. John Watson. Both characters became two of the most beloved and charming characters in English literature

The immense appeal of the Holmes character stems from traditional Anglo valorization of reason as the fundamental ingredient of civilization. The world of chaos is conquered by the gentleman who employs the Ariadne-like thread of logical rationality to solve problems that at first appear irrational or pathological in the murky labyrinth of criminality. In "A Study in Scarlet," Holmes says, "There's the scarlet thread of murder running through the colorless skein of life, and our duty is to unravel it, and isolate it, and expose every inch of it." This formula puts hard science to work for the first time in detective fiction.

Doyle's popular plot of Holmes reasoning backwards is loosely based upon the detective stories of London-educated Edgar Allan Poe. Being a physician, Doyle introduced forensic pathology, advanced psychology, and spiritualism to the detective genre. This threefold appeal, combined with backward reasoning, fascinated his readers and remains revelatory for his many fans.

A CONFEDERACY OF DUNCES
John Kennedy Toole
1980
Novel
Southern Gothic, Satire

A satiric novel set in New Orleans, A Confederacy of Dunces *mocks Southern bigotry and pretensions.*

The novel offers a picaresque in the tradition of Le Sage's *Gil Blas* (1735). Toole provides a Falstaffian personality who tries his hand at various jobs that lead to lunatic situations. Like the Russian comic figure Oblomov in the 1859 novel of that name by Ivan Goncharov, Ignatius Reilly, the anti-hero, is a fat, belching slob more in love with idleness than life. The dialogue in the novel brims with mischievous humor.

After an absurd night in a strip club with his mother (who drunkenly crashes her car) Reilly manages to find a job as a file clerk for Levy Pants. Forging Levy's signature, Reilly writes an amusing but abusive letter to a retailer.

Satirizing Freud, Reilly's Bronx girlfriend Myrna Minkoff, a Jewish hippie, thinks if they only had good sex, all of Reilly's problems would vanish since Reilly is obsessed with masturbation. Like Don Quixote, Reilly remains an absurd idealist with little connection to reality. Attempting to impress Myrna, Reilly leads African American workers on a strike with comic results. Reilly is fired.

Dressed in a pirate outfit, Ignatius becomes a hot dog vendor, consuming most of the hotdogs himself. With the girth of a Thomas Aquinas, Reilly prefers early medieval philosophy, especially Boethius. A firm Roman Catholic bigot, Reilly judges Mark Twain to be "a dreary fraud." Mr. Levy accosts Reilly about the forged letter and threatens to sue him. Reilly denies writing the letter, unfairly blaming an elderly lady.

Mrs. Reilly becomes angry at her son's inability to hold a job or be honest. She decides to marry Communist-obsessed Claude Robichaux and resolves to have her son, Ignatius, committed to an asylum. The Boeothian Wheel of Fortune, Lady Luck, suddenly appears in the form of Myrna Minkoff. Ignatius persuades her to rescue him. They depart for New York as the hospital ambulance pulls up. New Orleans is left in the dust with this deus ex machina ending.

The novel was published in 1980 and won a Pulitzer Prize in 1981. The frustrated, unpublished author had committed suicide in 1969.

CONFESSIONS
Saint Augustine
397-401
Nonfiction
Autobiography

Augustine explored the human personality and the nature of God in this vital Christian testimony.

Because he believed in the centrality of the Bible, Augustine interpreted his life according to his understanding of the Scriptures. The first 9 books of the *Confessions* concern God's activity in Augustine's life, both before and after his conversion to Catholicism. He attributed his earlier involvement with the heretical Manichees to a denial of biblical truth and his conversion to Catholicism to the scriptural explanations of Bishop Ambrose.

Augustine made it clear that nobody deserves God's favor, not even children. "I myself have seen and known a baby who was envious," Augustine wrote. "It could not yet speak, but it turned pale and looked bitterly at another baby sharing its milk." The teenage years are no more virtuous. Augustine recalled stealing pears when he was 16, only to throw them away. "All I tasted in them was my own iniquity, which I enjoyed very much," he confessed. By adulthood, he had left vandalism behind for fornication and devotion to a false religion. But God had mercy and sent Bishop Amborse to convert him to Catholicism.

Many testimonials would end here, but Augustine continued to confess his imperfections and God's grace. As grace is the theme of the first part of the *Confessions*, habit is the theme of book 10. According to Augustine, habit is so powerful that change is possible only through God's grace. He believed that conversion to faithfulness is an unending process.

In the last 3 books, Augustine contemplated the opening verses of Genesis. There he discovered that the meaning of life is in God's design for creation.

THE CONFESSIONS
Jean-Jacques Rousseau
1784
Nonfiction
Autobiography

Mature readers will find in the personal revelation of this noted eighteenth century social thinker the extraordinary record of a sensitive man's feelings over a half century.

Jean-Jacques Rousseau strove for a self-portrait "true to nature." Unlike the *Confessions* of Saint Augustine, this book does not attempt religious introspection and moral guidance for others, but Rousseau is like the early medieval saint in expressing his deepest convictions, though they are set forth more systematically in other books such as Emile and *The Social Contract*.

It is a fairly complete autobiography from Rousseau's birth in Geneva in 1712 to the year 1765, twelve years before his death. He frequently attests his weaknesses, such as the time when, as a boy serving in an upper-class household, he had a servant girl dismissed for his own petty theft, or his abandonment of a choir master, with whom he had been living, while the latter was suffering an epileptic fit.

Any other autobiographer would have suppressed such unflattering incidents, and Rousseau chides Michel de Montaigne, famous for his honest self-portrayal in his Essays, for having included nothing comparable. If Rousseau's facts are not always verifiable, his candor is certainly genuine.

He wrote out of a sense of his uniqueness, not of his greatness. Indeed, he believed in the uniqueness of all humans; it is simply that he knew his own story and his own self best. This conviction that the individual—good or bad—is worthy of account represents one of the author's major contributions to progressive social and political thought.

Although the revelations of a unique individual, the book has, contrary to its author's expectation, spawned many imitations in autobiography, fiction, and even poetry. His narrative skill and attractive informal style have been as much responsible as his frankness for his influence.

A CONNECTICUT YANKEE IN KING ARTHUR'S COURT
Mark Twain
1889
Novel
Satire

A blow to the head transports an average American from 1879 Connecticut to 528 England. Twain contrasts King Arthur's Camelot and his own time primarily to satirize several excesses of 19th century America.

Hank Morgan sees himself as the epitome of democratic principles and is shocked by life in feudal England. Proclaiming himself "the champion of hard unsentimental common sense and reason," he sets out to reform this society but creates chaos instead.

Taking advantage of an eclipse of the sun, Morgan supplants Merlin as the most powerful force in Arthur's court. Known as "The Boss," he sincerely intends to right wrongs by reforming the feudal system, reducing the power of the nobility and the Church, and creating industrial and other technological advances, but his successes blind him to his original goals.

He considers anyone who does not share his view of the world to be his enemy. His insistence upon reducing everything to financial terms causes him to reject the quest for the Holy Grail because there is no money in it. His own quest eventually leads him to employ a flooded moat, electrified fences, and guns to kill 25,000 knights in the name of reform.

The novel makes fun of chivalry and chivalric romances, but Twain is much more interested in addressing various evils associated with industry, technology, business, religion, slavery, war, and the idea of progress itself. Twain frequently interrupts his narrative with didactic asides about these and other matters.

Too often categorized as a children's classic, this cynical satire is much more than that. It is one of the best explorations of the ambivalent nature of the American character: inventiveness combined with self-destructiveness.

THE CONSOLATION OF PHILOSOPHY
Boethius
523
Nonfiction/Poetry
Philosophical

Philosophy, in the form of a wise woman, advises Boethius and the thoughtful reader on questions raised by a troubled spirit in a time of affliction.

This dialogue between the persona Boethius and Dame Philosophy dramatizes the interior struggle of one who feels strongly the injustices and indignities of life. Written during the imprisonment of the author, this work reflects the temptations to self-pity and despair of a person who deserves better and follows his progress toward overcoming these temptations.

Born shortly after the fall of Rome, Boethius served Theodoric as consul before falling from the Ostrogothic king's favor. Though a Christian and the author of theological treatises, Boethius here writes of the problems of evil, chance, free will, and God's omniscience from a philosophical rather than a religious standpoint. Clearly, however, Boethius shares with the later Scholastic philosophers the desire to harmonize the best Greek classical thought with Christianity.

Boethius has been called the last of the Roman poets, and this work in five books features alternating Latin prose and verse sections throughout. The former carry the discussion along, while the latter reflect lyrically on the subjects as they arise.

For more than a thousand years, *The Consolation of Philosophy* remained one of the most influential books in the Western world. Two of the most able monarchs of England, Alfred the Great and Elizabeth I, translated it, as did Chaucer, and it is indispensable to anyone who wishes to understand medieval and Renaissance habits of thought.

The work continues to appeal to those interested in pondering such problems as the relationship of God's foreknowledge to human freedom, of time to eternity. As Philosophy advises her questioner, "God views as present the coming events which happen of free will."

THE COUNT OF MONTE CRISTO
Alexandre Dumas
1845
Novel
Historical, Tragicomedy

One of the most widely recognized works of literature over the past millennia, The Count of Monte Cristo *is a tale of romance, betrayal, revenge, and the unforeseen consequences that affect all those involved.*

Alexandre Dumas' novel follows the life of the Frenchman, Edmond Dantès in the early 19th century. At the onset of the tale, Dantes' closest friends, jealous of his success in life, betray Edmond who is living a seemingly perfect life. The three conspirators—Danglars, Fernand Mondego and Caderousse—draft a letter accusing Dantès of treason, which leads to his arrest on the day of his wedding to his love, Mercédès.

While imprisoned, Edmond befriends an Italian priest, Abbè Faria. Faria educates Edmond on the finer arts throughout their time together, and upon his deathbed, Faria reveals to Edmond the location of a hidden fortune, buried on the island of Monte Cristo.

After escaping from prison in the priest's own body bag, Edmond uncovers the vast fortune believing it to be a gift from God. Disguised as an Italian priest, Edmond then travels to Marseilles where he makes amends with Caderousse, who has now become a poor innkeeper. Ten years later, Edmond suddenly appears in Rome using the title of the Count of Monte Cristo. He becomes a member of high society where his past identity is a secret to all except his former lover, Mercédès.

Implementing his long thought out plan of revenge, Edmond strikes first at Mondego, who had married Mercédès after the Count's disappearance. Edmond convinces the daughter of Mondego's former boss to testify that Mondego had betrayed and sold his boss's family into slavery. Her testimony thus ruins Mondego's reputation, forcing him to commit suicide after Mercédès leaves him. Edmond then gets his revenge upon Danglars by manipulating him into losing his fortune and his family.

Finally, Edmond uses his fortune to help Maximilian, the son of Edmond's kindhearted former employer. Helping Maximilian's love escape potential death at the hand of her mother, Edmond reunites the two of them on Monte Cristo. In the closing scenes of the novel, Edmond finally finds peace and love with the beautiful Haydee.

THE COUNTERFEITERS
André Gide
1925
Novel
Sociological

The only one of Gide's long fictions to be labeled by its author as a "novel," this book is notable both for its portrayal of character and for its continuing influence upon the development of the novel form.

Although a band of counterfeiters does in fact appear in the novel, the title functions intentionally at several levels, calling attention to the falsehood and hypocrisy of adult lives lived under the watchful, inquiring gaze of the often-disturbed children and adolescents who are, in fact, the novel's main characters.

Focusing primarily on the students and faculty of a small Protestant boarding school, the novel repeatedly contrasts the restless questioning of the youthful characters with the unquestioning smugness of their parents and other elders. For years, the students of the Pension Azais-Vedel have turned a deaf ear to the hollow, hypocritical platitudes of the pastor, Azais, and his son-in-law, Vedel, realizing that such advice does little to prepare them for the realities of life. Even the pastor's own children and grandchildren have had to fend for themselves, with often disastrous results. The opening scene, in which young Bernard Profitendieu runs away from home after discovering his illegitimacy, sets the tone for the entire novel; later, young Georges Molinier will steal a packet of love letters from his father's mistress to use as a form of blackmail.

Although somewhat confused in its organization, the action often hinging on improbable coincidence, the novel nonetheless manages to hold the reader's interest even as it explores the problems and possibilities of novel writing: Georges' maternal uncle, Edouard, a former teacher at the Pension who functions as the prime viewpoint character, is himself planning a novel of the same title that will doubtless never be written. In fact, the bisexual Edouard himself is one of the "counterfeiters" of the title, even as he remains somewhat more lucid, and honest with himself, than the other adult characters.

Notable in 1925 for its frank and open discussion of homosexuality, the novel remains so because of its exploration of the novel form, and also for such memorable characters as Bernard, the anarchist-counterfeiter Strouvilhou, and the utterly amoral, American-born Lady Griffith.

THE COUNTRY OF THE POINTED FIRS
Sarah Orne Jewett
1896
Novel
Regionalist

A young woman writer near the turn of the century spends the summer getting to know the inhabitants of an isolated Maine seaport. This novel celebrates the old folkways and mourns their passing as technology encroaches.

Deciding to spend the summer at secluded Dunnet Landing in order to work on her writing, the narrator finds the seemingly taciturn villagers only too willing to confide to her the important events in their lives and in the life of the community. The various character sketches establish the sense of place, a connection to nature, and the feeling of loss as story after story reveals a missed or thwarted opportunity.

The inhabitants of Dunnet Landing include both those who seem competent and fulfilled in life (such as Mrs. Todd, the herb-gatherer, and her mother, Mrs. Blackett, eighty-six years old but still youthful and open to life) and those who are not (such as Abby Martin who thinks she is Queen Victoria's twin because they were born on the same day, and Joanna Todd who has become a hermit after being jilted by her lover). The narrator's comments on their stories universalize the characters and their feelings.

The novel's plot emerges both from the narrator's stay at Mrs. Todd's house and from various past events in the lives of the characters she encounters. It is this interweaving which creates the texture of the novel and moves it away from the realm of a short story collection. Jewett's story primarily focuses on the women in the community and honors the lives of the elderly, but in a natural way since the loss of sea trade has limited work for the young. Despite the stagnation and decay present, the novel represents the old ways as worthy and important and their loss as lamentable.

THE COUNTRY WIFE
William Wycherley
1675
Drama
Comedy

In this naughty comedy of manners, Horner the dandy pretends impotence in order to woo and bed the wives of unsuspecting businessmen. Named for one of the victims, this play is an excellent example of the English comic style.

Returning Country Wife, Thefrom France, and with the collusion of Dr. Quack, Horner has it rumored that he has lost his manhood. Thinking their wives safe in Horner's company, Sir Jasper Fidget, Mr. Pinchwife, and others allow them to pursue whatever harmless pleasures are left to them. One by one the ladies are told the truth; their reputations, if not their honor, are safe. But Mrs. Pinchwife, newly brought from the country and anxious to enjoy all the pleasures of the city, naively threatens to expose the hoax. The ladies and the husbands, forced for their own reputations' sake to cover up the trick, let Horner get away with the wholesale cuckolding.

Restoration comedies of this kind claimed an instructive value, on the grounds that spectators seeing their follies exposed on the stage would avoid them in the future. In actuality, much of the enjoyment of The Country wife lies in the titillation of the situation, the double entendre of the language, and the then innovative practice of using women actors in female parts. The play provides for modern readers a rich source of information regarding the foppish habits of the time, the idleness of the idle rich, and the preoccupation with fine clothes (by men and women), a by-product of the French influence on English life-styles after Charles II's return from exile in 1660.

The play caused an uproar in English post-Puritan circles; criticism of its blatant sexuality led eventually to a more sentimental and moral drama in the 18th century.

CRIME AND PUNISHMENT
Fyodor Dostoevski
1866
Novel
Psychological

A nineteenth century Russian student learns that man, of necessity, must pay for crimes against others. The novel offers its readers intense psychological conflict, realistic depiction of life in St. Petersburg, suspense, and profound ethical insights.

Raskolnikov, an impoverished law student, plans to commit the perfect crime by murdering an old female pawn-broker. He hopes to gain money for himself and others and to demonstrate that he belongs to the portion of mankind not subject to conventional morality. Having studied the careers of men such as Napoleon Bonaparte, he embraces the theory that an elitist few are justified in pursuing their objectives through any means.

No sooner is the murder committed than events begin to call his theory into question. When the pawnbroker's half sister arrives unexpectedly, Raskolnikov kills her also. In his haste and confusion, he overlooks most of the money and is unable to use the small amount he does take. Following the crime, he rapidly sinks into physical and mental illness.

As the hero experiences intense guilt, other characters influence the course of his expiation. The cunning detective Porfiry discovers the truth early but waits until Raskolnikov is ready to accuse himself. Raskolnikov eventually realizes that he must choose one of two alternatives—confession or suicide.

Characters such as Luzhin and the sensual Svidrigailov defeat themselves by exploiting others for their own selfish ends. Svidrigailov's suicide demonstrates to Raskolnikov the futility of egoism. Other characters—Raskolnikov's sister, Dounia, his friend Razumihin, and Sonia, a young prostitute—willingly sacrifice themselves and suffer for others. Aided by Sonia, who grows to love him, Raskolnikov chooses life, confession, and punishment, without, however, achieving true repentance.

An intense psychological account, the narrative presents thoughts and emotions from each character's point of view. When the character is confused, the reader is also, for no authorial voice intrudes to clarify the situation. Unable to understand his own motives for the crime, the protagonist recognizes that one risks psychic disintegration by sweeping aside traditional morality.

CRITIQUE OF PURE REASON
Immanuel Kant
1781
Nonfiction
Epistemology, Philosophical

Kant explores, at great length, two interrelated questions: (1) What exactly can we know independently of sense experience? (2) Is metaphysics a true science that can answer questions of religion?

Kant begins with what he calls his "Transcendental Aesthetic," using the word aesthetic in its original meaning referring to sense experience. He wants to discover what happens as sensations such as the taste of an apple are accumulated and transformed into knowledge.

Kant's first important conclusion is that space and time are not things in themselves but rather aspects of our minds that process sensations and shape them into perceptions. The mind, then, is not passive but active, always shaping and ordering our world.

The next higher level of the mind's activity—what Kant called the "Transcendental Logic"—is the arrangement of perceptions into conceptions by means of such mental categories as causality and necessity. Perceptions mean little until the mind has winnowed them and sorted them out. Space and time, as well as cause, necessity, and other categories, are a priori. That is, they are fixed and permanent elements of our minds; they precede experience and are absolute and necessary.

The third stage of Kant's argument treats what he calls the "Transcendental Dialectic." Here Kant distinguishes between the phenomenon an object presents and its "noumenon." An apple displays redness and sweetness as phenomenal qualities, but what the apple is besides our perceptions of it we can never tell. The apple really exists and there is a "thing in itself," or a noumenon, which exists behind its appearance to our senses, but the universe of noumena is closed to our apprehension.

The Transcendental Dialectic thus provides the answer to Kant's original question about the ability of metaphysics to provide scientific answers to religious questions. The answer is no, it cannot, because our minds have no capacity for processing noumena, the things in themselves.

THE CRUCIBLE
Arthur Miller
1953
Drama
Historical

The 1692 Salem witch trials serve as a backdrop for this timeless drama of accusation, fear, betrayal, guilt, love, and honor.

As the play opens, the Reverend Samuel Parris is questioning his niece, Abigail, about his daughter Betty's mysterious illness. He discovered the girls dancing in the forest with Tituba, a slave from Barbados. Thomas Putnam's daughter is similarly afflicted. Mrs. Putnam fears witchcraft, even though she had asked Tituba to conjure the spirits of her dead children.

Parris calls in a witchcraft expert, the Reverend John Hale. Despite the common sense challenges of John Proctor and others, Hale forces Tituba to confess to witchcraft. Soon the entire town is in an uproar, and hidden resentments and land disputes become the real basis for the accusations.

Proctor's pious and unbending wife, Elizabeth, is accused of witchcraft. Mary Warren, their servant girl, is one of the accusers. Proctor makes her admit the truth: The girls had merely feigned possession by evil spirits. At the risk of disclosing his adultery with Abigail, the ringleader, Proctor forces Mary to testify.

By then Judge Danforth has arrived, who interprets any challenges or defenses as an attempt to overthrow the court's authority. In trying to save Proctor, Elizabeth condemns them both. Because she is pregnant, she is given a stay of execution.

Hale, sickened by the realization that Proctor and Mary were telling the truth, resigns from the court and tries to persuade the convicted to confess and save their lives, even though they are innocent. Elizabeth desperately wants Proctor to live. But she finally forgives him for his adultery, admits her own faults, and leaves him free to choose. When he learns that his confession will be made public, he elects the scaffold with the others who refuse to compromise their consciences and their souls. His good name is all he has to leave his sons.

The drama is based upon contemporary sources noted within the text but omitted in performance, as are explanations of the political significance of witch hunts, past and present. On stage, it is the compelling human tragedy that has made the play an American classic.

CRY, THE BELOVED COUNTRY
Alan Paton
1948
Novel
Sociological, African American

This account of racism in South Africa is both a hymn of praise to the natural beauty of a country whose people are subjected to an ugly social system and a testament to the potential good in humankind. The stylistic originality infuses the narrative with strength and conviction.

The story reveals how the practices of apartheid, as the system of racial segregation is called in South Africa, afflicts both blacks and whites in every aspect of their lives. Set in the late 1940's, the events point out that only forgiveness and understanding will break down the barriers and put in order the chaos that apartheid has created.

An old black minister travels from his village to Johannesburg, the nation's modern industrial city, to find his missing relatives. Wandering amid the black shantytowns and the great white-inhabited city which they encircle, he finds that his sister has turned to prostitution, his brother to rabble-rousing, and his son to murder. The son's victim was a white man determined to correct his country's racial problems and injustices.

Saddened, the old man returns to his village, which lies near the vast landholdings of the murdered man's father. So these two men, who have lost their sons, play out "a story of comfort in desolation," as the novel is subtitled. Through the intensity of their encounter emerges the compassion of which the human spirit is at rare times capable.

Such is the message of this work: Compassion will bring about forgiveness, love, and generosity, thus wiping away the evil that men do. Only then will "the beloved country" need "cry" no longer.

The novel made an impact at the time of its publication abroad, for it was the first widely distributed book to depict so graphically the cruel absurdity of apartheid. Yet history has proven that the solution Paton proposed has not worked. Although the ideas expressed have failed to stamp out apartheid—or any such form of separation along racial, national, or religious lines—that failure does not make the ideas any less valid.

THE CRYING OF LOT 49
Thomas Pynchon
1966
Novella
Mystery

This bizarre mystery story resembles a Moebius strip. Its protagonist, like the classic detective, finds clues that seem to add up to a vast conspiracy, but it is a conspiracy without closure, a metaphor, ultimately, of paranoia itself.

Oedipa Maas, a California housewife called on to execute the will of her former lover, the tycoon Pierce Inverarity, discovers that the estate seems consciously designed to reveal an extraordinary pattern to her. She discovers a secret: a centuries-old mail delivery system called Trystero that subsumes every conceivable pocket of disaffection in the new world—from disgruntled aerospace workers to Mexican revolutionaries to AC/DC, the Alameda County Death Cult. The more she investigates, the more evidence she finds that Trystero is everywhere, an unnoticed but terrifying presence in a troubled landscape.

In addition to being a metaphor for Oedipa's gathering paranoia, Trystero comes to suggest something more benign: an alternative to "the exitlessness that harrows the head of everyone you know" in affluent America. The Trystero is something that resists the cultural entropy that afflicts modern society—the deadly tendency to seek some level of minimal differentiation.

It is also Pynchon's model of the system, the scheme of significance, that humanity always hungers for. The modern world offers fewer and fewer verities, and absolute systems of value such as those traditionally found in religion have long since been debunked. Yet the world persists in embracing attempts at systematizing human experience, whether in scientific, religious, or cultural terms. *The Crying of Lot 49* reveals such systems as merely less obviously objectionable paranoid delusions. At the same time, it gives expression to a desperate yearning, on the part of modern civilization, for some new revelation, some new ordering principle that will redeem the post-Darwinian wasteland.

CUTTING FOR STONE
Abraham Verghese
2009
Novel
Family Saga

This bestseller by an Ethiopian doctor recounts the story of twins, born conjoined at the skull, but surgically separated. Their mother dies during the Caesarian childbirth, and their father flees. The novel becomes a quest for family reconciliation.

In 1954, Marion and Shiva Stone are born prematurely in Addis Ababa. Their mother, a Carmelite nun from India, dies during the delivery. Their British father, Thomas Stone, chief surgeon at the hospital, abandons his infants as he flees in shame, both from the woman's death and the illicit scandal. Marion narrates their story as the twins grow up at a Mission Hospital, cared for by two doctors and their wives, from Madras, India: gynecologist Kalpana Hemalatha and Abhi Ghosh who teaches himself surgery because the hospital now has no surgeon.

Although physically separated, the twins remain emotionally close, but at puberty they become rivals for Genet, the daughter of Rosina, a domestic helper in their households. Marion desperately desires to marry Genet, but Shiva manages to take her virginity. Marion feels betrayed by his brother. In anger at Genet's sexual activity, Rosina has Genet undergo genital mutilation. Genet's reaction embarrasses Rosina who commits suicide.

Marion attends medical school, while Shiva studies surgery under Hemalatha, who has a low opinion of medical schools. Shiva learns how to handle vaginal fistulas. Gosh becomes ill. He has two wishes before he dies: that Marion becomes reconciled with his brother, whom he hopes will become a successful doctor, and that Marion finds his father.

Genet joins the Eritrean Liberation Movement which opposes female mutilation. She participates in a 1979 airliner highjacking. Police discover Marion's name among her contacts. Warned, Marion departs for Nairobi, then New York. He lands a job as an intern surgeon at a Bronx Catholic hospital. For political reasons, Shiva also comes to America.

While Marion assists in an operation, a doctor enters the Bronx hospital room to witness a procedure. That doctor is Thomas Stone, visiting surgeon based in Boston, a liver surgery specialist. Discovering his biological father allows Marion to find Shiva and forgive him.

The book's title refers to a Hippocratic passage urging general practice doctors not to treat bladder stones by cutting, but to leave this operation for specialists. The novel contains medical information on many symptoms, diseases, and vivid descriptions of various surgical procedures.

All three Stone characters have been cut by family feuds and war. America is the healing specialist.

CYRANO DE BERGERAC
Edmond Rostand
1897
Drama
Historical

This play tells of a 17th century French soldier, swordsman, poet, playwright, and lover who has difficulty wooing his beloved because of his exceedingly large nose.

The play opens in a theater, where Cyrano has gone to prevent the leading actor from performing because he has made overtures to Cyrano's beloved Roxanne. After Cyrano shuts down the play, a marquis challenges him. While they duel, Cyrano composes a ballade, and at the end of the refrain, thrusts home.

Roxane, who has been watching, sends a message that asks Cyrano to meet her the next morning. He is encouraged to tell her of his love, but before he can do so, she confesses that she is in love with a handsome guardsman of his regiment and asks Cyrano to protect him. The guardsman, Christian de Neuvillette, is clever enough with men but hopelessly tongue-tied with women, and Roxane is an intellectual who must be wooed poetically. Cyrano persuades Christian to let him write speeches and love letters, which the latter will deliver. Thus Cyrano can make love by proxy.

When Christian insists on making love himself, he fumbles helplessly. Concealed by the dark, Cyrano then speaks in his own voice to Roxane. At his most eloquent, he wins her love, but it is Christian who weds her.

Though Cyrano has courage, wit, compassion, and integrity, he is undone by vanity; self-conscious about his appearance, he is afraid to woo Roxane on his own lest he be rejected. It is really Cyrano's soul that she loves; Christian would bore her within a few hours. Unable to declare himself openly, Cyrano, in trying to make Roxane happy, brings tragedy to all three of them. Despite the tragedy, the play has much humor, verve, and panache. A variation on the Beauty and the Beast tale, *Cyrano* is irresistible theater, full of wit, swashbuckling, pathos, poetry, and romance.

D

DAISY MILLER
Henry James
1878
Novella
Psychological, Regionalist

James's most famous and popular story takes its title from the heroine, Daisy Miller, a charming, somewhat naive American girl, whose tragic flaw is her social ineptness.

An early work, *Daisy Miller* is written in a simple style that avoids the ponderous and abstract vocabulary and syntax of James's later works. Also, like most of his early fiction, the tale has elements of a moral allegory and features a love triangle as the basis for the plot.

Here we have the prototype of a situation that James called the "international theme." Though he was American by birth, James spent most of his life abroad living in France, Switzerland, and England, finally becoming a British citizen. He found that his perspective on both American and European cultures could be employed in plots where characters from the new and old world interact. The international theme, in addition, was well suited to show his talents as a social historian and satirist.

Daisy Miller begins in the summer of 1875 in Vevey, Switzerland. Daisy is traveling in Europe with her mother and young brother, Randolph, trying to acquire the finish many nouveau riche Americans thought European travel would provide. She meets, without proper introduction, another American, 27-year-old Frederick Winterbourne, who has lived in Geneva most of his life. He is immediately fond of Daisy despite her laxity of deportment. After a few days of pleasant flirtation they part, agreeing to meet later in Rome.

Their reunion in January is not a happy one. Winterbourne's doubts about Daisy's morality are deepened by reports of her social eccentricities. Mrs. Costello, Winterbourne's stuffy aunt, remarks that Daisy acts as if she lived in the "Golden Age" before society had rules. One night Winterbourne discovers her in the Colosseum with an Italian admirer and decides that she is not the kind of girl he can respect. In a cutting adieu, he warns her of the danger to her physical health posed by the dank ruin. When she dies from Roman fever some time later, he learns that he was mistaken about Daisy; she was innocent and played the coquette only to attract his attention.

Despite the melodramatic denouement of a sweet young girl dying of a broken heart, qua Roman fever, the moral point of the story is serious: Naturalness and innocence are blighted by artificiality and sophistication.

DANDELION WINE
Ray Bradbury
1957
Novel
Science Fiction

Douglas Spalding, a boy of twelve, lives out the summer of 1928. This richly described book, drawn from the author's boyhood, affirms life and everyday experience.

Out looking for wild grapes with his father and brother, Douglas wakens to the fact that he is alive. He confides his realizations to his brother, Tom, and records them in a yellow nickel pad as they accumulate through the summer.

Life's bounty presents new tennis shoes, stories of buffalo stampedes by old Colonel Freeleigh, and the affection of and for John Huff, a neighborhood buddy. Family rituals provide another part of this goodness, especially the monthly gathering of dandelions for wine making. Grandfather Spalding supervises, but Douglas tends with eye, ear, and hand the mystery of preserving summer in the cellar. The bottles wait there to assuage winter's chills and colds.

Douglas wishes wonderful summer would stay put. It will not. Beloved John Huff moves away. Tennis shoes wear. The storyteller dies. Another vision assails the boy: Douglas Spalding will die some day.

Less a plotted story than a flaring of richly described episodes, the book depicts the birth of the artist as a Midwestern boy. As well, it portrays the isolation of selfhood. However full Douglas' experiences are, rupture jars them and creates anxiety. Life, initially so much a treasure, is open to doubt. Douglas utters "I hate you" to the disappeared John Huff, though he really addresses the fickleness of life. With determination, however, Douglas keeps his faith. The notebook fills up. Dandelion wine is gathered each month, an emblem of this faith.

The book works for the reader as a bottle of dandelion wine. The rich vintage of Bradbury's remembered Waukegan boyhood will vivify any reader's sense of his or her childhood. Anyone desiring to hear loud realistic acclaim for the cosmos that people mysteriously appear in and disappear from should not miss this book.

THE DARING YOUNG MAN ON THE FLYING TRAPEZE
William Saroyan
1934
Short Story
Collection

This title story from Saroyan's first published collection, at once both traditional in content and experimental in technique, tells of a destitute young writer's death by starvation.

The plot is traditional enough—a young writer, poor and starving, wanders the city streets in an attempt to stave off his hunger. He cannot find meaningful work and must sell his book to survive. In his vagaries, he dreams of food and of climbing out of his body. He finds a penny and brings it to his rented flat where he polishes it and dreams over it. Hallucinating because of his hunger, he dies alone, his imagination active to the end.

As in many of Saroyan's stories, the plot is loosely episodic, but there is a distinctly Russian flavor to this piece. The young writer's despondent wanderings about the heartless city are suggestive of Gogol's or Dostoyevski's starkly realistic portrayals of sensitive souls in conflict with an unheeding, indifferent society.

Such traditional material, however, is presented in the stream-of-consciousness technique. In the brief first part of the story entitled "Sleep," a series of dream images and associations flow through the sleeping writer's mind. This jangle of cultural, political, literary, and comic allusions all thematically suggest a cosmic imbalance, a world out of joint. Yet all is somehow unified or reconciled by the free-flight of the man on the trapeze, the writer and his imagination.

In the second part, "Wakefulness," the writer makes his rounds of the city looking for bread and work, his physical action alternating with his bitter attitude toward a society that offers him humiliation rather than life. In his room at the end, the writer withdraws into his mind, flying out of his body as easily and as gracefully as the daring young man on the flying trapeze.

DAVID COPPERFIELD
Charles Dickens
1849-1850
Novel
Victorian

One of the best-known and best-loved of Dickens' novels David Copperfield *is also the one in which Dickens reveals most about himself and the childhood experiences that marked him so deeply.*

Born to a gentle, helpless woman whose husband has died, little David is given an evil stepfather straight out of fairy tales when his mother marries the cruel Mr. Murdstone. Murdstone drives David's mother to an early grave.

Orphaned, David is sent off to school, where he encounters the additional cruelty of a tyrannical headmaster, but he also makes friends with the fascinating and Byronic James Steerforth. Put to work in the Murdstones' wine warehouse (like the blacking factory episode of Dickens' own youth), David runs away and is taken in by his eccentric aunt, Betsey Trotwood. Circumstances improve. He is apprenticed to Mr. Wickfield, his aunt's lawyer, and begins to practice law.

David introduces Steerforth into the fishing family of his old nurse, Peggoty. Steerforth seduces her niece, Em'ly, and they run away together, destroying the happiness of the family. Abandoned by her lover, Em'ly is finally tracked down and brought home by her father; Steerforth is drowned along with Em'ly's fiance, who had tried to save him. David, blind to the mature affection of Agnes Wickfield, marries Dora Spenlow, who is as pretty and childish as his mother. He becomes famous as an author. Even before Dora dies, David realizes his marriage has been a mistake.

Agnes' father has been caught up in the machinations of the villainous Uriah Heep, the apparently humble clerk who has designs on Agnes. But the plot is exposed by David and his friends, especially Mr. Micawber, and David marries Agnes.

DEAD SOULS
Nikolai Gogol
1842
Novel
Comedy, Epic

The protagonist, Pavel Chichikov, travels in a dreary Russian province buying up as many dead serfs (officially called souls) as local landowners will sell him. Since these dead souls are considered legally alive until the next decade's census removes them from the tax rolls, he intends to mortgage them before then and to settle comfortably with the money thus realized on some remote estate where his shady past would be unknown.

Dead Souls is one of literature's greatest comic epics, planned as a secular companion to Dante's *Divine Comedy* and also as a parody of the picaresque novel, with Gogol's hero ordinary and bland rather than racy and witty, and the book's episodic events commonplace rather than hazardous. While the subtlety of Gogol's humor invites comparison with Cervantes, his emphasis on provincial pettiness and paltriness, snobbery and stupidity parallels Jonathan Swift's and Gustave Flaubert's pessimistic views of human nature.

Chichikov is a pleasantly featureless hero, neither too fat nor too thin, too young nor too old, who begins the first part by arriving in a sleepy, dreary town and ends it by departing from that town. He ingratiates himself with a gallery of increasingly grotesque landowners, flatters them by his tactful conversation, is invited to visit their homes and, upon doing so, bargains more or less successfully for their dead souls.

His first transaction is with the sentimental, sugary Manilov, who mirrors Chichikov's affability. Then, he interviews the mistrustful, superstitious widow Korobochka, who echoes his slyness in business enterprise. Next, he sees the lying, disorderly Nozdryov, whose deceitfulness is a variant of Chichikov's; then the ill-tempered, brutish Sobakevich, whose calculating egotism copies the hero's; last and most horrifying, the degenerate miser Plyushkin, who dresses in filthy rags and hoards any and all trash for the sheer greed of senseless, sterile accumulation thereby representing the shadowy side of Chichikov's acquisitiveness.

Gogol's denunciation of Russia's social and moral meanness of soul dominates this book. Yet he occasionally interrupts his portraiture of emptiness and damnation with remarkably lyric digressions on his native land's future prospects for greatness among nations.

DEATH COMES FOR THE ARCHBISHOP
Willa Cather
1927
Novel
Historical

The missionary Archbishop Latour renews the Church's influence in the Southwest. His religious way of seeing makes for a spiritually profound, but not a preachy book.

After 300 years of neglect, the Catholic church decides in 1848 to reclaim the mission churches of New Mexico and Arizona. When Father Latour and Father Joseph arrive, they find rebellious priests, resentful Indians, and many humble faithful. Their mission is to bring this vast diocese, eventually including Colorado, securely into the Church.

The French priests feel lost in the desert Southwest, yet they make themselves welcome by good works and by the simplicity of their faith. They gain the confidence of various Indian tribes that live in tension with more recent settlers. They replace local priests who have betrayed their faith to gain political power, wealth, and sensual indulgence.

Their success separates the close friends; Latour becomes the Archbishop of Santa Fe, while Father Joseph eventually presides at Denver. Latour builds a cathedral while Joseph ministers to farmers and miners.

Though the novel does not preach Christianity, it sensitively portrays the religious vision of Father Latour. He believes that when one's perceptions become fine enough, then one sees and hears what is always present, the activity of Divine Love.

This belief helps him to understand and accept that the unique landscape of the Southwest will produce unique forms of faith. He is particularly sensitive to the value of tradition, to the importance of preserving the best from whatever past one has. Indeed, he sees Christianity, in part, as a kind of filter that can remove the destructive and transform the best in tradition. As a result, he is willing to accept the necessary complexity of grafting Christianity onto the ancient religious traditions of the Indian tribes, and he is willing to accept many uniquely Mexican expressions of Catholicism.

A DEATH IN THE FAMILY
James Agee
1957
Novel
Autobiographical Fiction

Inspired by the death of Agee's father in 1916, this compassionate and poetic novel focuses on the family of seven-year-old Rufus Follett in Knoxville, Tennessee, just before and just after the fatal accident of his father, Jay. In the hours and days that surround the news, Agee reconstructs a domestic routine charged with emotion by the catastrophe.

Jay Follett is called away by the message that his father, some distance away in the backcountry, is gravely ill. It will prove to be a false alarm, but another telephone call announces to Jay's wife, Mary, that Jay's car has gone off the road. The extended family gathers, but it is the children, Rufus and his younger sister, Catherine, who are the center of Agee's attention. As a sensitive but unsentimental portrait of childhood, with its full pain and sharp tactile and visual detail, its fleeting thoughts and lasting damage, this novel has rarely been equalled.

The plot, which ends with Jay's funeral, is not rich in events. What structures the book is the conflict between the parents, played out now within their son. After the death of Jay, who was never as interested in religion as his wife, Mary is seen to begin to move toward a heightened, compensatory piety, threatening to offer her children a rather unsympathetic minister, Father Jackson, as Jay's substitute. Rufus, like Hamlet, is torn between love for his mother and reverence for his father's memory. The battle lines form in him: between his mother's self-consciousness and his father's good heart, between her talkative religion and the silence of Southern masculinity, between the simple mountain people of the old South and the urban, educated middle class of the new South.

Gemlike in its precision, though it had to be pieced together by editors after Agee's own death, this novel exposes the ambivalence that made James Rufus Agee a great observer of himself and his time and echoes the yearning for communion with the South of his lost father that can be found in his other masterpiece, *Let Us Now Praise Famous Men.*

DEATH IN VENICE
Thomas Mann
1912
Novella
Philosophical, Regionalist

In this philosophical short novel, a staid German writer travels to Venice where he allows his stifled passions to run free in a pursuit of pure beauty.

The light narrative of Gustav von Aschenbach's stay in late 19th century Venice is inconsequential in itself. The events, though, serve to introduce ideas surrounding the nature of art and the artist. It is this symbolic presentation that lends the work richness and significance.

After years of uninterrupted writing, Aschenbach wishes to get away from Munich for a time. He goes eventually to Venice, a city entirely different. Although en route he meets the specter of death in various disguises, once settled in the elegant Lido hotel, he feels safe.

A Polish family staying at the same hotel has a 14-year-old son named Tadzio, whom Aschenbach beholds as the personification of pure and perfect beauty. His admiration turning to obsession, he follows the boy throughout Venice. Yet they never communicate directly. When cholera strikes the city, Aschenbach the pursuer (the artist) and Tadzio the pursued (art) move toward their inevitable doom.

It had been said of Aschenbach that he faced and lived life like a closed fist. To hold fast, to maintain discipline, and to synthesize his experience into art had forever served as his strict guides. While the outside world believes he keeps these standards to the very end, he had in secret finally loosened the strong hold on his passions when he set out in Venice to pursue pure beauty in the perfect form of Tadzio. On the beach watching Tadzio go into the waves, he at last witnesses at firsthand his ideal of beauty and attains the perfection which he had always sought. Once reaching this ultimate goal, the recorder of perfection (Aschenbach) and perfection itself (Tadzio) are ready for "death in Venice."

The struggle to understand the function and aim of art lies at the center of the work. So dense, so rich in texture and color, so abundant in symbols, Death in Venice almost reaches the perfection its hero seeks.

DEATH OF A SALESMAN
Arthur Miller
1949
Drama
Sociological, Tragedy

In the urban United States of the 1940's, an aging salesman desperately searches for personal dignity in his struggle against the unfortunate circumstances of his life.

Willie Loman is an ordinary man who embodies traditional American values of success. He has reached the age where he can no longer compete successfully in his chosen career, that of a traveling salesman. Faced with the termination of his job, he begins to examine his past life to determine its value.

At this critical point in Willie's existence, his oldest son Biff has returned home for a visit, and Willie's old desire for his son to be a traditional success in life is rekindled. But the old tensions between the two men are also renewed. Once again, to Willie's great disappointment, his son rejects Willie's values and aspirations.

In this rejection, Miller dramatizes the limited nature of Willie's values of material success and continual optimism. Willie is filled with illusions and self-contradictions which finally render him unable to function effectively in society.

When Willie's position at the company is terminated, he is driven to what seems to him to be his last opportunity for success: He decides to stage an accident in which he will take his own life so that his wife may collect on his life insurance policy.

This play ruthlessly explores the nature of the American dream for personal success. In Willie Loman's struggle to achieve personal dignity within the limited framework of his traditional values, he achieves an elevated stature which is an affirmation of the common man in American society.

THE DEATH OF IVAN ILYICH
Leo Tolstoy
1886
Novella
Psychological

This story presents a sober depiction of a dying man reluctant to renounce the false ideals by which he lived and to embrace a richer philosophy of selfless love.

Tolstoy's narrative opens with the revelation to a group of Ivan Ilyich's friends that Ivan Ilyich has died. As he presents the reactions of Ivan's friends and family to this event, Tolstoy exposes the hypocrisy and egocentricity that prevails in the cultured society of late nineteenth century Russia. He then provides an account of Ivan's life, showing how this ordinary individual, a kind of Everyman, became caught in the pursuit of material well-being and career success. Finally, Tolstoy narrows his focus to Ivan's psychology, closely examining the dying man as he tries to come to terms with his inescapable death.

Dominating this psychological portrait is Ivan's struggle against the inevitability of death. As he clings to life, and particularly to the kind of life he has led up to this point, Ivan finds himself in unbearable suffering. Only when he eases his grip on life and realizes that one must live a life of selfless giving, not selfish grasping, does he discover that dying is painless and that there is no death but merely light.

Tolstoy's story is a masterpiece of narrative art. The gradual narrowing of focus from the thoughts of Ivan's friends to the character's own psychology steadily draws the reader into the innermost realms of human experience. Tolstoy also fills his story with suggestive and symbolic detail; every element of the tale, including plot and setting, contributes to the message of the work, a message typical in Tolstoy's late fiction: One must live for others, not for oneself.

THE DECAMERON
Giovanni Boccaccio
1349-1351
Short Story/ Tales

These 100 tales, supposedly told by ten youthful narrators in ten days have the Black Death of 1348 as their macabre background. They collectively constitute one of the masterpieces of world literature.

The title, Greek for "ten days," refers to the time the fictional characters (three men and seven women) spend in telling tales to one another in the peaceful Tuscan countryside away from the plague-infested city of Florence. In the introduction Boccaccio, a firsthand witness to the Black Death, graphically describes the agonizing end that the bubonic plague inflicts on its victims and the ensuing social chaos that results from the death of so many citizens. The narrators' departure from the city represents a yearning to escape death, and the highly structured ordering of the 100 stories reflects a desire to restore order in a world gone mad.

Although each of the ten days covers a topic (such as "unhappy lovers" or "tricks wives have played on husbands"), two major themes characterize the book as a whole. The first exalts love, especially physical love, and initially appears in the work's subtitle ("Prince Galahalt"), a reference to the panderer who brought Guinevere and Lancelot together. Boccaccio dedicates his book to women and writes it in the service of love. The second theme emphasizes what man can accomplish by means of his intelligence. Foreshadowing Machiavelli, the author equates virtue not so much with piety as with cunning. The element tying these themes together and unifying the book is the realism with which Boccaccio tells his stories, whether of amorous monks at play or smart bourgeois merchants at work.

THE DEERSLAYER
James Fenimore Cooper
1841
Novel
Coming of Age, Western

The last of five novels called The Leatherstocking Tales, this book portrays the adventures of Natty Bumppo, the young Deerslayer, at the beginning of an almost mythical career as frontiersman and Indian fighter in the years before the American Revolution.

As with most of Cooper's novels, the plot is a complicated confection of chase, capture, and escape, combined with a romantic love interest. But the plot is relatively unimportant. What matters is the character of the hero—honest, God-fearing, straight-shooting, courageous, respected by his enemies, and morally superior to his peers. When, for example, the city-bred, sophisticated heroine, whose life Deerslayer has saved, offers herself in marriage, Deerslayer must courteously reject her. As the archetype of the ideal American hero, the moral embodiment of the true individualist, Deerslayer is a loner, apart from, yet superior to, the mores of an imperfect society.

Besides the character of Deerslayer, the novel contains some scenes of great narrative beauty. One such is Deerslayer's killing of his first Indian. The scene is elaborately choreographed and ritualistic, like a battle sequence in an ancient or medieval epic. When Deerslayer fatally wounds the Indian and offers the dying brave a drink of water, the warrior praises him and in his last breath bestows on Deerslayer a new name—Hawkeye.

For sheer inventiveness, the entire episode of the houseboat on the Glimmerglass is unmatched by anything else in the novels of Cooper. When the Indians attack this floating stockade, the reader follows breathlessly as, one by one, each brave attempts to get aboard. Though later mocked by Mark Twain, this scene shows Cooper's ability for fast-paced narrative action and for rendering the details of landscape with a vision approaching poetry.

DEMIAN
Hermann Hesse
1919
Novel
Coming of Age

In this psychological account of his growth to adulthood, a young German boy gains the strength to become an individual through the help of an older and wiser friend.

In this novel of development, Hesse writes a confessional novel about the struggles of Emil Sinclair, a sensitive young minister's son growing up in a small provincial German town sometime before World War I. Sinclair discovers the duality of life through the experience of being bullied by Franz Kramer, who extorts money from him until a strange new boy, named Max Demian, intervenes and rescues him. Demian (daemon, or "guiding spirit") has something timeless and unusual about him, perhaps the "mark of Cain," which sets him apart from the other boys. He befriends young Sinclair and teaches him to listen to the voice within himself.

Sinclair meets Demian again periodically throughout his adolescence, usually at some moment of crisis, when Demian offers encouragement and reassurance. Away at private school, Sinclair abandons himself to drink and dissipation until the memory of his friend calls him back to himself. He remembers how Demian had pointed to a heraldic emblem above the door to his house and said that it represented a sparrow hawk breaking free of its egg, a symbol of Sinclair's own struggle to find his destiny.

Later at the university, Sinclair meets the divinity student and organist Pistorius, a fellow seeker, who offers companionship until Sinclair finally rejects his sterile antiquarianism. Sinclair, still uncertain of his vocation and future, turns once again to Demian for advice, embarking on a search to find Demian and his mother, Frau Eva. Sinclair's infatuation with the beautiful and timeless Frau Eva suggests other unresolved psychological needs of which he is not fully aware.

Hesse's novel offers a fictionalized account of his own experiences with Jungian psychoanalysis and his struggles to become a writer. Clearly, Max Demian is something of an alter ego or "double," a dimension of the protagonist's personality that must be reintegrated in order for him to mature. Frau Eva perhaps suggests the narcissistic quality of Sinclair's self-absorption. This novel has a dreamlike quality in which both scenes and characters assume a vague symbolism. The characters may be read as external projections of struggles within the protagonist as he develops from child to adult.

DEMOCRACY IN AMERICA
Alexis de Tocqueville
1840
Nonfiction
Sociological

Alexis de Tocqueville, an aristocratic Frenchman, visited the United States in 1831-32 and observed the nature of its government and people. His analysis is still important, especially to readers interested in political and social science, economics, and history.

Since its publication in 1835 and 1840, *Democracy in America* has been noted for its insightful portrayal of the American character and democratic institutions. Initially, the French government commissioned de Tocqueville and Gustave de Beaumont to study the penitentiary system in the United States, but in their travels from the cities to the frontier throughout the young country, the two men kept detailed journals as they attempted objective observation of all phases of American life.

De Tocqueville wrote *Democracy in America* over a period of several years after his return to France and published the first pair of volumes in 1835. The work received immediate recognition as a significant study of social changes brought about by political freedom and equality. The scope of the work was much broader than originally projected and prophetic in many ways, one of which was prediction of the inevitable struggle to end slavery.

The first volumes focus on the evolution of the political order from aristocratic to democratic. De Tocqueville had to modify some of his original assumptions, one being that geographic isolation allowed the new country to thrive. He later attributed its prosperity to freedom of political institutions and equality of individuals.

Although complementary to the first part, the 1840 pair of volumes focuses more on the effects of democracy. De Tocqueville foresaw possible abuses of power, the greatest of which he considered to be tyranny of the majority. Democracy's greatest strength was also its greatest potential weakness: "Equality prompts men to indulge propensities very dangerous to freedom."

De Tocqueville's conclusions about democracy are still relevant and have implications not only for America but also for Europe and the rest of the world.

THE DESCENT OF MAN
Charles Darwin
1871
Nonfiction
Natural History

In On the Origin of Species, Charles Darwin had tried to show that species had not been created separately and that natural selection had been mainly responsible for the changes in them. The Descent of Man extends his arguments to cover the history of man.

Darwin spells out in his introduction his three-fold purpose. He will first consider whether man, like all other species, is descended from an earlier form. Then he will discuss the way man has developed. Finally, he will evaluate the differences among the human races.

Darwin develops his arguments through many examples from a wide range of sources. The first two chapters describe physical correspondences between man and the other vertebrates, concluding that to deny a common descent would be unreasonable. Only prejudice and arrogance, he says, would explain a rejection of this evidence.

Man's mental powers are compared at length with those of the other animals. Darwin finds many animals capable of some reasoning, and he also finds parallels between man's use of language and the cries of animals. Most significant, perhaps, are his tentative remarks about man's religious instincts and the instincts of animals.

Darwin devotes eleven chapters to the principles of sexual selection among animals and to their secondary sexual characteristics. The four chapters on birds give much information on the sexual functions of their plumage, their calls, and their behavior patterns.

The last three chapters are a special section on "Sexual Selection in Relation to Man." Much of the discussion in this part treats the role of beauty in determining marriages. Darwin also studies marriage customs among primitive people.

In conclusion, Darwin emphasizes that humans are descended from "barbarians." He compares our ancestors to the natives he had seen on Tierra del Fuego. Rather than being distressed by his findings, Darwin insists that man should feel pride at having ascended from lowly origins.

DESIRE UNDER THE ELMS
Eugene O'Neill
1924
Drama
Tragedy

Eben Cabot, determined to inherit his dead mother's land, buys off his two half brothers and cuckolds his father, impregnating his stepmother, who ultimately falls in love with Eben and smothers her baby to demonstrate her love for him.

Ephraim Cabot, a selfish skinflint, owns the best farm in the county. He has robbed his youngest son, Eben, of his birthright by taking land belonging to Eben's mother as his own upon her death. Eben swears to recover this land.

When Ephraim goes away, leaving his three sons in charge of the farm, Eben persuades his two half brothers, Simon and Peter, to renounce their claim to inherit in exchange for $300 each. Simon and Peter set out for California. Ephraim returns home with a new wife, Abbie.

Eben resents Abbie and is hateful to her. Meanwhile, she convinces Ephraim that they should have a child. She also seduces Eben, convincing him that he can get revenge on his father by making love to her.

Abbie bears Eben's child, whose arrival occasions a party. The celebrants realize that 76-year-old Ephraim is probably not the child's father. At the party, Ephraim taunts Eben with how Abbie has tricked him out of his inheritance. Eben confronts Abbie, who now loves him.

To show that Abbie really loves Eben, she smothers their child. Eben gets the sheriff, but then realizes that he loves Abbie. He falsely admits complicity in the infanticide. Both are arrested. Ephraim is left alone with his farm.

In this play, as in many of his other plays, O'Neill is much influenced by Greek tragedy, particularly by such plays as Euripides' *Medea* and Sophocles' Oedipus trilogy.

THE DIALOGUES OF PLATO
Plato
399-347 B.C.E.
Nonfiction
Philosophical

Although Socrates made no record of his own dialogues, they were recreated by his student, Plato.

Apology, Crito, and *Phaedo* depict the dialogues of Socrates, beginning with his trial in 399 B.C. and ending with his death. They illustrate both the thought and the integrity of Socrates.

In the fourth century B.C.E., it was no secret in Athens that the elderly Socrates doubted the wisdom of the city-state's leaders. So they brought him to trial in order to banish or at least to gag him. Formal charges: atheism and corruption of the city's youth.

The *Apology* recreates Socrates' defense at the trial. Socrates argued that he did believe in God and therefore was no atheist, and that he acted as a corrective to the corruption that permeated Athens. He said that God had given him the duty of questioning the beliefs, values, and behaviors he witnessed in Athens. Rather than punish him, Socrates said, the city should house and feed him because he performed a public service.

However, the court demanded unquestioning allegiance. So, because Socrates refused to be silenced, he was sentenced to death by poisoning.

Socrates accepted his punishment because he believed it was better to do right than to protect one's self-interest. His life on earth would be extinguished, but he would live nobly throughout eternity.

Socrates' only fault was his critical stance towards the powers that be in Athens. The oracle at Delphi had said that Socrates was unparalleled in wisdom, and Socrates confirmed this, he says, after interviewing the teachers, politicians, poets, and craftsmen of Athens. They pretended to know about matters of which they were ignorant. Socrates said that his wisdom lay in the fact that "what I do not know I don't think I do."

THE DIARY OF A MADMAN
Nikolai Gogol
1835
Short Story
Psychological

This famous story records the progression to madness of a minor clerk in a government bureaucracy. As the clerk begins to lose contact with reality, the reader becomes aware that the world around the madman is as insane as he is.

By using the diary form for his story, Gogol sets for himself the task of limiting the point of view to first person while, at the same time, showing the progressive nature of the clerk's madness and the reasons for it.

The clerk is a copyist living in poverty, subjected to and buffeted about by the whims of his superiors in the hierarchical order, without access to comforts or solace. Because of his daily frustrations, he withdraws to an imaginative world where he hears dogs speaking and reads their letters, where he fantasizes about his position, his goals, and his relationship with the director's daughter. Since his life is so circumscribed, he experiences feelings of terrible impotence magnified by his reading that a woman could accede to the Spanish throne. The "Spanish question" together with the clerk's questioning of his own identity and relevance trigger the final fantasy that the clerk is heir to the Spanish crown. Imaginatively caught up in his fantasies, the clerk loses all contact with reality. The dates of the diary move from entries normally made every few days to such nonsense recordings as "Year 2000, April 43" and "Martober 86. Between Day and Night." Ultimately, in his confusion, the clerk juxtaposes and then equates Russia, the Spanish crown, and the Inquisition with the madhouse where he finally resides. The powerful image created by this surreal juxtaposition extends at the end of the story to portray the whole world where "China is Spain."

The "diary" is not only a fine metaphor but also an apt device for telling this story. It allows for the fragmentation that mirrors the mind of the protagonist and the life he lives. It allows Gogol to present dramatically the various stages in the narrator's madness while staying within his perceptions. It also makes possible the remarkably contemporary tone characterized by pity and humor.

THE DIARY OF A YOUNG GIRL
Anne Frank
1947
Nonfiction
Biography

Written by a sensitive and perceptive adolescent, this real-life diary chronicles the daily activities of eight Jews hiding from the Nazis in Amsterdam in World War II.

When Otto Frank, a Jewish banker and merchant living in Amsterdam, decided to hide his family from the Nazis in the summer of 1942, the hiding place he chose consisted of a few rooms above his spice shop in an old section of the city. Here for over two years lived Frank, his family, and four other refugees. The story of their lives in hiding is told in the diary that Anne had been given by her parents on her thirteenth birthday.

Even in the impossibly cramped quarters of this secret annex, life goes on. Anne, in every sense a normal, healthy adolescent, records the mundane happenings in the lives of eight very different personalities. She speaks of her father's business partner, Mr. Van Daan, and of his troublesome wife; of their teenaged son, Peter, with whom Anne shares her first kiss; and of the bachelor Mr. Dussell, a Jewish dentist.

But juxtaposed with the timeless details of awakening maturity is the chilling and omnipresent threat of the Nazis. At any moment, the little band of refugees might be discovered and deported to the death camps. It is this tension between the mundane and the unimaginable that gives this slim volume much of its power.

Of the eight refugees, only Otto Frank survived the Nazi scourge. His daughter's diary, which had been found in the annex by his secretary after the Franks' deportation, was restored to him after the war. After careful deliberation, he followed Anne's wishes as expressed in the diary and published it. The book became a worldwide bestseller in the 1950's and prompted thousands of readers to write to Otto Frank to express their sympathy and admiration. During the same decade, *The Diary of Anne Frank* was successfully adapted for the Broadway stage and for the screen.

THE DIVINE COMEDY
Dante Alighieri
c. 1320
Poetry
Allegorical

Dante, the Pilgrim, journeys to God by way of the earth's center (the bottom of Hell), a mountain island in the lower hemisphere (the Mount of Purgatory), and the heavenly planets (or spheres of Paradise). This allegorical poem, representing the return of a soul to God, is a literary classic.

Dante called his Italian poem a "comedy" because it begins on a low or unhappy note (with the Pilgrim lost in the dark wood of sin) and ends on a high or happy note (with his contemplation of the Godhead).

An editor added "divine" to the title long after Dante's death, but the epithet has remained because of the work's lofty subject matter and the esteem in which readers hold the poem.

The author's stated purpose in composing the 14,233-line epic was to show the "status of souls after death." He wrote in the vernacular, rather than Latin, so that his work would be accessible not only to scholars but also to a wide reading public.

Through Hell Dante is accompanied by Virgil, symbol of Reason and Poetry and whose *The Aeneid* (book 6) was a model for the Dantean voyage to the underworld. As the two poets descend through the circles of Hell, Dante recognizes, in the gruesome but apt punishments assigned to sinners, sin's ultimate consequences. On Purgatory's isle, the two ascend a mountain where repentant sinners are purged of their sinful dispositions. At the mountaintop, Beatrice, symbol of Revelation, replaces Virgil as Dante's guide. She accompanies the Pilgrim through Paradise, home of the blessed, until St. Bernard, representing Contemplation, introduces the beatific vision.

DOCTOR FAUSTUS
Christopher Marlowe
c. 1588
Drama
Tragedy

Weary of his studies, a doctor of metaphysics seeks increased knowledge and strikes a deal with the devil to obtain it.

Doctor Faustus, a scholar famed the world over, thinks that he has reached the limits of knowledge in philosophy, medicine, law, and theology, and he hungers for power. Magic lures him with the offer of knowledge without work or study, and Faustus sells his soul to the devil in return for 24 years during which he will have everything he wants.

Faustus begins with grand plans: to free his country, to help the poor, and to make himself master of the world. In the scenes that follow, the reader never sees him even try to reach these goals.

Instead, he performs parlor tricks for the Emperor and plays practical jokes on the Pope. When he asks his servant devil Mephostopilis, the secrets of the universe, he gets what he calls "freshman" answers. Only at the end of the play does Faustus realize that he has tried to get something for nothing: knowledge without work and power without responsibility.

Marlowe's gorgeous language tends to hide the meanness of his character's desires. Time and again, Faustus begins to repent, only to be distracted by spectacle or frightened by threats.

Marlowe's play, first staged in 1592 or 1593, presents a figure who is a mirror: Each age sees Faustus in its own terms. Readers during the Romantic period, often more interested in the struggle than the goal, saw Faustus as an "overreacher," someone who pushes the limit of what humans can achieve. The very fact that he was doomed to failure only made him more interesting.

Contemporary readers are more likely to see Faustus as an example of "burn-out," a man whose life has become stale because he has no interests beyond himself.

DR. JEKYLL AND MR. HYDE
Robert Louis Stevenson
1886
Novella
Gothic, Horror

Dr. Henry Jekyll, a distinguished scientist and philanthropist, experiments with personality altering drugs which turn him into Edward Hyde, an evil, violent beast in this most bizarre of all Stevenson's tales.

The novelette is told from a variety of points of view and focuses on the search for the connection between the saintly Jekyll and the demon Hyde and concludes with the doctor's written confession of the experiments that ultimately render him permanently transformed into the Hyde figure. In his confession Jekyll admits that Hyde has taken over as his true nature and that he allows himself to be transformed. It is only after he discovers that he is unable to reassert control over the experiment, even though he is using ever stronger drugs, that he shuts himself in the laboratory and commits suicide by taking a lethal dose of poison.

More than a stock tale of science gone wrong, this work contains a serious discussion of the duality of human nature with the uncomfortable and inescapable conclusion that evil is not only more powerful than good but also more attractive. In the Hyde personality Jekyll is provided a welcome escape from the oppressive respectability of his life.

Stevenson attacks the rather heavy-handed morality and religious principles of the late Victorian world and charges that repression of natural urges can result in monstrosities as grotesque as those perpetrated by Hyde. Jekyll's need for freedom from conventionality is strong enough that he is seduced into not only experimenting with drugs but also into willingly succumbing to Hyde's persona. It is a disturbing tale which indicts the notion of progress through science while revealing a pre-Freudian glimpse of the beasts which hide within the human psyche.

DOCTOR ZHIVAGO
Boris Pasternak
1957
Novel
War

This complex, poetic novel treats great questions of human existence—love, freedom, death, immortality—against the backdrop of World War I and the 1917 Revolution in Russia.

Yury Zhivago perceives life with mystical, religious intensity. Keenly aware of his soul's intimations of immortality, Yury seeks out others searching for answers to life's mysteries.

After his parents' deaths, ten-year-old Yury lives with Uncle Nikolai whose philosophy of progress and mysticism touches the boy's poetic instincts. Later Yury lives with a professor's family and is inspired to become a doctor. He marries Tanya, the professor's daughter.

When war with Germany comes, Yury serves at the front as a surgeon. He is attracted to Lara, a married nurse, but the fighting separates them. Returning to Moscow, Yury finds family, property, and personal identity threatened by the Revolution's leveling force. Yury takes his family into the Ural Mountains.

Here he meets Lara and professes his love. The Communists capture Yury, forcing him to serve until he escapes. When Tanya returns to Moscow, Yury and Lara live together. Life is idyllic: Yury writes poetry about their transcendent love which puts them at peace with all creation.

When the townspeople label the lovers counter-revolutionaries, Yury forces Lara to escape with a protective Soviet official while he flees to Moscow. His wife and daughter have gone to Paris so he befriends his half brother, Evgraf. For several years he practices medicine and writes verse. He dies on the same day Lara comes to the capital. Later Evgraf publishes Yury's poetry.

Doctor Zhivago is slow but rewarding reading. The plot is less important than the characters' insights into their aspirations and compromises. Without denying life's frequent cruelty, Pasternak affirms the individual soul's power to transform itself by inward reflection and outward reaching.

A DOLL'S HOUSE
Henrik Ibsen
1879
Drama
Psychological

A woman discovers that she has given the best years of her life to a man who has treated her with indulgence and apparent love, but who nevertheless has prevented her from developing her own individuality.

Nora Helmer has been married for eight years. Her husband, Torvald, has assumed the typical male role of his age; namely, that of his wife's guardian, protector, and provider. On one occasion Nora has acted independently, however. Early in their marriage, Torvald was ill and could save his life only by spending some time in a mild and dry climate. Nora, who was aware of this fact, forged her father's signature in order to borrow money for a trip to Italy (at the time, women were barred by law from contracting debts on their own). Nora is proud of her action, however illegal, for she regards it as her life's sole expression of individuality.

As the play begins, Torvald Helmer has just become the manager of a local bank. The family's future (there are by now three children) is bright. Then Krogstad, a known embezzler from whom Nora had borrowed the money, presents himself. Excluded from polite society on account of his crime, he now hopes to rehabilitate himself by obtaining a position in Helmer's bank. He threatens Nora with exposing her forgery if she does not use her influence with Helmer in his behalf.

When Nora is unable to persuade her husband to offer a position to Krogstad, the latter writes a letter informing Helmer of Nora's forgery. This touches off a discussion which constitutes the central scene in the play, and where the theme of women's emancipation becomes most clearly visible. Helmer condemns Nora severely, and she becomes fully conscious of the fact that she has no chance of becoming an individual as long as she remains Helmer's wife. At the end she leaves her husband and children in order to find herself.

DON JUAN
Lord Byron
1819-1826
Poetry
Epic

This satirical poem interweaves the loves and adventures of its charming title character with the amusing opinions of its narrator, a sophisticate much like Byron himself.

Although the Don Juan of literary and operatic tradition is a coldly amoral seducer, Byron's version of the character begins as a sheltered youth but is progressively tarnished by his worldly experiences. A wellborn Spaniard, Juan is sent abroad when his mother and her lover, Don Alphonso, discover him to be having an affair with Alphonso's 23-year-old wife, Julia.

Don Juan's grand tour of Europe, from Greece, Turkey, and Russia to England, contains all the material of epic convention: storm and shipwreck, slavery, warfare, and political diplomacy. Most prominent among his experiences, however, is love. Juan's seduction by Julia is soon followed by an island idyll with a pirate's daughter, Haidee. Enslaved by the pirate, he is purchased for the pleasure of a sultana, makes a conquest of a pretty harem girl, and, after aiding in the Russian victory at Ismail, becomes the latest in Catherine the Great's parade of paramours. The poem ends at an English country house where three aristocratic beauties vie for his attentions.

The tale of *Don Juan* is a lively one, but much of the time only a pretext, a thread on which Byron strings the pearls of opinion. Byron's digressions—some serious, some lighthearted, some savage, but all eloquent—treat a wide range of subjects. Byron shares his religious doubts, political convictions, and poetic values. He describes what he has read, eaten, seen, and felt. He shares his preferences and fiercely attacks his enemies, especially William Wordsworth, the poet laureate Robert Southey, the British Foreign Secretary Lord Castlereagh, and Lady Byron, from whom he had separated. *Don Juan*'s candor scandalized some 19th century readers but tends to delight its modern audience.

DON QUIXOTE DE LA MANCHA
Miguel de Cervantes
1605-1616
Novel
Picaresque

This classic tale of the insane, self-styled knight-errant provides a satirical view of the author's society and has inspired other writers for more than three centuries.

Alonso Quijana, a Spanish country gentleman, is crazed by his reading of medieval romances. He resolves to go forth to right the world's wrongs and champion the downtrodden. Having himself "knighted" by an innkeeper who humors him, Alonso takes on a new name—Don Quixote de la Mancha—and a squire, the peasant Sancho Panza.

Seeking adventure, Don Quixote interprets everything he sees in terms of his chivalric fantasy. As a would-be righter of wrongs, he challenges many ordinary men who he imagines are committing injustices. Though sometimes victorious, he receives many beatings in these encounters. Some people also take advantage of his illusion to make him the butt of cruel jokes.

Through all of these mishaps, Sancho occupies an unenviable position. He ministers to his master's illusion while striving to protect him from its direst consequences. Sancho does not always succeed in this paradoxical role, but he does add cheer with his jokes and commonsense maxims.

A supreme challenge to three and a half centuries of readers has been how to interpret Quixote. Is he merely a ridiculous and pathetic victim of illusion, or a representative of all that was most noble in a bygone age? Another strong point of interest is the other characters' reaction to Quixote's madness. A few try to coax him out of his fantasies and back to the sensible, if dull, life of a country gentleman. Many more encourage him to continue, thus amusing them with his insane antics.

Some have called *Don Quixote de la Mancha* one of the world's two or three greatest novels. Others rate it much lower, citing its haphazard construction. In any case, this novel has remained a highly influential classic whose protagonists have become household words. *Don Quixote de la Mancha* has stimulated the work of later authors as diverse as Fielding, Dickens, Stendhal, Flaubert, and Dostoevski.

DRACULA
Bram Stoker
1897
Novel
Gothic, Epistolary

Vampire legends occupy a central place in European folklore and provide a resilient thematic resource for fantasy fiction. Dracula is the most famous of the fictional vampire creatures.

Jonathan Harker, a young English solicitor, travels to Transylvania to transact business with Count Dracula, for whom he has purchased an English country home. With business concluded, Harker finds himself Dracula's prisoner as well as his blood donor. Shortly thereafter, the Count sails for England, leaving Harker behind, a captive in Castle Dracula.

In England, Mina Murray, Harker's fiancee, visits her friend, Lucy Westenra, who is suddenly stricken with an unexplained illness. One night Mina follows Lucy during one of her sleepwalking episodes. In a churchyard, Mina finds a tall, thin man embracing Lucy, but the man disappears at Mina's approach. Upon waking, Lucy remembers nothing of the incident.

Lucy's condition worsens, and a local doctor, Dr. Seward, calls in a Dutch medical specialist, Van Helsing, who has studied the occult sciences as well as modern medicine.

When Harker returns to England and tells his story to Van Helsing, the doctor believes that Harker's Count Dracula was a vampire and that he and Lucy's assailant are one and the same. Despite their attempts to protect her from Dracula, Lucy dies as a result of the monster's blood lust. In order to save her soul from eternal damnation, Harker and Van Helsing are required to mutilate her body. They then pursue the fleeing Count back to his ancestral castle in Transylvania, where they are finally able to kill him by driving a knife into his heart and cutting off his head just as the sun rises.

This is the quintessential story of the vampire, thing of the undead who has haunted the memory of the European mind for centuries. Although a fantasy complete with open graves and Gothic trappings, the novel is also a fascinating study of suppressed sexuality, especially sublimated female sexuality. It also contains a critique of 19th century notions of social order and progress through science. Van Helsing must use his knowledge of the black arts in order to destroy Dracula; modern science is not sufficient.

Like other studies of the irrational written during the Victorian period, this tale exposes the dark side of human nature and reveals the marginal control exercised by the rational, scientific mind over the forces of evil and chaos.

DREAM OF THE RED CHAMBER
Cao Xeuqin
1791
Novel
Historical

Written in the middle of the 18th century, this novel, sometimes translated as The Story of the Stone, *remains one of the great novels in the Chinese canon. First printed in 1791, the first edition contained forty more chapters written by Gao E and Cheng Weiyuan, added to the original eighty. The dialect of the novel became the dominant language of spoken Chinese, Beijing Mandarin.*

The novel traces the fortunes of two aristocratic clans that live next door to each other. This partly autobiographical novel presents a melancholy memorial to the author's family and the declining Qing dynasty, especially for the women who were aristocrats, servants, and relatives. There are forty main characters and about five hundred minor characters.

The frame story presents a Buddhist parable about a sentient stone being incarnated to discover what the moral reality of human life is like. Grandfather's favorite, Jia Baoyu, born with a jade stone in his mouth, has just reached puberty when the novel begins. He falls in love with his two beautiful cousin playmates: Lin Daiyu, a romantic, rebellious, narcissistic lady of striking allure, accomplished in poetry and music, who has a respiratory affliction, and Xue Baochai who is more plump, reserved, and intelligent, possessing gracious consideration of others.

Through a family trick, Jia marries Xue Baochai and virtually goes insane; he really loves Lin Daiyu who dies shortly afterward from frustrated longing. Xue's brother acts as the archetypical Don Juan, hatching scandal after scandal.

Jia Yuanchun, Jia's older, accomplished sister, becomes a consort of the Emperor, who builds a gorgeous garden for her reception. When she dies, Jia is stripped of his rank, his grandmother dies, his properties are confiscated, and a nun in the family is abducted. Through the help of a monk, Jia resolves to reform and he passes the civil examination, ranking number seven. Although his wife is pregnant, Jia decides to leave her and become a Buddhist monk.

The story's excesses of romance and sexuality, to which many reformers object, functions as a moral warning about the illusory nature of virtuous or romantic love. The dominant theme of dream indicates the frail boundary between truth and fiction, and the terrain where fiction becomes truth amid the transient world of clouds.

Due to the delicacy of echoing linguistic nuance, there will probably never be a satisfactory translation into any Western language.

DUBLINERS
James Joyce
1914
Short Story
Collection, Regionalist

This collection of fifteen subtle, depressing stories presents the frustrations encountered at each successive stage of life by the lower-middle class citizens of Dublin at the beginning of the 20th century.

Joyce views his native city as a center of paralysis, denying its citizens opportunities to grow in understanding of themselves and the social forces that determine their lives. Through the successive stages of childhood, adolescence, adulthood, and public life, this theme of insufficiency of will is pursued: only the final story, "The Dead," brightens this gloomy portrait of a moribund society by the recognition of its humor and hospitality.

Each of these deceptively simple stories focuses on an epiphany (a moment of insight into character or society). The complex and brilliant handling of language and structure suggests levels of meaning beneath the dull surface of the texts. The effect of this technical virtuosity is to illuminate the historical, mythological, political, and social patterning which make all but impossible the assertion of psychological freedom in the Dublin of 1900.

The protagonists in these stories are caught in circumstances beyond their control, and they surrender pathetically to them. They are the victims of self-deception, clumsy educators, greed, laziness, colonialism, religious servility, and an excessive desire to be socially accepted. Only in "The Dead" does Joyce indicate that his native Ireland may have the spiritual resources to counter its malaise.

THE DUNCIAD
Alexander Pope
1728-1743
Poetry
Epic

This mock-epic poem, satirizing Pope's literary enemies as dunces and minions of the great goddess Dullness, grows into a prophetic warning of the triumph of mediocrity over civilization.

During the early days of Grub Street, a turbulent age of satire, party journalism, and personal attack, few writers had as many literary enemies as Alexander Pope. But amid this hurly-burly of hacks, critics, scholars, and publishers, the waspish, sickly Pope easily held his own, giving point to his pronouncement that "the pen is mightier than the sword." Like Dante in *The Inferno*, Pope salted away his enemies in *The Dunciad*.

Two versions of *The Dunciad* were required: a 1728 three-book version featuring Lewis Theobald Pope's rival editor of Shakespeare, and a 1743 four-book version with Colley Cibber—actor, playwright, theater manager, and poet laureate—as the hero who epitomizes mediocrity and bad taste. Both versions enroll dozens of other names in the catalog of dunces.

Written in heroic couplets (rhyming iambic pentameter) and recalling the epics of Homer, Virgil, and Milton, *The Dunciad* moves from a specific to a general perspective. In book 1, Dullness recruits the hero out of Grub Street and crowns him king of her empire. Book 2 provides a pause in the main action as the legions of Dullness celebrate their epic games, including such appropriate competitions as urinating, racing through filth, diving into sewer ditches, and staying awake while dull literature is read (all are lulled to sleep, including the readers).

In Book 3, the hero in dreams visits the underworld, where he meets the souls of past dunces, who prophesy the imminent victory of Dullness' kingdom. In Book 4 the conquest of Britain occurs, as the army of dunces overruns literature, politics, science, and learning, and "universal darkness buries all."

DUNE
Frank Herbert
1965
Novel
Bildungsroman, Science Fiction
This epic novel offers a thrilling adventure story, a multilevel examination of different philosophies and mythic patterns, and a detailed, comprehensive portrait of the planet Arrakis, known as Dune.

The center of this novel is Paul Atreides, a young man who grows to power and self-knowledge on the desert world Arrakis several thousand years in the future. Arrakis is a harsh world but also the only source of the spice melange, a highly prized substance in the intergalactic Imperial society.

Paul's family, the House of Atreides, has recently taken over Arrakis, but Baron Harkonnen, the planet's former ruler, attacks the newly arrived Atreideses, kills Paul's father, Duke Leto, and forces Paul and his mother, the Lady Jessica, to flee into the desert. Paul must make contact with the Fremen, Arrakis' native inhabitants, and enlist their aid in overthrowing the Harkonnen forces.

Paul must also develop and control his clairvoyant powers for they are the key to his success, enabling him to see the various forces that influence events. Through them, Paul becomes a leader of the Fremen and the founder of a new Fremen religion, giving him the military strength to fight the Harkonnens and, what is more important, providing him with the self-knowledge he needs to control his own destiny.

Beneath the adventure-story plot, with battles and intrigues, the novel explores the mythic patterns of the human mind. Paul's life conforms to that of the hero archetype with his noble origins, mystic powers, flight into the wilderness, contact with a foreign people, and avenging of his father's death. Herbert wished to show the disruption of a society by a messianic superman figure.

The novel is also a fascinating study of ecology, revealing the interdependent facets of Arrakis, from the climate to the Fremen religion. Part of Paul's development is his awareness that human society is as interconnected as a planet's ecology and that it is impossible to have complete knowledge or control of all the factors making up either. Allowance for the unknown and quick adaptability are the wisest measures because, as the novel reveals, the universe remains a mystery.

E

THE EARTHSEA TRILOGY
Ursula K. LeGuin
1968-1972
Novel
Trilogy, Science Fiction

From the time that Segoy spoke the First Word and raised the numberless isles of Earthsea from the depths, magic, grand and small, has been a natural part of everyday life. Yet, while knowledge of the original, secret names of things—and of people—can bring enormous power, the great equilibrium must be maintained, as even wizards may learn at their peril.

In *A Wizard of Earthsea,* when young Ged, known as Sparrowhawk, challenges a condescending oldster student-wizard to a test of strength, the talented yet prideful novice accidentally releases something horrible and dark into the world. The terrible thing first stalks him, yet eventually flees, until finally Ged realizes the truth: this darkness is but a part of him, and he must accept it to become whole.

The Tombs of Atuan follows lonely Tenar in her training as priestess to ancient spirits called the Nameless Ones. When Ged, now several years older, comes to Atuan seeking the other half of the ring of the great Erreth-Akbe, whose Lost Rune can bring peace to the world, Tenar eventually helps Ged, her enemy. The pair escapes the oppressive underground labyrinth and return to the Inmost Sea in triumph.

In *The Farthest Shore,* the experienced Ged, now Archmage of all wizards, must journey with the newly met but devoted Prince Arren of Enland, to find the evil that is draining magic from the world. In facing a necromancer, whose refusal of death upsets the great equilibrium, Ged uses the last of his power, and Arren finds his full inner strength; the old man then retires, and the youth ascends the throne of all Earthsea.

Weaving together not only wizards and dragons and the tales of heroes, but also the simplicity and beauty of nature, and the profundity of balance in the cosmos and, ultimately, in the human soul, LeGuin's Earthsea Trilogy remains a powerful and life-affirming masterpiece.

EAST OF EDEN
John Steinbeck
1952
Novel
Historical, Regionalist

This epic history traces three generations of two families—the Trasks and the Hamiltons—that settled the Salinas Valley in California during the late 19th and early 20th centuries.

The story is told by an intrusive narrator, the son of one of Samuel Hamilton's daughters, who lyrically describes the Salinas Valley during the early 20th century. The primary themes are those of jealousy and betrayal as well as loyalty and love set in the contexts of familial relationships. Steinbeck is particularly interested in the Cain and Abel myth, as he explores the interactions between two sets of brothers, Adam and Charles Trask and Adam's twin sons, Cal and Aron.

The novel begins with the difficult relationship between Adam and Charles, who grow up on a farm in Connecticut. Like the biblical Cain, Charles tries to kill Adam out of jealousy, and, when Adam falls in love and marries the amoral

Cathy, Charles sleeps with her. After Cathy and Adam move to the Salinas Valley to begin a dynasty, Cathy gives birth to twin boys, Cal and Aron, but deserts Adam and her newborn sons to become madam of a house of prostitution in the growing city of Salinas.

In this rich, extraordinary novel, Steinbeck explores a variety of themes. One is the civilizing of the American West, especially California, which begins with honest and hardworking homesteaders, such as the Irishman Samuel Hamilton who represents self-sufficiency, inventiveness, and goodwill. The wealthy Adam Trask, on the other hand, represents the decadent East. Although basically benevolent, Adam has difficulty making moral judgments and must buy the services of men such as Hamilton and his faithful and philosophical Chinese servant, Lee, to survive.

Steinbeck also explores the theme of inherited dispositions by creating innately immoral characters, such as Cathy and Charles, as well as naturally benevolent characters, such as Hamilton and his children, most of whom, in different ways, become successes. Instead of moral condemnation, Steinbeck treats all characters with respect and dignity, suggesting that humans, good and evil, interact to construct a complex social and moral tapestry.

Steinbeck's central message in this moralistic novel is the necessity of forgiveness and acceptance. Given that the human character can be formed for good and evil, humans must be willing to accept and to understand both.

EASTER 1916
William Butler Yeats
1920
Poetry
Lyric

A complex poem which simultaneously expresses admiration, tenderness, and grave misgiving, Yeats' "Easter 1916" commemorates the men and women who led Ireland in the brief, unsuccessful Easter Rebellion to gain independence from British rule.

The poem begins by paying tribute to the Irish people for leaving behind their previously mundane, trivial lives to dedicate themselves to the fight for independence. In lines which become a refrain, Yeats proclaims, "All changed, changed utterly: A terrible beauty is born."

The second stanza singles out individual martyrs, killed or imprisoned for their activities, among them his childhood friend Countess Markiewicz (nee Constance Gore-Booth) and Major John MacBride, the husband of Maud Gonne, the woman Yeats had loved long and unrequited. Although he had considered MacBride merely "a drunken, vainglorious lout," Yeats acknowledges that he too has been ennobled by his heroism.

Stanza 3 notes paradoxically that these martyrs are all changed in that they have become unchanging: their hearts, united by one purpose, have become unchanging as stone, in disturbing contrast to the living stream of ordinary human life. In a characteristic shift of mood, Yeats uses the stone metaphor to warn of the danger of fanaticism: "Too long a sacrifice can make a stone of the heart."

The final stanza raises but quickly abandons essentially unanswerable questions about the duration and value of the Irish struggle and the trustworthiness of England's promise of independence. Instead Yeats confines himself to the more modest task of paying tribute to the fallen patriots by naming them with the tenderness of a mother naming her child. While acknowledging the awful finality of death, Yeats proclaims the meaningfulness of their enterprise, in which they doffed the "motley" of their former clownish days to don green in a life both terrible and beautiful in its purpose.

With rare compression, Yeats not only succeeds in expressing his ambivalence about patriotism in general and about the Irish cause in particular, but he also allows the reader to follow sympathetically the shifts of thought and feeling in the troubled mind of a poet who is both critical and compassionate.

THE EDUCATION OF HENRY ADAMS
Henry Adams
1907
Nonfiction
Autobiography

Henry Adams never called this book an autobiography. Rather, he regarded it as a case study of the laws of history, with himself as the experiment and the book as a record of the operation of those principles upon his life.

Writing of himself in the third person to increase the sense of objectivity, Adams presents himself as one unable to cope with the multiplicity of the twentieth century. His education, rooted in eighteenth century rational humanism, had told him that the world is orderly. Yet his experiences had proved to him that chaos is the law of nature; order is the dream of man.

To establish this myth of failure, Adams distorts and deletes facts. He dismisses his monumental historical writings and his work for his father in the American embassy in London during the Civil War. He also skips over the twenty most productive years of his life (1872-1892). The style, too, is somber, the frequent passive constructions stressing Adams' vision of himself as a victim of forces beyond his control.

As a record of Adams' life, then, the work is not always trustworthy. It does, however, accurately reflect Adams' disappointments: He had longed for political power that eluded him, his sister had died tragically in 1872, and his wife had committed suicide in 1885.

The book also demonstrates Adams' lifelong quest for a unifying historical principle—that dream of order—to explain the movement from twelfth century unity (discussed in Adams' previous book, *Mont St.-Michel and Chartres*) to twentieth century multiplicity. Near the end of the *Education* he presents "The Dynamic Theory of History," arguing that changes occur with increasing rapidity and that the twentieth century is beyond man's ability to control. In his fear for the future of mankind, he expressed a concern common to his time—and to ours.

THE EIGHTY-YARD RUN
Irwin Shaw
1941
Short Story

Combining the themes of sports and mance, this vividly narrated story should appeal to readers of all ages, those who, like its hero Christian Darling, desire to recover a lost youth and those who have not yet lost it.

Christian Darling returns to the football practice field of a Big-Ten university where fifteen years earlier he experienced his greatest achievement in life—an eighty-yard run during scrimmage. Details of the moment when he felt invincible and invulnerable rush back to him, followed by the story of his subsequent career, all in a reverie.

Although Christian's girlfriend, Louise, had been impressed, his final two years as a starter produced no further moments of glory. The bid for stardom failed when another back, an All-American, joined the team after Christian's moment of triumph.

After marriage, Christian and Louise moved to New York, where he spent a few happy years as a sales representative for her father's company, until the crash of 1929 left him unemployed. Louise joined the editorial staff of a woman's fashion magazine, and Christian found solace in drinking.

Louise blossomed in her new environment, giving parties for artists, poets, intellectuals, and labor leaders. Although these events bored him, Christian could not entirely ignore his own inadequacy. Still in love with Louise, he took temporary sales jobs, and finally accepted one as a traveling agent for a custom clothier, a job that brought him back to is alma mater.

Recalling his triumph, Christian has a moment of insight, of recognition: He had not adequately practiced for New York City, for 1929, or for the change of a girl into a woman. His effort to relive the momentary invincibility that came to him fifteen years earlier astonishes a young couple who have noticed him on the practice field.

Narrated with admirable economy from Christian's point of view, the story touches upon the themes of lost youth, unfulfilled potential, and the alienation that develops in relationships when one partner outgrows the other.

ELECTRA
Euripides
413 B.C.E.
Drama
Classical, Mythology

Euripides presents an unusual variant to Electra's plot to kill her mother, Clytemnestra, and her mother's lover, Aegisthus, who have murdered her father, Agamemnon. Though not pure tragedy, the play has a marked psychological emphasis and a strong Freudian theme.

Though princess of Argos, Electra is give in marriage to an old Argive farmer to prevent her from bearing a son who might avenge Agamemnon's death. Still, this marriage serves Electra's purpose. It allows her to remain chaste and plot the double murder. She lives for her brother Orestes' return and remains intent on revenge. Obsessed by Agamemnon, Electra allows no man to touch her, not even her brother when he returns in disguise.

Electra often reveals a morbid attachment for her murdered father. Significantly, the old farmer, who becomes for Electra a father surrogate, eventually identifies Orestes, reunites him with Electra, and suggests the double killing. With delight, Electra plans her mother's death. Appropriately, the farmer plays a key role in the plot. He will announce to Clytemnestra the birth of his non-existent son. This will bring her to Electra's cottage and to her death.

Caught up in the scheme, Electra tells the farmer to guide Orestes to the place where Aegisthus performs sacrifices; there, Orestes will murder his mother's lover. Subsequently, a messenger announces that Aegisthus was killed as he was sacrificing to Zeus. Orestes returns, and he and Electra encourage each other in the murder of Clytemnestra despite unfavorable omens.

Clytemnestra enters only to fall by Orestes' sword. The play ends with the appearance of the Dioscuri, the stars Castor and Pollux, who stop the action by proclaiming the future of Electra and Orestes. The new marriage they foretell for Electra to Orestes' companion and foil, Pylades, is typical of Euripides' cynicism. It implies both the annulment of Electra's arranged marriage and her unsuitability to any other man.

EMMA
Jane Austen
1816
Novel
Manners

This perfectly constructed novel sympathetically satirizes the various pretensions of the citizens of the village of Highbury—including the wellborn, matchmaking heiress of Hartfield, Emma Woodhouse.

Emma is rich, beautiful, and clever, with time on her hands to devote to remaking the lives of others whom she regards as less fortunate and less clever. When her companion and former governess, Miss Taylor, marries a neighboring widower, Emma finds herself even more restless than usual. She takes under her wing young Harriet Smith, a pretty girl who admires Emma as a paragon of sophistication.

Emma sets her sights on marrying Harriet to a snobbish young rector, Mr. Elton, but he misunderstands her attentions and proposes marriage to her, instead. This defeat does not diminish Emma's matchmaking ambitions, which are given added encouragement when another young man, Frank Churchill, and a young woman, Jane Fairfax, appear in the small community. Emma's friend Mr. Knightly, the brother of her sister's husband scolds her for playing with other people's lives, but she refuses to listen to him.

In the end, the various couples are sorted out, according to social class and emotional inclination, and Emma discovers that she actually loves Mr. Knightly. She was wise enough, finally, to see the errors of her ways, and to reform. No longer will she consider the villagers as puppets for her amusement.

This witty, entertaining novel is also the most profound of Jane Austen's works. Written with complete technical control, it resonates with a deep understanding of human nature. Austen never blinked at the foibles that plague human beings, but she did not despise the men and women of her books because they were imperfect. She had that rare ability to portray the foolishness in a person without a loss of sympathy.

THE EMPEROR OF ALL MALADIES: A BIOGRAPHY OF CANCER
Siddhartha Mukherjee
2010
Nonfiction
Scientific

In this Pulitzer Prize–winning "biography," a practicing oncologist inquires into what humans have learned over four thousand years about this most dreaded of diseases, and considers whether we can hope to defeat it.

Cancer is not one disease but many diseases with a shared mechanism. The political and cultural contexts in which we have encountered cancer have profoundly shaped how we think about it. The nineteenth-century surgeon's inscription, from which Mukherjee draws his title, also calls cancer the "king of terrors"— characterizing not so much the disease, but how humans have experienced it. Mukherjee calls cancer a "shape-shifter," capturing both its medical nature and its nightmarish grip on our psyches.

Having planned to write a journal of his two-year advanced medical oncology training at the famed Dana Farber Cancer Institute and Massachusetts General Hospital in Boston, Mukherjee became immersed in a much broader quest to understand the disease through its history, beginning with the spare account in an Egyptian text dating from 2500 BCE. The book's chapters traverse several historical arcs preceding and following the emergence over the mid-to-late nineteenth century of a theory of cellular biology based on direct microscopic observation of the behavior of cells. The resulting recognition that cancers were the result of uncontrolled proliferation of cells led to advances in the understanding of the root mechanism of the many forms of cancer, despite their very different manifestations.

By the mid-twentieth century, further advances in research—and unexpected, even accidental breakthroughs— led pathologist Sidney Farber (the cofounder of the clinic in which Mukherjee labored) and others to believe that the "death" of cancer was imminent. Socialite Mary Lasker and her husband, advertising executive Alfred Lasker, joined with Farber in the early 1970s to launch a War on Cancer. Mary Lasker's formidable energy and organizing skills, and the fervor for finding a cure that she and Farber shared, gave the "war" the earmarks of a crusade. Politically, given the can-do, goal-oriented culture of the postwar years, their timing was impeccable, but their hopes for a quick cure proved to be tragically misplaced. The "war" mindset, however, lingered into the following decades, raising and often dashing the hopes of cancer sufferers.

Mukherjee came to believe that the "war" cannot be won; that the war metaphor itself fails to capture the intractable reality of the disease; and that the cellular distortions and mutations that result in cancer are, genetically, so intertwined with the very processes of cell replication that give us life and maintain it, as to be inseparable from our very biological nature.

Mukherjee's journey began with his patients, and his deeply felt tributes to their dignity and courage inform the book. Cancer's all-consuming physical, psychological, emotional effects on its sufferers and on those who treat them— the "dense, insistent gravitational tug that pulls everything and everyone into [its] orbit"—are constantly in view. An oncologist lives with death, and with what Mukherjee calls a "strange desolation."

AN ENEMY OF THE PEOPLE
Henrik Ibsen
1883
Drama

A rather trivial question of public health is used as the springboard for a discussion of the price that must be paid for truth and the conditions under which it may flourish.

Doctor Thomas Stockmann is the sole physician in a small Norwegian coastal town. One day he makes the surprising discovery that the local baths, which are well attended by people seeking to improve their health and which thus constitute a major economic factor in the lives of the townspeople, have been contaminated. Dr. Stockmann takes the position that the baths must be closed for the season or at least until the source of the contamination can be found and the problem corrected.

The doctor's view of the problem seems reasonable enough. He receives the support of the liberal town newspaper and a majority of the public but is almost immediately opposed by his own brother, Peter, the mayor of the town and the senior member of the Board of Directors at the baths. Peter Stockmann both questions the scientific accuracy of the tests used by the doctor and declares that, in any case, the doctor's concern for the public health must be subordinated to the economic well-being of the town. The conflict in the play is thus one between pure truth and the self-serving use of what passes for truth.

Dr. Stockmann loses all public support for his position as soon as the economic consequences of his discovery become known. He is ridiculed at a public meeting, and a mob marches on his house and stones it. In the end, he is forced to consider emigrating to America. People seem to be willing to accept truth only as long as their financial and power positions are unthreatened by it.

Despite this bleak view, there is hope in Doctor Stockmann's final position. He decides to remain in town, where he will establish a school for children of the lower classes and teach truth to those who have nothing to lose by accepting it.

THE ENORMOUS RADIO
John Cheever
1947
Short Story
Allegorical

Set in a New York City apartment house sometime during the 1940's, Cheever's story dramatizes both the actual surface quality of upwardly mobile middle-class life as it was lived by American couples of that time and, as well, the deeper anxieties that lurked beneath that placid surface.

The story focuses on Jim and Irene Westcott, an average couple in all but one respect, and that is in their fondness for music, which is to say, their fondness for harmony. When their radio breaks down beyond repair, Jim buys another as a gift for his wife. The machine's complexity, ugly gumwood cabinet, and "malevolent green light" trouble Irene. More disturbing is the radio's tendency to pick up interference. Wanting to hear music, Irene instead hears ringing telephones and the conversations and quarrels of her neighbors.

Soon, Irene begins to take pleasure in eavesdropping on her neighbors, but this perverse fascination soon gives way to an apprehensiveness and even defensiveness on the part of Irene, who too insistently maintains that she and Jim are innocent of the hypocrisy, fearfulness, and financial troubles that afflict their neighbors. Ironically, her knowledge of their lives and misfortunes eventually causes friction in her own marriage. Jim, it turns out, worries about growing old and wonders why he has not been as successful as he hoped to be. In a sudden outburst, he cracks Irene's "Christly" shell, exposing the lies, thefts, and even the abortion she has sought to conceal, indeed seems to have forgotten.

Although the story begins as a work of conventional realism, Cheever's plot and theme can be interpreted allegorically. "The Enormous Radio" can be seen as a retelling of the biblical story of man's fall from innocence and expulsion from the Garden of Eden, in this case, the American garden of middle-class respectability. In exposing Irene Westcott, Cheever in effect exposes the underside of the American life that she and her husband represent. The comforts of their middle-class life, Cheever suggests, cannot protect the individual against either the evil in the world or the evil in oneself. Tempted by the satanic radio, Irene falls into knowledge, out of love, and perhaps beyond the possibility of redemption as well.

THE EPIC OF GILGAMESH
Unknown
c. 2000 B.C.E.
Poetry
Epic, Mythology

The Sumerian poems collected as The Epic of Gilgamesh *extol the hero-king's quest for fame and immortality. Several of these orally transmitted poems parallel the biblical flood account, and all reflect Middle Eastern settings.*

The uncontrolled passion of Gilgamesh, ruler of the city-state Uruk, causes him to demand Uruk's brides before they consummate their marriage. The gods tame him with a companion, Engidu, whom a city prostitute seduces. Engidu thus becomes by stages nomad, shepherd, hunter, and the city dweller. He mirrors the development of an urban society. His arrival at Uruk brings a wrestling contest with Gilgamesh, who, because he loves his new friend so deeply, leaves the brides to their husbands.

Gilgamesh and Engidu journey to the cedar forest to acquire timber for Uruk's walls (this need for protection indicates both increased prosperity and further urbanization), but before doing so they must defeat Khumbaba, the forest's guardian, a primitive, nature deity. They know fear for the first time, triumphing only with help from the god Shamash's winds. Victorious Gilgamesh now rejects the passion goddess Ishtar, Engidu ridicules her, and she responds by sending the Bull of Heaven to devastate Gilgamesh's lands. Spurning Ishtar implies rejection of heterosexual passion, obviously wrong for continuing a heroic race of mortals.

When they kill the bull, Gilgamesh and Engidu also realize their mortality. Engidu is the first to die, and Gilgamesh first suffers deep depression, then undertakes a solitary journey to an underworld realm in search of immortality. Utnapishtim, human survivor of the great flood, tests Gilgamesh, but the hero fails and Utnapishtim cannot give him the secret. He does entrust Gilgamesh with a flower of immortality, however, which Gilgamesh loses to a treacherous serpent. He had wanted to share the gift with his townspeople.

These poems are of separate authorship, reflect different periods of composition, illustrate an eastern "culture hero," and because of oral transmission exist in sometimes contradictory variants. Still, they describe the progress of civilization, humanity's longing for eternal life, and its best hope, an earthly legacy.

EQUUS
Peter Shaffer
1973
Drama
Psychological

A teenage English boy who has inexplicably mutilated horses undergoes treatment by a psychiatrist and reveals the bizarre story of his devotion to a horse-god, Equus. This play vividly depicts the struggle between passionate belief and conformity.

Martin Dysart, an overworked psychiatrist, is given the case of Alan Strang, a stableboy who has recently shocked the country by blinding nine horses with a hoof pick. At first reluctant, Dysart becomes intrigued with Alan, whose contemptuous stare makes him feel "accused."

Meanwhile, Dysart questions Alan's mother and father and discovers that both parents, though well-meaning, have strong views: His mother is a pious Christian, and his father is an atheist and old-style Socialist. Repulsed by a lurid crucifixion that Alan has chosen to hang over his bed, his father one day replaced it with a calendar that shows a horse photographed straight-on that seems to be all eyes.

When Alan got a job as a stableboy, the owner suspected him of secretly riding at night. Dysart hypnotizes Alan and gets him to act out his naked midnight rides on Equus. The ride, which begins with religious ritual, ends in masturbation. This overpowering scene ends act 1.

Dysart confesses to the magistrate that he is envious of Alan's passion, but she reminds him that his job is to return Alan to the world of the "normal." Dysart begins asking Alan about the girl he worked with, Jill. One night after work,

Jill asked Alan to take her to a "skin flick." During the movie, Alan was aroused but spotted his father in the audience. An argument ensued, and Alan refused to go home with his father.

Jill took him to the stable where she attempted to seduce him. But Alan felt threatened by the presence of Equus and sent Jill away. In a rage, Alan blinded the horses.

Act 2 ends with Dysart's indictment of his own part in relieving Alan of his feeling, but Dysart admits that he is as much a slave as is a horse. "There is now, in my mouth, this sharp chain. And it never comes out."

Despite his crime, Alan is seen finally as a boy willing to risk anything for what he believes. Additionally, there is Alan's effect on Dysart, whose faith in eliminating individual passions and returning patients to normality is severely eroded.

Touching upon the mythical, religious, and moral, *Equus* is a meticulously crafted psychological detective story that is visually compelling (the horses are stylized humans) and reaches the spectator at the most basic level of emotions.

AN ESSAY ON MAN
Alexander Pope
1733-1734
Poetry
Philosophical

This work of Neoclassical poetry is a concise summation of eighteenth century philosophy, and is, therefore, an excellent introduction to the poetic tendencies and prevalent thought of Pope's Augustan age. In this masterwork of Neoclassical poetry, Pope looks at the bewildering human condition and searches for some principles to give it meaning. The four epistles that make up the poem examine man in his relation to the universe, to himself, to society, and to his final goal.

Pope's principle for understanding man is the Great Chain of Being, which orders all creation according to God's will. The disorders which man sees in the universe are actually parts of some larger perfection which man's limited knowledge cannot perceive. Man's prideful speculations, not the external universe, are the cause of his misery.

Within man himself, there is also an order based on the workings of self-love (the faculty of desire) and reason (the faculty of judgment). Right living depends upon the two working in harmony, since neither is good or evil in itself. Rather, good or evil arises out of their proper or improper use.

Human society also partakes of this universal order. The imitation of nature and rational self-love enable man to create a successful social order, but his favoring of a particular government or religion, instead of reliance on general principles, creates dissension and tyranny. Man's end—happiness—is attained when he submits to Providence and dispenses with pride.

Part of the essay's greatness is Pope's unity of structure and theme. The poem's orderly exposition of ideas, its concentration on universals rather than specifics, and its heroic couplet verses, reflect the ideas of balance, subordination, and harmony better than even the finest prose.

THE ESSAYS
Michel de Montaigne
1580-1595
Nonfiction
Philosophical

Montaigne richly deserves his reputation as a wise and honest man who in fulfilling his aim to portray himself also portrays human nature in general.

To essay is to "test" or "try," and Montaigne, thinking of his works as trials of his own judgment and capacities, succeeded in inventing the essay with a personal slant. While often personal, his essays are not confessional or confidential but achieve the universal quality of the greatest literature.

He investigates such topics as happiness, names, the education of children, solitude, repentance, and more than a hundred more. In length the essays range from one or two pages to one of more than a hundred pages.

Living in sixteenth century France, Montaigne had many opportunities to observe the disorder and cruelty that arose from intense religious conviction, and although he respected religion, he loathed religious excesses as begetters of vice. He cultivated a contrastingly skeptical approach, illustrated by his motto: "What do I know?" Even more than Socrates, he believed that the awareness of one's own ignorance is the basis of wisdom. Instead of insisting on the correctness of his ideas, he attempts to see his subjects from other points of view, including those of Mohammedans, cannibals, and even of cats.

His twin sources of ideas are books and experience. An extremely well-read man, he peppers his essays with quotations, but his style is relaxed, informal, and good-humored. At the end of his essay "Of Experience," Montaigne writes: "The most beautiful lives, to my mind, are those that conform to the common human pattern, with order, but without miracle and without eccentricity."

Although books of selected essays are also available, Donald M. Frame's translation of *The Complete Essays of Montaigne* is a most readable long book.

ESSAYS AND THE NEW ATLANTIS
Sir Francis Bacon
1624
Nonfiction
Utopian

According to the 19th Century historian, Thomas Babington Macaulay, Bacon's essays "...moved the intellects which have moved the world." Francis Bacon is credited with establishing the scientific method through inductive reasoning and, in The New Atlantis, *he creates the model for modern research institutions.*

The New Atlantis is part adventure fantasy, and part ethnographic speculation, as Bacon's vision of a utopian society. His story has him on a sea voyage that gets blown off course, landing on a heretofore, unknown island in the Pacific, called Bensalem. The story features Bacon's observations of this ideal society.

When the seamen are offered sanctuary at Bensalem, they try to offer gifts out of gratitude, but are refused. The society does not strive for money or treasure, but for perfect "light," which has been interpreted as truth or knowledge—acquired through systematic, rational thought. As the crewmen are healed and replenished, several, including Bacon, are invited to observe the "Feast of the Family" ceremony, which honors the patriarch with "thirty persons descended of his body." Bacon is later taken to meet the Father of Salomon's House, which is an institution of research and learning, considered the great "lantern" of the kingdom. The "father" of Salomon's House explains that their institution aims to learn "the knowledge of causes and secret motions of things," and includes everything from soils and plants, to "engine houses," "shops of medicines," and "perspective houses" for the study of light, color…and "delusions and deceits of the sight."

Bacon's "Essays" were originally for his own private use, and include his observations and speculations about a variety of subjects—fifty-eight in all—ranging from the highly esoteric, such as truth, love, and goodness, to more mundane topics like travel, innovation, and usury. Bacon's reputation as a great phrasemaker was generated from his essays, with aphorisms, such as "the folly of one man is the fortune of another," and "if the mountain will not come to Mohammad, Mohammad will come to the mountain." During his lifetime, Bacon saw his essays translated into French and Italian.

THE ETERNAL MOMENT
E. M. Forster
1928
Short Story
Collection, Fantasy

The cherished memory of an ecstatic experience set against the grim reality of the present turns an aging writer's visit to her beloved mountains into a period of disillusionment and questioning.

Subtle, witty, and elusive, this story is more concerned with the central character's personal sojourn inward than with her physical journey upward in the Italian Alps. Yet she arrives eventually at both destinations: the actual mountain resort and the symbolic country of the mind.

Miss Raby, now a well-known novelist, had set her first book in an obscure mountain village, which after the novel's publication and success became a popular tourist spot. When she goes back many years later to see how tourism has affected the village, she discovers only vulgarity in the plush hotels, ugliness in the other signs of prosperity, and disappointment in the unharnessed human greed.

She still cherishes her memories of the place, for on a hillside near the village a handsome Italian guide had declared his love for her one spring day. Although she had rejected him, she has always kept the moment alive, considering it the most perfect in her experience. Then on her return she meets the would-be lover, by now a fat, middle-aged, obsequious concierge in one of the grand hotels. How she confronts this destruction of her illusion brings the story to its dramatic yet understated climax.

When in Miss Raby's youth the dashing guide confesses his passion, she experiences that rare "eternal moment" aglow with beauty and joy and truth. No matter what occurs thereafter, the one who knows such a moment is richer for having embraced it. Even though the ugliness of progress and the degeneration of the lover cracks the shell of Miss Raby's illusion, the insight she had once gained remains intact for her.

The prominence of the youthful memory of the hillside encounter may appear exaggerated on the realistic level, but on the symbolic level it suggests a vision accessible to the one who stands ready and expectant. This vision might contain a key to the understanding of the individual's place in the universal scheme. It might offer the artist the awareness without which his work would fail. Or it might hold a hint toward the unraveling of the eternal mystery.

ETHAN FROME
Edith Wharton
1911
Novella

Ethan Frome, trapped by his bad marriage and lack of ambition, is awakened to the renewed possibilities of escape by the appearance of a new servant girl.

This claustrophobic novel centers on the triangle formed by Ethan, Zeena, his dour, hypochondriacal wife, whom he married to satisfy a sense of indebtedness to her for caring for his dying mother, and Mattie Silver, Zeena's poor but vivacious and younger cousin. Ethan and Mattie fall in love and plan to flee the bleak, New England world only to be stopped by Ethan's sense of obligation to his wife. In the end the couple attempt a double suicide which fails and leaves Ethan crippled and Mattie a hopeless invalid, ironically leaving Zeena to care for them both at the conclusion of the story.

Although atypical in setting for a Wharton novel, the tale recapitulates in condensed form one of her most obsessive themes, the question of freedom and entrapment within marriage. Each of the main characters exhibits strengths and weaknesses which contribute to the interlocking triangle to which they all belong. Mattie's youth and vulnerability play on Ethan's need to dream and to be protective; Zeena's hypochondria and conventionality touch Ethan's sense of duty and fear of change. Ethan in turn is bound to both women, two sides of the female nature, toward which he experiences both attraction and repulsion in equal parts enough to immobilize him.

The touching final scene of the three trapped, interdependent people in their secluded farm house is one of the grimmest in modern literature. It provides a fitting conclusion to Wharton's sparest and starkest piece of fiction, one which contains a distillation of her other work and has proved to be one of her most popular stories.

ETHICA NICOMACHEA
Aristotle
335-323 B.C.E.
Nonfiction
Philosophical

The most popular of Aristotle's books, it describes morality in terms of character traits and in terms of moderation between extremes of passion or action.

Long after he had studied under Plato and taught Alexander the Great, Aristotle developed the belief that everything has 4 causes: material (physical), formal (design), efficient (maker or ancestor), and final (ultimate goal). Thus, morality has to do with physical and emotional appetites, rationality, the social and political setting, and contemplation of truth.

According to Aristotle, a person is responsible only for voluntary deeds, not for deeds committed in ignorance or when forced. Truly bad acts are performed when irrationality overpowers reason, when persons act impulsively, or when evil is disguised as good.

Virtue, on the other hand, is the midpoint between the extremes of too much and too little. Courage in war is a virtue because it avoids the excess of rashness and the deficiency of cowardice. Likewise, temperance regarding physical desires is a virtue because it avoids the excess of licentiousness and the deficiency of insensibility.

In addition to courage and temperance, Aristotle names the following character traits as moral virtues: liberality and munificence (in regard to wealth), greatness of soul (in regard to social inferiors), gentleness, friendliness, and wittiness. The intellectual qualities of wisdom and prudence are virtues as well because they enable people to put moral principles into practice. An ethical person is one who is in the habit of enacting the virtues and of shunning cruelty and the loss of self-control.

The virtues are character traits, and as such can be acquired only by early training and constant deliberation and choice. Aristotle believed that character was molded by training and by the environment, particularly the legal system, so virtuous statesmanship is integral to moral conduct.

ETHICS
Baruch Spinoza
1677
Nonfiction
Philosophical

Spinoza was a rationalist who believed that the mind is capable of forming clear and distinct ideas that are true. In the Ethics *he elaborates a logical philosophy based on axioms and theorems. The* Ethics *is a difficult work modeled on the manner of reasoning of geometry.*

In part 1, "Concerning God," Spinoza reasons that God and the cosmos are the same; they are two different names for the one essential substance that makes up the whole universe. This substance is infinite but is revealed to us through the two attributes of thought and matter.

The forms in which the one substance comes into being in the world—such as in oak trees and spaniels—are called its modes. Every mode is what it is because that is what it had to be in God's creation. No end or purpose governs life; all things are simply interconnected manifestations of Nature, or God. Everything is determined by necessity.

Part 2, "Of the Nature and Origin of the Mind," tries to establish the parallelism between ideas and objects. The mind has no free will, Spinoza says, but is determined by a series of causes that regress to infinity. Knowing this, we should find peace in our understanding that we think what we think, do what we do, out of divine necessity. Furthermore, we should meet all that happens to us with tranquility.

In parts 3 and 4 Spinoza analyzes and defines the emotions. He argues that our human inability to control our emotions is a form of bondage, and that good and bad are but relative terms: To be good is to wish to align our desires with God's necessity; to be bad is to resist that necessity.

Finally, part 5, "Of Human Freedom," teaches that whatever power we can exert over our emotions is due to our understanding of divine necessity.

EUGENE ONEGIN
Alexander Pushkin
1833
Novel in Verse

A jaded Russian aristocrat rejects a country girl's affection, but he falls in love with her after she marries into high society. The novel blends poetic lyricism with dramatic storytelling.

The unhappy romance between Eugene Onegin and Tatyana Larin is narrated by a young man-about-Moscow who has complicated, contradictory reactions to his tale. The narrator alternately laughs, admires, despairs, and takes courage as the story unfolds.

Numerous love affairs have dulled Onegin's sensibilities. He retires to an estate where the inexperienced Tatyana imagines him a hero out of a romantic novel. She writes Eugene a long, adoring letter. He lectures her on the silliness of her emotions and flirts with her sister. The sister's fiance resents Onegin's attentions and challenges him to a duel. Onegin kills the fiance and leaves Russia.

Two years later, Onegin returns and meets Tatyana in Moscow. She has made a marriage of convenience. Finding himself passionately desiring Tatyana, Onegin becomes her devoted attendant. Soon he asks her to become his mistress. Although she confesses to loving him, she refuses to betray her vows.

The novel offers no resolution. It ends abruptly with Tatyana's elderly husband entering just as she refuses the stunned Onegin. The narrator offers no information on the characters' fates. Did Tatyana regret her decision? Did Onegin find another woman to desire? Readers, reviewing Pushkin's insights into the lovers' hearts, are left to ponder their destinies.

Eugene and Tatyana are among the great figures in Russian literature because they symbolize conflicting impulses in the national character: the desire to find something which fulfills the self, and the willingness to sacrifice that something when duty demands.

Pushkin combines the best of two genres. As novelist he depicts powerful dramatic scenes between characters. As poet, he probes the depths of desire, anxiety, and despair.

THE EVE OF ST. AGNES
John Keats
1820
Poetry
Narrative

In this narrative poem, which combines chivalric romance with erotic fantasy, a lovely virgin, Madeline, adheres closely to the ritual of St. Agnes Eve and retires for the night without supper, having prayed that her lover will appear in her dreams and awaken her to the reality of their shared bliss. Keats interweaves suspense and voluptuous imagery to create one of his most passionate verses.

Echoing Spenser's legendary romances of spiritual quest in verse form, diction, and plotting, Keats has Porphyro, Madeline's lover, sneak into the castle and, with the aid of her old nurse, spy on his beloved from the darkness of a closet. The blending of the spiritual and the erotic in Porphyro's awestruck voyeurism is the energizing principle of the entire poem. Keats works up a rich mixture of sense-impressions to render the sensual sublime.

After watching Madeline pray, Porphyro grows faint at the sight of her beauty when she disrobes. After she falls asleep, he leaves his hiding place and brings out dainty foods, exotic fruits, and candies that warm and perfume the winter chill of the virgin's chamber. As he softly plays his lute, she awakens. His erotic intentions fade into religious devotion as he falls to his knees; she in turn, begs him never to leave her.

The lovers, strengthened by the warmth of their passion and feelings, flee into the unpredictable future symbolized by the dark winter outside the castle walls, but they leave behind them the tensions and hatred of their warring families.

EVERYMAN
Unknown
1508
Drama
Morality Play

This most famous of the late-medieval morality plays uses allegory to achieve a statement of religious obligation as well as a psychological realism that rings true five hundred years later.

God sends the messenger Death to summon Everyman on a "long journey" at the end of which he must make a reckoning. Everyman does his best to stave off the duty, including an attempt to bribe Death. Told that he can bring company if he can find anyone willing to accompany him, Everyman turns to Fellowship, who amusingly vows to stand firmly by his friend—until he learns the nature of the journey. Kindred, Cousin, and Goods also refuse the invitation.

When it occurs to Everyman to ask his Good Deeds, he finds the latter weakened by sins and unable to make the trip, but she recommends her sister Knowledge, who vows to go by his side. After Knowledge leads Everyman to Confession, Good Deeds is able to rise from the ground and join him.

A final set of abstractions representing bodily attributes—Beauty, Strength, Discretion, and Five Wits (five senses)—accompanies him, but each leaves in turn as he approaches the grave. Eventually Everyman learns who is willing to go all the way with him to meet his Maker.

Like many other medieval works, Everyman uses the motif of the spiritual journey or pilgrimage to make a powerful statement of religious faith that also contains a warning to the spiritually lax in a period of increasing worldliness just prior to the Reformation.

Probably allegory has never worked more effectively than it does in *Everyman*. The play is an excellent example of the strengths peculiar to allegorical literature.

EVERYTHING IS ILLUMINATED
Jonathan Safran Foer
2002
Novel

A young American writer visits the Ukraine seeking the woman who saved his grandfather's life during the Holocaust and is guided on his search by a young Ukrainian and his grandfather

Jonathan Safran Foer's remarkable first novel explores Jewish life in the Ukraine during the late eighteenth/early nineteenth centuries and the 1930's/40's. Foer is also one of the protagonists, visiting the Ukraine in 1997 seeking Augustine, a woman who saved his grandfather, Safran, during the Holocaust. Safran's first wife, Zosha, died during the Holocaust and he met his second wife in a displaced-persons camp. Safran died suddenly shortly after immigrating to the United States. With a photograph of Augustine, he hopes to find her and Trachimbrod, the shtetl where his grandfather had lived.

The structure of *Everything Is Illuminated* is complicated. There are his translator's Alex's letters to Jonathan after the writer has returned to America, and the chapters narrated by Alex describing the search for Augustine. There are Jonathan's narratives about two of his ancestors, his great-great-great-great-great grandmother, Brod, and his grandfather, Safran. In 1791, when Brod is an infant, the wagon of her father, Trachim, tumbles into the river Brod, and only the baby is rescued. The shtetl holds a lottery for her custody, and she is won by the seventy-two-year-old Yankel, who names her for the river where she was found. Later, Yankel wins another contest and renames the shtetl Trachimbrod. Brod grows up thinking Yankel is her father.

Back in 1997, the search for Augustine leads Jonathan to Lista, whose husband was killed in a freak accident, and who became Safran's lover. The odd twists and turns of fate are another of Foer's concerns. Lista is the only survivor of Trachimbrod, and her home is filled with boxes containing the remains of the shtetl.

Everything Is Illuminated is highly self-conscious in the postmodernist vein. Alex inserts parenthetical comments about why he includes details in his narrative. Jonathan injects first-person intrusions into the Brod and Safran tales. When Yankel is awarded the baby, "We were to be in good hands." Because much of the Brod story has elements of Magical Realism, Jonathan even allows her glimpses of the future and of the Safran to come. On occasion, the two stories merge into one.

Foer plays seductive games with time. Because Alex's letters are written after Jonathan's visit to Ukraine, they often refer to events that have not yet taken place in the narrative. Trachimday is celebrated with such outbursts of sexual passion that the resulting glow can be seen from space by astronauts over 150 years later. This is also one of several literal and figurative illuminations throughout the novel.

Foer's method and style provide some necessary distance from the despair in the characters' lives but do not diminish their emotional impact. The scene in which Alex refuses to take no for an answer when Lista says she does not recognize anyone in the photograph of Augustine is wonderfully handled. It ends with her bursting into tears and admitting that she is all that is left of Trachimbrod. In her account of the day the Nazis came, Lista describes a pregnant woman who is shot but crawls away to safety. She lives but not the baby. Only much later does the reader realize that Lista is this woman and learn the identity of the father. The story is devastating the first time, and the realization of the complete truth is another jolt.

Everything Is Illuminated is an amazing debut novel. Foer makes Trachimbrod a living, breathing place. The novel is about guilt and responsibility, love and forgiveness, truth and illusion. It is also a commentary on the nature of art to transform or illuminate reality. Everything is not only illuminated but also connected. Despite its brevity, *Everything Is Illuminated* has an epic scope.

EVERYTHING THAT RISES MUST CONVERGE
Flannery O'Connor
1965
Short Story
Series, Southern Gothic
This 1965 posthumous collection of nine short stories is the last work of a noted ironic writer who died from lupus at age thirty-nine.

Parker, a college graduate living with and supported by his mother, daydreams of being a writer; he works as a part-time typewriter salesman, alienated and embarrassed by his uneducated mother who is oblivious, yet proud, of her son. His mother exhibits typical Southern racism and remains paranoid of riding a desegregated bus. They board a bus together on their way to the local YMCA. His mother meets a black woman with an identical hat. In Germanic folklore, meeting one's double prefigures immanent death; the story concludes with Julian's mother collapsed on the sidewalk. The third-person narrative presents a generational parable about the death of white supremacy.

The story "Parker's Back" provides a sequel to the title story. Parker, who has descended to Appalachian under culture, lives an aimless life of getting by with odd jobs. As an apple trucker, he meets and marries Sarah Ruth, yet he does not know why. His principle aim in life is to acquire tattoos, while his new wife is religious. With one bare spot on his back, he purchases a tattoo of a Byzantine Christ. Sarah sees this as a mocking, blasphemous exercise in idolatry, and beats him with a broom. Ironically, this marital sadism results in a Christian transfiguration and Parker's eyes are opened to religion.

"Greenleaf" satirizes pious hypocrisy. "A View of the Woods" offers a self-destructive portrait of Appalachian family life. "The Enduring Chill" presents a satire on the wish for martyrdom. In "The Comforts of Home" a mother attempts to marry her intellectual son to a young drifter with the end result that the young historian accidentally kills his mother. "The Lame Shall Enter First" mocks the destructive power of evangelism. "Revelation," the most accomplished and amusing story in the collection, dwells on the obscure theology of grace. "Judgment Day" explores the ironies of either race overcoming racism.

The collection's title phrase is a quote from the evolutionist mystic theologian Teilhard de Chardin. The sensibility reflects optimism that evolution itself continually gives rise to greater spirituality.

F

THE FAERIE QUEENE
Edmund Spenser
Books 1-3, 1590; books 4-6, 1596
Poetry
Epic

This influential 16th century epic successfully achieves the Renaissance ideal of both teaching and delighting. Related to a number of generic traditions, including the romance, historical poem, and courtesy book, The Faerie Queene *offers allegorical interpretations of religion, politics, and morality.*

In a letter to Sir Walter Raleigh, Spenser stated that his purpose in this epic poem was to "fashion a gentleman or noble person in vertuous and gentle discipline." Although Spenser may have intended to write twenty-four books, twelve concerned with private and twelve with public or political virtues, he completed only six books and *The Mutabilitie Cantos*, a fragment of a possible seventh book.

Spenser's first book focuses on the virtue of holiness and relates the story of Redcross Knight, also St. George of England, who hopes to liberate the parents of Una (Protestantism), the one true religion. Sir Guyon, the hero of the second book, is the knight of temperance who must withstand the temptations of the Cave of Mammon and the Bower of Bliss.

Books III and IV focus respectively on chastity and friendship. The central figure of both books is Britomart, the female knight of chastity, who seeks her promised lover, Artegall or justice. Britomart is chaste in an Aristotelian sense; she wants to be united with Artegall in honorable marriage, not to live as a celibate.

Artegall, the hero of Book V and knight of justice, sets out to free Lady Irena (Ireland) from Grantorto (Roman Catholicism) and to defend Belge (Netherlands) against her enemy (Spain). Book VI focuses on courtesy and the adventures of Sir Calidore and Sir Calepine, who try to restrain the Blatant Beast (slander).

In *The Mutabilitie Cantos*, Spenser revels the constancy of order which is obscured by the mutability of the natural and political world. An eclectic and fascinating work, *The Faerie Queene* represents Spenser's celebration of Elizabeth I and his analysis of 16th century civilization.

FAHRENHEIT 451
Ray Bradbury
1953
Novel
Dystopian

One of the most famous of contemporary dystopian novels, this story portrays a world in which books are illegal and subject to burning by firemen, one of whom comes to renounce his profession.

Guy Montag, a fireman whose job it is to burn books, begins to doubt his society's high-speed, hedonistic way of life when he meets Clarisse McClellan, a young girl whose family lives a slower, more graceful existence. Clarisse shares her values with him until the McClellans mysteriously disappear.

As Montag's dissatisfaction increases, he seeks out a retired English professor named Faber for support. However, Montag's chief, Beatty, correctly suspects Montag of being a secret reader and book collector. After Beatty burns down

Montag's house, he must flee civilization and, on Faber's advice, find a group of outcasts who have dedicated themselves to memorizing whole books while their society destroys itself in a pointless war.

Though the novel focuses on a book burner, it is more than a diatribe against censorship. Rather, it pictures a society, not far removed from our own, in which books and the leisure, thought, and tolerance necessary to enjoy them are no longer valued. The firemen simply enforce the will of a people who desire only conformity, unrelated facts, and immediate gratification. The most frightening aspect of the story is the portrayal of Montag's wife, Mildred, and her friends, who live through electronic entertainment devices.

The debasement of the quality of life through the misuses of technology and the neglect of literature is a persistent theme in Bradbury's fiction, but this novel remains his fullest treatment of the subject. The lyric power and symbolic richness of the book make this Bradbury's most satisfactory long fiction and a classic of speculative literature.

The title of the novel is derived from the combustion temperature of paper: 451 degrees Fahrenheit.

THE FALL
Albert Camus
1956
Novella
Philosophical

The third and final novel published by Camus during his lifetime is a somber and sardonic study in individual guilt and expiation.

The narrative is set in the red-light district of Amsterdam and is delivered during the course of 5 days by a man who calls himself Jean-Baptiste Clamence. He addresses himself to a Parisian lawyer who has wandered into a bar called Mexico City. Clamence ingeniously draws his listener into complicity with his own life, which he proceeds to outline.

Before becoming the expatriate barfly that he seems today, Clamence was a supremely successful and self-confident defense attorney in Paris. However, his faith in himself and in the social rituals he was enacting was forever subverted one night as he was walking alone across a bridge. Though he heard the splash of a young woman throwing herself into the river, Clamence continued walking, without making any effort to save her life.

That moment, which has haunted him ever since, marked his fall from innocence; it introduced an ineradicable self-consciousness that alienated him henceforth from his in-authentic social roles. He now lives in exile, compelled to recount his guilty story again and again to passing strangers.

Fond of heights and of islands that reinforce his sense of detachment, Clamence calls himself a "judge-penitent." He takes as his calling the expiation of personal guilt by implicating others. That is precisely what he is attempting to do through his narrative—which, he admits, he improvises each time to suit each successive listener.

During this particular performance, Clamence manages to fascinate his listener. On the fifth and final day, he persuades him to visit his apartment, where he reveals the stolen painting *The Just Judges*. Clamence thereby implicates the stranger in his own crime, thus temporarily overcoming the sense of doubleness that has haunted him since the drowning.

THE FALL OF GIANTS
Ken Follett
2010
Novel
Historical, War

The first book in a trilogy that spans roughly seventy-five years, Fall of Giants follows the progress of five separate, interrelated families from the four separate nations of Britain, the United States, Germany, and Russia, as they navigate the turbulent era of World War I. War and political machinations are not the only challenges the characters face. The Russian Revolution, women's suffrage, class struggles, and labor union strikes challenge long-entrenched beliefs.

As the young aristocrat, Earl Fitzherbert (Fitz) and his wife, Russian Princess Bea, prepare to entertain King George at their Welsh estate, young Welsh miner, Billy Williams' struggles to rescue fellow miners in a mine explosion. Mining widows and their children are turned out after the deaths; housing is an employee-only benefit. Billy's sister, Ethel, is a young housekeeper at the Fitzherbert estate—a position she loses after becoming pregnant with the Earl's bastard. Princess Bea is likewise pregnant. Ecstatic over having an heir, Fitz shunts Ethel and her bastard child to London.

Fitzherbert's sister, Maude, is a suffragette and civil rights activist, who has fallen in love with a German nobleman, Walter von Ulrich. They keep their love a secret, knowing their families will disapprove. When war breaks out between their two nations, they secretly marry. Walter's father, Otto, is an old-school nobleman, deeply entrenched in the ideology that Germany is a supreme nation. He supports the march toward war, feeling that Germany's sovereignty has been maligned. He is deeply humiliated by the war's outcome, but refuses to acknowledge his culpability.

In Russia, the brothers Lev and Grigori Peshkov struggle to survive. (They were orphaned as Princess Bea had their father hanged for grazing cattle on her family's land.) Lev is a hustler and a cad, staying just one step ahead of the law, while the older Grigori rescues him. In a heartbreaking instance, in order to save Lev's life, Grigori gives Lev his hard-earned ticket to America. Eventually, Grigori marries Lev's abandoned lover so she's eligible for wartime marital benefits, and raises Lev's child as his own. Grigori become a Bolshevik insider.

In America, Lev becomes a chauffer for Josef Vyalov, a Russian mob boss. Lev is nearly killed after impregnating Olga, Vyalov's daughter, thus ruining her chance to marry Gus Dewar—a young up-and-coming American statesman who works for the President.

Contrasting social entitlement and servitude, mindless prejudice and inconvenient love, Follett takes his readers from trench warfare to the White House, and from a Russian peasant uprising (from which the Fitzherberts barely escape) to the rising Labor Party in British Parliament, Follett documents the extraordinary changes in the early decades of the 20th century.

THE FALL OF THE HOUSE OF USHER
Edgar Allan Poe
1839
Short Story
Gothic

As a brother and sister fall into madness and death, their house collapses in a terrible storm. This complex, multilayered story is one of Poe's finest studies of metaphysical and psychological horror.

Whether one reads this story as metaphysical speculation on the identity of matter and spirit, or as a psychological study of the powerful influence a deranged mind may have on a sane one, or even simply as a Gothic horror chiller, it remains a genuine masterwork of American fiction.

The narrator of the story tells of an autumn visit to the House of Usher, the family home of his boyhood friend, Roderick Usher. He finds the house to be old and decaying, with a minute fissure zigzagging down from the roof to the waters of a stagnant tarn at its foundation. The gloomy landscape, the forbidding house, and the miasmic fog that hangs over the tarn depress the narrator and weaken his resistance to the mental atmosphere of the Usher family.

Roderick and his sister Madeline have been living relatively isolated in the house and have grown unnaturally close as she weakens with a terminal illness. After her death and burial in a sealed vault beneath the house, the sensitive and artistic Roderick becomes increasingly the victim of his fear and horror at his sister's death. As a storm roars around the house, he convinces himself that Madeline was buried alive and that she has forced her way out of the tomb and is coming to confront him.

The force of his conviction in mad harmony with the raging storm causes the narrator to share Roderick's hallucination, and he actually sees Madeline enter the room and die clutching the body of her fatally terrified brother. He rushes out into the storm as the house itself splits and falls into the tarn.

The interplay of solidly realistic detail and rich symbolic ambiguity gives the story an artistic texture of great intellectual as well as emotional force.

FAR FROM THE MADDING CROWD
Thomas Hardy
1874
Novel
Romance

This romantic story of a headstrong young woman farmer and the three men who love her in different ways shows Hardy's rich sense of life's unexpected ironies and disappointments.

This is the first of Hardy's Wessex novels, set in the timeless world of 19th century rural England. Central to Hardy's ironic tale of unrequited love are the characters of Bathsheba Everdene and Gabriel Oak. An honest shepherd and farm steward, Oak shows great loyalty and patience in his love for the beautiful and vivacious Bathsheba.

Farmer Oak unexpectedly meets Bathsheba on a country road and immediately falls in love with her. His marriage proposal rejected, he is forced to hire himself out for work after his sheep are killed in a freak accident. After helping to extinguish a fire at a nearby farm, he is offered a position at Weatherby Farm, which he discovers is owned by Bathsheda. Now he has become her hired man. A stubborn and impulsive young woman, she flirts with William Boldwood, a neighboring landowner, who soon falls in love with her. Yet Bathsheba is most attracted to Sergeant Troy, a dashing young soldier who has already seduced a young milkmaid named Fanny Robin. Bathsheba marries Troy against Oak's advice.

Bathsheba and Troy later separate when she learns of Fanny's death in childbirth, and Troy disappears and is reported drowned, but he is later murdered by Boldwood when he unexpectedly returns to his wife. All this time the long-suffering Oak has remained loyal to Bathsheba, who fails to appreciate his support.

Hardy dramatizes the capriciousness of a woman's love and its disastrous consequences for herself and others. His characters are vivid types drawn directly from English rural life, and his use of the natural world deepens this melodramatic tale of persevering love.

In this novel, the reader will find the blend of romance, pathos, irony, coincidence, and regionalism that distinguishes much of Hardy's fiction. The rivalry among Bathsheba's three suitors has a timeless and elemental quality about it, especially in the faithfulness of Gabriel Oak, who consistently serves his mistress and remains loyal to her despite her disdain.

A FAREWELL TO ARMS
Ernest Hemingway
1929
Novel
War

A love story set on the Italian front during World War I, this novel (partly drawn from Hemingway's experiences as an ambulance driver) is a moving commentary on mortality and on the desperate desire of human beings to establish a comity and commitment to each other that is so conspicuously lacking in the world-at-large.

Frederic Henry, an American lieutenant in the Italian ambulance service, and Catherine Barkley, an English nurse, fall in love while he is in the hospital recuperating from war wounds. The terrible waste of war has made Henry wary and sparing of his feelings, but the tough and bright Catherine appeals to his thoroughly unsentimental side. What he admires is what she does, not what she says; as he puts it, he likes the way she moves.

Behind Henry's attraction to Catherine is his disgust with words—or with the great abstractions that President Wilson used when he proclaimed that America was fighting to save the world for democracy. For her part, Catherine is drawn to Henry's steadiness and lack of cant. He does not deal with her deceptively and would not use a word such as love lightly.

The plot follows the development of their love in conversations that are remarkable examples of understatement. The crisp, economical dialogue is a brilliant counterpoint to the profligate expenditure of life in the war scenes—although even in the war episodes the author describes battles and landscapes with extraordinary lucidity and a thrifty use of language.

Without using the "big words," Hemingway is able to make his characters' love affair symbolic of an attitude, a philosophy of life. It is a bitter vision of existence; the novel ends with Catherine dying in childbirth and their baby, a son, stillborn. His desperate prayers unanswered, Henry leaves the hospital and walks back to the hotel in the rain.

FATHER GORIOT
Honoré de Balzac
1834-1835
Novel
Historical

This story of a wealthy Parisian flour merchant and the daughters on whom he squanders his fortune offers a portrait of many of the different economic and social strata of Parisian society in the wake of Waterloo and the restoration of the French monarchy.

The focus of this novel is less on the titular hero than on the young law student Rastignac, who lives in the same boardinghouse and befriends the aging Goriot, whom the other boarders mock and generally shun.

Rastignac's initiation into the world of wealthy aristocratic society is accomplished in part through the young man falls in love with Goriot's younger daughter. Torn by conflicting desires to act nobly or to serve his own interests, Rastignac finally stakes his own future on the fickle affection of this woman, who has abandoned her own father in order to rise in the social world of Paris in 1819.

Goriot, who wastes the final portion of his fortune to buy ball gowns for his daughters, succumbs to a mysterious ailment that has resulted from the ill treatment he has suffered at the hands of his ungrateful offspring. Rastignac spends the remainder of his own money to pay for Goriot's funeral expenses, then resolves to do battle with Parisian society as he overlooks the city from the hill in Pere Lachaise cemetery.

Among the greatest of the tales in Balzac's sequence on 19th century France, *The Human Comedy*, this novel initiates the reader into the Parisian world of which Balzac was the unparalleled chronicler. In addition, it introduces several of the principal characters whose further adventures will occupy the action of subsequent texts in the sequence: Rastignac, the criminal Vautrin, and Goriot's daughter Mme de Nucingen.

Modeled loosely on Shakespeare's *King Lear*, the novel blends pathos and irony in a manner characteristic of all Balzac's major fiction.

FATHERS AND SONS
Ivan Turgenev
1862
Novel
Tragedy, Family Saga

This is an account of a generational struggle between the "sons"—represented by the rebellious medical student Yevgeny Bazarov—and the "fathers," best typified by the conservative landowner Pavel Kirsanov. It stirred up an immense and acrimonious debate centering on the character and ideas of Bazarov, easily the most controversial protagonist in 19th century Russian letters.

In the spring of 1859, a middle-aged Russian gentleman, Nikolai Kirsanov, welcomes back to his estate his university-educated son, Arkady. The latter is accompanied by his fellow student Bazarov, whom he greatly admires. Bazarov soon finds himself engaged in fiercely ideological debates with Nikolai's brother, Pavel, who dresses in elegant English fashion, parades the most fastidious of manners, and defends the conservative views of the "generation of the 1840's" against the brusquely irreverent attacks of Bazarov's "generation of the 1860's." Bazarov meets and finds himself falling in love with a wealthy, refined but frigid widow, Anna Odintsov; Arkady meanwhile romances her younger sister,

Katya. Bazarov's relationship with Madame Odintsov ends abruptly when he declares his love for her and she retreats hastily, whispering, "You have misunderstood me."

At the Kirsanovs' residence, Bazarov is challenged to a duel by Pavel, wounds him slightly, and therefore finds further stay there impossible. He returns to the home of his old-fashioned parents and helps his father with his medical practice. While dissecting the body of a peasant who died of typhoid fever, Bazarov cuts and infects himself, finds no caustic available as antidote, and dies within a few days. Arkady marries his Katya, and Nikolai Kirsanov jumps the class barrier to wed his servant-mistress, Fenichka.

The meaning of the novel hinges heavily on Bazarov, who unites its various foci of interest. He proudly calls himself a "nihilist," yet is hardly a revolutionary: He has no coherent system, strategy, tactics, no opportunity or time for political action; his only ally, Arkady, soon abandons him. Bazarov's basic urge is to clear the rotten ground of the establishment's inertia and smug self-satisfaction, in order to replace it with a new improved society based on tough-minded individualism, hard work, scientism, and utilitarianism. "A decent chemist is twenty times more useful than any poet," is a characteristic Bazarovian statement.

Turgenev maintains a delicate balance in his characterization of Bazarov. He shows his hero's provocative rudeness, anti-aesthetic coarseness, and brusque cynicism, but he also portrays Bazarov's integrity, energy, passion, and valor. In a retrospective essay, he declared, "with the exception of Bazarov's views on art, I share almost all his convictions."

FAUST
Johann Wolfgang von Goethe
1790
Drama
Philosophical

In his quest for the meaning of existence, Faust risks eternal damnation by making a pact with the devil, Mephistopheles. Goethe's masterpiece, a 12,000-line dramatic poem in two parts, is one of the great works of world literature. It is also one of the few modern myths treating a universal theme as old as Adam, Eve, and the Garden, a central theme in Western culture: the risk of damnation by a desire for knowledge.

In prologue in Heaven, reminiscent of the biblical Book of Job, Mephistopheles bets God that he can corrupt God's faithful servant on earth, Faust.

Faust is a restless striver with an insatiable desire for experience and knowledge. He wagers that the devil can never cause him to be self-satisfied, or to wish any experience or achievement to last forever.

Mephistopheles tempts Faust with debauchery. Together they attend a witches' Sabbath. The devil restores Faust's youth and tempts him with the love of a woman, Gretchen. Faust becomes adviser to the Emperor and marries Helen of Troy, the world's most beautiful woman, but Faust finds none of these experiences ultimately satisfying.

In an effort to be useful to his fellowman, Faust drains a large tract of swampy land, making it productive for thousands of people. Though old and blind now, Faust imagines the fair scene he has created, and wishes for the moment to be prolonged.

With this expression of satisfaction, he loses his wager with the devil, who attempts to claim Faust's soul.

God, however, intervenes. Unquestionably, Faust has sinned: He has seduced and then abandoned the innocent maiden, Gretchen; he has caused an old couple who stood in the way of his reclamation project to be burned in their cottage. Still, God declares that while Faust made mistakes, he always strove to do good and therefore deserves salvation.

Goethe transformed a legendary medieval folk figure into a representative Western man, and a crude legend about a magician's desire for pleasure and power into a story of man's highest hopes and noblest aspirations.

FEAR AND TREMBLING
Søren Kierkegaard
1843
Nonfiction
Philosophical

Kierkegaard re-creates the biblical story of Abraham and Isaac to explain what it means to exercise real faith.

According to Kierkegaard, there are three stages of human existence. The most immature is the aesthetic, in which people are dominated by their physical, emotional, or intellectual desires. Gratification is fleeting, so the aesthete is never satisfied. The second stage is the ethical, in which people are dominated by a sense of right and wrong. Choices are often ambiguous, though, and sometimes people must choose between equally evil options, so those in the ethical stage remain as unfulfilled as those in the aesthetic stage.

The subject of *Fear and Trembling* is the third stage, the religious. But there are two types of religious persons: the Knight of Infinite Resignation, the person who has an awakened religious consciousness but who is bound by guilt; and the Knight of Faith, the person who lives in response to God, regardless of appearances.

Abraham is such a Knight of Faith. God had promised him that he would be the father of a multitude of nations, beginning with his son Isaac, who was born to Abraham and his wife Sarah, theretofore barren, in their old age. As a test, however, God commanded Abraham to sacrifice Isaac. An ethical person or a Knight of Infinite Resignation would have disobeyed God, because the command was not only for murder but also for an act that would negate God's promise. Abraham obeyed in what Kierkegaard calls a teleological suspension of the ethical—that is, obedience to a divine command which supersedes moral law.

In part, *Fear and Trembling* was Kierkegaard's explanation for breaking his engagement to Regine Olsen, the love of his life. Kierkegaard had to sacrifice Regine, but he could not regain her because of his guilty conscience. He was still a Knight of Infinite Resignation.

FICCIONES
Jorge Luis Borges
1944
Short Story
Collection

Published in translation in the United States in 1962, this landmark collection is representative of the author's career-long interest in fabulous themes and self-referential literary techniques. The stories of Borges introduced an international readership to the remarkable vitality of recent Latin American fiction.

The imagination of Jorge Luis Borges is a place of endless proliferation. His stories are filled with images of mirrors, masks, and mazes, and they abound with allusions not only to other literary texts but also to the whole range of intellectual history. Technically, they are endlessly intricate, as identities merge and fracture, actions multiply and repeat, and texts serve as testing grounds for the metafictional enterprise.

The narrative conventions of plot, character, and setting are redefined in these stories. They may more appropriately be seen as language problems or inquiries into the nature of how fiction is created and read. For example, "Pierre Menard, Author of Don Quixote" parodies literary criticism, as a pedantic reviewer analyzes the superiority of a verbatim twentieth century "reinvention" of the classic novel to its original.

Other stories, such as "The Library of Babel," "The Lottery in Babylon" and "Tlon, Uqbar, Orbis Tertius," present fantasticated worlds in which the boundaries between reality and illusion are erased. Another group, highlighted by "The Garden of the Forking Paths," "Death and the compass," and "The Form of the Sword," seem to turn plot into a conspiracy of form, so that the reader must double as detective, burrowing his way through layered identities and texts within texts. Or Borges will explore the possibilities opened up by impossible premises, as in "The Secret Miracle," whose heroes create for themselves the ability to author fate. Each story is its own elaborate dream system, an elegant game with its structure exposed.

A FINE BALANCE
Rohinton Mistry
1995
Novel
Historical, Political

This 1995 sociological novel by a Canadian author of Indian heritage nestles in Bombay during the Emergency (1975-84) when the Indian government curbed civil rights to augment regional control. A successful stage version of the novel was performed in London in 2006 and revived in 2007.

The novel chronicles the lives of four protagonists, from different ethnic backgrounds, who experience deep friendship living together in Mumbai (Bombay) when society was undergoing rapid modernization under the controversial rule of Indira Gandhi.

Dina, an independent-minded widow, refuses to live with her wealthy brother. She starts her own clothing business by employing Ishvar and Omprakash, uncle and nephew, as tailors despite their low-caste background as leather workers. Maneck, a young student from the North arrives in Mumbai to attend college. He lodges with Dina, a distant relative, when ostracized by other students for not being politically active.

The shantytown Ishvar and Omprakash occupy is bulldozed by the government without compensation. Like many others from the neighborhood, Ishvar and Omprakesh are arrested and sold into slavery. The Beggarmaster, head of local beggars, helps them to bribe their way out of the labor camp. The Beggarmaster assists and protects Dina whose little sewing business is in violation of zoning laws. The Beggarmaster is murdered, and Dina's landlord illegally evicts her.

At 18, Ishvar returns home with his uncle to look for a wife. Maneck returns home with a certificate rather than a degree. He finds conditions impossible: his father's small soda business is failing due to larger bottle distributors. Maneck takes a job in Dubai.

Ishvar and Omprakesh are seized by a government population control agency. They receive forced vasectomies; Ishvar's legs become infected, and then amputated; during surgery, Omprakesh is also castrated because he had offended the pride of a high caste acquaintance, by spitting in his presence.

After eight years, Maneck returns home for his father's funeral. His three sisters have serially hung themselves because their father could not provide a dowry. He visits Dina. Shattered at the news of his friend's fates as street beggars and his sister's deaths, he commits suicide by walking onto the train tracks.

The book's title refers to the precarious ledge that the downtrodden occupy in a society based more on greed than generosity or even common sense. Despite intense tragedy, the novel exhibits benevolent charm.

FINNEGANS WAKE
James Joyce
1939
Novel
Stream-of-Conciousness

A vast exploration of the myths underlying everyday experience, this work is written in a dream language. Thus, through symbol, allusion, and the splitting of language into its elements, the experiences of an ordinary Dublin family are fashioned to reveal all the history of the world.

Finnegans Wake takes place in the course of one night's dreams of the five members of a Dublin family: Humphrey Chimpden Earwicker, his wife Anna Livia Plurabelle, their twin sons Shem and Shaun, and daughter Issy. The fears, desires, conflicts, and confusions of these primary dreamers unfold to embrace social and political themes, so that their nightmares reveal the whole development of human history.

This development is imagined as cyclical, whereby all the experiences of life recur in every generation, and the large sweep of history returns upon itself to repeat previous patterns. Highly elaborated analogies between popular and intellectual culture, Irish and world politics, trivial incidents and momentous events are conveyed by means of an original "night language" drawn from dozens of languages impressed upon an English base. Every element in *Finnegans Wake* is meaningful and part of the total design. Thus, the title, borrowed from a comic Irish-American ballad, suggests etymologically that ends beget new beginnings.

Finnegans Wake is one of the most brilliant and complex literary works of the twentieth century. It has had a larger influence on writers than on the general public, but even the casual reader will find it a very funny book. Serious readers, however, are divided into devotees and those who consider its language too idiosyncratic to repay the committed study it requires.

THE FIRE NEXT TIME
James Baldwin
1963
Nonfiction
African American, Civil Rights Manifesto

Baldwin's eloquent manifesto, which calls on whites and blacks to avert the nightmare of a racial civil war originally appeared in The New Yorker *in 1962 as "Letter from a Region in My Mind," caused an immediate sensation, was quickly published in book form, and helped galvanize the widespread movement that resulted in the Civil Rights Act of 1964.*

Baldwin frames the substance of his sermon inside a dedicatory letter to his nephew, "On the One Hundredth Anniversary of the Emanciption." He advises the nephew to accept white Americans—and do so lovingly—even though they have established a society that considers most black men worthless. Why? Because, says Baldwin, son of a minister and himself a former boy evangelist, all men are brothers and America is the black as well as white man's house.

He then testifies to this text with an account of his youth and young manhood, covering events he previously narrated in essays collected as *Notes of a Native Son* (1955) and *Nobody Knows My Name* (1962), and in his autobiographical first novel, *Go Tell It on the Mountain* (1953). As a teenage preacher he finds himself active in the "church racket," which is only marginally superior to gambling, pimping, or trafficking in drugs. He soon becomes disillusioned with what he discovers to be a white man's God, in whose name white "Christians" behave arrogantly, cruelly, and self-righteously.

The next and more powerful temptation is represented by the Nation of Islam movement, headed by Elijah Muhammad and dedicated to the premises that, while Christianity is the white man's wicked rationale for oppressing blacks, the true religion is that of Allah; all white people are cursed devils whose sway will end forever in ten to fifteen years, with God now black and all black people chosen by Him for domination under the theology of Islam.

Baldwin describes an audience with Elijah: Muhammad is lucid, passionate, cunning—but he preaches a dogma of racial hatred that is no better than the reverse of whites' hatred for blacks.

Baldwin rejects it, saying to himself: "isn't love more important than color?" He recognizes that the American blacks' complex fate is to deliver white Americans from their imprisonment in myths of racial superiority and educate them into a new, integrated sensitivity and maturity. Should such an effort fail, then the words of a slave song may come true: "God gave Noah the rainbow sign, No more water, the fire next time!"

THE FIRST CIRCLE
Aleksandr Solzhenitsyn
1968
Novel
Historical

Winner of the Nobel Prize for Literature, Solzhenitsyn spent years as a prisoner in the Soviet labor camps, an experience fictionalized here and described more comprehensively in his work of nonfiction, The GuLag Archipelago.

The *First Circle* takes place at the Mavrino Institute outside Moscow in 1949, when Stalin's postwar frenzy of arbitrary arrests and detentions was at its height. As opposed to the hard-labor camps, Mavrino offers a relatively pleasant life to its highly educated "zeks." Like the wise pagan philosophers whom Dante consigned to the "first" or least horrible circle of his Inferno, they are the privileged inmates of the Gulag.

There is, however, a price for their privileges. A young minor diplomat, Innokenty Volodin, has tried to warn an eminent scientist, once his family physician, not to make an exchange of information with foreign doctors that will be used to accuse him of treason. The phone is tapped. Can the caller be identified from a recording of his voice? The prisoners of Mavrino are told to come up with a device that will identify telephone voices as surely as if they were fingerprints.

Among the central figures who are thus faced with a moral dilemma are Lev Rubin, a linguist and convinced Communist, and Gleb Nerzhin, a mathematician who, as Solzhenitsyn himself did, writes in secret. Watching the effects of Nerzhin's imprisonment on his relations with his wife, Nadya, we see how much each prisoner has to lose.

Under Stalinism, as Solzhenitsyn satirically observes, jailers and bureaucrats tremble as much as the prisoners themselves. Stalin himself, lost in fearful, deadly paranoia, is captured in an unforgettable psychological portrait.

In the end, Volodin is arrested, and Nerzhin, who has refused a job that would have led to his release and reunion with his wife, is transported back to an ordinary camp. Yet the ending is upbeat. This collective novel finds its real hero in the solidarity of the prisoners, who uphold moral principles despite their imprisonment and defeat.

THE FIVE-FORTY-EIGHT
John Cheever
1954
Short Story

This story of a psychotic woman's revenge brilliantly portrays the ways in which a successful and entirely selfish businessman protects himself from physical harm and, more important, preserves his baseless dignity.

The story begins when Blake, leaving work, steps out of an elevator and sees Miss Dent. In flashbacks, the reader learns that Blake had seduced the woman, a former mental patient, and subsequently abandoned her, taking the afternoon off while his company's personnel department fired her. Her sudden appearance and uncharacteristic look of determination turn the tables on Blake, who must face the fact of his own vulnerability. Nevertheless, Blake remains confident that he can outwit the woman and escape into the safety of the suburban community of Shady Hill.

It soon becomes clear that Blake's confidence in his own powers is as baseless as his self-importance, which appears to be founded on nothing more substantial than his willingness to act selfishly and to observe the "sumptuary laws" of the upper-middle-class society to which he belongs. It was Miss Dent's need for love that originally led her to Blake, and it is her need to reclaim some measure of self-respect that leads her to follow Blake to Shady Hill and to force him at gunpoint to grovel in the dirt at her feet. Having accomplished her task and having taught Blake a lesson, she walks off, a more dignified and certainly more merciful figure than he.

Cheever's ambiguous ending—"He got to his feet and picked up his hat from the ground where it had fallen and walked home"—leaves the reader unsure whether Blake has understood Miss Dent's lesson. Against the clarity of her message, one must weigh the fact that Blake, who may very well be Cheever's most unlikable character, is remarkable not only for his callous use of others but also for his capacity for self-deception and for confusing the sumptuary laws by which he lives with the moral obligations and human responsibilities to which Cheever subscribes.

THE FIXER
Bernard Malamud
1966
Novel
Political

Based on the actual case of Mendel Beiliss, a Kiev Jew accused of ritual murder, the story of Yakov Bok and his tribulations is a moving testimony to the greatness of the human spirit in durance vile.

Fed up with poverty, Yakov Bok decides to leave the shtetl and travel to Kiev in search of work. He attempts to leave behind an ethnic identity that has meant only hardship and suffering. For a while, he manages to pass for a Gentile and to hold a decent job. Unfortunately, however, a child is found horribly murdered, and Bok, exposed as a Jew, is accused of having drained its blood to make matzos.

Bok is imprisoned under terrible conditions; the authorities try to force a confession to spare them the embarrassment of a trial that will make Russian jurisprudence a world laughingstock. Initially no hero, Bok discovers the iron in his soul and refuses to confess—even when offered a pardon.

Bok's is a spiritual journey towards a recognition of responsibility to his fellow Jews. He realizes that no one—least of all a Jew—can opt out of history. He comes to see his prison cell, like the shtetl before it, as a microcosm of the much larger prison that is Russia under the Czar, and by the end of the novel he has become what he thought he could never be: a political man, capable of revolutionary violence.

The Fixer, then, is about a turning point in history. Malamud has constructed a parable about the birth of political consciousness in the early twentieth century. The fantasized act of political violence at the end of the novel, like the bombing of the carriage that is conveying Bok to his long-awaited trial, is a portent of the terrorism that would soon start World War I and end the reign of the Romanovs.

FLOWERS FOR ALGERNON
Daniel Keyes
1966
Novella
Epistolary

This 1966 picaresque science fiction novel exploits the theme of possibly increasing intelligence for the mentally disabled.

Algernon (named after the poet Swinburne) is a mouse who has, through experimentation, acquired increased intelligence. As a subject in the same experiment, Charlie Gordon, a mentally challenged 32-year-old man with an IQ of 68, is encouraged to keep a diary of his thoughts. At first, he writes his reports in phonetic spelling with naïve honesty, but after his experimental surgery, replicating the procedure used on Algernon, he writes with sophisticated style and acute insight. Charlie's post-surgery IQ is 185 (180 remains the maximum score). Once ridiculed for his lack of intelligence at his menial bakery job, Charlie becomes ostracized because of his high intelligence. Keyes satirizes the anti-intellectual strain in American culture as well as prejudice against the handicapped.

Charlie lives with Algernon (who is caged). Both resent being living experiments. Charlie attempts romance with his former teacher, Alice, the only character who appreciates him regardless of his intelligence. Their relationship fails, and he successfully rebounds with bohemian artist Fay who appears in Charlie's midtown Manhattan apartment at whim, via the fire escape, with her usual bottle of gin.

When sober, Charlie examines the biological procedure he has endured; he discovers a fatal flaw that indicates he may revert to his former disability.

Recalling his emotional abuse by his parents, and subsequent institutionalization, Charlie visits his parents. His mother suffers from dementia and his father, a barber, refuses to recognize him. Charlie's younger sister Norma accepts him. She asks Charlie to stay; yet he departs, promising financial support for their ailing mother.

Charlie's intelligence begins to fade. Terrified, Fay ends their relationship. With his reduced intelligence, Alice now accepts Charlie and briefly shares his bed with idyllic ecstasy, but their relationship concludes when Charlie's intelligence takes a severe nosedive. Algernon dies. No longer able to hold a job, Charlie once more becomes a student in Alice's class.

Charlie cannot endure the embarrassing pathos of being Alice's student. He moves into the Warren Home for the mentally disabled and regresses to his early primitive style in his near-daily diary entries, ironically called progress reports. In a final note to Alice, Charlie requests that she put some flowers on Algernon's grave, located in the backyard of their former romantic digs.

Like Mary Shelley's *Frankenstein,* the novel questions the science and philosophy of humankind's ambition to be God.

FLOWERS OF EVIL
Charles Baudelaire
1857
Poetry
Lyric

Baudelaire's brilliantly structured poems are often celebrated for their bold metaphors and bizarre juxtapositions of beauty and ugliness. Hothouse flowers, they celebrate a great range of unseemly sensual dependencies—an eroticism that strikes readers, even in a more permissive age, as perverse.

Although dismissed as morbid by many of his contemporaries, Baudelaire was actually lancing the boils of neurotic repression. He confronted images of gross flesh, the intoxications of strange touch and smell, forbidden sensual desires and fantasies; he celebrated exotic but voraciously consuming women, cats and tigresses who clawed their way to his heart. By flaunting such forbidden flights of fancy in an age of bourgeois respectability and hypocritical religiosity, Baudelaire was updating the liberating imperative of Romanticism.

He adopted the macabre from Edgar Allan Poe—a writer he introduced to his native France and whose influence on French literature has been immense—sexualized it, and then grafted it to the hauteur and defiance of Byronic independence.

Baudelaire was not merely glorifying art in the manner of the aestheticists who followed him later in the 19th century. His unique manipulations of Romantic ideas and attitudes broke important ground in the historical development of literary modernism. It is Baudelaire who must receive credit for much of what we have come to take for granted in modern poetry: stark and bold images sharply contrasted, richly textured lines that reward close reading with symbolic discovery, and a sense of form and control that seems to validate the modern artist's right to deal with matters usually considered too unconventional for public discourse.

The impact of Baudelaire's art has been immense; his influence on modern American poetry has been greater than that of any poet of his time.

FOR ESMÉ—WITH LOVE AND SQUALOR
J. D. Salinger
1950
Short Story
War

A chance encounter with a thirteen-year-old girl in England helps an American soldier deal with the tragedy of World War II.

The story is one of the best in Salinger's *Nine Stories*, a remarkable collection depicting varying responses to the meaningless hell that modern life has become for many people. It offers, with subdued sentimentality, a positive response to this hell.

In the first half of the story, the narrator, Sergeant X, meets Esme and her young brother Charles in a Devonshire tearoom just before embarking for the D-Day invasion. The children are orphans, their father having died in the war. Esme has great sympathy for the pain that the loss has caused Charles but shows no self-pity. She says she is training herself to be more compassionate. When she learns that X is a writer, she asks him to write a story for her about squalor.

In the second half, the war has ended, and X, stationed in Bavaria after five campaigns, is having a nervous breakdown. Esme has hoped that he would return from the war with all his faculties intact, but he has not. Borrowing from Fyodor Dostoevski, he defines that hell he is going through as the inability to love.

Then he receives a package from Esme mailed a few weeks after their meeting. She has sent him her most prized possession, her father's wristwatch. She also includes an affectionate message from Charles, whom she is teaching to read and write.

Esme's compassion, her ability to reconcile herself to the horrors of the real world, and her gift of love and time move a man who has felt out of touch with any emotions other than despair. If such compassion can exist, Sergeant X can find peace; he can write Esme a story not only with squalor but also with love.

FOR THE UNION DEAD
Robert Lowell
1964
Poetry
Lyric

This poem, a meditation on a Civil War monument set against the backdrop of contemporary Boston, unites past and present conflicts and images of personal and public decay into one of the most powerful contemporary poems.

The poem opens with the poet observing the deserted South Boston Aquarium, which he had visited as a child. The ruined building is symbolic both of his lost childhoood and of the decay of Boston, undergoing massive urban renewal, which disturbs such landmarks as the Statehouse and the statue of Colonel Shaw.

The statue causes the poet to think of Shaw, an abolitionist's son and leader of the first black regiment in the Civil War. Shaw died in the war, and his statue is a monument to the heroic ideals of New England life, which are jeopardized in the present just as the statue itself is shaken by urban renewal.

Images of black children entering segregated schools reveal how the ideals for which Shaw and his men died were neglected after the Civil War. The poem's final stanzas return to the aquarium. The poet pictures Shaw riding on a fish's air bubble, breaking free to the surface, but in fact, the aquarium is abandoned and the only fish are fin-tailed cars.

This poem is a brilliant example of Lowell's ability to link private turmoil to public disturbances. The loss of childhood in the early section of the poem expands to the loss of America's early ideals, and both are brought together in the last lines to give the poem a public and private intensity.

The poem is organized into unrhymed quatrains of uneven length, allowing a measure of flexibility within a formal structure. This style reflects the poem's combination of private and public concerns and gives substance to the poem's ideas.

FOR WHOM THE BELL TOLLS
Ernest Hemingway
1940
Novel
War

An American, Robert Jordan, fights for the Loyalist cause in the Spanish Civil War of the 1930's in a story which explores a man's commitment to himself, to his fellowman, and to the woman he loves.

Robert Jordan has been assigned the difficult military mission of blowing up a bridge behind enemy lines. After making contact with a small band of guerrilla fighters, he plans the bridge-blowing operation against the wishes of Pablo, the leader of the band. During the three-day period of the novel's action, Robert Jordan falls in love with Maria, a young woman living with the guerrillas. The two have an intense affair in which they become committed to each other.

The structure of the novel is centered on the bridge-blowing operation, with flashbacks and narrative subplots which reach out from this central focus to the larger incidents and issues of the war to create an epic scope.

Like other Hemingway heroes, Robert Jordan has a life filled with the enjoyment of simple, sensuous pleasures—the experiences of eating and drinking, the brotherhood of comrades dedicated to living life fully, the intense bond between man and nature. As the novel builds toward its climax, he also exemplifies the Hemingway ideal of commitment to meaningful physical action.

Although fatally wounded, Jordan completes his mission. In his very struggle to live life in the best possible way, whatever the cost, he achieves the status of a tragic hero, and thus he affirms our existence.

THE FORSYTE SAGA
John Galsworthy
1906, 1922, 1921
Novel
Trilogy
This fictional trilogy tells the story of the wealthy Forsyte family, while also chronicling the changes in British society from the late Victorian era through the first decades of the 20th century.

Written eover a period of four decades and covering more than 50 years of British history, Galsworthy's nine Forsyte novels (*The Forsyte Saga* is the name given only to the first three books) provide often trenchant social criticism of England's upper-middle class, represented in these novels by the landowning, mercantile Forsyte family. Galsworthy's underlying concern in this vast cycle of novels is the moral and spiritual decline of the social class embodied by the Forsytes, whose greed and blindness to social progress leaves them unprepared for the cataclysm of the 20th century.

Primarily a realist in his technique, Galsworthy at his best perfectly captures the social rituals and the physical settings that characterize the Forsyte way of life: the business meetings in bank offices, the receptions held in stuffy drawing rooms, the joyless weddings in expensive but lifeless houses. His characters are nevertheless types that are easily recognizable in real life: Soames Forsyte, the prosperous but unfulfilled man of affairs; his wife Irene, bored with possessions and in need of passion; Old Jolyon Forsyte, the dynasty founder; Soames' daughter Fleur, the new woman. Through the use of such a huge time frame, Galsworthy is able to convey the stark differences between the various generations treated in the novels, while also commenting upon the societal changes that are occurring around them.

Though the novels were immensely popular when they were first published, Galsworthy, along with his contemporaries Arnold Bennett and H. G. Wells, came under attack in the 1920's by Virginia Woolf, E. M. Forster, James Joyce, and other more characteristically modern writers who disdained the heavy and predictable realism of the older authors' work. But a whole new generation discovered the Forsyte novels when they were adapted for television by the BBC in the late 1960's.

FOUR QUARTETS
T. S. Eliot
1943
Poetry
Four closely related poems, three of which were originally published separately, form together the religious climax to the career of the best-known poet of the 20th century.

Four Quartets represents the culmination of Eliot's career as both a modernist and a Christian poet; he completes the spiritual quest that has been apparent in his work since his first published poem, "The Love Song of J. Alfred Prufrock." The conclusion of this quest is in what Eliot calls "the timeless moment," those points in life where the eternal and the temporal intersect, making meaning possible in an otherwise trivial world.

Eliot explores these timeless moments in four specific settings that have significance in his own life, three in England and one in New England. Among the themes common to the quartets is the need for escape from the tyranny of self and from the emptiness of a distracted and distracting world. Another, explored in the same section of each quartet, is the questionable ability of language, specifically poetry, to serve as a vehicle for meaning.

Eliot finds ultimate meaning in an emptying of self that makes possible recognition of a truer self in union with God, "the still point of the turning world." He seeks this union in the concreteness of his own life, realizing at last the optimism at the heart of faith—that, despite appearances, "All shall be well."

This work typifies Eliot's later style—it is more personal, symbolist, and philosophical than the poems that made him famous. It shows an Eliot who, while still struggling, has reached a new level of peace and acceptance. For some,

Four Quartets represents a falling off from Eliot's early greatness; for others, it is his best poetry and one of the landmarks of religious, philosophical poetry in the English language.

FRANKENSTEIN
Mary Wollstonecraft Shelley
1818
Novel
Gothic, Horror, Epistolary

Although it is often thought of as only a horror story, in part because of many melodramatic film adaptations, this novel is also a deeply philosophical study of how the pursuit of knowledge may both ennoble and damn man.

The plot revolves around Victor Frankenstein, who is dissatisfied with the limits of traditional knowledge and buries himself in scientific studies to discover hidden secrets of life and death. He succeeds brilliantly, ultimately becoming, like God, able to create life, but he pays a great price for his ambition, separating himself from nature, his family, and his fiancee.

Even the moment of his greatest success proves to be ominous. When his new creation comes to life, Victor is unwilling to face up to his responsibilities. He turns his back, spurning the being who should be his child or brother. As a result, the creature begins a life of alienation that turns him into a monster.

Ironically, the monster is articulate and sympathetic as he tells his own sad story. Although he is born in a state of innocence, constant mistreatment by everyone with whom he comes in contact makes him extremely bitter and causes him to strike back in a murderous rage at his creator, who turned him loose in a loveless world. The monster's revenge comes when he robs Victor of his loved ones.

From this point on, the monster and Victor are bound together, not as the brothers they should have been but as deadly enemies. The quest to create life is completely perverted as Victor chases the monster across the barren, icy wilderness of the North Pole, where both of them perish.

The novel is thus an effective critique of man's penchant for irresponsible creativity, his willingness to make scientific and technological experiments that may seriously threaten rather than serve his most important need for love, friendship, and tranquillity. But Victor and the monster are not so much villains as they are typically ambiguous Romantic heroes: Victor fails miserably, but his quest is inspiring; and the monster, though a murderer, is also a victim, and an eloquent and sympathetic rebel against forces that violate his basic rights.

FRANNY AND ZOOEY
J. D. Salinger
1961
Novel
Psychological

These two novellas about a sister and brother, Franny and Zooey Glass, continue the author's chronicle—begun in 1948—of an eccentric family with extraordinary creative and destructive energies.

Franny is in a state of nervous collapse. She has failed to fit in with the "collegiately dogmatic" atmosphere of schools such as Yale, where her boyfriend, Lane Coutell, pompously presides. After a disastrous weekend with him, in which she lets her disgust with phoniness rule all of her reactions, she returns home to her mother and father in a zombielike state.

Zooey is a successful television actor who still lives with his parents. Although Franny and he are famous for their intellectual abilities, having once been the stars of a popular radio quiz show, he refuses to go on for his Ph.D. As an actor he has freed himself to play any role he likes. It is his way of coping with the family's high expectations.

It is inevitable, then, that Zooey will confront Franny on home ground. With considerable humor, irony, and mimicry he demonstrates that the superior Glasses have set themselves too far apart from others. In the case of the eldest brother, Seymour, this superior attitude has evidently led to suicide.

Salinger makes Zooey a figure of great authority, for this actor has gone through the struggle which his sister is now experiencing: a quest for a distinct identity that will not cut her off from the society with which she must come to terms if she is to survive. This is a very funny and very wise work of literature.

THE FRENCH LIEUTENANT'S WOMAN
John Fowles
1969
Novel

The English author's third published novel is a richly detailed historical entertainment that probes the freedom of its characters and of its own narrative designs. Set in Wessex in 1867, it affords its readers a backward glance at an era that shared many of their own preoccupations.

While in Lyme Regis to visit his fiancee, Ernestina Freeman, Charles Smithson, a 32-year-old paleontologist, becomes fascinated by the mysterious Sarah Woodruff. A fallen woman said to have been jilted by a French officer, Sarah is a pariah to the well-bred society that Charles and Ernestina are a part of. While searching for fossils in a wooded coastal area, Charles encounters Sarah alone, and his curiosity and pity for her soon evolve into other emotions.

It is not clear who seduces whom, but when another opportunity presents itself, Charles embraces Sarah passionately. Shortly thereafter, Sarah disappears, having been dismissed from domestic employment by the tyrannical do-gooder Mrs. Poultenay. Charles finds her in a room in Exeter, where he declares and demonstrates his love.

Inspired by his image of Sarah as a valiant rebel against Victorian conventions, Charles rejects the constricting, respectable life Ernestina represents for him. He breaks off their engagement and is harassed with legal action for breach of contract. Meanwhile, Sarah vanishes again, and Charles spends 20 months scouring the world for her, finally tracing her to the lodgings of Dante Gabriel Rossetti in London.

Consistent with the author's playful intrusions throughout the novel, Fowles provides three possible conclusions to his story. He is intent on celebrating his characters' independence of the oppressive institutions of Victorian society, but he also concedes them freedom from their author, refusing to restrict them to any single plot he invents.

Through his wealth of literary allusions, digressions on 19th century England, and mocking anachronisms, Fowles also liberates his reader from imprisonment within either of two eras and within the author's own literary contrivance. When he shows himself sharing a railway compartment with one of his characters, Fowles flaunts the emancipated imagination. Even while borrowing its themes and techniques, he ridicules the limitations of the 19th century novel.

G

GENJI MONOGATARI
Murasaki Shikibu
1008-1021
Novel
Historical

Arguably the world's first novel, Genji Monogatari is a massive, fifty-four-volume tome of more than one thousand pages (in the English translation), written by Murasaki Shikibu, a lady-in-waiting for Empress Shōshi. Originally written at the request of the Empress, who had tired of existing fiction, Murasaki's masterpiece draws a vivid portrayal of court life, and the society of her time. The story follows the adventures of a tenth century prince named Genji.

Scholars agree that no other author, with the possible exception of William Shakespeare, has had the close scrutiny and flood of exegesis as Murasaki Shikibu. In addition to more than ten thousands books written about *The Tale of Genji*, entire dictionaries, concordances, encyclopedias, and textual commentaries attest to the difficulties of translating the text, which was written in obscure, antiquated court Japanese. Murasaki Shikibu is an accomplished poet, lacing poetry throughout her narrative, not unlike a contemporary stage musical cast breaking into song.

Adding to the linguistic barriers, the tale features nearly fifty major characters, many of whom are not named but are instead referred to by physical characteristics, actions, or public title. Neither does the narrative follow a chronological sequence.

The tale is one of romance and court intrigue, said to illustrate the correlation between beauty and sorrow. Genji is the Emperor's son, born to his father's favorite consort, Kiritsubo, who dies when the boy is just three. The bereaved emperor then marries Fujitsubo, a woman of high birth, who remarkably resembles Kiritsubo. (The author often uses physical likeness as a device to advance the narrative.) Genji is likewise drawn to Fujitsubo who so closely resembles his mother. He will later father a son with Fujitsubo, who will become Emperor Reizei.

While traveling, Genji meets Fujitsubo's ten-year-old niece, Murasaki. Enamored with the girl, Genji whisks her away to raise as his own, and marries her once she reaches adulthood. The charismatic Genji is exiled from court following a scandal after he is caught with a political rival's daughter. He welcomes this exile out of a sense of guilt, but also because he fears that Emperor Reizei's remarkable resemblance to him will be noticed (and the Emperor's secret parentage revealed).

A late chapter, titled "Vanished into the Clouds," is left entirely blank, and is thought to represent Genji's death. The final ten chapters occur after Genji's death, and feature his son and grandson.

GERMINAL
Émile Zola
1885
Novel
Sociological

Widely regarded as one of the greatest novels of the masses, Germinal is the story of an entire mining community struggling against unfettered capitalism and class exploitation.

Germinal is one of the twenty novels that make up the Rougon-Macquart cycle, an attempt by Emile Zola to put into practice the tenets he discussed in *The Experimental Novel* (1880). In that manifesto, Zola argued that the scientific method could be applied to the naturalistic novel. The novelist, then, could become a scientist, observing the human condition, forming a hypothesis, and exhibiting that hypothesis in the content of the novel. Believing that the course of an individual human life is wholly determined by heredity and environment, Zola thought that, with his writings, he could effect environmental change, resulting in significant changes in human behavior. Thus, novelist could become physician in both diagnostic and healer roles.

Germinal tells the story of Etienne Lantier, who takes a job in a mine in Northern France. An outsider to the community, Etienne has both the strength and intelligence to become a catalyst for the miners who are chronically starved and overworked. Etienne does rally them to strike, but he loses control of the workers when mob action triumphs over reason and terrible atrocities occur. At the end of the novel, the strike has been put down, the cowed workers are back in the mines, and Etienne leaves the village to take a post in the newly formed union.

Though a naturalistic novel, *Germinal* is constructed by Zola with careful attention to patterns of imagery that give the novel an aesthetically satisfying form and account for its tremendous effect and continuing popularity. The miners' cry for "bread" forms the base for one line of images that establishes the mine as a beast devouring the miners by shaft-loads, with its giant intestines capable of digesting an entire nation. Another dominant line of images is based on sexual activities, often bestial in their urgency. These two image-patterns coalesce in the castration of the grocer, Maigrat, an action that comes during the mob scene at the climax of the novel.

After the atrocities committed by the mob, management in distant Paris resorts to armed force to put down the rebellion, and the workers are forced to return to conditions that are worse than ever. Middle-level managers as well as stockholders also lose life and property in the monumental struggle. But, at the end of the novel, it is springtime again, and seeds are once again germinating. Thus, Zola leaves a final impression that seeds for a new strike and changing conditions have been sown and are growing, too, and will someday erupt through the earth.

GHOSTS
Henrik Ibsen
1882
Drama

A woman discovers that her son has inherited the syphilis of his father. To her, this becomes symbolic of how outmoded yet pernicious ideas from the past haunt the present.

Helene Alving, the widow of Captain and Chamberlain Alving, lives on a country estate in Western Norway. A sum of money, inherited from her late husband, has enabled her to construct an orphanage in his memory. The memorial is undeserved, however, for Captain Alving was a carnal lecher and a drunkard who transmitted his own syphillis to his newborn son, Oswald. Captain Alving also fathered a daughter, Regine, by the family maid.

Alving's behavior, when discovered by his wife, led her to want to seek a divorce. Dissuaded by the family's spiritual adviser, Pastor Manders, she consented to remain in her degrading marriage out of a sense of Christian duty, imposed on her by the Pastor.

The play begins on the eve of the dedication of the orphanage. Mrs. Alving, Pastor Manders, and Oswald are all present in the house. So is Regine, who is employed as the family's maid. Mrs. Alving first reveals the shocking truth of Regine's parentage to the Pastor; she then explains that she has begun to question her received faith and has become a reader of "freethinking" literature.

While the two are debating this issue, they overhear a flirtatious scene between Oswald and Regine. Oswald, who suffers from severe headaches, believes that his condition would be improved if Regine were his wife. At the end of the play, the orphanage burns and Oswald's inherited syphilis turns to insanity. First, however, he has given his mother some morphine tablets with which she has promised to take his life when his disease reaches its final stage. She must now decide whether to fulfill her promise.

THE GIFT OF THE MAGI
O. Henry
1905
Short Story

On Christmas Eve, in an $8-a-week furnished flat in New York City, an impoverished young married couple find the meaning of love in intertwined acts of self-sacrifice.

Della had saved only one dollar and eighty-seven cents with which to buy Jim a Christmas present. Though she has saved for months, the sum is not nearly enough for the chain which she wants to give him as a fitting complement to his most prized possession, his gold watch. Saddened, she decides to get the extra money by selling her most prized possession, her hair.

When Jim comes home that night, Della has tightly curled her shorn hair, hoping that Jim will still find her pretty. For a few moments, Jim is dumbfounded, incredulous. Then he hugs his wife and lovingly gives her a Christmas present: a set of combs she has always wanted. To buy them as a complement to her most prized possession, he has sold his own, his gold watch.

In spite of an old-fashioned talkiness, the story succeeds because it tempers sentimentality with humor and real insight. The trick ending, typical of O. Henry, is here not so much a contrivance of plot as it is a genuine irony found often in the deepest human relationships. Jim's selling of his watch and Della's selling of her hair are not merely examples of manufactured storytelling, but rather of a recognition of love's readiness for ultimate self-sacrifice, which is its own reward. In depriving themselves, Della and Jim enrich each other. They are, as O. Henry concludes, the true magi, the wisest of the wise.

O. Henry maintains a lightness of tone, the attitude of a genial observer, so that the story does not become overburdened with false pathos, and the trick ending appears as natural as the course of true love.

THE GINGER MAN
J. P. Donleavy
1955
Novel

Picaresque

Sebastian Dangerfield, an American living in Ireland, wants every bourgeois comfort but is unwilling to make any sacrifices. Attracted to the easeful life, he rejects the restrictions such a life places upon him.

A thorough rogue, Sebastian tries to justify his unjustifiable behavior. Devoid of any conventional morality, he evolves an infinitely flexible code of conduct.

Sebastian lives with his English wife and infant daughter while supposedly studying law at Trinity on the G. I. Bill. Barging from one Dublin neighborhood to another, he leaves unpaid bills, damaged property, and broken hearts in his wake. He steals a mistress' belongings, slugs his wife, and tries to suffocate his screaming child with a pillow.

Donleavy's goal is to shock the reader's moral complacency. Donleavy knows that Sebastian's outrageous acts are wrong but does not try to explain them away, leaving the reader to deal with them.

Self-pitying to an extreme, Sebastian sees himself as persecuted without realizing that he creates all his problems. Yet he is an attractive character in spite of himself because of the ironic, self-mocking way he is presented, the comic energy which invigorates his adventures, and his refusal to give in to the forces of conformity.

The novel is inspired by the fable of the Gingerbread Man, who escapes all his pursuers only to be eaten by a fox that he foolishly trusts. Sebastian is unwillingly to commit himself irrevocably to anyone or anything for fear of being devoured, and he flees from those who want something from him.

This plotless novel rambles from episode to episode with only Sebastian's bawdy personality holding it together. The first-person narration frequently slips into the third person as Sebastian steps back to observe himself in action, a device which heightens the novel's irony.

THE GIVER
Lois Lowry
1993
Novel
Children's, Dystopian

When twelve-year-old Jonas learns that the elders have assigned him the life-long occupation of "Receiver"—the most respected job in the community—little does he know that the pain he's been forewarned to expect will be that of isolation and grief, as the only keeper of collective memory and the horrible secrets that hold his society together.

The society Jonas was born into is perfectly predictable. There is no pain or discomfort, every citizen is even-tempered and polite, and each individual's life has been prescribed to follow a predictable path. Emotion and behavior are carefully monitored; problems are rare and easily corrected. There is no need to make difficult decisions. Those are all made by the Committee of Elders, which selects each citizen's occupation, spouse, and children. Children are born to professional birth mothers, and spend a year with professional nurturers, before they are farmed out to applicants—families who have requested a child (only one boy and one girl per family). All children celebrate birthdays on the same day, earning new privileges as they progress to the next age group. "Ones" are given their names; "Twos" are introduced to the "discipline wand." Nines get bicycles for the first time, and Twelves learn what professions they will spend their lives practicing.

Things go awry for Jonas however, when he is selected to be his society's all-important "receiver." Suddenly, the rules he has spent his lifetime learning—particularly obedience and honesty—no longer matter. In fact, his role requires him to lie. His job is to hold the collective memories of his people (without their awareness) the pleasure and the pain, joy and sorrow of humanity. His mentor, the "giver," is charged with transmitting all these memories to Jonas, who must now bear the lonely burden.

After witnessing his "nurturer" father "releasing" a newborn, Jonas realizes the horrible truth about his society, and he can't bear the deception. He and the giver plan for Jonas's escape to "elsewhere" where life is lived fully. The giver offers to stay behind to pick up the pieces when the population is left to experience hardship and pain for the first time.

Lowry wrote *The Giver* following a visit with her father who suffered from dementia. She realized that without his memory, he didn't suffer, and she began to visualize a society comprised of people with no long-term memories.

THE GLASS MENAGERIE
Tennessee Williams
1945
Drama

Tom Wingfield, in deciding between a life of adventure and the oppressive responsibilities of family life, dramatizes the universal conflict in every youth in this best-known and most-admired of modern American plays.

By means of a direct monologue to the audience, Tom reports that his father, "falling in love with long distance," has deserted the family, leaving Tom to care for Laura, a plain sister with a slight limp, and Amanda, the neurotic mother unable to let go of the genteel courting traditions of her Southern upbringing. In one of the most touching scenes in American theater, Tom describes to Laura his exciting night at the magic show, a symbol of all the life experiences Tom is sacrificing to care for his family.

Browbeaten by Amanda into bringing home a gentleman caller for Laura, Tom finally confronts Amanda with her illusions and storms from the house, knocking over Laura's delicate glass menagerie. The unicorn's horn is broken, and this event, aside from its possible sexual meaning, symbolizes the loss of magic that occurs in the household with Tom's departure.

Williams' play, which began his very successful career, is an archetypal example of a distinctly American combination of themes: the disintegration of the American family as a result of the inbred sense of adventure and exploration in the American soul. Transcending its Southern ambience, the play speaks to every family's struggle between generations. If Amanda presents her side of the struggle with unusual zeal and power, it is a tribute to Williams' skill at re-creating the universal mother in modern guise. Indeed, since the play's first appearance, the role of Amanda has become one of the most coveted parts on the American stage.

GO TELL IT ON THE MOUNTAIN
James Baldwin
1953
Novel
Autobiographical Fiction, African American
John Grimes, a black preacher's stepson, comes to terms with his stepfather and the heritage of his race. The spiritual quests of deep and passionate characters make this a gripping novel.

John Grimes wants to be a man standing on his own; at the same time, he wants his father, Gabriel, to love him. He feels oppressed by his father and by his circumstances as a black youth in New York during the Depression. To achieve manhood, he must either accept his heritage or embrace a world he instinctively feels is evil: the materialistic and oppressive white world.

In order to accept his heritage in the religious terms he understands, he must come to terms with his father, the prophet and preacher. To John, it appears that Gabriel loves neither John nor his mother. John both loves and hates Gabriel; he wants to kneel before God but not before his father.

Gabriel is a hard and passionate man who sees himself as chosen by God to found a long line of preachers of the true gospel. Gabriel has made himself hard in order to control his strong desires for worldly pleasure. If Gabriel does love his wife and stepson, it is with the stern love of a judging God rather than the forgiving love of Jesus. Gabriel seems to reserve tenderness for his wayward, natural son, Roy. Gabriel prefers that Roy continue the line of preachers and resents the fact that John is more likely to be a preacher.

In the third of the novel's three parts, John experiences a religious conversion. Though this conversion does not make his father love him as John hopes it may, it allows John to feel compassion for Gabriel and for all suffering people whose hearts' desires conflict with their souls' aspirations.

Baldwin has drawn on his childhood in Harlem to give authenticity to his story. Because John, Gabriel, and other family members are so fully and deeply portrayed, this is a powerful first novel. Though the religious experiences of these characters may seem sectarian, they are really universal. All of the major characters are trying to build and sustain community in the face of dehumanizing oppression. Their particular version of Christianity is an effective response to being captives in a racist culture.

THE GOD OF SMALL THINGS
Arundhati Roy
1997
Novel
A reunion of long-separated twins and a recollection of the events that ultimately destroyed their once-distinguished South Indian family are intertwined through a disjointed and shifting narrative.

This debut novel, which dwells on the cruelty of separation, opens with a reunion of twins Rahel and Estha, the youngest members of a ruined South Indian family. The psychological states of the brooding brother and unpredictable sister resemble the desolate house where they meet after their long separation. Yet their reunion, taking place in the present, does not provide the plot with its impetus. Rather, the past defines and formulates the immediate.

Allusions to other literary works and popular culture, mostly of Western origin, fill the text, suggesting how an anglicized family like the Ipes have one foot in the West, the other in traditional Indian culture. In fact, this conflict may partially account for their downfall.

One allusion drawn from South Indian Hindu culture, the Kathakali dance tradition, works effectively. The form of *The God of Small Things* itself is comparable to that exquisite form of pantomime where every gesture tells part of the story and where the dancers are costumed elaborately. Except for the tourists who watch truncated versions of

Kathakali at luxury hotels (a fact that Roy mentions in the novel), the viewers already know the story but take pleasure and find sustenance in its retelling. Roy expects much the same kind of attention from her readers, because she lays out the complete story at the novel's beginning, then tells it again and again in elaborate and ornate gestures to an audience which already knows the plot line.

The anguish that befalls each character might be the work of "the god of small things." Or perhaps this "god" serves as a refuge. For this mysterious deity's nature never emerges clearly, even in the dream sequence when the twins' mother meets a one-armed man, then asks who he is: "Who was he, the one-armed man? Who could he have been? The God of Loss? The God of Small Things? The God of Goosebumps and Sudden Smiles? Of Sourmetal Smells—like steel bus rails and the smell of the bus conductor's hands from holding them?" While the author need not explain a central symbol, the mystery in which Roy cloaks her "god of small things" typifies the novel's major fault: a self-conscious obscurity, which results from a tendency to bask in cleverness.

And while Roy, at times, succeeds in going beyond language's barriers and setting fictional conventions on their ear, these attempts don't always work. What Roy does best is tell a story, not a direct one, but a story that unfolds imperfectly. Her sense of time's fluidity lends the novel a quality of memory, where events reoccur in no particular order and where motivations do not always ring clear until all the pieces fall into place. There is something Faulknerian about Roy's method of narration, but William Faulkner knew his limits. When Roy lets the story proceed without any superfluous fancy dress, she shows an accomplished mastery of narrative technique. Likewise, she can look into the interior of her characters and express what she sees convincingly.

At its best, which is most of the time, *The God of Small Things* relates a chilling story that stems from those dark elements of the human condition that separate the individual from happiness: hatred, greed, jealousy, bitterness, resentment. The novel explores with sensitivity the cultural conflicts that afflict many people in post-colonial India.

THE GOLDEN COMPASS
Philip Pullman
1995
Novel
Children's, Fantasy

In the wake of her best friend's kidnapping, spunky Lyra Belacqua leaves her home in search of her friend and her uncle, and to unravel the mystery of "Dust." The Northern Lights *questions the authority of religion from a child's perspective.*

In a land similar to late 19th Century England, Lyra, a 12-year-old orphan, lives at Jordan College in Oxford, playing with neighboring children and Pan, her daemon or external spirit. Occasionally, her uncle, Lord Asriel, visits and inquires about her education. On one such visit, Lyra hides in the study and learns about Dust, a mystical substance that adults seem to attract, but not children.

At the same time, Gobblers are kidnapping children; Lyra's best friend, Roger, is one such victim. Lyra's worry is sidetracked by the arrival of the enchanting Mrs. Coulter, a respected female academic. Much charmed and fascinated by the woman, Lyra agrees to become her assistant. Her new life quickly looses its charm as Lyra learns Mrs. Coulter is quick to anger, and her white monkey daemon attacks Pan. Lyra learns that Mrs. Coulter is associated with the Gobblers, and runs away to search for Roger.

A band of Gyptians, travelers who reside on riverboats, rescue her and she joins their mission to find the stolen children, many of whom are Gyptians.

Lyra learns that Lord Asriel and Mrs. Coulter are her parents.

In the cold North, Lyra befriends a witch queen, Serafina Pekkala, the bear-like lorek, Byrnison, and an aeronaut, Lee Scoresby. Gobblers capture Lyra and she learns they are separating children from their daemons. The separation, known as intercision, is traumatic, leaving the children depressed and confused. It can also be lethal. Lyra finds her father, whom Mrs. Coulter had kidnapped, and discovers that he has been trying to break into the alternate universe in the Northern Lights, where Dust comes from, but he needs a huge burst of energy to do so. To Lyra's horror, he performs an intercision on Roger to harness the energy from the procedure. In the wake of her friend's death, Lyra decides to find Dust herself, and she enters the new world through the hole her father created.

Although the book is a young adult read, it questions the mature topics of religion, church authority, and what it means to mature, as Lyra steps out of childhood and learns to chart her own course.

THE GOOD EARTH
Pearl S. Buck
1931
Novel
Historical

The Good Earth *reads like a fable, following the life of Wang Lung, a poor farmer whose hard work and devotion to his land makes him a wealthy man. It demonstrates the power of a commitment to one's ideals, and the effects of neglecting that commitment. The novel examines the source of contentment, which cannot be found through wealth or high social standing.*

Wang Lung is a young farmer whose greatest dream is to till the soil, and bear sons. His father marries him to a slave—O-lan—from the great house of Hwang. She is not beautiful or charming. She is common and her feet are unbound, but she is hardworking, resourceful, and devoted to her duty as a wife. She proudly bears him two sons and a daughter, working alongside him in the fields. But fortune turns and a famine leaves them near death from starvation. Completely powerless, the family travels "south" to find food. While they eek out an existence, Wang Lung longs to return to his land. Fortune turns and, after looting a wealthy house, they return home with enough riches to purchase more land, the only thing that cannot be taken away.

Through resourcefulness and hard work, Wang Lung prospers and grows wealthy. O-lan bears him another son and daughter. However, to the extent that his wealth increases, he grows more restless and dissatisfied. Misfortune arrives in the form of a slothful and belligerent uncle, the uncle's wife and son. Out of his sense of filial duty, he takes in and provides for his relatives. Later, it is revealed that the uncle is a local crime lord who extorts Wang Lung's capitulation.

Wang Lung is always caught between the extremes of duty and the dictates of his soul. In fact, duty and the social code of his wealthier class often work against Wang Lung's contentment and prosperity. He sends his sons to school so they will never be ashamed of being illiterate. But their education takes them away from the land, and they fail to learn the value of the sacrifice and hard work that has made them prosperous. They become combative and greedy.

A sub-plot throughout the narrative is the inversely parallel fortunes of the great House of Hwang (from whom O-lan was purchased) and that of Wang Lung. As the story begins, the house of Hwang is like royalty, the pinnacle of social status. But their fortunes decline, and they fall into addiction and debauchery, far removed from the sources of their wealth. In time, Wang Lung purchases much of Hwang's land, even moving into the great house after Hwang has fallen. But Wang Lung's second, delicate wife, Lotus, his sons, and their wives, are greedy and demanding. The house is in continual strife, not unlike the great house of Hwang.

Eventually, Wang Lung returns to his country house to spend his last days alone and at peace, on his land.

A GOOD MAN IS HARD TO FIND
Flannery O'Connor
1953
Short Story
Southern Gothic

On the way to Florida for a vacation, a family from Georgia confronts the grotesque Misfit, a psychotic killer seeking meaning in his godless world. This often anthologized story illustrates O'Connor's use of irony, black humor, and religious themes.

The story begins with grandmother Bailey trying to dissuade her son from taking the family to Florida. Since she wants to go elsewhere, she shows her son an article about the southbound Misfit. This tactic fails to alarm Bailey, and the family, including Pitty Sing, a cat hidden in the grandmother's valise, begins the ominous journey southward.

Bailey reluctantly follows his mother's request to take a sightseeing detour to a plantation. Embarrassed upon remembering that the building is in another state, the grandmother kicks the valise. Pitty Sing jumps on Bailey, who, as a result, overturns the car.

The grandmother signals for help, but when a car stops in response, she realizes that the supposed rescuers are the Misfit and his gang. While the family members are methodically taken in pairs into the woods and executed, the grandmother and the Misfit discuss the meaning of life. The climax nears when the grandmother asks the murderer to bow and pray with her.

The grandmother's Christian love for the Misfit reflects an important religious theme within O'Connor's fiction—the perseverance of divine grace in the presence of evil. Frequently, O'Connor creates characters who are weak and only concerned with the material realm. She then places them in a position in which they experience the divine realm, usually resulting in painful sacrifice.

Violence is common in O'Connor's fiction; however, her emphasis is on the gains brought about by characters such as the grandmother who directly confront the world's evil with grace.

THE GOOD SOLDIER
Ford Madox Ford
1915
Novel

A wealthy American attempts to understand the characters and events that have led to two suicides and insanity. This complex novel explores the difference between appearance and reality.

The narrator, John Dowell of Philadelphia, begins what he calls "the saddest story I have ever heard" by comparing the breakup of the nine-year friendship between himself, his wife, Florence, and a wealthy English couple, the Ashburnhams, to events as unthinkable as the sacking of Rome.

Their friendship begins at a German health spa which the Dowells visit yearly because of Florence's heart problem. During these annual visits, the four spend all their time together, until Florence's sudden death on August 4, 1913. After Dowell returns to America to settle her estate, he receives two urgent request to visit the Ashburnhams' estate.

The visit to England changes life for everyone, especially John Dowell, who learns facts that shatter his beliefs and happiness. He finds himself and his world in chaotic darkness with no clear moral certitudes.

On one level, this is the subtly told story of two marriages and of the problems, passions, and misunderstandings that beset such relationships. On another level, it is a microcosm of Western civilization, gradually revealing the hollowness and sickness of its surface conventions and institutions. John Dowell, the passive, naive American, learns of the true sickness of the human heart almost simultaneously with England's plunge into the evil of World War I.

An acknowledged masterpiece, this fascinating story leaves the reader thinking, feeling, and seeing more clearly the complexities of human nature and society.

THE GOOD TERRORIST
Doris Lessing
1985
Novel

Focusing on the activities of a leftist commune in contemporary London, this novel meditates on the relationship between power, morality, and political commitment.

Like many of the protagonists of the realistic novels which established Doris Lessing as a major novelist, Alice Mellings is a talented woman struggling to resolve the tensions between her personal and political commitments. Involved in a long-term but sexless relationship, Alice and her companion Jasper are charter members of a splinter Communist group occupying an old house in London as "squatters." Eminently efficient, Alice sees to the practical details of communal living, while Jasper and several other commune residents pursue political fantasies that gravitate slowly toward terrorist activity.

Lessing emphasizes the naivete of the commune's political position by balancing sympathy and admiration for Alice with an acute awareness of her self-indulgence, particularly in relation to her mother and father, whom Alice exploits without qualms. Contrasting sharply with the shadowy but hardened presences of the Irish Republican Army, the Communist Party, and the British government, the commune radicals emerge as little more than rebellious children capable of annoying the police but not of effecting real change.

Written in the realistic mode of Lessing's five-novel sequence *Children of Violence,* with which it shares many concerns, this novel nevertheless reflects the philosophical perspective of her more recent and highly controversial "Sufi/science fiction" sequence, *Canopus in Argos.* Even as she portrays the suffering resulting from the failure to perceive the multiple levels of reality, Lessing challenges her readers to transcend the limitations of consciousness which render Alice a tragic heroine.

THE GRAPES OF WRATH
John Steinbeck
1939
Novel
Historical, Political

This story of the Joad family's journey to California is one of the most poignant sagas in American literature. It is a story of a people whose faith and determination endure even when their dreams of prosperity end in "boxcar" reality.

The Joads sell their farming equipment for eighteen dollars to flee the Dust Bowl drought. With Jim Casy, a preacher who stresses the holiness of all individuals, the family leaves Oklahoma to find work in California.

Hardship begins at once with Granpa Joad's death. Later, Granma dies in Ma Joad's arms during a night crossing of a desert leading into California. Ma conceals this fact until morning to prevent a delay in reaching their supposed Eden.

The Joads cannot find work since droves of "Okies" have fled to the same "promised land." The family is forced to live in poverty while slowly losing its individual members. Noah follows the shoreline of a river into oblivion. Connie flees his pregnant Rose of Sharon.

After leaving the haven of a government camp for migrants, the family loses Jim Casy, who is killed in his efforts to organize labor. Tom kills Casy's murderer and goes into hiding. The remaining family finds work picking cotton and make their home in a boxcar. Here, Rose of Sharon makes a sacrifice which provides the novel with a controversial ending, symbolizing the fortitude of the human will to survive.

The Joads represent Steinbeck's concerns with American farmers during the Depression. The intercalary chapters aid in relating the Joads' struggles to those of all farmers.

Within this novel, there is a progression from "I" to the collective "we" of Ma Joad. The self-centered Tom Joad is transformed into a person concerned with the rights of all individuals. This reflects a central theme, voiced by Casy, that every man and woman shares a unity with all humanity. Steinbeck suggests that in terms of "we," man can endure any adversity.

THE GRAVEYARD BOOK
Neil Gaiman
2008
Novel
Children's, Gothic

A precocious, baby boy crawls out the front door, and into the nearby graveyard on the night his family is brutally murdered. The story follows his childhood as he is raised by a community of ghosts, and one mysterious caretaker who is neither dead nor alive.

At the request of a newly dead mother's ghost, Mistress Owens—a ghost herself for several hundred years—promises to keep the woman's baby safe, with the support of a community of spirits that occupy the graveyard, which is fashioned after London's ancient Highgate Cemetery. The mysterious caretaker, Silas, offers to act as guardian for the boy, providing for his physical necessities such as food and clothing. The graveyard community names him Nobody Owens (Bod, for short) because he "looks like nobody but himself."

The cemetery's many inhabitants educate Bod in both common academic subjects and in supernatural skills, like "fading" (becoming invisible), and "dreamwalking" (invading another person's dreams). When Bod is about five years old (he never knows his actual age), he befriends Scarlet, whose parents think Bod is an imaginary friend. Bod introduces her to his world, but when her family moves, he loses his one human friend.

Bod experiences a series of misadventures: he is held hostage by a greedy pawn broker; kidnapped by a pack of ghouls, then rescued by his substitute guardian, Mrs. Lepescue, a "hound of God" who introduces him to some horrid beetroot-barley-stew; he attends school, but calls attention to himself when he confronts a pair of bullies and must use his supernatural skills to escape. When Bod is a teenager, Scarlet returns and the two continue their friendship, but Scarlet's new friend, Mr. Frost, turns out to be Jack Frost, a member of the Jacks of all Trades Brotherhood—the organization that murdered Bod's family and has searched for Bod ever since. (A prophecy claimed a boy like Bod would be their undoing.) Bod defends himself and defeats the Jacks, using his knowledge of the graveyard, and the many skills he has learned from his supernatural community. Finally, he learns that Silas and Mrs. Lepescue were members of "The Honor Guard," whose purpose has been to defeat evil, including the Jacks of all Trades Brotherhood.

GRAVITY'S RAINBOW
Thomas Pynchon
1973
Novel
Science Fiction

With its many characters and frequently elliptical style, Gravity's Rainbow is not easy to read, but like James Joyce's Ulysses, with which it compares in difficulty, it rewards careful analysis.

Pynchon takes as his subject the rapid development of rocket technology toward the end of World War II. To learn about the German V-2 (on which Pynchon confers mythic status by always calling it the Rocket), Allied Intelligence devises an experiment with an American army lieutenant named Tyrone Slothrop—an experiment conducted without his knowledge. Slothrop, however, becomes aware of the way he is being used and goes AWOL just as the war ends. Much of the book concerns his wanderings in stateless, postwar Germany, referred to simply as "The Zone," where he encounters an extraordinary farrago of strange characters, the human detritus of war.

The authorities select Slothrop for their experiment because of his strange sexual affinity with the Rocket: He experiences erections wherever V-2's strike around London. But he experiences these erections before the rockets strike, and this curious proclivity illustrates one of the novel's basic concerns—the inadequacy of the essentially Newtonian scientific model whereby most of us attempt to conceptualize physical reality.

Pynchon develops this theme in the conflict between Ned Pointsman, a Pavlovian scientist who seeks to account for physical phenomena—including Slothrop's erections—in terms of cause and effect, and a statistician named Roger Mexico, who embraces a science of statistical prediction congruent with the twentieth century physics of Planck, Einstein, and Heisenberg.

With this scientific agon as backdrop, Pynchon introduces numerous examples of the way modern scientists, especially chemists, have uncovered the secrets of physical reality only to violate and threaten the equilibrium of nature itself. The Rocket, its promise of transcendence (space travel) traduced by its employment in weapons systems, becomes the most terrifying example of this misguided application of the fruits of science.

GREAT EXPECTATIONS
Charles Dickens
1860-1861
Novel
Victorian

Great Expectations *tells the story of a boy, Pip, who helps a convict escape, accepts help from an unknown benefactor, learns to be a gentleman assenting to the values of a mercantile society, loses everything, and finally comes to understand the worth of real love and honest work.*

Blinded by love, Pip rejects his family and background, believing that he is being groomed to be Estella's husband by the eccentric Miss Havisham, Estella's guardian. Clinging firmly to his great expectations, Pip snobbishly rejects those who genuinely love him, Joe and Biddy, and aligns himself with such morally questionable characters as the lawyer Jaggers, the hulking Drummle, and the half-crazed Miss Havisham. In spite of his many blunders, however, Pip remains basically good and has the good sense to make provision for the future of his best friend, Herbert Pocket.

When Pip learns that his unknown benefactor is not Miss Havisham but Abel Magwitch, a convict, who intends to claim Pip as his own, Pip recoils in distaste, and his pride suffers a severe blow. But Pip and Herbert rally themselves to try to save Magwitch, who has reentered London under threat of death. In his futile attempts to save both Miss Havisham and the convict, Pip goes through a ritualistic cleansing by fire and water and is able to make atonement for his sins. Pip's consequent illness, which causes him to fall into a coma, is a symbolic death that makes redemption and metaphoric rebirth possible. Nursed back to health by Joe, Pip experiences new growth toward greater maturity.

Not many novels have two endings, but *Great Expectations* does. The original ending found Pip eleven years older, sadder and wiser, alone, but adjusted to his new life. However, Dickens changed his mind and wrote a happier conclusion in which Estella, herself greatly chastened after eleven years of suffering, comes back as a possible wife for Pip. The romantically happy ending is not farfetched. On one level, the novel is a projection of a fantasy wherein Pip envisions himself as a young prince destined to save an enchanted princess and inherit the kingdom. Fairy-tale elements in the novel foreshadow happiness for Pip just as surely as recurring elements of the nightmare world suggest that Pip will be haunted by past experiences throughout his life. Only the presence of "another" Pip, son of Joe and Biddy, intimates that a life without pain and suffering could be possible at some future time when criminality is not a condition of life and where the search for wealth without regard for others is not a commonly accepted mode of behavior.

THE GREAT GATSBY
F. Scott Fitzgerald
1925
Novel
Historical, Tragedy

Jay Gatsby, formerly a poor boy from the Midwest, acquires wealth for the sole purpose of realizing a romantic dream, that of winning back the love of Daisy Buchanan.

The narrator of the story is Nick Carraway, who has moved to New York from the Midwest. He rents a house in the town of West Egg, Long Island. Across the bay, in the more respectable East Egg, live his cousin Daisy and her wealthy, overbearing husband Tom Buchanan, whom Nick knew at Yale.

The most interesting character he meets, however, is his next-door neighbor, a mysterious rich man known as Jay Gatsby. After attending a lavish but ostentatious party at Gatsby's estate, Nick slowly becomes his one true friend. He discovers that Gatsby has long loved Daisy, and that he has dedicated his life to winning her from Tom. Gatsby (ne Gatz) has tried to make himself into the kind of sophisticated man he feels Daisy deserves, but his money has come from gambling and other underworld activities.

Nick recognizes the impossibility of Gatsby's dream but admires the inspired romantic imagination that has thus reshaped his life. Following the inevitable failure of Gatsby's quest, Nick returns to the Midwest, appalled at the sordidness and waste found beneath the alluring surface of the good life.

A perfectly constructed book, the novel is a masterpiece of narrative style. Nick reflects Fitzgerald's conflicting attitudes toward the wealthy, whom he found both glamorous and destructive. The book is also a testament to the power of the creative will to overcome, at least for the moment, the despair of everyday life.

GROWTH OF THE SOIL
Knut Hamsun
1917
Novel

A man moves into the wilderness somewhere in northern Norway, builds himself a farm, and then discovers that civilization closes in on him and deprives him of his way of life.

The protagonist of the novel is a man named Isaac, later surnamed Sellanraa after the farm he carves out of the wilderness in northern Norway. He is a man without a past, but also without any of the cultural baggage of contemporary life. As a pioneer, he is similar to many of the heroes of Western American literature.

The novel begins by detailing the growth of Isaac's farm as he clears the land, builds shelter, and acquires both farm animals and a wife, Inger. Disfigured by a harelip, she casts her lot with Isaac only because she lacks other suitors. Inger is fearful that one of her children will inherit her defect, which indeed happens to her third baby, a girl. Knowing the suffering that is in store for the infant, Inger kills her, later confesses her crime, and is sent to prison for five years.

During this time, she has an operation on her lip, is educated in modern life, and, in Hamsun's view, is spoiled by civilization. When she returns, she is no longer satisfied with the simple life on the farm. More settlers arrive in the area, and copper is discovered in a nearby mountain, which leads to the establishment of a mine with all of its attendant problems. At the end of the book, Isaac's (and Hamsun's) ideal way of life is, for all practical purposes, gone.

GULLIVER'S TRAVELS
Jonathan Swift
1726
Novel
Adventure, Satire

Swift's masterpiece of satire tells the story of Captain Lemuel Gulliver, who, through various misfortunes, is shipwrecked in four different lands, where he is alternately a giant, a pygmy, a sane man among crazies, and a lone human in a society ruled by horses.

Swift's jaundiced view of the politics and mores of the England of his day are elaborated in the form of four allegorical tales in which the narrator, Lemuel Gulliver, observes the local customs in foreign lands while becoming increasingly disenchanted with his own world. The transformation from the magnanimous benefactor of the Lilliputians (among whom Gulliver is a giant) to the misanthrope who can barely endure the company of his own family (preferring to live in his stable among horses) is accomplished with consummate narrative skill and a sure instinct for pretense and folly.

The first book, which focuses on Gulliver's stay in Lilliput, offers a thinly disguised version of political squabbles that would have been fresh in the minds of Swift's readers. The second book takes Gulliver to Brobdingnag, the land of giants, where his plans to provide the local ruler with cannons and gunpowder are viewed with contempt and horror. In the third section, Gulliver encounters the land of Laputa, the flying island, where a parody of the experimental science of Swift's day is raucously played out, including schemes for capturing the sunbeams trapped in cucumbers and for turning human excrement back into nutritious substances. The fourth book sends Gulliver to the land of the Houyhnhnms, horses who have the power of speech. The Houyhnhnms, who are distinguished by their virtue and their reliance on reason, to the exclusion of emotion, rule over a race of bestial creatures called Yahoos, who bear a dismaying resemblance to human beings.

Swift's humor remains as powerful today as when he wrote, and if the references to 18th century politics and history are now largely lost on us, the recognition that our own scientific experiments often resemble those of the Laputans makes us still Swift's contemporaries in many ways.

H

HAMLET, PRINCE OF DENMARK
William Shakespeare
1603
Drama
Tragedy

\Considered by many to be the greatest drama ever written, Hamlet is the story of a young prince who must decide whether the ghost of his murdered father is a true messenger from the dead or a product of his own grief-stricken imagination.

Hamlet, Prince of Denmark, has recently lost his father; his mother has entered into an overhasty marriage with the murdered man's brother, Claudius. Grieving at his father's death, and morally outraged at the hurried marriage, Hamlet broods about his helplessness, until a ghost appears on the ramparts, telling him his father was in fact murdered by his uncle, who poured poison in his ear while he slept. Gertrude, his mother, is indirectly implicated, but the ghost orders Hamlet to confine his revenge to Claudius.

In a series of delaying tactics, partly designed to obtain ocular proof and partly a result of Hamlet's natural hesitation to kill, he forces Claudius to react in public. Feigning madness, Hamlet waits for his chance to kill his uncle in hot blood (not a sin); the play ends in a duel of poisoned swords.

The complex nature of this play, together with the soaring poetry of the soliloquies, makes it the most often quoted play in all history. Hamlet's feigned madness, hesitation to action, demand for ocular proof, and final revenge are conventions of a formulaic dramatic form called revenge tragedy. What lifts *Hamlet* above its predecessors is the revelation of character by means of poetic diction. Through the device of soliloquies (internal monologues), we are privy to the anguished deliberations of a sensitive soul debating with itself the moral consequences of murder, weighed against filial loyalty, responsibilities of royal birth, and the human hesitation to perform irreversible acts whose consequences are unknown.

A HANDFUL OF DUST
Evelyn Waugh
1934
Novel
Satire

Driven abroad by his wife's adultery and his son's death, an aristocrat meets a bizarre fate in the jungle. This grimly humorous British novel satirizes the shallowness of upper-class mores.

Waugh uses the comedy of manners to depict the sterile lives of well-bred Londoners. Through terse dialogue and pointed description Waugh shows a world devoid of passion and commitment. Matters of life and death barely ripple the placidity of this smug society.

Tony Last, owner of ancient Hetton Abbey, loves his quiet estate. His wife, Brenda, does not. Pretending to study economics, she rents an apartment in London. Actually, she begins an affair with John Beaver.

Beaver is a witless youth more useful than romantic. He escorts Brenda to parties and can be shown off. Although Brenda's friends know of her infidelity, Tony remains blissfully ignorant. Then their son dies in a fall during a foxhunt.

After the funeral, Brenda requests a divorce. Tony at first agrees, until Brenda demands a financial settlement that would require Hetton to be sold. Giving Brenda a skimpy allowance, Tony leaves England.

Accompanied by the eccentric Dr. Messinger, Tony searches South American jungles for the legendary Shining City. Disease, mutinous natives, and a boat accident maroon Tony, who is nursed by an illiterate trader named Todd. Wanting Tony to read Dickens to him, Todd hides Tony from rescuers. Back in London, Brenda, deserted by Beaver, marries Tony's best friend.

The novel's minor characters are largely caricatures. The affluent Londoners fawn upon the manipulative Brenda; they blame the injured Tony for all unpleasantness. The reader comes to despise their inability to distinguish sincerity from pretense, morality from manners. Though the reader may sympathize with Tony, the man is infuriatingly feckless, an accomplice, a helpless cooperator in his own destruction.

THE HANDMAID'S TALE
Margaret Atwood
1985
Novel
Dystopian

Margaret Atwood's most popular novel is a cautionary tale about a brutal theocracy that represents a closed, elitist belief system. The protagonist, Offred, is challenged daily with the choice to rebel against the systematic repression, and risk her life in joining an underground rebellion, or submit to an oppressive society where trust, even of one's closest allies, can get one killed.

In the post-U.S. nation of Gilead, birthrates are alarmingly low. Handmaids are both revered due to their ability to bear children, and castigated because of the acts they are forced to perform in order to become pregnant. Offred is one such woman, captured with her husband and daughter as they attempted to escape to Canada. They are separated, and Offred is sent to a handmaids' finishing school, run by brutal headmistresses known as "Aunts," who use cattle prods to maintain discipline. Everything, from dress to a simple greeting, is proscribed and monitored. Stripped of her personal identity, the handmaid takes the name of her "commander." The sex act is ritualized in a "ceremony" involving a husband, wife and their handmaid. The wife holds the powerless handmaid as the husband essentially rapes her. Any sign of a personal thought or emotion, or any act made outside of prescribed decorum, can get one punished or killed. Offred's descriptions of the fear, brutality, and isolation are reminiscent of life in Nazi Germany.

Serena-Joy, the wife in Offred's case, realizes that her husband is infertile and offers to make a deal in order to get her baby. (Offred knows it could be a trap.) She arranges for Offred to sleep with the chauffer, Nick, in exchange for a picture of Offred's daughter (thus revealing that she has always known both the identity and location of the child.) Offred begins an ongoing sexual relationship with Nick, a sharp contrast to the clandestine, nighttime Scrabble sessions with the Commander, who is also at risk engaging in a forbidden act. (Handmaids are not allowed to read or meet with anyone outside of social boundaries.)

Margaret Atwood imposed one rule on herself while composing *The Handmaid's Tale*, and that was to only use social characteristics that have a precedent in actual human history. Every societal characteristic, from strictures about clothing to identify one's function and class, to forced maternity and public executions, has actually occurred.

THE HEART IS A LONELY HUNTER
Carson McCullers
1940
Novel
Southern Gothic, Regionalist

A pastiche of individual characters whose circles intersect, The Heart is a Lonely Hunter *demonstrates just how much people need each other. In a small mill town, a boy accidently shoots a tiny girl; a woman struggles to bring her father back into the family; her brother, an African-American man is critically injured by racist law enforcement; an educated physician urges his fellow African-Americans to take pride in their color, and to fight for social justice; one deaf-mute man goes insane, and another gentle deaf-mute curiously comes to fulfill his fellows' needs for intimate connection with one another.*

According to Carson McCullers, much of her writing developed around the common theme of the need to belong to something—to feel one's self a part of life. In *The Heart is a Lonely Hunter,* each of the characters suffers from a sense of isolation. For McCullers' readers, the few instances where characters do feel connection to another, that connection is based on a delusion or a lie.

McCullers felt that the central protagonist in the story was Singer—the kind, lonely, deaf-mute man whom a number of characters see as their "savior," or soul mate. Individual characters visit him regularly, spilling their most intimate secrets and dreams to this deaf man whom they consider to be such a good listener. Ironically, the only person Singer feels intimately connected to is the slovenly, narcissist, Antonapoulos who has gone insane and, in any case, is incapable of caring for anyone.

The story itself depicts pivotal circumstances in the lives of those who live in this small, southern, mill town. Fourteen-year-old tomboy, Mick Kelly dreams of her life as a great musician, but she has to work in a department store to help support her family. The Kelly family has been struck by tragedy when seven-year-old Bubber, accidently shoots a small girl. Though the girl lives, the incident leaves the family destitute. Dr. Benedict Mady Copeland is a stiff, repressed African-American doctor who lives alone, nearly estranged from his family, until the day his son is critically injured in a racist attack by law enforcement. Dr. Copeland wants to see his people take pride in their color, and to fight for social justice, but his incapacity for heart-felt compassion keeps him ineffective. Diner owner Biff Brannon is an observer, skirting the outsides of the lives of his patrons. Recently widowed, he bears an unsettling affection for Mick Kelly. Portia, Dr. Copeland's daughter, and housekeeper for the Kelly family is, arguably, the most self-contained and capable of the characters. She recognizes the isolation in the characters around her, and strives to help them.

The lives of these characters are shattered when, after learning the Antonapoulos has died, Singer goes home and puts a bullet through his chest, leaving all those who felt so close to him, shaken and, once again, alone.

HEART OF DARKNESS
Joseph Conrad
1902
Novella
Psychological, Thriller

One of Joseph Conrad's first great symbolic works, Heart of Darkness *is an exploration of the equivocal nature of evil. In subject matter, narrative technique, and emphasis on the psychological, the story anticipates later developments in the modern novel.*

The central story is related by Marlow, a sailor and adventurer who appears in other Conrad works such as Lord Jim. Marlow recalls his experiences as the captain of a steamboat in the Congo, far from the safety of civilization. There, at a station on the edge of the jungle, he hears rumors of a Mr. Kurtz, a remarkable, admired white man who operates a trading post located deep in the wilderness. The more Marlow learns of Kurtz, the more interested he becomes, for Kurtz has cut off contact with the outside world, and there are suggestions that he is seriously ill.

After numerous delays, Marlow steams up the winding, snakelike river toward Kurtz's trading post. Marlow feels that he is heading into a prehistoric time. Along the way, his boat is attacked by savages, and when they finally reach Kurtz's station, Marlow is shocked to see a display of human heads, the spoils of cannibal war. Kurtz himself is clearly demented and dying, and Marlow slowly realizes that the man is regressing to a primitive state, consumed by his own inner capacity for savageness.

Before Kurtz dies, he recognizes the extent of his change and is appalled. When Marlow returns to England, he lies to protect Kurtz's good name. Like Kurtz, Marlow has seen the heart of darkness within all men.

Conrad first published the story of Kurtz in 1899 as "The Heart of Darkness" for *Blackwood's Magazine*, but he revised it heavily for inclusion in *Youth: A Narrative, And Two Other Stories* in 1902. The tale has influenced writers as different as T. S. Eliot and William Faulkner, and it was the major inspiration for Francis Ford Coppola's 1979 Vietnam War film, *Apocalypse Now.*

HEDDA GABLER
Henrik Ibsen
1890
Drama
Psychological, Thriller

A woman chooses a course of negative and destructive action in order to relieve her boredom. In the end she finds that she is trapped and deems suicide to be her only option.

Hedda Gabler has married George Tessman, a scholar in the history of civilization. After a six-month-long honeymoon and research trip, the couple has returned home in order to settle into a comfortable middle-class existence. Tessman is counting on obtaining a professorship at the University.

It soon becomes apparent that Hedda is bored with everything in her life: her husband, his pretty bourgeois relatives, and the fact that she is pregnant. Her only amusement is practicing with two pistols inherited from her father, General Gabler. Judge Brack, the family lawyer, offers sophisticated company, but Hedda, who is mortified at the slightest hint of scandal, fears his intentions.

Then an old friend, Thea Elvsted, calls on her. Thea has left her husband in order to look after their former tutor, Eilert Lovberg, with whom she is in love. Lovberg, a gifted scholar in the same field as Tessman, has generally been given up as lost to drink, but has now been rehabilitated, has published one book, and has written another, which promises to be a masterpiece. Hedda, who several years earlier had loved Lovberg but refused to have an erotic relationship with him, now finds it amusing to undo his rehabilitation. She taunts him into getting drunk, destroys the manuscript of his new book, and gives him one of her pistols in order that he may commit suicide. After Lovberg's death, however, Hedda is linked to the suicide by Judge Brack, who attempts to blackmail her into taking him as her lover. Hedda now finds her situation utterly intolerable and uses her remaining pistol to shoot herself in the temple.

THE HELP
Kathyrn Stockett
2009
Novel
Historical, African American

Returning home from college in the early 1960s in Jackson, Mississippi, Skeeter Phelan, with the help of two maids, writes a book that challenges the racist treatment of domestic help in the South. Steering its readers from laughter to sadness, and doubt to hope, The Help *depicts one of the most fundamental battles for equality in United States history, from the perspective of women in the household.*

Recently graduated from Ole Miss, Eugenia "Skeeter" Phelan, a privileged daughter of a cotton plantation owner, returns home to Jackson, Mississippi with the goal of breaking into a writing career. Living in the South in the early 1960s, Skeeter is pressured to conform to the ideals of being a proper southern lady and securing a husband. Instead she snags her first job at a local newspaper, the *Jackson Journal*, writing the housekeeping advice column, despite her lack of knowledge on the subject.

Skeeter seeks the help of her friend's maid, Aibileen. It is common in the 1960s for a white household to hire an African-American maid to raise the children and clean for a small wage. But with Skeeter's direct experience of the Jim Crow laws and a letter from a New York publisher, Skeeter starts to write a more hard hitting story: the stories of the domestic servants of the South. Aibileen agrees to tell her story and recruits her friend Minny, a saucy maid who is repeatedly fired for back talk. While outside, the civil rights movement is just gaining momentum, the three meet in Aibileen's kitchen at night, documenting the experiences of the community's maids.

During her interviews, Skeeter is reminded of her beloved maid, Constantine, who had disappeared with no explanation before Skeeter returned home from college. She realizes the prejudice that she was brought up with and begins distancing herself from her old friends, who seem oblivious to the social inequity.

Eventually more maids agree to tell their stories and Skeeter publishes her book anonymously. The stories— ranging from instances of brutal abuse to mutual love—make her book a best seller, giving the African American maids a voice. Although many recognize that Skeeter wrote the book, she is able to deflect the social reproof and secure a job in New York City, while the community of Jackson is forced to acknowledge its inequality.

Unlike many stories about the civil rights movement that materialize in the southern streets and the public square, *The Help* is a story about the fight that took place in the privacy of the household. The characters are multi-dimensional, demonstrating both compassion and ignorance, love and hate within a single conversation.

HENRY IV, PART I
William Shakespeare
1598
Drama
Historical

Shakespeare's best-known history play chronicles the political troubles of Henry Bolingbroke after his overthrow of Richard II and the transformation of his son Prince Hal from a seemingly irresponsible idler to a valiant defender of the state. The play also features the dashing Henry Percy, called the Hotspur of the North, and Sir John Falstaff, the most beloved comic character of the Elizabethan stage.

Henry learns that independent lords who help one of their number to rebel against a king may turn against their former champion as well. Henry faces a headstrong group of former supporters, led by the powerful Percy family, who no longer trust his leadership.

The disorder of the state is paralleled by the private "riot and disorder" of Prince Hal among his disreputable cronies at the tavern. Sir John Falstaff, the old braggart soldier who earns a precarious living by an occasional highway robbery, beguiles the prince with a ready wit and jovial good fellowship, so foreign to the cold and often pretentious atmosphere of court.

When war actually breaks out, however, Prince Hal becomes his father's champion and offers Falstaff a chance to redeem himself as well by resuming his proper role as a soldier. The wily Falstaff misuses his new power and plays dead on the battlefield to avoid fighting. Prince Hal performs brilliantly, however, not only saving his father's life but also defeating the formidable Hotspur in single combat.

The play is a perceptive study of the meaning of honor and the requirements of kingship. Prince Hal must discriminate between the virtues and the flaws of several role models. He chooses the high seriousness but not the Machiavellian coldness of his father, the human understanding and wit of Falstaff but not his rascality, the bravery but not the foolish impetuosity of Hotspur.

HENRY IV, PART II
William Shakespeare
1597
Drama
Historical

Supporters of the now ailing Henry IV defeat his remaining enemies, and young Prince Henry ascends the throne. How does a companion of the incorrigible Sir John Falstaff face the serious business of ruling England?

Following the royal victory at Shrewsbury, there remain two determined opposing forces under the leadership of the Earl of Northumberland and the Archbishop of York, respectively. Prince John cleverly, if ruthlessly, brings the latter's forces to bay before they can unite with Northumberland's, and the realm is secured.

Meanwhile the king's concern over the moral character of young Henry continues, as the heir still consorts with the pleasure-loving Falstaff and his tavern friends. Contrary to the expectations of father and brothers, however, Prince Henry demonstrates, immediately upon the old king's death, the determination to govern prudently and wisely.

The carrying out of his vow, seemingly made in jest in Part 1, to banish Falstaff, is the most controversial action of this play. Set against Falstaff's great comic vitality, the new king seems cold and ungenerous, but Shakespeare establishes that Falstaff's main motive is not good-natured fun but the hope of future royal favors, and young Henry must reject the claims of a man so cowardly, self-indulgent, and irresponsible.

The terms of banishment are relatively mild: Falstaff must not approach within ten miles of court, the king guarantees him a pension, and he can expect advancement if he reforms. Falstaff, as might be expected, will never reform, and Shakespeare transfers him next to *The Merry Wives of Windsor,* a comedy where he can entertain without corrupting the kingdom in the process.

The play focuses on civil leadership and filial duty. Both require the eventual displacement of the father, and after experiencing the undisciplined life, young Henry must also reject the man who parodied his father in Part 1. High among the duties of leadership is justice, a theme that both comic and sober scenes progressively elucidate.

HENRY THE FIFTH
William Shakespeare
1600
Drama
Historical

The formerly madcap Prince Hal becomes Henry V, the ideal hero-king, by virtue of his shrewd statesmanship, his piety, and his inspiring military leadership.

Henry the Fifth completes a tetralogy of Shakespeare's history plays beginning with *Richard The Second* and continuing through *Henry the Fourth, Part One* and *Henry the Fourth, Part Two.* The Henry IV plays depict Prince Hal (the future Henry V) at first as a wild young man who runs with a jolly gang of thieves and drunks led by the fat Falstaff. But Hal resolves to change, acquits himself well in battle, and grows away from his dissolute companions, renouncing them entirely when he becomes king.

Henry the Fifth shows the finished product, the most popular king in English history (reigned 1413-1422). Henry V learnedly discusses religion and state with bishops and advisers. Then, after rooting out traitors, he leads a military expedition to France to claim territory he considers rightfully his. Inspired by Henry's leadership, the tired, outnumbered English forces defeat the French in a spectacular battle at Agincourt. Then Henry cements the peace by wooing Katharine, the French princess, as his bride.

A tribute to the possibility of human growth, Henry stands out, in part, in contrast to his earlier self, the unpromising Prince Hal. His old companions die, are hanged, or are beaten, marking an end to the former time—a change also marked by Henry's frequent expressions of piety.

The steady, unassuming Henry also contrasts with the vain and frivolous French, England's traditional enemy. *Henry the Fifth* thus celebrates not only the kingly ideal but also the patriotic ideal, Henry's downright Englishness: He is straightforward, just, and democratic—though modern audiences might consider him a bit bloodthirsty and the play chauvinistic.

HIPPOLYTUS
Euripides
428 B.C.E.
Drama
Tragedy, Mythology

The goddess Aphrodite orchestrates the death of a highly virtuous youth because of his failure to accord her proper worship. Generally ranked as one of Euripides' masterworks, this play should be considered obligatory reading for anyone seriously interested in classical Greek literature or its mythological components.

Phaedra, the young wife of the legendary Athenian king Theseus, falls passionately in love with her puritanical stepson, Hippolytus, and the ensuing conflict leads to the death of both parties, as well as to the emotional devastation of the king himself.

Aphrodite personally sets the plot in motion by formally announcing her intention to destroy Hippolytus as punishment for his sexual continence and for his inordinate devotion to the virginal goddess of the hunt, Artemis. Exercising her prerogatives as the goddess of love, Aphrodite causes Phaedra to become romantically obsessed with Hippolytus. Despite her moral qualms over this illicit passion, Phaedra agrees to let her maid act as an intermediary for the purpose of informing Hippolytus of her love for him. After learning that he had indignantly rebuffed her advances, Phaedra hangs herself. To protect her own honor, she leaves a letter behind accusing Hippolytus of having raped her.

Hippolytus defends himself eloquently even though he never reveals the content of his conversation with Phaedra's maid, since he swore a sacred oath of secrecy. Theseus refuses to accept his son's innocence and orders him into exile. Driving along the shore, Hippolytus is thrown from his chariot and mortally injured when his team of horses is frightened by a monstrous bull that suddenly emerges from the sea. This event occurs as the direct result of Theseus' plea to Poseidon that his son be annihilated. Meanwhile Artemis herself appears before Theseus and establishes his son's innocence. The dying Hippolytus is then brought home and thereupon has a tearful reconciliation with his remorseful father.

Since Hippolytus was the son of an Amazon mother and Phaedra was the daughter of the queen of Crete who gave birth to the minotaur, their disparate sexual proclivities were to some extent determined by heredity. Either extreme, however, constituted a gross violation of the Greek ideal of moderation as it was subsequently formulated in the Aristotelian doctrine of the golden mean.

THE HISTORIES
Herodotus of Halicarnassus
425
Nonfiction
Historical

This research presents a history in nine books by the world's first historian.

The telling of secular history, based on sources, came into being in the second half of the fifth century BC with this inquiry. Although some sources of Herodotus (525–484 BC) were not completely reliable, this learned traveler sought out the best available information of his day. He provides analysis of events, military strategy, geographical maps, religious background, ethnographical commentary, and his considered opinion.

Herodotus begins with demythologizing: he argues military conflicts were not the result of legendary rapes, but of pillage, empire, and various ambitions. The idea of Europe is a Persian concept to explain why Greeks are unlike other peoples.

Book One covers the conquests of Croesus of Lydia in Asia Minor and his defeat by Cyrus the Great. He describes the great wealth and customs of Babylon. In Book Two Cambyses succeeds Cyrus, yet most of the book describes the history and customs of Egypt from 3000–526 BC. Book Three treats the conquest of Egypt by Cambyses, the failed Spartan siege of Samos, the revolt of Magus, the death of Cambyses, the reign of Darius, and the Persian conquest of Samos.

Book Four investigates the conquest of Scythia and Libya by Darius. In Book Five Darius crosses the Hellespont, conquering Thrace. Athens subdues Thebes and Chalcis. Darius defeats the Ionians, Hellespont cities, Cyprus, and Greek cities in Asia Minor. In Book Six Darius imposes tribute. Athens and Sparta unite and defeat the Persians at Marathon (490 BC).

Book Seven begins with Darius raising another army, the revolt of Egypt against Darius, and the death of Darius. Xerxes prepares to invade Greece, but loses many ships to a storm near Thermopylae. The Thebans surrender. The Spartan 300 perish in glory.

Book Eight describes the indecisive naval battle at Artemisia. The Greeks abandon Attica. Themistocles persuades the Greeks to fight at Salamis where they defeat the Persians, and divide the spoils. The Persian fleet gathers at Samos.

Book Nine describes the Spartan march north, the Persian burning of Athens, the complexities of Greek intrigue, and the battle of Plataea where the Persians are defeated. The Greek fleet attacks the Persians at Samos, winning a great victory; Greeks sail to the Hellespont, reopening trade routes to the Black Sea.

THE HITCHHIKER'S GUIDE TO THE GALAXY
Douglas Adams
1979
Novel
Science Fiction, Humor

Douglas Adams' tale of an Englishman, his alien best friend, the two-headed president of the Galaxy, his human girl-friend, and a manic depressive robot traveling the galaxy together while already sounding wildly astounding, is full of even more surprises than one could ever imagine.

Seconds before Earth is destroyed by an interstellar demolition crew, Arthur Dent's best friend, an alien from Betelgeuse Seven, pretending to be an out-of-work actor, saves their lives by "hitching" a ride aboard the very same ship sent to destroy earth. Arthur soon finds out that his friend, Ford Prefect, actually works as an editor for the most famous book in the galaxy, *The Hitchhiker's Guide to the Galaxy*. Utilizing Ford's knowledge, and a lot of improbable events, the two friends escape the hostile ship and find themselves aboard the stolen ship of Ford's semi-cousin, and the president of the galaxy, Zaphod Beeblebrox.

Along with Zaphod, his human girlfriend Trillian and a manic depressive robot named Marvin, the five companions travel in search of a mythical planet called Magrathea. Legends tell that over five million years ago Magrathea had been used by the extremely wealthy in order to build custom-made planets. Once upon the planet, Arthur and his companions discover that the Magratheans had recently begun building a new Earth. While astonishing as that sounds, Arthur also discovers that the entirety of Earth's existence was an experiment run by ultra-intelligent lab mice. The story ends with Arthur and his friends narrowly escaping death on Magrathea, and heading for lunch at the Restaurant at the End of the Universe.

While primarily a science fiction novel, the hysterically funny *Hitchhikers Guide to the Galaxy* also delves into philosophical rants about the meaning of life. It is impossible for the first time reader to anticipate what is going to happen next, and this off the cuff absurdity is what truly makes Adams' work a classic.

THE HOBBIT
J.R.R. Tolkien
1937
Novel
Children's, Fantasy

The Third Age of Middle-earth holds wonder and mystery aplenty: elves and dwarves, goblins and dragons, wizards and necromancers. Small and ordinary creatures such as hobbits generally desire little else but a good meal and com-fortable surroundings, but one particular halfling finds himself swept into an adventure of travel, danger, and a magic ring.

J.R.R. Tolkien's saga of Middle-earth is a classic modern fantasy, and *The Hobbit* is the book that starts it all. Al-though Tolkien originally wrote the tale for his children, it is still well suited, both in action and in style, for adults.

Bilbo Baggins is a staid and respectable hobbit, or small human-like creature of portly build and furry feet, who nevertheless has a hidden streak of adventurousness. When legendary wizard Gandalf needs to recruit a fourteenth member for the treasure expedition of a boisterous band of dwarves—to forestall the bad luck incumbent upon thir-teen—he picks the dumbfounded Bilbo as their burglar.

And so begins a journey of strange creatures, and of locales little less strange: trolls that turn to stone by daylight, fierce goblins, gigantic spiders, and a gold-hoarding dragon, in wild wastelands, soporific enchanted woods, high crags, and the very roots of ancient mountains. During a strange subterranean encounter, Bilbo discovers a ring that, as it turns out, grants invisibility; at least in this book, though, the object is only another trapping, albeit marvelous, of the fantasy genre, seemingly in the same category as magic blades, impenetrable mail coats, and huge jewels. When Bilbo returns home at adventure's end, it seems as if nothing has really changed.

More than just a prequel to the justly revered *Lord of the Rings* trilogy, *The Hobbit* is its own solid tale of adventure and friendship, the lighter counterpart to later perils that will grow very dark indeed.

THE HOUSE OF MIRTH
Edith Wharton
1905
Novel
Feminist, Satire

While The House of Mirth *is rightly categorized a novel of manners, it is also a tragedy, and a searing indictment of upper crust America at the turn of the 20th century. The novel follows Lily Bart as she navigates the waters of turgid New York society, in a game requiring as much nerve, composure and strategy as a game of chess.*

Lily Bart, raised in the arts of wit, charm, and beauty, is left nearly penniless after her father's financial ruin, and her parents' subsequent deaths. She is left with a stingy aunt who sees her as a burden. Lily is quite at home in the country estates, mansions and yachts of the wealthy. Her primary goal is to marry a wealthy man so she can keep the lifestyle to which she is accustomed. She passes up several prospects, always thinking she can do better. In actuality, she and Lawrence Seldon are in love, but she could never marry him because he is not wealthy enough. Lily treats Seldon as a confident, and is more genuine with him than anyone. For his part, Seldon is an observer of society, and Lily's machinations in particular.

Lily's fortunes begin to decline as she racks up gambling debt. (Gambling at cards is a favorite pastime of the wealthy.) In an effort to keep up appearances, she asks her wealthy host, Gus Trenor, to "invest" her money for her, with the unacknowledged understanding, that he will help her from his own vast resources. But, when Gus calls Lily's bluff, the unacknowledged understanding is laid bare. Lily vows to herself to pay back the money. Rumors fly about her involvement with Gus. She escapes to the Mediterranean with the ultra-wealthy George and Bertha Dorset. Her real role is to keep George occupied while Bertha, has an affair. Lily knows the truth, and once the lovers are exposed, Bertha spreads a rumor that Lily had an affair with George. Bertha, who has tremendous social clout, sees that Lily is ostracized from society. Lily's reputation is ruined. Though others know she is innocent, they won't jeopardize their own standing. Lily's aunt disinherits her (based on the rumors) and Lily is left penniless. With no working-class experience, Lily falters under the burden. After confiding in Seldon one more time, she overdoses on a sleeping draft.

The novel's title is derived from Ecclesiastes 7:4—"…the heart of fools is in the house of mirth."

THE HOUSE OF THE SEVEN GABLES
Nathaniel Hawthorne
1851
Novel
Psychological, Romance

This is a story of guilt and retribution, of sins of the fathers visited on the children, of past wrongs righted in the present through marriage.

Clifford Pyncheon returns to his ancestral home, the house of the seven gables, after years of imprisonment for a crime he did not commit. He finds that his reclusive sister, Hepzibah, has opened a shop in the front of the house in order to supplement the fading family fortunes. Living with her is a cousin from the country, Phoebe, who is acting as a companion and housekeeper, and Mr. Holgrave, the local daguerreotypist and a distant relative of Matthew Maule, from whom the Pyncheons originally stole the property on which the house stands. The death of Judge Pyncheon, another cousin and the last in the line descended from the usurpers of Maule's property, provides Clifford, Hepzibah, and Phoebe with an inheritance of great wealth and a home in the country. At the end of the novel, they all prepare to vacate the old house and to celebrate the marriage of Phoebe and Holgrave, thus uniting the younger generation of the two feuding families and bringing the curse to an end.

Hawthorne intended the happy ending of his romance to lighten the darker elements of the tale and to give it what he called a sunshine ending. On first glance this may seem uncharacteristic of his fiction, but if one examines his work beyond the Puritan stories, there are more sunshine endings than are typical of the earlier, more somber works. Nevertheless, one of the enduring fascinations of this novel is the tension created between the ending and the rather dark nature of the body of the work.

THE HOUSE OF THE SPIRITS
Isabel Allende
1982
Novel
Family Saga, Historical

A ponderous, violence-filled generational novel set in South America and peopled by a cast of peculiar characters, few of whom are particularly appealing.

With the accidental death of her beautiful, green-haired sister Rosa, young Clara del Valle, whose psychic powers had warned her of imminent disaster, enters a period of self-imposed silence that lasts some nine years. Her first words then are to announce that she will marry her sister's fiance, Esteban Trueba, who has sought solace from his loss of Rosa by immersing himself in the revitalization of his country estate, building his fortune, and periodically raping any peasant girl who happens to catch his eye.

Oblivious of the illegitimate children resulting from his sexual excesses, Trueba marries Clara, determined to build a political career as the personification of the ideal Conservative Party family patriarch. Circumstances and his family conspire through the years to prevent this from being an easy task, as Trueba must contend with his suffragette mother-in-law, his somewhat unstable sister, his wife's calm acceptance of all manner of psychic phenomena, and his country's inevitable passage from the rule of chosen few to rule by the people and back again. His children further complicate his life: Blanca maintains an almost lifelong affair with a Socialist singer; Jaime ministers to the poor; and Nicholas pursues self-indulgence, dabbling in religious mysticism.

Only his granddaughter Alba seems capable of truly touching him, and yet even his eventual tolerance of her left-wing tendencies results more from his fear of ending his life as a lonely old man than from any deep love and unquestioning acceptance of her.

Death and violence proliferate the action which encompasses various natural disasters, political upheavals, and individual instances of human cruelty.

Supposedly derived from Clara's journals, the point of view shifts abruptly from this, to Trueba's rambling reminiscences and Alba's commentaries and back again with a disturbing lack of consistency.

Allende, a Chilean journalist, is a niece of the late Salvador Allende; this is her first novel. Her portrayal of the horrors of South American political disturbance may appeal to those with the patience to endure more than a half-century of the life of a self-centered, ill-tempered, chauvenistic tyrant.

THE HUMAN STAIN
Philip Roth
2000
Novel

The final volume of Roth's trilogy about postwar United States tells the story of how fatal sanctimony destroys a professor who had attempted to reinvent himself

The final volume in Philip Roth's trilogy, *The Human Stain*, links the tale of one man's fall from grace to the orgy of sanctimony in which the nation indulged itself during the year that a president of the United States was being denounced and impeached for his human stains. It was, writes Roth, "the summer of an enormous piety binge" that claimed Coleman Silk, along with Bill Clinton, as victims.

Narrator Nathan Zuckerman, the fictional novelist who appears in Roth's novels as early as 1974, undertakes to understand another man he has admired—this time, Coleman Silk in *The Human Stain*. "For all that the world is full of people who go around believing they've got you or your neighbor figured out," Zuckerman insists, "there really is no bottom to what is not known." Like the previous two volumes in the trilogy, *The Human Stain* is a character study that proceeds from the Gnostic premise that the full complexity of character can never be fathomed.

Silk is a dynamic, urbane dean and professor of classics at Athena College, a small, insular institution in the bucolic Berkshires. Silk's illustrious career comes undone six weeks into the semester, when he inquires about two students who have never attended class. "Does anyone know these people? Do they exist or are they spooks?" asks Silk, and the flippant question proves fatal. Though he is merely referring to the missing persons as phantoms, the word "spooks" is construed by political zealots as an abusive epithet, and the professor is accused of racism. In an atmosphere of ideological intimidation, no one dares rise to Silk's defense, and, appalled by the preposterous charge, he resigns in disgust.

Silk blames the vicious crusade against him for the sudden death of his wife, Iris. When he then takes up with a thirty-four-year-old cleaning woman, local gossip proliferates. One of the first important discoveries that Zuckerman makes about Silk is that the light-skinned professor is himself really African American, that he has for more than fifty years been passing as white—in fact, as Jewish. It is Silk who is the spook, a ghost of his true, black self. Silk's ethnic imposture has been so successful that not even his four grown children suspect their father's origins in a hard-working African American family in East Orange, New Jersey.

Silk fashions himself an expert on Greek literature, though he proves powerless to avert his own tragic fall. Silk's flaw is the unwarranted confidence that anyone can understand and control his or her own life. The curious directions that Silk's life took lead Zuckerman to ponder the Sophoclean enigmas of destiny and chance: "how accidentally a fate is made . . . or how accidental it all may seem when it is inescapable." Silk's life converges and collides with others who also believe in self-begetting. Faunia Farley, for example, flees an abused childhood into an abusive marriage and abandons that to become a menial laborer in Athena. Like her older lover, Silk, she, too, conceals secrets, redesigning herself as an eccentric, illiterate drudge.

The entire story is told by Zuckerman, who gathers his (incomplete) information from several sources. From time to time, Zuckerman becomes so absorbed in spinning Silk that the author's voice fades and what he imagines as the thoughts of others take over. Ultimately, readers are left with the tarnished image from which Roth's elegiac novel derives its name. *The Human Stain* is a sad, imperfect record of the insane urge to purify, by both Silk and his antagonists.

HUMBOLDT'S GIFT
Saul Bellow
1975
Novel
Psychological

Bellow vividly portrays poet-critic Delmore Schwartz through the fictional personage of Von Humboldt Fleischer in this novel notable for its intricate plot twists, its often rueful humor, and its depiction of American intelligentsia during the years before and after World War II.

The narrator, Charlie Citrine, is a somewhat diminished version of Bellow, a writer of fiction and nonfiction whose career and reputation have flourished during the same years that Humboldt's have declined. Even after death, the outrageous, eccentric figure of Humboldt looms large in Charlie's life, never far out of sight as Charlie grapples with a late-midlife crisis populated by agents, lawyers, accountants, gangsters, lovely ladies, and former wives (his own and Humboldt's).

Set mainly in Chicago in the early 1970's, with frequent flashbacks to an earlier New York, the novel in fact begins when Charlie's Mercedes is vandalized by an ambitious young hoodlum to whom he owes a small gambling debt.

The hoodlum, known variously as Ronald or Rinaldo Cantabile, soon intervenes in Charlie's life as a strange kind of "angel" bent on reacquainting him with the life of the common man. Here too the figure of Von Humboldt Fleischer looms, as Cantabile's wife is preparing a doctoral dissertation on Humboldt's life and work.

Haggling over children and finances with his former wife Denise, inevitably attracted to the treacherous young divorcee, Renata Koffritz, Charlie is again haunted by Humboldt's memory when he learns that Humboldt has bequeathed him some apparently worthless papers. Later, marooned in Madrid with Renata's young son after she has deserted them both to elope with a prosperous undertaker, Charlie will learn from the ubiquitous Cantabile that Humboldt's papers indisputably prove his and Charlie's authorship of a pirated script that has since been very profitably filmed. Although daunted by the prospect of further legal action, Charlie will in fact take steps to recover Humboldt's "gift," the tangible evidence of his warped but gifted personality.

James Atlas' life of Schwartz, published in 1977, revealed that many of Humboldt's more implausible actions were directly drawn from Schwartz's life, leaving the line between life and art even more blurred than before. The novel remains one writer's eulogy, testament, and testimony to a difficult but oddly rewarding friendship.

THE HUNCHBACK OF NOTRE DAME
Victor Hugo
1831
Novel
Tragedy, Romance

Hugo's romance has taken on mythic status largely because of the creation of the hunchback, Quasimodo, the central character whose hideousness evokes fear and revulsion but whose unrequited love for the beautiful Esmeralda elicits sympathy and pity, elevating the story to an archetypal retelling of the beauty-and-beast myth.

Through a series of tales of thwarted love, the novel reveals a tragic story of medieval Paris. The deformed Quasimodo, befriended by the Archdeacon of Notre Dame, Frollo, falls in love with the gypsy dancer, Esmeralda, who in turn is enamored of the aristocratic soldier, Phoebus, who once saved her life. Frollo, demented by his study of alchemy and the black arts, lusts after the dancer, too, and stabs Phoebus when the two lovers meet, allowing Esmeralda to take the blame. Destined for a public hanging, she is saved by Quasimodo, who carries her into the sanctuary of the cathedral. There he manages to fight off the mob of Paris, who, believing the gypsy is a witch, demand her death. Frollo, however, betrays Esmeralda to the crowd, and she is hanged. In revenge, Quasimodo throws the priest to his death from one of the towers of Notre Dame, after which the hunchback disappears from Paris. His whereabouts remain a mystery until years later, when, in a search of the vault where criminals were once buried, the bones of a disfigured man are found wrapped around the disintegrated corpse of a woman dressed as the gypsy.

It is not difficult to account for the popularity of this tale. The carefully drawn picture of the underworld of Paris, the various love triangles which interlock the classes and estates of the medieval world—all this provides a rich fictional tapestry. It is the tragic figure of Quasimodo, however, that gives the novel its mythic resonance, and his relationship with the gypsy forms the emotional center of the book, rescuing it from the banality of the conventional 19th century romance.

HUNGER
Knut Hamsun
1890
Novel
Stream of Consciousness, Psychological

Set in Christiania (now called Oslo), Norway, the first novel by the prolific Hamsun is an autobiographical account of a destitute young writer who is radically and willfully estranged from society. Organized into four sections, the book focuses on minute details of the anonymous narrator's solitary existence from one autumn through winter to the possibility of spring.

Wandering the streets with grandiose ambitions to write an opus on Philosophical Consciousness, the indigent narrator impetuously pawns his waistcoat to assist a beggar. He follows a strange woman whom he privately calls "Ylayali." He moves out of his boarding house and ends up sleeping in the woods. Though he sabotages his own attempt to get a job in a grocery, the first section concludes triumphantly, with payment of 10 kroner for a newspaper article.

Part 2 reverts to a mood of desperation and to the narrator's introverted fantasies. Registering as a vagrant with the police, he spends a bizarre night in jail. After his release, he is disappointed in his appeals to a clergyman and to friends. The section concludes with an acquaintance pawning a watch for him.

When the narrator tries to beg a candle, the clerk mistakenly thinks he has already paid for it and even gives him change. Later, he proudly returns the money. "Ylayali" pursues him, but he spurns her affection.

While trying to write a blasphemous play, the narrator observes cruelty within the ostensibly respectable family that runs his latest boardinghouse. After being evicted, he takes a job on a ship and prepares to depart for England. It is not clear whether the ending is auspicious or ominous, liberation or flight.

The novel's ambiguity is compounded by filtering everything through the febrile consciousness of a manic-depressive whose unreliability is manifest but who is also capable of great charm. His deliberately cultivated hunger, which marks him as an artist, sharpens his sensitivity and further alienates him from a complacent society of hypocritical thieves.

HYPERION
John Keats
1820
Poetry
Epic
This epic fragment derived from Greek myth, tells of the Titans' replacement by the Olympian gods.

Ever since the composition of *Paradise Lost*, English poets with epic ambitions have written under the shadow of Milton. *Hyperion*, Keats's effort along the Miltonic line, is powerful and extraordinary but a tour de force that he could not sustain.

As the poem begins, most of its action has already taken place. Saturn and the other Titans, with the sole exception of Hyperion, god of the sun, have been replaced by Jupiter and his fellow Olympians. Thus what occurs is not the issue. The questions to be raised are how and why benevolent gods have been overthrown. The difficulty of offering good answers combined with the static nature of the story to make *Hyperion* virtually impossible to complete.

Book I depicts, in sculptural detail, the throneless Saturn, whom Keats envisions as majestic, powerful, and beautiful—in fact, so thoroughly divine that it would be hard to imagine his superior. The second book brings Saturn to the gathering place of the Titans. Here, the deposed gods voice reasons for, and responses to, their great change of state. Oceanus, former ruler of the sea, advances the most convincing argument. The Titans are guiltless, he acknowledges, yet they have been superseded by beings yet more excellent—in a natural progression.

Book III bears out Oceanus' claim by presenting the young Apollo, who has not yet replaced Hyperion but who feels an aching eagerness to assume his divinity. Mnemosyne, the Titan goddess of memory, shows Apollo what he has not yet realized, that suffering and destruction precede creation, that life is change. This tragic "knowledge enormous" makes a god of Apollo, and the fragment breaks off as he undergoes his apotheosis.

Attempting to complete the poem, Keats transformed *Hyperion* into *The Fall of Hyperion*. In revising, he moved away from the influence of Milton and toward that of Dante. *The Fall of Hyperion* begins with an allegorical vision in which a dreaming poet enters a temple where the goddess Moneta reveals the story of Hyperion to him. Again, however, the epic remained unfinished.

I KNOW WHY THE CAGED BIRD SINGS
Maya Angelou
1969
Nonfiction
Autobiographical

This book is an autobiography written from the perspective of an African American poet, the first book in a series of seven volumes.

The narrative begins when Marguerite, aged three, and her brother Bailey, a year older, arrive in Stamps, Georgia, to live at her grandmother's house at the back of a general store: "High spots in Stamps were usually negative: droughts, floods, lynchings and deaths."

At the age of eight her father takes her and Bailey to live with their mother, Vivian, in St. Louis, Missouri. Vivian works in illegal gambling parlors. Vivian's boyfriend, Mr. Freeman, rapes Maya. Vivian sues in court. Mr. Freeman is mysteriously murdered.

Scarred by guilt and shame, Marguerite returns to Stamps where she endures a series of humiliating racist experiences. Her grandmother takes her to a white dentist who refuses to treat her, saying that he would rather put his hand in a dog's mouth than Marguerite's. At thirteen, Marguerite is returned to her mother, now in California. Vivian marries Clidell and for the first time, Marguerite experiences happy family life in San Francisco.

Marguerite spends a summer visiting her father in Los Angeles. His girlfriend, Dolores, calls Marguerite's mother a whore; they fight and Dolores stabs Marguerite with a sewing needle. Marguerite flees, spending a month living with homeless drifters in a junkyard before returning to San Francisco.

At the age of fifteen, Marguerite successfully defies the racist hiring policies of the city, becoming the first African American to become a ticket conductor on the fabled hills of San Francisco.

The next year Marguerite hides her pregnancy from her mother and graduates from the high school where they constantly practiced bomb drills. The narrative concludes with Maya exuding confidence, excited about being a mother to her newly born son.

The book's title comes from a line by the poet Paul Lawrence Dunbar, in a poem where the caged bird is a symbol for those imprisoned by slavery. The caged bird sings because it can't do anything else but use its voice to mark an imaginary territory.

THE ICEMAN COMETH
Eugene O'Neill
1946
Drama
Tragedy

This is O'Neill's bleakest drama, set in a squalid barroom in 1912 and concerned with a group of drunken derelicts who alternately feed and poison each others' illusions.

Harry Hope's saloon and rooming house are autobiographically derived from a lower Manhattan dive, Jimmy-the-Priest's, which O'Neill frequented between 1910 and 1912, and where he attempted suicide in the latter year. The play's theme is that humans cannot live without illusions, no matter how ill-founded those illusions may be.

Harry Hope's customers have seen better days, but they now blunt the pain of their lost lives with drink and dreams of "tomorrow"—the day they will renounce alcoholism and return to their former occupations. Harry subsidizes his guests in return for their supportive fellowship as he pretends to mourn for the wife he hated. The intellectual champion for these men of Tomorrow is Larry Slade, onetime anarchist, who has resigned himself to the conviction that life is lousy, man is doomed, and nothing matters.

Opposing the Tomorrow men is a hardware salesman, Hickey, who kicks away the crutches of their self-deceptions out of professed love for them and confidence that the truth shall set them free. In the last act, having made the derelicts hopeless with the horror of self-confrontation, Hickey delivers a long speech, revealing that he has slain his long-suffering wife, Evelyn, not out of love but out of a lifetime of hatred and self-loathing. Unable to face his authentic feelings, he then claims to have murdered her in a fit of insanity.

Relieved that they have been tricked by an apparent madman, the drunks relapse into their cherished fantasies.

THE IDIOT
Fyodor Dostoevski
1868-1869
Novel
Philosophical, Tragicomedy

In this novel, Dostoevski set himself the most difficult task in literature: to depict a supremely good man. The story suggests that people will consider a truly Christlike person to be an idiot. Such a person, though often attractive to others, will probably accomplish little in bettering the world.

Prince Lef Myshkin, the protagonist, is an impoverished nobleman lately released from a Swiss sanatorium where he was treated for epilepsy. He is so free of malice and so unfailingly kind that he inspires both love and contempt in his new friends in St. Petersburg. The most important of these are Parfen Rogozhin, a man of undisciplined passions, and Natasya Filipovna, a neurotic and helpless young person, generally believed to be a "kept woman."

Myshkin is drawn to Natasya because he recognizes both her essential innocence and her capacity for suffering. He proposes to her at their second meeting. She, however, impulsively rushes off with Rogozhin, who dramatically offers her a hundred thousand rubles for one night of love.

Through no fault of his own, Prince Myshkin becomes embroiled in several scandals. He successfully clears himself from charges of attempted fraud, then befriends the extortionist who wronged him. Returning good for evil only confirms his reputation as an idiot.

The novel ends in disaster: the murder of Natasya, prison for Rogozhin, and a return to the sanatorium with renewed attacks of epilepsy for the saintly protagonist.

Modern American readers are likely to find this story quite implausible. The point is well made, however, that a person who actually follows Christ's teachings will seem like a fool. Other elements in this most Russian of novels that may seem incredible or obscure to Western readers can be attributed to differences in national mores or temperament.

IDYLLS OF THE KING
Alfred, Lord Tennyson
1859-1885
Poetry
Narrative

This retelling of the legend of King Arthur and the Knights of the Round Table contains a vision of society particularly adapted for Tennyson's contemporaries. Those who appreciate narrative poetry and devotees of the Arthurian Legend will find this work enjoyable and intellectually stimulating.

Young Idylls of the KingArthur establishes his kingdom, marries Guinevere, and prospers for a time in Camelot. Sir Gareth, inspired by his King, is able to overcome significant odds to secure a maiden's release and win the hand of his beloved.

Soon, however, suspicion begins to divide the realm. Sir Geraint removes his bride Enid from Camelot to wander through the land and almost dies before he is convinced of his wife's fidelity. Twins Balin and Balan kill each other because the former fails to recognize his brother, who has been driven to madness by his knowledge of the Queen's infidelity with Lancelot. Merlin gives in to the wishes of the temptress Vivien, who imprisons him in an oak tree. Lancelot's refusal to put aside his adulterous relationship with the Queen to marry Elaine leads to her suicide.

The knights engage in a futile quest for the Holy Grail; the Round Table is decimated. Knights admitted to the fellowship to fill the void prove incapable, as the story of Pelleas illustrates. Finally, Camelot is turned upside down at the Last Tournament, where Tristram wins the prize for his paramour Isolt.

Open rebellion breaks out, causing Guinevere to flee to a convent, where she confronts her King and finally admits her mistake. Events have proceeded too far, however, and Arthur falls to Mordred in a final battle. His faithful knight Bedivere sees him taken away, but whether he dies or is removed to heaven remains a mystery.

The resurgence of popularity for the Arthurian Legend in 19th century England allowed Tennyson to use the story for his own purposes. This tale highlights specific Victorian virtues and vices. Spotless character is doomed to failure, as those less virtuous fail to recognize their duty to follow men like King Arthur. Adultery is the root cause of the failure of Arthur's kingdom, although one might argue that Arthur asks his followers to do more than is humanly possible in following the strict commands he places on them.

Though some of the character portraits are wooden, this exciting work provides excellent insight into the Victorian temperament, and is one of the finest examples of narrative poetry from the period.

ILIAD
Homer
750 B.C.E.
Poetry
Epic

This account of the Greek siege of Troy depicts the tragic struggle between the warrior Achilles and King Agamemnon, the anger of Achilles, and its consequences for the Greek army.

Homer's epic begins in the tenth year of the Trojan War, in which the Greek army besieges the walled city of Troy in Asia Minor. According to legend, the Greeks had sailed to Troy to win the release of Helen, wife of King Menelaus, who had been abducted by the Trojan prince Paris. The twenty-four books of the *Iliad* incorporate a body of legend that may date back to the twelfth century B.C. Rather than recount the entire conflict, Homer concentrates on the events which follow the feud between Greek warriors Achilles and Agamemnon.

After Agamemnon takes away Achilles' war prize, the maid Briseis, Achilles angrily withdraws from battle, and the demoralized Greek forces are pushed back almost to their ships. Achilles' friend Patroclus attempts to rally the Greeks, but he is killed by the Trojan hero Hector. Achilles then returns to battle, routs the enemy, and slays Hector in single combat on the plains of Troy. After Hector's death, King Priam is forced to plead for the body of his son, which has been mutilated by Achilles.

Homer's narrative presents a vivid picture of Bronze Age Greek culture. His warrior society lives by a heroic code according to which men were expected to show strength, courage, loyalty, and valor. Humans are at the mercy of capricious gods and goddesses, who intervene in battle to save their favorites. Even the great Achilles cannot alter his fate. Homer's genius lies in his ability to depict war in all of its brutal intensity and in his recognition that tragedy arises from flaws in human character. His depiction of the horror and fascination of war is as relevant today as it was to his own audience.

THE IMPORTANCE OF BEING EARNEST
Oscar Wilde
1895
Drama
Comedy
This satire on Victorian pretentions and the British class structure is a classic of comic construction and brilliant wit.

The two main male characters, Algernon Moncrieff and Jack Worthing, constrained by the rigid conventions of the Victorian upper class, have been leading double lives. Algy's alter ego is "Bunbury," while Jack has invented a fictitious brother named Ernest, whose loose behavior he claims to control but which he actually emulates. Jack falls in love with Gwendolyn Fairfax, Algy's cousin, and Algy falls in love with Cecily Cardew, Jack's ward.

Each of these ladies, moreover, is attracted to her respective beau on the assumption that his name is Ernest. Gwendolyn's mother, Lady Bracknell, is dissatisfied with Jack's account of his origins—he was an orphan—and thus forbids the relationship. Meanwhile, in order to marry Cecily, Algy makes arrangements to be rechristened Ernest.

The interaction of these four characters produces many delicious complications turning on the question of who is truly Ernest. Reversing her previous position when she learns the size of Cecily's fortune, Lady Bracknell consents to Algy's match. Jack, however, withholds his agreement considering Lady Bracknell's opposition to his match with Gwendolyn. The impediment to this alliance finally dissolves when it emerges that Jack is actually Algy's older brother and, moreover, named Ernest. This multiple coincidence resolves the differences between all parties.

This delightful comedy uses the devices of farce and cheerfully empty repartee to satirize the emotional shallowness of the English ruling class in the late nineteenth century. The elevation of style over substance, of words over reality, of earnestness over honesty of feeling, exposes the tendency toward triviality and pomposity in high society everywhere.

IN COLD BLOOD
Truman Capote
1966
Novel
Crime, Southern Gothic
This 1966 non-fiction bestseller recounts the 1959 murder of Herbert Clutter, his wife, and two of their four children in Holcomb, Kansas. Capote often adopts the point of view of the murderers, thus drawing public criticism.

On parole from the Kansas State Penitentiary, Richard "Dick" Hickock and Perry Edward Smith robbed the Clutter farm and, in the process, killed everyone at the farm, in an attempt to find the farm's safe. A former prison acquaintance who had worked on the farm, Floyd Wells, had told Hickock that Clutter kept great sums of cash in a safe. Clutter never had a safe; he paid all bills by check. Clutter was a successful, upright Methodist, popular with his more than dozen workers, as well as well-respected in his small community. The robbers planned to spend the rest of their lives living-it-up in Mexico.

After driving across Kansas at night, the robbers entered the Clutter household while everyone slept. They woke up Herbert and family. When no admission of the safe was forthcoming, Smith slit Herbert's throat, put a bullet in his head, then shot the wife and two children in the head, Kenyon aged 15, and Nancy, 16. Hickok steadfastly maintained that Smith performed all the killings, yet Smith claimed Hickok murdered the two women.

Wells provided the tip that led to the arrest of the murderers in Las Vegas on December 30, 1959. At trial, they both pleaded temporary insanity but were convicted during a one-week trial. The jury deliberated for only 45 minutes. Both criminals were hung in the wee hours of April 14, 1965 in Lansing, Kansas.

Capote travelled to Holcomb with novelist Harper Lee before the apprehension of the murderers. They interviewed many people the Clutters knew. While Capote provided a factual account of the investigation and murders, he took much artistic license with dialogue in the book. Many people have disputed or denied quotations, while others have challenged particular aspects of the investigation in Capote's description.

Attempting to get inside the minds of the murderers, Capote appears to identify and sympathize with their mental states as he continued to interview the killers in prison, finally appearing to accept their preposterous plea of temporary insanity, despite the book's title indicating otherwise. This type of journalism with novelistic techniques has subsequently been dubbed docu-fiction.

IN JUST

Edward Eslin Cummings (e. e. cummings)

1923

Poetry

"In Just—" is a poem about celebrating the first hint of spring with an attitude of innocence and joy.

The modern American poet who turned the English language on it's head, Edward Estlin Cummings (e. e. cummings) wrote poetry that defied the conventions of syntax, punctuation, and even typography, in eliciting feelings and impressions in his readers, that went beyond normal linguistic signifiers. Often characterized as a post-structuralist, Cummings used unusual combinations of words, extra or deleted spaces between words, and odd line breaks, to convey an impression beyond the mere meaning of his individual words.

"In Just—" is a poem about early spring. Cummings pairs words like "mud/luscious" and "puddle-wonderful," that evoke both the messiness of the season—it is usually wet (puddles) and muddy—along with the words "luscious and wonderful" to evoke a sense of the emotional richness in early spring—that sense of relief that the harsh weather is over. In combining the names "eddieandbill" and "bettyandisbel" he creates a sense of child-like belonging to a group, or at least to a pair. "eddieandbill" are not alone, and in fact share their excitement with "bettyandisbel." Reading these lines out loud demonstrates how quickly these combined names tumble off the tongue, much like excited children might run, finally free, in springtime.

Besides the children and the narrator, the poem includes a "goat-footed/ balloonMan," who "whistles/far/and/wee." The fact that the man is "goat-footed" draws a comparison with the mythic creature Pan, a satyr-like being that is half goat and half man. This image also hints at a touch of danger, not unlike the trickster, Pied Piper of Hamlin who lured children to their doom.

It has been said of Cummings' unconventional techniques that he startles readers into actually "listening," rather than just hearing his words.

IN MEMORIAM

Alfred, Lord Tennyson

1850

Poetry

Elegaic

In Memoriam is a long poem that developed from a number of separate lyrics that Tennyson composed over a seventeen-year period, following the death of his friend Arthur Hallam in 1833.

Considered in Tennyson's time his finest poetic achievement, *In Memoriam* has since lost some of its appeal, except to specialists in literary history. In the Victorian period, the religious issues raised in the poem gave it a special significance. Tennyson describes how grief and despair over Hallam's death and skepticism caused by new scientific theories led him to question his Christian faith. His account of how he won back his confidence in divine justice and belief in immortality in this poem prompted Queen Victoria, who no doubt spoke for many other readers, to say that next to the Bible, *In Memoriam* was her greatest comfort.

The length and subject of *In Memoriam* have been an impediment to modern readers who do not go to Tennyson's poem to shore up their religious faith. But for those who want to gain some insight into the mind of Tennyson and the Victorian Age as well as encounter a poem that is rich in imagery, rhythms, diction, and themes, there is no better source.

Beginning with a funeral and ending with a wedding, the poem is composed of 131 sections or elegies which, taken sometimes separately and often in clusters, comprise "a kind of *Divina Commedia*," as Tennyson said, that charts his spiritual autobiography through stages of grieving and doubting to eventual optimism.

The early sections (1-30) mark the impact of Hallam's death on the poet. The middle sections (54-56) constitute the "dark night of the soul," recording Tennyson's most acute sense of disbelief and alienation in a mechanistic universe. Later sections (94-95 and 103) record the turn toward hope that comes after Tennyson experiences a mystic trance and prophetic dream in which he communes with the spirit of Hallam.

Finally, Tennyson envisions a future age of progress and a higher race, of which Arthur Hallam was the prototype. Although Tennyson finds and gives reasons to hope, he confessed that the voice of *In Memoriam* was not necessarily his and that "this poem is more hopeful than I am myself."

INTERPRETER OF MALADIES
Jhumpa Lahiri
1999
Short Story
Collection

A first short-story collection from a talented young Indian American writer

Lahiri's almost self-effacing strengths are especially evident in the collection's opening story, "A Temporary Matter." The title refers to the disruption of electrical service. Shoba works as a proofreader and keeps fit by working out at a gym. Her husband, Shukumar, works at home on his dissertation on agrarian revolts in India. The power disruption forces them together, forces them to eat dinner together by candlelight rather than separately, as had become their custom. Awkwardness gives way to intimacy, but an intimacy fraught with as much risk as promise. Forced back on themselves and their severely depleted stock of emotional resources, they pass the time by telling stories they never told before.

The other eight stories play variations on the opening work's theme of disappointment and dislocation. What surprises is not that a young writer should be so narrow in range but that she should prove so adept at handling this theme with such complexity and from so many perspectives. The narrator of "When Mr. Pirzada Came to Dinner," for example, is a woman in her thirties looking back at events that took place in 1971 when she was ten. Her narrative focuses on a man she found both familiar and strange: Mr. Pirzada, a visiting scholar writing a book on the deciduous trees of New England who speaks her Bengali parents' native language but who is not, her parents insist, Indian. Rather, he is Pakistani, and, by story's end, Bangladeshi.

"The Interpreter of Dreams" takes up where the previous story leaves off. Here, a young, superficially Americanized Indian couple, while touring their nominal homeland, visit the Sun Temple at Kanarek under the watchful eye of their driver and guide, Mr. Kapasi. Although he is clearly dismayed by their ways, the reserved Mr. Kapasi begins fantasizing a chaste affair with Mrs. Das. In this way, the man who had once dreamed of becoming a scholar of foreign languages compensates for having had to settle for so little: first becoming a teacher of English in a local grammar school, then, in order to pay his dead son's medical bills, becoming his son's doctor's translator, an interpreter of patients' maladies.

The switch in perspective is even more pronounced in the two stories that adopt non-Indians as their center of consciousness. "Sexy" begins familiarly enough: "It was a wife's worst nightmare. After nine years of marriage, Laxmi told Miranda, her cousin's husband had fallen in love with another woman." The story then veers in a surprising direction. In "This Blessed House," the collection of Christian posters, statues, and key chains left behind by the previous owners become the source of comic conflict in the house in which the newlyweds, Sanjeev and Twinkle, begin their life together. Although the story ends with a compromise, there is an undercurrent of resentment on the husband's part and rebellion on the wife's that leaves the reader feeling uneasy about the chances that this marriage will survive. Even in the collection's two comic tales, "A Real Durwan" and "The Treatment of Bibi Haldar" (both set in India), displacement figures prominently.

In the closing story, "The Third and Final Continent," there is a welcome if uncharacteristic note of quiet triumph. The narrator, recalling his mundane odyssey from Calcutta to London in 1964 and then to Boston five years later, focuses on the short time he spent as a lodger in a cantankerous elderly woman's home where simple politeness on his part becomes an act of enormous kindness for her.

Because she traffics in "ordinary emergencies" and the domestic disasters and disappointments that erode her characters' fragile existences, Lahiri's fiction stakes out new territory for Indian and non-Indian readers alike. *Interpreter of Maladies* marks the debut of a quietly stunning new talent worth reading not just for what these stories promise, but for what they have so expertly and affectingly accomplished.

IN THE AMERICAN GRAIN
William Carlos Williams
1925
Nonfiction
Collection, Historical

William Carlos Williams applies his poet's intuition to interpret familiar American historical fact. The result is a stimulating tour of terrain not so familiar after all.

That the new world was never really "new" disturbs Williams. He shows the explorers asserting old identity, their inherited view, in a vast wilderness with names only Indians knew. The discoverers quite simply failed to understand what they had discovered. Williams portrays Columbus' inability to do more than open the door for crazed exploitation. With wry humor Williams sees Champlain's gentle frenchified mapping of the northern wilderness. The conquests—of Ponce De Leon, Cortez, and DeSoto—are shown as the blind and destructive acts that they were.

The colonizers ignored the spirit inhabiting this land. Conquerors and settlers destroyed the Indian. Puritans asserted their grim control, placing in stocks any white man who would prefer the maypole to their sermons. Their treatment of witches under Cotton Mather, Williams finds especially telling, and killing. The fear of touch was the earliest Americans' problem, compounded by an unwillingness to see what the Indians' culture was about.

Williams affirms some of our myths. He beautifully restates the treasure we owned in George Washington. Daniel Boone and Sam Houston remain authentic heroes. Benjamin Franklin, however, is seen in a harsh light: Williams cites his pragmatism and Poor Richard wit as a guise adopted out of fear of the New World's wildness.

Through energetic prose, Williams brings the figures on postage stamps to life. Often quoting directly from original sources, he adapts the tone of his writing to the quotation. Empathy, not iconoclasm, is the mode Williams uses in the book. He desperately hoped that America would recognize its genius and tradition as separate from English Protestantism and European culture. Thus the book aims not to debunk but to reveal, lovingly, our connection in the twentieth century with our founders. This connection is not a simpleminded patriotic nostalgia, but a living and problematic relationship.

INVISIBLE MAN
Ralph Ellison
1952
Novella
Psychological

This encyclopedic novel explores the psychological and political odyssey of an anonymous, black narrator who discovers, in his own words, "the beautiful absurdity" of American identity.

This book begins with a prologue in which the narrator explains why he has gone underground. Essentially, he has retreated from a society in which he could find no place for himself as an individual. From his subterranean hideout somewhere in the depths of Harlem he reflects on his past as a means of regrouping in the present and preparing for his future.

He tells an extraordinarily vivid story about his authoritarian Southern background; his confusing experiences as a naive student at a black college, where he meets a visiting white philanthropist; and his journey to New York City, where he becomes involved with various religious and political groups.

Ellison is a virtuoso stylist who manages to combine the graceful economy of Ernest Hemingway's best prose with the rather baroque imagination that William Faulkner exemplifies in many of his novels. Thus Ellison's narrator is thoroughly lucid even as he describes episodes that get at the mystery and confusion of the roles people play in their everyday lives.

Rinehart, a character who never actually appears in the novel, is regarded as the epitome of the role-player. When the narrator is mistaken for Rinehart, he realizes that ultimately he too will have to play many roles—that he has, in fact, already played many roles, from black college student to mental patient to revolutionary and counter-revolutionary.

In addition to being steeped in the themes of American identity that appear in the work of so many authors from Herman Melville to William Faulkner, Ellison also makes splendid use of his musical training by blending jazz lyrics and improvisational motifs that are characteristic of a specifically black culture.

IRONWEED
William Kennedy
1983
Novel
Historical, Regionalist

Former baseball player, Francis Phelan has spent the past twenty-two years running from the ghosts of his past—the ghosts of the men he has killed, of the thirteen-day-old infant who slipped from his hands and died, of the women he has loved. He is a "lost and distorted soul...too profane...humbl[ing] himself willfully through the years to counter a fearful pride in his own ability to manufacture the glory from which grace would flow."

Some might conclude that Francis Phelan is a bum by choice. He has a home, an understanding and compassionate wife, and children who love him. But he is driven away by demons, perhaps of his own making. He was a talented baseball player with the Albany Senators. He had a job working on the trolleys. But, two events (twenty-two years earlier) have him on the run: he dropped and killed his infant son, and he killed a "scab" during a trolley workers' strike. He takes up a vagabond's life, running from the ghosts that follow him, literally, as he holds whole conversations with them, treating them like old friends. He is not a man in obvious pain. Hero and anti-hero alike, Francis is compassionate toward those less fortunate than he, but he can't seem to take care of himself, and killing follows in his wake.

The story line has Francis returning to his former home, Albany, New York, to face charges of fraud after he registers as a Democrat twenty-one times, earning five dollars each time. Over the course of three days, Francis meets up with old friends and other street bums. In particular, he finds Helen, his partner of nine years, who is dying from a malignant tumor. Helen's story is likewise tragic, though she hasn't had the love that Francis has. Francis is resourceful, and earns some money doing odd jobs, in an effort to keep himself and Helen fed and out of the cold.

Ironweed is a study of street life in depression-era Albany, NY. The street code of love and responsibility is different from that of civilized life. Love can only be acted on, never spoken, just as kinship is an attitude rather than a familial imperative. Francis' children and wife are more strangers to him than the street bums with whom he shares a sandwich.

Running is a major theme in the novel. The narrator explains that "Francis began to run, and in so doing, reconstituted a condition that was as pleasurable to his being as it was natural: the running of bases... the running from accusation, the running from the calumny of men and women, the running from family, from bondage, from destitution of spirit... He had stood staunchly irresolute in the face of capricious and adverse fate. (75) The end of his story is ambiguous. Has he actually stopped running, or is a settled life with his family and home just another flight of fancy?

IVANHOE: A ROMANCE
Sir Walter Scott
1820
Novel
Historical, Epic

In England the publication of this 1820 novel stirred interest in the medieval period. This quest romance with realistic historic ambiance argues for the reconciliation of Saxons and Normans in creating a united England.

Wilfred's Saxon father, Cedric, disinherits Wilfred of Ivanhoe, due to his support for Norman King Richard (who speaks French), as well as Wilfred's love for Lady Rowena; Cedric had planned an arranged political marriage. Ivanhoe departs to fight for King Richard the Lionhearted during the third Crusade in 1188.

A debt dispute between a Jewish banker and a Holy Land palmer leads to a tournament resolution. On the first day, a masked knight (Ivanhoe) wins the tournament. As a reward, he claims the hand of Lady Rowena from Prince John. On the second day, Ivanhoe's side appears to be losing, but a masked knight, "Black Lazybones," aids him, yet Ivanhoe is severely wounded; the Jewish merchant's daughter, Rebecca, nurses him with herbs.

Abandoned by servants and guards, Ivanhoe and Rebecca, on their way to York, are taken prisoner by Cedric, whose party is then captured by de Bracy, who imprisons them at Torquilstone Castle. The Black Knight hears of their predicament, and raises an army with Robin of Locksley to besiege the castle. Ivanhoe's squire escapes.

Through a religious ruse, Cedric escapes with important strategic information. Richard, revealing himself as The Black Knight, storms and takes the castle, then pardons the captive de Bracy. Cedric rescues Rowena, whom de Bracy was about to marry. Ivanhoe is once more seriously wounded, yet rescued by Richard.

King Richard sends de Bracy to tell Prince John of the king's triumph and return. Bois-Guilbert had escaped Torquilstone with captive Rebecca, whom he puts on trial for her healing witchcraft. Rebecca claims the right to trail by combat. The Templar Grandmaster unexpectedly assigns Bois-Guilbert to fight Rebecca's yet to-be-determined-champion.

Cedric graciously agrees to marry Rowena to Ivanhoe. Rebecca's father pleads desperately for Ivanhoe to defend innocent Rebecca. Ivanhoe does, defeating Bois-Guilbert, who subsequently dies of internal wounds. Rebecca is vindicated. King Richard punishes all Knights Templar disloyal to him. Fearing religious persecution, Rebecca and her father depart for Grenada. Rebecca and Rowena tearfully part.

Ivanhoe and Rowena happily marry. After the death of King Richard, and Ivanhoe hangs up his sword. Although a hero, Ivanhoe is vulnerable; fundamentally, he's the ultra-English gentleman, Scott's greatest invention.

J

JANE EYRE
Charlotte Brontë
1847
Novel
Manners, Feminist

This classic novel, one of the most popular in all literature, presents what may be the first thoroughly developed female character in the history of the novel. Jane, orphaned early in life, becomes an individual who refuses to be stereotyped and who demands and gets what she considers her full due, not only as a woman but also as a complete human being.

One of the most striking characteristics of this novel is the voice of Jane Eyre herself, who tells her own story. Without that voice and the intimacy it provides for the reader, credulity would be strained, for the action of the novel is at times inadvertently ridiculous or far-fetched, and the characterizations are often simplistic.

Problems with credibility, however, recede into the background as Jane speaks directly to the reader, commenting on past actions or announcing events to come. On other occasions, she allows a scene to speak for itself but shifts from past to present tense to underline the force of the narrative and its emotional content. One of the most famous lines in all literature is the sentence, "Reader, I married him," which occurs after Jane returns to Thornfield to find the chastened, blinded, and maimed Edward Rochester, who becomes her husband.

The overall linear structure of the novel is quite straightforward: The first ten chapters treat Jane's childhood and education; the next seventeen chapters bring Jane to Thornfield Hall and introduce her to Rochester, carrying their relationship to the point of the collapse of their initial marriage plan; the next eight chapters detail Jane's flight and the developments that ensue with regard to the Rivers family, culminating in St. John Rivers' proposal of marriage to Jane; and the last three chapters detail Jane's return to Thornfield, including her marriage to Rochester and the beginning of their life together.

The second and third sections of the novel are dominated by male figures who symbolize opposing forms of love: Rochester, who stands for physical passion, and St. John, who stands for spiritual passion. At the end of the novel, Rochester, having passed through redemptive fires and having repented of his hubris, can embody the fully integrated masculine self, capable of both physical and spiritual passion.

Jane, too, must pay for her pride. Her flight from Thornfield Hall after the collapse of the marriage plans, her deprivations, her illness—these are the means by which Jane passes from youthful rebellion to a mature acceptance of the conditions of her life and an understanding of her own emotional and physical needs.

JOSEPH ANDREWS
Henry Fielding
1742
Novel
Comedy, Epic

An eighteenth century male servant resists the seductive advances of Lady Booby, his aristocratic employer. This richly comic picaresque novel captures the charming mix of earthiness and politesse that characterizes humor in the Age of Manners.

The novel's story and full title, *The History of the Adventures of Joseph Andrews, and His Friend Mr. Abraham Adams*, echo the first and greatest of all European novels, the story of Don Quixote and his squire Sancho Panza (Part One 1605; Part Two 1615). While Cervantes' novel burlesques the chivalric romances of his day, Fielding's is a parody of Samuel Richardson's *Pamela* (1740), a sentimental novel depicting the struggle of an honest serving maid to escape seduction by her master.

Joseph, whom Fielding makes a brother to Pamela, resists Lady Booby with the same virtue that enabled his sister to resist Squire Booby. Joseph's reward is dismissal. Without money or prospects but warmed by his devotion to his sweetheart Fanny, Joseph sets out from London determined to find her. En route he meets Parson Adams, his old tutor and friend. Under dramatic circumstances, they happen to encounter Fanny. Soon all three have a series of quixotic adventures.

Parson Adams is a totally ingenuous country cleric, simpleminded, good-hearted with a strong appetite for meat and drink and a wholesome disdain of selfishness, meanness, and hypocrisy. He is Fielding's primary vehicle for attacking affectation, and the parson's quick temper and physical courage make him a formidable adversary. Although he gets himself into one compromising situation after another, his essential goodness always shines through. In a magnificently farcical scene he is discovered asleep in Fanny's bed after an innocent attempt to protect her virtue.

The exuberance of this earthy and good-natured romance is reflected in its fictive playfulness, its blending of tale, parable, burlesque, parody, farce, and epic. Fielding was flexing creative muscles in this work, laying the groundwork for his brilliantly plotted masterpiece, *Tom Jones* (1749), often considered the greatest novel of the eighteenth century.

THE JOY LUCK CLUB
Amy Tan
1989
Novel

The story of four Chinese immigrants and their American daughters, examining the intricate nature of the relationship between mothers and daughters.

The Joy Luck Club opens with a woman leaving Shanghai for America, carrying a swan which she is determined to give to her yet unborn daughter, as a symbol of her high aspirations for her in the new land. In the immigration office, the swan is confiscated, leaving the woman with only one loose feather. *The Joy Luck Club* is about those things handed down from Chinese-born mothers to their American-born daughters; like the swan's feather, this legacy carries with it a mixture of both hope and disappointment, pain and love. More than a record of the cultural transition, The Joy Luck Club examines what daughters, in any culture, inherit from their mothers.

Eight women, each of four mother-daughter pairs, narrate the novel. Their common link is the Joy Luck Club, a weekly mah-jongg party. As the novel begins, one of the club's members has just died and her Americanized daughter June takes her mother's place. The rituals of the evening's game are at once familiar and mystifying to June, calling into relief the powerful cultural dissonance between the two generations and reminding June of those qualities in her mother which she had never fully understood. June also learns that the two abandoned daughters her mother had borne from a previous marriage have been located, and the aunties have arranged for June to go to China and tell these women all she can about the mother they never knew. "What will I say?" June wonders, "What can I tell them about my mother?" Dismayed but not surprised at June's response, the aunties see in her their Americanized daughters, just as ignorant and unmindful of the truths and hopes they have brought to America.

The Joy Luck Club becomes itself the means by which this connecting hope can be passed on to future generations. In the novel, June goes to China and tells her half-sisters all she knows of her mother, gathered from the shared text of each mother and daughter as they wove their meditation on this generational gulf and the struggle toward connection. What is seen through one pair of eyes is played back through another's; each time more is learned. Sometimes it is the same incident that is seen from different sides, other times it is an oblique reverberation, as when June receives a jade pendant from Suyuan, echoing the gift of the feather described on the opening page. The necklace is emblematic of the broken communication between mother and daughter. What one values, the other derides. Though their cultural differences make this rift particularly acute, the gulf that Tan describes is fairly universal. It is not only among

Chinese-American mothers and daughters that there is so much mutual disappointment, so many hidden resentments, as well as such a profound yearning for a greater love that can transcend the pain.

The mothers' hope is that their daughters will grow to combine the best of Chinese character with the best of American opportunities. Their pain is that much of the Chinese character seems to have gotten lost in translation. What gets passed on from mother to daughter? The question starts to be answered as similarities between June and her mother gradually take shape, as June finds herself growing territorial and hissing at the neighbors' cat just as her mother had done. Like the slowly developing Polaroid photo of June and her two half-sisters taken at the Shanghai airport, their images become clear, with not one of them is exactly like their mother, but together their likenesses conjure up Suyuan's as well.

The Joy Luck Club, is a brilliant first novel. Tan's characters are beautifully drawn, her language is graceful, her detail is strong. The one flaw is that the eight narrators are sometimes difficult to keep straight, but the richness of the book makes it well worth the effort to do so.

JUDE THE OBSCURE
Thomas Hardy
1895
Novel
Coming of Age, Tragedy

A poor young man plans to educate himself and enter the university at Christminster, but he is thwarted in his dreams by two young women with whom he falls in love.

Jude Fawley, a stonecutter's apprentice, teaches himself Greek and Latin and plans to go to Christminster to become a scholar. His plan is interrupted by Arabella Donn, a vulgar woman who tricks him into marriage. When the marriage fails, he makes his way to Christminster but is again kept from the university when he falls in love with his cousin, Sue Bridehead, an intellectual but emotionally cold woman.

When she learns Jude is married, she leaves him and marries the elderly Mr. Phillotson out of spite. Some time later, both Jude and Sue divorce their spouses and live together, unable to face the idea of marriage again. Financially burdened and socially shunned, Jude is unable to attend the university in whose shadow he now lives.

After the death of their children, Sue becomes extremely religious and leaves Jude to return to Phillotson, hoping in that way to atone for her behavior. Jude, deathly ill, is tricked again into marrying Arabella and dies in Christminster while she is out watching the boat races.

Sometimes criticized for its reliance upon coincidence to drive home its fatalistic message, the novel dramatizes Hardy's belief in the indifference of nature to man, but it also criticizes the Victorian social institutions of marriage and education. Jude's tragedy is one of missed fulfillment stemming from being denied entrance to the university and from his own natural impulses which lead him into two disastrous sexual relationships.

Hardy's novel is often regarded as a precursor of the modern novel in its presentation of the theme of failure and frustration. Angered and disillusioned when the book was greeted with severe criticism for its alleged immorality, he turned to poetry, never to write another novel.

JULIUS CAESAR
William Shakespeare
1601
Drama
Historical

The drama of the assassination of Julius Caesar in 44 B.C. becomes, through Shakespeare's art, a thought-provoking study of political ambition and its ramifications for both the individual and the republic.

The first scene of the play contains hints that Caesar's ambition and growing individual power may be suppressing the liberty of the people. Out of jealousy and fear of dictatorship, Cassius begins to conspire against Caesar, making every effort to gain the support of Brutus, one of Rome's most respected citizens.

Swayed by false documents prepared by Cassius and motivated by his love of Rome, Brutus joins the conspiracy against Caesar. While he agrees that Rome must be saved from Caesar, he opposes killing Caesar's supporters.

After murdering Caesar, the conspirators, Brutus insists, should bathe their hands in Caesar's blood to affirm symbolically that they are sacrificers, not murderers. His idealism eventually leads to the failure of the conspiracy.

Following the assassination, Brutus speaks to the mob and explains his complicity, winning their support. However, Mark Antony then speaks and turns the crowd against the conspirators.

Rome is then divided in two camps. Mark Antony, Octavius, and Lepidus pursue the conspirators to Philippi. In the ensuing battle, Antony and Octavius are victorious; Cassius and Brutus commit suicide. Unlike Caesar, Brutus, the man of ideals and words, ultimately has too little ambition to succeed in the corridors of power.

THE JUNGLE
Upton Sinclair
1906
Novel
Sociological

This muckraking novel portrays the misery and degradation of a Lithuanian immigrant family in the harsh world of Chicago's meat-packing industry at the end of the 19th century.

The Jungle presents the tragic story of Jurgis Rudkus, a Lithuanian peasant, and his family and friends, who are lured to America with promises of good wages and quick wealth. In Packingtown, they discover that Chicago is literally a "jungle" in which the non-English speaking immigrant is easily victimized by crooked and unscrupulous employers, political bosses, labor leaders, and real-estate hucksters. They are brutalized by an economic system that exploits them for their labor and then discards them when they are no longer productive.

When Jurgis and his family first arrive in Chicago, they are confused and bewildered. He goes to work at a packing house for $45 a month, but soon his father, wife, and relations must also find work to meet their expenses. Despite their best efforts, they find themselves slipping into poverty, disease, and squalor. When Jurgis is injured at work, he loses his job, his father dies, and his wife and child become ill. After serving a prison term for violence, he drifts miserably from job to job until one night by chance he hears a lecture on socialism.

Sinclair's bleakly deterministic novel was meant to dramatize the plight of the workers in the meat-packing industry, but the primary effect of his novel was to arouse his readers' indignation over the unsanitary conditions in which their food was produced. "I aimed at America's heart," he remarked, "and by accident hit it in the stomach." His novel was based on careful investigative journalism and provides a vivid account of the inhumane conditions that many immigrants faced in adjusting to American life.

As a naturalistic novel, *The Jungle* suggests that Jurgis is helpless in struggling against his social environment. Sinclair believed that socialism was the answer, but instead his novel led to reforms in the meat-packing and food-processing industries.

THE JUNGLE BOOKS
Rudyard Kipling
1894, 1895
Short Story
Children's, Collection

Of the 15 stories in The Jungle Books, *eight are about Mowgli, an Indian boy who is raised by wolves. Of the rest—a miscellany, not jungle stories at all—the best known are "The White Seal" and "Rikki-Tikki-Tavi."*

The Jungle Books were originally published a year apart as *The Jungle Book* and *The Second Jungle Book* but are now usually printed in one volume. The legend of the hero brought up by animals goes back to ancient times, and has been used more recently by Edgar Rice Burroughs in his Tarzan books. Thus, the Mowgli stories have deep roots. Mowgli, however, is a far more authentic character than Tarzan; his jungle world and its animal inhabitants are more fully imagined. The rhythms of Kipling's prose, and of the poems which introduce and follow each story, are hypnotic. Best read for the first time in childhood, these stories remain enjoyable for adults.

When Mowgli is about a year old, just able to walk, his parents abandon him in their haste to escape from Shere Khan, the lame man-eating tiger. This is a score which Mowgli will settle later. Meanwhile, he learns to hunt with the wolves, and he learns the law of the jungle from Bagheera, the Black Panther, and Baloo, the Brown Bear. He is kidnapped by a tribe of monkeys, the lawless Bandar-log, and rescued by Kaa, the Rock Python. Later, he leads the wolf pack against the Red Dogs, the most feared hunters in the jungle.

"Rikki-Tikki-Tavi" is about a mongoose who saves a family from Nag and Nagaina, the cobras; "The White Seal" retells the archetypal story of the flight—in this case from seal hunters—to the promised land. Other stories are about Eskimos, a Hindu holy man, baggage elephants, and a legendary old crocodile. These, and the Mowgli stories as well, have at their center heroic struggle guided by the rule of law, triumphant against the odds.

K

KIDNAPPED
Robert Louis Stevenson
1886
Novel
Adventure

This adventure novel, set in 18th century Scotland, describes the fortunes of young David Balfour as he attempts to claim his inheritance. Only after surviving the designs of his uncle, kidnapping, ambush, shipwreck, and a series of adversaries in the Scottish Highlands, does the hero return to regain his Lowlands estate.

When his father dies, David Balfour receives little beyond a letter of introduction to his Uncle Ebenezer of the House of Shaws. But shortly after David meets this suspicious, miserly old man, he finds that his life is threatened and that he has been tricked into boarding a ship bound for the Carolinas and slavery. An accident at sea brings on deck a dashing swordsman and supporter of the Stuart cause, Alan Breck. Despite their differing political loyalties (David is loyal to King George), the two quickly develop an alliance which enables them to survive all subsequent hardships.

First, the ship is blown off course and is wrecked off the Western Isles. As the pair travel together through the Highlands, they witness the murder of Colin Campbell, the "Red Fox," and are pursued as prime suspects. Their adventures take them east across the Highlands, where they are constantly in danger from redcoats, from Alan's Scottish enemies the Campbells, and from possible traitors among his own people. Finally, after crossing the River Forth, they contact David's lawyer and force his Uncle Ebenezer to yield his rightful inheritance to David. With this, the friends go their separate ways.

The theme of this romantic adventure story, a classic for young readers, is the value of physical courage and personal loyalty. Despite their many differences, David and Alan support each other through their common adversities. The novel has a sequel, *Catriona* (1893), which has never attained the popularity of its predecessor.

KIM
Rudyard Kipling
1901
Novel
Coming of Age, Colonialism

Set in late 19th century India, KIM *traces the struggles of an orphaned Irish boy in that exotic land.*

Kim finds himself torn between the Indian and British worlds which existed side by side during the days of the British Raj. His Irish blood and his Indian upbringing have created within him a crisis of identity as he approaches manhood.

Thirteen but wise beyond his years, Kim meets a Tibetan lama (holy man), and decides to lead the lama across India in search of a sacred river. At first, he considers the quest only another escapade, but soon he becomes a devoted disciple.

Filled with comedy, sadness, danger, and excitement, their wanderings span some six years. The compelling narrative paints vivid pictures of the infinitely varied Indian landscape, customs, and day-to-day life. When Kim encounters the British, who want to make him a gentleman, the imperialists are depicted with equal precision. All action points, though, to the lama's discovery and Kim's maturity, the foremost themes of the novel.

Both Kim and the lama have set out on a quest. The lama seeks the sacred river whose waters will deliver him at the end of his pilgrimage from the physical world and carry him to a state of spiritual bliss. Kim, on the other hand, desires to find himself in order to become a whole person. That realization of selfhood is the river he seeks.

To find their respective rivers, the lama and his disciple travel on the roads of India, which form an endless river of physical life. Sometimes they ride trains, but more often they follow the Grand Trunk Road that crosses the vast land or climb up the steep paths of the Himalayas. The roads and the sought-after river represent the two levels of man's existence: the physical and the spiritual. For the lama, the wandering on earthly roads has almost ended. For Kim, it has just begun.

KING LEAR
William Shakespeare
1605
Drama
Tragedy

When Lear, aged King of ancient Britain, divides his kingdom among his three daughters, he learns to his infinite regret that he misjudged all three. Driven mad in a storm, he recovers only to see his loving youngest daughter hanged and dies in an agony of grief.

King Lear, weary of rule, divides his kingdom among his three daughters, but he disowns his youngest and favorite, Cordelia, when she refuses to speak her love. The King of France, her suitor, loyally weds her.

Lear's two older daughters, Goneril and Regan, prove niggardly in their care of him; finally, accompanied only by his faithful Fool, he flees into a wild heath during a terrific storm. On the heath, he raves in a fit of inspired madness. Meanwhile, the two daughters plot against each other, and France invades England to rescue Lear. In the battle, Lear and Cordelia are captured and imprisoned, and Lear is unable to save her from hanging by her captors. His hopes blasted, he dies grief-stricken.

In a parallel subplot, Lear's faithful nobleman the Earl of Gloucester disowns his true son Edgar when he is deceived by his bastard son Edmund. When Gloucester aids Lear, Edmund informs on him, and in punishment Gloucester's eyes are gouged out and he is turned out to wander. Edgar, disguised as Poor Tom the madman, cares for him until Gloucester dies of a broken heart.

The intensity of elemental passions, the physical and mental cruelty, the enormous scope of the metaphoric cosmic language, and the depth of anguish in this play make it, in the judgment of many, Shakespeare's deepest tragedy. The play provides no clear answer to the question Lear raises: "Is there any cause in Nature that makes these hard hearts?"

THE KISS
Anton Chekhov
1887
Short Story

This is a poignant story about a shy young man who inflates an insignificant incident into an obsessive romance, only to return to a disillusioning and embittering reality.

The setting is a Russian village on a May evening. The officers of an artillery brigade are invited by a retired general to spend an evening dining and dancing in his residence. During the evening, one of the officers, Ryabovich, an inarticulate conversationalist, graceless dancer, timid drinker, and altogether awkward social mixer, wanders away from the other guests and strays into a semidark room. Shortly afterward, a strange woman enters the room, clasps two fragrant arms around his neck, whispers "At last!" and kisses him. Recognizing her mistake, the woman then shrieks and runs from the room.

Ryabovich also exits quickly and soon shows himself to be a changed man: "He wanted to dance, to talk, to run into the garden, to laugh aloud." He begins to exercise a lively romantic fancy, speculating which of the ladies at the dinner table might have been his companion.

The artillery brigade leaves the area for maneuvers. Ryabovich tries to tell himself that the episode of the kiss was accidental and trifling—to no avail. His psychic needs embrace it as a wondrously radiant event.

In late August, Ryabovich's battery returns to the village. He makes his second trip to the general's estate but this time pauses to ponder in the garden. He can no longer hear the nightingale that sang loudly in May; the poplar and grass no longer exude a scent; he walks a bridge near the general's bathing cabin and touches a towel which feels clammy and cold; ripples of the river rip the moon's reflection into bits. Ryabovich now realizes that his romantic dreams have been absurdly disproportionate to their cause: "And the whole world... seemed to [him] an unintelligible, aimless jest." When the general's invitation comes, he refuses it.

THE KITE RUNNER
Khaled Hosseini
2003
Novel

A debut novel which deftly weaves together recent Afghan history and its protagonist's journey from Kabul to California and from betrayal and guilt to atonement and redemption, The Kite Runner makes up part of the growing branch of Muslim American immigrant literature. Loosely autobiographical, The Kite Runner begins in the same well-off Kabul neighborhood in which the author grew up with his diplomat father and schoolteacher mother. The action then shifts to California, where the family resettled in the early 1980's after fleeing Afghanistan.

The Kite Runner begins with an act of betrayal. Part 1 focuses on the formative years of its narrator-protagonist, especially his relationship with Hassan, who is at once his servant and friend. The two boys are linked and divided in several important ways. Hassan's devotion to Amir is both a sign of his sweet disposition and, more troubling, the result of an ingrained servant-class mentality. Amir is, if not quite devoted to his playmate then certainly attached. Amir's relatively privileged life, however, coupled with Hassan's self-sacrificing devotion, makes Amir cruel, albeit in petty, even passive ways.

The crisis, and Amir's downfall, comes at the moment of what should be his greatest triumph, at the annual winter kite-flying competition. The kite flyers work in teams to use their strings, covered in tar and broken glass, to cut their opponents' lines. To win Baba's affection, Amir feels he must win the kite competition, but to do that he must rely on the very person he sees as a rival for that affection: Hassan. Amir must, in fact, rely on Hassan twice: as line feeder and as kite runner. The one who runs down the last opponent's kite will receive a highly coveted trophy, which Hassan will give to Amir and Amir in turn will give to Baba. Amir's triumph goes horribly wrong. Hassan does find the kite, but he is then found by Assef and his gang. Assef takes his revenge by sodomizing Hassan. Amir secretly witnesses Hassan's humiliation but does nothing. Experiencing the shame of his own cowardice as well as of Hassan's knowledge of it, Amir returns home to the paternal love he had long craved but now cannot bear, and betrays Hassan a second time, resulting in Hassan leaving the safety of Baba's home.

As Amir's personal situation deteriorates, so does the political situation in Afghanistan. Baba and Amir flee in 1981 and eventually settle in California, where they suffer a complete reversal of fortune. A phone call from a dying Rahim Khan in June, 2001, sets in motion the novel's final movement. "Come, there is a way to be good again," Rahim tells Amir, and Amir heeds the dying man's cryptic summons. In Peshawar he learns all that has happened since 1983 to his home, his country, his surrogate father Rahim, and above all to the friend he only now learns (and Hassan never knew) was his half-brother. Amir also learns that Hassan and his wife are dead, murdered by the Taliban, but that their son, Sohrab, is alive. The way for Amir to be good again is to find the orphan and rescue him from the hell that Afghanistan has become under the Taliban. Offered this opportunity to atone for his and his father's sins, Amir is at first reluctant, preferring to pay someone to rescue the boy, but Rahim is insistent, tricking Amir into thinking that once he finds the boy, Amir will have fulfilled his obligation.

The showdown between Amir and Assef is melodramatic and unconvincing because it is so predetermined. Overall, though, this part of the novel succeeds on the strength of Hosseini's depiction of Kabul and his handling of Sohrab's powerful but undeserved feelings of guilt and shame. After several delays, much anguish, many legal hurdles, and the boy's suicide attempt, Amir returns to California with Sohrab. While the novel ends happily, the happiness is qualified by the trauma Sohrab has suffered, by the lesson Amir has learned about making promises he may not be able to keep, and by the deep sense of loss which atoning for past wrongs cannot quite assuage.

The Kite Runner is a novel of conflict, and the conflicts range from warring armies, factions, worldviews, and ethnic groups to the conflicts between individuals, fathers and sons and Amir and Baba in particular. Underlying many of these conflicts, perhaps all, is the conflict between the masculine and the feminine. To call The Kite Runner a morality tale, or a tale of loyalty and betrayal, is not only to succumb to the power of its melodrama but also to miss the novel's greater significance and achievement.

THE KNOWN WORLD
Edward P. Jones
2003
Novel

A tour-de-force consideration of slavery in antebellum Virginia centers around the death of a slave owner, Henry Townsend, who is himself a former slave, The Known World employs a host of characters in its consideration of slavery, unrestrained power, morality, and racism.

By choosing a known but often overlooked historical truth—that some free black southerners owned slaves—Jones explodes the accountings of slavery that have become too familiar. He looks beyond the commonplace settings and stories to confront the dark truths of humanity that gave rise to the "peculiar institution." At the same time, the author does not fail to consider the evil of slavery itself, the way its existence, with one foot in racism and the other in ungoverned and unrestrained power over other humans, can corrupt everything and everyone it touches. In *The Known World*, Jones tells a series of stories of how slavery affects a whole battery of characters. Henry Townsend, the main character, is the owner of a plantation and "thirteen women, eleven men, and nine children." The stories of his wife, Caldonia; his teacher Fern Elston; his slave and overseer, Moses; his former master and patron in the ways of slave ownership, William Robbins; his parents; the sheriff John Skiffington; slaves like Elias, Stamford, Celeste, and Loretta; and a host of other characters all revolve around Henry's life and death.

The Known World makes the point that humans with almost limitless power over others can easily become corrupted, even when the inherent racism of the time, place, and social system is not a factor. When Henry first purchases Moses, he treats him more like an employee or a friend than a slave. While visiting, Henry's former master and mentor Robbins sees Henry wrestling and playing with Moses. "Henry," he tells him, "the law will protect you as a master to your slave, and it will not flinch when it protects you. . . . You are the master and that is all the law wants to know." However, he tells Henry, if he continues to be a "playmate" to his "property," then he "will have failed in [his] part of the bargain." Henry becomes a stern enough owner that he later sanctions the mutilation of runaway slave Elias's ear as punishment for his attempted escape.

In *The Known World*, the evil presence of slavery ripples out in unforeseen, hardly discernible ways. One could argue that by largely focusing on the tiny percentage of African Americans who owned slaves, Jones either is ignoring the real issues or is playing into the hands of apologists who feel pressed to assert that the evils of the nineteenth century United States were not restricted to white southerners. Such an argument misses the point of the novel. The recognition that free black citizens like Fern and Henry owned slaves does not reduce the horror of slavery. Rather, it shows how insidious slavery was; it reminds the reader that slavery was not the act of a single madman or tyrant. It was, instead, an open and legal social system sanctioned by the society it operated within—and that may be the most telling detail of all.

KRISTIN LAVRANSDATTER
Sigrid Undset
1922
Novel
Historical

This carefully researched three-volume novel, by a Nobel prize-winning author, tells of the private and religious life of an upper-class wife and mother in 14th century Norway.

Book one begins the story of Kristin, daughter of Lavrans Bjorgulfson, a wealthy landowner. Sober and religious, Lavrans lavishes love and attention on Kristin, who grows into a loving and gentle, yet stubborn and passionate woman. Kristin falls in love with a handsome but dissolute nobleman, Erlend Nikulausson, who has a bad reputation with women.

Erlend is not the sort of husband Lavrans wants for his daughter, and he refuses permission for their marriage. For two years Kristin stubbornly waits, refusing to marry anyone else. Finally, seeing Kristin's sorrow, Lavrans relents.

The second volume describes Kristin's life as wife and mother. Kristin's passion for Erlend cools somewhat during years of constant work, the birth of seven sons, and Erlend's imprisonment for political intrigue.

The last book tells of Kristin's later years, when, his lands forfeit to the crown, Erlend and Kristin return to her childhood home. Kristin hopes for a normal home like the one she experienced as a child, but Erlend is not happy, and eventually he and Kristin separate. Her sons grown, Kristin enters a convent.

Medieval religious attitudes fill this novel. To Kristin, God is the source of love and compassion, and through her hard experiences she learns that the love which her father had for her mirrors the Creator's love for His children. Like her own father, God does not compel his stubborn and willful children to obedience; rather he loves them and cares for them even when they make mistakes. The novel reflects Sigrid Undset's own search for God, which culminated in her conversion to Roman Catholicism in 1924.

KUBLA KHAN
Samuel Taylor Coleridge
1816
Poetry
Lyric

Both its music and its mystery commend this fragmentary poem to all lovers of poetry and to all those interested in the processes of the creative imagination.

Coleridge has described how as a young man in poor health he took a prescribed drug. While reading a popular travel book, he fell into a deep slumber and "dreamed" the poem in which a Mongol emperor orders a "stately pleasure dome" near a sacred river that has cut a deep chasm into the earth on its way to the sea.

Two thirds of the poem's 54 lines describe this strange setting. Then follows a vision of "an Abyssinian maid" whose song would serve the speaker—if only he could revive it—to reconstruct the exotic scene.

One theme of the poem is the nature of poetic inspiration. Coleridge makes use of the ancient tradition that poets are literally not themselves when composing but are possessed by a daemon or guiding spirit. The poet cannot control the daemon, only try to take advantage of it when it comes. This poem paradoxically voices the frustration of a poet whose daemon has departed.

"Kubla Khan" has attracted much criticism, including a classic study by John Livingston Lowes, *The Road To Xanadu*. Some critics have accepted Coleridge's explanation of an unconscious or semiconscious origin, while others have pointed to the poet's extraordinary command of meter and other sound patterns and even have discerned a logical structure that only a conscious and disciplined artist could achieve. To such critics, Coleridge is providing a carefully crafted picture of a wild creator with "flashing eyes" and "floating hair."

Whether the poem displays or only simulates wild inspiration, whether the poet is out of his mind or fully in control, "Kubla Khan" is a magical poem with a verbal richness approached only a few times by Coleridge and not often by any poet.

L

LADY CHATTERLEY'S LOVER
D. H. Lawrence
1928
Novel
Romance

Labeled obscene and banned for more than 30 years, this novel is now praised as a radical, courageous love story describing the kind of passionate relationship that Lawrence believed could redeem a fallen world.

The three main characters represent strikingly different attitudes toward love. Clifford Chatterley has been horribly wounded in World War I, paralyzed from the waist down and confined to a wheelchair. Even before the war he was repressed, but the war dramatically turns him into an obvious symbol of what repels Lawrence in modern life: the cold and dry life of the mind. As a captain of industry and an authoritarian technologist, Clifford ironically becomes an ally of the very forces that crippled him.

Connie Chatterley is repressed in a much more subtle way. She grows up in the household of elegantly aesthetic and casually radical parents, but her thoroughly modern independence is, according to Lawrence, superficial and evasive. Connie is the intellectual equal of the men around her, and she is liberated enough to indulge in various sexual affairs, but she always withholds rather than gives herself, and this leaves her free but perpetually unsatisfied.

Mellors, the gamekeeper on the estate, is the vital center of the novel. Although not without flaws, he is the exact opposite of his nominal master, Clifford, and the true lover and teacher of Connie. Mellors is passionate but marvelously self-controlled, at home with natural processes of birth and growth, and capable of great tenderness as well as fearless honesty. Through lovemaking with Mellors, described in explicit and intimate detail, Connie becomes vulnerable but also radiantly sensitive and alive. Lawrence's great hope is that this kind of lovemaking can forge peace and joy for mankind.

Lawrence is criticized by some for daring to write openly about private, sexual secrets and by others for pretending to liberate men and women but actually constructing a myth whereby women are forced to worship phallic gods. Nevertheless, Lawrence's honesty about sexual matters is bracing (and in any event not as shocking as it was years ago). His novel, whether we subscribe to his love ethic, is a powerful critique of a modern world that spends its energy on tyranny and technology rather than love.

LADY WINDERMERE'S FAN
Oscar Wilde
1892
Drama
Comedy

This witty play derives its comic impetus from the confusion of identity that exist between Lady Windermere and Mrs. Erlynne, a woman of questionable reputation, who, unknown to Lady Windermere, is her own mother.

Lord Windermere has given his wife a fan engraved with her name for her birthday, to be celebrated that night with a ball. That afternoon, the Duchess of Berwick calls and tells Lady Windermere that Lord Windermere frequently sees Mrs. Erlynne, about whom people gossip.

Lady Windermere refuses to believe this. She opens Lord Windermere's desk, rifles his checkbook, and discovers that he has given Mrs. Erlynne sums of money. She confronts Lord Windermere with her discovery. He upbraids her for not trusting him. She denounces his infidelity.

Lord Windermere demands that his wife send Mrs. Erlynne an invitation to the ball. When Lady Windermere refuses, he himself sends one. His wife vows to strike Mrs. Erlynne with her fan if she attends, but instead drops her fan, flees the room, and leaves her husband a note saying that she is leaving him.

Typical of Victorian irony, this is exactly what Mrs. Erlynne did years before to her husband, abandoning him and her child, now Lady Windermere. She tries to intervene, and goes to Lord Darlington's apartment, where Lady Windermere has fled.

Lord Windermere arrives unexpectedly, finds his wife's fan there, and is appalled. Mrs. Erlynne, coming out of hiding, claims to have taken Lady Windermere's fan accidentally. Lord Windermere and his wife are reunited, Mrs. Erlynne marries Lord Augustus Lorton, and Lady Windermere acknowledges Mrs. Erlynne as a good woman.

The play, crisp and witty, reflects typical Victorian attitudes about morality and portrays the hypocrisy of high society.

THE LAST OF THE MOHICANS
James Fenimore Cooper
1826
Novel
Historical, Adventure

A scout and his Indian friends try to rescue an English officer's daughters from Indian captors during the French and Indian War.

In this novel of forest adventure, Natty Bumppo joins with his Mohican friends, Chingachgook and his son Uncas, to escort the daughters of the commander to the besieged Fort William Henry. When the daughters are captured in the subsequent retreat from the fort, the three friends join with others to rescue them.

Magua, a renegade Huron, captures Cora and Alice in order to avenge an insult from their father, Munro. Because the spirited Cora proves attractive to him, Magua eventually decides to keep her as his squaw.

Magua takes his captives into Canada. Major Heyward joins the pursuers to regain his beloved Alice. Uncas has fallen in love with Cora. Natty and Chingachgook are loyal to Munro and to the ideals of filial piety. These motives suggest different thematic levels in the plot.

Of special interest is the problem of racial mixture. Natty often speaks of his pure white blood, implying that mixing races is evil. Cora, who has mixed white and black blood and who attracts Indian suitors, is an early example in literature of the tragic mulatto who has no place in a racist culture.

Cooper uses the American wilderness as a moral landscape. When the civilized English enter the wilderness, they must learn to read it like a book. Though the Indians are divided into good and evil forces, the British cannot tell them apart. They first choose an evil guide in the pagan Magua, but eventually find good guides in the Christian Natty and his "noble savage" Mohican friends. Without good guides, they would be lost in a moral as well as a physical wilderness.

These allegorical elements underline Cooper's belief that although evil cannot finally triumph, good men will often fall victim to evil if they are not courageous and skillful. Because so few men have the knowledge, skill, and integrity of Natty and Chingachgook, it is crucial to seek the protection of law and authority in civilization. The wilderness frees evil men to do their worst, requires good men to display heroic qualities, and teaches ordinary men the necessity of civilization.

THE LAST TEMPTATION OF CHRIST
Nikos Kazantzakis
1955
Novel
Revisionist

A humanized Christ struggles to overcome temptations of the flesh and the spirit on his way to his inevitable fate as mankind's Savior. This highly controversial portrait will stimulate readers who are interested in novelistic renditions of the Gospel story.

The town of Nazareth is the scene of numerous crucifixions of Zealots as the Jews struggle under the Roman yoke. The carpenter Jesus is reviled by his kinsmen for building crosses, but those around him do not know the inner struggles he undergoes as he tries to understand who or what is tempting him to embrace a public mission as the Savior of mankind.

Jesus encounters a variety of temptations: the prostitute Mary Magdalene, who wants to marry him; a group of ascetic monks who invite him to live with them away from the world's cares; the fiery Zealot Judas Iscariot, who wants him to lead a revolt against the Romans. Jesus' decision to assume a public role as a preacher confuses many around him, including his mother, who only wants him to marry and give her grandchildren.

Inevitably Jesus' actions bring him into conflict with the Jewish hierarchy and the Romans. He is convicted of treason and led off to be crucified. At the moment before he dies, he suffers his final temptation, but he is able to overcome it: He takes upon himself the sins of mankind, dying for others.

This novel is sure to cause readers to reevaluate their perceptions of the Gospel; many will reject Kazantzakis' portrait of Christ as heretical. Kazantzakis stresses Christ's humanity, making him an unwilling Savior. Further, he challenges the accepted interpretations of Gospel stories. His realistic portraits of Gospel characters are captivating and thought provoking. The theme of the novel is made clear throughout: God needs man, as much as man needs God, to bring about the redemption of humanity.

LEAVES OF GRASS
Walt Whitman
1855
Poetry

In some of the most striking poetry ever written, Whitman captures the spirit of America—natural, expansive, free-wheeling, down-to-earth, self-assertive, playful, and all-embracing.

When Whitman published his first edition, readers were astounded: It had no rhyme or meter, it used the language of contemporary America, and it presented a specific human being speaking of himself in physical as well as spiritual and mental terms. It appalled some readers but refreshed and delighted many others.

The book grew as Whitman grew, through six editions and several annexes that eventually added hundreds of poems to the original twelve. It became, as individual poems such as "Song of Myself" suggest, identified with the poet himself.

Besides depicting an individual man, the collection also depicts a nation, America moving into maturity with the harsh test of the Civil War and the subsequent expansion westward. Whitman writes movingly about the war in the "Drumtaps" section, drawing from his experiences in Washington, D.C. as a visitor and nurse to the wounded.

Other poems describe America's natural grandeur and the energy and drama of its people, from prostitute to politician, from pioneer to slave, from Indian to immigrant. Whitman's resonant, rambling lines amply embody the vitality of a growing nation and the unconfined natural world he observed so closely.

Yet his world was not all bright and fair. He could be critical of his country's shortcomings while singing its virtues. He also conveys the pain as well as the joy of love, both emotional and physical, especially in the "Calamus" poems, some of the greatest ever written expressing love for another man.

Even death finds a place in his scheme. He embraces it as natural and even beautiful, uniting human flesh with the eternal cycles of nature.

Reading *Leaves of Grass* is a richly uplifting experience. Often addressing the reader directly, Whitman himself leaps from the page, a living presence.

LEDA AND THE SWAN
William Butler Yeats
1924
Poetry
Sonnet

This sonnet concerns the rape of Leda, Queen of Sparta, by the god Zeus in the form of a swan. From this mythological subject, which held great fascination for Renaissance painters and sculptors, Yeats fashioned one of the great poems of the twentieth century.

Yeats expects his readers to recognize as archetypal the encounter between mortal woman and godhead. A gentler version of Leda's visit from the swan, after all, is the beginning of Christianity. Each event, for Yeats, constitutes the annunciation of a great cycle of history. As the impregnation of Mary by the Holy Spirit sets in motion the Christian era, so does Leda's union with the swan set in motion the heroic age. In conceiving the beautiful Helen of Troy and the vengeful Clytemnestra, Leda conceives love, war—even the evolution of justice. Her encounter with Zeus is the cultural genesis more fully chronicled in Homer's *Iliad* and Aeschylus' *Oresteia*.

To contain these ideas in a sonnet—a form requiring maximum economy of expression—is a challenge that the poet meets with great resourcefulness. For example, he artfully casts his account of the sexual consummation in language at once prophetic of the Trojan War and suggestive of defloration and orgasm: "The broken wall, the burning roof and tower." The full stop in line 11, along with the typographical break, represents the termination of sexual activity and the onset of post-coital lassitude (brilliantly captured in the half-rhyme of "up" and "drop"). The poem's energies seem to flag with the sated swan's.

The question that ends the poem—does Leda have access to the god's knowledge as she experiences his power?—calls to mind the nuances of "knowing." If Leda "knows" the god sexually, does she also "know" his mind?

THE LEFT HAND OF DARKNESS
Ursula K. LeGuin
1969
Novel
Science Fiction

In a distant future of near light speed interstellar travel, coupled with instantaneous communication via "ansible," the Ekumen links eighty-odd human worlds once colonized by the ancient Hainish. Reproduction on the most recently contacted planet, however, is different from anything previously encountered. What can this society teach about gender roles, governance, even humanity itself?

Underlying every aspect of *The Left Hand of Darkness* is the effect of a Hainish experiment unique in all known worlds: the natives of the harshly glaciated Gethen are androgynous except for a few days of *kemmer* during their monthly cycles, when gender is determined by chance. There are no expectations of male versus female behavior, and even childrearing may fall to any, not just a certain half of the population.

In inviting the nations of Gethen to join the far-flung Ekumen, Envoy Genly Ai of Terra finds "womanly" intrigue and betrayal in Karhide, and then the same in rival Orgoreyn. The banished Lord Estraven, Ai's former proponent in the court of the Kingdom of Karhide, rescues the Envoy from a gulag in the icy Orgoreyn wilderness, and the pair trek 800 grueling miles across the glaciers. Estraven eventually is killed in a type of suicide-by-police, but Ai already has followed his advice to signal the crew of the starship to come out of hibernation and land. Presented with a fait accompli, Karhide hurries to be the first nation to join the Ekumen, and Ai predicts that the others soon will follow.

Told with the interspersed reports of Ai, journals of Estraven, and Gethenian folktales and myths, the tale is richly introspective. Taoist notions—of yin and yang, of being rather than acting—run through the piece. Even scenes of physical danger focus less on the external than on mind and meaning. LeGuin's innovative novel, which once helped redefine science fiction, still raises important questions on the very nature of humanity.

THE LEGEND OF SLEEPY HOLLOW
Washington Irving
1819-1820
Short Story
Gothic

A schoolmaster loses the woman he is courting through a trick played on him by another of her suitors. Irving combines gentle humor with American folklore to comment on the importance of the imagination.

Early in the story, the reader encounters the legend of the headless horseman, a ghost with which the residents of Sleepy Hollow are familiar. Beheaded by a cannonball during the Revolutionary War, he searches nightly for his head. This anecdote—humorous in itself—provides the key to the trick by which the schoolmaster is driven from the town.

The schoolmaster, Ichabod Crane, is also the local singing master and, in that role, meets and falls in love with Katrina Van Tassel, the only child of a well-to-do Dutch farmer. In fact, Irving's complete catalog of the wealth of Baltus Van Tassel implies that Crane's desire to marry Katrina is partly monetary.

Crane has a rival, however, Brom Bones, whose ingenuity finally drives the superstitious schoolmaster away from Sleepy Hollow. Impersonating the headless horseman, Bones rides after Crane one night and finally throws a pumpkin, which Crane believes to be the horseman's head. The schoolmaster abruptly departs, leaving Bones to marry Katrina.

Irving uses this plot as a vehicle for commenting on the primacy of the imagination. Not only does the central story contain many references to legend and folklore, but also there is a frame around the tale that complements these references. As the story opens, the reader meets a nameless narrator whose description of Sleepy Hollow implies that it is a realm of the imagination, a retreat where dream and reality meet. A postscript explains how the story came to be known by a "Mr. Knickerbocker," the name of a fictional character in other works by Irving. By such devices the reader is constantly reminded that in this story—as, perhaps, in life—imaginative fiction exists side by side with everyday reality.

THE LEOPARD
Giuseppe Tomasi di Lampedusa
1958
Novel
Historical

A picture of Sicily at the time of Garibaldi's landing (1860), this novel is distinguished by its lyrical prose and elegiac tone. It was a worldwide best-seller, but highly controversial in Italy because of the allegedly reactionary tendencies of its author.

The Leopard concerns the passing of an era. It focuses on the impact of the Risorgimento—the reunification of Italy—on Sicilian society.

Don Fabrizio, Prince of Salina, recognizes that his class is doomed by its own decadence and by the rude energy of the new order. He knows, too, that the new order, whatever its pretensions, will bring with it no real change for Sicily's masses. A rapacious middle class will elbow aside the old families, which will succumb to a kind of moral and social entropy.

The symbol of the new order is the marriage between the aristocratic Tancredi, Don Fabrizio's nephew, and the beautiful Angelica, daughter of the newly rich but vulgar Don Calogero. Rank and pelf come together, but it is "a marriage which, even erotically, was no success." The calculation on each side dooms the match, and the larger social experiment fares no better. Morally compromised from the start, as one sees in the rigged plebiscite at Donnafugata, the Risorgimento itself is a failure. Rather than ushering in the just society which its apologists proclaim, it merely sets the stage for Fascism half a century later—and perhaps, in time, even Communism.

Lampedusa's account of the Sicilian aristocracy embattled by an aggressive middle class will appeal to all who enjoy the fictional treatment of the sweep of history. It has affinities with great historical novels such as Leo Tolstoy's *War And Peace* and Stendhal's *The Charterhouse Of Parma*, as well as with popular works such as Margaret Mitchell's *Gone With The Wind*.

LET THE GREAT WORLD SPIN
Colum McCann
2009
Novel
Historical

Set in New York City, the novel opens with a prelude anecdote of a tightrope walker, Philippe Petit, exemplifying the atmosphere of American life before 9/11: a life that was happy, whimsical, wondrous, and naïve. The novel's theme centers on a search for meaning in life amid various forms of fear, as well as the search for healing, and the effort to begin life again. This allegorical novel won the 2009 U.S. National Book Award for Fiction and the 2011 International IMPAC Dublin Literary Award, the most lucrative literary prize in the world.

Let the Great World Spin has several protagonists whose lives brush against each other, directly or indirectly, during these interwoven stories. Another unnamed protagonist is the reader who is meant to reflect on how the 9/11 tragedy affected the reader's life as we see vivid examples of characters whose lives have been altered by both Philippe Petit's caper—walking a tightrope between the twin towers of the World Trade Center in New York—and 9/11 with its destruction of those massive towers. It is as if all the characters are walking a tightrope of their own making, yet both magical antic and terrible tragedy recede in the memory of all these characters who witnessed both startling events.

With vivid conversation, the landscape of New York City is intensely invoked, as if the city were a small town. There's Corrigan, the Irish monk living in Bronx squalor, visited by his older brother Ciaran; Tillie and Jazzlyn, mother and daughter Bronx hookers; Carrie, the Park Avenue mom, and her husband, Judge Solomon Blain, who have lost their only son to the Vietnam War; African American Gloria who lives in Corrigan's building and belongs to the same grieving support group Carrie attends; Adelita, the nurse with whom Corrigan temporarily falls in love; Blaine and Lara who have fled drug addiction and the city by settling in the country, but return to the city for a visit where, on the FDR Drive, they crash into Corrigan's van, killing Corrigan and Jazlyn; a hermit tightrope walker who is never named, but is sentenced by Judge Blaine, just as he has sentenced Tillie and Jazzlyn; and finally, the photographer who photographs the tightrope walker.

The title of the novel derives from a line in a poem by Alfred Lord Tennyson, "Locksley Hall," which paraphrases some passages from a long sixth century Arabic poem, the "Mu'allaqat."

McCann, along with musician Joe Hurley, composed an album song-cycle based upon the novel.

LET US NOW PRAISE FAMOUS MEN
James Agee
1941
Nonfiction
Historical

A writer and a photographer depict the lives of sharecroppers in depression-era Alabama.

In 1936, James Agee and Walker Evans lived for a month with three impoverished farmer families—the Woods, the Gudgers, and the Ricketts. To protect their privacy, the families' real names were not used. These were people who lived as domestic beasts. Their houses were little better than cattle stalls. The men were harnessed for life in the straps of overalls. Under the strain of constant work the women grew old rapidly. Annie May Gudger looked 47 at 27. A child's tenderness disappeared as soon as he or she was big enough to drag a cotton sack down a row.

The book opens with Evans' now-famous photographs—houses, faces, groups of children, and a dusty grave. Agee's exhaustive analysis of the lives of these people follows. He records the sweaty taste of their food and water. He describes the interior walls, pine sheathing filled with bugs and no protection from heat or cold. He enumerates the mantel bric-a-brac, an assemblage that the ordinary eye would recoil from as being a pile of rubbish. He picks cotton and records sensations and emotions in the field with heartrending exactitude. One chapter is titled "Odors"; another is "Three women's dresses."

Yet Agee writes not to appall but to revere. Showing people stripped of everything, he paradoxically reveals their wealth. Wearing the curse of deprivation, they communicate, through Agee, a felt spirituality. His awe for his subject is so great that he confesses shame at his role as recorder.

Rather than argue for political reform to alleviate the problem, Agee articulates the significance of these lives. He clings to the principle that a life can reach such abjectness as to achieve fame. Agee's ability to penetrate material things and render them powerfully in description can shame the reader who has grown habituated to the world.

Anyone who reads this work with an open heart and an attentive eye will be rewarded and possibly changed. Evans' photographic contribution, like Agee's words, makes visible a glory of the world to which we have grown blind.

LIFE IS A DREAM
Pedro Calderón de la Barca
1635
Drama
Religious

In this great dramatic battle between the grace of God and pre-Christian superstition, a great prince learns how to rule his kingdom as though life is a dream from which death is the awakening.

King Basil of Poland, believing his astrologers' dire predictions, has imprisoned his son Segismund in a mountain fortress, where he lies in animal skins, visited only by old Clotaldo, who teaches him the natural sciences. When Rosaura, a wronged woman traveling in disguise, approaches Segismund's dungeon, he sees grace and nobility for the first time.

Basil orders Segismund to be drugged, dressed in sumptuous garments, and brought to the court; when he awakens, Segismund thinks he has dreamed his captivity and is in fact a prince. Untutored in the court's ways, he throws an ambassador out the window, attacks the women, and so alarms Basil that Segismund must be drugged again. Awakening in his cell, he is told that his brief day as a prince was only a dream. When he is once again given the opportunity to rule, he does so wisely, "as though life is a dream."

Underneath this improbable and complicated plot is the simple theme of the Spanish Golden Age: God's grace (here in the form of Rosaura) transforms bestial men into humans. Just as Segismund's animal skins conceal a man beneath, so his animal like behavior at court conceals a true prince, requiring only God's grace to reveal his nobility. Calderon, writing for the courts of Spain, pleased his patrons not only in the rich poetic insertions of set pieces and clever exchanges but also in the reinforcement of the basic principles of the divine right of kings, together with the lesson of Christian grace superseding pagan superstition, notably stargazing.

LIFE OF PI
Yann Martel
2001
Novel

A novel of more than physical survival, in which a sixteen-year-old boy and a Bengal tiger share a lifeboat for seven months

Life of Pi won the 2002 Man Booker Prize, Britain's most publicized and arguably most prestigious literary award. Although the dark horse, *Life of Pi* was much admired by reviewers, including fellow Canadian and former Booker winner Margaret Atwood: "a terrific book . . . fresh, original, smart, devious, and crammed with absorbing lore . . . a far-fetched story you can't quite swallow whole, but can't dismiss outright."

That protagonist is Piscine Molitor Patel, named for a Parisian swimming pool but, saddled with the moniker Pissing Patel, he reinvents himself as Pi. Pi becomes as enamored of religion as he is of science, but when priest, pandit, and imam each tries to claim him as his own, as his atheist science teacher previously tried, Pi balks, critical of their small-mindedness. When Prime Minister Indira Gandhi, brings down the local government, Pi's father, owner of the local zoo, decides that the family will immigrate to Canada.

On July 2, 1977, just eleven days after leaving Madras, the ship goes down. After 277 days in a 26-foot lifeboat, Pi and Richard Parker, a 450 pound Bengal tiger, arrive in Mexico, the sole survivors. At first, however, the lifeboat is a bit more crowded, its "ecosystem" more complex. The hyena eats the zebra and then the orangutan, before being eaten in turn by Richard Parker, who does not eat Pi. That he does not is as improbable as the tiger's name, only more ambiguously explained. The simple explanation is that Pi, the zookeeper's son, manages to master the beast. However, nothing is ever quite so simple in this artful fable, in which simplicity is invariably a means, not an end in itself. Man (or boy) and tiger, Pi and Parker, become dependent on each other: the tiger on Pi for food and water, Pi on the tiger for a strange kind of companionship that is as much spiritual as psychological.

At times, Pi sounds like a fortune cookie, at others like a mini-Salman Rushdie, practicing an art of restrained excess. Fantastical and ultimately metaphysical as his story is, Pi grounds it in the details of his severely circumscribed everyday reality. Precise descriptions of butchering a turtle, operating a solar water still, and taming a tiger alternate with brilliantly wrought comic scenes, skits, and shaggy dog stories: the arrival of the three not-so-wise men (pandit, priest, and imam), for example, and Martel's version of how the leopard got its spots. There is the scene, reminiscent of silent film comedy, in which Pi frantically encourages Richard Parker to save himself from drowning by swimming to the lifeboat only to realize, as the tiger climbs aboard, what he has just done, and then leaping into the ocean to save himself from the tiger he has just saved. Differently funny, more blackly humorous is the floating island which Pi first believes is his salvation and only later realizes is carnivorous. Mistaken first, and second, impressions are common in the novel, for the reader no less than for Pi, who steps on to a Crusoe-like island and right into a Swiftian satire.

Martel's intertextual range contributes to his larger purpose, turning either/or into both/and, undermining all forms of exclusivity by positing a more inclusive alternative. In the Peaceable Kingdom of *Life of Pi*, realism lies down with fabulation, the mundane with the miraculous, humor with despair, science with religion, past with present, storyteller with novelist. Released in Canada on September 11, 2001, Life of Pi is the perfect "literary novel" for the postironic age: earnest, uplifting, global. It is, as the *Nation*'s Charlotte Innes has noted, "a religious book that makes sense to a nonreligious person" and restores the reader's "faith in literature."

THE LIFE OF SAMUEL JOHNSON, LL.D.

James Boswell

1791

Nonfiction

Biography

Generally regarded as the best biography ever written in English, Boswell's The Life of Samuel Johnson *is a delightful and informative year-by-year study of the man who dominated English literature during the latter half of the 18th century.*

Though Boswell began the biography in 1786, shortly after the death of Johnson, he had been planning it ever since their famous meeting on May 16, 1763. He had therefore carefully recorded in his diaries and memory everything related to his subject, and he had acted as prompter and stage manager to draw Johnson out. Some of the most memorable episodes in the book, such as the Tory Johnson's meeting with the Whiggish John Wilkes, resulted from Boswell's manipulation.

To create what he called his "Flemish portrait" of Johnson, Boswell let his subject speak for himself through his letters and conversation, thus drawing on the techniques of drama and the epistolary novel to enliven his work.

Boswell does not gloss over Johnson's flaws. As he told Hannah Moore, "He would not cut off [Johnson's] claws, nor make a tiger a cat, to please anybody." Here are Johnson's prejudices, his stubbornness, and his frequent intellectual bullying.

Here, too, though, are Johnson's compassion for those less fortunate, his conviviality (led him to create a number of literary clubs), his common sense, and his brilliance.

Because Johnson knew all the important writers of the period, his biography also serves as a literary history of late 18th century England.

Johnson's writings would have earned for him a high place in English literature even if he and Boswell had never met. Without their friendship, though, Johnson's conversation—perhaps his most enduring and certainly his most endearing contribution to literature—and many details of his personal life would have been lost. Without Boswell, Johnson would still be respected. Because of Boswell he is loved.

LIGEIA
Edgar Allan Poe
1838
Short Story
Gothic

Poe's own favorite tale, "Ligeia" is a story told by a man who believes that his first wife's spirit returns to animate the corpse of his second wife.

Like Poe's other short fiction, "Ligeia" is told by a first-person narrator. The tale opens with an account of this narrator's marriage to his first wife, Ligeia, a woman from an ancient European family. Possessed with "great intensity," "fierce energy," and "immense" knowledge, Ligeia tutors her husband in arcane studies dealing with topics such as reincarnation and transcendentalism. Eventually Ligeia falls ill and dies with the words of Joseph Glanville, which also serve as the motto of the tale, on her lips: "'Man doth not yield him to the angels, nor unto death utterly, save only through the weakness of his feeble will.'"

The narrator then leaves the "dim decaying city by the Rhine" with his inheritance and purchases an abbey in a remote part of "fair England." There he marries "the fair-haired and blue-eyed" Lady Rowena Trevanion, of Tremaine. Unfortunately, the narrator's romantic thoughts, perhaps intensified by opium, are still of Ligeia, and after a few weeks of marriage, Rowena falls ill. One night the narrator thinks he sees three drops of a mysterious "ruby colored fluid" fall into the glass of wine that he gives Rowena, and very soon she apparently dies. On the third night of his bedside vigil, however, the narrator, his thoughts still of Ligeia, sees the corpse stir back to life, not as the blonde Rowena but as the dark-haired Ligeia.

The tale may be interpreted on several levels. The reliability of the narrator is questionable as his mental state is admittedly impaired by drugs; it is possible that he has murdered his wives and is attempting to rationalize his crimes. The allusive quality of the tale, however, suggests a more symbolic interpretation, perhaps a parable of the psyche.

"Ligeia" is a tale typical of Poe in that such ambiguities are left unresolved and that the real action is in the narrator's mind. It is also typical of the author's fiction in that it creates the Gothic effect of terror and horror and involves the death, in this case, of two beautiful women.

LIGHT IN AUGUST
William Faulkner
1932
Novel
Southern Gothic

Set in fictitious Yoknapatawpha County, Mississippi, this novel explores the lives of Lena Grove, Joe Christmas, and the Reverend Gail Hightower.

Each of these characters has embarked on a quest. Lena seeks the father of her soon-to-be-born child; Joe Christmas seeks his identity; Hightower attempts to escape the past. Lena's trusting nature allows her to become a part of the community, and she finds a worthy husband. Joe Christmas rejects both the black world and the white and can find peace only in death. Hightower, too, fails to free himself from the burden of the past, though he delivers Lena's baby and makes a gallant but unsuccessful effort to save Joe Christmas.

The lives of these three characters reveal a number of themes. Joe Christmas has been reared in a sterile, Calvinistic environment that Faulkner contrasts with the fertility and naturalness of Lena Grove. In part, Joe Christmas' plight results from his uncertainty of his racial identity, a matter of importance, Faulkner indicates, only in a racist society.

Hightower provides a warning against another aspect of the South: its worship of a dead past that bars it from facing the present. Hightower is so caught up in the Civil War exploits of his grandfather that he cannot attend to the needs of his wife or his congregation.

Like Christmas and Hightower, Lena is an outsider, but she is not fundamentally alienated from the natural order. Hence, only she succeeds in her quest.

Interweaving the tragedies of Joe Christmas and Gail Hightower with the comedy of Lena Grove, *Light in August* reveals the complexity of life. It also shows that compassion, community, and a love of the natural rhythms of life are essential if mankind is to endure and prevail.

THE LIME TWIG
John Hawkes
1961
Novel
Thriller

The Lime Twig *is a tautly controlled, highly imagistic novel about sexual repression and the compensatory and largely destructive fantasies to which the individual turns for fulfillment and power.*

Although he does not appear until the end of the long prologue, Michael Banks is the novel's focal character. A plain man married to a drab, nearly sexless wife, Banks has the satisfaction of having his fondest dream, that of owning a race horse, come true, only to see the dream transmogrify into his worst nightmare.

In order to live his dream, Banks has to act as front man for a gang of thugs led by Larry, a caricature of Freudian masculinity. From the beginning, then, it is clear that while this may be Banks's dream, Banks is not in control of either the horse, a stallion named Rock Castle, or the sexual power it represents. Although he gets his horse and his night of sexual abandon with the "venereal" Sibylline Laval (among others), the gang has his wife, Margaret, whom they beat and rape. The assault brutally fulfills her sexual fantasies, equivalent to the twisted fulfillment of Banks's dream.

Realizing what he has set in motion, Banks puts an end both to the fixed race and to the fantasy that has caught him in its web.

Parodying popular detective thrillers and more serious novels such as Graham Greene's *Brighton Rock, Lime Twig* is not a novel of plot and character (which Hawkes once called "the enemies of the novel") but instead an imagistic fiction, as nightmarish and surreal as the world of Banks's psychological imagination. Unlike Banks's fantasy, however, the novel remains very much in its creator's control. Hawkes, clearly understanding the consequences of both repression and release, writes a fiction that is at once innovative and free, yet aesthetically controlled. For Hawkes, it is art, not the repressed or the unbridled imagination, that redeems life.

LINES: COMPOSED A FEW MILES ABOVE TINTERN ABBEY
William Wordsworth
1798
Poetry
Lyric

This highly abstract and philosophical poem is both a meditation on the role of nature in human life and an inquiry into the powers of human memory.

Composed of 159 lines of blank verse (unrhymed iambic pentameter), this poem is narrated by a man who has returned after a five year absence to a ruined abbey on the banks of the Wye River. The tranquil scene prompts a meditation on the speaker's lifelong relationship with nature. As an adult, he must now come to terms with what nature has meant to him during the various stages of his life.

The speaker divides human life into three phases, each characterized by a distinct relationship to nature. A young child is at one with nature, bounding through the countryside like an animal. An adolescent feels a spiritual kinship, but this union is not yet affected by the intellect. An adult, however, has forever lost both these earlier stages of his life and must find recompense in remembering them.

The most significant portion of the poem deals with one fundamental question. Is the adult perspective on nature (and on life in general) a triumph or a loss? The poet refuses to give a pat answer, and much of the poem's greatness derives from its humane and serious analysis of the cycles of gain and loss that make up human life.

Important to the poem is the presence of the poet's dear friend (most likely Wordsworth's sister Dorothy), whom he addresses in the moving final stanzas. He wishes for her a feeling of unity with nature, and hopes that her memories of Tintern Abbey will be the richer for his presence. A difficult but rewarding poem, "Tintern Abbey" is one of the central documents of the English Romantic poets, exhibiting their preoccupations with nature, memory, and the human mind.

THE LITTLE PRINCE
Antoine de Saint Exupery
1940
Novel
Children's, Fantasy

After an aviator crashes his plane in the Sahara, he meets a Little Prince from a far off asteroid and hears the Prince's story about learning to grow up—A brilliant philosophical inquiry disguised as a children's fable that can be read at any age.

After crashing his plane in the Sahara, an aviator meets a young boy— the Little Prince. While the aviator tries to ration his water and fix his plane, he is distracted by the tale of the prince who traveled from a far away asteroid where he lived in solitude with just three volcanoes — two active, one questionably extinct— and a flower. His reason for leaving his home and coming to Earth was the distress from the sassy flower. Within the tale, the prince travels to six other planets meeting strange characters: a king, a conceited man, a drunk, a lamplighter, and a geographer. Each grownup thinks he is dealing with matters of great importance, whether it is drinking away sorrows or owning the rights of the stars, but the Little Prince finds each one's meaning of life ridiculous, and he concludes that grownups are odd.

Eventually he goes to earth where he meets a fox who tells him that creating friendship and love is what is important in life. After saying goodbye to the fox and telling the aviator his tale, the Little Prince decides he would like to go back to his asteroid to see his flower, keeping the fox's lesson in mind. Deciding there was no way to get his physical body to the asteroid, the Prince has a yellow snake bite him so he can finally return home. The aviator writes to readers six years after his encounter and asks them to let him know if they ever see the Little Prince.

The story of *The Little Prince* demonstrates the wisdom of childhood. Through his naïve eyes, the prince sees that the grownups have let their occupations overwhelm their existence, and he doesn't understand why none of them enjoy the beauty of the stars.

LITTLE WOMEN
Louisa May Alcott
1868
Novel

The story of four sisters, during and after the Civil War, this well-loved novel drew heavily on the author's own family history and personal experiences.

The March family, although suffering financially while the father, a minister, acted as chaplain in the war, was bound together by a deep love that transcended poverty. The four sisters—Meg, Jo, Beth, and Amy—had their disagreements but always helped one another in times of crisis. Their father and mother had taught them, through example as well as word, to be unselfish and caring.

The girls become friends with young Theodore (Laurie) Lawrence and his old grandfather. This wealthy family helps the Marches in times of trouble. John Brooke, Laurie's tutor, falls in love with Meg, and eventually they marry. Jo, always a "scribbler," turns seriously to writing. Young Beth, stricken with scarlet fever after tending the ill children of a poor widow, dies. Pretty Amy, the favorite of the sisters' well-to-do aunt, is invited on a European trip. The once close family breaks apart as the girls grow up and leave home.

Jo escapes her depression at the breakup of her family by moving to New York to pursue her writing career and work as a governess. There, she meets a German tutor, Professor Bhaer. Laurie marries Amy when she returns from Europe. Jo returns from New York uncertain what her life now holds. To her surprise, Professor Bhaer shows up and asks her to marry him.

Far from being a sentimental children's novel, *Little Women* is a realistic portrayal of strong and resilient people and their efforts to survive in an often bleak world. In large part, it is concerned with ideals, but these are integrated into the lives of the characters. Themes woven into the book include women's rights, the place of the woman in mid-nineteenth century America, war, and the importance of the family as a force to help individuals survive against all odds.

The importance of the family unit gives the book much of its power. Individuals suffer, struggle, and die, but the family endures. This extraordinary and vigorous novel presents a picture of human endurance that is both touching and inspiring.

THE LIVES OF A CELL: NOTES OF A BIOLOGY WATCHER
Lewis Thomas
1974
Nonfiction
Scientific

Pathologist, educator, and hospital administrator, Lewis Thomas was president of Memorial-Sloan Kettering Center for Cancer Research in New York City when Lives of a Cell *was published—a collection of twenty-nine essays originally written for his column of reflections on biology in the* New England Journal of Medicine. *Before being invited to contribute to that column, Thomas had published only a few poems decades earlier.*

In these succinct, gracefully written essays, Lewis Thomas distills his formidable scientific knowledge with the style and economy of a poet. He often works by exploring paradoxes, a method reminiscent of seventeenth-century author and physician Sir Thomas Browne, whose *Religio Medici* and other works—written, like Thomas's essays, at a time of great ferment in science and medicine—are among the few antecedents to these essays in tone and underlying intellectual daring. Many of Thomas's essays explore the question of what makes us human.

Thomas says our essential cellular functions depend on symbiosis with nonhuman forms of life: within the nucleus of each of our billions of cells, cell functions are directed by mitochondria with DNA and RNA quite separate from human DNA and RNA. Thomas accepts the idea that all life forms ultimately derive from a single cell, and speculates that viruses, which we associate only with disease, may actually ensure genetic diversity. He posits that the earth, with its teeming creatures, is like a single cell.

While the revelations of genetics have the disconcerting effect of undermining our biological uniqueness as a species, Thomas views symbiosis as inherently an optimistic mechanism, and he regards the presence of mitochondria and other cellular-level "strangers" within our cells as a "mystery." Thomas suspects that if he could understand how the mitochondria orchestrate cellular activities, he might begin to understand music—and here he circles back to the essential question of what makes us human, for music, in Thomas's view, is humankind's ultimate accomplishment. Music and art are "functions of the same universal, genetically determined mechanism" as language ("Social Talk"). We "engage in" language "communally, compulsively, and automatically," and Thomas suggests that to the extent that this is so, we humans are social animals in very much the same sense as ants and bees are social insects. Isolation is death for bees and ants, he points out ("Antaeus in Manhattan"); what might it be for humans?

In the first essay, Thomas declared Earth's atmosphere to be the "toughest membrane imaginable, opaque to probability, impermeable to death." The last essay in this collection—"The World's Biggest Membrane"—returns to the nature of a membrane, explaining that "it takes a membrane to make sense out of disorder," to catch the sun's energy and hold it. Our membrane of atmosphere holds oxygen in while keeping ultraviolet radiation and meteorites out. It is, Thomas says, the "grandest product of collaboration in all of nature."

THE LIVES OF THE NOBLE ROMANS
Plutarch
105-115
Nonfiction
Biography, Historical

This seminal work, a source of material for many modern authors, portrays in human terms a period of sweeping change in ancient history.

"Character is destiny." This saying, often attributed to the philosopher Heraclitus, sums up the outlook of the ancient Greek historian Plutarch, who sought to show how character shaped the destinies of both individuals and the state.

Plutarch, however, was not a true historian in the modern sense, but a moralist concerned to portray the distinctively Roman virtues. His subjects—especially Rome's builders, such as Fabius Maximus, Marcellus, and Cato the Elder—illustrate his themes of Roman valor and tenacity. Conversely, he suggests that it was the character of men such as Sulla and Antony that destroyed the Republic.

Plutarch's gauges of character include one's conduct in war, in politics, and in love. Thus Caesar, though power-mad, is praised for his mercy toward conquered enemies. The use of money was another important index of character; Plutarch disapproves of Antony for seizing others' property to indulge his spendthrift ways. (He also scorns Antony, the skilled strategist, for tolerating Cleopatra's ill-advised military decisions.)

Some of Plutarch's judgments may surprise modern readers. We condemn Brutus as a traitor for murdering his dear friend Caesar; to Plutarch, however, this was a noble act of self-sacrifice to preserve the Republic.

Another strong theme of Plutarch not found in modern historical writing is the way "Heaven" and "fate" influence important state decisions. Sometimes character seems to manifest these influences.

Plutarch paired each of his Roman biographies with that of a Greek whose life or character he thought comparable. Many modern translators, however, separate the biographies into two distinct sections, one for Greek and one for Roman.

In a sense, the first historical novelist, Plutarch, shared with his readers an interest in individual personality that has given his *Lives* an enduring popularity.

THE LIVES OF THE POETS
Samuel Johnson
1779-1781
Nonfiction
Biography

A collection of brief biographies of 17th and 18th century poets. These volumes will appeal to students of literary history and 18th century cultural and literary criticism.

In 1777, Johnson was commissioned to write brief lives as prefaces to a new collection of works of popular poets. He produced instead more than 50 biographies of English writers in vogue during the second half of the 18th century. While many of these authors are seldom read today, quite a few important figures are included. John Milton, John Dryden, Alexander Pope, Thomas Gray, and Abraham Cowley head the list of poets. Johnson also includes men who wrote poetry but who are acclaimed today for works in other genres: essayist Joseph Addison, satirist Jonathan Swift, and dramatists William Congreve and John Gay.

Johnson's method in most of these biographies is to chronicle the poet's life, then offer a critical assessment of his work. Drawing on many firsthand accounts and on his own prodigious memory, Johnson offers lively character studies of many important figures of the age. Equally important are his critical comments. His judgments display the particular prejudices of the century: Strong (but unforced) rhyme, high moral tone, and elevated language all receive high praise. Johnson shows great insight, however, into the strengths and limitations of most poets whose work he reviews. The significance of his commentary can best be seen in a single example. In his essay on Cowley, he dismisses the 17th century Metaphysical Poets as inferior artists. That judgment stood until T. S. Eliot's celebrated revaluation of the Metaphysicals in the early 20th century.

As interesting as the list of those included in the volumes is the roll call of those omitted. Readers in the 18th century took offense at what they considered the rough style and lack of decorum of many writers regarded today as masters of literature. Since Johnson wanted to please his contemporaries, he intentionally left out great poets such as Geoffrey Chaucer, Edmund Spenser, John Donne, and even William Shakespeare.

LOLITA
Vladimir Nabokov
1955
Novel
Sociological, Satire

This is a major work of fiction which unites wildly grotesque humor with the shock value of assaulting a major cultural taboo: the sexual inviolability of girls in their early teenage years.

The novel's middle-aged, Central European narrator, Humbert, traces his sexual obsession for girls between the ages of nine and fourteen to an instance of interrupted coitus he suffered when, at 13, he and a certain Annabel Leigh had the beginnings of their first affair forever aborted by her early death. (The allusions to Poe's poem and life are among a multitude of literary references in Nabokov's novel.) After a low-comedy marriage to a "life-sized woman" in Paris ends absurdly, Humbert emigrates to the United States, settling in a small New England town in the late 1940's.

There his nymphetmania leads him to Lolita Haze, a 12-year-old gum-chewing, Coke-swilling, comic book-addicted schoolgirl. Humbert marries her culture-vulturish mother to be near the daughter. All too conveniently for him, Charlotte Haze discovers his sexual perversity through reading his diaries, runs distractedly out of the house, and is killed by a passing car.

Humbert now undertakes the clumsy comedy of seducing his own stepdaughter, who, as it turns out, has already been sexually initiated by a boy at a summer camp. As Humbert complains, "It was she who seduced me....Modern co-education, juvenile mores, the campfire racket and so forth had utterly and hopelessly depraved [her]."

"Hum" and "Lo" engage in a parody of incest that takes them across the continent. As they traverse the neon-lit landscape of filling stations, motels, coffee shops, and highways, Humbert has to bribe Lolita to indulge his passion and makes a virtual prisoner of her. He finds himself genuinely enraptured by her in both a paternal and erotic fashion; Lolita, coolly acquiescent at times, peevishly self-centered at others, could not be more bored.

The couple is shadowed by a middle-aged playwright, Clare Quilty, who spirits her away from Humbert, has a brief liaison with her, then discards her. Several years later, Humbert manages to find Lolita again. Now seventeen, she is married, pregnant, poor, and plain. Finding that his love transcends his now-quiescent lust for her, Humbert begs her to return to him; she refuses, but gives him Quilty's address. He then murders the writer in a farcically protracted scene.

The novel works on many levels: a satire of billboard America, progressive-school education, and teenage mores; a commentary on Continental-American cultural relations; but above all as a moving love story, with Humbert captive to the cruel caprices of his indifferent child-mistress.

LONESOME DOVE
Larry McMurtry
1985
Novel
Historical, Western

Lonesome Dove chronicles the fortunes of a colorful variety of characters involved with or intersecting with a cattle drive from the Rio Grande to Montana

In *Lonesome Dove*, McMurtry has written an epic historical novel. Set probably in the late 1870's the work is a panoramic narrative centering on a cattle drive from the Rio Grande to northern Montana, spanning more than two thousand miles of frontier, and has a bit of everything: rustling raids into Mexico, stampedes, lightning and hail storms, river crossings, drought, deadly outlaws, gunfights, lynchings, murderous Indians, and Indian fights.

Full as it is of action, *Lonesome Dove* is essentially a novel of character. Leading the cast are Augustus McCrae (Gus) and Woodrow F. Call, owners of the Hat Creek Cattle Company in the town of Lonesome Dove on the Rio Grande. The genial and expansive Gus embraces life; the indrawn Call's accumulated frustrations have built up a store of suppressed violence.

The inspiration for the cattle drive comes from Jake Spoon, a former Ranger crony of Gus and Call. To collect a herd, Call undertakes a series of nightly raids into Mexico, from which he steals about three thousand head. To handle them, he hires on additional cowboys, most notably Dish Boggett. The rest of the outfit are a colorful crew: Deets, a black cowboy; Pea Eye, simpleminded but a persistent worker; Bolivar, a Mexican cook; Po Campo, who replaces him and creates unusual dishes; the O'Brien brothers, Irish immigrants who sing at night to the cattle; Lippy, former piano player; Jasper Fant, obsessed with a fear of drowning; Needle Nelson and Soupy Jones; and Gus's two pigs, who walk all the way to Montana.

Crossing the path of the cattle drive are numerous other characters. July Johnson, a naïve husband newly wed to a domineering wife; July's hopelessly incompetent deputy; the Comanchero Blue Duck, a cold-blooded and vicious killer who hates Gus and Call from their Texas Ranger days, and who abducts Lorena. After Gus rescues her, Lorena thinks that she is in love with him, though she is more terrified of losing his protection. Gus becomes increasingly devoted to her, but he thinks that he is still in love with Clara, whom he courted sixteen years earlier. If Gus is the most colorful character in the novel, Clara is the strongest. She and Gus have an affectionate reunion, but they cannot reverse their choices.

Among other things, the novel is an elegy for an era that was ending. For most of the characters the action is tragic. Many of them die violently, either murdered or the victims of accidents on the trail. The survivors are initiated into painful reality as they experience loss or disillusionment. Yet the overall impression is of the vitality of life.

The novel is full of energy. Its language, both in narrative and dialogue, is a lively vernacular, full of unexpected metaphors and turns of phrase, and there is a considerable amount of mellow, deadpan, and offbeat humor. *Lonesome Dove* chronicles both an epic journey and the picaresque adventures of other wanderers. The narrative shifts from group to group, connecting them in surprising but logical ways. Both McMurtry's storytelling verve and the vitality of his characters will catch readers and keep them deeply involved. McMurtry re-creates the details of Western Americana, geography, history, weather, and trail driving with such vividness and authenticity that the reader vicariously experiences the life of the 1800's. *Lonesome Dove*, winner of the 1986 Pulitzer Prize in the category of fiction, is not a formula Western but a major novel with a breadth, variety, and liveliness that recall Charles Dickens.

LONG DAY'S JOURNEY INTO NIGHT
Eugene O'Neill
1956
Drama
Tragedy

Combining the retrospective exposition of the past that he learned from Henrik Ibsen with the love-hate ambivalences of familial feelings dramatized by August Strindberg, O'Neill compresses the psychological history of his family into one August day of 1912.

The play is overtly autobiographical, with O'Neill calling his father James Tyrone, his mother Mary Tyrone, his older brother James Tyrone, Jr., and himself not Eugene but Edmund Tyrone—thereby assuming the first name of the youngest brother, who died in infancy when exposed to measles by the oldest. In the preface, dedicated to his third wife Carlotta, O'Neill thanks her for the "love that enabled me to face my dead at last and write this play—write it with deep pity and understanding and forgiveness for all the four haunted Tyrones."

Two events propel the action: Mary Tyrone, despite having recently been treated for drug addiction, relapses into her morphine habit; and Edmund learns (as O'Neill did) that he has tuberculosis and must enter a sanatorium. When other family members move urgently closer to Mary for her sympathy and support, she inexorably moves away from them into the fog of her illusions.

The family is shown as living in a closely symbiotic relationship, with each important attribute of one member affecting—usually for the worse—the behavior of the other three. The quartet is linked by resentment and guilt, but also by love and need. Anger and recrimination alternate with pity and understanding. Each character takes turns being victim and persecutor, aggressor and protector.

The drama rises above the confessional level to show the Tyrones as a universal family, whose soul-searing discoveries and dreams, loves and longings belong to us all. By critical consensus, this is O'Neill's greatest play.

LOOK HOMEWARD, ANGEL
Thomas Wolfe
1929
Novel
Autobiographical

This novel is a chronicle of a Southern family, the Gants of Altamont, as seen through the eyes of the youngest son, Eugene Gant, during the first two decades of the 20th century.

This vigorous, effusive, realistic novel focuses on a family of six children. The parents, W. O. Gant, a promiscuous, alcoholic stone cutter, and Eliza, a conniving woman who is greedy to own property, have a combative marriage. Eliza buys Dixieland, a boarding house, which she runs to support herself when she leaves her husband.

Wolfe understands well the interactions of the people about whom he is writing. He writes about himself with candor and insight, detailing his coming-of-age.

In contrast to his life at Dixieland, which he loathes, is Eugene's life at a private school run by the Leonards. Margaret Leonard recognizes Eugene's potential and fuels his love of literature. At 15, after four years at the Leonard's School, Eugene, now unusually tall, goes to the university at Pulpit Hill.

While he is there, his brother Ben dies. The material on Ben's death is some of the most sensitive in the novel. Eugene finally is graduated from the university, and as the novel closes, his father, now dying of cancer, is spending his last months in a drab room at Dixieland. Eugene goes off to graduate school. This book, huge in scope, is convincing in its realism and moving in its passion.

LORD JIM
Joseph Conrad
1900
Novel
Psychological

This story of lost honor ranks among the best of Conrad's tales of the sea, as interesting for its shifts in narrative point of view as for its mysterious and troubling plot.

Conrad introduces Jim as an able-bodied seaman with romantic ideas about his own courage. Those ideas change drastically, though, when a crisis strikes the Patna, a decaying steamer aboard which Jim serves as chief mate; the rest of the novel explores the complexity of Jim's character as he struggles to form a new conception of himself.

The steamer strikes a submerged object one night at sea and begins to go down, carrying a load of passengers. The unscrupulous captain and his drunken crew abandon the vessel immediately, and though Jim remains behind for a long while, he eventually jumps from the ship and joins the others in the captain's lifeboat. But the steamer does not sink; the passengers are rescued and Jim's actions become the subject of a legal inquiry, while the rest of the crew slips away unpunished.

It is at this inquiry that Marlow first appears, and he goes on to narrate much of the remaining story. Marlow helps Jim in his attempt to come to terms with the meaning of his actions and restore his lost honor. Marlow eventually finds work for Jim in a remote trading settlement, where, among the natives, be becomes known as Lord Jim. Here at last he arrives at some understanding of himself, though the dramatic conclusion of the novel challenges the depth of that understanding.

Conrad adds interest to the tale and complicates his themes of lost honor and self-knowledge by introducing Marlow as a narrator. Marlow becomes a kind of mediator between Jim and the reader, so that Jim's story can, at times, tell us as much about Marlow as it does about Jim. It is this added dimension—a Conrad trademark—that makes *Lord Jim* the profound exploration of human character that it is.

LORD OF THE FLIES
William Golding
1954
Novel
Psychological

English schoolboys, abandoned on a deserted tropical island as a result of atomic catastrophe, attempt to govern themselves while awaiting rescue. They soon discover the narrow line between civilization and barbarism.

The boys quickly divide into factions. Ralph, handsome and easygoing, is elected chief, but Jack Merridew, leader of a group of choirboys, repeatedly challenges Ralph's authority. Piggy, a fat asthmatic boy and the most intelligent of all, must necessarily support Ralph; his unprepossessing appearance prevents his own election to a position of importance.

At first, the rules of the civilized world prevail, reflecting the boys' unqualified acceptance of adult forms. The boys call assemblies with a beautiful conch shell. They decide to build shelters and maintain a signal fire. Jack and the choirboys become hunters, and the division of labor seems complete.

Conflicts soon arise, however, just as they had in the adult world now presumably in great part destroyed. Jack smarts from Ralph's decisive election and is jealous of Piggy's intelligence. The "little'uns" have nightmares and believe they have seen a "beastie." Ralph's helpers spend their days swimming rather than constructing shelters. The hunters, on the trail of wild pig, let the signal fire go out just as there is hope of rescue. In anger, Jack strikes Piggy and breaks one of the lenses in Piggy's glasses, which were necessary to light the signal fire.

Tribalism soon prevails, and Jack emerges as chief by default rather than election. He offers the boys day hunts, night revels, and wild dances around blazing bonfires. Ralph and Piggy find themselves isolated from the rest. Both become victims of Jack's tyranny.

The novel, written in the wake of Hiroshima's destruction and at the height of the Cold War, reveals that the Leviathan, the beastie, exists in humanity. Given the opportunity, such evil shows itself.

THE LORD OF THE RINGS
J. R. R. Tolkien
1955
Novel
Series, Fantasy

This 3-volume epic fantasy tells of the war against Sauron, the evil Lord of the Rings, and in particular of the hobbit Frodo's quest to destroy the Rings of power by throwing it into the fires of Mount Doom.

In *The Lord of the Rings*, the world that Tolkien has created is rich and real, complete with civilizations of men, orcs, trolls, dwarfs, elves, and hobbits, all fully imagined, with customs, traditions, and languages of their own. Full of quiet humor and high moral seriousness, the trilogy appeals equally to young and old, to aficionados of fantasy and serious students of literature.

In Part 1, *The Fellowship of The Ring*, the hobbit Frodo, his servant Sam, and his companions Merry and Pippin set out on the first stage of the quest to destroy the ring. They are joined by the wizard Gandalf and a mysterious man called Strider, later revealed as Aragorn, King of Gondor; these two are the most formidable of the heroes leagued against Sauron. Along the way they are hounded by the Black Riders, Sauron's agents, and the party splits up.

Part 2, *The Two Towers*, tells of the opening of the War of the Rings, in which the forces of Gondor defeat Saruman, the traitor wizard and minion of Sauron. It goes on to recount the journey of Frodo and Sam into Mordor, Sauron's black and blighted kingdom.

Part 3, *The Return of The King*, recounts the defeat of Sauron and the triumph of Aragorn, made possible by the fulfillment of Frodo's quest. *The Lord of The Rings*, which can be enjoyed both as an adventure story and as a profound exploration of the nature of good and evil, is a deeply rewarding work that invites rereading.

THE LOTTERY
Shirley Jackson
1948
Short Story
Dystopian

In an unidentified small rural community, the townspeople gather for their annual lottery. Although the event begins in a seemingly festive way, the reader is shocked when the winner of the lottery is stoned to death by the rest of the town.

This Lottery, Thestory is probably one of the best-known in 20th century American literature—not necessarily because it is philosophically profound or artistically excellent, but because its conclusion catches the reader unaware and horrifies him or her with its barbarity.

At first, one expects the usual convention of a lottery—that someone will win a desirable prize. However, as the reader progresses into the story, ominous details suggest that more is at stake. When Tessie Hutchinson draws the unlucky token and objects that "It wasn't fair," the townspeople urge her to be a good sport and accept her prize. All the townspeople join in the stoning, even her own children.

The basic social theme focuses on how people often hold on to customs, even when they are barbaric and have lost their earlier meaning. The idea of the lottery itself refers back to a primitive fertility custom of scapegoating; that is, choosing one member of the community to be sacrificed to appease the gods and assure a good crop.

What makes the story so disturbing is that it does not take place in a primitive society in the distant past but rather in America in the 20th century. Moreover, instead of being written as if it were a parable of man's primitive nature, it is presented realistically as if it were actually taking place. When "The Lottery" was first published, many readers wrote to Jackson demanding to know where such horrors were being tolerated.

LOVE IN THE TIME OF CHOLERA
Gabriel Garcia Marquez
1985
Novel

Florentino Ariza appears to win and then mysteriously loses the love of Fermina Daza, for whom he waits more than fifty years to have the opportunity to win her heart once and for all

Gabriel García Márquez won worldwide fame for himself and Latin American literature with his novel *One Hundred Years of Solitude*, 1970). *Love in the Time of Cholera* comes very close to the author's earlier masterpiece.

At seventeen, Florentino Ariza begins his courtship of Fermina Daza. After a two-year relationship, she accepts his proposal of marriage. Her father, takes her on a trip to forget Florentino, which she does not do, and the relationship grows as the lovers continue to correspond on the sly. On Fermina's return, however, she mysteriously rejects Florentino and marries Dr. Juvenal Urbino de la Calle, a prominent local physician. Florentino vows that he will win Fermina back and he patiently waits for her husband to die. When Dr. Urbino de la Calle does die, Florentino expresses his love to Fermina. She immediately asks him to leave and sends him an insulting letter. Undaunted after waiting so long, Florentino continues to pursue Fermina. The progress of his courtship is slow, but he finally manages to win her heart and in the process show her what love really is.

This novel, like García Márquez's others, are populated by a collection of wonderfully odd characters. Foremost is Florentino Ariza, whose obsessive love for Fermina Daza permeates the novel. The character most dissimilar to Florentino is the object of his enduring love, Fermina Daza. Dr. Urbino de la Calle's main role in the novel is that of the obstacle in Florentino's quest for Fermina. He is also a classic García Márquez character, a man who is said to be conscious of the size and weight of his internal organs, who attempts unsuccessfully to teach arithmetic and opera to his parrot, and who insists upon eating asparagus, even out of season, simply so he can "take pleasure in the vapors of his own fragrant urine." In spite of their strangeness, the characters of this novel, even the minor ones, never cease to be intensely human. Each and every character is, if not well developed, then at least presented with a wealth of details that give them individual identity and dimension.

Besides the collection of interestingly odd characters, other unmistakable García Márquez trademarks include the use of exaggerated and supernatural events, and the fact that the story of *Love in the Time of Cholera* is not told in a strictly chronological fashion. The text is full of radical changes in focus as García Márquez's narrator moves from the perspective and story of one character to those of another. There are also countless passages which digress from the subject at hand. Some shifts or digressions deal with one character's reaction to a situation just described from another character's perspective, while others provide a background story or simply treat—and often at considerable length—a subject that happens to come up in the narration. The constant changes in focus are not meant to confuse the reader but to provide the most complete story possible, a story told from multiple perspectives and veritably stuffed with information about the characters and the world in which they live. Because of this, García Márquez's novel presents a multilayered tale in which the reader can become fully immersed.

Love in the Time of Cholera presents a story that builds not toward a dramatic climax but toward a subtle one. Each part, each scene, each description is important, and "progress" is not as important as the "process" itself. The novel therefore requires a very patient reader, one willing to follow and be engrossed in the narrator's radical shifts of focus and long, detailed descriptions dealing with the activities, thoughts, and backgrounds of both major and minor characters. At times it almost seems that the reader must have the patience of Florentino as he waits for his second chance with Fermina. It is clearly a work in which the destination is not as important as the trip itself. The reader who accepts this interpretation will thoroughly enjoy the book.

THE LOVE SONG OF J. ALFRED PRUFROCK
T. S. Eliot
1915
Poetry
Psychological

A middle-aged man is unable to have a close personal relationship because of his emotional insecurity. His free-flowing, dramatic monologue is one of the most widely appreciated modern poems.

The reader accompanies J. Alfred Prufrock as he tries to resolve his emotional conflicts, to make a serious proposal to a woman, and to become reconciled with his approaching old age. The monologue takes the form of a mental rehearsal of the evening's excursion through a city's streets, his arrival at the woman's apartment, the small talk, the meal, to its climax in his proposal, and contemplation of its possible rejection.

As he reflects on these prospects, Prufrock constantly compares himself with negative aspects of the city or contrasts his ambivalence with the moral courage of various cultural heroes. His own lack of resolve is like the languid fog, the cultivated boredom of ordinary, passive citizens. Ironically, his education has only served to heighten his sense of failure: He is so different from figures such as Hamlet and John the Baptist.

His self-consciousness is conveyed in surprisingly, deliberately "unpoetic" images: He imagines himself being examined—and criticized—by sophisticated acquaintances, and so he takes refuge in thinking of himself as a solitary crab or a lonely beachcomber. Like Polonius in *Hamlet*, he is always near the action, never part of it; and he fears the risk of commitment, for like the imaginary pursuer of mermaids, he might for his efforts lose the half-life he has. So he continues to procrastinate.

The combination of psychological realism, free association, ordinary speech, sharp irony, anticlimax, and symbolism, and the juxtaposition of secular and religious allusions are all characteristic of Eliot's verse, and indeed of much modern poetry. For these reasons, as well as for its clarity and pathos, this work is one of the most influential of the 20th century.

THE LUCK OF ROARING CAMP
Bret Harte
1868
Short Story
Historical

This popular story is one of the best examples of the western local color writing made famous by Harte and his contemporary Mark Twain.

The story is set in 1850 in Roaring Camp, a mining settlement in California. Cherokee Sal, an Indian prostitute, dies shortly after giving birth to an infant boy. The men in the camp are joined together by a sense of responsibility for the orphan, although the child's actual father is unknown. The child's care is supervised by Stumpy, who uses the milk of an ass to feed the baby.

The intrusion of the infant into this rambunctious setting has a civilizing effect on its inhabitants. The greatest change takes place in Kentuck, an impoverished miner who feels a strong affection for the child, now known as Tommy Luck. Soon Roaring Camp and its people take on a new respectability and acquire an unexpected prosperity.

All ends, however, with a freak flood which destroys the settlement. The next morning, the survivors find Kentuck with the dead child in his arms. With a smile, he accompanies the spirit of Tommy Luck into the unknown.

Bret Harte wrote this story for the *Overland Monthly*, the magazine he edited. It pictured the realism of life in a mining camp but did so within a sentimental framework. His characters are stereotypes, and the resolution of the tale is undeniably maudlin. It remained for Twain to turn similar material into great literature.

LYSISTRATA
Aristophanes
411 B.C.E.
Drama
Classical

Lysistrata, an Athenian woman, brings about peace between Athens and Sparta during the Second Peloponnesian War by convincing the women of both city-states to deny sex to their husbands until an armistice is signed.

Lysistrata summons to Athens women from Sparta and the other city-states involved in the Second Peloponnesian War. She proposes to them that they use their feminine wiles to force an end to the prolonged conflict. Specifically, she suggests that they all swear an oath not to have sexual relations with their men until the armistice is achieved.

The women are horrified at the suggestion, except for Lampito, a Spartan woman, who agrees with Lysistrata that this solution is a workable one. Lampito helps Lysistrata persuade the women to take a sacred oath not to have physical relations with their husbands or lovers until the war is over.

Many of the women return to their native lands, but Lysistrata and a group of her female followers seize the Acropolis and lock themselves inside. The old men of Athens, the magistrates, build fires around the base, trying to smoke the women out, but the women retaliate by dumping water on the old men and holding their ground.

Eventually the sexually deprived men from the opposing sides gather but are reluctant to sign the treaty. Soon, however, they are enticed into doing so by the resolute women.

Lysistrata is high comedy, as popular and timely today as it was when it was written. The humor is broad and bawdy. Like much good comedy, the play holds up to ridicule contemporary conditions and situations.

M

MACBETH
William Shakespeare
1606
Drama
Tragedy

Derived from Holinshed's Chronicles of England, Scotland, and Ireland *(1577),* Macbeth *is the story of a Scottish general who secretly murders his king and then assumes the throne.*

Macbeth opens after the victory of Macbeth and Banquo, two Scottish generals, over rebels against the crown. Three witches appear and greet Banquo as the ancestor of kings and Macbeth as Thane of Cawdor and "king hereafter."

Emboldened by these prophecies and urged on by his wife, Macbeth murders Duncan, his king and kinsman, while Duncan is a guest in his home. After Macbeth is proclaimed king, he decides to forestall the prophecy of the witches by murdering Banquo's family. Haunted by Banquo's ghost, Macbeth awakens the suspicions of Macduff, who flees the country.

Warned by the witches to beware of Macduff, Macbeth proceeds to murder Macduff's family. He feels secure since the witches promise him that he will not be vanquished by anyone of woman born, nor will he be defeated until "Great Birnam wood to high Dunsinane hill" has come.

Lady Macbeth becomes insane and commits suicide. The enemy troops cut down Birnam trees to use as camouflage. Revealing that he was delivered in a Caesarian operation and so not of woman born, Macduff confronts the usurper Macbeth in combat. Macduff wins the battle and brandishes Macbeth's head on a sword. Duncan's son Malcolm is proclaimed king.

Shakespeare's dramatic mastery is fully mature in *Macbeth*. Even though Macbeth trespasses against the standards of human decency, he successfully claims our interest and understanding, his despair evokes our sympathy.

MADAME BOVARY
Gustave Flaubert
1857
Novel
Manners, Satire

Intended at least in part as a satire of provincial manners, the novel focuses primarily on the title character's dissatisfaction with her life as the second wife of an unambitious, incompetent rural physician.

Emma Rouault, a farmer's daughter, perceives herself as a romantic, a sensitive soul surrounded by clods and dolts. Addicted to wild fantasies nourished by popular literature and art, she longs for a grand passion that will somehow liberate her from her stultifying provincial existence. In time her reveries appear to affect her health, causing Charles Bovary to move his medical practice from the village of Tostes to the somewhat larger town of Yonville.

It is in Yonville that Emma, now a mother, will indulge her inclination towards a grand passion. From a chaste friendship with the mild-mannered law clerk Leon, in whom she perceives a kindred romantic spirit, Emma plunges headlong into a tawdry affair with the ruthless playboy Rodolphe, only to instigate a truly physical affair with Leon after Rodolphe has deserted her. By that time, her fantasies have led her into extravagance and crippling debt, leaving her open to blackmail on the part of her principal creditor. Charles Bovary, oblivious as usual, is caught totally unprepared by Emma's impulsive, yet slow and painful suicide.

In addition to the psychological portrait of Emma Bovary, the book is notable for its supporting characters, frequent memorable scenes depicting rural French society, and, above all, for Flaubert's painstaking attention to language, pattern, and coloration in forging his much-admired prose style.

MAGGIE: A GIRL OF THE STREETS
Stephen Crane
1893
Novella
Psychological

This story of a young Irish girl living in New York City slums in the late 19th century depicts the helplessness of victims in the face of a brutal social environment.

Maggie Johnson, the heroine of Stephen Crane's novel, is described as a flower blossoming in the "mud-puddle" of New York's Irish slum life. In her family and neighborhood, she has known nothing but violence and squalor, the results of poverty and deprivation. Her alcoholic father and mother fight constantly, and the children are terrified by their parents' brutality. Maggie's older brother Jimmie turns into a tough street urchin, and the baby Tommie dies of neglect.

Maggie grows up to be an attractive girl, but sees no way out of the trap of poverty and violence. Her alternatives are sweatshop exploitation or prostitution. When her mother and brother drive her out on the streets, she turns to Jimmie's handsome bartender friend Pete as the "knight" who will rescue her from her sordid life. At first Pete takes Maggie out to shows and clubs, but eventually he tires of her and casts her aside.

When Maggie returns home, her mother and brother hypocritically attack her as a fallen woman and turn her out. Homeless and without money, she appeals to Pete, who will have nothing to do with her. Desperate, she turns to prostitution, drifting slowly downward as she loses her good looks and men begin to avoid her. For Maggie, life offers few alternatives.

Crane's bleakly naturalistic novel shows the effect of a harsh and brutal environment on weak and pliable natures. He shows how economic forces deny freedom of choice for those at the bottom of the social scale. Maggie may be attractive and decent, but she cannot escape from her slum environment. Unfortunately, we only see Maggie from the outside, as a victim, rather than sharing in her thoughts and feelings, but Crane still makes her a sympathetic figure. He attacks the hypocritical religious attitudes that would blame the victim instead of trying to improve the social conditions that cause such misery. In *Maggie*, Crane tries to provide a true and accurate account of the sordid conditions of 19th century New York City tenement life.

THE MAGIC MOUNTAIN
Thomas Mann
1924
Novel
Coming of Age, Bildungsroman

This massive novel, rich with the depths of the human mind and soul, explores issues of time and action in the mysterious setting of a Swiss sanatorium.

Although grounded in a specific time and place—the years preceding World War I at Davos-Platz in the Swiss Alps—this novel has a quality of being timeless and not of this world. The setting is strange—a sanatorium for the tubercular in a town with a healthy but unpredictable climate. Also, because patients go there presumably to recover but basically to kill time in a world withdrawn from the pressures of real life, time moves differently, becoming a kind of eternity.

When Hans Castorp, the dreamy young German protagonist, arrives to visit his cousin Joachim, a matter-of-fact soldier, he is planning to stay three weeks. At first uncomfortable with the rigid routine and slow pace, Hans soon becomes accustomed to it and eventually enjoys it. When the doctor in charge finds in Hans symptoms of tuberculosis, the weeks turn into months and eventually into years.

Through its length, its story line, and numerous discussions by narrator and characters, the novel dislodges the reader's standard sense of time. The activities of the pre-war world below, though altering the world irrevocably, have no impact on the cloistered life of the sanatorium, except for such leisure-time innovations as the phonograph and the moving picture. This is its appeal for Hans, while Joachim yearns for that outside world, yet movingly must die apart from it.

The relationships in the sanatorium parody those in the real world, lacking permanence and commitment. Passivity wins over action. Hans's love for Clavdia Chauchat is frustratingly incomplete. His richest involvement is with the contentious Italian philosopher Settembrini, whose intellectual challenges galvanize Hans's often overly sensitive, even foolish, mind.

The entire novel involves the reader intensely in its feelings and ideas, provoking one to examine one's own responses to the challenges of life.

THE MAGUS
John Fowles
1965
Novel
Psychological

Originally hailed as pointing toward a new kind of ambiguous fiction, this lengthy tale of a young Englishman's unusual "sentimental education" has since lost some of its initial appeal. It remains, however, a tale well-told and has been successfully filmed.

Narrated in the first person by Nicholas Urfe, a cynical Oxford graduate who has drifted into teaching, the novel proceeds from bohemian London to the mysterious island of Phraxos off the coast of Greece. There Nicholas' quest for foreign adventure lands him in the clutches of the enigmatic Maurice Conchis. The magus or sorcerer of the title, Conchis is an alleged erstwhile Nazi collaborator who stages a series of unorthodox "encounters" ostensibly, yet inexplicably, aimed at awakening Urfe's true feelings.

Unable to fall in love, or even to sustain more than the most fleeting romantic attachment, Nicholas has chosen Greece over a recent involvement with Alison Kelly, an attractive yet vulnerable Australian seeking work as an airline hostess. Fleeing Alison, yet unable to break with her completely, Nicholas is still searching for true love. Having willed himself to fall in love with a young woman whom he has glimpsed on Conchis' property, he is vulnerable to the psychodrama that Conchis has prepared for him. This drama is replete with costumed actors and vertiginous plot twists that at times parallel the true (or invented) facts of Conchis' own life.

Thwarted, frustrated, even maddened by the tricks continually being played upon him by the mysterious mastermind Conchis, Nicholas loses his teaching job on Phraxos and begins to play detective, trying to strip away the masks of the people he has met there. Only toward the end of his grueling, mazelike search does Nicholas begin to detect some connection between his recent experiences and the abandoned Alison Kelly, long since presumed dead (thanks to Conchis). Apparently, all of Nicholas' recent trials have been mounted to cure him of selfishness and awaken his latent love for Alison—who will return to him only when and if he deserves her.

Set largely during 1953, the novel is notable not only for its dizzying plot structure—no mean feat in the "uninformed" first person—but also for its evocation of British society during the years of postwar transition.

MAIN STREET
Sinclair Lewis
1920
Novel
Satire

A young woman seeks to create a better and more beautiful life but is battered by a decade of disillusionments. This satire of her representative small American town is still timely.

Carol Milford, after college and jobs in Chicago and St. Paul, marries a doctor, Will Kennicott, from Gopher Prairie, Minnesota. Shocked by the gritty ugliness of her new home, she envisions a series of projects to make it more beautiful, but each is frustrated by narrow-mindedness, special interests, apathy, or pragmatism. Even her attempts to introduce joyousness, imagination, and culture into the town's social life are dismissed. She realizes that small-town life, far from being friendly and democratic, fosters tighter caste systems, more rigid conventions, and more prejudice against nonconformists and immigrants than the cities she has left.

In time, she finds her relationship with her husband faltering because she refuses to accept and admire the town as it is. After Will's attempts to make her happier with plans for a new home and an extended vacation fail, Carol takes their child and escapes to Washington, D. C. There she comes to a new understanding of herself, her marriage, and Gopher Prairie.

Lewis makes his attack on small-town America explicit in his preface. Massive details and recurring imagery underscore his urgent plea that America revitalize its belief in true democracy, personal integrity, and the nourishment of beauty to fulfill its promise. Otherwise, he suggests, America's hope of building a great civilization will be thwarted; it will become only a standardized, materialistic empire reflecting the worst of Main Street.

MAJOR BARBARA
George Bernard Shaw
1905
Drama
Comedy

Shaw is nearly always concerned with ridiculing conventional morality, and in this provocative comedy everyday pieties seem unrealistic and untenable even when compared to the outrageous guidelines for life proclaimed by a shrewd but apparently immoral munitions manufacturer.

The play revolves around the contrast between the Salvation Army, aiming to save the souls of men and women by preaching humility and submission, and the weapons factory of Andrew Undershaft, which provides its workers with a realistic escape from what would otherwise be a dreary life of poverty. Ironically, the model city standing alongside stockpiles of explosive materials is of more tangible help to the poor than the ineffective charity and hope for the hereafter offered by the Salvation Army. In short, the poor are better served by jobs than by prayers.

Major Barbara, Undershaft's daughter, is a powerful spokesperson for the Salvation Army and dominates the first part of the play. While Lady Britomart, her mother, and Stephen, her brother, are simply comic caricatures of unthinking, hypocritical morality, Barbara is articulate and compassionate in trying to spread the traditional virtues of love, honor, justice, and truth.

She is, however, no match for her father, who has turned these virtues completely upside down. His motto is "Unashamed," signifying that no moral caution deters him from making a profit from weaponry. Like most literary devils, Undershaft is a fascinating character, charming because he is honest, witty, and successful. When he visits Barbara at work saving souls, he convinces her that only his kind of power works in this world: Even the Salvation Army is supported by contributions from unscrupulous benefactors like himself.

Barbara's confrontation with her father is not so much a defeat as a revelation of her true character. Ultimately she is very much her father's daughter, receptive to the kind of vital life-force that makes him such an effective businessman.

The similarity to her father is confirmed at the play's end when she prepares to marry Adolphus Cusins, a foundling with no family ties and an unconventional upbringing, prerequisites to be the amoral heir of Undershaft's empire.

Like most of Shaw's plays, *Major Barbara* is an entertainingly comic and stageworthy battle of ideas. While he by no means urges everyone to get involved in the business of war, he does suggest that any truly effective plan for improving the lot of mankind must presuppose that conventional morality is a greater obstacle than a help.

THE MALTESE FALCON
Dashiell Hammett
1930
Novel
Detective

After his partner is shot and killed during a routine surveillance, San Francisco private investigator Samuel Spade finds himself embroiled in a desperate search for a priceless statuette.

Sam Spade, clearly the brains of the Spade and Archer detective agency, turns over to his plodding partner, Miles Archer, the case of a young woman client in whose presence he senses trouble. When Archer turns up dead not long thereafter, Spade is hardly surprised but proceeds to delve deeper into the case, uncovering a tangle of deceptions and false identities. The young woman's real name, it seems, is Brigid O'Shaughnessy, and it is not long before Spade links her to an international ring of criminals competing among themselves for possession of a priceless treasure known as the Maltese Falcon.

Supposedly, the football-sized sculpted bird, encrusted with rare gems, has been stolen and repossessed many times during the four centuries of its existence; in Hammett's hands, the unseen sculpture comes to symbolize the perpetuity of human greed, all the more so when the coveted object is unwrapped to reveal a worthless fake.

Central to the action is Spade's increasing involvement with Brigid O'Shaughnessey, whose deviousness and native intelligence compare favorably with his own. Spurning the affections of Iva Archer, who had been his mistress before her husband's death, Spade proceeds to fall in love with Brigid even while evidence suggests that she is in some way responsible for Miles Archer's murder.

As Spade proceeds to unravel the mystery, he encounters a memorable assortment of professional criminals, including the manipulative adventurer Casper Gutman and the blatantly homosexual Joel Cairo. Faced at last with the inescapable fact of Brigid's guilt, Spade incongruously but plausibly chooses honor over love, turning her over to the authorities even as she is kissing him; as he explains, he "may or may not" be waiting for her when she gets out of prison.

MAN AND SUPERMAN
George Bernard Shaw
1905
Drama
Comedy, Philosophical

This is one of Shaw's major dramas, consisting of two intertwined plays: a Victorian farce in four neatly arranged acts, and a long third act which is usually called "Don Juan in Hell" and often produced separately.

The action begins shortly after the death of Ann Whitefield's father. She has made certain that one of the two guardians designated for her in his will is John Tanner, a radical writer whose views are essentially Shaw's. While professing to be the most demure of young women, Ann is a predatory huntress who has set her cap for Tanner and stalks him relentlessly while he talks endlessly. She pursues Tanner across most of Europe, catches him in the Sierra Nevada, and triumphs over him through her irresistible sexual lure, which Shaw prefers to call the "Life Force."

The interlude in Hell is a dream vision that Tanner has while captured by bandits. It is a dazzlingly sustained discussion of ideas, with Shaw converting several of his leading characters from the core play into the cast of Mozart's opera, *Don Giovanni* (1787). Thus John Tanner becomes Don Juan, but an inverted, Shavian hero: His reputation as a heartless libertine is here ill-founded; he protests that he kept running away from women in fear and self-defense, as

Tanner ran away from Ann Whitefield. Ann is now Mozart's Donna Ana, as prudishly pious as Ann was adventurously avant-garde. Roebuck Ramsden, a reactionary foil for Tanner, becomes Ana's father, "The Statue." And the genially romantic leader of the Sierra brigands, Mendoza, turns into an equally affable Devil, respectable and democratic.

After a brilliant verbal duel in which Don Juan becomes Shaw's advocate of evolutionary progress through eugenic breeding, he and Ana repair to Shaw's Heaven, there to create a "Superman" in the "Life to Come." The dramatist's Heaven is a Puritan's delight, enshrining a "philosophic man" largely superior to the temptations of the flesh and organizing the highest sphere as a celestial workshop. Shaw's Hell, on the other hand, is the world as we know it, dominated by conventional illusions. Bored by Heaven, Ana's father prefers the Devil's companionship and descends to it in exchange for his daughter's and the Don's ascension.

MANFRED
Lord Byron
1817
Drama
Tragedy, Romance

This drama of an isolated, Faustlike magician embarked on a forbidden quest set in the Alps is a powerful portrayal of the brilliant, doomed Byronic hero of the early 19th century.

The magician Manfred summons a group of spirits to make him forget some secret, but they cannot. The next day, Manfred attempts suicide by throwing himself off a mountain, but a passing chamois hunter saves him. The hunter urges Manfred to repent of his secret sin, but Manfred claims that his sin is part of his destiny.

Manfred calls up the Witch of the Alps and reveals that the woman Astarte was destroyed by his love for her. Manfred then goes to the evil spirit Arimanes and demands that he summon the phantom of Astarte, who tells him that his torment will soon be over.

Manfred feels a great calm and prepares to meet his destiny. He encounters the Abbot of St. Maurice, who asks him to reconcile himself to God, but Manfred respectfully tells him that it is too late for repentance and that his fate is already decided.

Manfred, gifted, fiercely independent, and tortured by some secret guilt, is an excellent example of the Byronic hero, a figure which, based in part on Byron's personal mystique, exercised an enormous appeal throughout the Romantic period. Manfred's chief characteristic, in common with other Byronic heroes, is his pride; the play reveals this pride as both his glory, making him a great wizard, and his downfall, causing him to have a destructive love affair.

This pride alienates Manfred from human contact. His exalted life is a tormented search for escape from guilt. Yet Manfred's striving for self-determination invests him with a superhuman grandeur, making him an ambiguous, but all the more compelling hero.

MAN'S FATE
André Malraux
1933
Novel
Political

Written, like most of Malraux's fictions, from inside the situation portrayed and informed by the author's firsthand experience, this novel gives memorable form to the early years of the Chinese revolution, culminating in a 1927 attempt upon the life of Generalissimo Chiang Kai-Shek.

Notable for its vivid characters as well as for its action scenes, the novel focuses upon the dedication of a handful of Communist revolutionaries with little in common besides their cause. Kyo Gisors, the novel's central character, is a Eurasian married to a German-born physician; his French father, revered by Kyo's fellow revolutionaries as an adviser and ideologue, increasingly seeks refuge in opium from the pressures of a political situation that he can no longer understand or explain. Katov, a Russian veteran of the Bolshevik revolution, is perhaps Kyo's closest friend and ally.

Ch'en Ta Erh, a former student of the elder Gisors, is one of the first true terrorists to be convincingly portrayed in fiction; in this troubled young man, thought and action have become fused into a formidable, if not invincible, killing machine. Also closely involved in the plotting is Hemmelrich, a German-born phonograph dealer who arranges the transfer of coded information through specially rigged phonograph discs.

Kyo's wife, May, is another highly memorable character. Committed first of all to her medical career, May is a complex, often ambivalent figure; Malraux's portrayal of her relationship with Kyo foreshadows by some forty years the treatment of modern marriage that today's reader has to come to expect. Closer to caricature is Malraux's portrayal of the rich industrialist Ferral and his almost-liberated mistress Valerie.

Throughout the action, comic relief is provided by the Baron Clappique, a minor underworld character with a gift for striking poses. Ironically, it is Clappique whose unreliability proves fatal to the revolutionaries once they have decided to depend upon him. The revolution, however, will continue, and the rest is history.

MANSFIELD PARK
Jane Austen
1814
Novel
Manners

Set in the fictional village of Mansfield, Northamptonshire, England, this novel treats the contemporary life of the gentry as they attempt to find suitable spouses.

Of central interest are Fanny Price and her clergyman cousin, Edmund Bertram. At the age of nine Fanny had come to live with her uncle, Sir Thomas Bertram, and his family at Mansfield Park. Nine years later she has fallen in love with Edmund. He, however, loves Mary Crawford. Meanwhile Fanny is pursued, first jestingly and then earnestly, by Mary's brother, Henry.

Fanny recognizes that Henry and Mary are morally flawed. Her judgment is vindicated when Henry runs off with Marie Bertram after she has married Rushworth. Mary's refusal to condemn her brother reveals to Edmund that she would not be a suitable wife. With the Crawfords thus removed, Edmund and Fanny marry.

In a letter to her sister, Jane Austen wrote that the book is about "ordination." Edmund Bertram's choice of the church as a profession is indeed important in the novel, which explores the role of the clergy.

Ordination here is not limited to its clerical sense, though, for the novel, like all of Austen's fiction, concerns the proper ordering of society. The Crawfords and most of the Bertrams lack those principles necessary for civilization to survive. They have wit but lack wisdom; and, as Austen wrote to her niece in 1814, "Wisdom is better than Wit, & in the long run will certainly have the laugh on her side."

Such wisdom is not innate, and another concern of the novel is how to instill "that principle of right" that Fanny learns but the Crawfords and the Bertram girls do not.

Although the novel ends happily for Edmund and Fanny, the tone is somber. Writing at the time that Napoleon was upsetting the old order in Europe, Jane Austen warned that one violates conventions only at great peril to oneself and one's world.

THE MARTIAN CHRONICLES
Ray Bradbury
1950
Short Story
Science Fiction, Series

These classic short stories use man's contact with Mars and its mysterious inhabitants to reveal modern society's need to recognize and accept the dark side of man's nature.

In the late 20th century, Earth rockets begin arriving on Mars. The Martians try to defend themselves with their telepathic powers, at one point projecting the illusion of a town inhabited by the departed relatives of one rocket's crew, but they are eventually killed off by exposure to chicken pox, against which their bodies have no immunity.

Earthmen begin arriving on Mars and setting up communities. Their reasons for coming are different, but all see Mars as something that exists for their purposes. There are random encounters with the surviving Martians, but mutual misunderstandings render such contacts fruitless, as when a human and a Martian meet and each thinks that the other is a ghost.

Earth, however, is nearing atomic war. With the collapse of civilization imminent, the colonists must learn to adapt to the planet rather than adapt it to themselves. They must take on the Martian values in order to survive.

On one level these stories are a retelling of history in a futuristic setting. Mars is America, the Earthmen are European settlers, and the Martians Indians. The parallels between the colonization of Mars and the development of America allow Bradbury to show the ignorance, delusion, and brutality that was a part of our history. In addition, the Martians become supernatural figures, just as many displaced peoples became fairies and goblins.

On a deeper level, the Martians represent the imaginative, intuitive side of humanity. Martian culture unites science, art, and religion, whereas modern Earth culture emphasizes science over everything else. This imbalance makes the Earthmen vulnerable to Martian illusions and eventually leads to warfare on Earth. Only by accepting the Martian ideas of balance and wholeness can the human colonists live on after the atomic war.

THE MASQUE OF THE RED DEATH
Edgar Allan Poe
1842
Short Story
Horror, Gothic

Poe's tale of horror describes Prince Prospero's futile attempt to safeguard himself and a thousand favored subjects from the plague, the "Red Death" devastating his kingdom. All action occurs within Prospero's castellated abbey and its labyrinth of seven rooms.

Prospero takes extraordinary precautions against the plague's appearance. He fortifies his abbey with a lofty wall and iron gates. He also provides elaborate comforts for his favored subjects within. These include entertainments such as a masquerade ball.

The ball suite contains seven rooms, each a different color ranging from blue to ebony. Their number can represent the threescore and ten years of life, their colors life's stages. The black room has scarlet windows and a gigantic ebony clock against its west wall. It combines the color of death and mourning with that of blood and also time imagery with the location of the classical underworld. Only the boldest guests dare enter this last room, and its clock's chime silences the musicians and makes the ball guests grow pale.

Though he directs every detail of life within the walls, Prospero cannot control the Red Death's appearance as "guest" at the masquerade. The plague claims Prospero within the black western chamber, then one by one destroys the revelers.

Death's inevitable triumph fascinated Poe and recurs often in his work. That death appears in the splendor and comfort of Prospero's abbey makes its victory more ironic, and Prospero's name adds to the irony. Nevertheless, Poe's symbols are suggestive rather than rigid.

Poe's comparison of Prospero's ball to that in *Hernani*, an 1830 play by Victor Hugo, is a clue to Death's arrival. Hugo's protagonist kills himself upon the arrival of a black-robed figure. The ball guests of Poe's play in like manner fear the sinister stranger.

THE MASTER AND MARGARITA
Mikhail Bulgakov
1973
Novel
Historical, Satire

One of the greatest satiric and romantic novels in world literature, this maze-like hallucination exposes evil as it defends the religious imagination in an atheistic society.

Like Tolstoy's Anna Karenina, the novel features a dual plot. The primary plot is set in 1930s Moscow; the secondary novel is the historical story of the life of Yeshua of Nazareth who was crucified by Pontius Pilate. The hero of the primary novel—the Master—has written the secondary novel, but he burns it in a woodstove during a manic fit of despair; however, his insomniac mistress had secretly made a duplicate at night when the Master was sleeping. The historical (secondary) novel still remains compelling, containing deft parallels with the main story, in the face of contemporary archeology and textual analysis of the Gospels.

The main story describes a Kafka-like nightmare where the Master is condemned to a lunatic asylum run by the archly prophetic magician, Woland, who appears to be an incarnation of Satan, and is certainly a satire on Joseph Stalin. Woland, enjoys an entourage of colorful demons, (including a behemoth cat who loves guns, an albino assistant translator, a witch, a drooling assassin, and an angel of death), who enter the plot with mischievous and whimsical impunity. Joining Woland at a Walpurgis Night fete that celebrates evil, Margarita, as Queen of the Ball, achieves a Faustian bargain that saves the Master from certain Siberian exile—the same fate that befell the real-life poet, Osip Mandelstam.

The novel, written between 1929 and 1939, defends religion from a gnostic point of view: the world is mired in unremitting evil, yet good can evolve from suffering at the hands of evil beings. The novel's magical realism keeps the story surreal and dreamlike with the present as a miserable purgatory, the past as a vicious hell, and the future as a romantic utopian fantasy. This trajectory presents the greatest spiritual and political journey since Dante Alighieri's *Comedia*. The outrageous and ebullient sense of humor that carries the novel appears with unequalled vitality in repeated readings. Versions of the novel appeared in 1966-67, but a complete edition was not published until 1973.

THE MAYOR OF CASTERBRIDGE
Thomas Hardy
1886
Novel
Tragedy, Romance

A man of strong will and passions rises to prominence in Casterbridge, only to be ruined by a series of chance events and by his own stubbornness.

In a drunken fit, Michael Henchard sells his wife and child to a sailor. Twenty years later, a superficially changed Henchard has risen to be Mayor of Casterbridge. His wife arrives in town, bringing along a girl, Elizabeth-Jane, whom Henchard assumes to be his daughter. They remarry, though they keep their past a secret. A farming crisis causes Henchard to hire Donald Farfrae to manage the town's grain trade. The two men become rivals, and a series of chance mishaps and impetuous decisions cause Henchard's fortunes to wane while Farfrae's rise. When Henchard's wife dies, he tells his daughter he is her father. An old lover of Henchard's returns to town, but Farfrae wins her.

Henchard finally is forced to work for Farfrae, who becomes Mayor. The sailor who bought Henchard's family returns looking for his wife and daughter; Henchard must tell the girl that she is not his offspring. In disgrace, he leaves town. When Farfrae's wife dies, he marries Henchard's step-daughter. Henchard dies a bitter exile from his community.

Henchard is a man apparently beaten by circumstance (failed corn crops, letters found too late, coincidental appearances of figures from his past). His strong passion, however, causes him to be blind to his own weaknesses.

Hardy's main concern is to explore the nature of tragedy and the tragic hero. Elements of Classical, Renaissance, and Romantic drama are all woven into the work. The novel relies heavily on the notion of the Wheel of Fortune: as one man's fortune rises, so another's falls. Here, however, no omniscient deity controls the hero's destiny. Henchard seems to be a victim either of his own passion or of blind chance, indicating Hardy's concerns with the problem of godlessness prevalent in Victorian society. That issue had been accentuated by developments in science during the years immediately before, and during, Hardy's lifetime.

MEASURE FOR MEASURE
William Shakespeare
1604
Drama
Comedy

This dark comedy, often referred to as a "problem play," involves representatives of court, church, and city caught up in the crosscurrents of love, sin, justice, mercy, and forgiveness.

Shakespeare's study of judgment draws heavily on the biblical Gospels as well as on Italian writer Giambattista Giraldo Cinthio's prose tale of an obsessed governor who sets aside his rigid concept of justice to indulge his sexual passion. The drama of the play pits the inflexible, seemingly self-controlled Angelo against the virtuous novice nun Isabella, who pleads that her brother's execution for the crime of unchastity be commuted.

As the play opens, the ruling Duke of Vienna hands over absolute rule, including power of "mortality and mercy," to his deputy Angelo. The Duke, disguised as a friar, then observes, manipulates, and offers the final comment on the action. Some critics see the Duke as representing Divine Providence, while others perceive him as playing the artist's role in shaping the drama.

Angelo's test case involves judging Claudio, a young gentleman who has gotten his betrothed with child. Angelo, whose cold blood cannot condone or excuse the crime, condemns Claudio to death as testament to the fact that Vienna's old, unenforced laws are no longer to be flouted. The city's consternation is immense. The outcry even reaches the ears of Isabella in her nunnery, which she leaves to plead for her brother.

After an inconclusive first encounter, Angelo offers to trade Claudio's life for Isabella's virginity, a proposition she scorns. The execution is scheduled, but the Duke in his character of friar offers a plan. The former fiancee of Angelo, Mariana of the moated grange, can be persuaded to take Isabella's place in Angelo's bed. Angelo enjoys the lady he assumes to be Isabella, then hypocritically orders the execution to proceed. The Duke's intervention and subsequent judgment lead to a complex unravelling of identities and affections.

THE MEMBER OF THE WEDDING
Carson McCullers
1946
Novel
Historical, Southern Gothic

This short novel about growing up in the American South just before World War II realistically and poignantly delineates the pain, confusion, and loneliness of the transition between childhood and adolescence.

Twelve-year-old Frankie Addams, the protagonist of this novel, is one of the most provocative adolescent characters in American literature. Rebellious but inwardly frightened, she is a social outcast who secretly longs to be connected with a group. The novel tells the story of her scheme to run away to live with her older brother and his new bride, thus becoming a "member of the wedding."

Carson McCullers' third novel is short on conventional plot, concentrating instead on characterization and mood. Most of the book's events take place in the kitchen of Frankie's home, where she spends much of her time talking with the cook, Berenice Sadie Brown, and with six-year-old John Henry West. The three characters eat, play cards, and argue during the course of the long, hot Southern summer which is the novel's primary time frame.

Almost as important to the story as Frankie herself is Berenice, the only estimable adult character. Her love-hate relationship with Frankie and their arguments provide the basis for many of the novel's themes, among them the impossibility of mutual and lasting love and the essential loneliness of the human condition. Berenice is also representative of the oppression of blacks in a segregated South, a concern that runs through much of McCullers' work.

The novel is clearly divided into three sections, each dealing with a separate stage of Frankie Addams' emotional development. McCullers later adapted her best-known work for the stage, and it was a Broadway hit in 1950. Both the play and the novel deal delicately but honestly with the sad but necessary journey from childhood to maturity.

THE MERCHANT OF VENICE
William Shakespeare
1596-1597
Drama
Comedy

This romantic comedy containing the dark Shylock has the powerful atmosphere of a fairy tale. It celebrates the triumph of friendship, love, and mercy over hatred, revenge, and harsh justice.

The opening scene establishes the play's dominant theme—the Renaissance concept of friendship, which takes precedence even over romantic love. Antonio, a merchant of Venice, loans his bankrupt friend Bassanio money to woo Portia, the heiress of Belmont. To get the money, Antonio himself has to borrow it from Shylock, a usurious Jew who hates him and makes the collateral a pound of Antonio's flesh.

A dark figure of contrast, Shylock puts money above human values. He is so grasping and hardhearted that first his servant leaves him, then his daughter, Jessica. Jessica runs off with a Christian, taking jewels and ducats. Shylock is equally hysterical about losing Jessica and the ducats.

Bassanio journeys to Belmont and, by passing a shrewd test designed by Portia's dead father, wins Portia's hand: From gold, silver, and lead caskets, he chooses the one containing her portrait. Meanwhile, however, Antonio is forced to default on the loan, and Shylock demands his pound of flesh.

In a climactic court scene, Portia, disguised as a young judge, settles the case. Her learned decision, satisfying Shylock's call for strict justice, frees Antonio and condemns Shylock, but the court shows mercy by mitigating Shylock's harsh penalty and forcing him to become a Christian.

Even though Shylock seems to bring his troubles on himself, modern audiences have tended to see the treatment of Shylock not as a demonstration of Christian virtue but as hypocrisy and anti-Semitism. Similarly, they have tended to see Shylock as a character who began as a stereotype, captured the author's sympathies, and almost stole the show.

METAMORPHOSES
Ovid
8 C.E.
Poetry
Epic

In a series of some one hundred stories, Ovid provides a compendium of classical mythology. He imposes on these myths a chronological structure, moving from the creation of the world to the Rome of Caesar Augustus, and a controlling theme—the universality of change.

Metamorphoses is a handbook of classical mythology, containing such well-known stories as those of Pygmalion, Jason and Medea, Apollo and Daphne, Pyramus and Thisbe, and Hercules. Virtually all these legends were well-known before Ovid, but it is Ovid's version that is most familiar today.

This is so because Ovid is a brilliant story-teller, and his characters come alive. In earlier versions of the myths, human actors appeared to be mere pawns of the gods and hence lacking in realism. Ovid's characters, though, are motivated by love, fear, and hate. They thus seem three-dimensional, all the more so because they reveal their psychological states and their thoughts in dramatic monologues.

While one may open Metamorphoses at random and read with pleasure, Ovid envisioned the work as a unified whole. One source of unity is his chronological ordering of the tales, which begin with the emergence of the universe from primordial chaos and end with the prediction of the deification of Caesar Augustus.

Another unifying element is the theme of change. Gods change into animals, women change into trees and birds, heroes become constellations or divinities. Beneath these mythological accounts is the realization that in this world nothing endures; everything is subject to mutability.

Metamorphoses seeks to entertain rather than to instruct, despite the lengthy philosophizing in the final book. Yet it does suggest the proper way to live. True love can transform stone to flesh (Pygmalion; Deucalion and Pyrrha), while sensuality without love can effect the opposite change (the daughters of Propoetus). Love, then, is another unifying theme, for Metamorphoses is an epic not about heroic deeds but about true love, which at once links man to nature and allows him to transform it.

THE METAMORPHOSIS
Franz Kafka
1915
Novella
Magic Realist

A traveling salesman awakens one morning to find himself transformed into a hideous dung beetle in this bizarre, understated tale that is one of the few works published by Kafka during his lifetime.

For five years, Gregor Samsa has been an exemplary employee and a dutiful son and brother, the sole support of the family since the failure of his father's business. When an extraordinary physiological change prevents him for the first time from catching the early train to work, Gregor's manager is immediately outside his bedroom demanding an explanation.

Gregor's situation, like Kafka's universe, is inscrutable, and the story, presented in three sections, details the changing dynamics of Gregor's relationship to his family. Out of work and dependent on the goodwill of the others, particularly sister Grete, Gregor increasingly comes to regard himself as a repulsive burden.

In late March at 3 a.m., after three months of accumulated evidence that it would be best for all if he simply ceased to exist, Gregor expires. Father, mother, and sister acquire new vitality and celebrate with a trip to the countryside.

The metamorphosis of the title is not simply Gregor's dehumanizing mutation. It also refers to the changing status of his father, whose self-esteem bears an inverse relationship to his son's. Drawing on his own troubled filial ties, Kafka focuses on the violent tensions between father and son.

This novella is one of the supreme embodiments of early 20th century anxieties over the powerlessness and alienation of the individual in an irrational universe. Its intensity is heightened by a severely understated style and by presenting most details through Gregor's baffled but trustful point of view. It offers a distinctively Kafkaesque parody of salvation from individual guilt and solitude.

MIDDLE PASSAGE
Charles Johnson
1990
Novel
Historical, African American

A page-turning metaphysical sea story by the author of The Sorcerer's Apprentice *and* Being and Race: Black Writing Since 1970.

Charles Johnson's *Middle Passage* is several books in one. To begin with, it is the superbly told story of Rutherford Calhoun, raconteur, thief, and philosopher. In 1829, twenty-two years old and newly freed from slavery, Rutherford leaves Illinois for the exotic charms of New Orleans. Within a matter of months he finds himself deeply in debt and scheduled to be married to Isadora Bailey, a kind-hearted, well-educated, reform-minded, and very proper girl from a free Negro family in Boston. To escape this fate (he likes Isadora but has no desire to be married or to be reformed), Rutherford stows away aboard the *Republic*, a slave ship embarking for Africa on April 14, 1830. The book purports to be his retrospective journal of the voyage and its aftermath.

Once started, Rutherford's narrative is difficult to put down; with the twists of its plot and the sheer gusto of its telling, *Middle Passage* demands, on a first reading, to be devoured in one long, late-into-the-night session. It is a compelling adventure story with a Shakespearean villain, the despotic Captain Ebenezer Falcon, and a mystery at its center: the Allmuseri, an African people of great antiquity and wisdom. It is a meditation on the horrors of slavery and the experience of black Americans. It is also an exercise in literary legerdemain: By various devices (chiefly the use of anachronisms), Johnson allows his late-twentieth century voice to break into the narrative without destroying its fabric. At another level, this adventure story is a metaphysical parable revealing the attraction to Eastern thought that also informed Johnson's earlier novel *Oxherding Tale*. At yet another level, *Middle Passage* is Johnson's tribute to and argument with some worthy predecessors, among them Herman Melville's *Benito Cereno* and John Gardner's novella *The King's Indian*. The result is a rich, multilayered book which should win for Charles Johnson the larger audience he deserves.

MIDDLEMARCH
George Eliot
1871-1872
Novel
Victorian

Set in the 1830's, this rich and complex novel deals with the attempts of a group of young men and women to overcome the social and intellectual limitations of a provincial English town and to give moral purpose to their lives.

The principal plot line in this novel—there are at least four—recounts the sometimes misdirected efforts of Dorothea Brooke to give meaning to her life by dedicating it to some worthy and significant cause. Mistakenly thinking that he is a "guide who would take her along the grandest path," Dorothea marries Mr. Casaubon, a narrow and mean-spirited pedant. She is saved from the worst consequences of this marriage by Mr. Casaubon's timely death and eventually finds happiness in marrying Mr. Casaubon's nephew Will Ladislaw. However, Dorothea is able to exert her moral impulses only in very limited personal situations rather than on the large social scale of which she was potentially capable.

Balanced against this plot line is the story of Tertius Lydgate, a young doctor whose ambition to achieve significant medical reform is frustrated by his disastrous marriage to a beautiful but utterly self-centered wife. Other plot lines focus on Fred Vincy, a pleasant but rather aimless young man, who is led to some seriousness of purpose through his love for a sensible girl, and on Nicholas Bulstrode, an aspiring community leader who attempts—unsuccessfully—to conceal a past life as a dealer in stolen goods by conspicuous and assertive piety.

Unquestionably one of the finest achievements in Victorian fiction, *Middlemarch* combines a panorama of provincial society with a multitude of extraordinarily detailed and psychologically incisive portraits of individual characters. The struggles of these characters, limited by their own weaknesses, self-deceptions, and errors, as well as by circumstances beyond their control, illuminate the issues of social and moral responsibility that lie at the heart of George Eliot's fiction.

MIDNIGHT'S CHILDREN
Salman Rushdie
1981
Novel
Magical Realism

This magical-realist novel dramatizes the horror of partitioning India and Pakistan during 1947, and the subsequent difficulties. Told from the point of view of a Kashmiri Muslim, this tripartite novel won many literary awards, including the 1981 Booker Prize.

The book's title refers to children born between midnight and 1:00 a.m. on August 15, 1947, when partition went into effect; they are prophetic children of a new era, gifted with uncanny powers.

In Mumbai (Bombay), blue-eyed Saleem Sinai, born exactly at midnight with a cucumber-sized nose, is the first child of this new era. Due to a finger accident, it's discovered his blood type does not run in his family. From the hospital, he is sent to live with Uncle Hanif and Aunt Pia.

Saleem discovers Shiva (with whom he was switched at birth) was born with a pair of enormous knees, plus a gift for warfare. When Saleem returns to his parents, the distraught Hanif commits suicide. At the funeral, Mary, a midwife, confesses to having switched the infants.

Saleem's mother, Amina, flees from her husband Ahmed's alcoholism, taking Saleem and his younger singer-sister "Brass Monkey" to Pakistan, lodging with Emerald. Saleem observes Emerald's husband, General Zulfikar, stage a coup against the government. Zulfikar enforces martial law.

Four years later, Ahmed dies; Amina returns to Mumbai where Saleem has a nose operation to improve his breathing; his telepathic powers vanish, yet he gains a sense of smell that identifies people's emotions. When India loses its war with China, the family relocates to Pakistan, but during bombing raids from India, his mother is killed; Saleem suffers a head injury, erasing his identity.

Saleem is drafted as an army tracker. In Bangladesh, he witnesses massacres. Fleeing to the forest, Saleem befriends Parvati-the-witch, one of midnight's children, who helps him recover his identity, and enables his escape to India. Saleem telepathically reconnects to childhood friends and hundreds of midnight's children.

Saleem lives with Parvati in the magician's ghetto. Miffed that Saleem will not marry her, Parvati becomes pregnant from Shiva. Ostracized, Saleem agrees to marry Parvati. After their son's birth, the government bulldozes their ghetto; Parvati is murdered. Shiva arrests Saleem, and has him sterilized. Imprisoned, Saleem eventually discloses the names of all the midnight children who are then sterilized because their powers threaten Prime Minister Indira Gandhi. They are freed when Gandhi loses the election.

Saleem marries Padma, a guard at Mary's chutney factory.

A MIDSUMMER NIGHT'S DREAM
William Shakespeare
1595
Drama
Comedy

On a magical Midsummer Eve, two lovers, Hermia and Lysander, flee parental constraint and arrive in an enchanted forest where the activities of humans and fairies collide.

Four distinct circles of characters meet and overlap in this comedy of marriage, merriment, magic, and imagination. The occasion is the marriage of Duke Theseus of Athens to the Amazon Queen, Hippolyta. As lawgiver, Theseus must settle a romantic dispute. The young lovers Hermia and Lysander want to marry, but Hermia's father wants her to wed Demetrius instead. Helena, Hermia's dearest friend, loves Demetrius. Theseus supports the father's stance: Hermia is told to marry Demetrius or else decide between a nunnery and death.

Rather than obey, Hermia flees with Lysander. Demetrius sets off in pursuit of his betrothed, while the infatuated Helena follows. Far from the strictured world of court and city, the four lose themselves in a dream-dominated, spirit-haunted wood. The forest spirits are divided by a quarrel between Oberon, the king of the fairies, and his queen Titania. The dissension soon entangles the human lovers as well.

Oberon gives the mischievous sprite Puck a vial of magic potion to sprinkle into the eyes of Titania so that when she wakes she will be enamored of whomever she first sees. The fairy queen wakes to fall in love with Bottom, a weaver who has ventured into the wood with his fellow mechanicals to practice their play of Pyramus and Thisbe. Bottom, given an ass's head by the madcap Puck, is comic indeed. The sight of Titania caressing and crooning over this farcical monster softens Oberon, who frees her from the spell and sets the other lovers to rights.

With harmony in fairyland comes harmony in Athens. Out early, Theseus and Hippolyta come upon the waking lovers, and Theseus decides to overturn his first decision and pair the lovers as they desire. The comedy concludes with the three marriages solemnized, the long-awaited performance of Bottom and his fellow actors, and the fairies' blessing on the human couples.

THE MILL ON THE FLOSS
George Eliot
1860
Novel
Victorian

This nostalgic novel explores the emotional conflicts of Maggie Tulliver, an impetuous young woman whose attraction to two men conflicts with her loyalty to a family to which she is equally devoted.

The first sections of *The Mill On The Floss* are devoted to a rich evocation of the pains and conflicts of childhood. Maggie Tulliver, a child with a deep hunger for affection and approval, repeatedly acts in impetuous and careless ways that cause rejection by her narrowly self-righteous brother Tom and consternation among her opinionated aunts. As Maggie grows older, her problems intensify. When her father loses a lawsuit and subsequently suffers a stroke, the family is reduced to near poverty. Maggie's chief solace in these humiliating circumstances is meeting secretly with Philip Wakem, the son of the lawyer whom Mr. Tulliver blames for the loss of the lawsuit and for his financial difficulties. Tom discovers these meetings and harshly terminates them, blaming Maggie for disloyalty to the family. Tom is right according to the narrow terms of a family quarrel, but the sympathies of the author and reader clearly lie with Maggie.

Maggie transgresses more seriously when she allows herself to drift down the river with Stephen Guest, her cousin's fiance. According to the social code of the time, Maggie is hopelessly compromised by spending a night aboard a steamer with Stephen. By this indiscretion, she also brings unhappiness to her cousin Lucy and disgraces her family just when Tom's hard work is beginning to restore a measure of prosperity.

Maggie redeems herself—rather melodramatically—by her attempt to rescue Tom from the mill during a flood. Although both are drowned, the reconciliation of brother and sister is at least briefly achieved.

Although some aspects of the plot—especially the circumstances of Maggie's disgrace—seem remote from contemporary mores, the depiction of Maggie's struggle between the desire to do what is pleasant for herself and the demand to do what society and her family expect of her is powerful and moving. Eliot's portraits of Maggie's aunts—the Dodson sisters—brilliantly depict the rising middle class of early Victorian times.

THE MISANTHROPE
Molière
1666
Drama
Comedy

Blunt, misanthropic Alceste criticizes the shallowness and falsity of Parisian high society. This witty, ironic comedy of manners written in balanced rhymed couplets satirizes both Alceste and society.

Disgusted by fashionable society's effusive displays of politeness and phony affection, Alceste espouses honesty and plain speaking. His principles are immediately tested: The fop Oronte seeks Alceste's judgment of a sonnet dashed off in fifteen minutes. Alceste at first hedges, then criticizes the sonnet openly. Oronte is so offended that he takes Alceste to court.

A more serious test of Alceste's principles is his love for the coquette Celimene, the brightest ornament of fashionable society. Caught between his principles and his love, Alceste pursues a strange manner of courtship: He nags Celimene to change her ways.

Celimene, however, is not about to change; she too much enjoys being the center of attention and excelling at society's two-faced games, such as backbiting and coquetry. Even after her game seems up, when her other suitors expose her coquetry and walk out, she cannot abandon society. She turns down Alceste's proposal to marry and live together in the desert, so Alceste angrily heads for the desert by himself (though his friends hope to stop him).

No character represents a reasonable norm in *The Misanthrope*, not even Alceste's friends who compromise so easily and certainly not the fops or the jealous prude Arsinoe. The unhappy ending points up the ridiculous nature of Alceste's excessive reactions, while Celimene's unmasking underlines her folly.

The play's unhappy ending and lack of a character who embodies a reasonable norm illustrate Moliere's daring and complex art. Engaging one's mind, *The Misanthrope* is a mature comedy wherein folly provokes both laughter and logical consequences.

LES MISÉRABLES
Victor Hugo
1862
Novel
Historical

An essentially good man commits a series of petty crimes until an encounter with a truly holy man inspires him to a life of heroic self-sacrifice.

Jean Valjean, imprisoned for stealing a loaf of bread in late eighteenth century France, escapes years later and, after accepting the hospitality of a charitable bishop, absconds with the latter's silver. Under another identity, Valjean emerges as a village mayor who saves from the police a prostitute struggling to support her daughter Cosette. Pursued by the indefatigable Inspector Javert, Valjean confesses his true identity only when it appears that another man will go to prison in his place.

Valjean escapes again and assumes the care of the now-orphaned Cosette. When Cosette grows up to fall in love with Marius de Pontmercy, a young political activist who has drawn the pursuit of the same Javert, Valjean saves Marius' life by carrying the wounded dissident through the sewers of Paris to safety. Valjean must endure yet more rigors, however, before his goodness is acknowledged.

This long novel teems with minor characters and digressions, some of them captivating. No reader of the book will forget Gavroche, the Parisian street boy who lives by his wits, or Hugo's recapitulation of the Battle of Waterloo, though it is mere background to one relationship in the story.

While abounding in the farfetched coincidences and melodramatic scenes that nineteenth century readers relished more than their modern counterparts do, this 1862 novel avoids the sentimentality of its age. Furthermore, Hugo's firm authorial presence, his talent for making history live, his sympathy for the downtrodden, and, above all, his conviction of the capacity of human goodness to triumph against great obstacles will continue to endear him to new generations of readers. The relentless Javert, the noble Marius, the sweetly devoted Cosette, and the impregnable Valjean remain as fascinating as ever.

Norman Denny's translation for Penguin Books is an eminently readable modern English version of the novel.

THE MISMEASURE OF MAN
Stephen Jay Gould
1981
Nonfiction
Scientific

A thoroughgoing debunking of the errors of craniometry and intelligence testing as aspects of biological determinism and its social prejudices, The Mismeasure of Man *received accolades for its treatment of the controversies which perennially surround the testing and measurement of man's intelligence—and thus his "nature." It deserves reading and pondering for its scope, for its honesty of approach, and for what it exposes as prejudice and even deliberate deception, as well as a testimonial to the author's effort to see things as they really are, without the racist and sexist assumptions which have distorted so much human thought.*

In the midst of his technical and highly statistical summaries, Gould interjects anecdotes and observations about his own life, about his son's learning disability, and about his wife, his colleagues, and his students at Harvard. *The*

Mismeasure of Man is objective and impersonal where it needs to be but personal and human in overall tone and attitude. Gould's shifts in diction, from formal and technical scientific language to informal and even colloquial phrases and asides, make *The Mismeasure of Man* all the more accessible to the ordinary reader.

First, Gould sees science advancing by means of the replacement of ideas, not by the addition of them. Second, scientific debunking must truly increase knowledge and not merely replace one social prejudice for another one. An ailment such as pellagra, for example, can only be cured if it can be proved to be the result of a vitamin deficiency and not a genetic disorder inherent in poor people. Finally, as an evolutionary biologist, Gould believes that Darwin's central truth is the evolutionary unity of humans with all other organisms. Thus, man's narcissism and arrogance is much out of place.

Apart from his conclusion, and another historical chapter, Gould presents his case in five long, complex but provocative chapters. The first deals with American craniometry before Darwin, focusing on the scientific racism of Louis Agassiz as a theorist of polygeny, and Samuel George Morton as the empiricist practitioner. An ensuing chapter deals with Paul Broca's research at the height of the popularity of craniology. Broca, along with Francis Galton, speculated about the brain sizes and shapes and the characters of both eminent men and criminals. Gould then turns to the measurement of body types and Cesare Lombroso's farfetched but catchy theory of *l'uomo delinquene*—the criminal man—one of the most influential theories of criminal anthropology. Gould then investigates the related subject of mental testing, the work of Alfred Binet in IQ testing and the subsequent erroneous applications of his work by H. H. Goddard, who coined the term "moron" and resorted to trick photographs to prove his point; Lewis M. Terman, who began testing for IQ on masses of people and advanced some categorical assertions which he only reluctantly recanted; and of R. M. Yerkes and his grand scheme of utilizing soldiers to establish once and for all absolute degrees of intelligence—only to overlook obvious variables of the environment's impact on his subjects. A final chapter deals with the faked statistical evidence of Sir Cyril Burt and his staunch belief in the innateness and hereditarianism of intelligence—so biased a belief that even his collaborators were imaginary.

All in all, Gould unveils an amazing number of logical and procedural fallacies, a startling number of instances of outright prejudice and bigotry among allegedly objective researchers; and once again dramatizes how professional ambitions can skew data and results. Most of the instances of mis-measurement which Gould recounts can be regarded as nothing less than outrageous and, insofar as theory touched actual lives, regrettable, monumental mistakes.

Writing as both a scientist and a historian, Stephen Jay Gould takes a decidedly unconventional approach. His work is impeccably argued yet refreshingly humane, even if not very "scientific." Certainly future generations will benefit from Gould's detective work in *The Mismeasure of Man*. It is unfortunate that the scientists about whose work this book is written and their subjects and societies cannot do the same.

MISS JULIE
August Strindberg
1889
Drama
Tragedy

This play, generally regarded as one of the best examples of naturalism, demonstrates that people's characters and destinies are determined by their heredity and environment. It also contains what may be the most acutely concentrated portrayal of the sexual struggle in all of literature.

The plot combines sexual and social clashes. Miss Julie is the 25-year-old daughter of the widowed landowner of a large estate in the Swedish countryside. Her father's weak nature has taught her to despise men; her emancipated mother taught her to dominate and tyrannize them; her former fiance filled her with egalitarian notions that temper her arrogance; her strong libido checks her masculine inclination; her unconscious drives lead her toward dirt, degradation, and death.

The action has Julie flirt with and erotically provoke her father's valet, 30-year-old Jean, in the festive atmosphere of Midsummer's Eve. The dramatic design is that of a neatly executed crossover: Julie the social aristocrat condescends to Jean the upstart social slave; conversely, Jean becomes her sexual master; they meet on the leveling grounds of seduction, in the arms of that great equalizer, sex. The materialistic Jean then suggests that they avoid scandal at home by fleeing to Switzerland and running a hotel at Lake Como. However, the 35-year-old cook Kristin, engaged to Jean, prevents the lovers from leaving before the return of Julie's absent father.

In a conclusion open to contrasting interpretations, the desperate Julie begs Jean to order her to slash her throat. He puts the razor in her hand, and she "walks firmly out through the door," on her way to suicide. From a naturalistic perspective, her end signifies his triumph; he has defeated her sexually and is unscrupulous and opportunistic enough to advance his fortunes over opponents' bodies. From the perspective of Aristotelian tragic criteria, however, it is Julie who wins a moral victory through her honorable death. She may be morbidly masochistic, but she shows herself capable of assuming responsibility for her behavior and ending her flawed life nobly.

MRS. DALLOWAY
Virginia Woolf
1925
Novel
Psychological, Feminist

Following a single day in the life of a London society woman, juxtaposed with that of her double, a shell-shocked veteran, the novel explores the disparity between trivial external events and the rich play of human consciousness.

This novel follows Clarissa Dalloway on a June day in London as she takes care of last-minute arrangements for a party at her home that evening. An apparently happy, superficial society hostess, Clarissa is revealed through her thoughts as extremely sensitive to experience, aware not only of the beauties but of the horrors and dangers of daily life. Her day consists of small happenings to which the novel attributes major significance. She receives a surprise visit from her former suitor and reflects on her reasons for choosing her husband. When her husband accepts a luncheon invitation that excludes her, she feels resentful and alone. Learning of the suicide of a shell-shocked World War I survivor, Stephen Septimus Smith, she sympathizes with his defiance of authority figures who would force the soul. In accepting her emotional kinship with Septimus, Clarissa is able both to come to terms with death and to embrace life. With renewed vitality, Clarissa attends her party.

Contrasted with Clarissa's musings and mundane activities are the terrified hallucinations and apocalyptic visions of Stephen Septimus Smith. In a sense, however, Clarissa's and Septimus' thoughts show not only contrast but kinship: Stephen's conviction that the skywriting of an airplane is a secret message is removed only by degree from Clarissa's vision of an old lady extinguishing a light as a reminder of death. For Clarissa, as for Septimus, the world threatens to dissolve at any moment; and so, she sews material together, assembles people, and organizes events.

Accompanying both Clarissa and Stephen throughout the day are reminders of mortality. Their thoughts are punctuated by the chiming of Big Ben, which notes the passing of external time, impervious to human experience and oblivious of death. In addition Clarissa keeps remembering the line from Cymbeline, "Fear no more the heat o' the sun," which, as a reflection on death, both frightens and comforts her. Through the use of these recurrent motifs and of a narrative voice that moves into and out of diverse minds, the novel develops that theme that the individual life, like the art that records it, is but a fragile human construct, a thin envelope to contain the formless if fascinating tissue of experience.

MOBY DICK
Herman Melville
1851
Novel
Adventure, Philosophical

Although literally an adventure novel about whaling, Moby Dick *is in fact a metaphysical romance about the nature of reality and man's place in the world.*

The novel focuses on Captain Ahab's complex quest to find and kill the huge white whale, Moby Dick, that has physically robbed him of his leg and metaphorically deprived him of his manhood, of his sense of individual importance and identity. Set in the mid-19th century during the heyday of American whaling, the story is told by Ishmael. His own quest for "the ungraspable phantom of life" parallels Ahab's for the white whale. His style of storytelling, which includes action, meditative passages, exposition on whales and whaling, dramatic scenes modeled on Shakespeare, high tragedy and low comedy, is as various and as unstable as Melville's watery world.

As Ahab becomes increasingly drawn to and obsessed by the whale, Ishmael becomes similarly attracted to the monomaniacal captain, who is at once a tyrant and a tragic hero. Ahab's greatness arises from his insatiable need to do battle with and to know the most dangerous and the most legendary of all whales, a natural as well as supernatural creature that Ahab comes to view as the embodiment of evil in the world. To accomplish his goal, the wily Ahab first has to seduce his crew into accepting his quest as their own.

Of the Pequod's crew, only Starbuck, the first mate, withholds his support, attempting unsuccessfully to convince Ahab of the wrongness of his quest (since his antagonist is a mere brute) and of the essential goodness of creation. Failing to heed Starbuck's appeal, Ahab dies, his neck caught in his own whale line, caught, that is, in the fate he has unwittingly yet inexorably fashioned for himself by defining too narrowly the white whale and the world of which it is a part.

Ishmael, on the other hand, survives because unlike Ahab he achieves a healthy balance of Ahab's skepticism (even nihilism) and Starbuck's faith, of the tragic and the comic, of self and society. For Ishmael, as for Melville, life is an unending series of voyages out, whose meaning lies beyond the comprehension of even the noblest of men.

A MODEST PROPOSAL
Jonathan Swift
1729
Nonfiction
Satire

Swift's wickedly ironic essay satirizes the often brutal treatment of Ireland by England during the early 18th century, in part by creating an unforgettable fictional character who is rational, well-intentioned, and yet shockingly inhuman.

The essay begins innocently by establishing the speaker as a concerned citizen genuinely sympathetic to the Irish poor, whose suffering he describes in moving detail. Most readers no doubt find the voice of this speaker strikingly familiar: Like a politician, social scientist, or committee chairperson, he presents himself as sensitive, knowledgeable, and confident in his ability to resolve a serious problem by rational analysis.

The reader's confidence in the speaker vanishes quickly after the first few paragraphs, however, as Swift engineers one of the most shocking moments in all of English literature. The modest proposal, humbly presented and drafted at great length, argues for the many advantages of the Irish people raising their children as food to be sold at great profit to the landlords throughout the kingdom. Far from being horrified by this suggestion, as the reader surely is, the speaker continues to imagine himself as a disinterested patriot offering his countrymen a practical and almost miraculously effective way to reduce poverty, overpopulation, and an unfavorable balance of trade with England.

The most powerfully ironic aspect of this essay is rather obvious. The modest proposal is of course anything but modest: It is savage, frightening, perhaps even insane. But other subtle ironies and satiric targets may be overlooked if the speaker is simply dismissed as an extravagant madman. Most important, Swift characterizes him as rational and calculating in order to show that these qualities are dangerous when taken to an extreme: People who rely on speculative reason to solve problems may end up thinking the unthinkable rather than following what should be more natural and humane impulses of common sense and compassion, and those who treat humans as numbers rather than as living beings—recall how often the speaker in the essay computes and quantifies—are only one short step away from making it easier to murder them.

MOLL FLANDERS
Daniel Defoe
1722
Novel
Picaresque

The subtitle of this early English novel is its own best summary: Moll was "born in Newgate, and during a life of continued variety, for threescore years, besides her childhood, was twelve years a Whore, five time a Wife (thereof once to her own brother), twelve years a Thief, eight years a transported Felon in Virginia, at last grew rich, lived honest, and died a penitent."

Besides encapsulating the plot, the subtitle also provides a clue to the book's moral irony: Moll is one of the few literary figures who has her cake and eats it too. Far from being punished for her crimes, she is instead rewarded for them.

Purportedly Moll's memoirs, written in a lively, plain, and colloquial style, the narrative is an example of the picaresque novel, a series of rambling, often disconnected episodes concerning the picaro, a young, homeless scamp who lives by his wits on either side of the law as the opportunity arises.

As a female picaro, Moll survives the perils of the outcast in 18th century London. She steals, she seduces, she marries if necessary. The realism of Moll's adventures and of her character is the secret to the book's greatness. For all her materialistic ambitions, for all her hardheaded concern for things—watches, handkerchiefs, silks, petticoats, coins—Moll is filled with vitality; life is never depressing but strangely exciting and exhilarating.

Her gusto is largely the reason for her success; when she finally attains respectability, Moll can enjoy the luxury of repentance. Thus Defoe offers an ironic commentary on the rise of the middle class.

THE MOONSTONE
Wilkie Collins
1868
Novel
Detective

In this prototypical detective novel, the memorable Sergeant Cuff of Scotland Yard pursues myriad clues to trace the disappearance of the fabulous Moonstone.

The Moonstone diamond, stolen by John Herncastle at the fall of Seringapatan, India, in 1799 and bequeathed to his niece, Rachel Verinder, gives the novel its title. Its history, value, and disappearance prompt much of the work's action.

When Franklin Blake, Rachel's distant cousin, brings the moonstone to her for her birthday, it disappears. The list of suspects includes Franklin, Rachel herself, who obstructs the investigation to shield Franklin, and a trio of Indians sworn to return the stone to its sacred setting.

Rachel's engagement to Godfrey Ablewhite ends abruptly when his gold-digging motives surface. Sergeant Cuff helps expose Ablewhite as an opportunist. Cuff also traces the diamond to a pawnbroker, a murdered sailor (Ablewhite in disguise), and clears the Hindus; but he does not recover the gem.

Collins gradually reveals, through a succession of narrators, that Rachel saw Franklin take the gem while he was sedated. Franklin gave it to Ablewhite to hold, and forgot he had done so once he awoke. Years later, once Franklin and Rachel have been married for some time, a traveler reports having seen the gem in the forehead of an Indian idol.

Collins not only fashioned the first highly wrought detective novel but also developed a prototypical figure in Sergeant Cuff, whose passion for growing roses gives him the touch of eccentricity characteristic of many of the most famous fictional detectives. Collins' skill in plot construction, complete with the obligatory Victorian cliff-hanger chapter endings, is matched by his individualization of characters such as Cuff, arguably his most fully realized creation. Rachel vies for top billing in the novel: She is a spirited, intelligent, articulate, independent woman, a rare presence in nineteenth century fiction. Collins' other characters, especially the feckless Franklin Blake and the opportunistic Godfrey Ablewhite, play superb supporting roles in this drama of mystery and love.

LE MORTE D'ARTHUR
Thomas Malory
1485
Novel
Arthurian, Historical

This classic wellspring of English Arthurian literature chronicles the legendary birth, coming to kingship, life, exploits, and passing of Arthur, the once and future king.

Sir Thomas Malory, knight, adventurer, and soldier, composed this series of tales during nearly twenty years of imprisonment (ca. 1450-1471) and rendered into English the varied 13th century French stories of Merlin, Arthur, Camelot, the knights of the Round Table, and the Holy Grail. In so doing, he created a national treasure and a narrative central to English literature.

The work is filled with action in battle, passion in love, and wisdom in governing. At its center is an event that marks the beginning of the Round Table's breakup, the Quest for the Holy Grail. Galahad and Percival achieve the Grail Quest; Lancelot, because of his unworthiness, does not; Bors returns with Lancelot to tell the tale, and the fellowship loses two of its best knights, Galahad and Percival. Then follows Gawain's accusation against Queen Guinevere in "The Poisoned Apple," and the dissolution of the fellowship accelerates until the final battle, in which Arthur is mortally wounded.

Magic and the supernatural pervade the work from its outset, when Arthur pulls the sword from the stone, through the mystic adventures of the Grail, to the mysterious passing of Arthur, who some say shall yet come again.

Malory combines heroic and epic elements to celebrate England's golden age of chivalry, national ideals of unity, power, and civility, and the high code of knightly conduct.

MUCH ADO ABOUT NOTHING
William Shakespeare
1598
Drama
Comedy

This play, set in Messina, Italy, and dealing with mistaken identity, deceit, and cunning, stands out as one of the wittiest and most beguiling of all of Shakespeare's comedies.

From its opening lines to its final scene, *Much Ado About Nothing* is a feast of wit and verve. The play's humor runs from slapstick to subtle wordplay, and it features Shakespeare's wittiest couple, Beatrice and Benedick.

The plot consists of two interwoven love stories: those of Beatrice and Benedick, and that of Claudio and Hero. Claudio, accompanying his friend, Don Pedro to Messina, is smitten with the lovely Hero, daughter of Leonato, governor of Messina. To help his friend, Don Pedro assumes Claudio's identity at a masked ball and woos Hero. In the meantime, Don John, bastard brother of Don Pedro, does his worst to undermine the love affair by convincing Claudio that Hero is unfaithful.

Benedick, another friend of Don Pedro, has arrived in Messina a confirmed bachelor, ridiculing men who succumb to marriage. Equally opposed to marriage is Beatrice, Leonato's niece, the verbal jousting partner of Benedick. The fireworks between these two spark the play. Don Pedro, Hero, Claudio, and Leonato all conspire to bring this unlikely couple together.

The plot speeds to its climax on Hero and Claudio's wedding day as Don John's deceit convinces all but Beatrice and Benedick. When Don John's evil plot is exposed in a hilarious report by the constable, Dogberry, Claudio is led to believe that his foolish acceptance of Don John's lies about Hero has led to her death. One remaining plot twist awaits the repentant Claudio. After he consents to marry Leonato's niece, he learns that Hero in fact is alive. A double wedding ensues.

MURDER IN THE CATHEDRAL
T. S. Eliot
1935
Drama
Historical

This treatment of Archbishop Thomas Becket's murder in the 12th century offers rich insights into the nature of faith, temptation, and martyrdom.

Written in an engaging mixture of styles and tones, this play begins with a chorus and several priests heralding Thomas Becket's return from France to Canterbury. England has clearly suffered hardships during Becket's absence, but the action of the play is intended to show how suffering can be redeemed when it is seen as part of a divine pattern, how it can be an act of devotion.

Upon his return, Beckett quickly confronts the wiles of four tempters. Their temptations include sensual pleasures, political power, and revenge against the King, all of which Becket promptly rejects.

The fourth tempter's lure is more subtle: He offers Becket the glory of his own martyrdom. In this crucial moment, Becket recognizes that his actions and motivations must be subsumed within the will of God, and that the most grievous sin would be to will his own death and his own glory. Becket surrenders himself completely to the divine pattern that governs the world, and thus escapes the final temptation.

This theme of individual and divine will dominate the second part of the play, in which Becket overrules his priests' entreaties to bar the assassin knights from the door of the church. Becket calls upon his followers to trust in divine will and look beyond the earthly consequences of human actions. It is this wisdom, which is contrasted to the knights' deceptive (and entertaining) justifications for having killed Becket in the end, that forms the center of this rewarding and varied work.

MURDER ON THE ORIENT EXPRESS
Agatha Christy
1934
Novel
Detective

Years after the kidnap and murder of three-year-old Daisy Armstrong, a group of the bereaved hatch a plan to see that her killer meets justice. In an extraordinary act, they literally stage an elaborate plan that would have gone off without a hitch had Detective Hercule Poirot not boarded the train.

When Detective Hercule Poirot boards the Calais Coach on the Orient Express in an unexpected, spur of the moment, journey to London, he finds that all the first class berths have been taken—something unheard of during the winter months. It appears that the train's passengers are from all walks of life, every socioeconomic class, and from a striking array of nationalities.

Early in the journey, Mr. Samuel Edward Ratchett approaches Poirot, asking for his protection and help in determining who is threatening to murder him. Poirot refuses, claiming, "I do not like your face Mr. Ratchett." On the second night of the journey, Ratchett is found murdered—stabbed twelve times—and the train is at a standstill, stuck in a snowdrift. Poirot must determine who committed the murder— someone still aboard the stranded train.

Through an extraordinary act of sleuthing, Poirot determines that Ratchett was the infamous Cassetti, who kidnapped and murdered sweet little Daisy Armstrong. Poirot then interviews each individual aboard the train, and determines that each of the passengers has a secret identity, or was in some fashion, closely associated with the Armstrong family. With scant evidence, Poirot deduces the identity of Ratchett's killers.

Several real-life, historical events influenced Agatha Christie's plot. The Armstrong case reflects the kidnapping and murder of Charles and Anne Morrow Lindbergh's son in 1932, just a few years before the book's publication. Christie herself traveled aboard the Orient Express, and was stranded for twenty-four hours due to weather. Christie penned the novel while visiting Istanbul, Turkey.

THE MURDERS IN THE RUE MORGUE
Edgar Allan Poe
1841
Short Story
Detective, Gothic

In what is usually considered the first detective story, Poe's famous French detective, C. Auguste Dupin, solves, through logical analysis, a double homicide that baffles the Parisian police.

The first of three of Poe's tales involving Dupin, "The Murders in the Rue Morgue" is set in Paris, primarily on the fictional Rue Morgue. Poe begins the story with some observations on logical analysis by analogy to games such as chess and checkers; he continues the theme by having Dupin display his thought processes, which have the "air of intuition," as he appears to read the narrator's mind while they talk. This long introductory passage with its numerous allusions and obscure references prepares readers for Dupin's solution to the murders which confound the Parisian gendarmes.

Dupin and the narrator first learn from an evening newspaper of the atrocity, the murders of Madame L'Espanaye and her daughter Camille. Newspaper accounts the next day carry depositions by acquaintances of the victims and people in the vicinity where the crime took place; these conflicting accounts and the absence of evidence lead the narrator and the police to consider the crime insolvable.

Dupin, however, places a cryptic advertisement in a newspaper after having inspected the house where the woman and her daughter died. When a sailor in search of a missing orangutan responds to the newspaper advertisement, Dupin has his solution to the murders. Then, for the benefit of the perplexed narrator, the police, and the reader, he explains the clues that led him to the solution.

Dupin's analytic method of solving the crime has made the tale a classic in the detective-mystery genre. As the first detective in fiction, Dupin is the prototype of Arthur Conan Doyle's famous sleuth, Sherlock Holmes.

MUSÉE DES BEAUX ARTS
W. H. Auden
1940
Poetry
Mythology

A meditation on a 16th century painting by Pieter Brueghel the Elder, Auden's poem explores the relationship between the ordinary and the extraordinary in human existence.

The first section develops a general observation: that the Renaissance master painters understood the modest place of agony in the scale of experience. In deceptively casual lines, Auden suggests the utter apathy of most people toward the dramatic events of history. Significant happenings tend to occur in obscurity, while most humans are preoccupied with their own petty affairs.

The second section applies this general thesis to the specific case of Brueghel's *Icarus*. That painting depicts the moment in Greek myth when Icarus, the son of Daedalus, plunges into the sea after having flown too close to the sun with the wax wings fashioned for him by his father. The poet notes that, though the fall of Icarus is something very special, Brueghel, like the characters in his painting, treats it as a minor background detail.

The poem consists of two unequal stanzas, the first of 13 lines and the second of 8. The meter is irregular, the lines are of varying length, rarely end-stopped, and the style is conversational—consistent with the poem's theme of nonchalance toward the spectacular.

Written during the early stages of a devastating world war, the poem uses colloquialisms such as "anyhow" and "behind" (as an anatomical noun) to reinforce the sense of universal ingenuousness, of widespread ignorance of and indifference to the cunning forces of history.

MY ÁNTONIA
Willa Cather
1918
Novel
Historical, Regionalist

In this moving, realistic portrayal of the pioneer experience, Antonia Shimerda's struggles in reaching womanhood on the Nebraska frontier are narrated by her childhood friend Jim Burden.

Antonia immigrates as a girl with her family from Bohemia to a homestead on the open plains. The hardships of attempting to farm the raw land drive her sensitive father to suicide, and, as a young teenager, Antonia is forced to endure hard physical labor in helping to work the farm.

Like many other daughters of the farming immigrants, Antonia becomes a servant girl to an established family in the small town of Black Hawk, with her wages sent to her older brother to help support her family on the homestead. In town, she is able to participate in social activities such as dances and parties, and these gatherings become the focus of her life. She meets a man who works as a conductor on the railroad, and she runs away with him in the belief that he will marry her. However, he deserts her with child, and, in shame, she returns to the grueling hard work of her brother's farm.

Willa Cather's portrayal of the great presence of the prairie, which is converted during Antonia's lifetime from open expanse to productive farmland, serves as a powerful background to Antonia's struggles. Although Antonia faces severe hardship, she remains strong, responding openheartedly to her simple life, which centers on child rearing and family concerns. At the close of the novel, Jim Burden visits her after a twenty-year absence, and he discovers her happily married to a local farmer and caring for her large family. Her courage has enabled her to become a mature woman of dignity and strength.

MY NAME IS RED
Umberto Eco
1998
Novel

Part murder mystery, part sexy romance, but mostly an engaging meditation on the clash of Eastern and Western artistic traditions

That *My Name Is Red* is mostly about a character called Black is the kind of irony that characterizes this whole novel, a murder mystery set within a very confined group of miniaturists, who were in their twilight period in 1591. These painters and craftsmen work for the Ottoman sultan Murad III, illustrating the manuscripts that glorify his victories and rule. Murad III was a munificent patron of their art, however, the golden glow of the era comes from the sun setting on an artistic tradition that had spread, along with the precious secret of red ink, from China across Central Asia to Turkey over the course of many centuries and countless wars. Now the miniaturists' traditions are under attack, and murder is the least of their problems. They are a doomed lot, and the book provides a "melancholy elegy to the inspiration, talent, and patience of all the masters who'd painted and illuminated in these lands over the years."

This storyteller sits calmly at the heart of this novel, which has no single "storyteller," but a series of narratorsm. Characters pass the story from one to the next, and back again. They address the reader and point out the inconsistencies and implausibilities of the story, as one would expect in a postmodernist work. It is not just the dead that talk directly to the reader, but the color red, as well as series of drawings, all of which are given voice by the coffeehouse storyteller. It just so happens that these are the same images that the miniaturists were painting for the sultan's secret project. Thus, in a way, the novel in the reader's hands *is* the secret project. Pictures are not the only representational art, after all. Storytelling, too, is deeply distrusted because it replaces the Creator's world with the writer's, which is seen as a blasphemous challenge to Allah.

Murder opens the book and throws the reader right into the quagmire of human nature and its relation to evil. Black, returning from the long wars that have finally brought peace to the empire, thinks of the sultan's workshop of miniaturists and artisans as a kind of paradise he was ejected from because of love. Black retains some of that original innocence, which is why Shekure loves him, initially, yet he presents his uncle with the brass inkpot—"Purely for red"—that will later be used to kill him.

Throughout the novel, the narrative voice is lively and engaging, but the characters are not always easily differentiated, especially in the portions of the book taken up with historical and aesthetic argument. Because of the repetition and overlap, these long stretches often slow the story down. The focus on ideas means, too, that the workshop-centered world of the miniaturist is not rendered as vividly as it could have been. Fortunately, there is considerable drama inherent in the romance, especially since it is not at all certain whether Black will end up with Shekure or in the hands of the Sultan's executioners. Pamuk, who has graced one of the boys with his own name, writes about children very convincingly and uses them to add even more tension to the plot. The story becomes bogged down in so much discussion that, by the end, it may not really matter who the murderer is, but everyone should be happy that Black and Shekure manage to have a long and happy marriage, as these things go.

Unfortunately, miniaturists were not so lucky and were eventually banished, a fact the book is unabashedly laments. "Thus withered the red rose of the joy of painting and illumination that had bloomed for a century in Istanbul. . . . It was mercilessly forgotten that we'd once looked upon our world quite differently."

THE MYSTERIES OF UDOLPHO
Ann Radcliffe
1794
Novel
Gothic

An avaricious nobleman imprisons an orphaned girl in a remote castle and forces her to cede him her estate. This tale established the Gothic novel as a popular literary form.

Mrs. Radcliffe was the first important novelist of terror, but her fiction is less sensational than that of later Gothic writers. She employs the same devices (characters trapped in remote locales, threatened with physical violence, prey to fears of the unknown and of mysterious events) but focuses on the heroine's shifting emotions. Often in danger but seldom in dire peril, heroine (and reader) share thrilling adventures that always end well.

Orphaned at eighteen, Emily St. Aubert lives with her aunt and plans to wed Valancourt. When her aunt marries Montoni, Emily's engagement is abruptly broken.

Montoni carries aunt and niece to the ancient mountain fortress of Udolpho. He intends to force both women to surrender their fortunes to him. Udolpho becomes a place of terror, full of strange sights, eerie sounds, and threatening events. After her aunt disappears and is reported to be dead in a dungeon, Emily accedes to Montoni's demands.

Finally rescued, Emily lives with friends at Villefort chateau, a structure as isolated and mysterious as Udolpho. Again strange events unfold, including Valancourt's apparent addiction to gambling.

All ends happily, however. The authorities arrest Montoni and return Emily's deeds. The Villefort mysteries are solved. Valancourt explains his erratic behavior, enabling Emily to marry him.

Radcliffe rationally explains all the terrifying and mystifying events that befall Emily but not until her heroine experiences the accompanying emotions. Radcliffe depicts the course of the heroine's psychology: the original tranquillity disturbed by something unexpected, the curiosity growing into anxiety and fear, the momentary terror when doom seems inevitable, and the flood of relief when Providence, hero, or novelist intervenes.

N

THE NAME OF THE ROSE
Umberto Eco
1980
Novel

A murder mystery motivated by a theological dispute and solved by the tools of logic and scholasticism, The Name of the Rose combines a murder mystery with the historical novel and succeeds brilliantly with them both.

The Name of the Rose begins with a modern hoax, as Eco presents his novel as allegedly his "Italian version of an obscure, neo-Gothic French version of a seventeenth-century Latin edition of a work written in Latin by a German monk toward the end of the fourteenth century." There is considerably more of this literary detective work in the introduction, all of it bogus, but it helps prepare the reader for Eco's blend of ratiocination, erudition, and scholarship and the formal style of the fiction to follow, and it lends a pretense that the narrative is authentic.

The narrator of the story is Adso, an aged monk looking back on the days when, as a young Benedictine novice, he was sent from Melk to an abbey in Italy. There, he came under the direction of a middle-aged Franciscan, Brother William of Baskerville, reknowned for having the finest library in Christendom but now under suspicion for harboring heretics. Adso's role as "scribe and disciple" to William is a device that allows the Franciscan to explain to the novice many things that the reader must also know; in addition, it allows Adso to play Dr. Watson to William's Sherlock Holmes.

Though the action of the novel is confined to the unnamed abbey, the narrative embraces a much larger sphere. William has come to the abbey as mediator between the Holy Roman Emperor and the notoriously corrupt Pope John XXII. He must also turn detective, for a monk has died mysteriously, and the abbot assigns William to solve the case. The sense of apocalyptic terror was endemic to the time, for the novel takes place early in the 14th century and the Black Death, when Christendom lived under a sense of impending doom.

The whodunit element is only a small part of *The Name of the Rose*. The narrative is richly textured with discussions of the often violent controversy between the Papacy and the Empire and the Papacy versus innumerable groups of alleged heretics. There are debates over poverty, the coming and identity of the Antichrist, the nature of illusion and reality, the elusiveness of truth, and such questions as whether there should be limitations to learning and whether Christ laughed. Eco provides a wealth of detail on almost every aspect of medieval life, and the narrative is an intellectual tour de force that appeals to both readers of mysteries and of historical fiction.

The story unfolds with seven seeming murders in seven days; the plot's twists and turns are difficult to follow. The climax and the motivation for murder are ingenious but perhaps overly so; despite a morbid fanaticism that will stop at nothing to preserve its version of orthodoxy, seven deaths to suppress the evidence in question are extreme even for an insane zealot. Finally discovering the cause of the killings, the reader may ask whether that is all and question whether the cause is not insufficient for the consequences.

Even so, *The Name of the Rose* provides abundant intellectual adventure to accompany the mysterious events at the monastery. In his first novel, Umberto Eco has given a virtuoso performance. Compelling as it is, it is not light reading for the casual escapist; the reader must work almost as much as William of Baskerville to fathom the intricacies of thought as well as of events.

NARRATIVE OF THE LIFE OF FREDERICK DOUGLASS
Frederick Douglass
1845
Nonfiction
Autobiographical, Historical

This 1845 autobiography recounts a life of slavery, in a factual yet artistic manner, becoming the most famous abolitionist book of its era.

The narrative opens with the declaration that the author—like any slave—does not know the day he was born. This anonymous condition of mental punishment serves to diminish self-confidence. Douglass recalls watching his aunt Hester being bloodily whipped. At about the age of seven, his mother dies and he speculates that his owner likely fathered him. Anecdotes of humiliating rapes and beatings, even casual murder, depict the slave's subservient and brutal life.

After his mother's death, Douglass is sent to Baltimore, Maryland, as a house slave. Mrs. Auld teaches Douglass the basic rudiments of reading, yet she is harshly reproved by her husband when he finds them out. Douglass realizes the importance of reading and, in secret, struggles with difficulty to master reading. Understanding the meaning of abolition provides him with hope.

When Master Auld dies, Douglass discovers that he is ranked as property like cattle. At fourteen or fifteen, Douglass is sent to St. Michael's to live with Thomas Auld. His new Methodist master is especially cruel and nearly starves his slaves. Douglass is turned over to Mr. Covey, a slave-breaker. Due to a minor hand wound, Douglass is whipped daily. While working in the fields, Douglass collapses into unconsciousness and is awakened by a fierce beating. A few days later, Covey attempts to tie Douglass up for a whipping, but Douglas fights back and overcomes him. Douglass is not punished, as this would stain the slave-breaker's reputation.

Douglass is transferred to another plantation where he teaches other slaves how to read. Douglass and his new friends plan an escape but their plans are discovered. After serving two years in jail, he is sent to Master Hugh in Baltimore where he works as an apprentice in the shipyards. After Douglass is severely gang-beaten by four whites after work, Hugh refuses to send him back to the shipyard until Sophie Auld attends Douglass' injured eye. Master Hugh attempts to find a lawyer to sue, but no white man will accept the case.

Working as a shipyard caulker, Douglass gives all his wages to Master Hugh, but he eventually finds himself a job; he lives anonymously as he saves money to escape north, which he finally accomplishes. Douglass manages to locate his fiancée and becomes an orator in the abolitionist movement.

NATIVE SON
Richard Wright
1940
Novel
Sociological, African American

This pioneering novel of black protest shows the oppression of Northern urban blacks during the 1930's. Bigger Thomas, who commits two gruesome murders, exemplifies the psychic disorders that such conditions can produce.

Bigger Thomas, a 20-year-old black man, lives in Chicago's South Side ghetto with his long-suffering mother, his younger sister Vera, and his younger brother Buddy. Unemployed, Bigger hangs out with his pals; they occasionally commit petty crimes to get spending money and prove their manhood. Bigger expresses his pent-up feelings mainly through violence.

Bigger gets a chance for a better life when the Daltons, a family of rich white liberals, hire him as a chauffeur. Disaster strikes on his first night on the job. He carries the Daltons' drunken daughter, Mary, to her bedroom, where, to prevent being caught, he accidentally smothers her with a pillow. He burns Mary's body in the furnace, then conceives a kidnap scheme for which he recruits the help of his alcoholic girlfriend, Bessie. When Mary's bones are discovered, Bigger kills Bessie to keep her quiet.

Bigger is soon apprehended and put on trial for his crimes. His white, communist lawyer, Boris Max, battles a racist prosecutor, Buckley. Connecting Mary's death with Dalton ownership of the slums that bred Bigger, Max projects Bigger's case as a paradigm of black revolution, with future armies of Biggers swarming out of the ghettos. Bigger, however, makes a pathetic revolutionary model, and Max himself is no more convincing than the other stereotyped whites. What does persuade is the novel's depiction of black frustration: Wright's portrayal of Bigger has a gripping intensity that recalls Dostoevski's *Crime And Punishment*.

THE NATURAL
Bernard Malamud
1952
Novel
Allegorical

A baseball player's fall, rise, and fall are presented in a heavily symbolic novel which uses ancient and modern myths to examine the nature of good and evil.

This novel, which retells the story of Percival, the Grail knight, and his quest to restore plenty to his desolate land, chronicles the efforts of Roy Hobbs to lead the New York Knights baseball team to the pennant.

At the beginning, Roy, nineteen, is on his way to Chicago for a tryout with the Cubs when he meets the mysterious Harriet Bird. When he can explain his purpose in life only in terms of self-interest, Harriet shoots him.

Fifteen years later, Roy attempts to comeback with the Knights and quickly establishes himself as the greatest slugger in baseball history—with the help of his magical bat, Wonderboy, suggestive of the tree of fertility, Percival's lance, and Excalibur, King Arthur's sword.

When he gives in to the temptations of the corrupt Memo Paris, however, Roy goes into a slump. He recovers through the influence of Iris Lemon, representative of fertility, life, and responsibility, but he ultimately rejects her and sells out to Memo's gambler friends. He has one more chance to redeem himself.

The wasteland-Holy Grail legend is combined with baseball history and lore, including the 1949 shooting of Eddie Waitkus, the 1919 Black Sox scandal and the consequent disgrace of Shoeless Joe Jackson, Babe Ruth's career, and "Casey at the Bat," to depict the moral complexities of contemporary American life, the opportunities for heroism offered by America, and moral obligations placed on the hero.

The sufferings of the Christlike protagonists in Malamud's novels are the ultimate tests of their humanity. Roy Hobbs fails as a hero because he does not recognize Iris's goodness or his own selfishness. He fails to grow up morally, a growth necessary to revitalize a decadent society. He fails as a baseball hero, yet his suffering can make him succeed as a man.

NAUSEA
Jean-Paul Sartre
1938
Novel
Philosophical

Presented as the fictional diary of Antoine Roquentin, Sartre's first book is a brilliantly spare existentialist probe of the themes of personal identity and the power of art.

After varied experiences throughout the world, the 30-year-old Roquentin has spent the past three years in Bouville, a dull, provincial French town. He is there to use its library, which houses the papers of an obscure 18th century figure, the Marquis de Rollebon. Roquentin intends to write Rollebon's biography and thereby find some justification for his own existence.

Roquentin's austere, solitary routines are relieved only by encounters with the Self-Taught Man, a fellow scholar who fatuously believes he is accomplishing something by devouring everything in the library in alphabetical order, and Anny, a former lover. In the four years since they last met, Anny has become bitterly disillusioned, and she cruelly mocks the love that Roquentin believes they once shared.

Roquentin also loses faith in his biographical project, convinced now that another human being cannot justify his miserable existence. Utterly distraught, he is about to abandon Bouville, when, sitting in a cafe, he hears a recording of the jazz song "Some of These Days." He is entranced by the music's ability to transcend the contingencies of space and time.

Roquentin vows to create a work of art that will similarly triumph over the pettiness of his life by immortalizing it. He will write a novel, and Sartre's book concludes with the possibility that it is a self-begetting novel, a narrative that recounts its own genesis. But the diary remains a fragment, and an editor's note indicates that it was discovered among Roquentin's papers. Perhaps its author is indeed dead and never succeeded in writing his novel.

Sartre's disturbing and droll novel concludes with the wryly ambiguous "Tomorrow it will rain in Bouville"—a buoyant promise of purification, or a fatalistic recognition that the *Ville De Boue* (city of mud) that is the human condition will only become murkier.

NICHOLAS NICKLEBY
Charles Dickens
1838-1839
Novel
Victorian

In this novel about a penniless young man and his sister who try to make their way through the hazards of early 19th century London, Dickens exposes the abhorrent conditions that plagued English schools of the time.

When his father dies, Nicholas Nickleby travels to London with his mother and sister, Kate, to seek help from his uncle, Ralph Nickleby. Uncle Nickleby, a hardened and unscrupulous moneylender, grudgingly secures Nicholas a position at Dotheboys Hall, run by Wackford Squeers, a dishonest, cruel, and greedy schoolmaster.

Exploited by Squeers and his wife and pursued by their unattractive daughter Fanny, Nicholas berates Squeers for his abuse of Smike, a retarded boy, and leaves, taking Smike with him.

Nicholas and Smike are protected by Newman Noggs, Ralph's secretary. Nicholas confronts his uncle, who denounces him and refuses to support any who have anything to do with him. To shield his mother and Kate, Nicholas takes Smike, leaves London, and joins a theatrical company.

Forced to attend a dinner party give by her uncle, Kate is subject to the unwelcome advances of Sir Mulberry Hawk and attracts the admiration of Lord Frederick Verisopht. Ralph refuses to discourage Hawk. Noggs, in desperation, sends for Nicholas, who confronts Hawk. Verisopht, realizing Kate's integrity, fights a duel with Hawk. Verisopht is killed, but Hawk is forced to flee England.

Nicholas is employed by the Brothers Cheeryble, philanthropic twins, and falls in love with Madeline Bray, befriended by the Cheerybles when her father is in debt. Nicholas is horrified to discover that his uncle, scheming to defraud Madeline of her inheritance, has arranged for her to marry the aged Arthur Gride. To save her father, she agrees, but Nicholas and Noggs rescue her.

Kate is courted by Frank Cheeryble, the brothers' nephew. Feeling that they cannot marry the wealthy Frank and Madeline, Kate and Nicholas retire to Devon with the dying Smike, who they and Ralph discover is Ralph's son, abducted years ago. His crimes catching up with him, Ralph commits suicide. The Brothers Cheeryble reunite the couples.

Nicholas Nickleby appeared in serial form when Dickens was only twenty-six. While the novel is a success story with a happy ending, its portrayal of education, poverty, and greed make it one of Dickens' more realistic and mature works.

NIGHT
Eli Wiesel
1960
Novella
Historical, Holocaust

While not entirely autobiographical, Night is the retelling of Elie Wiesel's experience as a prisoner in Nazi Germany's Auschwitz and Buchenwald prison camps. The novel is fundamental in the genre of holocaust literature.

In the opening paragraphs of Night, the character Moshe the Beadle claims "every question possessed a power that did not lie in the answer… man raises himself toward God by the questions he asks Him." With those lines, Wiesel directs his readers toward an essential element in the book—to answer the question "why?" Though the book was never intended as an autobiography, it is easy to identify the main character, Eliezer, as Wiesel. Their circumstances were so similar that some controversy has erupted through the years as to whether or not the book should be classified as fiction.

The story is based on Wiesel's experiences in 1944-45, when he was imprisoned at Auschwitz and Buchenwald concentration camps. Opening with some background on Eliezer's family life and religious training, the story conveys the utter disbelief, even as it is happening, that the Jews are being rounded up, imprisoned and murdered, en masse. At every turn, from being forced to wear a yellow star, to being herded into ghettos, the Jews are in denial. By the time they are systematically herded onto cattle cars and shipped to the camps, it is too late. Filled with gruesome images of brutality and deprivation, the story documents Eliezer's horror and suffering, that strips him and his fellow prisoners of all human dignity or sanity.

Throughout the novel, Wiesel uses the imagery of darkness, fire, and smoke, whether it is spewed from smoke stacks, or in the "little faces of the children, whose bodies [he] saw turned into wreaths of smoke." Foreshadowed in early scenes of the cattle car ride, where the deranged Madame Schachter screams "Jews, listen to me! Fire! I see fire!" at all times of day or night, Eliezer later claims these fires consumed all of his faith, and turned his life into one long night.

NINETEEN EIGHTY-FOUR
George Orwell
1949
Novel
Dystopian

Written in 1949, this story tells of a society in which men and women live in bondage to Big Brother, who regulates their every thought and emotion.

Instead of a glorious future of freedom and dignity, George Orwell imagines that despair, slavery, and numbing hopelessness will be mankind's fate. The slogans of the new order—War is Peace, Freedom is Slavery, Ignorance is Strength—adequately convey the bleakness of the world that Orwell envisioned. The inhabitants of this future society live under the watchful eye of Big Brother, leader of a government whose power is enforced by Thought Police and diabolical informants.

The novel's protagonist, Winston Smith, a member of the outer ring of the Party, finds himself slowly evolving into an independent thinker who writes anti-Big Brother slogans in his diary. He eventually encounters individuals who appear to share his disdain for the Party. First, Julia comes into his life, a winsome woman who anachronistically speaks of love and with whom Winston shares many encounters in a rented room above Mr. Charrington's antique shop. Winston also encounters O'Brien, a member of the Inner Party, but one who, Winston deduces, is not in sympathy with Party aims.

Winston subsequently discovers, however, that except for Julia all those whom he had trusted as confidants and fellow dissidents were in fact Party operatives, seeking to entrap Winston and Julia in their "conspiracy" against Big

Brother. The disturbing climax of the novel exemplifies the dehumanizing effects of totalitarian control on the individual person.

A key ingredient in this chilling documentation of eroding human freedom is its depiction of a corrupted language, "Newspeak," Orwell's brilliant rendering of that degraded language of politicians and sophists which hides rather then reveals truth.

As a true anti-utopian novel, one in which the horrors of totalitarianism are amply illustrated, *Nineteen Eighty-Four* serves as a poignant reminder of the preciousness of free thought and an open society.

NO EXIT
Jean-Paul Sartre
1944
Drama
Existential

No Exit is a play about a modern hell for selfish, malicious, but otherwise rather ordinary people. The setting is a conventional living room containing three hideous sofas and some tasteless bric-a-brac. Yet, the interaction of the three sinners confined there effectively reveals the nature of hell on earth.

The three are initially strangers to one another, but soon learn each other's worst secrets. Equally malicious, they invariably confirm the sense of guilt each has acquired in life. Cradeau, the French newspaperman, was shot for collaborating with the Germans and fears the implication of cowardice. Inez gradually poisoned a young woman's mind against her lover in order to use the woman for her own lesbian needs. Estelle killed her newborn baby by a lover so that her rich old husband would not discover her infidelity. She is horrified that the room contains no mirror, for she is unsure of her own existence unless she can see her reflection.

The play is sometimes misunderstood as being unrelievedly negative about human companionship: At its climax, Cradeau exclaims, "Hell is other people!" Sartre has said of this play that "...many people are encrusted in a set of habits..., that they harbor judgments about them which make them suffer, but do not even try to change them." Such people, he says, are already dead. While he does suggest that it is difficult to know oneself initially except through the eyes of other people, mature living demands that one renounce self-chosen hells and accept responsibility for oneself and others.

The best commentary on the moral implications of this work is Sartre's discussion of patterns of bad faith in his *Being and Nothingness*. In spite of its relatively heavy philosophic intent, however, the play is gripping in dramatic terms.

NORTHANGER ABBEY
Jane Austen
1818
Novel
Satire

Published the year after Jane Austen's death, Northanger Abbey burlesques, and ironically parallels, the plots and devices of the popular Gothic romances that had appeared in the 1790's—most particularly Ann Radcliffe's The Mysteries of Udolpho *and* The Romance of the Forest.

Catherine Morland, the protagonist, is an enthusiastic reader of Gothic novels. She expects her life to be like those she reads about, despite the fact that she is no storybook creature—neither beautiful nor clever nor rich, just a country parson's daughter in a large, happy family.

Like the maidens in romances, though, Catherine ventures away from home. Instead of some exotic locale, she visits Bath, where she enjoys ordinary resort pleasures with amiably normal English folk. Of her new acquaintances, the most agreeable are a witty young clergyman, Henry Tilney, and his sister. Catherine is delighted when their proud father, General Tilney, invites her to stay at their country house, which is, she is thrilled to learn, an abbey.

In spite of its antiquity and monastic origins, Northanger Abbey turns out to be both comfortable and convenient. Catherine's education in the difference between life and literature continues when she discovers a mysterious document in an old chest, broods all night over what dire tale it may relate, and at daybreak finds that she has lost sleep over a laundry list.

Catherine's new experiences may not be what the Gothic novelists describe, but they are not simple, direct, or dull either. General Tilney, though not the wife-slayer Catherine had idly fancied him, is a brutal and calculating man. On learning that she is not the heiress he had supposed, he packs her off to her parents. But Catherine does not have long to mull over the harsh lessons of real life. Henry Tilney, outraged by his father's behavior, rushes to her and proposes. The Morlands approve, and the general comes to decide that his clerical son could do worse than marry a clergyman's daughter.

NOTES FROM THE UNDERGROUND
Fyodor Dostoevski
1864
Novella
Existential

Dostoevski's novella is the misanthropic diatribe of a 40-year-old retired civil servant. Alienated and anonymous, the exasperating Underground Man both excoriates and celebrates himself, insisting finally that we are as loathsome as he is.

Set in St. Petersburg, the narrative consists of two parts. The first contains the Underground Man's general pronouncements on the hollowness of 19th century civilization. Despite the ostensible triumph of reason, he contends that human beings are fundamentally perverse, that they will seek pleasure in a toothache simply to assert free will.

The sight of snow leads the Underground Man to the second part, which he titles "A Propos of the Wet Snow." It is the memoir of an incident when he was 24 that helps to explain how he became the morbidly self-conscious recluse he is in part 1.

The Underground Man insists on attending a farewell dinner for a foppish former schoolmate, though he is not at all close to him. Ill at ease and quarrelsome, he is thoroughly humiliated, though he seems to enjoy both the humiliation and the recounting of it.

At the conclusion of the dinner, the Underground Man follows the others to a brothel, where, instead of enjoying himself, he sets himself the challenge of reforming a young prostitute named Liza. Lecturing her on the horrors of the path she has chosen, he succeeds in eliciting her confidence and her remorse.

Several days later, Liza makes a surprise visit to the shabby rooms that the Underground Man shares with his disdainful valet, Apollon. He now insults her, but she responds with sympathy for him. He cannot abide her pity and humiliates her so thoroughly that she walks out on him forever.

The Underground Man is alternately as considerate and caddish toward the reader as he is toward Liza. An anti-hero who wallows in self-examination, he questions his reliability as narrator. Yet, as much as he castigates himself and antagonizes us, he insists that we are akin.

O

O PIONEERS!
Willa Cather
1913
Novel
Historical

This account of a young Swedish girl and her family who settle on the virgin Nebraska prairie in the 1880's depicts the hardships, courage, and determination of the early pioneers.

The heroine of Willa Cather's novel is Alexandra Bergson, whose family farms a bleak homestead outside the little town of Hanover, "huddled on the windblown Nebraska prairie." One cold winter day, Alexandra and her little brother Emil go into town to pick up a prescription for her father, who is ill. As they prepare to leave, Carl Lindstrom, another Swedish boy, rescues Emil's kitten from atop a telegraph pole. That winter, Alexandra's father does not recover, and finally, on his deathbed, he calls the family together and tells his sons to listen to Alexandra after he dies.

A strong and capable girl, Alexandra is the smartest and most businesslike in her family and knows how to manage their farm. The two middle boys are slow and thick-witted, and Emil, the youngest, is an artist and dreamer. A handsome young man, Emil is attracted to Marie Shabata, a pretty and vivacious Czech girl married to a jealous and possessive husband. Alexandra admires Carl Lindstrom, her childhood friend, who has left for Chicago to become an engraver.

The high prairie country is hard to farm and after a few bad years the settlers begin to sell out, but Alexandra has promised her father to stay. In buying more land while the price is low, she shows the courage and imagination of a true pioneer.

After sixteen years, Alexandra and her brothers have prospered by staying when others left. Her brothers have both married, but they fail to appreciate Alexandra's talent and ability. When Carl Lindstrom comes back to visit her, they are suspicious and warn her not to marry him. Emil, now twenty-one, returns from the university and flirts with Marie Shabata. He finds that he is still in love with her and the two manage to meet despite her husband's jealous watchfulness. Realizing that the situation is hopeless, Emil decides to travel to Mexico City about the same time that Carl leaves for the Alaskan goldmines. Alexandra remains loyal to the land that has nurtured her.

AN OCCURRENCE AT OWL CREEK BRIDGE
Ambrose Bierce
1891
Novel
War

This grim tale of a Southern collaborator during the Civil War provides both a gripping account of a doomed man's thoughts while awaiting execution and a tantalizing, suspenseful example of controlled prose narrative.

The anonymous protagonist stands on a railroad bridge, awaiting execution. The preparations are meticulously described. As he awaits death, his thoughts carry him back in time.

The man, we learn, is Peyton Farquhar, a well-to-do Southern planter. A civilian, he wanted to do something to help the Southern cause. A stranger passing through his property stops for water and mentions that the Owl Creek Bridge is crucial to the advancing Northern troops. The reader understands that Farquhar is being hanged because he attempted to destroy the bridge.

He is hanged; the sensations of the hanging are told in precise detail. He seems to survive the hanging, a freak accident sending him into the river below where he manages to escape the soldiers' bullets, as well. He seems to find his way home again after the ordeal on the bridge and in the river. But, at the end, we discover that he is dead, that he never actually escaped from the hanging. Everything so carefully described occurred only in his mind, in the split second before he ceased to live.

Bierce was the master of closely observed, meticulously related detail. The power of the tale derives from this straightforward technique. Even the understated title helps to seduce the reader into a false sense of security. The photographic description of the scenes and locations builds up a basis of naturalistic realism that is in direct contrast to the dramatic conclusion of the tale.

The ironic tale, influenced by the brothers Goncourt and Gustave Flaubert, was a particularly apt vehicle both for Bierce's technical skill and for his bleak view of life.

THE OCTOPUS: A STORY OF CALIFORNIA
Frank Norris
1901
Novel
Historical, Western

Frank Norris was the first American novelist to follow in the footsteps of Emile Zola's revolutionary sociological realism. This novel and its 1903 sequel, The Pit *dramatized the economic mechanisms of inequality and the corporate structure that justifies repression.*

The primary novel in an uncompleted, projected trilogy (*The Epic of Wheat*) this 1901 novel depicts the struggle of farmers in California to produce wheat while opposing the monopolistic machinations of the railroad industry. Presley, a poet from the East, visits Magnus Derrick's family in the San Joaquin Valley where farmers have leased lands from the railroad, and meets several disgruntled ranchers. He discovers that since the farmers have improved the land, the railroad plans to reclaim the land they have leased, with the aim to monopolize the wheat industry, then the beef industry. The railroad enjoys complete political control of the state, as well as the support of newspapers.

After a train kills sheep on the tracks, Annixter, whose broken fence was responsible for the accident, organizes farmers in a league against the railroad. A veteran engineer for the railroad, Dyke, quits his job rather than accept a pay cut; he farms, but goes bankrupt due to a hike in freight rates. He robs a train, is apprehended, sentenced to life in jail. Lowering his literary ambition, Presley composes a popular political ballad, "The Toilers," to support the farmers, but realizes that poetry is useless in the political arena.

The farmers' league place Magnus' son, Lyman Derrick, a corrupt San Francisco lawyer, on the state commission, but he betrays the farmers and orders them evicted. In armed resistance many farmers, including the heroic Annixter, are killed in a bloodbath. Sunk in poverty and humiliated, Magnus is a broken man. His wife manages to find a job teaching.

The evil antagonist, Behrman, who manages the railroad, dies ironically from a loading accident, when his foot, caught in a rope, drags him to be smothered under bags of wheat he had dishonestly acquired. Presley visits the railroad president, an urbane and civilized man who espouses modern laws of economic progress. Lyman Derrick's election as state governor appears likely. Presley departs for India.

Although the octopus-like railroad has been victorious, the novel concludes with a tongue-in-cheek moral addendum: greed and injustice is short-lived, that from a larger perspective truth and progress will eventually triumph.

ODE: INTIMATIONS OF IMMORTALITY
William Wordsworth
1807
Poetry
Lyric

One of the most famous and important works of the English Romantic period, this profound philosophical poem at once bemoans the loss of childhood and celebrates the wisdom that comes with maturity.

Like so many of William Wordsworth's poems, the *Ode* illustrates the concerns with childhood and human psychology that were central to English Romanticism. The speaker of the 203-line poem catalogs the gains and losses of growing older, at the same time making some profound observations about the effect one's childhood has on adult life.

The poem can be divided into three parts. The first (roughly stanzas 1 through 4) details the loss of the glory of childhood. No longer is the poet able to see the earth, as he once did, through the visionary eyes of childhood. While nature still holds wonders for him, he realizes that he can never again behold the life around him as he did in years gone by.

The middle section of the poem (stanzas 5 through 8) elaborates the process by which all human beings suffer this loss as they mature. Growing from childhood to adulthood, says the poet, involves gradually forgetting the glory that we knew in paradise before birth. As the sensory pleasures of earth replace the spiritual pleasures of preexistence, the child gradually forgets the glories that once were his. Thus childhood is a truly blessed state, retaining as it does some vestige of "celestial light."

The poem ends with a celebration of the recompense that comes with maturity. These new pleasures are the products of what the adult remembers of his early life. Thus, the adult intellect is tempered by recollections of early childhood to remind us of our spiritual nature.

The "Intimations Ode" is a complicated and highly abstract work, a poem to be read and reread. It probes the very nature of the spiritual plane of human existence.

ODE ON A GRECIAN URN
John Keats
1820
Poetry
Lyric, Mythology

Through imaginative description of a richly ornamented Grecian urn, Keats contrasts art's timelessness with the natural world's prevailing transience.

"Ode on a Grecian Urn" is one of the loveliest and most richly puzzling of English lyrics. In five short stanzas of ten lines each, Keats vividly presents the scenes adorning an ancient urn, which he personifies and addresses directly as "still unravished bride," "Foster child of silence and slow time," and "sylvan historian."

The urn's frieze eloquently if wordlessly proves that art offers a permanence impossible in the real world. The pictured trees beneath which a piper forever plays will never lose their spring leaves. The "bold lover" pressing his suit will never stop loving, nor will his lady cease to be fair. On the other hand, the kiss sought can never be granted, the melodies can never be heard, the trees can never bear summer fruit—so the changeless state conveyed by art clearly has its drawbacks.

Having reflected on the living moments frozen into decorative "attitudes" on the urn—love, flight and pursuit, music making, ritual sacrifice—Keats backs away to view the urn as a whole. The "cold pastoral" of the urn lives forever precisely because it has never lived. However the reader chooses to interpret the poem's cryptic final lines, which because of a punctuation discrepancy in early editions permit sharply different readings, the urn's message of "Beauty is truth, truth beauty" is a statement of triumph and limitation entirely valid in the realm of art where the urn exists.

ODE TO A NIGHTINGALE
John Keats
1819
Poetry
Lyric

Conceived as a poet's address to a singing nightingale, this 80-line poem explores the relationship of art and real life and questions the seemingly clear divisions between imagination and reality.

One of Keats's six great odes, this poem is a lyric meditation narrated by a poet who is tempted to forsake the real world of human suffering for the ideal world of art. As he listens to a bird's song, the speaker becomes more and more enraptured by it, and increasingly disgruntled with the mortal world of pain and death.

The poet begins by describing his current listless mental state, contrasting it with the beautiful and carefree song of the nightingale. He wishes for freedom from earthly cares and longs for the fairyland of art, represented in the poem by the nightingale. Life on earth is too full of sorrow, despair, and disappointment, and the only escape from it is through poetry.

Death, says the poet, has long been a temptation for him, and the bird's song temporarily strengthens his death wish. He admits that the quiet of the grave seems preferable to life on earth. But just as he is about to abandon himself to the nightingale's song, the poet realizes that in death he would be unable to hear the bird's song.

The ode's concern with death is often attributed to the death of Keats's brother in 1818, but the poem, like so many of this great Romantic poet's works, is really an affirmation of human life. The poem was written in 1819, a year that witnessed the composition of some of Keats's greatest poems (among them five more odes and "The Eve of St. Agnes"). He died less than two years later at the age of 25.

ODE TO APHRODITE
Sappho
Sixth century B.C.E.
Poetry
Lyric

One of the earliest examples of intensely personal lyric poetry in Western literature, and certainly the earliest by a woman, the "Ode to Aphrodite" centers on the emotional and religious experiences of Sappho of Lesbos.

Probably the only complete surviving composition of Sappho, this poem of seven quatrains is written in a Greek lyric meter called the Sapphic stanza. The poem illustrates the three traditional parts of a prayer: the invocation, the sanction, and the entreaty.

In the invocation, Sappho calls on Aphrodite in a colorful, descriptive address to the goddess. Referring to Aphrodite respectfully as mistress, Sappho acknowledges with anguish and emotion Aphrodite's control of the human souls that she subdues with distress and grief.

The central part of the poem moves from the poetic present to the past. This section represents the sanction of a prayer, a recognition of a god's earlier relationship with a mortal. Here Sappho focuses on divine epiphany, on her own previous relationship with Aphrodite. The goddess omnisciently guesses the motive for Sappho's prayer: Sappho's passion for another woman, whom Aphrodite promises will soon love Sappho "even unwillingly." (Much of Sappho's poetry reveals a similar lesbian orientation.)

In the last four lines, Sappho returns to the poetic present and ends her prayer with an entreaty, a request. Sappho here begs more calmly for a second epiphany, for release from the pains of love. Aphrodite is described as Sappho's "companion-in-arms," her ally. This military metaphor emphasizes the strength of Aphrodite and of the emotion she oversees: Humans are powerless before this goddess and before this force.

The formal structure of the poem suggests a detached self-analysis; the tone, however, implies personal experiences and feeling. Verbal and thematic links between the first and last quatrains poetically express the answer to Sappho's prayer: Intense emotion at the beginning of the poem is displaced by calmer, more rational speech at the end. Sappho's prayer is thus a source of spiritual comfort. The poem, the experience itself, is the answer to her prayer.

ODYSSEY
Homer
725 B.C.E.
Poetry
Epic

The Odyssey, *a Greek oral epic about the homecoming of the hero Odysseus, is both a timeless adventure story and a sophisticated literary work which has strongly influenced the development of later epic and novel forms.*

The *Odyssey* begins in the tenth year of Odysseus' wanderings following the Trojan War. The first four books, called the Telemachy, focus not on Odysseus, but on his son Telemachus, who undertakes a journey of self-maturation in search of his missing father. These books establish the reputation of the hero before he is introduced directly. They also underscore the plight of Odysseus' family in his absence and the need for the hero's return.

The main plot, Odysseus' homecoming, is introduced in books 5-8 by the hero's departure from the island of the nymph Calypso. Odysseus' later experiences on the island of Phaeacia are highlighted by his encounter with Nausicaa, a Phaeacian princess, who aids the shipwrecked hero and leads him to the court of her father, King Alcinous.

At Alcinous' palace, Odysseus recounts, in the form of a flashback, his adventures from the fall of Troy, ten years before. This narrative, books 9-12, includes the memorable episode with the Cyclops Polyphemus and Odysseus' journey to the Land of the Dead. Both events illustrate the wrath of Poseidon, god of the sea, who delays Odysseus' homecoming for ten years.

The second half of the *Odyssey*, books 13-24, deals with the hero at home on the island of Ithaca. Disguised as a beggar, Odysseus enters his house and prepares his eventual revenge on the suitors. Homer presents the hero in a series of progressively more important recognition scenes, climaxed by Odysseus' revelation to the suitors by means of a special bow and to his wife via their marriage bed.

Disguise is just one aspect of the crafty, deceptive, and suspicious nature which Odysseus shares both with Penelope, who deceived her suitors for many years, and with his patroness, Athena, goddess of wisdom. Hero, wife, and goddess thus create a bond of intelligence which guarantees the safe return and successful vengeance of Odysseus.

OEDIPUS AT COLONUS
Sophocles
401 B.C.E.
Drama
Classical, Mythology

Chronologically the middle play of the Oedipus trilogy, this play tells of the later years of Oedipus, banished king of Thebes, who blinded himself when he learned that he had killed his father and married his mother. He spent his exile in Colonus near Athens.

Oedipus and Antigone, his daughter, have wandered far since his banishment. Finally they come to an olive grove in Colonus, over which Theseus, King of Athens, rules. The grove at which they have stopped is one which the Furies hold sacred. Most men fear it, but Oedipus feels comfortable there.

The patriarchs of Colonus, learning that the stranger in their midst is Oedipus, whose horrible story they know, try to drive him away. He is able to calm them, implying that he has special powers and will bring good to the land that provides him refuge.

Ismene, Oedipus' other daughter, comes to Colonus with news that her two brothers, Polynices and Eteocles, have struggled for power in Thebes and that Polynices, the loser, has been banished.

Meanwhile, King Theseus, sympathetic to Oedipus, offers him protection. The Delphic Oracle foresees that Thebes will suffer greatly if Oedipus is not returned and buried there. Creon, Thebes' villainous king, comes to Colonus and seeks to return Oedipus by force. Theseus prevents this.

Creon abducts Antigone and Ismene, his nieces, but Theseus has them rescued. Oedipus remains in Colonus and dies there, blessing the land. Antigone and Ismene return to Thebes, attempting to prevent conflict between their brothers.

This was Sophocles' last play, written when he was almost 90 years old and first performed after his death. Like *Oedipus Tyrannus* (429 B.C.) and *Antigone* (441 B.C.), it examines the prevalent Greek theme of hubris (pride).

OEDIPUS TYRANNUS
Sophocles
429 B.C.E.
Drama
Classical, Mythology

This most celebrated of ancient Greek tragedies recounts the terrible story of Oedipus, King of Thebes, who discovers that he has murdered his father, and married his mother, fathering four children by her.

A plague has swept Thebes. Apollo's oracle reveals that plague will continue until the murderer of King Laius is apprehended. Oedipus, the present king, orders a relentless search for the murderer of his predecessor.

Teiresias, a blind seer, hesitates to tell Oedipus what he knows, that Oedipus' true parents are not Polybus and Merope. Oedipus soon realizes that a man whom he killed in his youth was Laius.

Going to Thebes after killing Laius, Oedipus had answered the riddle of the Sphinx, and upon doing so was declared king. He married Jocasta, the former king's widow.

Jocasta had borne Laius one child. Because a seer predicted that Laius would be killed by his child, a shepherd was told to take Laius' offspring to an isolated mountain and leave it to die. But the shepherd disobeyed his orders and gave the child, Oedipus, to a messenger, who in turn gave him to Polybus.

On learning this news, Jocasta hangs herself. Oedipus discovers her body, pulls the gold brooches from her dress, and puts his eyes out with them. Blind and bloodied, he appears before the Thebans to declare himself the murderer of their former king. He flees into exile at Colonus, a broken man.

Oedipus Tyrannus, chronologically the first play of the Oedipus trilogy, which includes *Oedipus At Colonus* (about 407 B.C.) and *Antigone* (about 441 B.C.), was actually written after *Antigone* and is generally considered the best of Greek tragedies.

OF HUMAN BONDAGE
W. Somerset Maugham
1915
Novel
Autobiographical

In this bildungsroman, young Philip Carey grows to adulthood in late 19th century England, gaining a cosmopolitan viewpoint and abandoning his illusions. This straightforward, third-person narrative offers its readers a realistic account of life, a varied and lively array of characters, a pellucid style, and philosophical reflections.

Following his mother's death, Philip becomes the ward of his uncle, the Vicar of Blackstable, a rural parish in Kent. Philip, also oriented toward a clerical life, attends the King's School, Tercanbury, where he finds himself isolated, lonely, and unhappy. He is by nature shy, and a clubfoot severely limits his participation in usual school activities.

Before completing his schooling, he decides against the clergyman's life and travels to Heidelberg, where he absorbs German philosophy, culture, and art. The remainder of the novel largely concerns Philip's efforts to establish a career and to discover the meaning of life. It chronicles his growth and clarifies the understanding he gains from experience, as he seeks to become first an accountant, then an artist, and finally, a physician. He succeeds in medicine after abandoning accounting for lack of interest and painting for lack of talent.

It is, however, the necessity for controlling his emotions that Philip learns most painfully—a lesson taught him by his long and unrequited love for Mildred Rogers. By the novel's end, he can make sense of his life by accepting a philosophical position that reconciles suffering and pain with the quest for happiness. From a piece of Persian rug given him by an eccentric poet, he discovers the meaning of life.

The novel reflects the author's fundamental values and interests—a clinical detachment, a skeptical attitude, a distrust of passion, a belief in tolerance, a cosmopolitan point of view, and an essentially existential outlook on life.

OF MICE AND MEN
John Steinbeck
1937
Novella
Historical

In this brief, tightly structured work, two drifters find their special bond destroyed by their inability to cope with the human frailties of hate, jealousy, and loneliness.

Brusque, friendless George Milton has been taking care of big, strong, slow-witted Lenny Small for so long that each has become as brother to the other. Lenny's great physical strength, coupled with his childlike innocence, has gotten him into trouble in the past. George has always been quick to save him, later threatening to deprive him of his share of their longed-for land, their own little place where they will be beholden to no one.

George's threats to Lenny's (and his own) vision of a better life are cathartic, curative, and loving. George needs Lenny as friend, family, and devoted partner. Each is fighting his own type of loneliness: Lenny, the loneliness of brutish incomprehension in a hard world; George, the loneliness of the essential solitary.

When they begin a new job on a ranch, other human conflicts begin to destroy their relationship. Curley, a little man and a bully, takes an immediate dislike to Lenny.

One day, Curley's wife, bored and lonely, flirts with Lenny in the quiet of the barn, and Lenny, in his innocent strength, accidentally kills her and flees. Curley forms a posse, but George, knowing where Lenny is hiding in the woods, borrows a gun and goes to him. In a final, loving rebuke, George recites for Lenny their vision of a better life and shoots him, saving him once and for all from the punishment of the world's cruel justice.

OF MICE AND MEN typifies Steinbeck's ability to tell a simple tale invested with elements of myth and symbol. The opening scene in the woods, for example, in which Lenny reveals his innocence, is mirrored at the end when, innocence threatened, Lenny is killed in the same wood, the Edenic garden lost to him—and to George—forever.

THE OLD CAPITAL
Yasunari Kawabata
1987
Novel

In The Old Capital, *Kawabata, the only Japanese artist to receive a Nobel Prize, evokes the meeting of new and old in postwar Japan with extraordinary beauty and pathos.*

To the Western reader casually acquainted with things Japanese, Yasunari Kawabata's *The Old Capital* strikes an intensely foreign chord. Set in Kyoto, *The Old Capital* is the story of the lovely Chieko, adopted daughter of a kimono designer who is beginning to look to artists such as Paul Klee for inspiration.

Despite this and other postwar influences, however, Chieko is a delicate, old-fashioned girl. Her life revolves around the many seasonal festivals at the various shrines in and around Kyoto. Deeply moved by the hues and scents of nature, Chieko is also prey to melancholy born of her conviction that her real parents abandoned her (contrary to her adoptive parents' story that they stole her from under the cherry blossoms in a moment of supreme desire).

What surprises in this superbly written and well-translated novel is not so much the unusual twist in plot that changes Chieko's perception of herself forever as how it is conveyed. Chieko's discovery is not resolved in the manner of a conventional Western novel; nor is it left hanging in the way that contemporary short-story writers seem unable to resist. Instead, her emotions—and those of the other characters as well—are conveyed through half-spoken sentences and the subtlest of signs. The result is as exquisite and alluring as Chieko herself.

THE OLD MAN AND THE SEA
Ernest Hemingway
1952
Novella
Coming of Age

This parablelike story of the heroic struggles of an old Cuban fisherman to land a giant fish embodies the values of courage, self-control, and endurance that Hemingway proposes as a guide for modern living.

The story focuses on old Santiago and his two most important relationships: to a young boy, and to nature. Santiago has not caught a fish in many days when the story opens, and his young companion has been forced by his parents to fish on another boat. His love for the old man, however, prompts him to look after his needs nonetheless.

Santiago goes further out than usual and hooks a giant marlin. The major part of this brief and very spare work traces the three days that Santiago fights against this mighty fish. We see not only his courage, strength of will, and knowledge of his craft, but also his deep respect for and understanding of nature.

Santiago defeats the fish, which he addresses as a comrade and fellow-sufferer throughout the struggle, but loses his catch at the end to sharks. The old man returns to port exhausted and with only the skeleton of his great fish.

Hemingway suggests, however, that the old man cannot ultimately be defeated because he conducts himself with dignity and self-respect, no matter what the external circumstances. The young boy lovingly receives him back, heart-broken at Santiago's suffering but glad for the vindication of the skills of his master.

The story lends itself to many symbolic interpretations. Some see it as an allegory of Hemingway's life as an artist, laboring alone to realize the elusive prize of art, only to have his efforts torn apart by shark like critics.

Others emphasize the distilled expression here of the famous Hemingway code: courage, endurance, suffering without complaint, and the like. If so, the code has been expanded somewhat to include humility, pity, loyalty, and love—though life is no less killing for these things.

OLIVE KITTERIDGE
Elizabeth Strout
2008
Novel
Psychological

In thirteen interlocking short stories, Elizabeth Strout presents a portrait of Olive Kitteridge, a tart-tongued, difficult woman who makes people uncomfortable but who is also capable of immense depth of feeling and emotional under-standing. Cumulatively, the stories have the density of a novel. The individual stories provide, on their own terms, piercing insights into Olive and those around her. The book achieved wide acclaim upon its publication, becoming a 2008 finalist for the National Book Critics Circle Award, and winning the 2009 Pulitzer Prize for literature.

The book opens with Henry Kitteridge thinking about his wife, a math teacher in the small town of Cosby, Maine. Henry is a retired pharmacist who harbors deep-seated anxieties regarding his loud, volatile wife, and whatever mental instabilities he may have inherited from his overbearing mother. He remembers when their only child, Christopher, approached adolescence, frequently clashing with Olive. Henry had taken refuge in the orderly world of the pharmacy and in fantasies about his new, married assistant. The young woman's husband died in an accident, unleashing a welter of emotions that Henry could never quite relinquish. Olive also grieves for a lost love—a colleague who died in a car crash. Neither Olive nor Henry ever acknowledges their shattering grief, but each apprehends the other's loss. They remain warily devoted to one another.

Fellow townsmen hold the main stage in some of the stories that follow. One of Olive's former students is ready to commit suicide until Olive stops to speak with him, and notices a girl falling into the turbulent ocean. The suicidal young man swims to rescue her, and finds himself bound to life once more. In another story, Christopher marries, but when Olive overhears her daughter-in-law suggesting that Christopher views his mother more negatively than Olive knows, Olive breaks into a nearly deranged fit. The couple moves to California, which devastates Olive and Henry. Christopher divorces shortly afterward, yet chooses to stay in California, wounding his parents further. Shortly after learning of the divorce, a stroke paralyzes Henry, and it becomes clear that he will never regain consciousness. Olive is bereft. Later, Christopher asks 72-year-old Olive to come to New York City to help his new, pregnant wife. The visit ends badly, with a fight. Olive and Christopher become estranged. The final story, a year and a half after Henry's death, has Olive hoping to die—grieving for Henry and for her son, blaming herself for time "squandered"—but instead she realizes that life still baffles her, a thought that, unexpectedly, renews her desire to live.

OLIVER TWIST
Charles Dickens
1837-1839
Novel
Victorian, Adventure

This lively and moving chronicle of an orphan's adventures in early-Victorian England is famous for its many memorable characters and for the impetus it gave to the reform of the harsh and cruel Poor Law of 1834.

Oliver Twist, a rich tapestry of English society in the 1830's, has two distinct strands. In the first chapters, Dickens satirizes Victorian social institutions. Born in a workhouse, the young protagonist of unknown (but genteel, as it turns out) parentage is arbitrarily given the name Oliver Twist. His subsequent experiences of charity at the hands of the parish beadle Mr. Bumble, the workhouse directors, the magistrates, and the household of the undertaker to whom he is apprenticed sharply indicate the hypocrisy, stupidity, and cruelty of the so-called respectable world.

Running away to London, Oliver finds himself in a warmer though not actually kinder milieu—the urban underworld of thieves. In depicting the wily old Jew Fagin and his gang—the Artful Dodger, brutal Bill Sykes, Nancy, and others—the narrative becomes more sentimental and more humorous than in the early chapters. Though Dickens' moral ties are with Oliver and the virtuous middle-class characters (Mr. Brownlow and the Maylies), his interests and sympathies seem to lie with the outlaws.

Throughout the novel, Oliver himself is a mere pawn. Fagin tries to make a thief of the naive boy, who is rescued, recaptured, and saved again. The mysterious Monks, who turns out to be Oliver's half brother, would like the child to go bad: If debased, Oliver will lose his share of their late father's estate. Oliver, however, proves passively incorruptible. The novel ends with nearly everyone where he or she should be. The genteel characters live together in a country village that is heaven on earth; the criminals are dead or punished. Only in the case of Nancy, viciously murdered for passing information to Rose Maylie, is conduct not appropriately rewarded.

Oliver Twist's plot is intricate and governed to an improbable degree by coincidence. The book's chief excellences are its vivid descriptions of London and its remarkable exploration of the criminal mind. The complexities of the satanic but amusing Fagin, the dishonest but engaging and resourceful Dodger, and Nancy, a woman of intelligence and good intentions trapped by her social circumstances and her love for an evil man, fascinated the book's contemporary audience and continue to engage readers.

ON LIBERTY
John Stuart Mill
1859
Nonfiction
Philosophical, Political

As the middle classes became dominant socially and politically in mid-Victorian England, their morals and manners created a climate of "decided opinion" that Mill feared would stifle freedom of expression. On Liberty is not a response to any specific repressive act, but is the result of Mill's conviction that the pressures of conformity in a mass society would lead to mediocrity and uniformity of opinion and conduct.

Mill's object in writing this essay was to assert the principles that should govern the relationship between individuals and the collective authority of church and state. Following the utilitarian maxim that a good society is one where the greatest number of persons enjoy the greatest amount of happiness, Mill sought to ensure that individuals would be able to think and act freely, thus creating the maximum of happiness.

Mill bases his argument for the usefulness of airing all points of view on three premises. First, an opinion that is suppressed can turn out to be valid, as in the case of the teachings of Socrates and Christ. Secondly, even if an opinion is false, its discussion will cause us to test the validity of our own opinion and thus strengthen it. Finally, a counter opinion may contain part of the truth because the truth is complex and often lies between two opinions.

Mill, however, advocates more than simply a free exchange of ideas. He maintains that an individual should be permitted to act as he pleases in order to pursue the fullest self-development. He does not, however, defend irresponsibility; a person is free to act as he pleases only in matters that affect him alone. The state has the right to intervene in cases where individual conduct does harm to others.

Mill's *On Liberty* stands with Milton's *Areopagitica* as one of the classic statements in English literature on the issue of freedom of expression. The present-day relevance of Mill's protest against the interference of groups and governments in the affairs of individuals is a testament to the acuity of his ideas.

ON DEATH AND DYING
Elizabeth Kubler-Ross, M.D.
1969
Nonfiction
Psychological

On Death and Dying is a groundbreaking treatise based on Dr. Kubler-Ross's observations and research into the process of dying. Using first-hand accounts, Dr. Kubler-Ross reveals a universal progression, from denial through acceptance that has changed how the western world approaches the taboo topic of death.

It is no accident that Kubler-Ross's seminal book about death and dying coincided with Britain's Dame Cicely Saunders' groundbreaking hospice movement. At a time of "free love," and the crumbling of many social barriers, Kubler-Ross, a pioneer in modern thanatology, provided the world with a much-needed breakthrough in how humanity, and western culture in particular, approaches death.

She identified a problem—a cultural failure to acknowledge death as an integral part of life—and posited the notion that one does not stop growing, emotionally or intellectually, when one's own death is eminent. Through a process of interviews and scientific observation, Kubler-Ross and her students identified a five-stage progression toward accepting death, that include denial, anger, bargaining, depression, and acceptance. This progression is commonly referred to as the grief cycle.

ON THE NATURE OF THINGS
Lucretius
60 B.C.E.
Poetry
Philosophical

Lucretius explains the world's origins and operations in terms of atomoi, minute particles which, variously arranged, constitute all matter. He intends to disprove the need for religion and supernatural causality and thereby free humanity from these constraints.

Lucretius weds the philosophical system of Epicurus (born 341 B.C.) to the atomic theory of Democritus (born 460 B.C.) and from their marriage, derives a new philosophical perspective.

The poem has six books. The first establishes that matter renews itself and is composed of atomoi. These infinitely small particles periodically recombine and are the sole constituents of all matter—animal, vegetable, or mineral.

Book Two describes the shapes, combinations, and movements of the atoms, that is, how they swerve in random fashion to create the differences which exist in matter. These are also purely material, the roundest and finest atoms. Necessarily, the soul dies with the body when the atoms recombine.

The fourth book describes the films all atoms produce. These strike the senses and account for sense perception. Book Five notes the destructible nature of the world, since it too arose from spontaneous generation. Similarly, civilization becomes savagery through recombinations of atomic particles. The strongest atomically—namely, the "fittest"—survive. The last book focuses on thunder, lightning, rain, and on natural calamities—earthquakes, volcanic eruptions, floods, and epidemics.

Lucretius saw himself as an enlightened missionary bringing truth to a world riddled with superstition and fear. His book found acceptance among educated Romans ready to abandon mythic explanations and religion based on superstition. His was not a new philosophy; rather he offered an ingenious synthesis of Greek thought.

ON THE ORIGIN OF THE SPECIES
Charles Darwin
1859
Nonfiction
Natural History, Scientific

Often referred to as "the book that shook the world," Charles Darwin's treatise on the origins and evolution of life on Earth had an extraordinary impact on humanity's perceptions of its place in the cosmos.

Darwin's postulations about the origins and progression of life on the planet engendered a new paradigm in human thought. Until the late 19th century, the accepted Platonic worldview presupposed that life is an imitation of the ideal form from which it sprang. Someone or something designed and created all life forms. Darwin's observations suggested that terrestrial life has been perfected over time through variation and mutation, and not as a created imitation.

Today, many of Darwin's groundbreaking theories are considered common knowledge. His most revolutionary assertions include the idea that all life has descended from a common ancestor; that beneficial characteristics accumulate and survive over many generations, while the less beneficial or unused characteristics fade from a species, over time. (This is known as natural selection.) All instincts and physical characteristics are variable, and the struggle to survive helps to preserve each profitable deviation, each new or changed characteristic.

At the time, the laws of inheritance were still unknown, yet Darwin surmised that "the most frequent cause of variability may be the male and female reproductive elements"—a notion supported by Darwin's contemporary, Gregor Mendel in his experiments with pea plants.

On the Origin of the Species created a firestorm upon its publication. Though the concepts inherent in evolution had been postulated before, Darwin's treatise provided scientific data to back up his assertions. In addition, Darwin was one of the first scientists to write for the lay population, rather than for other scientists. Among the most incensed detractors were Creationists who saw the theory of evolution as a direct affront to their religious beliefs. Regardless of the scientific support for evolution, pockets of Creationists still see Darwin as a heretic, and evolution as an affront to their beliefs.

ON THE ROAD
Jack Kerouac
1957
Novel
Sociological

The story of a reckless and hedonistic drive through the United States and Mexico, this rambling narrative is at once a celebration of America's diversity and an indictment of the post World War II consumer culture.

Jack Kerouac's most famous book was withheld from publication for six years while editors vainly attempted to persuade the author to delete or rewrite potentially shocking portions. But this formless and irreverent novel was an instant success and remains a best-seller. It placed Kerouac firmly at the center of the literary movement he helped to found, and to this day it is one of the two or three works most closely associated with the Beat generation.

The novel's two principal characters are the narrator, Sal, and his companion and hero, Dean Moriarty—thinly veiled versions of Kerouac and his friend Neal Cassady. The book unfolds as a loosely connected series of episodes that document the pair's adventures during a drunken and drug-ridden odyssey through the United States. Along the way, they meet and befriend an unforgettable gallery of American types: jazz singers, drug addicts, hitchhikers, and drifters. Their journey culminates in a revealing and darkly humorous stay in Mexico.

Much of *On the Road* is barely disguised autobiography, a document attesting to the alienation felt by Kerouac, Cassady, and other members of the Beat group in Eisenhower's America. This group, which also included the poets Allen Ginsberg, Lawrence Ferlinghetti, and Gary Snyder, and the novelist William Burroughs, sought to transcend the conformist values of the 1950's through such diverse channels as sex, drugs, alcohol, Eastern mysticism, and the poetry of William Blake. Their works were meant to shock the middle-class establishment, by which these writers felt beaten down and disenfranchised.

Though *On the Road* is basically apolitical, it and other Beat writings had a profound influence on the countercultural movements of the 1960's. Kerouac himself did not survive that decade, dying at the age of 47 in 1969.

THE ONCE AND FUTURE KING
T. H. White
1958
Novel
Arthurian, Romance

This popular, modern rendition of the story of King Arthur, presented in four parts, will appeal to readers young and old. Fantasy and political commentary are expertly woven into the classical tale.

White's version of the Arthurian legend consists of four stories. "The Sword and the Stone," the best known of the four, is the account of the young Arthur's education for kingship. The magician Merlin changes him into various animals so that he may better come to understand human emotions. The middle stories, "The Queen of Air and Darkness" and "The Ill-Made Knight," detail the rise of the King's fortunes. The King creates his Round Table so that might might serve right, and, for a time, his ideals are realized. At the same time, the seeds of Arthur's downfall are sown: Morgause and her son Mordred plot against him; and Lancelot, his best knight, suffers from an incurable love for Arthur's queen. Boredom, too, infects the knights and Arthur creates the quest of the Holy Grail to give his knights a cause worthy of their attention. In the final tale, "The Candle in the Wind," the relationship between Lancelot and Guinevere is discovered, and Arthur is obliged to enforce laws that are technically correct but seem morally unfair to him. Civil war breaks out, and Arthur goes off to die, entrusting the legacy of his kingdom to a young boy whom he charges to keep alive the spirit that had been created at Camelot.

White's Arthurian story has been adapted for the stage (*Camelot*) and for the screen (Disney's *Sword and the Stone*), attesting its appeal as a love story and a child's fantasy. Nevertheless, the novel is filled with political allusions and is, in fact, a scathing commentary on modern man's inability to achieve perfectibility. The animal characters all serve to illustrate human qualities, good or evil. Similarly, the traditional events of the Arthurian legend are given contemporary significance, and the purposes of knighthood are redefined in modern terms. White's philosophy borders on the pacifistic; he is clearly against war, especially war designed to subjugate peoples or to attain advantages for a minority. His portraits of politicians and military men are particularly unflattering.

ONE DAY IN THE LIFE OF IVAN DENISOVICH
Aleksandr Solzhenitsyn
1962
Novella
War

This powerful novel of muted hope follows a Russian prisoner through a typical day in a Stalinist labor camp.

The story opens with Ivan Denisovich (Shukov) rising in the frigid, predawn Siberian darkness and ends with his return to his bed after what he considers a very good day.

That very good day consists of earning a few extra portions of bread and diluted soup, getting a few drags on the butt of someone else's cigarette, beating another brigade back to camp from their work assignment, smuggling a piece of scrap metal past the guards, not getting sick, and the like. If this does not sound like much to celebrate, that is exactly the point.

The novel is intentionally not sensational. It is an expose of Stalinist labor camps, and of the Soviet system generally, but it accomplishes this through understatement and indirection.

This work, however, is much more than a political indictment. Its power derives from its depiction of a man retaining his humanity under inhumane conditions. Shukov is not a heroic figure, but he wins our admiration for his cleverness, his endurance, and his simple integrity.

Through Shukov, Solzhenitsyn suggests that there are certain qualities which must be retained no matter what the circumstances if we are to maintain our humanity. Primary among these is self-respect. Shukov works constantly to increase his odds of survival, but there are definite things, lying and begging among them, which he will not do.

The pivotal scene in the novel, the building of a brick wall, demonstrates not only Shukov's sense of worth, but also the importance of human solidarity and cooperation in the face of evil. The novel's ambivalent conclusion, however, precludes seeing it as a simple celebration of human endurance. Solzhenitsyn takes evil too seriously for that.

ONE FLEW OVER THE CUCKOO'S NEST
Ken Kesey
1962
Novel
Psychological

Set in a mental hospital and narrated by one of the patients, this novel is one the classic protests against a regimented society to be written in the 1960's.

This novel is narrated by Chief Broom, the son of an Indian chief, who pretends to be a deaf mute as a protection against a society which denies him dignity as a human being. Many of his comments on conditions in the hospital ward and in society, while not literally true, are accurate metaphors for the social regimentation against which the novel protests.

The action of the novel begins with the arrival of Randle Patrick McMurphy, a rambunctious and free-spirited roisterer who has chosen to come to the mental hospital to avoid completing a sentence at a prison farm. He is instantly and deliberately in conflict with Nurse Ratched, "Big Nurse," whose object is to reduce the patients on her ward to abject conformity. As many of these patients have deliberately chosen to stay in the hospital to avoid the pressures of life outside, she has met with little resistance until McMurphy's arrival.

Almost immediately McMurphy becomes a focus of hope for the patients who have been emasculated by Big Nurse and by their fears of the outside world. Passage after passage suggests that Kesey envisions McMurphy as a Christ figure who must sacrifice himself to bring life to the other patients.

McMurphy's efforts to give the other patients a sense of joy in living culminates with a drunken party he arranges on the ward; a featured guest is a prostitute who provides Billy Bibbit, a painfully shy and insecure man aged 30, with his first sexual experience. When Big Nurse discovers Billy with the prostitute, she overwhelms him with guilt, causing his suicide.

McMurphy attacks Big Nurse, but he is pulled away and lobotomized. When McMurphy is returned to the ward, Chief Broom smothers him so that he cannot be used as a trophy of Big Nurse's victory. He then throws a huge control panel through a window and escapes, an action symbolizing his restoration to manhood and independence through his contact with McMurphy.

ONE HUNDRED YEARS OF SOLITUDE
Gabriel García Márquez
1967
Novel
Magical Realism, Family Saga

This 1967 novel is largely responsible for its author's claim to the 1982 Nobel Prize for Literature. The story follows seven generations of the Buendias family, the city of Macondo's founding family, and examines the loss of innocence that comes with developing technology.

José Arcadio Buendía and his wife and first cousin, Ursula Iguarán, leave Riohacha, Columbia on a search for a better life. After a vision of a city of mirrors that reflect the world, José Arcadio Buendía founds the town of Macondo—a city based on José Arcadio Buendía's beliefs and perceptions. He is a curious man, interested in technology and discovery, and many people respect and follow him even though they do not necessarily agree with his ideals. This leads to Macondo's isolation from the rest of the world, for a time, except for the wandering Gypsies who amaze the town with "modern technologies" like ice.

Each new Buendia generation experiences its own kind of love, pain, happiness, and sorrow. The town is constantly facing strange and fantastical occurrences that impact the multi-generational Buendía family, which is unable to escape the series of unfortunate events that include insomnia and ghost appearances. The city's solitude eventually ends when it contacts other towns and war breaks out.

An American-owned banana plantation settles in the city. Its mistreated workers strike and thousands are massacred, their bodies dumped into the sea. Five years of rain flood and destroy Macondo. The city and the family fall into solitude once again. At the end, the last Buendía family member translates an encryption that informs him of all the fortunes and misfortunes the family has faced, and he realizes that the family was just living out a predestined cycle of the beauty and terror of life.

One Hundred Years of Solitude examines whether modern technology and the pursuits of intelligence are necessarily progressive. José Arcadio Buendía loses his happiness with these pursuits and, as a result, sends the city into chaos and misery. In the end, the city regresses into isolation with its history written in ancient text.

THE OPEN BOAT
Stephen Crane
1898
Short Story
Adventure, Philosophical

In "The Open Boat" Crane's talents as a storyteller and interpretive writer are fully displayed. Subtitled "a tale intended to be after the fact," this short story describes a misadventure that Crane actually experienced after a shipwreck while running guns to Cuba.

The main conflict is the classic one of man against nature—in this case, the sea. Crane gives a detailed account of thirty hours spent in a ten-foot dinghy by four men—a cook, a correspondent, the Captain, and Billy Higgens, the oiler, who is the only character called by name, though the correspondent is obviously Crane himself.

The four men make up the entire cast of characters; there is no single protagonist. The point of view is that of an omniscient narrator, and the use of plural pronouns through much of the story enforces the impression that their predicament is a collective experience.

While the men are adrift off the coast of Florida, they learn two important lessons. First, the natural world is at best indifferent to man, if not hostile, as the high, cold winter star, the roaring waves, and a menacing shark symbolically suggest. Second, if they are to survive, they will have to rely on themselves alone since they can expect no benevolent intervention from either God or nature.

Even though Crane writes that "shipwrecks are apropos of nothing," he conveys with almost poetic prose a conception that was at the heart of his vision as an artist: The true nature of man's perilous position in the naturalistic universe dictates that he must form "a subtle brotherhood," composed of those who truly understand the way things are. The men in the open boat show us that compassion for one's fellows, stoic endurance, and courage are the true moral standards in an amoral cosmos.

The cynical view of human society reflected in Crane's earlier story "*The Blue Hotel*" is here replaced by a more optimistic outlook; although Crane still regards the universe as inhospitable, he sees hope in human solidarity as a means of mutual salvation.

THE OPEN WINDOW
Saki
1914
Short Story
Comedy, Satire

"The Open Window" typifies the classic Saki short story, the main ingredients being an oddly-named, somewhat priggish adult, a bluffly impertinent child, and a confrontation between them resulting in a surprise ending.

Armed with a letter of introduction, Framton Nuttel is visiting Mrs. Sappleton's country estate for a "nerve cure." Mr. Nuttel is greeted by the niece, Vera, a polite "self-possessed young lady of fifteen," who begins telling him about her aunt's great tragedy. Pointing to the open French window, Vera (Latin, meaning "truth") spins a yarn about her aunt's husband and two brothers who went out through the window on a hunting trip through the moors fifteen years earlier and never returned. The aunt keeps the window open in expectation of their imminent return.

Suddenly the aunt enters. Over the civilities of tea and polite conversation, she alludes to the hunting trip, and Mr. Nuttel becomes gradually unnerved. When, indeed, the hunting party returns, Nuttel, as if he had seen ghosts, flees. The niece, we learn, had told the truth about the hunters, but had made up the part about their disappearance. They had simply gone out that morning, but, says Saki, Vera was incorrigible. "Romance at short notice was her specialty."

At first glance the story appears to be a mere joke; but "The Open Window" can be reread with pleasure because of its masterful tone—a finely honed, polite restraint with only a hint of a smirk on the authorial face.

Finally, the narrative works as a parody of the traditional ghost story. Vera's yarn has all the trimmings of the standard mystery—the journey on the moors, the mysterious disappearance, even Mr. Nuttel's role as scared listener. In the end, the tradition is subverted. Romance is but a prank.

THE ORESTEIA
Aeschylus
458 B.C.E.
Drama
Classical, Greek

The Oresteia is a trilogy of plays dramatizing a curse on the ruling family of Mycenae and a social change from ancient clan justice to the more objective civil justice of the Greek city-state.

In the first play, *Agamemnon,* the protagonist of that name returns home from the Trojan War with his beautiful prize of war, the Trojan princess Cassandra. Agamemnon's wife Clytemnestra pretends to welcome him home gladly, but when he steps from his bath, she folds him in a large robe and stabs him to death. The helpless Cassandra, a prophetess of Apollo, foresees the fate of her master and her own murder as well, but no one understands her ravings. Clytemnestra flaunts her deeds before the chorus of elders as revenge for Agamemnon's sacrifice of their daughter Iphegeneia to gain favorable winds to sail to Troy.

The second play, *The Libation Bearers,* focuses on the return of Orestes, Agamemnon's son, his reunion with his grieving sister, Electra, and their plot to avenge the death of their father. When Orestes kills his mother, however, the Furies, terrible avengers from the underworld, drive Orestes from the scene in a fit of insane horror.

The third play, *The Eumenides* (Benevolent Ones), is the trial of Orestes, who has sought the protection of the goddess Athena. She convenes a jury of 500 Athenian citizens to try the case. The god Apollo, who had goaded Orestes to avenge his father, defends the matricide. Orestes is acquitted, and Athena performs the more delicate task of persuading the resentful and dangerous Furies to assume a new role as honored protectors of the family.

The first two plays reveal how violence begets violence, each avenger mistakenly believing that he or she has restored moral order in the world. The last play is more philosophical, suggesting a reconciliation between the old gods and men and a more compassionate approach to complex moral situations.

THE ORPHAN MASTER'S SON
Adam Johnson
2012
Novel
Political, War

Set in North Korea, this 2012 picaresque novel won a 2013 Pulitzer Prize in fiction for the author who once visited North Korea. This dystopian novel examines the psychological interconnections between fascism and Orwellian propaganda.

The novel has two parts: Part One presents an omniscient narrator furnishing a biography of Pak Jun Do, a homonym for John Doe, an ordinary everyman; Part Two offers the confessions of Commander Ga, Pak Jun Do's father (whom Pak Jun Do impersonates) a military hero and rival of Kim Jong II.

The book contains many interludes of loudspeaker broadcasts that provide phony, fantastic, or manipulative news. The only first person narrator in the novel is a canny torturer who believes his work accomplishes good because the confessions he extracts, whether true or false, save lives.

Raised in a state orphanage, Long Tomorrows, run by his father during famine, Jun Do is sheltered from the outside world, though he is harshly treated by his father, Ga; Sun Moon, his mother, rumored to be a singer of such ethereal beauty that she has been kidnapped and air-lifted to Pyongyang, is Ga's wife.

Shunted into the military during his teens, Jun Do trains in the blind midnight of tunnels under the demilitarized zone. Assigned to shrimp poaching, he graduates to kidnapping Japanese vacationers on remote island beaches. Attempting to abduct a girl from a pier, he accidentally drowns her. Deemed uncoordinated for such activity, he's sent to learn English by listening to tapes and typing out what he hears. He does well enough that he's assigned to work in radio intercept. Promoted, he is flown to Texas as part of a spy team that visits a wealthy Senator's surreal ranch.

Part Two of the novel takes the reader through the streets of Pyongyang where sadism bounces like a roulette ball. In a quest to locate his mother, Jung Do assumes a fabricated identity—that of his father, General Ga—thus becoming a living fiction in an imposter's uniform. He becomes a "replacement husband" for Sun Moon. Initially, she makes him live in a deep hole in the yard, but eventually allows him to join her other children.

Dear Leader offers Jun Do the job of guarding an important American hostage. Like many writers, Jun Do commits imaginary treason.

Parallels to American culture—like, "Interrogators never go to prison,"—invite the reader to identify playfully ironic, amusing similarities. There's a labyrinthine echo to the book.

OTHELLO
William Shakespeare
1604
Drama
Tragedy

This tragedy chronicles the jealous rage of its soldier-hero, who, manipulated by a demonic villain, eventually kills his faithful wife and himself.

Othello, the drama's vain hero, is a Moor—traditionally interpreted as a black man—who wins the heart of Desdemona with his rollicking tales of battle and adventure, much to the dismay of her father and the Venetian court of which they are a part. Othello is a military man, ill at ease with public pomp and circumstance. The plot speeds up quickly when Iago, a subordinate of Othello, vows revenge after he has been passed over for promotion.

What follows is a series of intrigues in which Iago slowly convinces Othello of Desdemona's infidelity with Cassio, the lieutenant to whom Othello had given the position Iago had sought. Othello's inability to relate to individuals on a personal basis makes him a poor judge of character and highly susceptible to the ruthless Iago's machinations.

Oblivious to Iago's scheming and the transparent innocence of his wife and lieutenant, Othello is ultimately a victim of his own naivete and implacable ignorance. The final verdict upon Othello's character, despite what he claims in his final speech, is that he loved neither "wisely" nor "too well."

OUR TOWN
Thornton Wilder
1938
Drama
Magical Realist

Wilder's first full-length play, which won for him the Pulitzer Prize in 1938, is set in a small New England town in the early years of the 20th century and tells of the simple and tender love between George Gibbs and Emily Webb.

Influenced Our Townboth by German expressionism and by the French "purism" of Jacques Copeau and others, Wilder opens the play on a bare stage, allowing the audience to visualize the (nonexistent) scenery as it is evoked and described by the omnipresent Stage Manager.

The Stage Manager is surely one of Wilder's most memorable and masterful creations, a paternal and even godlike figure whose homespun speech and easygoing manner lend an air of simplicity and naturalness to what is, in fact, a rigorously structured, carefully contrived three-act play.

Set initially in 1901, the play telescopes in time to 1904 and eventually to 1913, ostensibly depicting everyday life in the mythical town of Grover's Corners, New Hampshire. Although almost all conditions of life are portrayed, the spectator's attention is gradually directed toward George Gibbs and Emily Webb, who eventually will fall in love and marry.

Because of its range, the role of Emily provides an excellent challenge and showcase for aspiring young actresses, which may account for much of the play's popularity with amateur and student groups.

The play's principal appeal, no doubt a function of its deceptive simplicity, is the ease with which the spectator is invited to identify with the characters portrayed. Just barely sharper than flat stereotype, the villagers of Grover's Corners help to remind spectators of what makes Americans different from other people; the play's setting, meanwhile, serves to remind them of a simpler life-style which, even by 1938, had retreated behind the mists of nostalgia.

OUT OF AFRICA
Isak Dinesen
1937
Nonfiction
Autobiography

A famous author's experiences as a coffee plantation owner in Kenya from 1914 to 1931 are turned into a lyrical account of her perception of the land and people of Africa.

Out of Africa is not a conventional autobiography but rather a selective collection of the author's impressions of her life in Africa that have been turned into a pastoral idyll through her art. The book focuses on the land and people of Africa and on the significance they had for her. Though Dinesen is present throughout the work, the real protagonist of the autobiography is Africa itself.

For Dinesen, Africa is separated from the everyday Western world by more than geographical distance. It is a world untouched by various social and scientific changes. The land, not yet domesticated by technology, is the shaper of human destiny. As a consequence, the people, whether native or immigrant, must be courageous, imaginative, and capable of dealing with the unknown.

Dinesen describes at great length these people, filling the book with such portraits as the destitute but vivacious Old Knudsen, the Englishmen Berkeley Cole and Denys Finch-Hatton, her servant Kamante, and Masai chief Kinanjui, the actor Emmanuelson, even the gazelle Lulu. These figures, Dinesen explains, are aristocrats who live outside of rigid systems but have a keenly developed sense of ritual that grows from their imaginative response to life.

The book ends with the failure of Dinesen's farm and, with it, the passing away of the old Africa, symbolized by the deaths of Kinanjui and Finch-Hatton. Yet this Africa would live on in the stories that Dinesen had begun to write on her farm. The values of Africa form an integral part of Dinesen's writing, of which *Out of Africa* itself is one of the finest examples.

THE OUTCASTS OF POKER FLAT
Bret Harte
1869
Short Story
Western

Several social outcasts—a gambler, a prostitute, a drunk, and a madam—are run out of a small Western town. When they become snowbound in the mountains with an innocent young couple, they reveal their inner nobility.

The simplicity of the story is a result of the too-easy transformation of such characters as "the Duchess," a prostitute who reveals a "heart of gold," and "Mother Shipton," an old reprobate who gives up her food, and thus her life, so that the innocent Piney Woods can live. The unlikely combination of the innocence of the young couple and the "sin" of the outcasts forms a sympathetic human community.

The story's sentimentality reaches its climax when Piney and the Duchess are found frozen to death and all "human stain, all trace of earthly travail, was hidden beneath the spotless mantle mercifully flung from above." One cannot tell which is the innocent virgin and which is the sinful prostitute.

The gambler, John Oakhurst, is the most interesting and complex character in the story, even though he too, in his philosophic attitude toward reality, is more a cliche than a fully embodied person. Although he stoically accepts his fate throughout the story and reveals his basically noble nature, at the tale's conclusion he takes his own life rather than await death by freezing and starvation. Thus he is called the strongest and yet the weakest of the outcasts of Poker Flat.

Oakhurst approaches life as his profession dictates, basing his actions on his awareness of luck; knowing when it will change is what makes a man, he says. His suicide at the end can thus be attributed to his knowledge that he has "hit a streak of bad luck"; he "cashes in his chips" before he "loses the game" of life.

THE OUTSIDER
Colin Wilson
1956
Nonfiction
Philosophical, Existential

This book is an immensely popular and influential study of the alienation of modern man and an attempt to arrive at an objective religious solution to the central problem of Western civilization.

Written while its young author was spending his nights in a sleeping bag on Hampstead Heath and his days reading and writing in the British Museum, this book exploded onto the literary scene of the mid-1950's, making Colin Wilson at the age of twenty-four one of the most widely read and discussed writers of his generation. Although his worldwide celebrity led to savage critical attacks on his second and following books, his reputation was established, and his first book remains one of the major books of the last half-century.

Wilson, who never attended college but was an omnivorous reader, found himself drawn to the experience of certain key figures of the modern world: Vincent Van Gogh, Vaslav Nijinsky, Friedrich Nietzsche, and T. E. Lawrence.

They are Outsiders, men whose lives of undisputed genius and often self-destructive violence set them apart from the ordinary. All stood for truth, but the sensitivity and awareness that enabled them to discover the truth also caused them great suffering. All had low "pain thresholds" (a term Wilson borrowed from William James) which prevented them from slipping into the spiritual sleepiness that pervaded their civilization.

Studying these men (and the lives and works of many others, such as Fyodor Dostoevski, Leo Tolstoy, Henry James, Hermann Hesse, G. I. Gurdjieff, H. G. Wells, and Jean-Paul Sartre), Wilson defined the Outsider as the one man who knows he is sick in a civilization that does not know it is sick. The suffering Outsider seeks an essentially religious answer to the crisis of value and the loss of individual worth in a secular society.

The book is both a study of the Outsider's predicament and an impassioned call for the creation of a healthy new existentialism which will produce a satisfactorily objective religious understanding of the nature of life. The Outsider who begins that long effort may finish it a saint.

THE OVERCOAT
Nikolai Gogol
1842
Novella
Comedy

This is a satiric view of the bureaucracy of czarist Russia, the indifference of people generally, and the misery of life at the lower levels of the social hierarchy.

A poor man in Saint Petersburg, after many years of labor as a government clerk, scrapes together enough money to buy a much-needed overcoat. He wears it proudly for one day, only to have it stolen from him on a dark street that night.

The ironic humor of this tale about Akaky Akakyvitch, confined to interminable copying of government documents both by society and by his own narrow preferences, contrasts sharply with the stark social realism of the action.

Akaky never recovers his prize possession. He appeals to the general, identified as a "Person of Consequence," but receives only a humiliating reprimand for not showing proper respect for rank. The distraught Akaky, crushed by the petty tyrant, who was only showing off his power before a friend, catches pneumonia on the way home and dies soon after.

The story ends with a seriocomic bit of Gothic fantasy. A corpse haunts the frigid night streets of Saint Petersburg, snatching fine overcoats off the backs of passersby. The ghost does not rest until, at last, he steals the luxurious fur coat of the terrified Person of Consequence who had humiliated him.

Although Nikolay Gogol was not particularly revolutionary in spirit, this tale had considerable influence on mid-nineteenth century Russian writers of the Critical Realism school, those interested in revealing the pitiable state of the "little man." Fyodor Dostoevski once remarked that all Russian writers came from under Gogol's "Overcoat."

Gogol combined humor, symbol, and social message in several other works, as well, including a comic play, *The Inspector General* (1836), which also satirizes bureaucracy, and a novel, *Dead Souls*, which describes a con game in the provinces.

OZYMANDIAS
Percy Bysshe Shelley
1818
Poetry
Sonnet

Shelley's powerful sonnet describing the wreck of a monument intended to memorialize an ancient ruler is a deeply ironic commentary on how the arrogant wishes of a tyrant may be crushed by forces far beyond his control.

The poem's narrator presents the reader with a stunning vision of the tomb of Ozymandias, another name for Rameses II, King of Egypt during the 13th century B.C. Shelley emphasizes that to a modern viewer this tomb tells quite a different tale than that which Ozymandias had hoped it would. The king evidently commissioned a sculptor to create an enormous sphinx to represent his enduring power, but the traveler comes across only a broken heap of stones ravaged by time.

Enough of the original monument exists to allow Shelley a moment of triumph over the thwarted plans of the ruler. The face of Ozymandias is still recognizable, but it is "shattered," and, though his "sneer of cold command" persists, it is obvious that he no longer commands anyone or anything. The vaunting words carved into the stone pedestal can still be read: "Look on my works, ye Mighty, and despair!" Yet he is to be pitied, if not disdained, rather than held in awe and fear: The broken-down tomb is set in a vast wasteland of sand, perhaps Shelley's way of suggesting that all tyrants ultimately end up in the only kind of kingdom they deserve, a barren desert.

Shelley's sonnet, however, would not be the great poem it surely is if it were only a bit of political satire. The irony of "Ozymandias" cuts much deeper as the reader realizes that the forces of mortality and mutability, described brilliantly in the concluding lines, will erode and destroy all our lives. There is a special justice in the way tyrants are subject to time, but all humans face death and decay. The poem remains primarily an ironic and compelling critique of Ozymandias and other rulers like him, but it is also a striking meditation on time-bound humanity: the traveler in the ancient land, the sculptor-artist who fashioned the tomb, and the reader of the poem, no less than Ozymandias, inhabit a world that is "boundless and bare."

P

PALE FIRE
Vladimir Nabokov
1962
Novel
Satire

This novel offers an imaginative study of a madman's attempt to extract unique personal meaning out of the poetic creation of another.

The novel consists of a long, elegiac poem written by a poet named John Shade and a rambling commentary on the poem produced by a Professor Charles Kinbote. Comparing Kinbote's commentary with Shade's poem, one immediately discovers a strange disparity. Shade's poem is a touching, emotional work portraying the poet's attempt to understand the reality of death, the poignancy of loss, and the redeeming power of love in human life. Kinbote's commentary, in contrast, interprets the poem as a veiled saga about the exiled king of a fabulous realm named Zembla. As he develops his commentary, Kinbote plunges deeper and deeper into his personal tale of Zemblan manners and intrigue, ultimately suggesting that he himself is that marvelous Zemblan king, Charles the Beloved.

Nabokov's novel presents a humorous and unusual portrait of subjective reality. Kinbote's extravagant attempts to project his fantasy onto Shade's poem reflect an important theme in Nabokov's fiction—that the creation of one's inner vision is more real to an individual than the reality of the external world. Reading further into Kinbote's commentary, however, one discovers profound links between Kinbote's and Shade's concerns. Both men attempt to deal with such concepts as suffering, loss, and love, and each tries to find order in the seemingly chaotic world of human experience, Shade through the structured processes of genuine art, and Kinbote through his anxiety-ridden tale of royal exile and persecution.

The unfettered forces of imagination, the ability to treat life as fiction and fiction as life, combine in *Pale Fire* to create a dazzling novel of wit and high seriousness.

PALE HORSE, PALE RIDER
Katherine Anne Porter
1938
Novella
Collection, Tragedy

The three novellas gathered in this volume range from the tragic tale of a Texas farmer who accidentally kills a man, to the complex stream-of-consciousness story of a young woman who loses her lover to influenza during World War I.

Old Mortality centers on Miranda's memories of childhood. She remembers especially how her family idealized Aunt Amy, making her a legend of Southern womanhood after the Civil War. Ironically, Amy is shown to be a free-spirited woman who was trapped into a conventional marriage. When Miranda sees how Amy is trapped, her faith in romantic legend is shaken. Miranda wants to be free of convention. She wants to be an airplane pilot, to know the truth about her own life, and still to be loved by her family. This short novel shows the degree to which Miranda is caught between these contrary desires.

In *Noon Wine*, Mr. Thompson's good luck seems to begin the day he hires Mr. Helton, a strange, quiet, and very competent Swede. Thompson is failing because dairy farming offends his sense of dignity and order, but Helton takes everything in hand. Years later, Mr. Hatch, a bounty hunter, comes to take Helton back to the North Dakota insane asylum from which he escaped. Trying to protect Helton, Thompson kills Hatch. Thompson wants to believe that killing Hatch was right, but he cannot. Oppressed by inescapable guilt, Thompson finds his family and his life falling apart. Powerless to restore their lost happiness, Thompson commits suicide.

Pale Horse, Pale Rider is the most complex of these three novellas. In 1918, Miranda feels she has lost everything and, therefore, that she will lose her beloved Adam, too. She nearly dies in the influenza epidemic which kills Adam. Even though she does not know he is dead, she is tempted, during her delirium, to give up her life. War and plague point to a fundamental chaos that she believes rules life. After her recovery, she is still torn between the need to erect illusions, such as the legend of Aunt Amy, as a defense against chaos, and her desire to face squarely the truth about life.

PAMELA
Samuel Richardson
1740-1741
Novel
Epistolary

Parrying her master's sexual advances, a servant girl wins his love and becomes his wife. Often described as the first English novel, Pamela *remains an intriguing account of the battle between the sexes.*

Richardson poses as the editor of numerous letters passing between the major characters in the novel. Most of the letters are devoted to Pamela's account of her efforts to avoid seduction and rape.

Pamela is a servant at an estate whose owner, Mr. B., becomes enamored of her beauty. From stealing kisses, he progresses to outright seduction. He makes Pamela a prisoner to force her to become his mistress. When Pamela resists, B. unsuccessfully attempts rape.

Pamela proves resourceful in defense of her virginity. With logic she destroy's B.'s rationale for dalliance. By fainting and faking suicide she stymies his physical assaults. By writing letters she rallies the help of friends and family.

Pamela's virtuousness eventually changes B.'s attitude. As his lust turns to love, her defensiveness melts into deference. When he proposes, she gratefully accepts. The match is not easily accepted: His family resents her social background, her family fears a false marriage. Pamela's goodness and B.'s fervor win over the doubters.

Richardson's novel was daring for its time. The public debated the sensational sexual theme. Readers responded to Richardson's original technique of "writing to the moment," that is, of depicting events through various letter writers, for whom the thoughts and emotions regarding these events were supposedly still fresh.

Some readers have found objectionable Pamela's willingness to marry her tormentor. Did she preserve her virginity for virtue's sake or for a better offer? Others admire Pamela's plucky defense, both intellectual and physical, of her sense of self.

PARADISE LOST
John Milton
1667
Poetry
Epic

Centering upon Adam and Eve's fall from grace and their restoration to God's favor, the epic narrates the Christian scheme of time from Satan's rebellion until Judgment Day. In twelve books of ornate blank verse, the poem reveals the story of all things, a mythical account from a Protestant Christian perspective.

To carry out his prime aim of justifying God's ways to man, Milton clarifies Satan's motives by showing his machinations in Hell following his rebellion against God. The effort to subvert man having been determined, Satan journeys to Earth, arriving in Eden, where Adam and Eve dwell in perfect happiness.

Knowing Satan's purpose, God sends the angel Raphael to instruct Adam so that he cannot plead ignorance as an excuse for disobedience. Raphael narrates an account of war in Heaven and explains God's purpose in creating men—to provide other beings to fill heavenly places left empty by Satan's defeat.

Despite the warnings to Adam, Satan induces Eve to taste the forbidden fruit. Adam, unwilling to live without Eve, accepts the fruit from her hand, thereby breaking his covenant with God.

The final books reveal Adam and Eve's restoration to grace. The archangel Michael shows Adam all that will result from his sin, both good and evil, so that Adam understands and accepts God's will. Because God promises redemption through Christ, Adam departs from Eden assured that the will of God will prevail.

In presenting the Christian story in epic form, the poem adapts classical conventions to its narrative purposes, usually associating the classical elements with the demonic. Milton's ideal hero, unlike the warfaring classical hero, suffers and endures, like Christ and Adam.

The style—enriched by allusion, repetitions, Latinate diction, and numerous figures of speech—has never been surpassed for its grandeur. The densely textured narrative includes vast distances in time and space, long journeys, dreams, and allegorical fiction. To Milton, the central narrative represented historical truth; he had no doubt that it justified God's ways to man.

PARADISE REGAINED
John Milton
1671
Poetry
Epic

Based upon New Testament accounts of the temptations of Jesus following his baptism, the poem offers readers a highly individualistic interpretation of this episode in the life of Christ, who represents a suffering hero of faith and a model for Christians.

As the poem opens, neither Christ nor his followers understand his messianic role. Having fasted in the desert for 40 days, he is approached by his adversary Satan in disguise. Satan has heard the voice of God proclaiming Jesus His son and seeks to discover the meaning of the declaration.

Satan tempts Christ to assuage hunger, first by seeking to have him turn stones into bread and then by presenting an elaborate banquet. Recognizing his adversary, Christ refuses the blandishments.

In a second sequence, Satan tempts Christ by offering him wealth, power, and imperial sway. These would, presumably, enable him to exercise his role as Messiah, which he has not yet done. Rejecting all offers, including the wisdom and art of Athens, Christ prefers to wait for guidance from God.

After attempting to terrify Christ with a storm, Satan spirits him through the air to the pinnacle of the Temple, where the temptation is to cast himself down and be rescued by God's power. Christ's reply causes Satan to fall instead and signals that both characters have recognized his divine power. As angels minister to him, Jesus returns quietly to his mother's house.

Having triumphed over Satan, Milton's Christ is prepared to begin his public ministry. He has learned from the episode which roles the Messiah must reject. At the same time, he has been genuinely tempted, as a suffering human being who might have succumbed, and has remained steadfast in his faith. The poem suggests that this survival of temptation represents Christ's real triumph over Satan, even though man's salvation requires his death and resurrection.

A PASSAGE TO INDIA
E. M. Forster
1924
Novel
Psychological, Colonialism

Set in India in the last decades of the British Raj, this story of an Indian falsely accused of attempting to rape an Englishwoman crystallizes the political, racial, sexual, and philosophical issues raised by the confrontation of West and East.

Aziz, a Moslem doctor, shows off one of few sights of the region, the Marabar caves, to two visiting Englishwomen: Adela Quested, who has come out to marry an English official, and Mrs. Moore, the fiance's mother. Something happens to Adela at the caves, but both the alleged assault and the philosophical meaning of the Caves, with which Adela's experience is associated, remain mysterious. The philosophy is centered in Mrs. Moore, an old woman who is merely bored by the fuss being made over Aziz, and in the Hindu Professor Godbole, who also finds questions of individual guilt and innocence irrelevant. The critique of colonialism is centered in Fielding, who becomes friends with Aziz and breaks ranks with the English in order to support him.

The case is won when Adela collapses and retracts her accusation, but the friendship between Aziz and Fielding cannot hold out against the harsh fact of Empire. And the largest issue, Forster suggests, may not be the relation of East and West at all.

In a sense it is the alien, inhuman landscape, throwing the values and certainties by which both Fielding and Aziz live into question, which is Forster's hero. Like the birds who circle the events of the novel from above, Forster retreats from the comedy of manners and the social plot into a nihilistic detachment, which has as much to do with the Mediterranean pastorals of his earlier novels as with Hinduism. Although the Hindu festival of the novel's last section introduces an affirmative note, its affirmation is impersonal. The belief in "personal relations" that had inspired Forster's novels is gone.

PATERSON
William Carlos Williams
1963
Poetry
Williams' answer to T. S. Eliot's The Waste Land *and the other great long poems of American Modernism, this book-length poem employs the city of Paterson, New Jersey, as an extended metaphor for a man's life.*

Originally conceived in four parts, William Carlos Williams' longest poem was left unfinished at the time of the poet's death in 1963. Williams had by then realized that a poem that sought to include the poet's entire world was ultimately unfinishable. The first section was published in 1946, the fifth in 1958. Notes for a sixth section were found after Williams' death.

The poem's main character, Dr. P., is both a poet and a physician, as was Williams himself. His journeys through the city of Paterson take him to a park, to a library, and to the bedside of his patients. Minor characters abound. A brutalized black girl, a woman poet called "Cress," and the poet Allen Ginsberg (called "A. G.") all figure prominently in P.'s world.

As important as any human character in the poem is Paterson itself: Williams quotes liberally from documentary sources, re-creating imaginatively the history and legendry of the city. Also central are the Passaic River and the Falls, which take on several symbolic and allegorical meanings in the poem.

Like Eliot's *The Waste Land* and Ezra Pound's *Cantos* (both of which are alluded to in *Paterson*), the poem is a collage made up of quotations from other sources and the poet's own lyric musings. Like many of Williams' shorter works, it is characterized by innovative prosody and typography. *Paterson*, along with the poems mentioned above and Hart Crane's *The Bridge*, is one of the best-known and most significant long poems written by an American in the post-World War I era.

PAUL'S CASE
Willa Cather
1905
Short Story

The subtitle of this story—"a study in temperament"—provides a clue to its naturalistic focus: Paul's unsuccessful attempt to escape from his background and to live in the rarefied world of money, status, and class.

The story opens in Pittsburgh, a city of hardheaded, steellike reality, where Paul, a boy from a middle-class family, is dismissed from high school because of his impertinent attitude and bearing. Paul sees his case as special. He perceives himself as above the middle-class ethic and bourgeois values of his neighborhood.

In asserting his superiority, Paul seeks to live in the world of the arts. He loves the theater, the opera, and music, even though he is not particularly artistic. The world of art and its external trappings—luxury hotels, midnight champagne, the finest clothes—represent Paul's inarticulate aspirations, his desire to escape from his environment.

When Paul embezzles some money and flees to New York for a week of luxurious living, he both puts into action his own aspirations and sows the seeds of his own destruction. Once his crime is discovered, his father comes to New York to bring him back home. Paul realizes the futility of his flight, the impossibility of escaping into a better world. Despairing of a return to a world he loathes, Paul plunges back, by his suicide, into "the immense design of things." It is this "design of things" that determines Paul's fate.

PEARL
Unknown
Latter half of the fourteenth century
Poetry
Elegiac

Pearl *blends the grief of bereavement, religious piety, and a vision of heavenly glory in a quietly beautiful and fascinatingly intricate poem.*

The narrator, a "jeweler," is lamenting the loss, in a garden, of a "pearl," which symbolically represents the death of his young daughter. He falls asleep and in a marvelous dream finds himself in a paradiselike setting beside a river. Across the stream he sees a maiden both familiar and strange in a white gown set with pearls and wearing a splendid crown. It is his child, grown to maturity.

They converse across the river, he trying to understand the deprivation of his present life, she trying to reveal the mysteries of God's will to him. She suggests that the "pearl of great price," referred to in the biblical passage Matthew 13:46, is presently unavailable to him, for it is part of the eternal realm beyond the river. The rest of the poem presents the transformation of his grief by faith, the outcome of his desire to join her and the other blessed, and the ultimate acceptance of his loss.

In its form, PEARL is one of the most complex poems in the language. All but one of its twenty sections contain five twelve-line stanzas. The stanzas have an elaborate scheme of rhyme and alliteration, with those in each section linked by repeated words and phrases. Section 15 contains an extra stanza, giving the poem 1,212 lines, of which the last echoes the first. Thus, the poem is circular, like the pearl itself, and the structural use of the number twelve evokes the number symbolism of the Book of Revelation, such as the twelve gates of the New Jerusalem.

A contemporary of Chaucer, the Pearl Poet composed in a more difficult dialect. Brian Stone, Margaret Williams, and Marie Borroff are among those who have translated this poem into modern English while striving to retain the form of the original.

PEER GYNT
Henrik Ibsen
1876
Drama
Picaresque

An irresponsible young man abandons his sweetheart, spends his manhood traveling through the world, and arrives at old age, only to discover that his self has been lost along the way.

Peer Gynt is a lazy but charming Norwegian farm boy. A liar and boaster, he causes himself to be outlawed by stealing the bride at a wedding and then casting her away once he has seduced her. The latter action is motivated by his having met the young Solveig, who becomes his love ideal. In Solveig's absence, however, he commits even grosser erotic sins. Consorting with a mysterious woman dressed in green, a supernatural creature modeled on folk belief, he fathers a troll bastard, and later he is taken into the mountain, where he is to be married to the daughter of the resident troll king. Here he is asked to make certain promises which signify his making utter selfishness his rule of life.

After Peer's banishment, Solveig comes to join him in his forest cabin. A brief period of happiness ensues. Then Peer is confronted with his troll offspring and flees. A lifetime of various activities follows, among which are participation in the American slave trade and gunrunning in the war between Greece and Turkey.

After a period in North Africa and a stint at an insane asylum in Cairo, Egypt, where the other inmates make him their emperor, Peer finally returns home. Shipwrecked off the coast of Norway, he has to travel to his native valley on foot. En route he encounters a mysterious character named the Button Moulder, who states that since Peer has no visible personality he is now destined to have his soul melted down into nothingness. Peer frantically searches for a witness who can testify to the fact that he indeed has a self. None can be found until Peer reaches the cabin where Solveig, now an old woman, lives alone. She assures him that in her mind and love, he exists in a state of wholeness.

PENSÉES
Blaise Pascal
1670
Nonfiction
Religious

Pensées is a religious classic composed of fragmentary reflections on the human condition without and with God.

Pascal is a significant figure in the history of science and mathematics whose most important legacy is this collection of what are essentially notes for a formal defense of Christianity, which he never completed.

Many of Pascal's most powerful entries poignantly explore the tragedy of the human condition if there is no God. He depicts mankind as lost in an alien and inhospitable world, in consequence of which it gives itself over to the baubles and distractions of human society.

Pascal finds the solution for the human dilemma in the grace of God as manifested in Jesus Christ. He does not, however, offer this as an effortless solution. Part of Pascal's enduring appeal is his very modern awareness of the difficulty of religious faith in a scientific and skeptical world.

Pascal felt caught between two contrary forces: the rationalism of rising 17th century science, and skepticism about all human efforts, reason included, as epitomized by his French predecessor Montaigne. He sought an approach to life that avoided the arrogance of the former and the cynicism and moral passivity of the latter.

In this sense, Pascal's situation anticipates the modern one. How does one justify faith in a rationalistic, skeptical world? One aspect of Pascal's response is his famous "Wager," in which he argues that belief in God, while not certain, is less a risk than unbelief when one considers the consequences of betting wrongly.

Pensées is a timeless work indispensable for anyone with religious sensitivity or curiosity.

A PERFECT DAY FOR BANANAFISH
J. D. Salinger
1948
Short Story

Seymour Glass, a hypersensitive, alienated young man, cannot reconcile himself to the demands of a vulgar world. This brief, arresting story introduces Salinger's preoccupation with the plight of the dedicated idealist in the modern world.

J.D. Salinger's America is a loveless place that provides little opportunity for romantic or spiritual achievement. Seymour Glass is a poetic saint caught in a stifling marriage to Muriel, whom he has dubbed "Miss Spiritual Tramp of 1948." Their honeymoon only emphasizes their separateness and the impossibility of real intimacy between them: While an unfeeling Muriel concerns herself with drying her nails and gabbing on the phone with her mother about her new husband's questionable sanity, Seymour roams the beach. There he meets and courts the affection of a little girl, Sybil Carpenter, whose innocence and natural sympathy for his loneliness both please him (he plants a kiss on her ankle) and force him to weigh a child's warmth against the bleakness of the adult responsibilities that face him.

The story's title refers to a tale which Seymour relates to Sybil about mythical fish that presumably swim into holes deep in the ocean floor where bananas are hidden; once there, the bananafish gorge themselves until they are too fat to escape the holes, thereby sealing their doom. Likewise, Seymour is a victim of gluttony: He is so vulnerable to sensation, so overwhelmed by the mysteries of his universe, that he cannot return to society again—especially not as that society is defined by the small-minded concerns of his wife and his mother-in-law.

The shocking end to the story exemplifies what dedicated readers of Salinger have come to appreciate as the intricate relationship between humor and misfortune. On one page, we are laughing at Seymour's caustic encounter with a woman in the hotel elevator, and on the next we are confronted with his calmly methodical suicide, Seymour's "banana fever." Seymour is but one of Salinger's perceptive, feeling heroes surrounded by people who limit themselves to artificial gestures and shallow desires. It is a perfect day to purge himself of participation in such company.

PETER PAN
James Barrie
1904
Drama

In this classic children's tale, Peter Pan, embodiment of eternal youth and fun, leads Wendy and her brothers through exciting adventures in Neverland. Older readers enjoy the story's charm, fantasy, sly humor, and its exploration of adult ambivalence about growing up.

On a serene Friday night in suburban London, Peter Pan disrupts the Darling household by flying into the nursery window to listen to bedtime stories. Soon Wendy and her brothers take wing, following Peter to Neverland, where time stands still.

Cocky Peter Pan captains his new guests and his crew of six lost boys through the dangers of his island domain—wild beasts, mermaids, Indians, pirates. Wendy readily assumes the role of surrogate mother, in charge of storytelling, darning, and maintaining order. Harrowing adventures such as being trapped on Marooner's Rock, rescuing Princess Tiger Lily, and narrowly escaping the snares of villainous pirate leader, Captain Hook, spice the flow of childhood fun.

On the Night of Nights, pirates discover the children's underground house; a pitched battle occurs, and all but Peter are captured, trussed, and scheduled to walk the plank on Captain Hook's ship. Through a clever ruse, Peter is able to sneak aboard and demoralize Hook's crew. At last, Peter goes sword to sword with the infamous Hook. The Captain meets his fate, not on Peter's sword, but in the jaws of the ticking crocodile, which has pursued him as tirelessly as time itself.

Peter, Wendy, and all the boys return to the security of the Darling nursery, where school, jobs, and adulthood inevitably ensue. Peter, however, refuses adoption and returns to Neverland because he wants always to remain a boy and have fun. To Wendy's daughter, to her daughter's daughter, generation after generation, Peter Pan reappears ever cocky, ever a boy, to touch each child with the fairy dust which will spark her life with magic.

Peter Pan is best known as a rollicking bedtime story, but beneath its surface gaiety and innocence lie our fears of sex and death, our desires for dependence and independence, and our aversions and attractions to authority. This book remains a classic exploration of the tensions between staying a child forever and growing irrevocably into maturity, a parable of the fierce battles and fragile interdependence of the child and the parent within each of us.

PHAEDRA
Jean Racine
1677
Drama
Neoclassical

Essentially an adaption of Euripides' Hippolytus, this play also serves as a vehicle for the expression of the author's own commitment to the Christian doctrine of predestination. While Neoclassical literature has but a limited appeal for most English-speaking readers, Racine's masterwork deserves the widest possible audience by virtue of its paramount importance in the repertory of the French theater.

In this drama, Phedra, the young wife of the legendary Athenian king Theseus, struggles valiantly, albeit unsuccessfully, to control an illicit passion for her stepson, Hippolytus, and his unresponsiveness leads to the tragic death of both principals.

As the play opens, Theseus has been absent from his domain for more than six months. During this period, Hippolytus, who enjoys a reputation for being indifferent to women, discovers that he is in love. The object of his affection is Aricia, the sole surviving child of Theseus' archrival for the kingship of Athens. He dares not make a proposal of marriage, since Theseus has decreed that she must remain unwed to safeguard the dynastic rights of his own children by Phedra. At the same time, Phedra herself is struggling to repress her own romantic obsession with Hippolytus.

The situation changes abruptly when news of Theseus' purported death arrives. Hippolytus declares his love for Aricia, and Phedra, at the prompting of her maid, confesses her own love to Hippolytus. While Aricia is receptive, Hippolytus reacts with indignation. To everyone's surprise, Theseus now appears, and Phedra's maid feels obliged to protect her mistress's honor by informing him that Hippolytus had attempted to seduce the queen. In defending himself, Hippolytus chooses not to betray Phedra's confidence, but informs his father that he is really in love with Aricia. Refusing to accept his son's innocence, Theseus banishes Hippolytus and calls upon Neptune to annihilate him.

Phedra herself is now on the point of admitting the truth to Theseus. When her husband informs her of Hippolytus' claim to be in love with Aricia, however, she remains silent out of jealousy. Hippolytus, meanwhile, has been thrown from his chariot and dragged to death after his horses were frightened by a sea monster as he drove along the shore. When his corpse is returned home, Phedra is stricken with remorse and takes poison. Before expiring, she confesses her guilt to Theseus. To appease the shade of Hippolytus, Theseus announces that he will henceforth treat Aricia as though she were his very own daughter.

Phedra is by no means wicked, for she struggles fiercely to control her emotions. From a pagan perspective, she is simply a victim of Venus. There is, however, every reason to believe that Racine himself viewed her in terms of the Jansenist theology of predestination. She was, in short, an essentially virtuous person from whom redeeming grace had been withheld.

One of the singular beauties of the play lies in its use of rhymed alexandrine couplets to establish a Baroque tension between content and form.

PHANTOM OF THE OPERA
Gaston Leroux
1911
Drama
Gothic

A great fan of Edgar Allan Poe and Sir Arthur Conan Doyle, Gaston Leroux wrote his classic as part horror story, and part detective fiction, with scenes reminiscent of Dante's descent into hell, when the Vicomte's "Persian" guides him through the labyrinth far below the opera stage, to rescue his love, the opera diva, Christine Daaé.

Vicomte Raoul de Chagny overhears a man's voice in his love, Christine Daaé's dressing room, entreating her with "you must love me." Raoul is stricken with jealousy, so as soon as Christine leaves, he surreptitiously enters to confront the man, but finds the room empty. So begins the Raoul's quest to learn the identity of this "phantom," and to rescue Christine from his grip. At the same time, a murder has occurred, and the new managers of the opera, Richard and Moncharmin, receive strange demands from a mysterious source—demands for money and, most importantly, to keep "Box 5" reserved for this unknown patron. Various opera employees claim it is the opera ghost, but Richard and Moncharmin think it must be a practical joke. However, they learn that not honoring these demands is dangerous. Despite their best efforts to learn this man's identity, he remains a mystery.

Christine Daaé was a deeply devoted daughter and, after her father's death, she looks for his "Angel of Music" whom he promised to send, to instruct her in voice. When the mysterious Eric, who wears a mask to hide his facial deformities, meets Christine, he teaches her, claiming to be the anticipated "Angel of Music," thus winning her trust. Eric falls deeply in love, becoming jealous of Raoul who is successfully wooing Christine. He kidnaps Christine but sets her free long enough to break off all ties with Raoul. Raoul and Christine make secret plans to run away, but the phantom overhears. Christine mysteriously disappears during her last performance. With the guidance of the mysterious "Persian" (also known as Daroga) Raoul finds his way through vast underground structures, into the phantom's torture chamber, where they learn that the phantom plans to destroy them all, including the opera house, if Christine refuses to marry him.

In the final chapter, the Persian reveals that Christine, in an act of great compassion, kisses the phantom and melts his rage. That one act of love, through her own free will, is enough to sustain him, and he lets her go to marry Raoul.

PICKWICK PAPERS
Charles Dickens
1836-1837
Novel
Comedy

Pickwick Papers *follows the adventures of Samuel Pickwick and three of his fellow members of the Pickwick Club as they travel through England between 1827 and 1829.*

With only *Sketches By Boz* to his credit, Dickens asked his publisher to allow him to present a free "range of English scenes and people," and in *Pickwick Papers*, his first novel, he does just that. There is little coherence to the Pickwickians' journey. As they wander through the country, they repeatedly get into trouble because of their innocence. Pickwick in particular is the embodiment of simplicity and innocence—an angel in gaiters—and hence easily victimized. Yet his benevolence triumphs; he redeems both spiritually and financially those who seek to prey upon him.

Dickens reveals a masterfully light touch: The various incidents are comic in themselves, and the work itself is a comedy, presenting the triumph of goodness. Indeed, the work has a fairy-tale atmosphere.

Occasionally a darker tone does intrude. The nine interpolated stories present visions of poverty, madness, and drunkenness unrelieved and unredeemed by any benevolent angel in gaiters. Pickwick and his friends are able to leave debtor's prison, but most of the inmates are not so fortunate. Legal chicanery, political corruption, and religious hypocrisy also cast their shadows across the landscape.

"Like another sun," Pickwick keeps these shadows small, though, and the book is filled with cheerfulness. Dickens' first and happiest novel, it hints at the themes that would preoccupy him for the remainder of his life.

THE PICTURE OF DORIAN GRAY
Oscar Wilde
1891
Novel

An aristocrat remains eternally youthful while his portrait absorbs the effects of his dissipations. This late 19th century masterpiece espouses the claims of art and the individual over those of society and morality.

The opening chapter of this fascinating story establishes a milieu in which leisured aristocrats indulge exquisite aesthetic tastes. Dominating this world of luxury is the cynical and brilliantly witty Lord Henry Wotton. He introduces Dorian Gray, a wealthy young man of mysterious background, and Basil Hallward, a renowned artist. Filled with admiration, Basil paints a striking portrait of Dorian. Seeing it, Dorian exclaims that he would sell his soul to remain always youthful while the portrait ages in his place. He gets his wish.

Dorian then embarks upon a hedonistic life, developing every intellectual, aesthetic, and sensual appetite to the utmost. Despite his look of innocent beauty, he exerts a corrupting influence over many acquaintances. At least two later commit suicide. Yet except for his irrational (and undetected) murder of Basil—who realized the truth about Dorian and tried to make him repent—Dorian's sins remain unspecified. He tries to confess them to Lord Henry, who, however, refuses to take anything seriously.

Meanwhile, Dorian's portrait grows more horribly ugly with each new sin, until in a fit of remorse he destroys it and, unwittingly, himself.

The Picture Of Dorian Gray was a controversial masterpiece of the 1890's Aesthetic movement. (Wilde defended it against charges of immorality by saying that vice and virtue are to the novelist what colors on a palette are to the painter.) Yet the novel's appeal far exceeds that of a mere period piece. Despite the dark theme, it gives us the peculiarly Wildean brand of flashing wit and paradox, and finely wrought descriptions of color, sound, and even scent.

PICTURES FROM BRUEGHEL
William Carlos Williams
1962
Poetry

The poet's last collection of poems, this book will inspire the reader to see the world anew. On the brink of the grave Williams advises his reader to cherish love and the imagination.

These poems record the poet's looking at things, both visible and invisible. Whether examining the paintings of Brueghel or the love for his wife Flossie, it is with an eye and a mind conscious of their decay. They look inward upon their own extinction, with grief, yet forcefully continue to affirm life.

Williams champions Brueghel for his artist's grasp of life in a world twisted by distortion. The Dutch peasants in the wedding painting dance vigorously, despite their loutishness. Brueghel shares with Williams the imagination which sees through death to life. Poetry, like painting, Williams declares, is a spring activity, even if its subject is winter or old age.

After ten poems on Brueghel, the book flowers with poems on diverse subjects, both conventionally poetic and randomly prosaic. Trees share space with dead sparrows, the poet's family with anonymous figures seen by Williams on the street.

A poignant desire to be heard is felt in the poems. His faculties in ruin from strokes, Williams reaches out from his physical isolation to loved ones. To type the poems, he lifted his paralyzed arm with his usable arm and dropped it on the typewriter's electric keyboard. Do not close up the mind, he says, again and again. Love is a marvel, he sings, so use it to forgive.

Williams' poetic technique works to create the sound of a real voice speaking. The voice in these last poems is a teacher's voice and a lover's voice, which says that to know and to love are the same thing. Loving the world, Williams grants it pardon for gradually silencing his poet's speech. He painfully surrenders his power to say. But praise and thanksgiving for all he has felt, and yet partially feels, is the dominant message.

THE PILGRIM'S PROGRESS
John Bunyan
1678
Novel
Allegorical
This allegory of Puritan devotion illustrates the trials and rewards of Christian spirituality.

Bunyan's two-part allegory covers the spiritual lives of a Christian convert and his family. The main character, Christian, is converted by Evangelist, who instructs him to leave the City of Destruction through the wicket gate on his way to the Celestial City. Christian's family misunderstands him and his neighbors attack him, but Christian leaves his home with a burden on his back and a book in his hand.

Before finding the wicket gate, Christian succumbs to the Slough of Despond and Mr. Worldly Wiseman, who leads him to comfort in the village of Morality. Fortunately, Evangelist steers him to the wicket gate, where Christian climbs a hill to a cross. There Christian loses the burden and is outfitted for travel to the Celestial City.

On his way there, Christian encounters the Hill of Difficulty, Humiliation, Vanity Fair, and By-Path Meadow. Christian gets lost at Doubting Castle, where the giant Despair imprisons him. Remembering his key of Promise, Christian escapes and ascends the Delectable Mountains, where he first sees the Celestial City.

One more temptation awaits Christian: He almost drowns in a river when he contemplates his sins. He is rescued by Hopeful, and the two of them enter the Celestial City together.

In the second part of this allegory, Christian's wife and sons, who had refused to accompany him to the Celestial City, are converted at his death and decide to journey to the Celestial City themselves. They take the same path but have different experiences because by this time there are more pilgrims to help them. They find help in Mercy, Mr. Greatheart, Mr. Honest, Mr. Valiant-for-Truth, and Mr. Steadfast, among others. They encounter their fair share of temptations, but their journey is easier than Christian's because his courage was inspirational and instructive.

THE PIT AND THE PENDULUM
Edgar Allan Poe
1842
Short Story
Gothic
The narrator of this tale finds himself in a rat-infested dungeon facing annihilation.

"Terror is not of Germany, but of the soul," said Poe in the preface to his *Tales of the Grotesque and Arabesque*. In other words, Poe rejected the conventional trappings of the Gothic horror tale and tried, instead, to create the effect of terror by leaving much to the imagination, while at the same time giving minute details which create verisimilitude.

A victim of the Inquisition, the narrator of "The Pit and the Pendulum" finds himself confined in a torture chamber. He escapes by plunging into a pit, only to face further terror in the form of a swinging pendulum with a razorlike blade that descends closer to his body with each swing.

The entire plot consists of the narrator's responses to this plight. He endures a series of dreadful predicaments which hasten the disintegration of his mind and body in this living death. Despite the seeming futility of his condition, he absurdly struggles to save himself from each dilemma, only to face a yet more horrible situation. At various times, hope revives, and his mind becomes calm, attaching itself to a trifle or matter-of-factly calculating the dimensions of the prison. At other times, his mind plunges into despair and his senses betray him, especially toward the end when he perceives the shape of the room changing.

The tale ends with the unexpected deliverance of the narrator from the scene of terror. On the literal level, he is liberated by the enemies of the Inquisition, but the real story is one of the mind saved from annihilation or madness.

THE PLAGUE
Albert Camus
1947
Novel
Allegorical

The second of the three novels that French author Camus published during his lifetime in a grim allegory of the human condition as an unremitting struggle.

Set in Oran, in Camus' native Algeria, during the 1940's, the book chronicles the onset and duration of a bubonic plague. An alarming rate of casualties induces the authorities to declare an epidemic and to quarantine the city. The closing of Oran's gates causes the separation of families, friends, and lovers. Such is the case for Dr. Bernard Rieux, whose wife happens to be out of town when the quarantine is imposed.

Rieux takes a leading role in assisting the victims of the plague, though it is not clear that medical aid makes any difference whatsoever. He is joined in his stubborn efforts by Tarrou, a solitary figure who keeps a diary in a very understated style, and by Joseph Grand, a meek civil servant intent on writing a single perfect sentence.

Rambert, a French journalist stranded in Oran and separated from his lover, abandons efforts to escape the city and makes common cause with those resisting the plague. Cottard takes personal advantage of adversity by profiteering in smuggled goods.

In the second and fourth of the novel's five sections, Father Paneloux delivers a sermon in the Oran cathedral. His first sermon excoriates the townspeople for the sinfulness that must surely be responsible for the divine retribution of a plague. By the time of the second sermon, however, Paneloux has come to accept unprovoked suffering as a cosmic mystery, and his righteous indignation gives way to humble compassion.

The plague departs as inscrutably as it arrived, oblivious to collective human efforts to combat it. Yet those futile labors are portrayed as valuable in themselves. In its final pages, the text suddenly abandons its pretense of detached objectivity when one of the characters reveals that he has been the narrator all along. The novel's narrative structure is another representation of the struggle to overcome isolation and idiosyncrasy, to affirm solidarity.

THE PLAYBOY OF THE WESTERN WORLD
John Millington Synge
1907
Drama
Comedy

A young man arrives at an inn on the west coast of Ireland and announces that he has killed his father, and is surprised when the inn's patrons laud him for the deed.

The story of Christy Mahon, the play's main character, is at once comic, pathetic, a bit sordid, and frightening. Its diversity reflects the richness of human nature that Synge observed in the people around him.

Christy arrives at Flaherty's pub, bringing with him the story of how he has killed his own father in the fields. By the end of the day, he is at least a local hero, the object of much gossip and many a batted eye from the ladies, while the men hold his athletic prowess in high regard. Synge's comedy focuses on how easily Christy's supposed crime is overlooked in favor of his novelty, his singularity, for which the crime is in fact a kind of symbol.

Finally, Christy's reputation suffers a dramatic decline, and the people who were once his admirers—his idolaters even—nearly become his executioners. The Flahertys and the other Mayo countrymen who populate the play end up looking rather foolish, but they are never merely ridiculous. For Synge, these people are characterized by an imagination that is the source both of their vitality and of their limitations. The play stands in the end as a celebration of this quality, a mixed virtue for the characters of the play and a source of great enjoyment for Synge's readers.

PNIN
Vladimir Nabokov
1957
Novella
Satire

Nabokov's most charming and accessible novel, Pnin *concerns an emigre professor and his comic attempts to adjust to American life and the English language.*

The plot unfolds as a series of droll vignettes in which Professor Timofey Pnin tries to find suitable living quarters, teaches class, does research in the library, receives visits from his former wife and her precocious son, summers with fellow emigres at a country house, and, thinking that he will finally be able to settle down, gives what he calls a "house-heating" party.

Those critics who complain of the novel's episodic structure have missed the architectonic detail, characteristic of Nabokov, that ultimately makes *Pnin* such a cohesive fiction. This detail is visible in replicating motifs (squirrels, reflections, gardens and floral imagery) that may or may not contain meaning but demonstrate continuously the control of the artist responsible for the novel.

Nabokov comments on his own activity by introducing a number of artist figures into the action, including an emigre painter named Gramineev, an art teacher named Lake, and Lake's star pupil, Victor Wind (son of Pnin's former wife). There is also the novel's sly and manipulative narrator, who is not to be confused with Nabokov himself, despite a superficial resemblance. The closest of these figures to their creator is Victor Wind, and the reader who studies the author's account of Victor's artistic activity will gain much insight into Nabokov's technique.

Like many of Nabokov's fictions, this one concerns the condition of exile. With his odd mannerisms and his labored locutions, Pnin is a funny and pathetic figure. Yet he is also tragic, and it is Nabokov's balancing act between these extremes that makes reading the novel an extraordinarily entertaining and moving experience.

POETICS
Aristotle
334-323 B.C.E.
Nonfiction
Philosophical

Generally considered to be the first extant work of literary criticism, the Poetics *is also without a doubt the most influential piece of criticism ever written.*

Plato, who was Aristotle's teacher, had criticized poetry as both subversive (the Greek myths were full of immorality) and delusive. The carpenter copied the concept of the table; the artist's picture of the table was only a copy of a copy. Hence poets were liars, and should be banished from an ideal commonwealth. Without mentioning Plato directly, the *Poetics* answers both charges.

The key term of Aristotle's answer is plot. The plot of a tragedy or epic is a means of ordering the chaos of events and exploring their meaning. In this sense, poetry does not merely imitate appearances, as Plato thought, but discovers through its form the reality of process hidden within them. Penetrating to universals, poetry is more philosophical than history. Character is inessential to this task; what poetry needs is a unified action.

In order to make poetry moral, Aristotle suggested that only certain types of characters could be responsible for certain types of actions. Slaves could not be noble; tragic heroes could not be utter villains. In later centuries, these and other suggestions were codified into rules of literary decorum, like the so-called "three unities" of time, place, and action, for which Aristotle himself is not responsible.

Along with its classification of the genres (the section on comedy is unfortunately missing), the *Poetics* is perhaps best known for the notion of "catharsis" or purgation. In Aristotle's view, poetry did not move men to action, as Plato feared, but rather stirred their emotions only in order to purge them.

After its rediscovery in the Renaissance, the *Poetics* was central to the theories of neoclassicism, and it continues to inspire many critics in our own day.

THE POETRY OF DICKINSON
Emily Dickinson
1890
Poetry
Collection

Filled with odd images, eccentric rhyming, and an often playful tone, Dickinson's poetry penetrates into the depths of the human soul and mind with infinite insight.

In contrast to many of her contemporaries Dickinson had minimal experience with the world, spending almost every day of her life in a single house in Amherst, Massachusetts. Yet her poetry displays a range of perception and emotion that few poets have matched.

She might be called a miniaturist, since most of her poems have fewer than 30 lines, yet she deals with the profoundest subjects in poetry: death, love, humanity's relations to God and nature.

Her poetry impresses by its constantly amazing freshness and vitality. Not only does she approach her subjects in unique ways, but her use of language itself is highly idiosyncratic. She makes nouns serve as verbs, adjectives as nouns, and abstractions as concrete objects.

Her images startle by their unexpectedness and their supreme rightness as well. For her, death can be courteous ("Because I could not stop for Death") or terrifying ("I felt a Funeral in my brain"): it can be perceived through what the dead person has left undone ("How many times these low feet staggered") or through the trivial details one might focus on while dying ("I heard a Fly buzz when I died"). Nature has its terrors (the snake in "A Narrow Fellow in the Grass") as well as its glories ("The Day came slow") and sensual delights ("I taste a liquor").

Her dramatic monologues, always with herself as persona, convey rich complexities of human emotion—elation and depression, faith and doubt, hope and despair.

Her direct, first-person voice makes much of her poetry easily accessible, yet her unusual word usages and oblique approaches to a subject call for multiple readings and sometimes multiple interpretations. Her density and imaginativeness hark back to the Metaphysical poets of the 17th century, while her play with language and her psychological and philosophical insights, many quite unusual for the largely conservative 19th century, brought her a wide audience only posthumously.

A PORTRAIT OF THE ARTIST AS A YOUNG MAN
James Joyce
1914-1915
Novel
Autobiographical Fiction, Kunstlerroman

A young boy grows up and finds his true vocation as an artist. This novel popularized the stream of consciousness technique.

Young Stephen Dedalus goes away to school and suffers greatly from his shyness and poor eyesight. Christmas at home is unpleasant because of the political arguments which divide his father and aunt, as they do all Ireland. Back at school, Stephen earns acclaim from the other students for speaking out against his unjust punishment.

Winning a literary award, he shares the money with his family and then buys his first sexual experience, which turns out unsatisfactorily. While on a religious retreat, he begins to believe that the experience with the prostitute will damn him and he seeks out a confessional. Relieved of his guilt, Stephen turns to intense study, denying all forms of sensual experience. Although successful in his religious studies, as he grows older he begins to doubt.

Eventually he decides to become a writer and cuts himself off from family, friends, church, and country in order to cultivate his art. He decides that he must leave Ireland now that he has found his true vocation as a writer.

Joyce's quasi-autobiographical novel has at its center the issue of sin and its impingement on the human soul. It expands the topic to cover all the ways the individual may be limited in his quest for fulfillment, by family, friends, and social and national institutions. The novel is particularly noteworthy both in its use of the interior monologue and in its presentation of life in Ireland at a time of unrest. Here, in contrast to the usual novel of adolescence, the primary emphasis is placed upon the spiritual, emotional, and intellectual development of the protagonist.

THE POSSESSED
Fyodor Dostoevski
1871-1872
Novel
Allegorical, Political

This novel includes two major themes. First, it develops the spiritual forlornness of a man destroyed by his rejection of God. Second, it analyzes the mentality of the Russian revolutionaries known as nihilists.

Dostoevski had worked for several years on a novel to be called "The Life of a Great Sinner." This became *The Possessed*, the story of Nikolai Stavrogin, a spiritual nihilist.

The account of Stavrogin's degradation is fused with a "pamphlet novel" describing the machinations of a group of political radicals. Taken together, the two plots give a bleak picture of human alienation—from God, from country, from fellow humans. Dostoevski's Christian ethic and love of Russia are felt everywhere in *The Possessed*.

Dostoevski got the idea for a novel about political radicals from the murder in 1869 of a young Moscow student named Ivanov by a group of revolutionaries. The rebels were inflamed by a leftist agitator named Sergey Nechaev.

In *The Possessed*, Nechaev becomes Pyotr Verkhovensky, who takes over an innocuous liberal discussion group from his father and urges the members to perform acts of unrest and incendiarism. One feature of the plot is the disgrace of the writer Karmazinov, intended to represent the great Russian author Ivan Turgenev, who also wrote about Russian nihilism.

Another important revolutionary is Shatov, a devout Russian nationalist crippled by his lack of genuine religious faith. Shatov's opposite is the engineer Kirillov, who rejects his Russian heritage for Western values. Together, Shatov and Kirillov dramatize the tension in nineteenth century Russia between Slavophiles and Westerners.

While the fate of the revolutionaries is working itself out, Stavrogin, the man who rejects God, behaves more and more enigmatically. Despite his estrangement from life, he is a powerful, charismatic figure whose fate richly complements this anatomy of Russian nihilism.

THE POSTMAN ALWAYS RINGS TWICE
James M. Cain
1934
Novel
Mystery

An itinerant handyman and a frustrated housewife plan and carry out the "perfect" murder. This short but graphic novel shocked readers with its darkness and pessimism when it was first published.

Narrated by Frank Chambers, a drifter who has been brought to ruin by a beautiful woman, this tale is set in the Southern California of the 1930's. Having no better offer before him, Chambers accepts a job in a roadside cafe operated by Nick Papadakis, a Greek immigrant, and his beautiful wife, Cora.

Chambers is plunged into a chaos of greed, lust, and murder. Cora is an extremely ordinary person pushed to the breaking point by the tedium of her everyday life. Chambers is persuaded by her to take part in the murder of the kindly but dim-witted Papadakis. Hitch after hitch foils their plans, and soon they grow to hate each other. A series of plot twists keeps the reader in suspense about what will finally happen to this pair of outlaw lovers.

Typical of Cain's work is a terse, uncluttered style, which is characterized by little description, much realistic dialogue, and brief chapters with suspenseful endings. Because of the first-person narration, the reader is forced to share in Frank Chambers' increasing horror and bewilderment as he sinks ever deeper into an abyss of murder and deceit.

James Cain's novels have already been adapted with great success for the screen; at least three film versions of this novel have been made. Like the crime novels of his contemporaries Raymond Chandler and Dashiell Hammett, Cain's tales of obsession and murder are especially well-suited to that dark cinematic style of the 1940's known as film noir.

PRAGMATISM
William James
1907
Nonfiction
Philosophical

This very popular and influential work is a major American philosopher's still provocative statement of his thinking about questions of belief, meaning, and truth.

The word "pragmatic" has come generally to mean a way of behaving that is practical, success-oriented, and businesslike with little regard for moral or other philosophical questions. Nothing could be further in spirit from the pragmatism of William James. Strongly influenced by the American philosopher C. S. Peirce's essay, "How to Make Our Ideas Clear" (1878), this book attempts to develop a method of seeing things straight, so that one's own peculiar vision may function meaningfully in a pluralistic and wide-open universe.

Facts, James says, are not true; they simply are. We may, however, have true ideas, those that we can assimilate, validate, corroborate, and verify. Ideas are instruments used to take account of reality, as maps or diagrams do. They may (and, in fact, must) be changed when they cease to allow us to live meaningfully. In order for an idea to be true and meaningful, it must make a difference in our lives. This necessary and practical difference allows us to determine which of our ideas are true. True ideas, then, become invaluable instruments of action, and truth becomes not something objective and distant from everyday life but an active daily force and a species of the good.

James thought that individuals testing their ideas against reality by acting in the world for the good were literally engaging in the act of creation. The individual, by growing and reaching turning points in his or her life, may actually be the workshop of being, where fact may be caught in the making and the world's life turned in its course.

THE PRAISE OF FOLLY
Erasmus
1511
Nonfiction
Satire, Philosophical

The spokesperson of this work is Folly, a female goddess (the off-spring of Plutus, god of riches, and Youthfulness), who argues that all good in the world is attributable to her. Written in a week while Erasmus was convalescing from an illness, The Praise of Folly *was considered a minor work by its author. Yet it was immensely popular when it was published and still speaks to audiences today.*

The opening is lighthearted as Folly catalogs the boons which she bestows on humans: It is she who allows the human race to procreate, since nobody can be solemn about sex; further, she provides solace for husbands deceived by their wives, since they are usually so foolish that they do not even recognize their wives' adulteries. The tone changes in chapter 31, however, as she lists her other beneficiaries: grotesque old men and women who try to deceive others into believing them still young. From this section on, the tone shifts back and forth between banter and serious—often biting—satire.

About three-fourths of the way through the work, Erasmus turns his satire on theologians and monks whose religious views serve to divide rather than unite Christians. This section of *The Praise of Folly* was especially controversial when it was published. Finally, the work dwells on the virtues of Christianity, which, according to Folly, look like madness to the world: Even Christ, she says, was a divine fool to sacrifice himself for humanity. As the work draws to a close, Folly remarks that she has been carried away in her speech and ends with the hope that the audience, followers of Folly, will applaud, live, and drink.

This satire had special meaning for a Renaissance audience, especially in its criticisms of specific religious sects and practices, but it appeals to modern readers in its satire of universal human foibles and its scathing indictment of war.

A PRAYER FOR OWEN MEANY
John Irving
1989
Novel

John Wheelwright achieves a sense of religious commitment through the eccentric agency of his tiny best friend, Owen Meany

A Prayer for Owen Meany details the friendship—from childhood in the 1950's to Owen Meany's death in the late 1960's—of two boys who grow up in Gravesend, New Hampshire, at opposite ends of the social scale: Owen's reclusive family owns the local granite quarry, whereas John's family boasts of Mayflower origins and is local gentry. Their roles are reversed and confused, however, when Owen, a diminutive boy who never grows more than five feet tall, and whose voice is a prepubescent squeak, becomes a Christ figure with powers over life and death, whereas John Wheelwright leads a rather uneventful adult life, even remaining a virgin, having been convinced by Owen's prescience and his sacrificial death that there is in fact a purpose to life—and to death.

The novel is narrated as a memoir by John Wheelwright, who teaches English in Toronto. His routine, almost monastic existence in Toronto contrasts sharply with the frequently tumultuous years of his friendship with Owen, whose energy, intelligence, and sense of purpose belie his childlike stature.

Imagery and actions identifying Owen Meany with Christ begin early in the novel and accumulate rapidly to the climactic scene of his death: his size as a child seem to the other children a "miracle"; he is cast as the Christ Child in a church Christmas pageant; Owen's father tells John that Owen's was a virgin birth; Owen "plays God" to save John from being drafted during the Vietnam War by cutting off one of his fingers; and Owen has a recurrent dream that he will die saving small children.

Yet *A Prayer for Owen Meany* is far from being a solemn theological tract. John Irving's characteristically ebullient humor erupts throughout the novel in slapstick scenes and boyish pranks.The importance of the family is a major element in *A Prayer for Owen Meany*, and as in Irving's earlier novels, family includes not merely the traditional nuclear family, but any group of bound together by mutual love and respect. *A Prayer for Owen Meany* is a *Bildungsroman*—a story of initiation into adulthood, of quest for meaning and pattern in adult life. Yet there are multiple ironies to complicate these stories. John's lifelong virginity contrasts sharply with Owen's involvement with John's sexually aggressive cousin. The diminutive Owen struggles successfully to join the Army during the Vietnam War, sure that his destiny includes such service, whereas John is spared the draft by Owen.

In addition to its thematic emphasis on the value of friendship and faith in troubled times, *A Prayer for Owen Meany* re-creates substantial portions of American cultural and political history from the early 1950's through the 1980's. It novel can be read as a social history of the period from the point of view of one who believes that the 1950's were the last decade of a kind of American innocence, which ended dramatically with the assassination of President John E Kennedy in 1963. John Wheelwright and Owen Meany turn twenty-one in 1963, so too ending their innocence.

A Prayer for Owen Meany is a mixture of realism and fabulism, of commentary on contemporary American society and evocation of the magic of childhood and friendship. Religious imagery permeates but does not overwhelm the novel, which takes its tone from the narrator's slightly self-mocking stance and his obvious delight in recalling the "miracle" of Owen Meany. The novel is indeed a "prayer" for, and to, Owen, who, in refusing to flinch from his own destiny, has given John Wheelwright the courage to face his own life with equanimity.

THE PRELUDE
William Wordsworth
1850
Poetry
Autobiographical, Epic

Originally planned as an introduction to an ambitious philosophical poem explaining the poet's views of the interlocking condition of man, nature, and society, this long poem now stands as a colossal fragment—fourteen solid "books" devoted to an account of the development of the poet's own mind and heart.

Wordsworth's blank-verse narrative, often achieving Miltonic sublimity, is punctuated by hauntingly recalled "spots of time" which Wordsworth links to intimations of his future poetic calling. These "spots" include the earliest moments of moral and spiritual awareness and are usually associated with an intensely felt response to nature.

In the first two books, "School-Time," Wordsworth concentrates on the pleasures of sports, mountain walks, and relationships with schoolmates and supportive adults. "Residence at Cambridge" records the impact of the first important intellectual influences in his life, while the "ministries" of nature are reaffirmed by "Summer Vacation," a book that also conveys his first self-consecration to the poet's task. Books contrasting an Alpine excursion with the overpowering density of London lead the poet to his discovery of the interface between man and nature, the "Love of Nature leads to Love of Man."

The poem now rises to the challenge of the French Revolution, which Wordsworth confronts as a great cataclysm in the moral history of mankind. Man's essential nature is revealed anew. Returning to England and desperate over his native country's declaration of war against the Revolution (which he felt was already endangered from within France itself), Wordsworth finds strength in his own ripening powers as a poet. *The Prelude* concludes with a magnificent hymn to the Imagination, "Reason in her most exalted mood."

Begun in 1799 and finished in 1805 when Wordsworth was thirty-five, the poem was not published until after his death in 1850 by his widow. The 1850 version is a more Christian poem than the original of 1805, in which Wordsworth's strange mixture of pantheism and idealism shines with unique force.

PRIDE AND PREJUDICE
Jane Austen
1813
Novel
Manners, Family Saga

This witty portrayal of English country life contains one of the most perfectly satisfying courtships in literature.

When Pride and Prejudicea novel focuses on the day-to-day life of a family with five young unmarried daughters, the subject is certain to be romance. *Pride and Prejudice's* depiction of Jane, Elizabeth, Mary, Kitty, and Lydia Bennet is something richer, though. As its title hints, the novel is a shrewd and subtle psychological study. Pride and prejudice are the double defects shared by the heroine and hero, spirited Elizabeth Bennet and Fitzwilliam Darcy, a rich, aristocratic young man she meets when his friend Bingley rents the estate next to the Bennets'.

In the course of the story, Darcy becomes more flexible in his social views and learns to recognize excellence (notably Elizabeth's) in the ranks below his own. Similarly, Elizabeth becomes less rigid in her judgments, more aware of the many virtues of Darcy, whom she had at first dismissed as cold and haughty. Elizabeth and Darcy's growing love delights the reader because everything about the two—their minds, tastes, appearances, and words—shows them to be ideally suited.

Pride And Prejudice contains less brilliant variations on the marriage theme as well. Jane Bennet, the serene oldest sister, and easygoing Charles Bingley, a couple whose engagement is for some time thwarted by Darcy and the Bingley sisters, are equally well matched if less dashing. The Reverend William Collins, the pompous cousin who as next male relation will inherit the family estate on Mr. Bennet's death, hopes to marry Elizabeth, but on being rejected, settles for her plain and practical friend Charlotte Lucas, a woman aware of his foolishness but in need of the security his situation can provide. The fourth match made in the novel is between a charming but amoral officer, George Wickham, and pretty, empty-headed Lydia, the youngest Bennet sister. Wickham first attracts Elizabeth, then elopes with Lydia. Only when Darcy intervenes is he persuaded to marry the silly girl.

Supplementing this cast of characters is a wonderfully imperfect gallery of human types. The selfish and cynical Mr. Bennet, his ill-bred wife, their priggish daughter Mary, and the domineering Lady Catherine de Bourgh are all people a reader would walk far to avoid in real life. But they are figures delightful to encounter in Austen's satirical novel.

THE PRIME OF MISS JEAN BRODIE
Muriel Spark
1961
Novella
Comedy

Set in the 1930's, this story of an eccentric Edinburgh school teacher is both an entertaining comedy filled with unforgettable characters and a penetrating study of the nature of moral judgment.

The novel focuses on Jean Brodie, a teacher at the Marcia Blaine School for Girls, who dedicates the years of her prime to six students: Sandy Stranger, Rose Stanley, Mary Macgregor, Eunice Gardiner, Jenny Gray, and Monica Douglas. She hopes to mold their lives into her own unique pattern, and her teaching includes comparative religion, Fascism, and the details of her love life.

This naturally causes friction between Miss Brodie and the more conventional faculty. The headmistress, Miss Mackay, continually searches for some grounds on which to dismiss Miss Brodie. Meanwhile, Miss Brodie's efforts to dominate the lives of her girls increase as when she tries to arrange an affair between Rose Stanley and the singing master Teddy Lloyd.

As the Brodie set grows older, Miss Mackay begins questioning them unsuccessfully, hoping that one girl will betray her friend and teacher. Finally, Sandy Stranger comes to realize that Miss Brodie's influence may ruin the lives of her students and must make a choice between her personal loyalty to Miss Brodie and her newly awakened moral perception.

Jean Brodie is a remarkable comic figure, by turns admirable, sinister, and ludicrous. As the story presents new sides of Miss Brodie, she is by turns a benevolent teacher, a calculating Fascist, and a silly, frustrated spinster. Each of these shifts in perception is presented from the viewpoint of Sandy Stranger, so that the reader goes through the same learning process as Sandy does. Finally, like Sandy, the reader recognizes the complexities of moral judgment.

THE PRINCE
Niccolò Machiavelli
1532
Nonfiction
Political

In this Renaissance study of the methods of effective government, Machiavelli, an experienced diplomat, offers a realistic assessment of the operations of city-states in 16th century Italy.

Machiavelli outlines the various forms of principalities in his country and explains what princes must do to govern them well. Much of the volume surveys the successes and failures of historical figures; he is careful to point out the lessons that princes can learn from history, both ancient and modern. He follows his survey with chapters on the qualities that the successful prince must have. Among these qualities are a willingness to deal ruthlessly with those who oppose him, a determination to act cruelly when necessary, and an insistence that real-world concerns should always outweigh ideals.

The Prince has long been considered the most succinct statement of the political philosophy that "the end justifies the means." Machiavelli makes no pretense at idealism; he argues that his work is designed to show princes how to succeed in the real world, not how to strive in vain to build a Utopian society. As a result, Machiavelli himself has become the symbol of deceit, of the win-at-any-cost attitude that ignores the feelings and human worth of those who are governed. That rulers such as Mussolini and Hitler found much of value in *The Prince* has further added to the notion that the work is anathema for those dedicated to democratic principles.

While it is clear that Machiavelli found little value in democracy, one must remember that he was basing his advice to princes on what he saw around him in Italy, and on his reading of history. Whatever ideological faults the work may contain, its penetrating realistic analysis marks it as one of the few political works that has insisted that leaders see things as they are before trying to change them.

THE PRINCE AND THE PAUPER
Mark Twain
1881
Novel
Historical

By imagining King Edward VI exchanging places with a pauper from the London slums, Mark Twain examines the oppressive politics and economics of Tudor England.

On the same day on which a son is born to Henry VIII, occasioning much celebration, a son is born to John Canty in the squalor of Offal Court. While Edward Tudor is reared as the Prince of Wales, Tom Canty survives on the streets and learns literacy and Latin from a friendly priest. Reading about royalty, he organizes games in which he plays the prince. One day in Westminster, Tom sees the real prince in the palace grounds. When a guard tries to drive Tom away, Edward intervenes and invites Tom to play with him.

To their amazement, they look like twins. To complete the impression, Edward has them exchange clothes. Seeing a bruise which Tom received from the guard, Edward goes to reprimand him, and the guard, thinking him the pauper, drives him from the palace.

Tom is assumed to be Prince of Wales, and when he insists on his real identity, he is thought insane. Shortly thereafter, Henry VIII dies, and the Prince becomes King, only it is the pauper who sits on the throne. Gradually, Tom functions as monarch and by his common sense and feeling for justice rules wisely and well.

Meanwhile, Edward is forced into John Canty's band of thieves. Mocked by a mob when he insists that he is the king, Edward is saved by Miles Hendon, a soldier of fortune. Canty recaptures the boy and takes him into the countryside, where the king learns of the hardship and suffering of the common people. When, with Hendon's help, he is restored to the throne, he becomes a better ruler from his experience as a pauper.

An ardent advocate of democracy, Twain shows that a poor boy can be as good a ruler as the son of a king and that a king rules better after living among the poor.

THE PRINCESS BRIDE
William Goldman
1973
Novel
Children's, Fantasy

A quirky love story set in a Renaissance-era world, in which a poor farm hand must defeat a group of mercenaries and, eventually, his nation's own prince, in order to win back the love from his youth, Princess Buttercup.

Presented as a frame story in which a grandfather reads the tale to his sick grandson, Goldman's comedic adventure about a love that could overcome any obstacle begins with Westley, a poor farm hand, and a beautiful woman named Buttercup who lives on the same farm. Buttercup consistently berates Westley with verbal abuse yet, every time, Westley simply responds with, "As you wish." After discovering each other's undeniable love for one another, Westley leaves Buttercup's farm in hopes of finding fortune so he can marry her.

Upon eventually hearing of the death of Westley at the hands of the Dread Pirate Roberts, Buttercup reluctantly agrees to marry the future king, Prince Humperdinck. However, before the wedding, Buttercup is kidnapped by the three mercenaries Vizzini, Inigo Montoya, and Fezzik. As the four of them travel, they notice a man in a black mask has been following them. Eventually, the man catches up to the mercenaries and, upon defeating Inigo and Fezzik in separate bouts, he finally reaches Vizzini and Buttercup. The man in black quickly outwits Vizzini whom he tricks into drinking a lethal dose of poison.

With the Prince and his men right behind him, the man in black flees with Buttercup. After being taunted about never truly loving her former farm hand, Buttercup pushes the man in black down a ravine just as she discovers his true identity as her love, Westley. Eventually, Humperdinck captures the lovers and Westley is tortured to near death. Upon being rescued by Inigo and Fezzik, Westley and his companions save Buttercup and make a daring escape on horseback.

Perhaps the most unique aspect of *The Princess Bride* is that Goldman presents the novel as an abridgment of the larger story by S. Morgenstern, thus allowing Goldman to add asides throughout the novel, as he comments on Morgenstern's work.

PRIVATE LIVES
Noël Coward
1930
Drama
Comedy

One of Coward's most popular plays, Private Lives *is a series of misadventures created by a swap of husbands and wives.*

Sybil and Elyot are in Paris on their honeymoon. Elyot has been married previously to Amanda, who happens to be living in the suite next door, across an adjoining terrace. She has taken Victor as her would-be second husband, but as the scenes move back and forth between Sybil and Elyot and Amanda and Victor, it becomes clear that these couples are wrong for each other.

Sybil is timid, submissive, clinging; Elyot is wickedly arch, independent, and insulting. Amanda is really Elyot's counterpart; she is sly, clever, independent, while Victor in his courtly way is more akin to Sybil. In the course of the play, Elyot drifts away from Sybil and rekindles his relationship with Amanda, while Victor and Sybil draw closer together.

Near the end of the play, Victor remarks angrily to Elyot about his "damned flippancy," to which Elyot responds that flippancy is meant to cover a real embarrassment. "We have no prescribed etiquette to fall back upon," he says. Elyot's lament points to his loss of faith, his lack of connection with a meaningful tradition. In the post–World War I world, flippancy is a major means of survival.

Thus, Elyot provides a crucial clue for understanding the frivolous repartee that is basic to *Private Lives*. The play is essentially talk—amoral chatter, broken only by heated argument and physical grappling. The talk disguises the private lives—the empty, faithless relationships, the pain beneath the glittering surface. Clearly, Elyot and Amanda love each other, but their love survives only amid their conflicts, thrives only on their arguments, their insults.

PROMETHEUS BOUND
Aeschylus
c. 460 B.C.E.
Drama
Tragedy, Greek

*Aeschylus' * Prometheus Bound *is the sole surviving play of a trilogy which also included* Prometheus Unbound *and* Prometheus the Firebringer. *Set in the wilds of the Caucasus Mountains, it describes the Titan's confrontation with Zeus over the latter's decision to destroy the human race and create another less likely to challenge his authority.*

Prometheus has given fire and useful arts to humanity. For this, and for not revealing to Zeus which among his consorts will give birth to the son that destroys him, Zeus orders his henchmen Force and Violence and the god

Hephaestus to chain Prometheus to a rock. Prometheus' punishment reveals Zeus's insecurity as founder of the new Olympian dynasty.

Io, a nymph who is another victim of Zeus, appears in the form of a heifer. To avoid discovery of his affair with Io, Zeus had transformed her thus, but his wife Hera had known of the seduction and sent a stinging gadfly to pursue the maiden. Prometheus tells Io of the sufferings she must yet face and how Hera, will continue to persecute her before she ultimately finds contentment.

Hermes, traditionally Zeus's messenger but here his lackey, enters arrogantly to demand the consort's name from Prometheus. Prometheus bravely refuses, though his decision will mean punishment from Zeus's eagle, which will daily devour the Titan's liver. The final scene contains violent earthquakes, windstorms, thunder, and lightning, all meant to terrify the unyielding Prometheus.

The play concludes as Prometheus asks his goddess-mother to witness the injustice of his sufferings, though it seems Prometheus and Zeus resolved their arguments in the final plays of the trilogy. Prometheus, by modern interpretation, can be a savior, creator, victim, prophet, angel, thief, or rebel. In the Middle Ages, he was the mystical symbol of Christ's passion. The myth has inspired numerous literary treatments.

PROMETHEUS UNBOUND
Percy Bysshe Shelley
1820
Drama
Lyric, Mythology

Chained for years to a rock by Jupiter for giving fire and knowledge to man, Prometheus, the Titan, defies all expectations of anger or bitterness. Gradually, he forswears all revenge, insists that he wishes no living thing harm, and claims to have forgotten his original curse against his tormentor. Nevertheless, Prometheus knows that Jupiter will fall. Out of this strangely passive attitude on the part of his epic hero, Shelley builds a great dramatic song of cosmic love which has moved readers sensitive to his ethereal music.

Utilizing a greater variety of verse forms than appear together in any major English poem, Shelley celebrates the change of heart in Prometheus by demonstrating that his hero's discovery of love triggers its affirmation throughout the entire universe. Not only is Asia, Prometheus' wife, raised from her cave in the Caucasus and freed to rejoin her husband by the power released through his loving heart, but even the moon and earth dance in their orbits in heavenly sympathy and self-discovery.

Jupiter is overthrown by Necessity, embodied in the terrifying Nemesis of Demogorgon, who rises in the form of Jupiter's own child to cast the tyrannical father from his throne. Demogorgon coincides his judgment on Jupiter with Prometheus' declaration of universal love. Necessity is not the instrument of revolutionary destruction, determinism, or any rational critique; necessity is the unfolding force of love.

Shelley's great song of liberty and love is his answer to 18th century rationalism as well as a rebuttal of Aeschylus' intention in his unfinished trilogy on the story of Prometheus. The great Greek tragedian had planned to reconcile Prometheus and Zeus (Jupiter) through the Titan's revealing of the secret that the head of the gods feared: that Zeus's son, born of his marriage to Thetis, would overthrow him. Shelley could imagine no such understanding between love and evil. *Prometheus Unbound* is one of Romanticism's greatest contributions to the doctrine that "Love Conquers All."

THE PRUSSIAN OFFICER
D. H. Lawrence
1914
Short Story
Gothic

This story, set in the period before World War I, centers on the violent conflict between two men who represent opposing views of life is told in a powerful and richly evocative prose style, making it a masterpiece of Lawrence's art.

The primary characters are a Prussian cavalry officer conducting his men on maneuvers and his young orderly. The officer is a haughty, self-disciplined aristocrat, frustrated both in love and in his career. The orderly, Schoner, is a peasant with an easy, natural grace.

The officer is profoundly affected by the warm animal spirits of the orderly, but his personal code requires that he deny these feelings. Soon he comes to hate Schoner and to harass and arbitrarily restrain him. The orderly himself begins to feel an unaccustomed anger toward the officer.

Eventually the officer becomes so enraged at the orderly that he savagely beats him. This action destroys the young man's sense of wholeness and awakens in him a murderous desire that leads inevitably to the death of both men.

This story portrays the destruction of man's instincts by an overemphasis on his rational, conscious nature. Schoner reacts to life directly, at an instinctual level, while the officer has suppressed all of his emotions in compliance with his aristocratic and military station. As a result, he is an isolated figure with no close ties and stands in contrast to the orderly, who feels a oneness with all things.

THE PURLOINED LETTER
Edgar Allan Poe
1845
Short Story
Detective

This is the third and last of Poe's tales featuring the famous detective, C. August Dupin.

As he did in "The Murders in the Rue Morgue" and "The Mystery of Marie Roget," Dupin outshines the police in solving a seemingly insoluble crime.

Unlike the other two tales, which involve gruesome murders of women, "The Purloined Letter" presents only petty thievery and deception as the crime. The tale's mock heroic tone is suggested even by the title's description of the missing letter not as "stolen" but as "purloined."

The Prefect of the Parisian police, Monsieur G——, actually knows the identity of the thief, the Minister D——, but the letter itself must be found in order to protect the honor of a lady being blackmailed. Despite an exhaustive search of the culprit's apartment over a three-month period, the Prefect has not found the document and appeals to Dupin for assistance in the matter.

As in "The Murders in the Rue Morgue," Dupin's strategy is to match wits with the culprit. Dupin and the Minister D——are, in many respects, alike. Both are poets and mathematicians who tend to think in a similar fashion, both find the letter in plain sight, and, significantly, both use the letter for personal gain. The Minister uses it for political advantage, while in the end Dupin extracts a large reward from the Prefect.

Dupin claims the reward by handing the letter in question to the Prefect after a search of the Minister's apartment that involves some deception and trickery. Dupin then explains to the incredulous narrator the reasoning which led him to discover the letter: His reasoning in the matter was superior to the Prefect's elaborate search because too much concentration on minute detail can obscure obvious truths.

PYGMALION
George Bernard Shaw
1912
Drama
Sociological

Shaw's popular study of English class distinctions depicts the rapid rise of Eliza Doolittle once she is tutored in speech by the eccentric Henry Higgins.

In this comedy of morals, Shaw tilts at two particularly English windmills, the class structure and an inadequate alphabet. Using the myth of the sculptor Pygmalion, who fell in love with his marble masterpiece, Shaw introduces phonetician Henry Higgins to the Cockney flower-seller Eliza Doolittle. Eliza, kept firmly in her place by her appearance and particularly by her lower-class accent, would love to become genteel and sell flowers in a "proper shop."

When Higgins demonstrates his skill at placing any English person by his or her neighborhood accent, he amazes the bystanders sheltered from the rain under the columns of St. Paul's. Higgins berates Eliza, a product of Lisson Grove slum, for her gutter English—a disgrace to the language of Shakespeare and Milton. Later, the girl bravely appears at Professor Higgins' Wimpole Street home to ask for lessons in speech, and Higgins wagers that he can transform her into a young woman able to pass as a duchess.

The professor threatens and bullies his pupil, nearly driving her mad with his perfectionism. Soon Eliza's accent is correct, but her topics of conversation are wildly unsuitable for the average ruling-class drawing room. Higgins must rapidly explain her utterances as "the new small talk." With a series of comic social coups, Eliza becomes a darling of the fashionable world.

Shaw consistently undercuts any idea of romance that might cling to this tale of transformation. While Higgins, Eliza, the talkative dustman Mr. Doolittle, and the callow Freddy Eynsford-Hill are well-realized characters, it is their social dimensions that interest Shaw. If class and accent rather than individual merit determine one's place in society, then society is vulnerable to the satirist's pen. And if the reader expects Higgins in his role as Eliza's Pygmalion to fall in love with his creation, Hollywood's *My Fair Lady* is the place to look.

R

A RAISIN IN THE SUN
Lorraine Hansberry
1959
Drama
African American

The five members of a black family living in a run-down Chicago apartment are dissatisfied with their lives. The play examines the hopes and traps that the American Dream offers to all, regardless of race.

The Youngers are desperate, in varying degrees, for change and are presented with the means necessary for change in the form of a $10,000 life insurance payment which they are to receive following the death of the head of the family. Disagreements about what to do with the money, however, threaten to alienate them from one another.

Walter Lee Younger, a chauffeur with a wife and son, wants to buy a liquor store. Beneatha, his younger sister, wants to go to medical school. Lena, their mother, wants to buy a decent house in an all-white neighborhood. Lena decides to compromise and split the money between them, but Walter is robbed by a business partner. After Walter makes the conflict worse by accepting money from a representative of the white neighborhood for not moving there, he changes his mind, realizing he would be sacrificing his manhood.

The problems which might have destroyed the Youngers have unified them, made them stronger as individuals and as a family because they have gained self-knowledge and learned to love one another more.

The first of the two full-length works which Hansberry lived to complete, the play is one of the most widely known literary creations by a black American. She makes the Youngers more than typical American blacks; they are members of the universal family of those who strive to realize their dreams.

THE RAPE OF THE LOCK
Alexander Pope
1712
Poetry
Mock-Epic

This mock-epic poem about an audacious young lord's theft of a beautiful young lady's lock of hair satirizes the vanity and frivolity of fashionable English society in Pope's day.

As the beauteous Belinda sleeps toward noon, a guardian sylph warns her in her dreams of a dire event to occur that day. Undeterred, she rises to her makeup table as usual, then sails off down the Thames for a tea party at Hampton Court. Here the world quite properly admires her, but then the "rape" occurs: An amorous young lord (the Baron) snips off one of the two curls carefully trained to dangle just so down the back of Belinda's lovely neck.

Belinda screams in horror, and a loud scene ensues. The party chooses sides; women slay men with frowns and revive them with smiles. Meanwhile, the lock of hair is lost in the scuffle, but the invisible sylphs observe it as it mounts heavenward to take its shining place among the stars.

Pope gives this fluffy action epic proportions: the Invocation, the Argument, the supernatural interventions, the epic similes, the epic combat, the set descriptive pieces—Belinda's makeup to do battle, the voyage down the Thames, a card game, the tea service—recall the epics of Homer, Virgil, and Milton, especially Milton's *Paradise Lost*. (Pope at the time was also translating Homer's *Iliad*.) An epic sums up a culture: To the fashionable English world, Belinda is a cultural heroine, the loss of her lock a significant action. (*The Rape of The Lock* was based on an actual event which caused two families to fall out.)

Pope makes the comedy abundantly clear through his heroic couplets (rhyming iambic pentameter lines). As delicate, balanced, and carefully trained as Belinda's two bouncing curls, Pope's urbane verse likewise sums up his age.

RASSELAS
Samuel Johnson
1759
Novella
Philosophical

Johnson's tale of the Abyssinian prince who searches the world for happiness will interest students of literature and appeal to those who are intrigued by stories with strong philosophical overtones.

Rasselas, Prince of Abyssinia, tires of the Happy Valley where he lives in seclusion while waiting to assume the throne. With the poet Imlac as their guide, Rasselas, his sister, and her maid leave the Valley and travel throughout the Middle East in search of a happy life. His experiences in both city and country offer Rasselas no satisfaction; nowhere can he find a pleasant existence. He comes to understand that life is an experience that must be endured, and whatever happiness comes to man does so only fleetingly. Finally weary of his journeys, Rasselas decides to return to the Happy Valley.

Johnson's story has been described as a moral tale. Throughout, the emphasis is on the lessons Rasselas and his companions learn. These lessons are bitter ones. Rasselas begins his search for happiness by leaving an Edenic locale, where all sensual pleasures are fulfilled. Yet nowhere outside the valley does he find anyone truly happy; those who seem to be so are either lying or mad. Earthly happiness occurs only when change enters one's life; one's only real hope is to find eternal happiness after death.

In the process of destroying notions of earthly Utopia, Johnson systematically penetrates the facades that had grown up around certain ways of life. For example, he exposes the sham of the pastoral tradition by portraying shepherds as ignorant and displeasing buffoons. The work also provides a wealth of insight into Johnson's personal and literary philosophy; Imlac's discussion in chapter ten of the function of poetry is an important summary of 18th century literary theory.

REBECCA
Daphne du Maurier
1938
Novel
Gothic

A darkly brooding middle-aged widower marries a young, awkward woman and takes her to his estate where she is haunted by the memory of his beautiful first wife, Rebecca.

Told in the first person, this novel reveals the powerful psychological pressures on a very young, inexperienced woman who lives in the shadow of her husband's dead first wife, the brilliant and sophisticated Rebecca.

When the young woman first meets Maxim de Winter in Monte Carlo, she is working as a paid companion to an obnoxious, loud, and vulgar American socialite. Almost without being aware of it, the young woman drifts into a romance with de Winter, marries him, and returns with him to his sumptuous estate, Manderley, on the Cornish coast.

Once at Manderley, the young woman's awkwardness becomes more marked as she compares herself to Rebecca, who drowned in a sailing accident less than a year before.

The mansion is filled with mementos of Rebecca: the statuary she selected, the rooms she decorated, and the luxuriously scented clothes and furs which still fill the closets of Rebecca's bedroom—the most beautiful room in the house.

Every detail of daily life is just as Rebecca ordered it, from the sumptuous daily meals to the menacing housekeeper, Mrs. Danvers, who came to Manderley with Rebecca.

When de Winter's preoccupation with the estate makes him seem distant, the young woman assumes that he is comparing her, unfavorably, with Rebecca. She thinks that her clothing and makeup are wrong and that besides the memory of Rebecca she must appear very plain and ugly. Finally, after a disastrous costume ball, the truth about Rebecca is slowly and compellingly revealed.

Critics reviewed *Rebecca* favorably, some even saying it was a 20th century *Jane Eyre*. Whether this comparison is deserved, Rebecca is certainly one of the best of the perennially popular romantic novels.

THE REBEL
Albert Camus
1951
Nonfiction
Philosophical
Albert Camus gives a very qualified yes to the central question of this book, "Is murder permissible?"

Rebellion, according to Camus, is the attempt to overcome the contradiction between the human mind, which relentlessly strives for clarity, and the world, which is essentially meaningless. Camus' contribution to moral philosophy is his argument that the act of rebellion against suffering in the world brings out the qualities of justice, love, and joy in human consciousness.

Although rebellion can lessen human suffering, as often as not it causes the very evil it seeks to abolish. Rebellion fosters evil when it is fueled by idealism and doctrine. The idealistic belief that evil is temporary, that it can be vanquished, leads to totalitarianism, and doctrinal formulas inevitably find expression in a police state. The enforcement of a doctrine of total goodness requires violence, and violence tends to breed rather than dissipate. Evil persists.

A just rebellion is neither idealistic nor doctrinaire. It is moderate. A good rebellion always opposes suffering, so it will try to fight injustice, always mindful that the struggle itself can create injustices. This makes killing a dubious tactic. Violence may be necessary to fight colossal injustice—the Nazis in World War II, for example—but violence must always be a last resort, a choice of the lesser evil. The strategies of a just rebellion are always difficult choices in the light of concrete situations; they are never the simple embodiment of formulas.

Camus was no pacifist, but neither was he a warmonger. By advocating both moderation and rebellion, he was able to take a stand against repression without committing himself to any particular political party. Camus preached allegiance to rebellion against injustice, not to a political or philosophical system.

THE RED AND THE BLACK
Stendhal
1830
Novel
Psychological
This classic novel of ambition pitted against social barriers in the reactionary climate of France after Napoleon's fall will speak to any modern reader who still believes in the power of individual will.

The son of a simple carpenter, the headstrong and egocentric hero of this exuberant novel idolizes the lost leader, Napoleon. The Corsican adventurer who crowned himself emperor and humbled the aristocracy and the Church is Julien Sorel's alter ego. Like Napoleon, whose brilliantly ruthless strategies in war and politics brought him great power, Sorel campaigns relentlessly to achieve his goals.

His first conquest is Madame de Renal, the pious and dutiful wife of Julien's employer, the mayor of the village, who hires the intelligent and reputedly pious carpenter's son to be a tutor to his children. When the affair is exposed, the mayor rushes Julien off to a seminary in Besancon, where Julien continues to rise by attracting the attention of a powerful aristocrat, the Marquis de la Mole, who hires Julien as personal secretary. Once settled in the great nobleman's Parisian estate, Julien first charms and then dominates the Marquis' daughter, Mathilde. When she becomes pregnant, the Marquis overcomes his fury and, to make the penniless young upstart a suitable husband for Mathilde, gives Julien a title and a commission in the army.

Julien is now within reach of his Napoleonic goal. He has traveled from the obscurity of the Church's first attention (the Black) to the splendor of military rank (the Red). Also like Napoleon, however, Julien has his Waterloo—Madame de Renal. When she exposes his past to the Marquis and dashes all of Julien's splendid opportunities, he takes revenge. That revenge and its denouement constitute one of the most bittersweet moments in all nineteenth century fiction.

If Napoleon is Julien's consciously chosen hero, the poet Byron—the legacy of his work and personality—provides the model for the balance of coldness and emotion, rational detachment and unbridled passion, that make Julien such a compelling hero. Stendhal's ambivalence, the conflict between his dedicated liberalism and fascination with aristocratic hauteur, as well as the clash between his icy and realistic powers of psychological observation and his love of Romantic excess and posing—all this is splendidly Byronic. A "cult" writer ever since the 1880's, when he was rediscovered by writers such as Henry James, Ivan Turgenev, and Gustave Flaubert, Stendhal provides a bridge between the Romantic and modern sensibility.

THE RED BADGE OF COURAGE
Stephen Crane
1895
Novel
Historical, War

Stephen Crane's story depicts the experiences and more especially the impressions of a young soldier during a few days of the American Civil War as he undergoes an ironic initiation into manhood.

Leaving his widowed mother alone on their New York State farm, Henry Fleming, his head filled with visions of the heroic deeds of epic literature and popular myth, joins the Union Army only to enter the decidedly unheroic world of the military camp: the boredom of daily drills and the anonymity of military life. The "youth," as Crane prefers to call him, persists in his delusions as well as in his fear that he will not measure up to his grandiose and utterly unrealistic vision of himself as a hero.

Dismayed by reality's failure to meet his expectations and frightened by the chaos that swirls around him, Henry runs from his first battle. Hit on the head by another fleeing Union soldier, Henry receives the ironic wound, his "little red badge of courage," that gains him reentry into his regiment, with no questions asked. On the second day, Henry fights like a "wildcat," earning the admiration of his fellows and the praise of his lieutenant.

The "quiet manhood" that Henry gains in the final chapter is another of his delusions, one which the reader may mistakenly come to share if he fails to note Crane's subtle irony. The back and forth movement of Crane's plot, the pendulumlike swings toward and away from battle, with experience at one pole and reflection, especially rationalization, at the other, parallel the back and forth movement of Henry's impressionistic perceptions about reality and about himself.

His misperceptions derive literally from the obscuring smoke of battle but figuratively, or psychologically, from his insatiable need to see himself and his world as meaningful even as experience teaches him quite the opposite lesson, that the world is flatly indifferent to man. The discrepancy between Henry's self-portrait of the young man as hero and Crane's depiction of him as a small, vainglorious, and nearly nameless cog in the military machine (or more generally in the meaningless, mechanistic world) serves as the measure of the author's ironic vision.

THE RED PONY
John Steinbeck
1937
Novella
Series

This brief, episodic novel presents a series of four linked stories about a young boy growing up on a ranch in the Salinas Valley of California during the early part of this century.

The central character in this collection of four loosely connected tales is Jody Tiflin, a shy, ten-year-old California ranch boy who wants to be treated as a grownup. The Tiflins live far from any neighbors, and, as an only child, Jody has only the ranch-dogs and the cowhand Billy Buck as companions. His father is too strict to show much affection for the boy, and his mother is usually preoccupied with her kitchen chores.

In the first story, "The Gift," Carl Tiflin brings home for his son a red pony and saddle which he has bought at an auction in town. Jody names the pony Gabilan, meaning "hawk," and lavishes attention on his new friend. He relishes his new responsibilities and takes good care of the pony until he unwisely leaves it out in the corral during a fall rainstorm and the pony develops "strangles." Jody and Billy Buck desperately try to nurse the pony back to health, but the boy learns that nature can be cruel and indifferent to human wishes.

The second tale, "The Great Mountains," tells the story of an old paisano named Gitano who returns, when he becomes to old to work, to the Tiflin Ranch where he was reared. Jody's father cruelly refuses to take the old man in, offering him only one night's shelter, but he discovers the next morning that Gitano has disappeared into the mountains with a decrepit old horse.

In "The Promise," the third story, Jody is given an opportunity to raise another colt to replace the red pony, but first he must have the mare Nellie bred to a neighbor's stallion and then take care of her during the year of her gestation. Jody loyally cares for Nellie until she is ready to deliver her colt; once again, he learns that nature has no respect for his desires.

In the last story, "The Leader Of The People," Jody witnesses his father's meanness towards his grandfather, who loves to relate how he led a group of pioneers westward to California. After Carl Tiflin insults his father-in-law, Jody offers the old man lemonade to soothe his injured feelings.

During the course of these stories, Jody Tiflin learns that growing up can be a frustrating, confusing experience, and that adults are neither infallible nor always kind in their treatment of one another. He develops some maturity as he understands his father's shortcomings and slowly becomes less dependent upon his father's approval. Through these four experiences, he grows from innocence to experience and adulthood.

THE RED TENT
Anita Diamant
1997
Novel
Revisionist

This vibrant reimagining of the biblical story of Dinah (DEE-nah) has been characterized as a feminist reading of the violent events recounted in Chapter 34 of the Book of Genesis, in which Dinah herself is silent.

Dinah, the daughter of Jacob and Leah, is the only surviving daughter among Jacob's many children. Leah and Rachel, the legitimate daughters of Laban, are Jacob's wives; Laban's illegitimate daughters Zilpah and Bilhah are Jacob's concubines. Cherished by all of the women, Dinah inhabits a female sphere profoundly separate from that of the men. In Jacob's household the men have complete dominion over the women, whose lives are circumscribed by a variety of customs embodying their subservience. As she matures, Dinah is initiated into the female society of the red tent, where women are sequestered during menstruation, childbirth, sickness, and the approach of death. Female rituals and the women's relationships among themselves offer their deepest emotional satisfactions. The novel opens with Dinah's retelling of the history of her four "mothers" along with her own; only by being passed down from one generation to the next are women's stories preserved. Rachel becomes a midwife, and she teaches Dinah her skills.

After years of tending Laban's flocks, Jacob returns to Canaan and eventually moves to lands near the city of Shechem. Dinah and Rachel are called to assist at the childbed of a concubine of Hamor, Shechem's king. Dinah meets and immediately falls in love with Shalem, a prince of Shechem, and he with her. Dinah and Shalem later consummate their love. Shalem declares Dinah his wife, and Hamor offers Jacob a royal bride price. Jacob's sons, however, ask that all the men of Shechem be circumcised so that the two peoples can live as one. As is recounted in Genesis, when the king complies, Dinah's brothers Simon and Levi and their servants enter the city and kill all the men of Shechem as they sleep.

Genesis presents Dinah's relationship with the prince as a rape and has no more to say about Dinah's fate. But the novel carries her story forward as she flees to Egypt with Re-nefer, the queen, and gives birth to a son, Re-mose, who is brought up as Re-nefer's son. Befriended by the midwife Meryt, Dinah returns to the practice of midwifery. After Re-nefer's death, she and Meryt go to live with Meryt's son in the Valley of the Kings. There, Dinah marries Benia, a master carpenter. Summoned to attend at the birth of the vizier's son, she discovers that the vizier is Joseph, her favorite brother. Having learned of the murder of his father, Re-mose threatens to kill Joseph, a capital offense. Dinah convinces him to accept exile in punishment; she does not see him again.

Years later Joseph persuades Dinah to return with him to Canaan to be reconciled with their dying father. She finds that although Jacob and her brothers have forgotten her, her story is alive among the women, in the red tent. Content, Dinah returns with Benia to Egypt, where she lives out her days.

REMEMBRANCE OF THINGS PAST
Marcel Proust
1913-1927
Novel
Autobiographical

Narrated in the first person, this novel in seven volumes tells of the youth, maturity, and advancing age of a French bourgeois whose vocation as a writer is delayed by his desire to enter the salon society of the Parisian aristocracy.

Proust's narrator, Marcel, recounts the events in his life and the characters he has come to know up to the moment when he discovers that his long-awaited career as a writer is upon him. The subject he is to take up in fiction is more or less the novel we have just finished reading, which ends with Marcel's resolve to tell his own story and the stories of the characters whom we have come to know in the preceding seven volumes.

Too intricate to recount in full, the plot turns around several major episodes: Marcel's extortion of a good night kiss from his mother; Marcel's walks in the country around his parents' residence at Combray; the love affair between Marcel's family friend Charles Swann and the cocotte Odette de Crecy; Marcel's lengthy amorous involvement with a young lesbian, Albertine; Marcel's entry into the social circle of the Duchess de Guermantes; Marcel's stormy but ultimately friendly relations with the homosexual Baron de Charlus; and finally, Marcel's removal from and return after many years to Parisian society.

Told with the chronology of events disrupted, shifting abruptly back and forth in time, Proust's novel is less a story than an extended meditation on the themes of literature and art, love and jealousy, snobbery and social ambition. Its rich verbal textures, captured successfully in the generally excellent English translation, make this novel a splendid reading experience for those with leisure to devote many hours to it at a stretch. Its lack of action may, however, not be to everyone's taste.

REPRESENTATIVE MEN
Ralph Waldo Emerson
1850
Nonfiction
Philosophical

This collection of philosophical essays by 19th century America's most important intellectual is an inquiry into the relationship between genius and the common man, a discourse on the relevance of the past to present needs.

Knowing that each age must produce its own geniuses, Emerson offered these essays to the nation as examples from past ages, trying to explain the attraction of these men and to understand their contributions. He called them *Representative*, by which he did not mean average. Each genius came forth to stand above all others in his field; each was representative of what could be accomplished; each illustrated and characterized the age that produced him; and each was an abstract ideal given solid form. In form, each essay begins with a philosophical premise concerning some aspect of man's endeavor which the genius at hand particularly illustrates. Then Emerson interweaves historical background with the man's biography before analyzing the specific traits which mark the man's genius.

The six examples range from the purely abstract mind to the intensely practical: Plato, the philosopher; Swedenborg, the mystic; Montaigne, the skeptic; Shakespeare, the poet; Napoleon, the man of the world; and Goethe, the writer. Each is man in his most prized mode: man thinking. Plato gives us clear thought; Swedenborg, mystic insight via scientific knowledge; Shakespeare, infinite invention producing beauty; Napoleon, practical action necessary for the times; and Goethe, consummate scholarship, mastering all and transforming facts into art.

The result is Emerson, at the height of his rhetorical and philosophical powers, speaking to the cultural interests of a country which he feared was on its way to mere materialism.

REPUBLIC
Plato
388-368 B.C.E.
Nonfiction
Philosophical

Plato's most influential book describes an ideal state by which actual states can be judged. The ideal state is ruled by a philosopher king who maintains social harmony through careful control of the state's educational institutions.

The best society, according to Plato, is a harmonious one, the result of rational coordination of the populace by carefully selected and trained rulers.

Plato identified three classes of citizens who, if they are to live in harmony, must be satisfied with their position on the social hierarchy. At the bottom are the artisans and laborers, who supply the material needs of the state. Next are the soldiers, who defend the state. At the top are the rulers, the few who are selected at birth to be taught how to organize best the state's social life.

These three classes of citizens correspond to the three parts of human beings as Plato understood them. The first of these is appetite, the physical needs and desires of individuals. The second is spirit, the emotional core of individuals. The third is reason, which gives unity to the human personality. Artisans and laborers are dominated by appetite, soldiers are dominated by spirit, and rulers are dominated by reason.

The ideal state is characterized by community, or harmony. Plato opposed private property and individualism because they can fragment a society, advocating instead communal property, housing, and work—even communal sex and childrearing. In a like manner, because education should foster social harmony, poets and fiction writers who question the state must be censored.

The type of government closest to the ideal state is what Plato called timocracy, or rule by the principles of military honor. The next best is oligarchy, or rule by a few. Government by the people, democracy, ranks third, surpassing only tyranny, or dictatorship by one individual.

THE RETURN OF THE NATIVE
Thomas Hardy
1878
Novel
Psychological, Romance

The Return Of The Native *is one of Hardy's early and most memorable novels about the fictional world of Wessex, a rural area in southern England. It is a love story in which the two central characters play out their tragic destinies against the timeless pastoral world of Egdon Heath.*

Thomas Hardy's works reflect the impact of 19th century evolutionary thought and naturalistic doctrines. He saw man as an alien in an impersonal universe, at the mercy of environment, heredity, and blind chance. Most of his fiction poignantly presents tragic human situations, and thus Hardy earned a reputation for pessimism.

The theme of this novel reflects Hardy's concept that human fate is shaped by accidents and natural forces over which there is no control. The heroine, Eustacia Vye, is a smoldering, unfulfilled girl who is motivated by a desperate desire to escape from the desolate heath region where she feels trapped. She first pins her hope for getting away on Damon Wildere, the local ladies' man, but he throws her over to marry Thomasin Yeobright. When Clem Yeobright returns from Paris to attend his cousin Thomasin's wedding, Eustacia becomes interested in him as a way to leave Egdon Heath, and shortly afterwards they are married over the protests of Clem's mother.

Clem, who has become disillusioned with the civilized life of the city, decides to stay on the heath and live among the simple, virtuous peasant folk, much to Eustacia's chagrin. Events take a tragic turn as Eustacia becomes estranged from her husband and resumes her affair with Damon Wildere. While attempting to elope in a storm, both lovers drown in a flooded weir. Their fate reinforces a dominant idea of the book, that those who do not adapt to their habitat will perish.

At every turn in the novel, chance plays a sinister role. The characters' desires are thwarted by unforeseen events, and their dreams are incompatible with reality. In the end, the omnipresent heath remains, a stolid and somber witness to the fate of hapless mortals.

RICHARD THE SECOND
William Shakespeare
c. 1595-1596
Drama
Historical

This account of the fall of an incompetent English monarch offers intense human conflict, a study in the exercise of political power, and a Renaissance perspective on English history of the late 14th century.

In the opening scene, King Richard the Second confronts two feuding noblemen—Mowbray and Bolingbroke, the king's cousin—who accuse each other of treason and demand a resolution by combat. The king's irresolute and theatrical handling of this episode indicates his weakness and inability to rule. Instead of permitting combat he vacillates and then banishes both men.

Needing revenues for a military campaign in Ireland, the king initiates schemes of taxation and confiscation of property which alienate both the nobility and the commoners. While Richard is in Ireland, his banished cousin, Bolingbroke, returns to claim titles and property seized by the king. Discounting Richard's view of divine right, the entire populace flocks to Bolingbroke's banner, an indication that the real power in England belongs to him. Lacking support against Bolingbroke, Richard agrees to abdicate and Bolingbroke ascends the throne as King Henry the Fourth.

Following his imprisonment, Richard recognizes the extent of his misrule and his flaws. His understanding through suffering and his vain attempt to save his life during an attack by assassins arouse the reader's sympathy for a hero too weak and self-indulgent to be genuinely tragic.

Essentially a one-man play chronicling the king's fall, the work incorporates strongly contrasting characters—Richard and Bolingbroke. Richard—emotional, willful, theatrical, poetic—prefers words to actions, whereas Bolingbroke, a taciturn, unimaginative, tough, and astute realist, understands by nature how to acquire and wield power.

From the beginning, Bolingbroke's triumph seems inevitable, yet the outcome creates uneasiness rather than assurance, for, as prophecies in the play make plain, convulsions and chaos followed in a society that deposed a rightful king. From a Renaissance perspective, these disorders seemed greater evils than any attributable to Richard. A spirit of intense nationalism permeates the play, reflected particularly in some of the most passionately patriotic speeches found anywhere in Shakespeare.

RICHARD THE THIRD
William Shakespeare
c. 1592-1593
Drama
Historical

This historical drama chronicles the rise and fall of the evil, humpbacked, King Richard and celebrates the rise of the Tudor monarchy.

As the play opens, Richard announces his evil intent: since his deformity will not let him be a lover, he will be a villain. In spite of his villainy, however, there is an ingenuity and bravado in Richard that compels the audience's admiration.

In order to take over the throne from his brother, Edward IV, and his rightful heirs, Richard has one other brother killed; woos and marries Anne, the Earl of Warwick's daughter (even though he had earlier killed her husband and father); and, after Edward's death, has his two young nephews murdered. Toward the play's close, after Anne has died, Richard is trying to arrange a marriage with his niece, Edward's daughter, so that there will be no rival claims to the throne. Before Richard can achieve this goal, however, Henry of Richmond defeats him in battle.

Throughout this play, an Elizabethan audience would have been aware of the Wars of the Roses, an event of comparatively recent history. In that bloody dispute between the houses of York and Lancaster for the throne, Edward IV's reign was a triumph for the house of York, but Henry, Earl of Richmond, was a Lancastrian, and his defeat of Richard and later marriage with Elizabeth of York finally united the families in peace. Richmond ushered in the Tudor dynasty culminating in the rule of Elizabeth I. On this level, the play, with its closing speech promising prosperity and an end to civil strife, is Shakespeare's compliment to his queen.

The melodramatic events of this play are complemented by Shakespeare's early, highly theatrical style. There is an abundance of wordplay, for example, a style Shakespeare would later abandon for more natural speech. Touches of the supernatural also add to the theatricality of this play: The last act shows Richard and Richmond on the eve of battle, being visited by the ghosts of Richard's victims, each of whom blesses Richmond and damns Richard. Such theatrical scenes make this play one of Shakespeare's most arresting character studies.

RIGHTS OF MAN
Thomas Paine
1791
Nonfiction
Philosophical

Addressed to the general reader, this political tract is the classic defense of republicanism, written in a clear, readable, forceful style.

This philosophical argument written in two parts published separately in 1791 and 1792, answers Edmund Burke's vituperative attack on the French Revolution in *Reflection on the Revolution in France* (1790) by justifying the principles of modern republican governments. Paine attempts not only to justify the French Revolution but also to use the United States as a primary example of democracy in action.

In Part I, Paine attacks the notion of monarchy and privilege. Unlike Burke, who supported hereditary privilege, Paine argues that each generation has the right to establish its own system of government. No nation can legally be ruled by a hereditary monarchy. The French people, therefore, could rightfully depose Louis XVI and establish a republican regime. Government is for the living, not the dead, so hereditary power is by definition illegitimate. No generation has the right to establish a government binding on future generations, so Burke's argument for hereditary power is essentially bankrupt.

In Part II, Paine uses the example of the American Revolution and the new American constitutional government to demonstrate the superiority of a republican over a monarchical system. Monarchies foster wastefulness and courtly excesses while republics encourage frugality and fiscal responsibility. Monarchies lead to war, republics to peace. Framed by elected representatives and approved by the people of a nation, constitutions form the basis of all legitimate governments.

This tract is an example of 18th century positivism. Paine argues throughout that humankind can reach its full potential under republican governments which allow individuals to live free of privilege and caste.

Like Rousseau and Locke before him, Paine believed that environmental influences create the individual and that a benevolent form of government can bring about human happiness. This basic assumption continues to inform our political debates today.

THE RIME OF THE ANCIENT MARINER
Samuel Taylor Coleridge
1798
Poetry
Narrative
A Mariner relates his tale of a fantastic voyage in which spirits vie for the lives of men. Lovers of narrative verse and students of Romantic poetry will be captivated by this poem.

On his way to a wedding, a young man is stopped by an Ancient Mariner who insists on relating a strange tale of adventure at sea. The Mariner reveals that years ago he had sailed from his home to the South Pole and beyond. While the ship lay becalmed near the Pole, he shot an albatross which had been following the vessel. Initially praised by his shipmates, the Mariner is eventually reviled because the deed seems to being bad luck; the albatross is hung about his neck. A spectral ship, carrying two figures, approaches the Mariner's vessel; Death and Death-in-Life play dice for the Mariner, and the latter wins. The other crew members aboard the ship die, but the Mariner lives on. Alone, he contemplates the heinous crime he has committed. Noticing the beauty of the sea creatures following the boat, he blesses them. Almost immediately, the wind picks up, the ship sails forward, and a band of spirits descend to inhabit the dead crew, aiding the Mariner to return to his homeland, where his ship goes down. He is rescued, but is compelled to tell his story to others as penance for his deed.

Coleridge's poem is characteristically Romantic: Set in a strange locale, containing accounts of the supernatural, it uses the elements of the fantastic to highlight a universal human problem. The Mariner commits a motiveless crime, but it becomes an occasion for the poet to explore the notion of guilt and repentance. Fittingly, the act of contrition involves a recognition of the beauty of nature, another Romantic axiom. Further, the Mariner is forced to share his experience with others; this, too, characterizes Romantic poetry, whose practitioners felt that poetry was a vehicle for sharing experience as well as conveying ideas. Like many Romantic heroes, the Mariner is exiled from society by his crime, and returns to it only when he feels within himself a brotherhood with other creatures of nature.

THE RING AND THE BOOK
Robert Browning
1868-1869
Poetry
In June, 1860, in Florence, Italy, Browning found an old yellow book of documents concerning the murder of the seventeen-year-old Pompilia Comparini by her husband, Count Guido Franceschini, and four accomplices. Over the next eight years, Browning turned the sordid tale of domestic violence into the crowning achievement of his poetical career.

Consistent with the epic tradition, Browning divides his poem into twelve books. After an introductory Book I he allows various participants and observers to offer their views on the murder and the subsequent trial. Guido, his lawyer, and "Half-Rome" defend the murder as the husband's legitimate revenge for his wife's betrayal. "The Other Half-Rome," Giuseppe Caponsacchi (the priest who tried to save Pompilia), Pompilia, her lawyer, and the Pope portray the young wife as a martyred saint, and the spokesman for "Tertium Quid" regards neither Guido nor Pompilia as totally innocent or guilty.

Browning's sympathies are clearly with Pompilia, whom he identified with his recently deceased wife. Throughout the poem he explores the metaphysical reasons for Pompilia's suffering, which he regards as the symbol of conflict between good and evil. In the execution of the murderers he finds grounds for cautious optimism about the ultimate triumph of goodness, and in the transformation of the murder into poetry he suggests the redemptive power of art to "suffice the eye and save the soul beside."

RIP VAN WINKLE
Washington Irving
1819-1820
Short Story
Fantasy

This tongue-in-cheek tale of a simple country bumpkin who escapes his shrewish wife by going into the woods and sleeping for twenty years is regarded as the first American short story.

"Rip Van Winkle," published as the end of the first installment of Irving's *Sketch Book*, purports to be "A Posthumous Writing of Diedrich Knickerbocker"—Irving's imaginary chronicler of the early Dutch history of New York.

The story itself could hardly be simpler. Rip, a good-natured, lazy fellow, is henpecked by his wife, whom he escapes by taking daylong jaunts with his gun and dog into the Catskill Mountains. One evening, having scrambled onto one of the highest peaks, he is hailed by a stranger dressed in "the antique Dutch fashion," who without speaking asks Rip to help him with a keg he is carrying. Rip complies, and the stranger leads him to a hollow where a whole company of similarly dressed men is playing a ninepins.

Rip begins to drink along with them, falls asleep, and awakes to find himself alone with an old rusty gun beside him. When he gets home it emerges that he has slept right through the American Revolution; his wife is dead, so, happier if no wiser, he goes back to his old idle ways and is "reverenced as one of the patriarchs of the village."

On one level the story is a gentle satire on politics: Freedom to Rip has nothing to do with King George or George Washington, but is simply a matter of being out from under his wife. "Rip Van Winkle" is also a wish-fulfillment fantasy. Its charm however, lies mostly in Irving's invocation of "the magical hues and shapes" of those "fairy mountains," where the ghosts of Henry Hudson and his crew play at nine-pins and make the thunder.

THE RISE OF SILAS LAPHAM
William Dean Howells
1885
Novel
Tragicomedy

Silas Lapham's special formula for paint brings him financial success, but poor business practices coupled with bad luck bring about his eventual ruin.

Helped along by pluck and luck, Silas Lapham has traveled the road from poor farmer to successful businessman. He has made his fortune by manufacturing a useful product (paint) and by selling it at a fair price. Having tasted success, Silas grows greedy. He squeezes his partner, Rogers, out of the business and then rationalizes his action as having been for the good of the company. Lapham subsequently turns from the hard work that has contributed to his rise in the world to stock speculation, an activity that will contribute to his downfall.

Written during a time of unprecedented growth and vulgarity in America, *The Rise of Silas Lapham* dramatizes the moral dilemma that Howells found at the heart of that change. Silas is representative of the self-made man, the rugged individual as entrepreneur, so prevalent in the boom times of late-19th century America. Like those he represents, Silas finds himself between states: the old and the new, rural Vermont and cosmopolitan Boston, and more especially between the Puritan morality of his wife Persis and the social Darwinism of the robber barons.

If Rogers and Persis represent Silas' past, the original sin and his guilt over that sin which taints his present success, then the house he builds in Boston's Back Bay area represents his ambiguous future. On the one hand the house suggests the worst in Silas: an expression of the parvenu's faith in conspicuous consumption. On the other hand, it implies a latent aesthetic sensibility still in need of considerable guidance and refinement. Silas' attraction to the Coreys, part of Boston's Brahmin class, is similarly complex; while Silas envies the Coreys' social standing and admires their civilized taste, Howells also make clear that he possesses the stamina and spunk that they have lost.

Silas' social and financial rise ends as abruptly as it began but is not without its own compensation, a MORAL rise. Faced with the collapse of his paint business, Silas entertains but finally rejects those expedients that would enable him to gain the world but that would cause him to lose his soul. His material wealth evaporates, his house accidentally burns to the ground, and Silas returns to Vermont, wiser and morally much stronger for his experience.

THE ROAD NOT TAKEN
Robert Frost
1915
Poetry
Narrative

Considered one of Frost's greatest poems, "The Road Not Taken" is often read as an endorsement of independent and courageous thinking, or a treatise on self-reliance. However, in truth, Frost composed the poem in jest, with ironic, even whimsical intent, as an observation that humans are inclined to give meaning to even the most trivial choices. Some critics characterize the poem as an ironic poet's failure at irony.

Robert Frost himself characterized "The Road Not Taken" as a "tricky" poem that he wrote for his Welsh friend and fellow poet, Thomas Walker. Apparently, it was quite common for Walker, in his excitement over all the wonders he wanted to share with Frost, to choose one direction, then express remorse that he hadn't taken Frost a different direction. Sadly, Walker took Frost's poem quite seriously, considering it the impetus he needed to join the fighting in World War I. Walker died two years later at the Battle of Arras.

In the poem, the narrator walks in a "yellow wood," and comes to a fork in the road where he must choose which direction to take. The two roads are virtually equal, "just as fair," neither having been trodden that morning. Neither road has been more or less traveled. Yet, he claims to take the "the one less traveled by…" Frost surmises that years hence, he will recall his trivial choice with "a sigh," thus hinting at the hyperbolic importance of his decision.

Interestingly, the title belies the poem's purpose or total effect. The reader is left to ponder "the road less traveled by," and what it means to go the way less traveled, yet the title suggests the poem is about the road he didn't take. The more traveled road is never considered.

ROBINSON CRUSOE
Daniel Defoe
1719
Novel
Adventure

This fictionalized account of one man's survival after being shipwrecked alone on a tropical island has become the prototype of all exotic tales of adventure.

The third son of an English merchant family from York, Robinson Crusoe rejects the comfort and security of his home and against his father's advice embarks on a life of adventure. "Bent upon seeing the world," he sets sail from London aboard a ship bound for Africa. En route, he is captured by Turkish pirates and sold into slavery. After managing to escape, he sails to Brazil aboard a Portuguese trader. There he buys a small plantation, but, once again feeling restless, he sails to Africa for slaves. On this voyage he is shipwrecked and finds himself marooned on a small island off the South American coast.

There for the next 24 years he learns to survive by using his ingenuity and resourcefulness to contrive the necessities of life. Much of Crusoe's story reads like a diary of his life as a castaway, but he is such an appealing narrator that he holds our interest. His greatest adventure comes in his 24th year when he discovers a strange footprint on the beach.

Finding that cannibals have come ashore, he plans to ambush them and rescues one of their prisoners, whom he names Friday. The two men exist as master and servant as Crusoe gradually civilizes his new companion. Eventually they free two other captives, Friday's father and a Spaniard.

As well as being an exciting tale of adventure and survival, Defoe's story celebrates the sturdy, self-reliant English-man character who can learn to exist under the most unfavorable circumstances by using his native wits and common sense. Readers have always enjoyed the details of how Crusoe slowly transforms his uninhabited island into a produc-tive homestead. He overcomes his isolation and despair through his faith in God and his knack for keeping busy with his daily work.

Along with John Bunyan's *Pilgrim's Progress*, this book stands as one of the great moral allegories of Protestant literature. Though written for adults, it has become one of the perennial favorites in children's literature for its example of the self-reliant individual who triumphs over adversity.

THE ROCKING-HORSE WINNER
D. H. Lawrence
1926
Short Story

This ironic fantasy illustrates what happens when a young boy's power of divination helps him win large sums at the races.

Paul, the protagonist of this haunting story, is a sensitive boy who would do anything to gain and keep his mother's love. Though she is beautiful, talented, well-bred, and blessed with three lovely children, she is preoccupied by her lack of luck. Luck, to the mother, is what brings you money. Father is not lucky, for the family does not have the means to live in style. The anxious children, especially the morbidly perceptive Paul, hear their house whisper, "There must be more money."

Paul longs to silence the house and his mother's creditors. After discussing racetrack lore with the family gardener, Paul furiously rides his rocking-horse. During the wild, rhythmic plunging, the nearly hypnotized Paul "knows" the name of the horse that will win big at the next race. With the trustworthy gardener to place his bets, Paul rapidly ac-cumulates a heady sum.

With his uncle's help, Paul arranges a birthday surprise for his mother—one thousand pounds annually for the next five years. He eagerly watches his mother open her mail only to find that she wants, and gains, all five thousand pounds at once. The voices of the house go mad as the mother redecorates, fills the rooms with flowers and the nursery with new toys. "There must be more money" becomes a scream, not a whisper.

Paul returns to his frantic late-night rides. He feels that he must "know" for the Derby because his mother, still cool, remote, and dissatisfied, longs to live in greater style. Even she realizes that something is wrong with Paul, who has grown overwrought and feverish. Entering his room late at night, she hears the rhythmic plunge of the rocking-horse. Paul collapses in a brain fever as he mutters over and over "Malabar," the name of the horse to win the Derby. The gardener bets Paul's money as planned; his mother is 80,000 pounds to the good. "I am lucky," are Paul's dying words.

ROMEO AND JULIET
William Shakespeare
c. 1595-1596
Drama
Tragedy, Romance

This late-16th century play about young people struggling for love in a world filled with hate will always be cherished as one of the greatest romances of all times.

This love story, though familiar even to those who have never read or seen a Shakespearean play, reveals fresh depths and nuances when experienced directly because of the beauty and precision of Shakespeare's language and his brilliant perception of character.

The brawl that opens the play reveals at once the violence that racks Verona. The enmity between the city's two leading families, the Capulets and the Montagues, is laid to rest only in the final scene, when Capulet and Montague reach reconciliation through the tragic death of their children.

Romeo, a Montague, moping for the love of Rosaline at the beginning of the play, falls in love with Juliet at a ball give by Capulet, her father. That Juliet feels the same about him he discovers by eavesdropping as she talks to herself on the balcony overlooking the Capulets' garden. This balcony scene offers some of the most memorable love poetry ever written, with an abundance of phrases and images that have become a permanent part of our cultural heritage.

The chain of unhappy events that follow constitutes a tragedy of errors, as the antagonism between the two families leads to the death of Romeo's friend Mercutio and Juliet's cousin Tybalt, slain by Romeo himself.

Yet the mood of the play is not heavy. Shakespeare includes much comic byplay between Romeo and his friends and between Juliet and her Nurse, thus enriching the texture of the play as its characters appear in diverse lights.

It is incredible that Romeo and Juliet are actually on stage together for only about twelve minutes, for these two adolescents have become the Western world's most memorable lovers.

A ROOM WITH A VIEW
E. M. Forster
1911
Novel
Romance, Historical

A Room with a View *is a love story that reflects the social evolution from staid Victorian mores, to the more freeing, exploratory Edwardian, with its emphasis on self-exploration.*

The story follows Lucy Honeychurch and her older, spinster cousin, Charlotte Bartlett, to Florence, Italy where the two have been promised adjoining rooms, with nice views. When they discover their rooms face an inner courtyard, they are rescued by the Emmersons—a father and son duo who offer to exchange rooms. During this holiday, two men vie for Lucy's affections—Cecil Vyse, an upper class snob who hopes to rescue Lucy from the social mediocrity of her birth, and George Emmerson, a passionate dreamer, whose father has taught him to stay true to the dictates of his soul. George rescues Lucy after she swoons from witnessing a bloody altercation between two Italian men. Lucy realizes George's kindness after she discovers he has thrown her recently purchased pictures into the river. They had been splattered with blood.

On the other hand, the self-absorbed Cecil, can offer Lucy social status, exposing her to society's elite, though she will have to live with Cecil's constant scrutiny and judgment, not only of her family and friends, but also of herself. Life with Cecil would "estrange her a little from all that she had loved in the past." After rejecting him twice, Lucy finally accepts Cecil's proposal of marriage following a scandalous kiss from George Emmerson, who has thrown himself at Lucy.

Upon returning home, just when she thinks she is free from the confusion she experienced following George's kiss, Lucy learns that George and his father have, unbeknownst to them, rented a cottage near the Honeychurch home, (ironically, due to Cecil's machinations to keep a set of dowdy spinsters out). Lucy is faced with the overwhelming dilemma of choosing to follow her heart and break off her engagement with Cecil, even if it means never marrying, in order to admit to and explore a burgeoning attraction to George.

The novel ends one year later, when the newly married Lucy and George stay at the pension Bertolini where they first met.

A ROSE FOR EMILY
William Faulkner
1930
Short Story
Southern Gothic

Faulkner's story tells of Miss Emily Grierson, a Southern woman who murders her lover and keeps his body in her house until her own death.

Miss Emily met Homer Baron, a foreman with a construction company, when her hometown was first getting paved streets. Her father had already died but, not before driving away her eligible suitors. As rumors circulate about her possible marriage to a Yankee, Homer leaves town abruptly. During his absence, Miss Emily buys rat poison.

When Homer returns, the townspeople see him enter Miss Emily's house but not leave. Only when she dies do the townspeople discover his corpse on a bed in her house and, next to it, a strand of Miss Emily's hair.

This Gothic plot makes serious points about woman's place in society. Throughout the story, the reader is aware that these events are taking place during a time of transition: The town is finally getting sidewalks and mailboxes. More important, values are changing. The older magistrates, for example, looked on Miss Emily paternally and refused to collect taxes from her; the newer ones try, unsuccessfully, to do so.

Caught in these changing times, Miss Emily is trapped in her role as genteel spinster. Without a husband, her life will have no meaning. She tries to give lessons in painting china but cannot find pupils for this out-of-date hobby and finally discontinues them. If Homer is thinking of abandoning her, as his departure implies, one can understand her desire to clutch at any sort of union, even a marriage in death.

The theme is developed through an exceptionally well-crafted story. Told from a third-person plural point of view, it reveals the reactions of the town to Miss Emily. As this "we" narrator shifts allegiance—now criticizing Miss Emily, now sympathizing with her—the reader sees the trap in which she is caught, and the extensive but unobtrusive foreshadowing prepares the reader for the story's final revelation without detracting from its force.

ROSENCRANTZ AND GUILDENSTERN ARE DEAD
Tom Stoppard
1966
Drama
Comedy

This witty but serious play puts two minor Shakespearean characters center stage for an exploration of contemporary anonymity and aimlessness.

In William Shakespeare's *Hamlet*, Rosencrantz and Guildenstern are ordinary gentlemen of the court, spying, fawning, and never really performing any action. In Stoppard's play, they are quintessentially modern men, impotent and averse to action, updated and somewhat more intelligent versions of Didi and Gogo in Samuel Beckett's *Waiting for Godot*.

Thrust into a complicated situation that they do not understand, they are torn between opposing factions—Claudius, Gertrude, and Polonius versus Hamlet. The play's action follows that of its source, but always from the perspective of these two characters.

Hamlet's principals, who in Stoppard's play speak only lines taken from Shakespeare's original dialogue, here are seen as supporting characters in Rosencrantz and Guildenstern's lives, yet they are the ones involved in important actions, while Rosencrantz and Guildenstern are mere pawns, never able to understand what they are doing or why. Sometimes they even forget which of them is which.

They are not helped in their dilemma by a troupe of players also from Shakespeare's original play but with their function and character greatly expanded. Through them, Stoppard explores questions of reality and the meaning of death.

To give themselves the impression that they exist and can accomplish something, the title characters engage in constant, almost dizzying wordplay, for which Stoppard is noted. This, his striking theatrical devices, and the fascinating central idea—common to most of his later plays as well—have caused him to be recognized, along with Harold Pinter, as one of Great Britain's preeminent living playwrights.

RUBÁIYÁT OF OMAR KHAYYÁM
Edward FitzGerald
1859
Poetry
Philosophical

The Rubaiyat *of Edward Fitzgerald consists of what he called his transmutation of a selection of the rub'ai or quatrains left by the 11th century Persian poet, philosopher, and astronomer, Omar Khayyam.*

Containing 75 quatrains in the first edition, some 100 in later editions, Fitzgerald's collection imposes an organization, both philosophical and artistic, on the otherwise random ordering of Khayyam's poetry. Such an arrangement stresses the materialistic side of Khayyam's thought by eliminating the more spiritual of the rub'ai, and it earned for Fitzgerald's Omar the reputation as a hedonist and religious skeptic, explaining somewhat his place as a cult figure of Victorian England.

Fitzgerald's Khayyam advocates that humankind make the most of life through intense sensual living within a world of moral ambiguity and religious doubt. Allied with such heretical beliefs is Khayyam's constant use of the image of wine as a symbol linked with themes of escape and celebration—hence the reputation of the *Rubaiyat* for wine, women, and song.

The extent of Fitzgerald's knowledge of Persian culture, especially the history and conventions of its poetry, is questionable. He did not aspire to produce a scholarly or literal translation but rather to achieve literary excellence—which he did, even in places outstripping the lyricism of the Persian. Moreover, he produced a volume of poetry which exerted a powerful influence on artistic circles of the late 19th century and helped to reinforce the vogue for Orientalism in both English and American society of the period.

S

SAILING TO BYZANTIUM
William Butler Yeats
1928
Poetry
Lyric

Yeats's four-part lyric is characteristic of his later work, both in its technical assurance and mastery, and in its concern with the conflict between body and soul, youth and old age.

In "Sailing To Byzantium" the aging poet confronts his own mortality and describes the triumph of art and the soul over the decaying body.

In the first two sections of the poem, the poet tells of his quest for a song of the soul rather than the body, an eternal song rather than a song of what is passing. He hopes to learn that song in Byzantium because, for Yeats, ancient Byzantium represented a culture whose various arts were the product of a single idea, a single image, and thus contributed to one vast and eternal design.

Part three of the poem is an invocation to the sages of Byzantium, calling upon them to instruct the poet in the song of the soul. Finally, Yeats presents an image of the poet removed from nature, his soul no longer "fastened to a dying animal," his song encompassing past, present, and future at once. The poet is now an emblem of eternity, a golden figure hammered into shape by some ancient, anonymous craftsman.

"Sailing To Byzantium" becomes a richer poem when placed in the context of Yeats's other writings, both poetry and prose. Rather than standing as any final statement on the nature of the poet, it represents one stage in a conflict that lies behind many of Yeats's best poems. And no summary can do justice to the poem's principal virtue, the grace and vitality of its language, which combines conversational ease with lyric intensity.

SAINT JOAN
George Bernard Shaw
1923
Drama
Historical

This interpretation of the life, trial, and death of Joan of Arc is Shaw's most admired play. It celebrates Joan's visionary gifts, criticizes institutional religion, and sees in her spirit the germ of Protestantism and modern nationalism.

The action of the play takes place during the Hundred Years War between France and England. Northern France is controlled by the English, and the forces of Charles VII of France are demoralized. The teenage peasant girl from Lorraine, against all likelihood, gains the confidence of a local squire, then Charles himself, in her military leadership.

Joan has all along claimed a special mission from God, communicated to her by means of inner voices; and the miracles which aided her as a French soldier now provide her enemies with a basis to destroy her. Thus, after some significant successes in the field, she is captured by the English and tried by the Inquisition as a witch. She stoutly holds to her convictions, however, and is eventually burned at the stake.

Shaw's Joan is a natural, determined, and charismatic young woman. But she also has divine gifts which are either unrecognized or feared by her political and ecclesiastical opponents. His play develops her character with feeling and complexity. It has a wide range of dramatic effects, from light comedy to high drama (as in the trial scene) and poetic lyricism (as in the epilogue).

Yet the play is most effective for its dramatization of the conflict between individual genius or inspiration (represented by Joan) and social, historical, and ecclesiastical necessities (represented by the Inquisitor). In this way, it avoids romanticism, piety, and positivism, and advances a view of saints and miracles which is modern, yet respectful of traditional religious values.

SAMSON AGONISTES
John Milton
1671
Drama and Poetry
Tragedy

Based on the biblical story of Samson and modeled on the structure and conventions of Greek tragedy, Samson Agonistes *depicts a hero whose tragic fall turns into a victory when he allows himself to be guided by God's Providence.*

Because Samson AgonistesMilton was blind when *Samson Agonistes* was published, the drama is sometimes interpreted biographically by critics who perceive Samson as a spokesman for Milton's own feelings. The work, however, may have been composed as early as 1646-1648 and revised much later for publication.

As Milton indicates in the preface, this dramatic poem was never intended for performance. The first great "closet drama" in English, *Samson Agonistes* questions the justice of God's treatment of Samson and by extension his treatment of all men.

Prior to the play's action, which takes place over a twenty-four-hour period, Samson, overcome by Dalila's wiles and by his own pride, disobeys God. The Philistines blind Samson to render him helpless. During the action of the play, Samson is visited by his father Manoa, his wife Dalila, his enemy Harapha of Gath, and finally by a Public Officer, who encourages the blind hero to join the festival. The Chorus of Hebrew Elders discusses these visitors with Samson.

The play concludes when Manoa returns, joyful at having ransomed Samson; a messenger appears who relates the final catastrophe. His strength renewed, Samson has pulled down the pillars of the temple, ending the lives of many Philistines, but sacrificing his life as well.

One of the last great works of the Renaissance, *Samson Agonistes* represents a successful effort to synthesize classical, Hebraic, and Christian traditions. Samson suffers from pride, the Greek tragic flaw, but faced with temptations of the spirit and flesh, he refuses either to distrust God or to run away from his suffering.

SANCTUARY
William Faulkner
1931
Novel
Detective, Regionalist

This story of a Southern lawyer's vain attempt to restore order in his life and to bring a criminal to justice presents Faulkner's bleakest view of mankind.

Caught between a Prohibition gangster and Southern customs, Horace Benbow tries to bring a vicious criminal to justice and save the life of a local moonshiner. At Lee Goodwin's moonshine farm, Horace stumbles unwittingly into the insidious world of Popeye, an impotent gangster, who holds Temple Drake, a flirtatious but innocent coed, semi-captive. Benbow, unable to deal with his own family, is ill prepared for the barbarous rape of Temple which follows the murder of the feebleminded Tommy.

When Lee Goodwin is falsely accused of the murder, Benbow undertakes his defense. To save Goodwin, Benbow must first locate Temple, who has been put by Popeye into a Memphis brothel, and he must then get her to tell the truth in court. In the process of the story's complex conflicts, Benbow is stripped of all faith in humanity, shaken to his moral foundations. By the novel's ironic end, the gentle lawyer has no defenses left against the world's evil. All he can say is, "Lock the door."

The novel becomes an ironic satire on the cliched heroine and traditional values. Temple Drake is no temple of innocence, and there is no sanctuary from evil—not the blatant evil without nor the evil hidden within the society. Popeye's evil at least is pure compared with the hypocritical attitudes found in the "good" Southern people. Horace, the ineffectual lawyer, repeats a phrase that runs ironically through the novel: "There ought to be a law." The Law, however, is no better than the people who live under it.

THE SATANIC VERSES
Salman Rushdie
1989
Novel
Magical Realism

This novel presents linked stories about the eternal struggle between good and evil, within an Islamic context.

This frame story tells of two immigrant actors, Gibreel Farishta and Saladin Chamcha, in England, who are current incarnations of good and evil. The dreamlike magical realism of the style reflects the dramatic experience of listening to actors perform fantastic monologues.

A hijacked airliner explodes and the two main characters fall out of the sky. Traumatized by the fall, both characters struggle in dreams to recall and restructure their lives. Farishta takes on the personality of the archangel Gibreel, while Chamcha takes on the persona of the devil.

Three long narratives constitute much of the novel, the first being the episode of the Satanic verses. These were passages said to have been dictated by the devil to Mohammad. In those verses Mohammed endorsed the pagan gods Baal and Allat, whom was said to reside inside the Ka'bah stone and is presented as the co-consort goddess of Allah. This theme parallels the late night obscene phone call Chamcha makes to Farishta.

The second hallucinatory narrative dramatizes the story of the peasant girl Ayesha who claims to receive messages from the angel Gibreel. She leads an apocalyptic religious pilgrimage to walk across the Arabic Sea to Mecca. Some reports assert the pilgrims all drowned, while other reports claimed they successfully walked on water.

The third narrative, written in the vein of Zola's sociological realism, portrays a devastating satire on the lifestyle that Ayatollah Khomeini led in Paris before he overthrew the Shah of Iran.

The novel concludes with traditional reversal: Farishita kills his beloved English mistress Allie in India and then commits suicide; Chamcha learns to reconcile with his father and return to his family in India: thus the apparently saved are damned, and the damned are saved. Throughout the novel the perceptions of the reader are constantly turned upside down.

In some parts of the Islamic world the novel was deemed blasphemous and the Ayatollah Ruhollah Khomeini issued a fatwa for the author's assassination.

THE SATYRICON
Petronius Arbiter
66 AD
Novel
Comedy

Following the young student, Encolpius, through a series of misadventures, most having to do with food, sex, or curses, Petronius's mock epic is a scathing parody of Roman society, and is remarkably refreshing for such a vulgar story

Whether this novel's title was derived from the word "satura," translated as a "mixed dish" and the root of the word "satire," or "satyr," a mythological beast with pronounced virility, both are fitting. One of the earliest known works of fictional prose, the novel's existing pages are but fragments of a much longer work that was at least sixteen volumes long. (The extant fragments are said to be from the fifteenth and sixteenth volumes.)

A bawdy picaresque tale of the misadventures of the young man, Encolpius, and his sprite-like, slave boy lover, Giton, who seems to steal everyone's' hearts, The Satyricon is a curious mix of both high comedy, with its deft references to, and clear parallels with Homer's Odyssey; and low comedy—the narrator's name is Encolpius, which translates as "the crotch." Just like Odysseus, Encolpius is fleeing an offended god named Priapus, the god of lust or fertility) whose grove he has "disturbed." Later in the story, Encolpius seeks the help of a witch in overcoming his impotence.

The plot has Encolpius and Ascyltus, who are former lovers, vie for Giton's affections as the three wend their way through loosely related episodes of mischief. In the largest fragment of the novel, the three attend a dinner host by a freed slave named Trimalchio. An elaborate affair, Trimalchio's surprises grow more and more absurd—Petronius's scathing parody of Roman class and manners. (Some conjecture that Trimalchio is actually a caricature of the emperor, Nero)

Petronius had been a member of Nero's inner circle as the arbiter elegantiae (translated as the "director of elegance" or "director of good taste") until a rival accused him of being in collusion with a group seeking Nero's assassination. Though he was innocent, Petronius committed suicide rather than wait for judgment.

THE SCARLET LETTER
Nathaniel Hawthorne
1850
Novel
Historical

Set in 17th century Puritan New England, this historical romance concerns questions that are still significant today: To what extent is the individual responsible for his or her own actions, and to what degree does the community have authority over its members?

The novel begins with the "Custom House" section that pretends to explain Hawthorne's discovery of the scarlet letter that led to his narrative of the life of Hester Prynne, an adulteress—so judged by her community and compelled to wear the symbol of her iniquity. The author gives the letter itself a tangible feel, as if he could actually experience the passions that provoked Hester and her minister, Arthur Dimmesdale, to become lovers. Hawthorne's purpose is to make readers identify with human emotions that transcend historical contexts and different value systems.

When Hester is first observed in public taking her punishment, she seems more of a Romantic than a Puritan figure. She is defiant and gloriously individual. Later, she even speaks of her affair with Dimmesdale as having had a "consecration of its own."

Yet for all his criticism of his Puritan ancestors, one of whom took part in the Salem witch trials, Hawthorne is not unmoved by the Puritans' strong sense of community. Only such values enable a society to control the anarchy inherent in rampant individualism. Hester is a lost soul who doubts the validity of her lonely stand; the Puritans, for all their hardness, are shown to be forgiving and fair-minded within the limits of their religion.

Hawthorne insisted in the "Custom House" and elsewhere that he was a writer of romances, by which he suggested that for all the historical authenticity of his work, he was not a realist but rather a symbolist, a romancer who probed beneath the daylight aspects of things into the darker, shadowy motivations of human beings. A master of ambiguity, he is one of the honored forebears of modern fiction, and *The Scarlet Letter* is his finest achievement, a perfectly constructed work of art remarkable for its exquisitely balanced handling of moral issues and conflicting human personalities.

SCHINDLER'S ARK
(Released as Schindler's List in the U.S.)
Thomas Keneally
1982
Novel
Historical, Holocaust

This 1982 novel by an Australian writer originally appeared as Schindler's Ark, and won both a Booker Prize and the Los Angeles Times Book Prize for fiction. Steven Spielberg's 1992 movie adaptation was nominated for twelve Academy Awards, winning seven.

German businessman, Oskar Schindler, a typical hard-drinking Nazi Party womanizer, employs Jews at his factory. After witnessing a brutal expulsion of Jews from the Polish ghetto in Krakow, Schindler experiences a wave of guilt: an officer casually shoots the father of a little girl in a red coat, then paternally pats her on the head.

Schindler bribes high-ranking SS officers with cash and booze to exempt his mechanics and metal workers at his enamelware factory from concentration camps. In doing so, he becomes friendly with several of his loyal workers, especially Leonard Pfefferberg.

In portraying Schindler, Keneally avoids adulatory heroism: Schindler is a simple man (who keeps a careful eye on profit and solvency) with a normal heart. He takes calculated chances walking a schizophrenic tightrope, knowing that his fall would result in ignominious death. The force of Schindler's extroverted persona allows Schindler to succeed among local Nazis, especially with Commandant Amon Goeth, whose hobby is rifle-sniping Jews from his front porch.

Keneally endows the story of various workers with resourceful suspense that avoids melodrama, as Schindler skirts unexpected encounters and inspections by Nazi superiors, during which workers engage in improvised theater. Schindler even steals medical supplies for his workers. Because the narrative drive remains so emotionally intense, this docu-novel became Keneally's best book.

As the result of a chance encounter, Keneally bought Schindler's actual list (which contained the names, occupations, ages, birthplaces, and religions of Schindler's workers) from a Los Angles boutique owned by Pfefferberg, who owed his survival to Schindler. During the course of an hour, Pfefferberg urged Keneally to write the obscure story of Oskar Schindler and how he saved a thousand Jews. Pfefferberg travelled to Krakow with Keneally, visiting specific places mentioned in the novel, and interviewing surviving Jews from the list. The novel is dedicated to Pfefferberg, who eventually prevailed upon Steven Spielberg to produce the film.

After the war, Oskar Schindler was spat upon in the street as a traitor; he ended up living and dying in Jerusalem. In 2007, Keneally published Searching for *Schindler: A Memoir*.

THE SEAFARER
Unknown
960-980 C.E.
Poetry

The Seafarer is an Anglo-Saxon poem in the form of an old sailor's monologue. His lifelong acceptance of loneliness, his contempt for the luxuries of those on land, and his yearning to set out on another voyage are both starkly imagined and resonantly Christian.

The sailor begins with the reasons for his sorrow. His only home has been a ship constantly encountering indifferent forces, the sea and the cold. The prosperous man situated on land does not know the icy feeling of exile, the feeling of being cut off from one's loved ones. The sailor's joy has been the cry of sea birds instead of the laughter of men. On the sea, he says, there is no protector for men. Those on land, flushed with wine, are incapable of believing in his suffering.

Nonetheless, the sailor maintains that the heart's desire is to venture forth on another journey. At the same time, he warns, there is no man so brave he can escape the anxiety that accompanies seafaring. His thoughts are not of music, riches, or women, but of his own longing. Not satisfaction, but dissatisfaction urges his heart and mind "over the stretch of seas."

This yearning leads him to the "joys of the Lord," which are not earthly. There are three things that are always uncertain until they come: illness, old age, and hostility, each of which entertains the possibility of death. Why then, he wonders, should one wish for earthly fame? One should rather seek fame among the angels.

The best days and their joys, he concludes, are gone, and weaklings have come to power. When a man dies, none of his former joys will have meaning. Thus it is foolish not to fear the Lord, but one is blessed who lives humbly—as presumably the seafarer has done. The poem ends with an exhortation to the reader to consider where his real home is and how to proceed there.

The Seafarer provides interest because it was obviously composed at a pivotal time when north European stoicism was giving way to Christian forbearance and hope. The poem has the feeling of both, and though the Christian feeling is uppermost, most readers remember the poem's austere, impressionistic images of life at sea.

THE SEAGULL
Anton Chekhov
1896
Drama
Comedy

The Seagull *tells of young Konstantin Treplev's efforts to become a great writer and gain the love of Nina Zaretchyn, an aspiring actress.*

Madame Arkadina, an aging but accomplished actress, entertains assorted friends and relatives at her country estate; her guests include the famous novelist Trigorin and a lovely neighborhood girl named Nina. Arkadina's son Treplev has written a play in the new Symbolist style. When it is presented with Nina in the lead role, the visitors laugh, sending Treplev into fits of rage and artistic despair. Nina, disenchanted with Treplev, falls in love with the dissipated Trigorin, already Arkadina's lover, and elicits from him a promise to sponsor her acting career in the city in exchange for becoming his mistress.

Chekhov draws his portraits in great detail, mercilessly revealing flaws and showing the fragile, exposed egos beneath the surface. The penultimate scene, between a broken Treplev and a fallen Nina, stands for man's inability to regain the zeal and passionate integrity of youth.

After one false start, the play was successfully staged by the Moscow Art Theatre, which took the sea gull as its symbol in honor of the playwright and the new dramatic approach the play initiated. All of today's realistic drama owes a debt to the innovations of Chekhov's work: naturalistic dialogue without obvious construction, a loosening of strictly Aristotelian rules of dramatic structure, and condensed, psychologically convincing characterization.

THE SEA-WOLF
Jack London
1904
Novel

Like The Call Of The Wild, *which was based on London's experience of the Klondike gold rush,* The Sea-Wolf *draws on what he had learned of sealing and smuggling before his sudden rise from sailor to best-selling author.*

The story is told by Humphrey Van Weyden, a dilettantish and comically over-civilized literary critic. When his ferry boat sinks in San Francisco Bay, Van Weyden is picked up by the Ghost, a sealing schooner, and carried off into the Pacific against his will. He is appalled by the cruelty of the schooner's captain, Wolf Larsen, but also fascinated by Larsen's physical power and spiritual magnetism. A self-taught philosopher who echoes much of London's own reading in Herbert Spencer and Friedrich Nietzsche, Larsen is amused by trials of wit with this gentleman, whom he renames "Hump" and sets to work as cabin boy.

Hump's attempts to escape and the crew's attempts to revolt are ruthlessly thwarted by the seemingly omnipotent Larsen. Nevertheless, Hump, promoted to mate, is learning to adapt to the struggle for survival that he had ignored in his protected life on shore.

Then another shipwreck victim is rescued, the beautiful poet Maud Brewster. One night Hump finds Maud struggling in Larsen's arms. Before he can act, Larsen is struck by a sudden, mysterious headache. Hump and Maud escape in an open boat and finally manage to go ashore on an island off the Alaskan coast. There they learn to fend for themselves. Months after their escape, Larsen is washed up in the Ghost. Though blind and dying, he still almost succeeds in frustrating their efforts to repair the schooner. After his death they sail off, united by their shared return to self-reliance.

Yet this is less the story of their romance than of Larsen himself and of the self-destructive isolation, symbolized by his fatal sickness, behind his ruthless climb to success. Like *The Call of the Wild*, this novel takes its power from London's mixed feelings about his own metamorphosis.

THE SECRET GARDEN
Frances Hodgson Burnett
1911
Novel
Children's, Historical

When Mary Lennox, a homely, bitter British girl in India, is sent to live with her uncle in Yorkshire, England. A locked-up garden, a mysterious hallway, and unexpected friendship transform her into a kind and beautiful girl, and give life to her cousin, Colin, and his grieving father. Originally published as a series, the novel has been adapted for film and the stage numerous times

Mary Lennox is a disagreeable ten-year-old girl whose father works for the British government in colonial India. Skinny, homely, and mean, she is forgotten when cholera sweeps through her home, killing everyone except her.

She is sent to live in Misselthwaite Manor in Yorkshire, England with her uncle, Mr. Archibald Craven. Spoiled, she throws tantrums when she isn't pampered. Martha, a young housemaid, teaches her how to be a "normal" child by encouraging her to play outside. There she meets gardener Ben Weatherstaff, a kindred spirit, and becomes enchanted by "the secret garden," locked up for ten years since it belonged to Craven's deceased wife for whom he is still grieving. Mary wants to bring it back to life. Martha enlists her little brother, Dickon, a sweet boy with an incredible knack for gardening, to help. He and Mary become friends.

In the large, seemingly empty house, Mary often hears crying in the hallway but no one will tell her its origin. She explores and finds a boy her age in a wheelchair. The boy, Colin, is her cousin who has been kept isolated since birth because he was deemed an invalid, and because his resemblance to his mother upsets Mr. Craven.

The servants agree that Colin has met his match in Mary; she is the only one who is able to calm his tantrums. They become friends and devise a plan to take him out to "the secret garden." Realizing there is nothing wrong with Colin, they discover that he can stand, and he and Mary gain weight and get stronger by playing outside and eating more each day. They accredit their transformations to "magic," which is a combination of friendship, nature, and positive self-affirmations: "Magic is in me! Magic is making me well!"

Mr. Craven, who has been absent on a trip, is compelled to come home after a letter from Susan Sowerby, Dickon's mother. He finds Mary and Colin, alive and well as ever, in his late wife's "secret garden," and everyone's spirits are restored and awed when they see "Master Colin walking."

THE SECRET SHARER
Joseph Conrad
1912
Short Story
Psychological

Set in the Gulf of Siam, this story describes a young sea captain's determination to help Leggatt, a sailor who has killed a man, avoid detection. In Leggatt, the inexperienced captain increasingly recognizes his possible alter ego.

The captain has held his first command for only two weeks. His responsibility is imposing: to sail his ship from Southeast Asia to Europe. Except for the second mate, he is the youngest man on board. Moreover, he does not know his crew members, who have served together for eighteen months.

The chief mate seems to question even the captain's simplest observations; the second mate, so the captain believes, is often implicitly contemptuous of his new master. In short, the captain is insecure and believes that his crew is repeatedly testing his judgment.

Partly to gain his crew's support, the captain dismisses his men and assumes the night watch himself. He thus takes on the job of common seaman, with which he feels more at ease. During his solitary patrol of the deck, he discovers a rope ladder carelessly left dangling over the side and at its end a sailor who has escaped from another ship.

Leggatt, nearly drowned in his escape, tells the captain that he had strangled a sailor who refused to obey his orders, and the captain immediately recognizes the similarity of their situations. He gives Leggatt a sleeping suit identical to his own, hides him in his own cabin, and plans his escape to shore, all without the knowledge of his crew.

Conrad describes what Sigmund Freud had called the encounter of the ego and id, the outer and inner self. The insecure captain's decision to help is an act of courage which fills him with new-found assurance.

SEIZE THE DAY
Saul Bellow
1956
Novella
Psychological

This is the tragicomic story of a man searching for acceptance and respect in a society that only accepts and respects successful people—those who make money.

Tommy Wilhelm is a loser. He is divorced, unemployed, broke, undereducated, self-indulgent, and dependent (on pills and his father, among other things). He lives in a hotel in New York City and wants desperately to put his life in order. Tommy, like all Bellow protagonists, has trouble determining how to cope with the modern world.

One of the symbols of Tommy's problems, and those of modern society generally, is his relationship with his father. Tommy's father lives in the same hotel and is disgusted with his son's weakness. He refuses to give the one thing Tommy wants most—sympathy.

Tommy makes one last grasp for success by investing in the commodities market under the dubious influence of Dr. Tamkin. His money quickly evaporates and with it his hopes.

At this lowest point, however, Tommy has an epiphany. He accidentally happens into a church during a funeral, and, after looking at the body of a man he does not know, breaks into uncontrollable weeping.

Tommy weeps for the man, for himself, and for the human condition. He is transported beyond his own particular problems to a cathartic suffering for all mankind.

Bellow sees the problems of the modern world as essentially matters of the spirit. In a high-pressure, pluralistic, threatening, materialistic world, people must find a way to live and to remain human. Tommy does this by recognizing that human beings, for all their weaknesses—or perhaps because of them—must accept and share one another's burdens.

Bellow offers this important response to the modern condition in a comic tale that is a contemporary classic, one which later helped win for him the Nobel prize.

SENSE AND SENSIBILITY
Jane Austen
1811
Novel
Manners

This witty domestic novel follows the fortunes of two pretty, marriageable sisters of contrasting temperaments.

Sense and Sensibility is, as its title suggests, a study of opposites. The novel centers on two sisters, Elinor and Marianne Dashwood. The first is serene and reasonable, the second impetuous and emotional; but they are devoted to each other and to their mother and younger sister. Since their father's death and their half-brother's succession to the estate, they all have retired to Devonshire.

There Marianne meets Willoughby, a charming but amoral gentleman. She falls ecstatically in love. He trifles with her affections, runs off to London, and engages himself to an heiress. Marianne bears her disappointment as befits a representative of sensibility: with tears, swoons, and tragic postures.

In the meantime, Elinor has her own share of love and sadness, both of which she handles in a manner markedly different from that of her sister. Elinor admires her sister-in-law's brother Edward Ferrars, a less dashing but more scrupulous man than Willoughby. Ferrars hesitates to voice his love for Elinor because of an imprudent earlier understanding he had formed with a woman of low degree, Lucy Steele. On hearing of his secret pledge, Elinor honorably and unselfishly conceals her feelings until Ferrars' mother discovers his unsuitable promise to Lucy and disinherits him in favor of his younger brother, who then becomes the victim of the fickle and mercenary Lucy.

Austen's study of manners and morals ends, as her other novels do, with appropriate marriages rewarding and defining the chief characters. Elinor marries Ferrars, who has obtained a small church living that will support him and a wife of her practical sort. Marianne, who has paid the penalty of her sensibility, also gains a mate. Educated by her suffering, she realizes that Colonel Brandon, a rich, kind man who has long loved her and who has experienced romantic disappointments of his own, is a suitable husband despite his wearing flannel waistcoats and being an " old man" of five and thirty.

A SENTIMENTAL EDUCATION
Gustave Flaubert
1869
Novel
Historical, Coming of Age

When a young man's passion for an older woman is thwarted, he turns to the more practical matter of furthering his career; in the process he loses his innocence and becomes a disillusioned cynic.

A young man from the provinces, Frederic Moreau comes to Paris and dabbles in law, literature, and painting, supported by a private income and then an inheritance. His one real passion is for Madame Arnoux, who looks to him like a woman out of romantic novels. He pursues her with devotion, but when her son falls ill, she fails to appear at the decisive tryst where he had hoped to seduce her. Frederic consoles himself by going off with Rosanette, the mistress of Madame Arnoux's husband. Thus, he both loses the reward of his romantic passion and, on the same day, misses the heroic uprising that begins the overthrow of the monarchy.

Out of sync with history, Frederic enters a period of cynical disillusionment. His illegitimate child dies in infancy. He neglects Rosanette in order to further his career by courting the wife of the wealthy capitalist Dambreuse. Dambreuse dies, and his widow proposes to Frederic. He is ready to marry her, but then it is discovered that her husband has left his money elsewhere. Frederic declines the proposal.

The novel's one hero is Dussardier, who is shocked into joining the Revolution by the cruelty of government reprisals against the people of Paris. Dussardier is contrasted to Senecal, a dogmatic revolutionary who becomes a factory manager and then a police agent. In the coup d'etat of 1851, Senecal murders Dussardier while the latter is crying "Vive la republique!" The revolution is crushed, and Frederic's fellow townsman Deslauriers marries the heiress Louise, to whom Frederic had been engaged before his passion for Madame Arnoux. A new regime of soulless, unprincipled opportunism has arrived.

Frederic and Madame Arnoux finally meet again and confess their passion, but for him it is now defunct. Her hair has gone white, and as she leaves she kisses him on the forehead like a mother.

The last words of the novel are even more ironic. Frederic and Deslauriers look back nostalgically to their visit, as boys, to the local brothel. Unconsummated and humiliating, this episode now seems to represent all the innocence Frederic has lost.

A SEPARATE PEACE
John Knowles
1959
Novel
Coming of Age, Bildungsroman

In his last year at a New England boys' prep school during World War II, Gene Forrester learns that the real enemy is inside himself.

This book opens with Gene Forrester's return to Devon school after World War II to revisit the place where he believes he fought his war. He remembers his last year at Devon, when he became friends with his roommate, Finny.

While Gene is thoughtful and unsure of himself, Finny is filled with confidence. This confidence is based on a physical prowess which makes him the best athlete in the school. While Gene is capable of earning the top grades in his class, Finny is the undisputed class leader. Finny's constant invention of pranks and games and his insistence on fun and good fellowship remind the boys, who have many kinds of trouble on their minds, that the joy of living should be valued above all things.

Gene comes to feel that there is a secret rivalry between him and Finny, he even suspects that Finny's midnight larks are part of a plot to prevent him from getting the best grades. When he realizes that he is mistaken and that he has projected his own insecurity onto Finny, he is unable to accept this fact. Suddenly presented with a chance to hurt Finny, he causes an "accident" which results in a crippling compound fracture for Finney.

Most of the novel deals with Gene's attempts to come to terms with his act. Finny does not suspect Gene, so Gene must deal with himself in moral isolation. Though Gene tries to confess, Finny will not listen to him. Only when their classmates hold a mock trial, do Finny and Gene face what Gene has done. Perhaps as a result of the trial, Finny re-breaks his leg and dies in the resulting operation. Before the operation, in a secret visit to Finny's hospital room, Gene learns how much he has hurt Finny and how truly innocent Finny has always been.

Though often discussed as a novel for young people, *A Separate Peace* is rich enough to interest adult readers. Gene's discovery that the real enemy is not across the ocean but in his own soul is convincing and moving.

SEVEN GOTHIC TALES
Isak Dinesen
1934
Short Story
Collection, Gothic

Forever entertaining, at times fantastic, and often chilling in their revelations, the tales all the while present a discourse on the darker side of life.

The Seven Gothic Taleselegantly written narratives, each independent of the others, treat stages of 19th century aristocratic life in Europe. Their adventures frequently transcend the ordinary, for theirs is a Gothic world in which the unreal often appears more substantial than reality itself.

"The Deluge at Norderney," the opening tale, recounts how four people, each one eccentric, spend a night in a flood-surrounded barn and pass the time by revealing their secrets. In "The Old Chevalier," an aging baron recalls a youthful and disastrous encounter with a prostitute in Paris. "The Monkey" takes up an arranged courtship between an unmatched couple whose meeting brings about a catastrophe.

When a Danish count in "The Roads Around Pisa" sets out to search for an Italian noblewoman's runaway granddaughter, he meets some peculiar travelers at an inn and becomes involved in a proposed duel. "The Supper at Elsinore" tells of a mysterious reunion between a long lost brother and his two spinster sisters.

"The Dreamers" is a story about three men passionately in love with elusive women, who turn out to be one woman given to disguises. "The Poet" reveals how a young genius' rejection of his mentor leads to disaster. The tales employ a narrative style reminiscent of an earlier time, an approach which allows them to be openly instructive while they entertain.

Their Gothic qualities, which embrace darkness and grotesqueness, permit them to strip away the murky side of humankind—its undefined desires, inexplicable passions, love mixed with hate, and sexual repression. Layered with meaning that goes far beyond their outward air of adventure and mystery, the tales try always to unravel the more important mystery of human nature.

They depict, as well, the end of an age. The decadent aristocrats of these tales stand doomed as their world crumbles, feudalism giving way to democracy, aristocracy to equality. Yet the characters manage to retain their dignity as they face the destruction that awaits them.

SHE STOOPS TO CONQUER
Oliver Goldsmith
1773
Drama
Comedy

When two young men mistake their host's home for a country inn, confusion ensues, but, typical of comic drama, the play concludes with enlightenment, reconciliation, and the prospect of marriages.

Charles Marlow, bashful with women of his own class but uninhibited with those of lower rank, is traveling to meet Kate Hardcastle, his prospective wife. He is accompanied by Hastings, who loves Constance Neville, a niece and ward of Kate's mother.

When they stop at an alehouse for directions, Tony Lumpkin, Mrs. Hardcastle's son, directs them for lodging to a supposed inn, which really is the Hardcastle home.

When they arrive, Hastings sees Miss Neville and learns that Tony duped them; however, he does not tell Marlow, thus setting the stage for Marlow's pursuit of Kate, whom his father has chosen for him, but whom he thinks is a servant.

Hastings and Constance want to wed, but her aunt hopes to match Tony with the girl. Since Tony does not want to marry, he helps orchestrate Constance's elopement.

In the final act, Tony again demonstrates that though illiterate, he is not an oaf, and he cleverly forestalls his mother's attempt to remove Constance to another aunt for safekeeping. The arrival of Marlow's father also moves the plot to its proper conclusion, for he and Hardcastle confront the young man with the real identity of the girl he has been wooing.

Mrs. Hardcastle finally releases Constance's inheritance when Hardcastle's revelation that Tony is of age enables the young man to renounce Constance as his prospective wife. All are reconciled and look forward to the two marriages.

Goldsmith's play is a rejection of the morally uplifting sentimental comedy popular through much of the 18th century and a return to the older tradition of laughing comedy. Therefore, it is more closely related in subject matter and technique to Shakespeare's comedies and those of the Restoration than to its 18th century predecessors.

SHIP OF FOOLS
Katherine Anne Porter
1962
Novel
Satire

A German ship sailing from Veracruz, Mexico, to Bremerhaven, Germany, in 1931 is a microcosm of a troubled world moving inexorably toward war.

Porter explains in an introductory note that the novel's title is taken from a 15th century German allegory, *Das Narrenschiff*, by Sebastian Brant. She read the book in 1932, soon after her first voyage to Europe. She wrote her novel over a period of years and finished it in 1962.

The passengers and crew of the ship Vera represent the whole spectrum of humanity, from good to evil. Many of the passengers, most of the crew, the ship's doctor, and the Captain are German. Also traveling on the ship are several

Latin passengers, including a zarzuela company, a few Americans, a Swiss family, a Swede, and uncounted and mostly nameless steerage passengers.

The novel has little plot, but a troubled love affair between two American artists, Jenny Scott and David Brown, provides a thin story line. A climactic festival near the end of the voyage offers insights into particular individuals, developing character traits suggested earlier. Despite the lack of plot, lively incidents and colorful characters make the novel entertaining and thought provoking.

Although the author's point of view is omniscient, she remains unobtrusive and objectively presents the characters in their strengths, weaknesses, folly, and, occasionally, their repulsiveness. Her keen insight pointedly reveals the destructive potential of racism, particularly in the Captain's personality. Both the author's and the reader's inescapable hindsight, provided by knowledge of World War II, makes this conventional topic unconventional.

THE SICKNESS UNTO DEATH
Søren Kierkegaard
1849
Nonfiction
Philosophical, Treatise

In this densely argued work contrasting despair and faith, Kierkegaard analyzes human nature and the process of self-realization. Like many of his books, it was published under a pseudonym—in this case, the name Anti-Climacus.

The title of this book is taken from a passage in the Gospel of John in which Jesus responds to the news that Lazarus is sick: Jesus says, "This sickness is not unto death, but for the glory of God, that the Son of God might be glorified thereby."

Kierkegaard begins by noting a paradox: Lazarus did in fact die. It is true, he adds, that Christ then raised Lazarus from the dead—"for the glory of God"—but, after all, Lazarus ultimately had to die again. The real point of Christ's statement, Kierkegaard says, is not that Lazarus was going to be raised from the dead but rather that for all Christians, even death itself is not "the sickness unto death."

The fears that trouble the natural man should not trouble the Christian: The Christian, however, fears a threat of which the natural man is not even aware: a "sickness of the spirit" which Kierkegaard calls despair, using the word in a special, narrow sense. Despair is the sickness unto death.

Kierkegaard's intention, then, is to analyze the psychology of despair, showing how it grows out of the conflict between man's eternal soul and his earthly condition. Only when man begins to recognize the claims of the eternal is he subject to despair.

The antidote to despair is faith, the state of abandoning oneself to the mercy of God in full confidence that God forgives one's failures. The leap of faith actualizes a person's human potential. Only by choosing to abandon despair and self-reliance for trust in God can a person become fully human.

SIDDHARTHA
Hermann Hesse
1922
Novella
Biographical

This novel presents the story of a Brahman's son who forsakes his family and religion in order to embark on a lifelong search for the way of truth, wisdom, and enlightenment.

Siddhartha (literally "he who has achieved his aim") is a handsome young Indian Brahman who is restless and unhappy with his comfortable village life, and so he decides to become a seeker. Along with his friend Govinda, he becomes a samana, or wandering ascetic. He quickly masters the self-discipline and meditations, but he becomes dissatisfied with the ascetic life, and comes to the village of Savathi to hear the illustrious Buddha preach. Siddhartha is much impressed with Buddha's teachings but decides that he cannot be content as a disciple and must find his own "way."

Leaving his friend Govinda to become a Buddhist monk, Siddhartha abandons the monastic life and returns to a large town, where he meets the beautiful courtesan, Kamala. In order to become her lover, he decides to work for a wealthy merchant named Kamaswami. Though Siddhartha is quite successful in business, his real devotion is to Kamala. He learns the arts of love from her and cultivates his taste for sensual pleasures. Gradually he loses his ascetic detachment from the world and comes to love wealth and luxuries for their own sake. He becomes a compulsive gambler and abandons himself to the thrill of winning or losing for high stakes.

One morning, he awakens from a dream unhappy and depressed. He realizes that the pleasures of the world can become as much of an illusion as asceticism. He decides to return to the ferryman on the river and lead a simple life there. Through the old ferryman's example, Siddhartha finds contentment not through renunciation or sensuality but through love and acceptance of the things of this world.

In Hesse's religious novel, he offers his own interpretation of Buddhism through the character of Siddhartha, a name often given to the Buddha himself. The proud Siddhartha can never be content in a disciple's role, but must seek out truth and wisdom himself through his own experience. After the old ferryman Vasudeva teaches him the secrets of the river, the simultaneity, unity, and timelessness of all that exists, Siddhartha achieves the peace he has always sought.

SIGNS AND SYMBOLS
Vladimir Nabokov
1948
Short Story

Two elderly Russian refugees, now living in America, determine to bring home their institutionalized, suicidal son. However, given the sadness and suffering depicted in the story, the son's urge to "tear a hole in [the] world and escape" is not at all a symptom of madness.

The parents attempt to deliver a birthday gift to their son who has been committed to a mental institution. He is suffering from "referential mania," a state of mind in which "the patient imagines that everything happening around him is a veiled reference to his personality and existence." Unfortunately, their visit is preceded by the son's second suicide attempt, and they are forced to return home without seeing him.

Later that night, the mother looks through an old photo album. Even as a baby, her son looked, she notices, "more surprised" than most babies. The photos provide overwhelming evidence of their humiliation and pain in exile: the many cities, the friends and relatives exterminated by the Germans, her son's vicious classmates. Reviewing her son's life she sees, in retrospect, his fear growing until he "hardened," becoming "totally inaccessible to normal minds."

After midnight, the father appears, unable to sleep. He cries that he is "dying" and insists that they bring the boy home; the mother agrees. At this point they are frightened by the ringing telephone, but it is the wrong number.

They resolve to bring their son home the next day, and the phone rings again. The mother patiently explains to the caller that he is dialing the letter O instead of a zero. Having decided on a course of action, the father examines the basket of ten jelly jars that had been meant as a present for his son. Just as he reaches the fifth jar, the phone rings again, and the story ends.

Much of the story's power derives from the ambiguity of the ending. Is the final call another wrong number, or is it a call confirming what they fear most, that their son has succeeded in killing himself? Although the author leaves the story unresolved, he does provide clues that point to the latter interpretation.

Their son's decline into madness and his wish to escape is at least consistent with a hostile universe, while his parents cling precariously to an existence that offers no reward for endurance—only more fear, debility, poverty, and eventual darkness.

Despite its pessimistic worldview, "Signs and Symbols" emerges as a superbly poignant story told through a scrupulously objective narration; its theme of displacement and victimization is a powerful one.

SILAS MARNER
George Eliot
1861
Novel
Victorian

This story of a linen weaver in early 19th century England demonstrates the author's conviction that devoted human relationships can take the place of religious beliefs in giving meaning and purpose to life. The novel also implies a criticism of Victorian materialism.

In an incident briefly recounted at the beginning of the novel, Silas Marner is cruelly betrayed by his best friend, who steals some money and contrives evidence suggesting that Silas is guilty. When a trial by lots conducted by Silas' narrow Protestant sect confirms his guilt, Silas is bitterly disillusioned with divine, as well as human, justice. Moving to a rural village in central England, he isolates himself from all contact with the community and, by his assiduous weaving, accumulates a substantial sum in gold coins.

Silas' lonely and miserly life is disrupted when his gold is stolen by Dunstan Cass, a son of the most prominent local landowner. The void which the loss of the gold leaves in Silas' life is unexpectedly filled when a small child, the daughter of Dunstan's older brother Godfrey by a secret marriage, wanders into Silas' cottage. Rather than invite social disgrace by admitting his sordid marriage to a drunken barmaid, Godfrey fails to acknowledge the child. Silas undertakes the responsibility of rearing her.

Much of the significance of the novel turns on the contrast between the gold and his adopted daughter Eppie as successive centers of Silas' life. In simplest terms, the gold isolated Silas, whereas Eppie brings him into cordial contact with the community. The child, George Eliot suggests, is like the angels who, in ages of religious belief, led men away from "threatening destruction" and toward a "calm and bright land."

Silas attains his reward—and George Eliot asserts the moral of her fable—many years later when Eppie rejects Godfrey's belated claim of paternity and chooses to remain with Silas.

THE SILENT DON
Mikhail Sholokhov
1928-1940
Novel
Epic, War

World War I and the Bolshevik Revolution threaten the traditional life of the Cossacks. This Nobel prize-winning novelist presents a panorama of the Soviet Union's violent birth in two volumes.

This Silent Don, Themodern epic recounts Gregor Melekhov's stormy growth to manhood. Simultaneously it describes the ordeal of the people living along Russia's greatest river. These Cossacks find their unique identity swept away by war and revolution.

In *And Quiet Flows the Don* (the first section of the novel) Gregor lives by the old ways. He learns to fish the river, till the land, and fight from horseback. He learns too about his passionate, independent Cossack nature. He falls in love with a married woman; when his family marries him off to Natalya, Gregor deserts his bride for his lover.

When war with Germany comes, Gregor enlists. He fights bravely and is wounded. Returning home, he finds that his lover is now another's mistress; he reconciles with Natalya, who soon bears him twins. At the front, Gregor witnesses the army's collapse. After the October Revolution, unsure whether the Whites (who support the old order) or the Reds (who support the revolution) will prevail, Gregor fights first for one side, then the other.

In *The Don Flows Home to the Sea* (the second section) the Red Army invades Cossack lands. Gregor fights the invaders, but the Cossacks are overwhelmed. The victors brutalize the vanquished, prompting renewed fighting. Revolt is futile; Gregor saves himself by joining the Communists. Sickened by their harshness, Gregor leads an abortive uprising before returning home to his son. His parents, wife, daughter, and mistress are all dead; Gregor faces a hopeless future. Gregor's life and the Cossacks' fate are tragic, but in what sense? For some, the tragedy is one man's doomed quest for a third way between re-creating the past and embracing the future; to others, the tragedy is that an alien philosophy destroys a culture.

SILENT SPRING
Rachel Carson
1962
Nonfiction
Nature

After its miraculous control of wartime outbreaks of parasite-borne malaria and typhus, DDT became a postwar panacea for health workers, farmers, and suburbanites alike. As Carson thoroughly yet eloquently explained, however, the indiscriminate use of powerful chemicals was destroying far more than noxious pests.

For a decade and a half following the Second World War, victorious American technology in the form of DDT and other "wonder" chemicals promised to eradicate the deadly scourge of malaria, expensive agricultural losses due to countless insect pests, and even the annoyance of gnats and houseflies. In an era before the creation of the Environmental Protection Agency, former U.S. Fisheries and Wildlife biologist Rachel Carson detailed the way pesticides such as DDT were used without regulation, often at the encouragement of the U.S. Department of Agriculture. Aircraft sprayed vast tracts of forests and even croplands as casually as homeowners sprayed their gardens and baseboards.

Although scientific articles and anecdotal evidence kept appearing on the damage that DDT and its ilk did to wildlife, livestock, and humans alike, it took Carson to draw together the disparate strands in a quietly impassioned book for the unknowing public. Such poisons, Carson asserted startlingly, were not just "pesticides" but actually "biocides," killing off huge populations of desirable insects, birds, and mammals. And yet while many pests developed resistance, once-minute amounts of toxins increased dramatically in concentration as they spread higher up the food chain and, ultimately, into the human body.

Despite the urgency of her argument, though, Carson never simply railed against chemicals per se but instead advocated for caution based on the complexity of the ecosystem. Even strong poisons have their place in necessary spot treatments, she explained, as should biological solutions such as using natural predators to keep down pests.

In a time when the spray nozzle alone was touted as near magic, *Silent Spring* revolutionized the conversation, and began modern environmentalism.

A SIMPLE HEART
Gustave Flaubert
1877
Novella

Felicite, a poor, uneducated servant in rural Normandy, lives a rich and full life because of her simple heart.

The orphaned Felicite is treated badly in her youth, first by a cruel master and later by jealous fellow servants. Disappointed in love at age 18, she leaves her neighborhood to become cook and general servant for a widowed mother, Madame Aubain. In that position, she lives a life filled with duty, devotion, and affection. Flaubert tells the story in a simple manner which emphasizes the value of Felicite's humble life.

At Madame Aubain's, Felicite enters a routine which makes her life seem orderly. By conscientious work, she makes herself necessary to the family. Most important to her happiness is her increased freedom to love.

She loves Madame Aubain's two children, Paul and Virginia, courageously saving them from an angry bull. She accidentally discovers a lost sister whose family she helps from her tiny income and whose son, Victor, becomes a favorite. Victor and Virginia both die young. Felicite's grief at their loss is as great as Madame Aubain's for her daughter. The two women first express simple affection for each other when they one day go through Virginia's long-kept clothing.

When the children are gone, leaving only Madame Aubain for Felicite to love, she begins to collect objects which remind her of them, such as Virginia's felt hat. Her prize possession becomes Loulou, a parrot which reminds her of

Victor because it came from America, where he died. The parrot becomes so important to her that, upon its death, she has it stuffed. She eventually becomes deaf and loses Madame Aubain. In her increasing isolation, she clings to the image of the parrot, which becomes for her an image of the Holy Ghost, a symbol of what she has loved and of her power of loving simply.

SIR GAWAIN AND THE GREEN KNIGHT
Pearl-Poet
Fourteenth century
Novel
Arthurian, Romance

Written in about 1375, in a difficult provincial dialect by an anonymous poet, Sir Gawain and the Green Knight *is the greatest of the English medieval romances. The long alliterative poem tells of Gawain's efforts to uphold the honor of King Arthur's Camelot by fulfilling his pledge to trade blow for blow with the redoubtable Green Knight. The rich characterizations, vivid descriptions, and sophisticated narrative techniques rival Geoffrey Chaucer at his best.*

Camelot, described as the hallmark of courtesy and chivalry, is ablaze with the New Year's festivities as the poem begins. The festive atmosphere is abruptly broken by the entrance into King Arthur's hall of a gigantic green knight, who derides Arthur's knights as mere boys and challenges anyone to trade blows with him. He will take the first blow, but in a year and a day the assailant must receive a blow in return. The only knight to accept the challenge is Gawain. With one blow, Gawain decapitates the Green Knight, but the headless knight picks up his head, adjures Gawain to find his way to the Green Chapel to receive his blow as agreed upon or be disgraced, and rides out of the hall, holding his head aloft.

After a perilous journey, Gawain happens upon a beautiful castle the following Christmas Eve and is hospitably received by the lord and his lovely lady. On successive days, the host goes hunting, leaving Gawain alone with the lady, who tries to seduce him. Resisting her charms, Gawain does accept from her a girdle, or belt, supposedly having the power to protect the wearer from harm. Later at the Green Chapel, it is revealed that the host is the Green Knight, who at the behest of the enchantress Morgan le Faye had sought to test the pride of Camelot. Gawain is disgraced for having kept the girdle in defiance of a vow to exchange with the host what each would receive on the days of the hunts. His life spared, Gawain keeps the girdle as a reminder of his weakness. Finally, back at Camelot, Gawain publicly confesses his shame, and the members of the Round Table resolve to wear a green belt in honor of their worthy comrade.

Sir Gawain and the Green Knight has been frequently translated into modern English and is readily available in literary anthologies.

SISTER CARRIE
Theodore Dreiser
1900
Novel
Coming of Age

One of the pioneer works in the naturalistic movement in modern literature, this vivid novel tells the tragic story of a naïve young country girl who finds hard work, poverty, and unhappiness in the American big city of the 1890's.

Carrie Meeber, a poor and inexperienced young woman, leaves her hometown in Wisconsin to live with her sister and find work in Chicago. Life soon becomes a grind of never-ending labor for mere survival. Falling ill and losing her poor-paying job, she accepts money from Charles Drouet, a man whom she met on the train when she traveled to the city. Eventually, she becomes his mistress.

Drouet's friend, G. W. Hurstwood, is fascinated by Carrie's charm and beauty. Carrie and Hurstwood fall in love and begin an affair. Mrs. Hurstwood threatens that unless he leaves Carrie, she will sue him for divorce. Faced with social and financial ruin, Hurstwood steals several thousand dollars from his employer and takes Carrie to Montreal. Given the opportunity to return the money, he does give back most of it, but his life is changed forever.

Hurstwood and Carrie marry under the name of Wheeler. She does not realize that the ceremony is not legal. They move to New York, but he cannot find work and they continually flee creditors. Carrie finds work as a chorus girl and eventually becomes well-known as an actress. She leaves Hurstwood and succeeds on her own, becoming rich and famous. As his fortunes decline, hers rise.

During the famous streetcar strike of the time, Hurstwood works as a scab, but soon he degenerates into a bum. He visits Carrie and gets some money from her, but he never goes back to her again and finally dies. Carrie, invited to perform in Europe, sails without knowing that Hurstwood is dead. Although she is now materially successful, her soul has been damaged and she is alone and unable to find happiness.

The book is a startlingly real picture of the social history of the time, a stark indictment of the ruthless nature of capitalism. Dreiser believed that men are inevitably crushed under the wheels of the giant machinery that keeps society moving. People use one another, mercilessly, and have no regrets for those who fall by the wayside. The message is a grim one, but the impact of the novel renders it unforgettable.

SIX CHARACTERS IN SEARCH OF AN AUTHOR
Luigi Pirandello
1921
Drama
Comedy

This drama of ideas examines the creative process, the theater, art and life, and illusion and reality when six fictional characters invade a play rehearsal and attempt to perform their story.

Six fictional characters rejected by their author interrupt a rehearsal of Pirandello's *Mixing It Up* and, after much mix-up, persuade the theater company's manager to let them act their story instead. The prompter will record a script in shorthand, and the company's actors will also look on to learn their parts.

The confusion continues. The characters' sensational story comes out piecemeal and disjointed, mainly through narration—about a man who gives his wife to her lover, then years later is tragically reunited with her and her children. Only two scenes are acted: the man's tryst with a prostitute who turns out to be his stepdaughter (possibly his daughter) and the deaths (by drowning and suicide) of two younger stepchildren.

The characters' play-within-a-play is cheap domestic tragedy, but their bustling interaction with the theater company results in brilliant intellectual farce. The unruly characters with their uneven story suggest the author's messy creative process, his unsuccessful attempt to mold his material. Another object of satire is the theatrical world—its tawdry tastes, its prudish censorship, the actors' hackneyed interpretations, the practical but insensitive manager's concern for staging, box office, and time.

The farcical action also raises philosophical questions about art and life, illusion and reality. The illusions of art (the characters) are truer than the reality of life because they are timeless and unchanging: whereas real people (the actors) change so much that they cannot even define their identity. Thus, Pirandello adapts the old metaphor of the world as a stage to the modern world of relativity, anticipating the methods and message of the Drama of the Absurd.

SLAUGHTERHOUSE-FIVE
Kurt Vonnegut
1969
Novel
Science Fiction, Tragicomedy

This radically unconventional and absurdly comic novel focuses on a poor innocent, Billy Pilgrim, as he wanders passively back and forth through the crucial moments of his life: his horrifying wartime experiences, his desperately empty upper-middle-class marriage and career, and his fantastic adventure on the planet Tralfamadore.

Like Vonnegut, who speaks in his own voice in several places to confirm that much of the novel is based on his wartime experiences, Billy Pilgrim lives through the firebombing of Dresden during World War II. From the beginning of the book, war is presented as both comically and horrifyingly absurd. Billy and his comrades, American and German, are ludicrously inept as soldiers. As the subtitle of the novel indicates, they are children on a gamelike crusade, manipulated by inscrutable forces.

Yet the game is deadly: The destruction of Dresden, a city of no strategic importance, populated only by Germans too old or weak to fight and prisoners of war such as Billy, is senseless but inevitable. Because of the shock of this event, Billy becomes a perpetual prisoner of war, returning again and again in his mind to this scene. Vonnegut's message is especially powerful as he reminds the reader that the destruction of Dresden is no isolated occurrence: *Slaughterhouse-Five* was written during the Vietnam War era and alludes frequently to a new generation of Billy Pilgrims and Children's Crusades.

More than simply a war novel—or, more precisely an antiwar novel—*Slaughterhouse-Five* is a captivating science fiction story. Scenes from World War II alternate with Billy's life on exhibition in a kind of zoo on the distant planet Tralfamadore. What little solace or pleasure Billy experiences comes at the hands of the Tralfamadorians, whose calmly fatalistic philosophy seems wise when compared to normal human stupidity and irrationality.

Vonnegut's style is disjointed and the novel is composed of short vignettes and fragments rather than a fully developed sequential narrative, but this style is purposely unsettling and helps Vonnegut accomplish several key objectives. Billy Pilgrim's time traveling, his habit of jumping quickly from present to past to future as if they were all simultaneously existing moments, makes him seem odd, even crazy, at first glance. But as the novel progresses, the reader acknowledges more and more that this is the natural way the human mind works. Everyone daydreams, remembers, and fantasizes, and these activities become especially important when a person lives in a world that is highly in need of such imaginative remaking.

SOMETIMES A GREAT NOTION
Ken Kesey
1964
Novel
Historical, Western

Ken Kesey's second novel offers a Faulknerian panorama of the Northwest that portrays the inner conflict, betrayals, and rivalries of a patriarchal family.

Written primarily from first-person perspectives, this cubist-like novel, set in Oregon during the early 1960s, dramatizes the foibles of the Stamper family who exhibit rugged, resourceful independence. Although the style of the novel remains realism peppered with lively dialogue, an embedded perspective permits the reader to understand the interior life of each character. The novel's title comes from a line in Huddie Ledbetter's hit song "Goodnight, Irene." The subsequent line in the song is: "To jump into the river…an' drown." A fickle river, with its unpredictable rages, functions as a major character in the novel as felled trees float downriver to the mill. The fictional Wakonda Auga River becomes more than a symbol as it approaches deistic personification.

Despite a loggers' union strike for higher pay, the Stamper family is defiant, supplying the local mill with timber. The patriarch of the clan, Henry Stamper, behaves like an obdurate rock. His motto is "Never give an inch" as the river threatens even his house, which becomes a peninsula in the river.

Henry's son, Hank, is also strong-willed, though he lacks his father's monumental self-confidence. After the death of his first wife, Henry marries young Myrna. Later, her son, Leland, witnesses his mother, Myrna, having intercourse with his older half-brother, sixteen-year-old Hank.

After high-school, Leland departs for Yale University, yet this educated man returns home seeking revenge against his father, Henry and half-brother, Hank. Hank's wife, Viv, gradually grows disenchanted, with the Stamper family on the brink of self-destruction. The character Indian Jenny addresses the plight of Native Americans in their stolen land.

In this novel of Oedipal and sibling rivalry, the dominating will of Henry becomes somewhat tempered as the epic concludes with a looming showdown between Hank and Leland, thus implying that male sibling rivalry remains an eternal human predicament.

THE SONG OF HIAWATHA
Henry Wadsworth Longfellow
1855
Poetry
Epic, Western

Through his portrayal of the adventures of Hiawatha, Longfellow presents numerous Indian legends and captures the Indian way of life that was already vanishing in 1855.

The poem opens with a great Indian parley held on the shore of Lake Superior. Gitche Manito, the Indian divinity, has summoned the tribes to unite under a prophet whom he promises to send.

That prophet is Hiawatha, son of the West-Wind and Wenonah. Hiawatha brings corn to the Indians, destroys Pearl-Feather (who brought disease), and teaches the Indians how to keep pictographic records and cure illnesses.

He cannot, however, save his wife, Minnehaha, from death in a famine, nor can he prevent the coming of the white man, who will soon scatter the Indian tribes. Realizing that his world is ending, Hiawatha sails westward after making a vague promise to return someday, like King Arthur, to lead his people once again.

Although Longfellow wrote the poem in approximately a year, it is the product of at least two decades of interest in the legends of the Indians. Recognizing that these stories were in danger of disappearing, Longfellow sought to preserve them within the framework of an epic poem.

The Indians are American, but the poem reflects the European legend of the noble savage and the classical conventions of the heroic poem. Longfellow's Indians are fierce, even savage, but they are also brave, stoic, loving, and patriotic. Indeed, they bear a strong resemblance to the Greeks of Homer and the Trojans of Virgil.

In celebrating the Indian, Longfellow also extols the American West, which he regards as his inspiration and which he describes in some of the loveliest passages in the work. Thus, even though he borrows epic conventions from the classics and takes his rhythm from the Finnish *Kalevala* ("Land of Heroes"), he has created a truly American epic that is both a tribute to and an elegy for the Indian way of life.

SONGS OF INNOCENCE AND OF EXPERIENCE
William Blake
1789
Poetry
Romantic, Lyric

The fifty-four poems that make up this volume of poetry were the result of merging Songs of Innocence *(1789) with a later group of poems,* Songs of Experience *(1794), which together envision what Blake called the "two contrary states of the human soul."*

These naive and childlike poems belie their complex form and content. *Songs of Innocence and Experience* is one of the most remarkable books ever issued. Blake employed here for the first time his unique method for publishing poetry; he wrote the text, drew the designs to illustrate it, engraved the plates, and handpainted the printed volumes with water colors.

Underlying theme in *Songs of Innocence* is the all-pervading presence of divine love and sympathy. Such lyrics as "The Lamb" show the confidence that a child has in the goodness of God and the creation. In "The Little Black Boy" the child's innocent acceptance of racial differences is celebrated. In poems such as "Holy Thursday," which describes a procession of charity children into St. Paul's church, Blake employs irony, implying that the children are too innocent to recognize that they are repressed. Likewise, in "The Chimney Sweeper" the urchin's dream of release from his life of dirt, danger, and drudgery provides a satiric comment on child labor customs.

Songs of Experience, the complementary work to *Songs of Innocence*, there is a growing sense of gloom, mystery, and evil. Blake depicts the actual world of human suffering in lyrics such as "London," where the economic, social, and political doctrines of the 18th century are indicted. In the cryptic poem "The Tyger," the speaker asks the same questions about the creator as in "The Lamb," but here there is no reassuring answer; rather, it is suggested that the creator is savage and malefic.

Many of the poems in these two collections present parallel situations from opposite sides of the coin. The shift from innocence to experience can be seen in change from lamb to tiger, childhood to adulthood, rural to urban scenes, and generous love to selfish sexuality. These are the dominant symbolic patterns that Blake uses to show the differences between the contrary states of the human soul.

SONNETS OF SHAKESPEARE
William Shakespeare
1609
Poetry
Sonnet, Collection

In a sequence of 154 sonnets addressed to an aristocratic young man and an erotic but somewhat common "dark lady," Shakespeare describes his undying love for both.

Shakespeare was the most unconventional of the Elizabethan sonneteers. The typical lovesick sonneteer, imitating the Italian Petrarch, idealized his fair lady in highly wrought, artificial language featuring metaphor and oxymoron. Shakespeare not only poked fun at this conventional language (see Sonnet 130) but also declared his love for a younger man and a rather sluttish "dark lady." He also used a simplified sonnet form, three quatrains and a rhyming couplet.

Sonnets 1-126 address the young man, whom Shakespeare idealizes but also advises and corrects. The first seventeen urge the young man to marry and procreate, but the main group develops Shakespeare's own emotional relationship with the young man, who also becomes involved with Shakespeare's mistress and a rival poet. Sonnets 127-154 treat Shakespeare's relationship with his unfaithful mistress, the dark lady.

Can the speaker of these poems be identified in every particular with William Shakespeare, the man? Critics continue to disagree about this question. The publication of the sonnets in Shakespeare's time caused no scandal, and no one has definitely identified either the young man or the dark lady.

All such questions aside, Shakespeare's sonnets deserve their fame for their unsurpassed expression of life's transience, moral ambiguities, and entanglements.

SONNETS FROM THE PORTUGUESE
Elizabeth Barrett Browning
1850
Poetry
Sonnet, Collection

This book recounts the love story of Elizabeth and Robert Browning in a sequence of forty-four sonnets, the forty-third of which ("How do I love thee? Let me count the ways") is one of the most widely known love poems ever written.

Despite its title, this sequence of love poems is not a translation, but a very personal telling of the love story of Elizabeth Barrett and the poet Robert Browning. Elizabeth, who had been living in virtual seclusion with only her spaniel, Flush, as a companion in a home dominated by an iron-willed, classically Victorian father, received a fan letter from Browning which led to their meeting, to their falling in love, and ultimately to their elopement and marriage. The poems, which she wrote privately for her lover's eyes alone, were published after their marriage at his urging. To maintain some privacy, she wanted to call them Sonnets from the Bosnian, but Robert suggested that she substitute Portuguese as the appropriate language of their imaginary origin.

The poems were very popular during the poet's lifetime, and they remain so today.

They are in many ways typically Victorian with their tone of gloom and sorrow, their almost morbid sensitivity to illness and death, their great outpouring of feeling as love develops, and the force and intensity of their passion. Elizabeth had been in frail health since childhood, and she fully expected to live alone until an early death. The lover in the poems, as Robert did in her life, brings about her resurrection from a living death, giving her faith in herself and the courage to live fully in the wide world beyond her father's house.

The poems, because of the universality of the feelings they express and their complex patterns of religious symbolism, carry meaning far beyond the personal story and its Victorian identity. They are deservedly still admired and still read.

SONNETS TO ORPHEUS
Rainer Maria Rilke
1923
Poetry
Lyric, Mythology

Addressed to the mythical poet who charmed trees, rocks, and beasts, this cycle of fifty-five sonnets celebrates the oneness of life and death.

Rilke, the preeminent German poet of the early 20th century, invokes the name of Orpheus as a means of renewing the myth of the singer who experiences death of a love one yet is able to transform loss and sorrow into song of transcending power. Memory of the divine singer lightens the modern poet's lamentation over our ephemeral existence and enables the poet to praise the frail beauty of art and the natural world.

Yet modern technology and urban societies threaten to destroy nature and obliterate the past. Only a quiet and humble reconnection to venerable traditions and the divine sources of our being can counteract the youthful arrogance of scientific knowledge and the noise and senseless speed of the industrial age. By invoking Orpheus and his healing song, the poet appeals to the deeper, enduring levels of wholeness and creativity in human experience.

Rilke thus turns to images of natural objects, innocent individuals, and ancient monuments to express his vision of a restored intimacy with the external world. The extolling of such typically Rilkean figures as the rose, ripe fruit, the dancer, his beloved cousin Egon von Rilke, the tapestry of the virgin and the unicorn, a Russian stallion, Egyptian temples, and Roman fountains and tombs is an attempt to transform transitory phenomena into a language of pure subjectivity.

The thematic difficulty of the sonnets is in part offset by their poetic musicality. Striking sound patterns combine with variable rhythmic configurations to break open the formal restraints of the traditional sonnet. Despite the challenges they may pose for the contemporary reader, the sonnets are a major monument in the history of the form.

SONS AND LOVERS
D. H. Lawrence
1913
Novel
Coming of Age

This novel about the maturing of Paul Morel, an English coalminer's son living in the industrial Midlands during the early 20th century, portrays his ardent desire to escape from his unhappy family life and from his mother's possessive dominance.

The protagonist in Lawrence's autobiographical novel is Paul Morel, a talented young artist who is caught in the bitter domestic battles between his uncouth coalminer father and his refined, neurotic mother, who has married beneath her class. Unhappy with her marriage, Mrs. Morel lavishes her affection on her sons, first William and then Paul. She wants a better life for her sons and encourages Paul to develop his artistic gifts, turning him against his father. These domestic struggles dramatize the intense class consciousness that Lawrence himself felt.

Paul's life is dominated first by his overly protective mother and then by two unhappy love affairs, first with the repressed and passive Miriam Leivers, a farmer's daughter, and later with Clara Dawes, an older woman married to a blacksmith. Neither relationship satisfies Paul, and he feels guilt over his mother's disapproval. Paul nurses her as she is dying of cancer and gives her an overdose of morphine to end her misery. After her death, Paul makes his peace with his father and reconciles Clara Dawes with her husband before setting out to find his own life.

Lawrence's novel dramatizes his fears of maternal domination and his determination as an artist to find a new basis for relations between men and women, free from sexual guilt and repression, life-affirming, and unbound by class snobbery. A sickly youth, Paul is further "crippled" by his unhealthy Oedipal attraction to his mother. He lacks the paternal balance of respect and esteem for his father, and he cannot become fully son or lover until he has escaped from his mother's possessive influence. By the end of the novel, Paul learns to value his father's frank heartiness and to free himself from his neurotic ties to his mother and to Miriam. At first, Paul feels helpless without his mother's emotional support, but he gradually realizes that he must find the strength to continue within himself.

SOPHIE'S CHOICE
William Styron
1979
Novel
Historical, Holocaust

Although the central story is fictional, this work, which is set within the tragic climate of what has come to be known as the Holocaust, is based on Styron's extensive research and travel, on his own experience as a writer, and on his continuing effort to take the largest subjects of historical significance as the novelist's province.

Stingo, the narrator and one of the principal characters, comes from the South to live in a Brooklyn rooming house where he hopes he can learn how to become a writer. He soon becomes passionately involved in the lives of his neighbors—Sophie, a Polish Catholic and concentration camp victim, and Nathan, her manic-depressive and paranoid Jewish lover.

The novel is as much about Stingo's education as it is about Sophie's tragic European life and Nathan's ambivalent reactions to it. She is a victim, but she has also collaborated in various ways with the enemy. Her own father had been a party to the anti-Semitism sweeping Europe, and Nathan alternately absolves and accuses her and Stingo of infidelity and deceit that arises out of his acute sense of how dreadfully human beings have betrayed one another in the Holocaust.

Stingo has to learn how to read both of these complex characters and to sense how their lies about themselves are also expressions of deeper truths about the human personality. He falls in love with Sophie, but her loyalty is to Nathan—not only because he has saved her once after a complete physical collapse but because his erratic behavior somehow sums up the ordeal of history which she has experienced.

Occasionally, in passages which read like essays, Styron seems to lean too much on his historical research, but the way he is able through his characters to call every human motivation to account is an impressive achievement. He does not simply dwell on the tragic human waste of the Holocaust; rather, he explores the human responsibility for it.

THE SORROWS OF YOUNG WERTHER
Johann Wolfgang von Goethe
1774
Novel
Epistolary, Psychological

A young man writes letters to a friend chronicling his own love for an unattainable woman. Though the effusiveness of these confessions occasionally strains modern sensibilities, the dramatic vitality of the portrayed emotions can still arouse interest in most readers.

Werther, a man of some means, flees the complexities of life by taking refuge in the countryside. There he indulges his exuberant imagination by immersing himself in the idyllic delights of his natural surroundings. His happiness reaches new heights when he meets Lotte, a charming young girl who is, however, engaged to a likable but unimaginative local official. Werther's ecstatic love soon tortures both himself and Lotte as it begins to conflict with the norms of polite society.

When his overwrought sentiments make his stay more and more untenable, Werther accepts a position at the court of one of Germany's small principalities. Yet bureaucratic narrow-mindedness and social snobbery soon drive him back to Lotte. Unable to compromise his desperate emotions in any way, Werther prepares himself for the unavoidable catastrophe, which is reported by the fictional editor of Werther's letters at the end of the novel.

For decades, this comparatively short book, the first psychological novel in German literature and its first international best-seller, mesmerized young people all over Europe. It succeeded in articulating the social predicament of a whole generation that found itself cut off by an antiquated political system from channeling its high sentiments into the arena of social responsibility. As Werther's fate exemplifies, unbridled emotions divorced from any impact on reality have to become self-destructive.

What gives this novel its continuing appeal, in contrast to so many similar books of that period, is that Goethe allows readers to view his hero from the perspective of a sympathetic but not uncritical detachment. The sufferings of young Werther are not idealized as a desirable way of life; they are displayed both as a warning to the young and a protest against their elders.

THE SOT-WEED FACTOR
John Barth
1960
Novel
Picaresque, Parody

This parody of the 18th century picaresque novel features an intricate plot, bawdy humor, and iconoclastic treatment of America's national beginnings.

Barth examines ideas about innocence and experience in this novel. Its protagonist, Ebenezer Cooke, travels from London to the Edenic new world, where he enacts an Adamic lapse, loses his patrimony, and then must go through numerous painful trials to regain it. Also drawn to the new world is Henry Burlingame, Eben's friend and tutor. Burlingame, a foundling, engages in a search for his father, who turns out to be the half-breed son of one of Captain John Smith's companions.

Henry and Eben represent contrasting attitudes to experience. Eben, the archetypal innocent, prides himself on his double calling as poet and virgin. The more admirable Henry, on the other hand, embraces every kind of experience, especially the sexual experience that Eben foolishly avoids. In traditional terms, Burlingame is the foul tempter, but in Barth's revision of the familiar myths of innocence and experience, this "serpent" is a Blakean incarnation of redemptive sexual energy.

He is also, without overt anachronism, an embodiment of 20th century thinking. He describes the world and humanity's place in it in modern, existential terms. He is continually engaged in creating and modifying his own identity.

In *The Sot-Weed Factor*, then, Barth brilliantly attacks the traditional valuation of innocence as a Christlike virtue. Eben's pretensions to virginal purity cause suffering for himself and others, and thus his understanding comes when he reproaches himself for "the crime of innocence, whereof the Knowledged must bear the burthen. There's the true Original Sin our souls are born in: not that Adam learned, but that he had to learn—in short, that he was innocent."

THE SOUND AND THE FURY
William Faulkner
1929
Novel
Stream of Consciousness, Gothic

The main events in the decline of a Mississippi family are told from four points of view. Most critics agree that this difficult novel requires multiple readings to be understood.

The Compson family consists of Jason III and Caroline; their children, Quentin, Caddy, Jason IV, and Benjy; the black servants, Dilsey and her relatives; and eventually Caddy's illegitimate daughter, Quentin. By 1928, when most of the novel takes place, Jason III has drunk himself to death; his son Quentin has drowned himself; Caddy has married, divorced, and left her child with the family; and Jason IV rules the family.

Between the children's earliest remembrance and 1928, the family has gone from domination by Caddy's special gift for loving to domination by Jason IV. Jason IV, who believes that Caddy's failed marriage to a banker has deprived him of success, revenges himself on her through her daughter.

The novel has four sections and an appendix which tells what happened to Caddy after 1928. The first three sections are internal speeches by Benjy, Quentin (male), and Jason IV. The retarded Benjy, in his inarticulate but moving way, feels the loss of the only person who ever loved him, Caddy. On the day he commits suicide, Quentin shows that he is unable to accept Caddy's growing up. Jason reveals his petty paranoia on the day he finally drives Caddy's daughter away. With her departure, he loses further opportunity for vengeance and also loses his ill-gotten savings, which she has taken with her.

In section four Dilsey and Benjy attend an Easter Service. There Dilsey experiences the communion in love which the Compson family has lost. Because of this experience, she can continue loving this family despite its lovelessness.

THE SPANISH TRAGEDY
Thomas Kyd
1586
Drama
Tragedy

A Spanish nobleman, Hieronymo, seeks revenge for the murder of his only son; thwarted by the ruthlesness and courtly power of his adversaries, he feigns madness and successfully plots their deaths.

Bel-Imperia, niece of Spain's king, is loved both by Horatio, a war hero, and by the captured Portuguese prince, Balthazar. Her brother Lorenzo aids Balthazar and together they murder Horatio. The murdered man's father Hieronymo seeks revenge; he must first identify the murderers, then use guile to trap them. Distracted by grief, Hieronymo pretends madness to hide his bloody intent.

Finally Hieronymo arranges a play to entertain the visiting Portuguese king; it is a short tragedy in which the actors are his enemies and the murders are not pretended but are real. As their fathers watch and applaud, Lorenzo and Balthazar are killed and Bel-Imperia kills herself; Hieronymo then gloats over his revenge before biting out his tongue and stabbing himself.

Kyd's highly popular play established on the Elizabethan stage the revenge tragedy, a genre which included William Shakespeare's *Hamlet*. Kyd introduced many of the stock features of the type: classical quotations and allusions, allegorical characters and ghosts, rhetorical verse style, play-within-the-play, dumb show, real and feigned madness, and a bloody ending.

SPRING SNOW
Yukio Mishima
1969
Novel
Historical

An eighteen-year-old school boy's obsessional love for a girl betrothed to the Imperial Prince puts both of them in conflict with family and society. A rich prose picture of the changing mores of 20th century Japan frames the tragic story of star-crossed lovers.

In 1912 Kiyoaki Matsugae, the handsome only son of an old and very wealthy samurai family, is one of the most privileged young men in Tokyo society. Sensitive and prone to melancholy, however, he feels alienated from his family, insecure, and unmotivated. Although powerfully drawn to Satoko, a twenty-year-old girl with whom he was reared, he is too fearful to declare his love.

Tradition demands that Satoko's family find her a husband. Because the love between her and Kiyoaki remains unacknowledged, she must commit herself to marriage to the Emperor's son. Kiyoaki, finding his courage or perhaps stimulated by the rivalry, confesses his desire, and he and Satoko become lovers. As the intricate political and social machinery of the betrothal proceeds inexorably, their secret affair intensifies. When Satoko becomes pregnant, the lovers find themselves in a trap from which they cannot escape. Both are doomed.

In their culture, their romance is at once social anathema and political treachery. The novel dramatizes the clash between private and public lives and the collision of past and present, as Japan emerges from its long isolation. On another level, we see that the individual is captive to his own emotions and imprisoned by the social structure in which he lives. The young lovers, in the spring of their lives and the bloom of their love, cannot escape the snow-cold reality of their world.

Mishima embodies this bleak, existential drama in a vibrant poetic style, lavish with word paintings of the workings of nature, body, and mind. An entire panorama of personalities and social classes serves as backdrop to the love story and offers us a fascinating glimpse of another time, another culture.

STEPPENWOLF
Hermann Hesse
1927
Novel
Psychological

A middle-aged intellectual undergoes a painful self-analysis. This compellingly written account of a personal and cultural crisis in the Germany of the 1920's should appeal to a wide range of readers.

The novel opens with Harry Haller, a man in his late forties, who rents a room in a respectable neighborhood. Barely a year later, this polite but remote and eccentric tenant mysteriously disappears, leaving behind a manuscript detailing his personal travails.

Haller has been trying to escape from the throes of a severe marital and professional crisis. He is appalled by the disintegration of traditional values around him. His solitary existence, at the same time, makes Haller aware of his own divided personality, in which a calm and rational exterior is constantly mocked by streaks of an irrational, wolfish aggressiveness. This seemingly hopeless duality drives him into bouts of depression, anger, and alcoholism.

On his way toward recovery, Haller begins to realize that he contains within him a much richer spectrum of possibilities and that he must allow all parts of his personality to express themselves. Most of all, he is asked to respect and come to terms with those aspects of his self which, up to now, he had simply lumped together as the wolfish side of his character. In the process, he is forced to forgo the deadly seriousness of his mental despair in favor of a more lighthearted tolerance of himself and others.

Hesse, who won the Nobel Prize for Literature in 1946, creates a most memorable vision of cultural pessimism, while still affirming the viability and continuity of the Western tradition. His style, in which a linear development of plot is counterbalanced by scenes of surrealism, allows the reader to view the events with an increasingly humorous detachment, a perspective which not only restates the novel's theme but also contributes to the continuing appeal of its wisdom.

THE STORY OF LUCY GAULT
William Trevor
2002
Novel
Historical, Gothic

When seven-year-old Lucy Gault is told she and her family will have to leave Lahardane, she is heartbroken, and decides to run away. The consequences of that decision change the course of her life, and the lives of everyone she touches.

In 1921, during the Irish struggle for independence, three Irish boys try to burn the Gault home to get the Gaults to leave. Heloise Gault is English. They are discovered and Everard Gault fires a warning shot, but accidently hits one of the boys. The Gaults decide their only choice is to leave, for safety's sake. Heartbroken, seven-year-old Lucy decides to run away. Deep in the woods, she breaks her ankle. However, her coat and shoes are discovered beside the sea—she had lost them weeks earlier—and everyone assumes the worst. In their grief, after weeks of mourning, Everard and Eloise decide to leave Ireland and their painful memories.

The household caretaker, Henry, discovers Lucy, nearly dead. He and his wife, Bridget, nurse her back to health. They and the Gault's solicitor, Aloysius Sullivan, do all they can to locate the grieving parents, but Heloise and Everard have taken special care to close the door on their past. Living off of cashed investments, with no connection to anyone, personally or through business, they remain exiled in their grief. Henry and Bridget raise Lucy, a solitary girl who isolates herself as punishment for creating so much pain. A young tutor, Ralph, accidently comes upon Lucy's home. The two fall in love, but Lucy refuses his proposals, feeling that she has no right to happiness, and that she only brings grief to those she loves.

Heloise dies from influenza and grief, never knowing that her daughter did not kill herself. Eventually, Everard returns to find Lucy alive.

In the meantime, the Irish boy—Holohan—who had been shot, cannot live with his guilt for destroying the Gault family. He tries to apologize, but eventually goes insane and lives in an asylum. Following Everard's death, Lucy begins visiting Holohan, but he doesn't know who she is. Lucy lives out the rest of her life alone.

This novel explores the caprice of fate, where small choices—a little girl's decision to run away, and a young boy's act of vandalism—can have consequences that last a lifetime. Another important theme is that of the futility of self-imposed exile. Heloise and Everard try to run from their grief, and Holohan runs from his guilt, only adding to their grief.

STRANGE INTERLUDE
Eugene O'Neill
1928
Drama
Psychological

Nina Leeds, thwarted by her father in her desire to marry Gordon Shaw, who is subsequently killed in the war, enters into a loveless marriage with Sam Evans after a fleeting period of promiscuity. She bears Edmund Darrell's child, who is reared as Sam Evans' son. When Sam dies, she is too old to marry any of her real loves.

This convoluted play brings stream-of-consciousness techniques to the modern stage, achieving this effect through asides and soliloquies, which fill to some extent the role of the chorus in Greek plays.

Nina Leeds wished to marry Gordon Shaw, but her possessive father prevented it. Gordon's death in the war leads to Nina's promiscuity with soldiers.

Her father's friend Charles Marsden, much her senior, wants to marry her, but his aged mother stands in the way. Dr. Edmund Darrell is attracted to Nina, but marrying such a neurotic woman would damage him professionally. When her father dies, Nina marries Sam Evans, scion of a well-to-do family, at the urging of Marsden and Darrell.

On becoming pregnant, Nina learns of insanity in Sam's family. She aborts the child. She then becomes pregnant by Darrell, bears his child, and passes it off as Sam's, naming it Gordon after her first love.

Fatherhood helps Sam's self-image, and he becomes immensely successful, as do his backers, Marsden and Darrell. When Sam dies, Nina cannot marry Darrell. She turns to the aging Marsden for companionship and with him replicates the father-daughter relationship she had rankled under with her own father.

O'Neill explores the questions of unfulfilled love and heredity in this play. He explores people's inability to control their destinies and hints at Nietzsche's theme of eternal recurrence that concerned him earlier in *Anna Christie*.

THE STRANGER
Albert Camus
1942
Novella
Psychological

Set in his native Algeria, Camus' first published novel is a case study in radical anomie.

Narrator Meursault begins with one of the most famous opening statements in modern literature: "Mother died today. Or, maybe, yesterday; I can't be sure." Meursault is not so much callous as affectless, utterly disconnected from social conventions. He attends his mother's funeral but fails to conform to the rituals expected on such an occasion.

The next day, he goes to the beach and picks up a woman named Marie. The two become lovers, but Meursault is unable to make any long-term commitments. He is also befriended by a petty hoodlum named Raymond.

The following week, Raymond invites Meursault and Marie to join him at the beach. While walking alone along the shore, Meursault confronts a hostile Arab. The sun flashes in Meursault's eye while he finds himself with Raymond's revolver in his hand. Before he is aware of anything, he has fired five shots into the Arab's body.

The novel is divided into two almost equal parts; the second focuses on Meursault's trial for murder. The prosecutor builds his case upon what he argues is a pattern of consistently selfish, cynical behavior. The defense attorney uses the same circumstantial evidence to attempt to depict Meursault as fundamentally sympathetic.

Meursault rejects the specious games of both and the premise that there is a meaningful pattern to any individual's existence. Uncomfortable with the facile abstractions that distort the gratuitousness of actions, he offers himself as a martyr to the truth.

Written in a severe, understated style, the novel mocks grandiose claims for coherence among discrete, immediate events. It questions traditional assumptions about moral responsibility and about the individual's role in society.

STRANGER IN A STRANGE LAND
Robert A. Heinlein
1961
Novel
Science Fiction

What would a hypothetical "Man from Mars" think about humanity's rarely questioned customs, moralities, even religions? In a novel that ushered in the 1960s, Heinlein employs the trope literally, enabling him to question everything from God to monogamy.

"Once upon a time," begins *Stranger in a Stranger Land*, "there was a Martian named Valentine Michael Smith." An orphan of the lost first Terran expedition to Mars, Smith was reared by Martians until brought to Earth twenty-five years later by the crew of the next Mars mission. After nurse Gillian Boardman, girlfriend of crusading journalist Ben Caxton, unthinkingly offers Smith a glass of water—a solemn and binding ceremony on arid Mars—she ends up helping the imprisoned Smith escape from his guarded hospital suite.

Smith may be childlike in his reaction to unfamiliar situations and idioms, but he has been schooled by the long-dead but still-present "Old Ones" of Mars, and possesses telekinetic powers, including the ability to make disappear any object or person he groks, or understands, as wrong. After hiding out from the corrupt world government at the estate of writer Jubal Harshaw, and learning what he can from his crusty, iconoclastic old host, Smith finally journeys out to experience the totality of human life firsthand.

Ultimately, Smith founds the Church of All Words, a commune-like organization espousing brotherhood, free love, and the notion "Thou art God." At the novel's shocking conclusion, an outraged mob kills the Christ-like figure as he calmly preaches, after which his disciples, understanding that mere "discorporation" is not the end, prepare a ritual meal of his flesh—a sacred Martian ritual. Smith, now termed the Archangel Michael, then turns up in an ironic sort of Heaven alongside his former religious adversaries.

Heinlein's most famous novel, more about questioning than providing answers, remains as stimulating as it was at the beginning of the 1960s counterculture movement. The United States Library of Congress included *Stranger in a Strange Land* on its list of "Books that Shaped America."

A STREETCAR NAMED DESIRE
Tennessee Williams
1947
Drama
Southern Gothic

The clash of appearances with reality and of antebellum manners with blue-collar crudity leads to violence and insanity in this Pulitzer Prize-winning play.

The play begins with Blanche DuBois visiting her sister Stella and her brother-in-law Stanley Kowalski at their home in the French Quarter of New Orleans. Blanche says that she is there on vacation, but in fact she has lost the family mansion, Belle Reve, and her teaching position because of her sexual indiscretions, the last one with a 17-year-old boy.

Blanche is clearly an emotionally disturbed individual. When she was very young, she married a homosexual. When she found out, she accused him, and he shot himself. Afterwards she earned a reputation for sleeping with men indiscriminately, all the while pretending to be a Southern belle.

From the moment Blanche arrives, Stanley suspects that Blanche's manners are a facade and is angered by Blanche's constant insults of his vulgar ways. Stella, however, tries to satisfy both her sister's and Stanley's desires.

The climax comes when Stella goes to the hospital in labor. Stanley confronts Blanche with her concealed past, and Blanche replies, "I don't tell truth, I tell what ought to be truth." Stanley then puts on the pajamas he wore on his wedding night and rapes Blanche.

In the final scene, Blanche is clearly insane; a psychiatrist and a nurse are on their way to take her to an asylum. Blanche told Stella about the rape, but Stella refused to believe her. "I couldn't believe her story and go on living with Stanley," Stella says. Clearly she chose to believe a lie in order to stay happy—the same choice that her sister had made.

SUMMA THEOLOGICA
Thomas Aquinas
c. 1265-1273
Nonfiction
Epistemology

In keeping with the revival of Aristotle in the 13th century, Aquinas wrote the first formal system of theology. In so doing, he placed theology among the human sciences.

Human areason, according to Aquinas, is capable of proving or clarifying a number of Christian beliefs which are based on faith. Reason can prove that God exists, for instance, as well as discern certain of God's characteristics. Reason can do this without the help of faith.

Reason is limited, however, because it must rely upon knowledge gained through the senses. By making inferences from the material world, reason can discover that God is the basis of all reality, that God is the source of all truth, and that God is the cause of everything good. Revelation provides knowledge of things that cannot be derived from the senses. It is through revelation that human beings learn of the Trinity, the Incarnation, and the Resurrection.

In *Summa Theologica*, Aquinas applied this understanding of reason and revelation to the Christian faith. He wrote the *Summa* in three parts. The first explains divinity: the nature of God, the Trinity, creation, and providence. The second explains ethics: theological virtues from Paul (faith, hope, and love) and cardinal virtues from Aristotle (prudence, justice, courage, and temperance). The third explains Christology: Christ, the sacraments, and eternal life.

Aquinas made his place in history by synthesizing Christian theology and non-Christian philosophy. For Aquinas, Christianity is not the antidote to civilization as it was to New Testament writers. Rather, Christianity is the complement of civilization. The good of the world is the result of human reason; the best of the world will be the result of reason cooperating with faith.

THE SUN ALSO RISES
Ernest Hemingway
1926
Novel
Historical

American and British expatriates live lives of quiet—and sometimes noisy—desperation in France and Spain during the 1920's. Lean prose and understated feeling distinguish this unsparing portrait of modern alienation.

Jake Barnes, like nearly every other Hemingway hero, suffers from a terrible wound. His wound—he has suffered emasculation as a combatant in World War I—is emblematic of the sterility and impotence of modern man. Modern woman fares little better, as Hemingway shows in Brett Ashley, whose sexual excess is merely another form of sterility. These characters and their joyless friends live in a moral and cultural Waste Land, and indeed critics have discovered in this novel a prose analogue to T.S. Eliot's poem of that title.

Hemingway is particularly harsh in his indictment of those who pretend that the old truths remain operative. Hence the stupidly romantic Robert Cohn, who makes trouble for himself and others by embracing an obsolete ethic of chivalry, becomes the book's least attractive character.

Barnes salvages some dignity by his stoicism, but the only character who seems wholly admirable is the bullfighter, Pedro Romero, who has ordered his life by mastering a sport that ritualizes and thereby orders the world's violence. As Barnes remarks, "Nobody ever lives their life all the way up except bullfighters."

Hemingway celebrates sports, especially blood sports, because they provide a welcome fiction of order. They also teach the adept to function with "grace under pressure"—as existential humanity must function if it is to survive.

When Romero has an affair with Brett Ashley, he jeopardizes his simple integrity. In an unselfish gesture, Brett breaks off with him, hoping she has not done too much damage. She cannot, however, save herself. The novel ends where it began, the expatriates locked into their meaningless round of dipsomania, erotic frustration, and creeping anomie.

THE SWIMMER
John Cheever
1964
Short Story

Cheever's story concerns that desperate search for meaning and importance that underlies all human life, especially in the modern age, when man's acts may at first glance appear either comic or absurd.

"The Swimmer" begins as a comic fiction written in the realist mode. As Cheever's well-to-do suburbanites sit around the Westerhazy's pool, complaining that they drank too much the night before, one of their number, Neddy Merrill, decides to swim to his home, eight miles away across affluent Westchester County, New York, via his neighbors' pools. As Neddy begins his odyssey along what he calls the Lucinda River (named for his wife), the reader is struck by Neddy's strength, determination, and youthful exuberance. No longer one of the story's comically hungover, exurbanites, he becomes an explorer and mythic hero.

In the first few pages of Cheever's story, Neddy covers four miles in one hour swimming in eight of the fifteen pools. Gradually, however, the pace of the story and of the swim slows, and the pools grow farther apart as Neddy's energy and optimism drain away. Motion turns into contemplation, joyous adventure into painful ordeal. Appropriately, the light comedy gives way to a darker, more somber mood as the realism turns imperceptibly into mythic nightmare. The brightness and freedom of the first pages turns into the darkness and confinement of the last.

At the journey's and the story's end, Neddy finally and wearily arrives at his house, only to find it empty and boarded up. His mythic swim across the county and ahead in time has actually been a journey back into Neddy's past and down through his unconscious mind. His attempt to regain all he has lost—his youth, money, wife, and family—ends in failure, leaving the reader to ponder whether the attempt has been mythically noble or childishly ridiculous.

Neddy is clearly a latter-day Rip Van Winkle, one who longs to escape from the painful facts of his actual existence and to return to an earlier, more hopeful, more innocent period. Having lost his world, Neddy, however, gains a certain measure of tragic dignity, standing as naked and dispossessed in Westchester as Shakespeare's Lear howling on the storm-ravaged heath.

T

A TALE OF TWO CITIES
Charles Dickens
1859
Novel
Historical
This complexly plotted, action-filled novel, set against the passion and turmoil of the French Revolution, is crowded with some of the most fascinating and memorable characters in English literature.

Mr. Jarvis Lorry, an agent for the Franco-British banking house of Tellson & Co., brings young Lucie Manette from London to Paris to find her father. He was imprisoned in the Bastille for 18 years, but is now being kept above the wine shop of Mme. and M. Defarge until he can be taken safely back to England.

Back in England, Lucie becomes engaged to Charles Darnay, the nephew of a murdered French aristocrat much hated by the revolutionaries in France. Lucie and Charles are married and have a child. During the revolution, Charles returns to Paris to save an old family servant imprisoned by the revolutionaries. Charles, however, is seized and brought to trial. Denounced by Defarge, he is condemned for the crimes of his family against the people.

A close friend of the family, Sydney Carton, who strongly resembles Charles and secretly loves Lucie, now acts to save Charles. Through deceit, he gains entrance to the prison and has Charles carried away, while he remains behind, in his place. The Defarges also try to denounce Lucie and Dr. Manette, but they manage to escape. Lucie and Charles return to England, but Sydney Carton dies at the guillotine, choosing to sacrifice his life to secure the safety of his friends.

Although well researched, this book—Dickens' only historical novel—is popular chiefly because of the momentum of its ingenious plot. Seldom in literature are so many interesting characters swept along at such a pace.

THE TALENTED MR. RIPLEY
Patricia Highsmith
1955
Novel
Thriller, Detective
At the request of Herbert Greenleaf, Tom Ripley travels to Italy to visit "Dickie" Greenleaf, Herbert's son, to convince him to return to the U.S. to be with his ailing mother. Tom does more than relay the father's request; in a spontaneous act of brutality, Tom murders Dickie, and assumes the man's identity. The story follows Tom's cat and mouse game to live Dickie Greenleaf's life.

Though Tom admits to Herbert Greenleaf that he doesn't know Dickie, Herbert's son, well, Herbert insists that he try to convince the recalcitrant son to move back home. His mother is sick. Herbert finances the trip, providing Tom with a generous stipend. Upon meeting Dickie, Tom immediately envies his confidence, his easy-going social grace, wealth, and free lifestyle. But Tom is a narcissist whose sense of self is directed by what he perceives others think of him. He is careful to be all that he perceives Dickie might want from a friend. In the moments when Tom thinks he is failing, he hates this man whom he also envies. While the two are vacationing in San Remo, Tom murders Dickie, ties an anchor to his ankle, and drops him into the ocean. The move was as spontaneous as it was brutal. He tells Marge, the friend with whom Dickie has spent most of his time, that Dickie has decided to move to Rome, and not to contact him while he tries to figure out his life. (Marge has been in love with Dickie, though the feeling is not mutual. Marge assumes he is contemplating their relationship.)

Because of their physical resemblance, Tom uses Dickie's passport, and adopts his mannerisms, speech patterns, and handwriting. He forges Dickie's signature to collect checks from Dickie's trust account. Tom pulls it off with nary a hitch, until several worried friends arrive to see Dickie in person. Tom finds it necessary to murder one of them. The cat and mouse game intensifies.

Police begin to suspect that Tom Ripley has met with foul play after police find the bloodstained boat Tom scuttled after murdering Dickie. The police question "Dickie" (that is, Tom impersonating Dickie). Tom feels it's necessary to make an appearance as Tom so police will stop looking for him. Finally, the police are concerned because "Dickie" has vanished. Ultimately, Tom is able to convince everyone that Dickie committed suicide, leaving a will bequeathing all his worldly goods to Tom Ripley.

TAMBURLAINE THE GREAT
Christopher Marlowe
1587
Drama
Tragedy

Christopher Marlowe's first play, which tells the story of a Scythian bandit who has an insatiable thirst for power, began a fashion in poetic language that lasted through the English Renaissance and gave Shakespeare the blank verse form that he was later to perfect.

The story of the poor shepherd who becomes the conqueror of kings must have been attractive to Christopher Marlowe, son of a carpenter. In two parts, the plaly depicts Tamburlaine's rise from humble beginnings to his death, not in battle but from disease.

Marlowe's Tamburlaine yearns for conquest, not because he has any plan for progress or improvement but simply to glorify himself. That the 16th century could have seen such a man as heroic tells us much about that time. The play gave its audience a political model just as the first English empire was being formed.

Part of the play's appeal was the spectacle it presented: A famous scene brings Tamburlaine on stage in his chariot drawn by vanquished kings.

More important than the story, however, is the way that Marlowe tells it. This was the first English play to use blank verse, a ten-syllable line with the rhythmic alternation of weakly and strongly accented syllables. Some critics have called the language of the play bombastic, yet it created a sensation among playgoers and writers. Marlowe himself was to do better in later works, and the great dramatists who succeeded him found blank verse a suitable form for their histories and tragedies.

THE TAMING OF THE SHREW
William Shakespeare
c. 1593
Drama
Comedy

Shakespeare's robust comedy of courtship and marriage demonstrates one man's unorthodox technique of wooing and winning a headstrong woman.

Old Baptista of Padua has a problem. His much-courted, demure younger daughter Bianca is surrounded by suitors, but he has resolved not to give her in marriage until the elder, Katherina, the shrew of the play's title, is wed. Though Kate is well-dowried and fair, her temper is legend. Father, sister, and suitors writhe under the lash of her tongue.

Hortensio, enamoured of Bianca, explains his predicament to Petruchio, a witty and wise young man of Verona who has come to "wive it wealthily in Padua." The description of Kate fails to daunt him; he has the intelligence to perceive the woman as both puzzle and prize.

Though Hortensio's plan avails him naught—he loses Bianca to Lucentio disguised as a schoolmaster—he sets Petruchio in motion. In a scene perhaps better dramatized than read, the sparks fly as Petruchio ventures to woo Katherina. He pretends to have heard nothing but good of her. As she insults him, he compliments her courtesy. This is only a skirmish in the battle between the sexes; later, Petruchio comes late to the wedding, wears tattered clothes, and rides a pathetic excuse for a horse. He swears at the priest, smacks a loud kiss on the bride, and hurries her off without the comfort of a wedding feast.

Once Kate is installed in her new home, Petruchio's antics grow even madder. Nothing is good enough for his Kate, so the food is thrown out, the bed flung asunder, her new gown returned to the tailor. Exhausted, hungry, and wary of her husband's unpredictable temper, Kate finds that gentleness and agreeability, once foreign to her nature, transform Petruchio into a man fit to live with, which was his plan all along.

The comedy ends with a marriage feast for Bianca and Lucentio. A merry debate on marriage ends with the new husbands testing their brides for gentleness and obedience. The results puzzle the banqueters but not the reader of this tale of unfolding mutual respect and understanding.

TAO TE JING
Laozi
Fourth Century B.C.E.
Nonfiction
Sacred Text, Philosophical

The eighty-one sections of this evocative and practical classic (jing) of Chinese philosophy outline a way of living in harmony with the Tao, or natural order. The most widely translated work of Asian literature, this book is as stimulating, popular, and useful today as ever.

For Laozi, the legendary author of the enigmatic aphorisms in this brief work, the Tao is the name for ultimate reality, yet the eternal Tao defies all names and descriptions. Images can only suggest its vast and mysterious creative potential. It is like water, giving and sustaining life, always moving, yet never striving.

While the essence of the Tao remains elusive and beyond our comprehension, we may observe the Tao as it reveals itself in the natural development of things. By stripping away our selfish desires and fears and accepting the world as it is, we can imitate the Tao and discover in ourselves Te, or natural virtue and moral strength.

The person at one with the Tao gives unselfishly and effortlessly to others without trying to control their actions. Modest, yielding, tolerant, impartial, and patient, the sage lives a simple and tranquil life and realizes the principle of wu-wei, working without effort, accomplishing without concern for reward or results.

Written during the age of political anarchy and social decadence known as "The Period of Warring States" (5th-3rd centuries B.C.E.), the Tao Te Jing addresses problems of wise government as much as right personal conduct. Humility is the mark of a wise leader, who rules by virtuous example rather than by interference with other countries or in the lives of the people. With a minimum of laws and regulations and without fear of punishment and harsh taxes, people will order themselves according to their own nature and innate virtue. Ruled with a light hand, they will live long lives of few needs and in peace with their neighbors.

TARTUFFE
Molière
1669
Drama
Comedy

Among the most polished of Moliere's sophisticated comedies, this play is notable also for its serious overtones and for the skillful portrayal of the complex title character, whose name has become a synonym for hypocrisy.

Despite his central role, Tartuffe is not the play's principal character. That dubious distinction belongs to Orgon, the wealthy bourgeois who has befriended Tartuffe and is almost willingly gulled by the latter's machinations.

The character of Tartuffe himself does not appear onstage until the third of the play's five acts, by which time his entrance has been amply prepared by grumblings among the various members of Orgon's household. A most selfish and demanding houseguest, Tartuffe has turned the household upside down, disrupting any semblance of order and routine. Orgon, meanwhile, staunchly defends his guest as a man of rare piety and probity, a truly religious individual from whom the others could learn much if only they would follow his example.

Like Moliere's other comedies both high and low, this one builds upon a base of stock characters drawn from early Italian comedy. Here, as in his other high comedies, Moliere develops the featured characters (such as Orgon) well beyond stereotype, observing also the classic rules of construction and development established for French tragedy by Pierre Corneille. Tartuffe himself is a highly individualized and extremely complex character, not without some true sincerity even as he tries to relieve Orgon of both his money and his wife, Elmire. The play's ending, quite frankly artificial and contrived, functions at least in part as a parody of artificial endings on the stage, underscoring the play's self-conscious theatricality.

Orgon, onstage throughout the action, emerges from stereotype (the gullible bourgeois) as he grows and develops toward the end, truly learning and profiting from his mistakes. Tartuffe, in contrast, remains locked in character, however fascinating that character may be.

THE TELL-TALE HEART
Edgar Allan Poe
1843
Short Story
Gothic, Horror

A murderer buries his victim's body beneath the floor, and when the police come to investigate, the murderer thinks that he can hear the beating of the dead man's heart.

A nameless, first-person narrator tells, in initially cool but increasingly desperate tones, the story of his calculating murder of an old man for whose care he was responsible. His reason for telling the tale is to prove to the reader, whom he addresses directly, that he is not insane. In the telling, however, he demonstrates a perversity that not only reveals his mental imbalance, but also confronts the reader with the possibility of evil at the core of every human being.

"The Tell-Tale Heart" exemplifies perfectly Poe's notion of "unity of effect," the conviction that every line of a story should contribute to a single, unrelieved effect on the reader. This is illustrated, as Poe insisted it should be, in the very first line: "True!—nervous—very, very dreadfully nervous I had been and am; but why will you say that I am mad?"

Poe precedes Dostoevsky and modern writers in exploring motiveless evil. The narrator quickly informs us that he killed the old man for none of the usual reasons but only because he could not stand the look of the man's blinded eye.

Poe's primary interest, however, is not evil in the theological sense but as a species of psychological obsession. His fascination is with the working of the human mind, with the relation between hyperrationality and madness, and with a bent in human nature that all our reason cannot explain away. All of these are connected in the story with the incessant beating of the old man's heart that even death cannot still.

THE TEMPEST
William Shakespeare
1611
Drama
Romantic

An exiled duke employs magic to recover his domain. This eloquent, highly crafted play marked the culmination of Shakespeare's dramatic career.

At the center of the play's action, and controlling it from the island where he lives in exile, is the wise magician Prospero. He conjures a storm to shipwreck his brother Antonio, usurper of his ducal throne in Milan. Prospero engineers a marriage between his daughter and the son of an enemy, King Alonso of Naples, who accompanies Antonio. The marriage would end the feud and allow Prospero to regain his dukedom.

The portrayal of the villainous characters presents a contradiction between seeming and being. Reportedly they have victimized Prospero; yet on stage we see them as Prospero's victims. The shipwreck leaves them helpless, stranded, and separated; Alonso grieves when he thinks that his son has died in the storm.

Over all is Prospero—reportedly the victim—manipulating others' perceptions. In the end, he reveals Alonso's son as still living, secures the king's repentance for supporting Antonio the usurper, and regains his dukedom.

As Prospero manages the perceptions of other characters, Shakespeare manages those of the audience, often to its confusion. For example, though Prospero is supposed to be the stock figure of the benevolent magician, Shakespeare makes him address his daughter and servants with unneeded harshness that seems out of character. Again, the stock dramatic plot calls for wrongdoers to repent, yet two who planned Alonso's murder are pardoned without repenting. Even a Christian audience might have trouble forgiving their lack of remorse. Such conflict is a typical effect of watching Shakespearean drama.

Scholars see *The Tempest* as Shakespeare's farewell to the stage. Prospero's speech beginning "Our revels now are ended ..." seems to sum up both the play's action and the playwright's estimate of human life. Besides a philosophically challenging situation, the play contains some of Shakespeare's best poetry, songs, and comic scenes.

TEN DAYS THAT SHOOK THE WORLD
John Reed
1919
Nonfiction
Political, War

John Reed's intense, personal account of the Bolshevik uprising of October, 1917, is perhaps the best firsthand reaction to the Russian Revolution and arguably the best single study of any of the political insurrections of the 20th century.

Using a chronological narrative of fictional intensity, Reed weaves together the events preceding and during the takeover of the Russian state from the czarist government by leftist political parties, led by the Leninist-dominated Bolshevik party. Tracing the social as well as political antecedents to the events of October, the volume outlines the gradual political collapse of the Russian government, beginning with the Czar's abdication and culminating in Aleksandr Kerensky's ineptitude in handling the power thrust upon him to form and hold together a coalition of disparate social and economic groups.

Interspersing accounts of his personal experiences with excerpts from public documents such as newspapers, press releases, speeches, interviews, and broadsides, Reed creates a documentary montage of the chaotic progress of the revolution. Written close enough to the actual events to retain their immediacy, the narrative also does not sacrifice its objectivity. The result is a book of genuine historical insight and value.

Although Reed was a socialist himself and an open admirer of both Lenin and Trotsky, his professionalism as a reporter kept this study from becoming an uncritical apologia for the Bolshevik cause. He saw the repressions and excesses of the new government and was later critical of what he perceived as further and unnecessary repression of individual liberties by the Bolshevik party. Nevertheless, Reed was convinced by the justness of the cause to downplay actions which in later accounts would assume a greater significance. In spite of its theme and period, however, the volume holds up remarkably well both as a work of history in the making and as a piece of dramatic personal journalism.

TENDER IS THE NIGHT
F. Scott Fitzgerald
1934
Novel
Gothic, Psychological

Fitzgerald's most ambitious work, this book explores the moral failure of a group of Americans living in Europe between the two World Wars. Through them, Fitzgerald illustrates the tragedy of wasted lives and abandoned dreams.

The main characters in the book are Richard (Dick) Diver, a respected psychiatrist, and his wealthy wife, Nicole. In appearance they seem the perfect couple: attractive, loving, and successful. They conduct their lives as one continual celebration, surrounded by their friends, with Dick always in control.

The Divers are, in fact, not as happy as they seem. Nicole suffers from schizophrenia, the result of a brief incestuous relationship with her father. Dick first meets her as his patient and is attracted to her, in part, because of her dependency on him. It is suggested that he never wants her to be completely cured. Moreover, although Dick is regarded as a brilliant doctor, he has never fulfilled his early promise and has begun to devote more of his time to the social life he and Nicole enjoy than to his work.

The book details Dick's moral collapse. The story is told in such a way as to make Dick appear charming to the reader; he seems to be the master of any occasion. After an introductory section, however, Fitzgerald employs a lengthy flashback to explain the truth of Dick and Nicole's relationship and to show that neither is what he or she seems. The remainder of the novel traces the unraveling of their marriage as Nicole learns to live on her own terms, and Dick follows his private downward trajectory.

This extremely complex and thoughtful work, Fitzgerald's last complete novel, draws heavily on his marriage to Zelda Fitzgerald; in particular, it utilizes Zelda's mental illness and Fitzgerald's own sense of failure and self-betrayal. Critical opinion of the book remains mixed, but most readers recognize it as a brave and splendid accomplishment, and many consider it one of the great novels of the 20th century.

TESS OF THE D'URBERVILLES
Thomas Hardy
1891
Novel
Victorian

In the late 19th century, an innocent young woman living in rural England falls prey to an unscrupulous man and is thereafter drawn inexorably toward tragedy.

One of the most sympathetic heroines in literature, Tess is tricked by Alec D'Uberville into leaving her impoverished home to come to work as a poultry tender for Alec's mother. In a situation where fate intervenes, Tess is raped by Alec—a man she never loves—and then submits to him for a brief period. Fleeing him, she returns home where her child is born, and where she endures the shame of motherhood out of wedlock.

After her child's death through illness, Tess again leaves home to work, this time as a dairy maid. On the dairy farm, she meets the love of her life, Angel Clare. Against the pastoral background of Hardy's famed Wessex, Tess and Angel's love blossoms with an innocent passion which culminates in marriage.

Tess is totally committed to Angel in her happiness, but once again, fate intervenes. Tess had communicated her past life to Angel in a letter before the marriage, but he never received the letter. When Angel learns of Tess's past after their marriage, he leaves her. Angel fails Tess because of his idealism: In Tess he sought the Victorian ideal of the virgin bride, and this idealism is both his and Tess's undoing.

Tess survives Angel's absence until the needs of her destitute family force her once again to Alec D'Uberville; at that point she believes that Angel will never return. When Angel does, indeed, reappear, the hand of fate deals its final blow to Tess in Hardy's great tragic ending.

The design of the novel may be compared to classical tragedy with its emphasis on fate controlling the protagonist's destiny. One difference should be noted; Tess's character is elevated through her actions, but her great misfortune is not brought about through a flaw in her character. Rather, in his subtitle to the novel, "A Pure Woman Faithfully Presented," Hardy indicates that Tess's character remains one of innocent integrity.

THEIR EYES WERE WATCHING GOD
Zora Neal Hurston
1937
Novel
Historical, African American

The first feminist novel about an African-American woman, Their Eyes Were Watching God, *is a story of triumph for a woman determined to make her own choices. Her first choice was to insist on loving the man in her life.*

Before she can die, Janie's grandmother—who has raised Janie—insists on Janie being wed. Janie is appalled at the prospect, especially if there is no love, but for Nanny, respectability is key. The seventeen-year-old Janie has no choice but to marry the widowed Mr. Logan Killicks. Though he treats her well, she feels he expects too much from her.

One day, the charismatic Jody Starks walks by with wads of cash in his pocket, and the two become friends. Janie runs off with Jody to marry him, and start a new "colored town" with Jody's cash. They succeed in the venture, but after Jodi is selected Mayor of Eatonville, he expects Janie to act like a mayor's wife, rather than be herself. Through the years, his jealousy and hunger for power, and her hunger for love, separate them and they become estranged after Janie defies him.

Following Jodi's death, Vergible Woods (also known as Tea Cake) a young drifter, sweeps the widowed Janie off her feet, even though she is twelve years older. They get married and leave the people of Eatonville who had become too judgmental of Janie, saying she didn't appreciate Jody. Janie and Tea Cake are truly in love even though Janie often doubts his love for her and fears he might be after her money. They make a life on "the muck" (the Florida everglades) and, for the first time, Janie feels truly loved for who she is.

As the two flee a hurricane, Tea Cake rescues Janie from an angry dog, but is bitten in the face. Weeks later, Tea Cake becomes sick with rabies. In his rabid madness, Tea Cake tries to kill Janie who is then forced to shoot him. She is tried for murder, but deemed innocent under the circumstances. She returns to Eatonville and relays her extraordinary story of courage, self-discovery, and love to her best friend, Pheoby.

THINGS FALL APART
Chinua Achebe
1958
Novel
Historical, Colonialism

Set in a Nigerian village during the 1890's, Chinua Achebe's tale illustrates the consequences of European colonialism on the people of Africa. Okonkwo, the village strong man, finds himself facing an ever-changing social landscape as Christian missionaries enter his ancestral home.

Okonkwo, disturbed by his late father's reputation as a weak and untrustworthy man, has centered his entire life around the values of strength, masculinity, and the traditions of his village, above all. These values have led Okonkwo to become one of the most respected warriors in his village, Umuofia, where he lives with his three wives and many children. Seemingly guided by ill-fate, Okonkwo is eventually exiled from Umuofia for killing the village oracle's son when his gun accidently goes off during that same oracle's funeral salute.

Upon returning to Umuofia seven years later, Okonkwo finds his village under the control of Christian missionaries, and he formulates a plot to restore the traditional social structure of the village. After burning the local Christian church down, Okonkwo and the other leaders of Umuofia are taken into custody. Still attempting to repel the Europeans after his release, Okonkwo murders a Christian messenger before realizing his fellow villagers had lost the will to fight. The novel ends with the white men coming to take Okonkwo to trial for the murder only to find him dead, having hung himself.

Okonkwo's suicide represents an ironic end to a man so obsessed with maintaining the traditions of his people, that he commits the gravest of sins in their eyes. Achebe also uses Okonkwo's death to symbolize the sense of futility experienced by the African communities attempting to maintain their traditional way of life, yet eventually falling to the influence of the Europeans. *Things Fall Apart,* while telling the story of a single African village, works as a representation of the African experience with colonization across the continent, and the death of thousands of distinctive cultures.

THE THINGS THEY CARRIED
Tim O'Brien
1990
Short Story

A work about the need to tell the story of Vietnam and about the difficulty of telling that story. The Things They Carried *is self-examining in ways and to the extent that no work on the same subject has been. Neither polemical nor sentimental, it is a brilliantly and disturbingly obsessive work whose actual subject is not the war but the difficulty of writing about it.*

The Things They Carried takes the form of a list struggling to become a litany, a secular enumeration yearning for wholeness and spiritual redemption. Artfully contrived yet following no clearly discernible pattern, it catalogs the "things" the men of Alpha Company carried, everything from flak jackets to fear; above all they carried the knowledge "that they would never be at a loss for things to carry and the opposing dream of "lightness," of being "purely borne" (a punning condensation of their twin desires of being carried and being reborn). Like O'Brien's act of remembrance, the dream stands apart. Instead of either fulfillment or even a "sense of developing drama," the reader finds what the characters do, chapters/stories/parts oscillating back and forth in time and space. The repetition of information from one section to another creates a sense of stalled action and Sisyphean doom or, more optimistically, the need to go over the same ground again and again in the faint hope of finding the missing link that will allow the action to develop dramatically, to imagine a different end. Lacking this sense of developing drama, individual stories tend to dissolve, leaving the reader with an apparently random collection of individual images: Rat Kiley and Curt Lemon playing catch with a smoke grenade, until the latter steps on a booby- trapped artillery round; or Azar detonating the Claymore mine to which he had strapped a puppy and then responding to the others' horror with a line that rings all too true: "I'm just a boy." There is Norman Bowker, mustered out and back home, driving around and around a lake, the village they burn because Ted Lavender has been shot, the dancing of the fourteen-year-old girl whose entire family has been killed in an air attack, and the triple-canopied jungle, mist-filled and ominously silent. The starkness of these and other images parallels the simple fact that as the stories progress and the number of casualties increases, the sense of causality declines.

The Things They Carried differs from other books about Vietnam by laying claim to a very different "greater truthfulness" by insisting upon its status as fiction, O'Brien problematizes the connection between word and world and, indeed connections of all kinds. Both essay and fiction, "How to Tell a War Story" insists: "This is true," and another generically ambiguous chapter, "Good Form," begins: It's time to be blunt. I'm forty-three years old, true, and I'm a writer now, and a long time ago I walked through Quang Ngai Province as a foot soldier. Almost everything else is invented."

The Things They Carried does not offer the quick fix provided by the Vietnam War Memorial; it offers, instead, the most thorough examination yet to appear of the failure not simply to understand but even to find an appropriate means for depicting what has been insufficiently described as the American experience in Vietnam—that burden of guilt, confusion, and silence carried then, carried still.

THREE PLAYS
Seán O'Casey
1924-1927
Drama
Tragicomedy

This volume collects Seán O'Casey's greatest plays: two Dublin plays treat local war with Realism; The Silver Tassie provides an expressionist anti-war play addressing the syndrome of imperial wars.

Juno and the Paycock (1924) recounts the story of Juno O'Boyle, a mother, who works to support her family while her husband, Jack, exercises his elbow in a bar with his lay-about buddy, Joxer. Daughter Mary, on strike, languishes at home while her brother Johnny, an invalid who lost an arm in WWI, fears an indiscretion. Lawyer Bentham informs the family of a cousin's death; they will inherit. Parading his luck, Jack purchases a new suit, a furniture suite, and a gramophone, on credit.

Bentham impregnates Mary, botches the execution of the will, and flees England. Jack's purchases are repossessed. Mary, disowned by her father, is shipped to a relative. Johnny, murdered by the IRA for being an informant, receives a notable lament from Juno who leaves Jack. Unaware of developments, Jack, drunk with Joxer, arrives home; he manages to drop his last coin before passing out. Joxer cops the coin, and departs.

The Plough and the Stars (1926) limns chaos amid the 1916 Easter Monday Rebellion. Nora and Jack Clitheroe vegetate at home when Captain Brennan of the Irish Citizen Army delivers orders to "Commandant Jack," informing him his battalion must attend a meeting with James Connolly. In a local bar, amid patriotic speeches, women bicker; Bessie—a Protestant street vendor—literally fights with Mrs. Gogan. Jack Clitheroe and Captain Brennan arrive Sunday evening flaunting the flag of revolution—the plough and the stars—vowing to die for Irish independence. On Monday morning, Bessie relishes news: the rebels appear defeated. Nora fruitlessly sends messages to Jack to cease fighting, and then goes into labor which ends with a stillbirth. Brennan arrives, announcing Jack's death. Nora in delirium remembers a day she and Jack strolled through the woods. Soldiers arrive to arrest Brennan. Nora rushes to a window, calling Jack. Bessie pulls her back; she is shot in the back, supposedly mistaken for a sniper.

The Silver Tassie (1927) portrays athlete Harry in the prime of life. At the battlefront he finds that cynicism reigns among fellow soldiers. Seriously wounded, Harry lies in a hospital with other disillusioned veterans. Disabled and repatriated, Harry plunges into deep alienation: obtuse civilians don't understand war or its consequences.

Portraying strong women, O'Casey was the first effective anti-war playwright, and, arguably, the best English-language playwright since Shakespeare in portraying authentic characters.

THE THREE SISTERS
Anton Chekhov
1901
Drama

One of the masterpieces of modern theater, this touching drama portrays the thwarted ambitions of three educated, sensitive sisters who demonstrate strength of character and endurance, despite their disappointments.

Originally from Moscow, the three sisters moved years before to a provincial town with their now dead father. Olga, the eldest, is a teacher in the local school; Masha is married to a man whom she once thought clever, but now realizes is foolish. Young Irina dreams of great things. All of them long to return to Moscow.

The sisters pin their hopes on their brother Andrey, but he falls under the spell of Natasha, a vulgar local girl. Masha, a woman of deep emotions, falls in love with the handsome Vershinin, the new battery commander of the local brigade. It becomes evident that they all are becoming increasingly trapped in this hated town.

Olga is promoted to the job of headmistress at the school and Irina gets a job in the telegraph office. Andrey loses all ambition and Natasha takes over the household, dominating everyone in the family and driving away old friends and servants. Although the sisters still dream of escape to Moscow, in their hearts they know that escape is impossible.

While many of the characters in the play are weak-willed or foolish, they remain sympathetic. Each character struggles desperately to cling to a dream, a vision, some remnant of beauty. Although Vershinin and Masha are separated by his neurotic wife and her ridiculous husband, their frustrated love is both poignant and beautiful. The sisters are generous, even in adversity; they believe in the importance of hope, even when there seems to be little reason for it.

The end of the drama offers no hope for these characters. Masha must say goodbye to Vershinin, and the three sisters know that they are trapped in this provincial town. Nevertheless, they voice their conviction that they must keep trying because someday the world will be a brighter place. Perhaps they themselves will not live to enjoy that time, but they will, at least, help to make it possible.

THROUGH THE LOOKING-GLASS AND WHAT ALICE FOUND THERE
Lewis Carroll
1871
Novel
Children's, Fantasy

This long-popular sequel to Alice's Adventures in Wonderland *tells of Alice's strange and wonderful experiences in a looking-glass world.*

Analogous to a chess game, the fast-paced events of this fantasy carry Alice from the security of her own home through a dizzying sequence of moves until, at last, she is crowned queen. The looking-glass world in which she finds herself is one of opposites and contrasts, with no one quite what he or she seems.

Upon crawling through the mirror in her sitting room, Alice discovers the Red Queen and King and the White King and Queen in a state of agitation. Trying to discover the problem, she picks up a "looking-glass book," which is written in mirror image, and finds the poem "Jabberwocky."

Moving through a garden of talking flowers, she surveys the countryside beyond, which is laid out like a vast chess board, in alternating squares. The Red and White Queen draft Alice into their game, rushing her breathlessly across the landscape—and introducing her to a bizarre group of characters. These include the looking-glass insects (such as the rocking-horse fly), Tweedledum and Tweedledee (who recite the poem of "The Walrus and the Carpenter"), and the imprisoned Mad Hatter (here known as the King's Messenger).

One of the most perplexing of Alice's encounters is with Humpty Dumpty. This chapter of the book has been quoted countless times, both for its wit and for its brilliant discussion of the nature of language. Soon Alice is swept away into a battle, where she meets the clumsy, ineffectual White Knight, who quite charms her. Finally, she reaches the eighth square, where she finds a golden crown, and becomes Queen Alice.

Being queen, however, is not what she expected it to be, and the fantasy turns into a nightmare from which she, mercifully, wakes up. Alice's adventures through the looking-glass have become an important part of Western literature, providing humor and food for thought for successive generations of readers.

THUS SPAKE ZARATHUSTRA
Friedrich Nietzsche
1883/1884
Novel
Philosophical

Zarathustra comes down from the mountains, where he has pondered for ten years, announces the death of God, declares Christianity a spiritless slave morality, and teaches the doctrine of the Superman. This work summarizes the thought of one of the great and increasingly influential figures in modern German literature and philosophy. Familiarity with this work is essential for anyone wishing to understand the history of Western thought since the late 19th century.

Writing a vivid poetic prose resembling that of the Old Testament prophets and psalmists, Nietzsche mounts a bold critique of 19th century bourgeois culture. Rationalism, Christianity, and democratic tendencies he argues, are the root causes of degeneration in modern society. Conventional values and attitudes—belief in an afterlife, humility, self-sacrifice, equality, compassion—belong to a slave morality suitable only to weak, inferior people.

Speaking through the persona of his poet-prophet, Zarathustra, Nietzsche calls for voiding the old commandments that reflect slave morality and for replacing them with their opposite.

The superior man affirms life in this world through aristocratic values based on pride, heroism, instinct, and strength. The superior man freely wills the constant development of his body, mind, and total personality.

Instead of despising life and this world, Zarathustra teaches, people should despise their conventional notions about virtue, rationality, and the good life, and try to surpass themselves.

Reflecting Darwin's theory of evolution, Nietzsche views man as only a transitional stage to something greater—the Superman. Like a tightrope walker crossing an abyss, man is on a dangerous passage from his animal nature to his higher self.

Misreading him, the Nazis of the 1930's and 1940's tried to justify their brutal policies by claiming Nietzsche and his Superman for their camp. Nietzsche had opposed the nationalism, imperialism, and especially the racism of his time.

THE TIME MACHINE
H. G. Wells
1895
Novella
Science Fiction

This "scientific romance," as Wells himself termed it, vividly portrays a late-Victorian scientist's journey to England in the far-distant future.

The Time Machine, the first and arguably the finest of H.G. Wells's science fiction novels, begins in the comfortably prosperous world of the Victorian professional classes, where a scientist proposes the possibility of traveling in the fourth dimension—Time. Wells wisely never tries to explain how the scientist's time machine works but instead describes its appearance and the sensation that time-traveling produces.

Whatever the principles behind it, the machine succeeds in taking the Time Traveler to A.D. 802,701. England of that age seems to be paradise—an uncultivated yet weedless garden inhabited by the Eloi, a delicate, androgynous people oddly lacking in curiosity and intelligence.

Besides depicting the future world, Wells shows the scientist's clear, logical mind judging it and attempting to fathom its workings. Reasoning from Darwin's evolutionary theories, the Time Traveler surmises that, having perfectly controlled the environment, mankind has lost all need for intelligence and initiative. Then he encounters a second race, the Morlocks, who live underground, retain some remnants of technological skill, and eat meat. At first the Time Traveler suspects that mankind has diverged into two races: The descendants of capitalists living on the surface, the long-distant offspring of laborers existing below and serving the Eloi out of instinct. Later he learns the stark truth of the relationship: The Morlocks are shepherds, the Eloi their sheep.

Having seen how the human race has, in the act of perfecting its world, committed suicide, the Time Traveler departs. His scientific passion for knowledge takes him yet farther into the future. After returning and reporting his discoveries to his friends, he travels off on the machine yet again, leaving behind only two strange, withered flowers: proof that his adventure was real and symbols of man's future fate.

THE TIN DRUM
Günter Grass
1959
Novel
Satire, Grotesque

A mental patient recounts his bizarre life of prolonged childhood and his subsequent attempt to become an adult. With its fantastical welter of details and a narrative bravado which brazenly assaults conventional tastes, this novel should prove immensely enriching for the experienced reader.

From earliest infancy, the unnaturally precocious Oskar Matzerath is so appalled by the cruel absurdities of life that he refuses to grow beyond the age of three. Choosing the perspective of infantile curiosity, he instead proceeds to unmask the world of the adults around him: the small-mindedness of his German father, the sensuality and guilt of his mother, and the weakness of her ineffectual Polish lover. Compensating for his own vulnerability with sly aggressiveness, Oskar becomes at least partially responsible for their unhappy fates.

During the 1920's and 1930's, Oskar's hometown of Danzig (now Gdansk) was precariously perched between German and Polish spheres of influence. His deteriorating family life represents, therefore, not only a private tragedy but also the historical collapse of Danzig's German-Polish symbiosis under the impact of Nazism and the horrors of war. An amoral will to live makes Oskar survive the catastrophe by alternately practicing strategies of accommodation and rebelliousness.

At the end of the war, possibilities of a new beginning in West Germany entice him to grow again. As these hopes are quickly crushed, his body revolts by developing a hump. Infantile desires and fears reassert themselves, and Oskar finally agrees to be committed to a mental institution.

Though the hero's childish fascination with what is revolting, perverse, and sacrilegious scandalized many readers, Grass's first novel was immediately recognized as a major event in postwar German literature. The shocking absence of moral restraint in Oskar's fight with adult reality is, on the one hand, an indictment of that reality's moral pretensions; on the other hand, however, it is also meant to challenge existing morality to come to terms with this fictional world, which offers few signposts for moral orientation and yet seems in such desperate need of them.

TO KILL A MOCKINGBIRD
Harper Lee
1960
Novel

Children's, African American

A girl growing up in a small Alabama town during the 1930's learns the importance of tolerance. Though often read by young people in school, this amusing and sometimes tense novel offers pleasure to all ages.

Between the ages of 6 and 9, Scout Finch has doubts about whether she wishes to grow up to be a lady. She much prefers the free, boyish life she enjoys with her older brother, Jem, and his friends. She also enjoys an open relationship with her widowed father, Atticus, a local attorney and perennial legislator.

Though many of the family's adventures are told, Scout's life during these years centers on two events, her developing relationship with Boo Radley and her father's defense of Tom, a black wrongly accused of raping a white woman.

Scout discovers that while the mentally deficient Boo Radley has been a curiosity to her, he has been lovingly caring for her. She and her friends watch the house where his family keeps him hidden and speculate about him, sometimes cruelly. Various signs show Scout that Boo's interest in them is friendly and protective. Scout becomes sure of his goodness when Boo saves her and Jem from a murder attempt.

This lesson in tolerance is often repeated in the novel. Tom's trial reveals the degree to which the whole town needs to understand what Scout learns. Because he proves the likelihood of Tom's innocence, Atticus must endure scorn, anger, and the attempted murder of his children. Despite Atticus' successful defense, the jury recommends the death penalty.

Scout's innocent perceptions reveal how family, class, race, region, and religion can be barriers to tolerance and sympathy. The openness to experience that Atticus cultivates in her helps her to look closely at people and to withhold judgment until she understands them.

TO THE LIGHTHOUSE
Virginia Woolf
1927
Novel

Victorian, Feminist

Demonstrating the primacy of personal thoughts and relationships, this novel focuses on the daily life of an English family on vacation and revisits the family ten years later, after World War I and personal crises have changed their lives.

At the center of this novel is Mrs. Ramsay, the beautiful, mysterious, nurturing wife and mother of an English family, headed by an autocratic, but remotely loving father, renowned in the late-Victorian world as a philosopher. The couple, modeled on Virginia Woolf's parents, Sir Leslie and Mrs. Stephen, vacation in the Hebrides, surrounded by their children and friends, who both admire and criticize them.

The proposed action of the first part of the novel is an excursion to the nearby lighthouse, which does not take place until ten years later, after the death of Mrs. Ramsay. In actuality, the novel presents almost no external action. Rather, the entirely subjective narrative moves in and out of the minds of the various characters, both major and minor, who interpret the nature and actions of the other characters in private symbols and thus reveal their own biases and personalities. In this way, Lily Briscoe, an artist and spinster, sees Mrs. Ramsay as a "wedge-shaped core of darkness," and Mr. Carmichael, a sour bachelor and failed philosopher, sees Mr. Ramsay as followed around by a hen and chicks. Occasionally, individual characters experience moments of epiphany, in which they have a visionary glimpse of truth. In such a moment, Mrs. Ramsay sees herself symbolized in the stern radiance of the lighthouse.

This insistence on the supreme value of the individual self collapses in the middle section of the novel, in which the vacation home falls into decay, as nature obliterates all trace of the Ramsays. This reversal is reflected in the way in which the narrative reports critical events in the life of the Ramsays: in parenthesis.

In the final section, remaining Ramsays and friends return to the house and make a pilgrimage to the lighthouse in an effort to understand and make peace with the past. The excursion, while reasonably successful, is shadowed by the deaths of Mrs. Ramsay and her oldest daughter, who closely resembled her. Thus the novel points out the fragility of human relationships, for these are always threatened by the chaos of the waves.

TOM JONES
Henry Fielding
1749
Novel
Historical

This influential English novel, one of the first to present everyday life in realistic detail, tells of the bawdy adventures of a young man, wrongly accused and much abused, in the early 18th century.

Tom Jones, a foundling, is reared by Allworthy, a wealthy Somersetshire squire. He has all the good qualities possible except prudence (which Fielding considers the supreme rational virtue) and suffers as a result; his desire to experience all that life has to offer constantly gets him into trouble, making him seem inferior to the falsely pious Blifil, Allworthy's nephew. When Jones becomes drunk celebrating Allworthy's recovery from an illness, Blifil conspires to have him expelled from the estate. Jones is thus separated from his beloved, Sophia Western, who is promised to the hated Blifil.

Setting out on the road to London, Jones is immediately robbed by Black George, whose poor family Jones has helped. This is the first of many such incidents which lead Jones, believing he has committed incest and murder, to prison to await hanging.

The novel's plot is one of the most complex ever contrived, with all the many characters and events being connected. This structure reflects Fielding's belief in the ultimate design and order of the universe. The novel's lively characters, its inventive plot, and Fielding's self-mocking digressions, however prevent the underlying moral seriousness from dominating.

The most entertaining and aesthetically pleasing of 18th century English novels, the book has had a profound influence on the development of the novel because of Fielding's ability to combine vividly drawn characters, narrative technique, and explorations of almost all areas of human interest.

TREASURE ISLAND
Robert Louis Stevenson
1883
Novel
Children's, Adventure

This classic adventure story tells how a young boy, Jim Hawkins, finds a pirate treasure map in his parents' inn and with several adult friends sets sail to a South Seas island to search for the treasure.

Stevenson based *Treasure Island* on the boy's adventure tales of the time. It has what the standard piratical potboilers lacked, however—graceful lucidity, richly imagined physical settings, and above all one of the most fascinating of all villains in Long John Silver—and it continues to provide grand entertainment today. Since it contains only one minor female character—Jim's mother—its primary audience is male, from about ten years old on up.

The novel, set in the 18th century, falls into three stages. In the first, a "brown old seaman" with a sabre scar takes up lodgings at The Admiral Benbow, Jim's father's inn. This man, Billy Bones, is pursued by other sinister characters, led by the blind Pew. When Bones dies (Jim's father in the meantime has also died), Jim and his mother search the seaman's chest and discover the map.

The treasure-hunting expedition now sets out aboard the Hispaniola from Bristol. What the good characters do not know, however, is that Long John Silver, the one-legged sea-cook they have engaged, was one of the pirate Flint's chief lieutenants. Silver, having got wind of the treasure, has also persuaded the ship's captain to sign on a number of Flint's pirates as hands. Shortly before the ship reaches the island, Jim overhears the pirates' plot. The remainder of the book recounts the struggle on the island between the good and bad characters, and the search for the treasure.

Treasure Island, lacking the pell-mell pace of most pirate stories, was unsuccessful when it first appeared as a serial. The novel contains a number of wonderful set pieces, however, and is imbued with an appealing boyish innocence: The good characters are all good, the bad all bad. It benefits moreover from its complete lack of pretension. It is a small, happy, timeless book.

A TREE GROWS IN BROOKLYN
Betty Smith
1943
Novel
Historical, Family Saga

A precocious eleven-year-old, from the tenements of Williamsburg, Brooklyn, Francie grows from an observant, scrappy eleven-year-old into a self-sufficient young woman, wise beyond her years, who learns the value of perseverance and love in overcoming the poverty and hardship of her environment.

The Nolan family lives in abject poverty, in large measure due to Johnny Nolan's alcoholism. But other factors contribute to the Nolans' hard life. There is prejudice, especially from those more well to do; superstition, often with religious overtones; and, ignorance, where attending school is a luxury for the poor, whose children have to work to help support a family. Both Nolan parents, Johnny and Mary, realize that the best chance for their children, Francie and Neely, to overcome their low station, is through education. Francie is an avid reader who carves out her own private sanctuary, sitting on the fire-escape, hidden from view by her "umbrella" tree—a tree that comes to symbolize the strength and richness of character acquired only through hardship. The tree grows as no other tree can, in cement cracks where there is little soil.

A Tree Grows in Brooklyn could easily be categorized as feminist—perhaps one reason the novel has endured as a classic. The hardship is real. The women are strong, resilient, and determined. They make their own way, sometimes through deception, to take care of themselves and their children. The men in the story are victims. Johnny's alcoholism is a harsh taskmaster he never overcomes. When Francie is accosted by a pedophile, it's her mother who pulls the trigger. After Johnny succumbs to his alcoholism and despair, and Mary is pregnant, Francie finds work to support their family.

When published in 1943, *A Tree Grows in Brooklyn* created a sensation, as one of the first novels about a working class family, intended for a working class readership. The novel is largely autobiographical. The story's plot could be trite in less skilled hands, but Smith's writing is driven by details, both grimy and sublime, with a cumulative effect of a tour de force.

THE TRIAL
Franz Kafka
1925
Novel
Dystopian

A man tries to learn why legal charges have been leveled against him. The story's barely hidden terror and bewildering uncertainty have made this one of the most mysterious novels of the 20th century.

On the morning of his thirtieth birthday, the bachelor Josef K., a career-oriented bank employee, wakes up to the unsettling news that he is under arrest. Uninformed as to the crime he is alleged to have committed, K. receives a summons to appear before a judge a few days later. Yet neither this nor a subsequent visit to the curiously irregular court provides him with any clarity about his case.

Left stranded in his efforts to communicate with the legal authorities, K. finds his daily life invaded by grotesque reminders of guilt and punishment. Soon a debilitating sense of doom begins to destroy the normalcy of his existence.

In order to advance his case and to justify himself, K. turns to ever more unlikely helpers. A famous lawyer is dismissed when he counsels procrastination as the safest course of action. The inside information K. hopes to gain from a portrait artist in the employ of the court and from its prison chaplain only entangle him further in a world of legal subterfuge.

Worn out by his futile search, K. shows no surprise when, on the eve of his thirty-first birthday, two executioners come to his apartment. Willingly he submits to their authority as they lead him to his death.

For some critics, the German-Jewish author from Prague has foreseen the nightmare of totalitarianism that was to descend on Europe under the reign of Nazism. Others see K.'s fate as a parable on the price man must pay if he refuses to acknowledge his peculiarly modern in-authenticity. Most readers, however, are captivated by Kafka's claustrophobic visions of a horrid and yet faintly ridiculous world without feeling the need to arrive at a definition of its menacing spell.

TRISTRAM SHANDY
Laurence Sterne
1759-1767
Novel
Satire

A zany recounting of the life and opinions of one Tristram Shandy, a member of the English gentry, this book is a long satire on the foibles of the philosophically and theologically inclined. It is notable chiefly for the liberties it takes with conventional narrative forms and for being one of the first works of fiction to employ stream-of-consciousness technique to tell its story.

The novel opens with an account of the moment of Tristram's conception. How Tristram came by this knowledge is never made entirely clear. He claims that this moment was primarily the cause of the sorrows of his subsequent life, since the proper environment for the process was disturbed by an inadvertent coitus interruptus. Other accidents attend Tristram's birth, christening, and subsequent events in his life, most of which are narrated with a ribald self-mockery that reflects the oddity of the author's view of himself—indeed, of the entire world.

The novel has no plot in the conventional sense of the term. It is, rather, a random sticking together of events and stories that bear in one way or another on Tristram's unhappy life. We are told about his Uncle Toby's amours; his father's views on naming, cursing, classical authors, the proper method for delivering infants, and much else; about

Tristram's travels in France, and so on. The point of all this good fun is to consider what the world looks like once one accepts John Locke's conception of the mind as an empty receptacle for sense data devoid of organizing structures or principles. The world looks very odd indeed.

Sterne's humor, like that of his avowed master Rabelais, is often bawdy and scatological, as was more common in the 18th century novel than would be the case in the 19th or even the 20th, but the length to which he takes some of the jokes has provoked commentators to speculate on the soundness of Sterne's own mind. His contemporary Samuel Johnson, while laughing heartily at many of the jests, thought it the product of a diseased imagination.

THE TROJAN WOMEN
Euripides
415 B.C.E.
Tragedy, Greek

A powerful piece of antiwar literature, this 5th century, B.C. Greek tragedy depicts the aftermath of the Trojan war and the enslavement of the Trojan women.

The dramatic setting is the city of Troy, just captured by the Greeks after a bitter, ten-year war. With the exception of Talthybius, the Greek herald, and Menelaus, the Greek husband of Helen, all the mortal characters in the play are Trojan women, prisoners of war who face cruel servitude in Greece.

The tragedy is noted not for suspense-filled, dramatic scenes but for passages of powerful lyric lamentation. The pathetic solo song of Hecuba, queen of Troy, leads into an elaborate passage sung by both the queen and the chorus of Trojan women. This lyric tone intensifies in later scenes, with the solo songs of Hecuba's daughter Cassandra, the duet between Hecuba and her daughter-in-law Andromache, and a final song between the queen and the chorus sung as their city burns to the ground.

Neither the audience nor the Trojan women are offered any moral solace in this play. The criminal Greeks are not punished. Rather, the play focuses on the sufferings of the innocent victims of war. Andromache, widow of Hector, is forced to become mistress of the son of her husband's slayer. Her infant son, Astyanax, is cruelly hurled to his death from the walls of Troy. Cassandra, who is chosen to become the mistress of Agamemnon, leader of the Greek expedition, offers the women their only legitimate hope for vengeance, but, ironically, she is not believed. The Trojans interpret Cassandra's true prediction of Agamemnon's impending death as a sign of Cassandra's madness and another reason for lamentation. Yet Helen, whose seductive and sinister charms caused the war, receives a reprieve in the play from the execution the Trojan women hope for her. For the victims of war in this tragedy, there is no justice, only suffering.

TROPIC OF CAPRICORN
Henry Miller
1939
Novel
Stream of Consciousness

This visionary novel, banned in the United States until 1961, tells the story of a man's liberation from the imprisoning values of modern civilization by means of a sensual and imaginative awakening.

If Henry Miller's first novel, *Tropic of Cancer*, can be seen as a modern version of Dante's *Inferno*, then this novel is clearly Miller's version of Dante's *Purgatorio*. The earlier book describes a world of sex and surreal violence without love. This novel opens in a similarly hellish environment, but the central character (a fictional version of the author) recognizes its nature, passes through a series of purgatorial punishments, and emerges possessed of an angelic or paradisiac vision.

The book opens with Miller living in New York and working as personnel manager of the Cosmodemonic Telegraph Company. He describes himself as a clown living in an insane world, dominated by his deadly business life, violence at home in a loveless marriage, and crazy random sex. With the lesson of his father's broken spirit before him, he dreams of the imaginative freedom he finds in books but sinks into a torpor of despair at the life around him.

The only force that keeps him from giving in to his despair is the sensuous power he finds in sex. The middle portion of the book is a catalog of sexual encounters, present and remembered, all explicitly described in Miller's uniquely explosive language. This sexual landscape is purgatorial, filled with suffering and betrayal and loss, but ultimately liberating.

The book is dedicated to "Her," a woman like Dante's Beatrice who opens to him a vision of life beyond the wheel of destiny. He achieves resurrection from the tomb of the telegraph company in a vision of life as love. He calls himself Gottlieb Leberecht Muller, a God-loved and loving, right living man who has baptized himself anew. In his new angelic identity as a man who has walked out on himself, a happy rock in the divine stream of life, he meets Mona (Her) and begins a new life as an artist with both death and birth behind him.

THE TURN OF THE SCREW
Henry James
1898
Novella
Gothic, Horror

Two young children and their governess, alone except for a housekeeper in an isolated country house, are threatened by ghosts—perhaps real, perhaps figments of the governess' diseased imagination—in this classic tale of the supernatural.

Since *The Turn of the Screw*, is told in the first person by the governess, everything hinges on whether she is a reliable narrator. An innocent, susceptible young woman, the daughter of a minister, she has been hired by a wealthy bachelor to look after Miles and Flora, his orphaned nephew and niece.

There is no question of the governess' good will, at least on a conscious level, and her honesty—she reports what she thinks she sees—but she has fallen desperately and hopelessly in love with her employer, and would like nothing better—as she herself admits—than to earn his gratitude by rescuing the children from some danger. Moreover, the atmosphere at Bly, the employer's country house, is Gothic and vaguely sinister from the first—excellent circumstances for seeing ghosts, whether there are any to see or not.

The ghosts are those of Peter Quint, the employer's former valet, and Miss Jessel, the former governess, who apparently died while giving birth to an illegitimate child. In life, these two had been sent away because they threatened the social order (sexual immorality, in particular, could not be tolerated); in death, the governess believes, they are trying to avenge themselves by claiming the children for their own.

The story centers on the struggle between the governess and the ghosts for the children's souls, with the added hint that the real evil may lie in the governess' possessiveness. The evil is real—that much at least is clear, in this deliberately ambiguous tale which has haunted the imaginations of generations of readers.

TWELFTH NIGHT
William Shakespeare
1600
Drama
Comedy

Named after a midwinter Christian festival (Feast of the Epiphany), this comedy mixes romance and revelry in a carnival spirit: jollity, love, and life triumph over gloom, repression, and death.

Twelfth Night develops its theme on two levels. The main plot, written mostly in blank verse, shows the nobility in pursuit of love. The subplot features lower characters, who speak in prose and pursue drunkenness and mischief.

In the main plot, the twins Viola and Sebastian are shipwrecked on the Illyrian coast and separated; each presumes the other dead. Disguised as a young man, Viola joins the court of Duke Orsino, falls in love with him, and becomes his favorite. Orsino loves the lady Olivia, who refuses his attentions because she still mourns her dead brother. When Orsino sends Viola to woo Olivia for him, Olivia falls in love with Viola.

In the subplot, Sir Toby Belch, Olivia's uncle, and Sir Andrew Aguecheek, a ridiculous suitor to Olivia, fall out with Malvolio, Olivia's puritanical steward, who condemns their revels. With the help of Maria and Fabian, Olivia's servants, they trick the self-serving Malvolio into thinking Olivia loves him, then they confine him for insanity. Sir Toby also persuades Sir Andrew to challenge Viola to a duel.

These plots untangle when Sebastian appears, marries Olivia, and whips Sir Andrew and Sir Toby. Viola throws off her disguise and accepts Orsino's proposal of marriage. Freed, Malvolio stomps out vowing revenge on them all.

Symbolically opposed to Malvolio is Feste, the wise clown. He fools Olivia out of her mourning and Orsino out of his lovesickness—both self-indulgent, sterile behaviors, like Malvolio's self-love. Shakespeare implies that people should open themselves to celebration and love, even if it makes them appear foolish, since it is truly foolish to deny these life forces.

TWENTY THOUSAND LEAGUES UNDER THE SEA
Jules Verne
1870
Novel
Science Fiction

In this pioneering science fiction novel, world shipping is menaced by the mysterious sinking of a number of vessels. Accounts by survivors suggest that they were attacked by an unknown sea monster.

The United States government prepares an expedition to seek and destroy the suspected sea monster, enlisting the aid of Professor Aronnax of the Museum of Natural History in Paris. Aronnax theorizes that the creature is a giant narwhal. The expedition therefore includes harpooner Ned Land, a Canadian. After months of fruitless search, they sight an immense marine object. It turns out to be a giant submarine, which sinks them.

Only Aronnax, his servant Conseil, and Land survive, to be captured and taken on board the submarine Nautilus. There they meet Captain Nemo, who, because he will never release them, reveals to them the Nautilus' wonders.

Aronnax discovers in Nemo a congenial fellow scientist but also a misanthrope who has vowed never again to set foot on inhabited land. At first Aronnax is fascinated by such wonders as scenes of the ocean from the submarine's window, explorations of the sea bottom in diving gear, a funeral in an undersea coral cemetery, Atlantis by night, and an underwater volcanic explosion. Ned Land, however, grows moody and discontented, constantly planning escape.

When they are nearly trapped under ice at the South Pole, Aronnax agrees to flee at the next opportunity. The Nautilus then travels northward and, when approaching the coast of Norway, is drawn into a maelstrom. Aronnax, Conseil, and Land regain consciousness on an island, and the Nautilus has disappeared. Whether it escaped, they do not know.

TWO YEARS BEFORE THE MAST
Richard Henry Dana, Jr.
1840
Nonfiction
Autobiography

To regain his health, a young man in the 1830's signs on as common seaman aboard The Pilgrim, an American merchantman. His two-year voyage of adventure begins in Boston, travels around Cape Horn, then up the storm-tossed Pacific coast, and finally along Spanish California.

This personal narrative contains the two truths of all great autobiography—the truth of time and place, and the truth of character.

The descriptions of the day-to-day routine of life "before the mast" are recorded in a solid, colloquial English, a non-bookish style that persuades the reader of the author's honesty and accuracy. The high adventure of fighting squalls and escaping ice floes is counterpointed by the drudgery of tending sail, of keeping watch, of tarring and scraping and cleaning. Dana's account of his two-month duty ashore in California drying and curing hides, his pictures of sleepy Monterey and busy San Diego and the barren beaches of Southern California, capture exactly a time and place, history being lived rather than merely recorded.

Dana's ability to depict human character is the second great truth of the work. The book is rich in journalistically concise portraits, such as the happy-go-lucky Sandwich Islanders who worked only until they made enough money to live idly for a month or so; or Tom Harris, who knew more about sailing than any man alive and who taught the young author more about human nature than "many hours to be passed in study." The most memorable delineation is that of Captain Frank Thompson, a harsh, mean-spirited tyrant who flogs a sailor partly out of discipline and partly out of sadistic pleasure.

The secret of the book is its honesty. Its power was evident to Herman Melville who was deeply influenced by it. Melville's *Moby Dick* (1851) rendered experience before the mast in more symbolic terms.

ULYSSES
James Joyce
1922
Novel
Psychological, Stream of Consciousness

Joyce's technical virtuosity in bringing together a dazzling array of structural, stylistic, mythological, and realistic elements makes this the most influential novel of the 20th century.

The novel focuses on the events of June 16, 1904, in Dublin, Ireland, in particular on the day's experiences of Leopold Bloom, an advertising salesman, his wife Molly, and Stephen Dedalus, an artist in search of a subject. Although he has abundant intellectual and educational resources for the task, Stephen is burdened by a weak father image, a debilitating guilt over his recently dead mother, and insensitive and untrustworthy companions. Leopold Bloom, on the other hand, is an average citizen carried along in the flow of everyday life: We observe his every move, thought, sensation, and fantasy throughout the day, from his preparing breakfast for his indolent wife to his return to their bedroom at 2 a.m. on June 17. Among his many trials during the day is the awareness that Molly betrays him with an impresario named Blazes Boylan.

Thus Stephen and Bloom complement each other as spiritual son and father, and their eventual meeting toward the end of the day produces an ambiguous resolution of their respective problems. The novel concludes with the famous soliloquy of Molly as she lies abed reflecting and speculating on the day's events.

Every detail in this richly textured novel carries with it a weight of philosophical, mythological, or literary reference, so that it can be read on several levels simultaneously. The most explicit of these is implied in the title: The major episodes of Homer's epic *Odyssey* are replayed in the apparently trivial incidents of an ordinary day.

THE UNBEARABLE LIGHTNESS OF BEING
Milan Kundera
1984
Novel

A brilliant, perverse "novel of ideas," The Unbearable Lightness of Being *is a novel in which reflective thought plays an unusually prominent role, and one that has a "polyphonic" structure. Polyphony, as Kundera defines it, is the fusion of "philosophy, narrative, and dream" and "the specifically novelistic essay" into "a single music."*

The Unbearable Lightness of Being is divided into seven parts: part 1, "Lightness and Weight"; part 2, "Soul and Body"; part 3, "Words Misunderstood"; part 4, "Soul and Body"; part 5, "Lightness and Weight"; part 6, "The Grand March"; and part 7, "Karenin's Smile." Each part is divided into numbered subsections of varying length; this suggestion of theme and variation seems to invite the reader to find a musical analogy.

While unhesitatingly affirming the cognitive authority of the novel to "shed light on existence" Kundera is, however, equally emphatic in his seemingly contradictory insistence that "The novel…is a territory where one does not make assertions; it is a territory of play and of hypotheses. Reflection within the novel is hypothetical by its very essence." Kundera's first paragraph reads:

The idea of eternal return is a mysterious one, and Nietzsche has often perplexed other philosophers with it: to think that everything recurs as we once experienced it, and that the recurrence itself recurs ad infinitum! What does this mad myth signify?

This is an extraordinary way to begin a novel. Who is speaking? It seems that the novelist himself—not a character or a "narrator" in the conventional sense of the term—is speaking here, addressing the reader with a compelling directness, yet Kundera never resolves the uncertainty which the reader feels after the first paragraph concerning the status of such reflections. Kundera maintains that only if events were to recur would they have significance, weight: "If the French Revolution were to recur eternally, French historians would be less proud of Robespierre....There is an infinite difference between a Robespierre who occurs only once in history and a Robespierre who eternally returns, chopping off French heads." That which is "ephemeral, in transit"—in other words, "light"—cannot be submitted to moral judgment, Kundera asserts: "In the sunset of dissolution, everything is illuminated by the aura of nostalgia, even the guillotine." This move accomplished, Kundera gives his argument a final twist. He recounts "a most incredible sensation" that he experienced while leafing through a book about Adolf Hitler. Certain portraits of Hitler, Kundera says, reminded him of his own childhood, and he was touched.

Some feel that Kundera's moral perversity is revealed in the deliberately provocative tone of his fiction. In any case, the opening chapter introduces the metaphorical opposition between "lightness" and "weight" that organizes much of the book, in particular the notion of "the unbearable lightness of being." The interlocking stories of the novel's main characters all are presented in terms of the conflict between traditional concepts of moral choice and destiny ("character is fate") and the radically opposed perspective that Kundera introduces.

Such reflections, meditations, and arguments are as integral to the novel as the stories with which they are interwoven. Indeed, the characters themselves are schematically presented—explicitly so. "It would be senseless for the author to try to convince the reader that his characters once actually lived," Kundera writes. Yet, by the grace of fiction, his characters live in the reader's mind—particularly Tomas and Tereza, the novel's principal pair.

UNCLE TOM'S CABIN
Harriet Beecher Stowe
1852
Novel
Philosophical, African American

The most popular novel of its day, adapted successfully for the stage and later for the cinema, is much more than an antislavery tract. Stowe exhibits a shrewd combination of social commentary and character typing.

Although Stowe was both attacked and lauded by her contemporaries for her exposure of the evils of slavery and Southern injustice, her purpose seems to have been larger: to indict the nation for its inadequate efforts to improve life among "the lowly." On the one hand, Simon Legree, the brutal slavemaster, is a New Englander who has gone South only to indulge in his baser instincts. On the other hand, St. Clare, the benign slaveowner, is an ineffectual but morally sensitive Southerner forced to split apart a black family because of his economic losses.

Standing in the middle between these two representative characters is the slave Uncle Tom, the author's Christian hero. The term "Uncle Tom" has become synonymous with passive, servile behavior, but Stowe's character is dynamic. He saves the life of Little Eva, St. Clare's daughter, and scares Legree, who is desperate to crush Tom's courage and fortitude.

Although melodramatic elements often simplify the novel's treatment of complex social and psychological problems, much of the author's story remains relevant to individuals faced with the threat of overwhelming force in any situation. Her work concerns a fundamental question: To what extent can the world be swayed by the force of a moral example?

UNCLE VANYA
Anton Chekhov
1899
Drama
Tragicomedy

Exploring the changing moods of isolated rural people, this alternatingly desperate and comic play foreshadows the complexities and vulnerable hopes of modern life.

The central character is Ivan Voynitsky, or Uncle Vanya, who gradually comes to an awareness of the folly of his life's ideals. Dedicated for many years to advancing the career of Professor Serebryakov, the husband of his dead sister, Uncle Vanya comes to realize that the professor is a fraud; that the years devoted to making the family estate produce extra income for his brother-in-law's expenses in the city not only required the sacrifice of his own ambitions, but also stifled the hopes of Sonya, the professor's daughter.

Uncle Vanya tries to find a release for the pain of lost illusion by seducing the old professor's bored, young, beautiful, and equally disillusioned second wife, Yelena. She rejects his advances but is charmed by the attentions of Doctor Astrov, a friend of the family secretly loved by Sonya, who is too shy and resigned to express her love openly. Astrov, like the professor, is also somewhat of a crank; however, his enthusiasm for the cultivation of trees is a life-affirming ideal in contrast to the dead ideas of the old professor.

All this hopelessness and human waste is finally challenged by the crazed and absurd revolt of Uncle Vanya. When the professor decides that the estate should be sold and the money invested to raise more income for his city life, Uncle Vanya reacts in maddened horror and insists that the estate belonged originally to Sonya's mother and must pass on to Sonya. Yelena tries to get her husband to apologize to Uncle Vanya, but the professor's attempt to make amends is met by comic violence. Uncle Vanya shoots at him twice, missing both times.

It would be an error to interpret this "shooting scene" as a climax. Chekhov's plays lack conventional dramatic structure; there is no developed action or plot, and one cannot make too much of any conflict between the characters. What matters in Chekhov is the deeply insightful revelation of what makes his ordinary people feel, dream, and live the way they do. The fluid action provides greater opportunity for the characters to reveal their innermost thoughts and impressions. Chekhov seems to be telling us that any life transcends the time, space, and action that determine its direction.

UNDER MILK WOOD
Dylan Thomas
1954
Drama
Comedy

This play for sixty-three voices dramatizes a typical day in the life of the people of the fictional Welsh fishing village of Llareggub. Humorous and lyrical, it combines extravagant language and hilarious caricature to form a very entertaining portrait.

The narrator takes the listeners on a tour of the dreams, memories, songs, gossip, arguments, and work routines of the villagers during one complete day in spring. The play has no main action, but a series of episodes in three parts: night and dreams, waking and morning, afternoon and dusk.

The narrator introduces and comments on each character and episode. Each character, such as the postman, preacher, butcher, prostitute, organist, various drinkers, housewives, children, and deceased, represents an aspect of the culture of the village: its parochialism, sentimentalism, naivete, pettiness, and passion. From this array of characters, two emerge as thematically significant: Captain Cat, the retired, blind sea captain, whose dreams are of life's experiences, of love and lust; and the Reverend Eli Jenkins, who waxes poetic as he asks God's mercy on this place he loves. Polly Garter, whose sex life is the occasion of much of the village gossip, has one of the moments of real pathos in her lament for her lost true love.

The play's chief merits are its musical language, its rhetorical variety, and its Dickensian caricature. Its humors are bawdy, black, impassioned, lyrical, hilarious, and nostalgic. On the other hand, it lacks emotional depth, and substitutes playfulness for development of situation and character.

UNDER THE VOLCANO
Malcolm Lowry
1947
Novel
Stream of Consciousness

This modern masterpiece, a troubling exploration of the theme of commitment, questions the individual's ability to continue to function as a human being in the face of tragic events and seemingly inescapable doom.

Set in Quahnahuac, Mexico, in the late 1930's, the novel is governed by the mind of Geoffrey Firmin, an alcoholic British consul. He has recently resigned his post and is in despair over the loss of his wife, Yvonne, whom he cannot believe will be his again—even when she returns after their divorce.

The continuity of Firmin's thinking is often hard to follow and seems at the mercy of how much he has had to drink, but if his life is in ruins, so is the world which is tearing itself apart in conflicts like the Spanish Civil War.

Given his disappointment in human beings, Firmin's stubborn probing of how people treat one another is heroic. He simply will not let go of ethical issues even though his debilitation seemingly disqualifies him from being taken seriously. As the consul quite rightly insists, he is battling for "the survival of the human consciousness."

Firmin forgets nothing. Other people pretend "not to know" about the causes of volcanic eruptions, which, in their built-up pressures, are so like the political history of the 20th century, but he realizes that, both in the cases of individuals and nations, people have interfered with one another and explosions are the result. Ultimately it is Firmin's surprising integrity of character and language, his way, as he says, of stretching a point, that makes this novel an indispensable exercise of the modern imagination.

U.S.A.
John Dos Passos
1937
Novel
Historical, Trilogy

U.S.A., which comprises the novels The 42nd Parallel, 1919, *and* The Big Money, *is a documentary and fictional history of America in the first three decades of the 20th century. In terms of both content and style, the trilogy offers an innovative and provocative look at the problematic American idea of progress.*

Each novel is divided into four distinct ways of comprehending history. The Newsreel sections report on the public events of the day (wars, scandals, political trials, and the like). The Camera Eye sections are reflective of the author's deeply personal experience and are written in a highly subjective and elusive manner that requires careful concentration. The episodic sections concern the biographies of individuals who are often alienated from the youthful hopes for their lives. Finally, highly condensed and brilliantly ironic biographies of famous figures (Woodrow Wilson, for example) are interspersed in the narrative to give examples of successful but gravely flawed Americans.

In *The 42nd Parallel*, Dos Passos tells of the rise of characters such as J. Ward Moorehouse, a public relations executive, and Charley Anderson, a former aviator who becomes a wealthy airplane manufacturer, dramatizing the growth of both business and labor at the beginning of "the American Century," as one of the Newsreel sections calls it.

1919 focuses on the political consequences of the development of capitalism and shifts attention away from inventors such as Edison featured in the first novel to radicals such as Joe Hill and John Reed.

The Big Money explores the enormous impact of the mass media and Hollywood in capsule biographies of Rudolph Valentino and William Randolph Hearst and in the lives of characters such as Margo Dowling, who enjoy only the brief success that a movie career usually affords.

A steady theme throughout the trilogy is the erosion of individual liberty. In war and at peace, the country seems increasingly corrupted by a mania for self-aggrandizement and a concentration of political and economic power that thwarts the integrity of individual lives.

UTOPIA
Sir Thomas More
1516
Novella
Utopian

A two-part treatise which takes readers to More's ideal realm, Utopia. The contrast between the customs of 16th century Europe and the fictional land illustrate More's ideals. This account defined a new genre, utopian fiction.

When *Utopia* first appeared, many people thought More was relating an incident that had actually happened. To make the realistic framework of the story convincing, More includes himself as a character. He and his friend Peter Giles meet Raphael Hythloday, a Portuguese seaman who has been to the New World.

More, Giles, and Hythloday engage in a conversation concerning the value of entering a king's service in order to promote the public good. This discussion leads to an analysis of the economic and social ills in the Europe of the 16th century.

Book II, actually written first by More, contains Hythloday's description of the representative government, communistic economy, and religious toleration of the Utopians. Although individual Utopians are fallible, the Utopian state is organized upon rational and humanistic principles.

Much controversy concerning *Utopia* has arisen because the Utopians, whose imaginary state is described in Book II, have abolished private property. Marxist critics have claimed More as an early forerunner of Karl Marx, interpreting *Utopia* as a critique of bourgeois capitalism.

More was canonized as a Catholic saint in 1935. His canonization has intensified speculation about the orthodoxy of *Utopia*. Since the Utopians practice mercy killing and divorce, some critics have argued that More did not regard Utopia as a good place. Other critics have insisted that *Utopia* should not be taken seriously, that it is a witty joke.

Modeled in certain respects on Plato's *Republic, Utopia* is an important touchstone for subsequent works which describe imaginary societies.

V

A VALEDICTION: FORBIDDING MOURNING
John Donne
1633
Poetry

Addressing a lover, the greatest of the 17th century English Metaphysical poets argues that although distance or death may separate them, their souls will remain united in love. Donne's poem is of interest to anyone wishing to understand the peculiar blend of passion and logic characteristic of the Metaphysical poets, who have influenced 20th century poetry through the mediation of T.S. Eliot and the New Critics.

Donne's poem is a closely reasoned farewell consisting of a premise and a conclusion that inevitably follows. The first five stanzas establish the premise: The love that unites the souls of Donne and his lover is spiritual and not physical in nature. Therefore, the last four stanzas conclude, physical separation, since it does not alter the spiritual oneness of their souls, is no cause for mourning.

Donne supports this argument by two striking comparisons. In the first, their souls do not separate, but undergo "an expansion,/ Like gold to airy thinness beat." In the second, even if their souls are logically two, they are united like the feet of a drawing compass. His lover's soul, the "fixed foot," occupies the center of an imaginary circle. If Donne's soul, the other foot of the compass, moves outward, his lover's soul "leans and harkens after it."

The exploration of this metaphor in minute detail results in a conceit, a comparison elaborated at considerable length. In this celebrated conceit, one of the best known in English poetry, the feet of the drawing compass function as the "objective correlative" (Eliot's phrase) for the lovers' souls.

The poem's structure resembles a logical argument, but the logic supports an essentially irrational texture consisting of lovers' souls likened to beaten gold and to the feet of a drawing compass. This combination of rational structure and sensuous texture illustrates the characteristic interplay, in Metaphysical poetry, of thought and feeling, ingenuity and emotional intensity.

The ideational lyric of the 20th century, at once controlled and unbridled, cool yet impassioned, is much indebted to this poem and others by Donne.

VANITY FAIR
William Makepeace Thackeray
1847-1848
Novel
Manners, Satire

The subtitle of this dissection of Regency society states that the narrative is "without a hero." Nevertheless, generations of readers have been fascinated by its "heroine," the indomitable social adventuress, Becky Sharp.

From the moment she throws Johnson's *Dictionary,* the patronizing graduation gift of her teacher, out the window of the Sedley coach, to her final pose as respectable philanthropist at novel's end, Becky bluffs, lies, and extorts her way through life.

Becky's foil is her schoolmate, Amelia Sedley, Jos' sister, who is as vapid and passive as Becky is electric and aggressive. Ironically, the seemingly gentle Amelia hurts her secret, patient, and self-effacing suitor, William Dobbin, as thoroughly as rascally Becky victimizes the Osbornes, the Crawleys, and the Sedleys.

Thackeray's fashionable world is populated by "puppets" carved so true to life that his satire almost persuades us that shallowness defines all of humanity, that banality is the great social truth. Because society as a whole fails the moral test, Becky's struggle to climb to the top of so worthless a heap seems more futile than evil and more a waste of her magnificent energy than it does an immoral act deserving moral condemnation.

Becky's pluck renders her ambition charming. By scaling barriers of poverty, class, arrogance, and stupidity, she acquires the aura of a revolutionary figure. She is the scourge that British materialism and complacency deserves.

THE VARIETIES OF RELIGIOUS EXPERIENCES: A STUDY IN HUMAN NATURE
William James
1902
Nonfiction
Religious

Originally written and presented as a series of lectures delivered at the University of Edinburgh, Scotland, in 1901 and 1902, James's expressed purpose was to "use human standards to help us decide how far the religious life commends itself as an ideal kind of human activity..." He examines religious history as it reflects an evolutionary gestalt of human thought; his purpose is to explore "survival of the humanly fittest applied to religious beliefs."

William James makes it clear from the start that he is not concerned so much with institutional religion, theology, or doctrine—what he calls "outer" religion—as he is with individual religious experiences, and the common characteristics shared by those individual experiences. James clearly discusses "religion" in this context, as a state of mind that does not necessarily rely on belief in a deity, or adherence to any doctrine. (In fact, he explains that atheism itself can be approached with religious zeal.)

He begins with basic temperament, or disposition, distinguishing the healthy-minded from the sick soul, and suggests that, for most individuals, one's sense of self is divided between the two. He describes "conversion" as a type of integration and internalization of religious consciousness. In James' words, "religious ideas, previously peripheral in his consciousness, now take a central place...form[ing] the habitual centre of his energy."

James identifies saintliness as a "fruit of religion" that includes an expansive consciousness of things beyond everyday experiences, a sense of continuity with an ideal that provides a great sense of freedom, and a shift of focus toward helping others. Common characteristics of the mystic state include ineffability—experience that defies description; is usually considered a state of knowledge; is fleeting and passive—the individual has no control over the occurrence, or the duration of the mystical experience. Finally, most religious belief has included the notions of sacrifice, confession, and prayer.

Religion is different from philosophy in that with religion, there is "a willingness to close our mouths and be as nothing in the floods and waterspouts of God," providing a "new sphere of power," and "the soul's liberation from oppressive moods."

For James, science does not negate belief, but removes dogma and theology that are proven "absurd or incongruous."

THE VICAR OF WAKEFIELD
Oliver Goldsmith
1766
Novel
Romance

Dr. Primrose, the vicar of Wakefield, is a proud but lovable churchman, as naively unworldly as he is genuinely good and gentle of heart. He suffers all the woes of Job before his children are finally redeemed, his own wealth restored, and his faith in human goodness vindicated. His resilience and undaunted hope have charmed readers for generations.

Dr. Primrose rejects a suitor for his daughter's hand because the man has lost his fortune and seems to live in near poverty. What the Vicar does not discover until the end of the novel is that the impoverished Mr. Burchell is actually Sir William Thornhill, the uncle of Squire Thornhill, a man the vicar respects but who in the course of the novel does him and his family great evil.

The good Vicar does not see things very clearly, but the warm humor of this first-person narrative—the vicar tells his own story—lies in his many trusting and moral observations. The way he sees the world is nowhere near the way it is, but neither is his goodness completely foolish. He wants all the right things for his children: humility, civility, and true simplicity. Instead, they are seduced and jailed. Nevertheless, Dr. Primrose is not rendered absurd by his trusting ways. He is too easy a mark, and his near destruction by the vicious Squire is too easy a victory for evil to enjoy.

Goldsmith's book was admired by sages such as Goethe for the way it made goodness respectable. The Age of Reason had sunk to depths of cynicism and despair, perhaps best expressed in Voltaire's *Candide* (1759). Goldsmith's gentle fable has a philosophical depth as tough-minded as Voltaire's famous fable is savage. A writer who can please us with his wit and charm us with his characters and scene painting has the right to ask us to deem his belief in human goodness credible.

A VINDICATION OF THE RIGHTS OF WOMAN
Mary Wollstonecraft
1792
Nonfiction
Feminist, Philosophical

A major source of inequality in 18th century England was the restriction placed on women's legal and social rights. The feminist movement began with Mary Wollstonecraft's courageous attack on prejudices and conventions that were the cause of numerous injustices imposed on women.

As an expression of protest, *A Vindication of the Rights of Women* seems mild today. Wollstonecraft, following Rousseau on the subject of female education, was mainly concerned with gaining for women the right to be educated so that they would be fit companions for men and have a chance to become equally accomplished intellectually.

Her essay, however, goes beyond arguing for an equal education for women. It is also an expose of numerous injustices to women, such as the denial of the right to vote, to hold office, to own property, or to perform any but the lowest jobs. The impact of the essay stems from examples of abuses drawn from the author's experience rather than from abstract arguments.

Though she makes her case for women's rights with passion, Wollstonecraft nevertheless provides a clear analysis of the problems facing women at that period in history, refuting such traditional views as those of John Milton, who held that women were designed to manifest their attractions in order to gratify the senses of men while docilely obeying them.

Unfortunately, Mary Wollstonecraft was so unconventional—she believed in sexual freedom, open marriage, and birth control—that the scandalous aspects of her life obscured her message during much of the 19th century. In our time, *A Vindication of the Rights of Women* has found its rightful place in the history of feminism.

A VISIT FROM THE GOON SQUAD
Jennifer Egan
2010
Psychological, Thriller

Although considered by its author to be a novel, A Visit From the Goon Squad *resembles a collection of short stories akin to J. D. Salinger's* Nine Stories, *comprised of the interlocking, non-chronological narratives of record executive Bennie Salazar, his assistant Sasha, and the many people in each of their social circles. The reader learns Sasha and Bennie's pasts through a series of their interconnected relationships.*

The first story follows Sasha on a first date with Alex, a newcomer to New York City. She steals a woman's wallet and then returns it to her, revealing her pathological kleptomania. Ironically, her date, Alex, tries to find the thief

(Sasha). Later, in Sasha's future, it is revealed: Sasha had run away to Italy as a teen; her best friend at New York University, Rob, drowned after following Drew, her eventual husband, into the Hudson River; her father left when she was six; she has two kids, Alison and Lincoln, the latter of whom is autistic.

Bennie was once a Bay Area punk musician and mentee of Lou, who formerly held Bennie's position at the company; was married to a public relations protégé of infamous publicist La Doll; and got the famous rock band, The Conduits, off the ground.

The stories come from various perspectives and mediums; some peripheral characters, such as Sasha's friend Rob, and Bennie's high school friend Rhea, narrate in the first person; Sasha and Bennie are experienced from a third-person perspective; and Alison, Sasha's daughter, produces a chapter of slides from a Microsoft PowerPoint slideshow about her family.

The book explores the theme of time, which sometimes presents as an actual character. The phrase "Time's a goon," stated by Bosco, a musician, and later, Bennie, sums up the book well; it's a matter of perspective whether the people or time itself has won the story. Ironically, the novel demonstrates that chronology may not be necessary to understand a complete story.

VOLPONE
Ben Jonson
1605
Drama
Satire

This tightly knit, acerbic comedy set in early 17th century Venice satirizes the debasing effect of human greed.

The aging, corrupt magnifico Volpone (Italian for sly fox) operates a profitable con game. Rich and without heirs, he pretends to be on his deathbed, thereby attracting legacy hunters as carrion attracts flies. The lawyer Voltore (vulture), the old gentleman Corbaccio (raven), the merchant Corvino (crow), and the English lady Madam Would-Be woo Volpone with expensive gifts and favors, each hoping to become his sole heir. They also hope for his early death.

Assisted by his servant Mosca (fly), Volpone plays the suitors against one another. At Mosca's suggestions, Corvino offers his beautiful young wife Celia to Volpone; and Corbaccio, disinheriting his son Bonario (good-natured), makes out his will to Volpone (in expectation of soon getting everything back). These schemes are foiled, however, when Bonario rescues Celia.

To protect themselves, gullers and gulls alike conspire to accuse Bonario and Celia of adultery and plotting murder. The play takes a near-tragic turn when, swayed by Voltore and lying witnesses, the court's verdict goes against the young couple, but still in store are a number of other reversals which leave the couple cleared, the conspirators conspiring against one another, and the fox outfoxed.

Contributing to the play's carrion-breeding atmosphere are its exuberant Renaissance language, imagery, and symbolism. Jonson sacked the annals of Roman decadence, such as Petronius' *Satyricon*, for menus, home remedies, and other sickening details of distorted values. For example, Volpone greets his gold like the morning sun and keeps the dwarf Nano, the eunuch Castrone, and the hermaphrodite Androgyno for entertainment. Jonson's moral purpose is to inspire not only humor but disgust. In this, he succeeds memorably.

WAITING FOR GODOT
Samuel Beckett
1952
Drama
Tragicomedy
This play about two tramps with a dubious appointment is at once philosophical speculation, vaudevillian routine, and metatheater, and it has grown to become one of the world's most influential and widely produced plays.

Vladimir (Didi) and Estragon (Gogo) meet near a tree beside a country road to wait for the arrival of the ambiguous Godot. In order to pass the time, the two companions complain of physical and spiritual ailments, wonder about the likelihood of salvation, abuse and comfort each other, try in vain to remember their past and present purposes, and consider the merits of leaving or of hanging each other. The first act concludes with the arrival of a little boy who brings Godot's regrets: He cannot come today, but he will certainly come tomorrow. The second act, in which the tramps go through the same routines (perhaps a bit more desperately), concludes with the same disappointment. They decide to leave, but neither can move.

Beckett has dramatized the act of waiting, showing how hope can be sustained even in the face of the dimmest prospects. It becomes increasingly clear that Godot, whatever he is or represents—God, death, meaning, or simply an end to waiting—will never come, and that Vladimir and Estragon themselves do not know what to expect of him or how to recognize him if he did come. Yet together they sustain the fiction of purpose and take what little comfort they can in their common predicament.

Two other characters arrive to help the tramps occupy themselves: Pozzo, a pompous slavedriver, and Lucky, his decrepit servant. At Pozzo's brutal command, Lucky rouses himself from his stupor to produce a crazy monologue of mangled learning until he is tackled back into silence. They travel off, leaving the tramps a chance to play at mimicking master and slave; at their second appearance, Pozzo is blind and Lucky mute. Little is remembered. No cause is clear.

The events of this play are singularly uneventful, and it is repetition, rather than progress, which keys the action. It is as if we were witnessing actors who were forced to extemporize eternally while dreaming of the day their script might be delivered. In short, Beckett captures the existential condition of modern man.

WALDEN
Henry David Thoreau
1854
Nonfiction
Nature
These autobiographical essays, notable for their reflective wisdom and beautiful prose style, are an engaging blend of social criticism, philosophical discussion, and nature description.

Anxious to get away from the pressure and clutter of modern civilization, the twenty-seven-year-old Thoreau built a shack on the shore of Walden Pond, a mile or so from Concord, Massachusetts. Though he occasionally had visitors and often visited Concord, he basically lived alone for two years and two months, beginning on Independence Day, 1845.

While there, he kept a journal (as he had begun doing years before), recording his observations of the natural world, his criticisms of the society he had abandoned, and his speculations about the meaning of life. Upon returning to the regular company of mankind, he developed this material into a book.

To give his experience a coherent shape, he incorporated two years into one, so that the book could begin in the summer, descend into autumn and winter, and then emerge into spring, signifying the perpetual regeneration that was his dominant theme.

Like his mentor and fellow Transcendentalist, Ralph Waldo Emerson, Thoreau believed that every man had to find his own way. All around him people were following courses that others had laid out for them and were consequently living lives of frustration rather than of fulfillment. Too often, people were enslaving themselves to the quest for material goods and allowing no time for pursuits of the spirit.

Thoreau sought to correct his age's focus on ephemeral matters, from fashion to news, by making people aware of what was more permanent—the beauties of nature endlessly renewing themselves.

His style and language amply embody his themes. He delves beneath the surface of words and makes cliches fresh. His abstractions become concrete through parables and details of plant and animal life. He addresses the reader directly, not so much as a preacher but as an often wryly comic village raconteur.

THE WALL
Jean-Paul Sartre
1937
Novella

Lending its title to Sartre's only collection of short stories, "The Wall" deservedly has been anthologized frequently and remains among the most widely disseminated of Sartre's published works. Although Sartre stopped writing fiction rather early in his career, "The Wall" still stands as a landmark in the developing technique of the short story.

Set amid the confusion of the Spanish Civil War, which was in progress at the time of its composition, *"The Wall"* documents the capture, imprisonment, and eventual execution of three leftist revolutionaries through the eyes and voice of one of their number, who eventually identifies himself as Pablo Ibbieta. As Pablo recounts his experiences, the wall against which prisoners are lined up to be shot by the firing squad comes to symbolize the absolute boundary between life and death, presaging the later development of Sartre's existentialist philosophy. As Pablo prepares to die, he becomes so detached from his own life and experiences that he no longer seems alive, or even human. That Pablo survives to tell the tale at all, because of ludicrous coincidence, is one of the more skillfully managed ironies in all of modern fiction.

Notable for the economy and occasional coarseness of its language, *"The Wall"* also illustrates what would become Sartre's criteria for the evaluation of fiction written by others: The story is told, in the first person, by an "unprivileged" narrator whose narrative is limited to what he sees, feels, and remembers; the narrator, moreover, is "engaged" in a political cause, and the tale is told entirely from inside the situation being described. In the first few years after its publication, this story was hailed as an example of "authentic," almost primitive fiction. By now, however, it is easy to detect the artifice involved in the production of such evident simplicity, and to sense the hand of the omniscient Sartre behind the words and actions of the supposedly authentic Pablo.

Notwithstanding, the story continues to survive its author, having long since outlived his own brief interest in the writing of narrative prose.

THE WANDERER
Unknown
c. 900
Poetry
Elegiac

Written during the decline of Anglo-Saxon society, this 10th century poem offers a poignant retrospective on a pagan and tribal way of life being supplanted by Western Christendom. Caught in changes which he cannot control, the speaker evokes nostalgia for the past, although the poem acknowledges the moral superiority of the civilization replacing it.

Essentially a monologue set within a frame, this poem of 115 lines creates two personae—the anonymous author who gives a brief introduction and conclusion, and the Wanderer, an aging warrior who roams the world seeking shelter and aid. The Wanderer's monologue divides into two distinct parts, the first being a lament for his exile and the loss of kin, friends, home, and the generosity of his king. In nature he finds no comfort, for he has set sail on the wintry sea. Poignantly the speaker dreams that he is among his companions and embracing his king, only to awaken facing the gray winter sea and snowfall mingled with hail.

In the monologue's second portion, the Wanderer reflects more generally on man's fate, urging resignation and control of emotion as ways of meeting adversity. From the ruined walls and cities he encounters his travels, he witnesses the destruction that has befallen societies other than his own. This portion of the poem introduces the ubi sunt theme, as the Wanderer questions what has become of the things he has known and realizes that many have vanished and all else is fleeting.

The poem, like much other Anglo-Saxon poetry, links pagan and Christian values in an uneasy combination. The authorial voice begins and concludes the poem, referring to God and stressing the importance of faith, themes absent from the Wanderer's speech. The Wanderer's lament, even in the voice of an outcast, upholds Anglo-Saxon tribal values, notably loyalty, generosity, courage, and physical strength. It reflects an overriding concern with the grim and somber aspects of nature and with the power of fate, against which an aged man can pit only resignation and inner restraint. Written in unrhymed Old English alliterative verse, the poem is most readily accessible in modern prose translations.

THE WAPSHOT CHRONICLE
John Cheever
1957
Novel
Family Saga, Series

Cheever's first novel, an episodic tale of various members of the eccentric Wapshot family, is a lyric evocation of a love of nature, of a sense of place and tradition, and of a ceremonial style of life.

The story opens on Independence Day in St. Botolphs, a declining New England seaport on a silted-up river, where live the descendants of Ezekiel, the 17th century progenitor of the present-day Wapshot clan. Honora, the wealthiest member of the family, sends her nephews, Moses and Coverly, out into the world to earn their inheritance by getting jobs and producing children. The death of their father, Leander, the visionary center of the book, brings Coverly, now a father himself, back for the funeral on another Fourth of July, which closes the action of the plot.

The lyric contents of Leander's journal entries, which celebrate the joys and significance of the town's Puritan traditions and sense of the past and his appreciation of nature, are contrasted with the vagaries of modern life as experienced by the boys. The follies of contemporary existence are counterpointed against the deliberateness and ceremoniousness of life in St. Botolphs. Lost innocence, human loneliness, and corruption in the modern world are all redeemed, even if only momentarily, through Cheever's lyric vision of life.

The novel does not ignore the dark side of human existence, however, and its lyricism is underscored by a sense of loss and corrupted innocence. Even the episodic nature of the narrative, which has bothered critics of the novel, contributes to its fragmentary sense of reality, and the book's nostalgia is rescued from sentimentality by Cheever's sharp-eyed observation of the terrors and chaos of life lived even in a quaint, small town. The final note remains, however, that life lived with proper recognition of tradition and nature can offset the confusion of existence in a disoriented and rootless modern world.

WAR AND PEACE
Leo Tolstoy
1865-1869
Novel
War

A protean effort, considered by many to be the greatest novel ever written, WAR AND PEACE offers a panorama of Russian life during the Napoleonic wars.

War and Peace, once read, impresses on the mind a vast tapestry, rich in color and variety that seems the very stuff of life; it shows not only relationships among people in society both in and out of family groups but also relationships between people and families and a nation's destiny.

Eschewing the "great man" theory of history, Tolstoy shows how events are determined by large numbers of people whose actions coalesce at any moment in history to determine the course of events. Arguing that the closer people are to a situation the more they believe they have exercised free will, and the farther away people are from that situation the more they realize that their actions were already determined by past events, Tolstoy demonstrates the theory by means of the characters and actions of his immense novel.

True to the theory, *War and Peace* has no single protagonist. Rather, from among the more than five hundred and fifty characters, both real and imagined, several major families interact with one another: the Rostovs, the Bolkonskys, the Kuragins, the Drubetskoys, and Pierre Bezuhov, the natural son of a Russian nobleman. From among these families, a few male and female characters emerge who become focal points for the narrative: the men—Nikolay Rostov, Andrey Bolkonsky, Boris Drubetskoy, Anatole Kuragin—and the women—Natasha Rostova, Marya Bolkonskaya, and Helene Kuragin. If the reader must narrow the cast of characters even further, the two who stand at the very center from the beginning of the novel to its end are Pierre and Natasha, who after many tribulations are finally married at the novel's conclusion. Other important characters are Kutuzov, the great Russian general who drives Napoleon (the French) out of Russia by understanding that he must allow events to happen as they will, and the Russian peasant, Platon Karatayev, who teaches Pierre much the same lesson.

As the title suggests, the novel is built upon a series of contrasts. Tolstoy balances nonmilitary actions with military actions even to the point of interweaving peaceful interludes during the time that all Russia is at war. Balanced also are alternations in mood: Rapture is balanced with despair, joy with care and trouble, and death with birth.

In the novel, Tolstoy makes the point that there can be no beginning to an event, for one event always flows without interruption out of another. Consequently, *War and Peace* begins in medias res and concludes with youthful dreams for the future.

THE WAR OF THE WORLDS
H. G. Wells
1897
Novel
Science Fiction

Martians invade the Earth in this story that provides the first and definitive picture of the ruthless, aggressive alien being.

Thinking about an account of the discovery of Tasmania by Europeans, Wells's brother suggested the idea for this story: What if other creatures, as superior to humans as Europeans were to Tasmanians, were observing us with plans of conquest?

From that germ came the idea for this, the fourth of a group of early novels that established Wells's fame and popularity.

Soon after the observation of flashes of light on Mars, strange cylinders fall to earth around London. The spaceships and the small craft they send forth destroy Earth's most modern armies with weapons beyond human science.

Told from the point of view of a man living near London, the story is in the form of an eyewitness account of the Martian landings and attacks. The scenes of devastated cities were to become real less than twenty years later in the wreckage of World War I. The heat ray of the Martians sweeps all before it.

Wells depended on the scientific theories of his day for his story: In keeping with the notion that Mars was an older planet than the Earth, the Martians have evolved further than humanity. Their bodies show the effects of this evolutionary specialization: They cannot even digest food but must drink the blood of other creatures. They have become, in a sense, prisoners of their machinery. Without their vehicles, they are nearly helpless in the Earth's heavier gravity.

After human science fails to stop the invaders, the Martians' own "progress" defeats them. Having no resistance to earthly bacteria, they succumb to disease. Since the appearance of this landmark novel, humans have gained a new view of the universe: The possibility of intelligent life in the depths of space becomes (and remains) a captivating idea.

WASHINGTON SQUARE
Henry James
1880
Novel
Psychological
A plain and subdued heiress has a battle of wills with her domineering father over her love for a shallow fortune hunter.

In mid-19th century New York, Dr. Sloper, a fashionable physician, resents his daughter Catherine because her mother died in childbirth and the girl lacks her mother's wit and beauty. Catherine has never had a beau until a handsome, charming young man named Morris Townsend makes advances to her. When she falls overwhelmingly in love with Morris, Dr. Sloper investigates and finds that the suitor is a penniless fortune hunter who hopes to gain Catherine's considerable inheritance.

The doctor orders her to break off the relationship; but, though ordinarily dutiful, she refuses. Dr. Sloper, who scorns his daughter, is at first amused by her resistance. To his surprise and increasing exasperation, she remains firm in her attachment to Morris, even when her father takes her away to Europe. Part of the doctor's opposition to Morris is the fact that they are much alike, and indeed Dr. Sloper got most of his wealth not from his practice but from his wife.

Resisting her father, Catherine develops a will of her own and stands up to him. Unable to love her himself, the doctor considers his daughter unlovable. Gradually becoming aware of this, she clings all the more to Morris, only to have him jilt her when the doctor threatens to disinherit her. Unwilling to let her father dominate her, Catherine refuses to promise not to marry Morris, though she is now through with him, and she is disinherited except for a moderate income from her mother. When Morris returns years later and tries to win her back, she rejects him.

One of the first and best American psychological novels, *Washington Square* was popular on stage and screen as *The Heiress*, and it remains one of James's most accessible and compelling works.

THE WASTE LAND
T. S. Eliot
1922
Poetry
Embodying the widespread disillusionment that followed World War I, Eliot's 433-line poem provides a vivid portrait of the spiritual malaise of the modern age.

At first glance, *The Waste Land* appears fragmentary, even incoherent. The themes of the cruelty of physical existence and the unreality of modern life which dominate the poem's difficult first part, "The Burial of the Dead," give way to the simpler but no less horrifying portrayal of upper and lower-class life in "A Game of Chess": the materialism and fearful ennui of the one, the abortions and physical decay of the other. Parts 3 and 4 are more deeply and overtly ironic. In "The Fire Sermon," the reader finds neither the spiritual love that Buddha and Augustine advised nor the sexual passion that they warned against but only perfunctory sexual encounters that leave the partners as separate and unfulfilled as they were before. In "Death by Water," Eliot turns the symbol of physical and spiritual life into yet another form of death in an age given over to dying.

"What the Thunder Said" is at once the most hopeful and the most pessimistic of the poem's five sections. The fact that it ends with the Hindu word Shantih ("the peace that passeth understanding") repeated three times may be construed (like the thunder heralding the needed, life-bringing rain) as a sign of recovery or as yet another of the many fragments that Eliot and his narrator have shored against their—not the reader's—ruin, a ruin which grows more pervasive, more total throughout the poem.

The ambiguity of the final section of Eliot's dense and difficult poem is appropriate in that Eliot wishes to leave the reader not with a moralistic solution but with a difficult and necessary choice: either the spiritual life that the reader finds so conspicuous by its absence or the spiritual death that Eliot chronicles so exhaustively. Composed as a literary collage and narrated as a stream of consciousness by the blind and androgynous seer, Tiresias, of Greek myth, *The Waste Land* depicts a secularized world in need of spiritual redemption.

Eliot not only wishes to describe the waste land; he wants the reader to experience it, to feel the alienation and the absence as well as the presence of some deeper level of meaning. Eliot's allusions to composers, writers, holy books, and so forth underscore the abiding presence of this deeper level. More importantly, so, too, does the poem's underlying plot, drawn from the legends of the Fisher King and the Holy Grail. The presence of this mythic subtext implies both the fallen, confused state of the modern age and Eliot's alternative to it.

WATERSHIP DOWN
Richard Adams
1972
Novel
Children's

This classic fantasy-adventure story featuring anthropomorphized rabbits that speak the invented Lapine language, became a surprise international best seller. The first-time author from Berkshire, England, wrote twenty more books. Critics have identified references to the Odyssey and Aeneid in the novel.

A young rabbit from Sandleford Warren, Fiver has a prophetic vision of apocalyptic destruction. When the Chief Rabbit won't take him and his brother, Hazel, seriously, they escape with a band of five other males. Hazel becomes their leader. They skirt dangerous castes of warrior rabbits.

Cowslip invites them to join his cozy warren, but after Bigwig is temporarily caught in a snare then rescued, they realize that there are too many rabbit snares in the area and they move on.

Fiver's vision had promised a safe haven and, after wanderings, they settle on the hill of Watership Down. Holly and Bluebell arrive, telling of the complete destruction of their former warren by humans. In search of female rabbits, these male rabbits send four ambassadors to Efrafa Warren, asking for females.

Meanwhile, Hazel leads a raid party on nearby Nuthanger Farm Though Hazel is wounded and rescued by Fiver, they triumphantly return from the Hampshire farm with two does and a buck. The returning ambassadors recount that Efrafa is a dangerous military dictatorship, and that the doe, Hyzenthlay, wished to leave, and promised to recruit other discontented does. Hazel and Bigwig plan a cunning sneak raid on Efrafa, returning with several does.

The warriors of Efrafa, led by Tyrant Woundwort, attack Watership Down, but Bigwig's courage and Hazel's cleverness foil the attack by unleashing the Nuthanger Farm watchdog. The dog kills Woundwort, yet his body is never found. Hazel is almost killed by a cat, but the farm girl, Lucy, saves him. A myth evolves among some Efrafans that Woundwort never died.

The warren of Watership Down prospers.

Several years later, in the epilogue, Hazel wearily dozes in his burrow on a chilly March morning. El-ahrairah, the renowned rabbit folk-hero (whose name means "The Prince with a Thousand Enemies") appears. He is endowed with a silver halo around his ears. He politely invites Hazel to join his legendary warren. Abandoning his now useless body in a ditch, Hazel departs Watership Down with the spirit-guide. Their spirits sprint through the woods amid the first blooms of primroses.

THE WAVES
Virginia Woolf
1931
Novel
Psychological

This experimental novel brilliantly combines dramatic, lyric, and narrative techniques to express the range of human consciousness.

The novel begins with a description, set in italics, of the sea at morning. Then six children in a nursery school, three boys and three girls, present their individual personalities and relationships in a series of soliloquies. The author continues to alternate short italicized accounts of the sea from morning to night with sections devoted to the six at successive stages of their lives.

They are united by their common admiration for a friend named Percival, who emerges only indirectly through their words. In a later section, the friends, grown middle-aged, reunite in a restaurant; in the final section, one of them, Bernard, reflects in old age on the meaning of his own and their lives.

Though the characters differ considerably, from farmer's wife to university don, they all speak in very much the same stylized way throughout. They reflect on youthful hopes, the competition among them, the forging of a personal identity, the death of a loved one (Percival), and fulfillment or the lack of it.

The six characters may also be understood as various aspects of one person contemplating life. Thus, Woolf suggests that each person contains the male and the female, the married and the unmarried, the fulfilled and the unfulfilled.

Woolf had intended to call this novel *The Moths* but changed her mind, no doubt because she believed that the rhythm, regularity, and relentlessness of ocean waves were more appropriate symbolically to her theme. The author thereby resolves, at least artistically, the ancient dispute between those who see permanence and change, respectively, as the basic reality. The waves are both, and the pattern of people's lives—including the mysterious pattern of each life—continues as individuals change.

THE WAY OF ALL FLESH
Samuel Butler
1903
Novel
Satire

A milestone in the history of the English novel, The Way of All Flesh *tells the story of Ernest Pontifex, who manages to break free of the stultifying Victorian value system into which he was born.*

Although written in 1885, The Way Of All Flesh was not published until one year after Butler's death in 1902. Largely autobiographical, the novel is said to have dealt the Victorian ethos its final blow and pulled England into the 20th century. Through the story of Ernest Pontifex and his godfather, the novel's narrator, Overton, Butler attacks institutions that the Victorians held sacred, such as the Church, traditional family structure, and the educational system; in addition, he promulgates such new ideas as "creative evolution," "life force," and "unconscious memory," thus anticipating such thinkers as Henri Bergson, Sigmund Freud, C. G. Jung, and George Bernard Shaw.

As narrator and friend of the Pontifexes from his earliest youth, Overton is in a position to tell the story of five generations of the Pontifex family. Ernest, Overton's favorite, is fourth generation Pontifex, and his experiences during his formative years reflect the experiences of his father before him, as each son struggles in his own way against the dictates of society as embodied in parents and surrounding institutions. Ernest breaks the vicious cycle by providing foster parents for his own children and an atmosphere he considers more conducive to their mental and physical health.

Although Ernest liberates himself from the strictures placed on him by Victorian sanctimony, it takes him many years, several occupations, a jail term, a bigamous marriage, the subtle guidance of Overton, and a substantial inheritance from an aunt to emerge from his struggle against cant and hypocrisy and move toward individuation, liberty, and truth.

Although *The Way of All Flesh* is not as closely knit structurally as such other great 19th century initiation novels as Charles Dickens' *Great Expectations*, George Eliot's *Adam Bede*, and Thomas Hardy's *Jude The Obscure*, neither is it formless or lacking in novelistic interest, as earlier critics maintained. Rather, its form is more subtle, being expressed not so much in linear plot as in counterpoint and ironic juxtaposition; also, its satire is delivered in short thrusts rather than in well-developed, artful scenes. Characterization of both major and minor figures is excellent, though of all the characters, Overton is most clearly developed, since his consciousness is ultimately the shaping force of this classic novel.

THE WAY OF THE WORLD
William Congreve
1700
Drama
Comedy

In this witty Restoration comedy, an urbane, man-about-London schemes to gain his beloved's hand in marriage despite the opposition of her aunt.

Mirabell, the play's hero, wants to marry Millamant, but her aunt, Lady Wishfort, opposes the match. Though Lady Wishfort cannot prevent their marrying, Millamant will lose half her fortune, six thousand pounds, unless she can secure her aunt's approval. Neither Mirabell nor Millamant is mercenary, but neither wants to be cheated. Hence, Mirabell devises a series of intricate schemes to trick Lady Wishfort into consenting. All of these plots apparently fail, however, when Fainall, who has married Lady Wishfort's daughter, threatens to expose Mrs. Fainall's affair with Mirabell unless Lady Wishfort turns over to him her fortune and Millamant's six thousand pounds.

Mirabell has one last trick, though. Before marrying Fainall, Lady Wishfort's daughter had conveyed her entire estate to Mirabell; Mirabell produces the deed of conveyance. Having no money of his own, Fainall discovers that he is dependent upon the good will of his wife and Mirabell and so must yield. Lady Wishfort is so grateful that her daughter has escaped disgrace that she consents to the Mirabell-Millamant wedding. Thus, true love overcomes greed, and Mirabell proves himself worthy of Millamant by overcoming Fainall in their battle of wits.

With its complex plot, disguises, and sudden reversals, the play might seem like an improbable farce. Yet it is very much tied to the real world in that it explores whether one can live honestly amid corruption. Mirabell and Millamant see the unhappiness of the Fainalls and the folly of Lady Wishfort, who, at fifty-five, seeks to rival her youthful niece. By their actions and language, particularly in the famous Proviso scene in the fourth act in which the lovers draw up a set of rules for civilized marital behavior, they prove that they have the intelligence and good nature to accommodate themselves to the way of the world without being tainted by it.

WHAT IS THE WHAT:
THE AUTOBIOGRAPHY OF VALENTINNO ACHAK DENG
Dave Eggers and Valentino Deng
2006
Novel
Autobiographical, War

The story of the Lost Boys (and Lost Girls) who fled the Second Sudanese Civil War is presented as a 2006 autobiography. Northern Arab bandits plunder, rape, and massacre peaceful tribal villages in the Christian south on a massive scale. Deng, a young victim, must find his way to safety and freedom, against all odds, as he grows to realize the importance of "possibility."

The book opens in the middle of a robbery: Deng is tied up and beaten with a rifle butt in his Atlanta apartment. The robbery experience is layered with memories of Deng's home village and upbringing: the burning down of his village, the abduction of his sisters, and murder of his relatives, his escape, the march through desert while escaping either Arabs or Southern militia, his near starvation and dehydration, his loss of walking companions to lions, Arabs, bombs, and his eventual arrival in an Ethiopian refugee camp where he spends three years as a cook before he becomes one of the few to be brought to America. In America, Deng manages to find work and graduate from college.

The book offers a double critique of both the Sudanese and Americans, identifying virtues and flaws, cultural assets and deficiencies, anecdotes of heroism and cowardice within their respective cultural norms. Interlaced into the narrative are the stories of numerous Southern Sudanese in the United States: their foibles, industry, problems, failures, and achievements. Deng's romance with Tabitha turns tragic when another Sudanese man murders her and attempts to commit suicide by jumping off a bridge. With great irony, after surviving such extraordinary dangers, Deng is beaten and robbed by American thugs, and then guarded by a small boy who sits and watches television, and in whom Deng recognizes something of himself. Deng tries to tell him his story, but the boy refuses to listen.

As in Homer's *Odyssey,* the theme of lying and exaggerating plays a substantial role in the narrative. The reader is asked to judge, ethically, what has happened in the lives of numerous people. A disarming honesty, accompanied by an appreciative astonishment of life's unexpected ironies, provides suspenseful energy.

The book's title refers to the Dinka tribe's creation story in which God gives man a choice of gifts—cattle or the "What." When man asks God What is the What, God replies he won't explain, but man must decide now. The Dinka man chooses cattle, a definite known quantity. While at first, Deng sees The What as a dangerous, irrational entity, representing unknown evil, gradually, in telling his story, he realizes it may refer to knowledge, possibility and freedom.

WHAT'S BRED IN THE BONE
Robertson Davies
1985
Novel
Psychological, Trilogy

After growing up in a provincial Canadian town, Francis Cornish moves into the larger world where he hopes to succeed as a painter. Davies' account of Cornish's triumphs and trials provides for a novel that is witty, rich in detail, and varied in settings and characters.

Cornish has already died when the narrative opens, and his official biographer admits that he has failed to discover the significance of his subject's life. Two spirits then appear; one of them is Cornish's "Daimon"—a kind of guardian angel—who reveals what the biographer has missed. At times, the spirits interrupt the quickly paced narrative to comment on how particular events affected Cornish.

Although Cornish's childhood in Canada appeared outwardly dull, those years formed a basis for the life to come, and on the surface, it seemed a rich life. After preparatory school in Toronto, Cornish went to Oxford University where he gained distinction. Wealthly through inheritance, he then traveled on the Continent to pursue his artistic ambitions and to serve as a British spy. This combination led him into a number of adventures, including one close to prewar Nazi Germany.

When the war ended, Cornish decided to return to Canada. He was by then a respected authority on art and a famous collector. He had, however, failed as a painter, because his two materpieces were in truth fakes.

So what had Cornish truly accomplished? Were his years distinguished by anything special? Did he make any worthwhile contributions to art? Through the voice of the Daimon, Davies considers these questions and draws conclusions regarding the life and times of Francis Cornish. In his search for answers to Cornish's riddle, Davies reaffirms the joy of living. On one hand, he shows that life brims with contradictions: happiness and sorrow, beauty and ugliness, triumph and disappointment, significance and triviality. At the same time, though, he shows that those very opposites lend life its delight, its zest, its meaning.

WHO'S AFRAID OF VIRGINIA WOOLF?
Edward Albee
1962
Drama
Tragicomedy

This violent, often powerful, drama is rich with symbols and black humor, using the apparently restrained world of the academic community to represent the emotional and philosophical turmoil in the United States of the early 1960's.

From the opening of the front door at 2 o'clock in the morning, to the final knock-down-and-drag-out battle hours later, the events of this play sweep the audience along in a maelstrom of savage humor and emotion.

George, a history professor in his 40's and Martha, his somewhat older wife, have returned from a party with her father, the president of the college at which George teaches. Nick and Honey, a young instructor and his wife, join them for after-party drinks. The rest of the drama centers on the confrontations that occur among these four characters.

There is much talk about George and Martha's son, who is to be twenty-one the next day. Eventually, however, it becomes clear that the son is fictitious, the product of a perverse game that George and Martha have played during the years of their turbulent marriage. It also becomes evident that although they quarrel violently, they are just as violently dependent upon each other. So, although Martha tries to cheat on George with Nick, and they are often cruel to each other, in the end they are tied by bonds that can be broken only by death.

Nick and Honey have their own secrets, including the fact that Honey trapped Nick into marriage. They are four hurt and vulnerable people, who wound each other because they have nothing better to do. As the four characters continue to drink and challenge each other, more protective layers are stripped away. Finally, each of them stands exposed and exhausted. The audience lives through the experience with them, reaching a kind of emotional catharsis at the end.

Albee has a powerful ability to manipulate the audience, unleashing a flood of conflicting emotions. Although the play is very derivative of August Strindberg, particularly *The Dance of Death*, it is one of the most powerful American plays of the second half of the 20th century. Albee has not lived up to the promise of this play, but it stands as a powerful vision of the inner chaos that many people see at the root of contemporary American society.

THE WILD SWANS AT COOLE
William Butler Yeats
1917
Poetry

This book of poems serves as a transition between the increasingly spare, personal, and public poems of the middle of Yeats's career and the great mythic poems of the later Yeats.

The title poem, "The Wild Swans at Coole," contains the most important themes of the collection and is one of the landmark poems of modern poetry. The speaker stands contemplating the wild swans that float on the water at the country estate of Lady Gregory, Yeats's patron. They cause him to reflect on the years that have passed and the changes in himself since he first saw these swans, seemingly the same ones, nineteen years before.

The speaker's reverie suggests attitudes about death and eternity and the possibility of immortality. The poem is essentially romantic, with a distinctly modern obliqueness, in its treatment of these themes, and in the movement between external nature and the inner longings of the poet.

Many of the poems of this collection were written during the time of World War I, a period of great personal as well as international turmoil. One of the personal tragedies of Yeats's life was the death of the brilliant Major Robert Gregory, the only son of his patron and a symbol for Yeats of a kind of enlightened aristocracy which he felt was crucial to Ireland's future.

Yeats wrote a number of powerful poems on Robert Gregory's death, genuinely lamenting him and, at the same time, using the occasion to meditate on death in general.

The transition to Yeats's important later poetry begins in this book with the introduction of poems based on his theories of the mask, cones, gyres, phases of the moon, and so on—as later detailed in his book, A VISION (1925).

Yeats infuses personal aspects of his private life, such as the restored tower which he seeks to make his home, with great symbolic and universal meaning in a foreshadowing of his later efforts to wed the temporal and transcendent worlds in a unified whole.

THE WIND IN THE WILLOWS
Kenneth Grahame
1908
Novel
Children's

The Wind in the Willows—in structure more like a group of related short stories than a novel—is by turns an idyll, a slapstick farce, and a mock-heroic adventure as it relates the riverbank exploits of Rat, Mole, Badger, and Toad.

The charm of *The Wind in the Willows* lies in the timeless physical world Grahame has created—"The River Bank," "The Open Road," "The Wild Wood," to quote the first three chapter titles—and in its principal characters: the powerful and phlegmatic Badger; the steady and loyal Water Rat; the impulsive and volatile Mole; and, above all, the vain, feckless, yet lovable Toad. This is one of the those rare classics which appeals equally to adults and children.

The chapters cut back and forth between several main story lines. At the outset Mole, weary of his humdrum underground life, ventures to the river and makes friends with Rat. Later, one winter day, Mole incautiously sets out alone to explore the Wild Wood, full of sinister weasels and stoats and ferrets, and has to be rescued by Rat; both take shelter in the spacious burrow of Badger.

Meanwhile Toad, a wealthy animal who lives in the "finest house on the whole river," as he modestly puts it, involves Mole and Rat in his most recent enthusiasm, rambling about the countryside in a horse-drawn "gipsy caravan." The caravan is wrecked by an automobile, and now Toad is wild about motoring. After a number of misadventures he is imprisoned for auto theft; by the time he escapes, Toad Hall has been usurped by the stoats and weasels, whom Toad and his friends must evict by force of arms.

The characters, especially Rat and Mole, are held by the delights of home, drawn by adventure and the open road, just as children desire simultaneously to remain dependent and to grow up. To this *The Wind in the Willows* owes much of its universality.

WINESBURG, OHIO
Sherwood Anderson
1919
Short Story
Collection

This book, the best by the most influential American storyteller of his day, reveals and celebrates the lives of men and women in a small Midwestern farm town.

The central character, insofar as the book has one, is George Willard. This young reporter for the Winesburg Eagle draws the confidences of many of the lost souls who, misunderstood or ignored by their fellow townspeople, are mostly silent and invisible. When George leaves town at the end of the book, he plans to become a writer—to give voice to the voiceless, as Anderson does here.

Of the twenty-five stories in *Winesburg, Ohio,* among the most striking are "Hands," "Adventure," and "The Untold Lie." Each is also typical: Anderson's stories are plotless, depending for their effects not on action but on moments of revelation. In "Hands," for example, hardly anything happens. A man named Wing Biddlebaum tells George Willard that he must not waste his life—he must "begin to dream"—and George is struck by the expressiveness of Wing's hands. Then the reader learns that Wing had been an inspired teacher who was fired for innocently putting his hands on his pupils. A wasted life is poignantly revealed in a few pages.

All that happens in "Adventure" is that a young woman named Alice Hindman, abandoned by her lover years earlier, runs naked out of her house into the rain. This small event, the culmination of a long period of growing restlessness, leads her to try "to face bravely the fact that many people must live and die alone."

In "The Untold Lie," a farm hand named Hal Winters confesses to Ray Pearson, a fellow worker, that he has gotten his girlfriend pregnant and asks if he should marry her. Ray, who knows Hal's duty but feels trapped by his own marriage, remains silent. "Whatever I told him would have been a lie." Anderson's stories, simply and sympathetically told, are timeless in their revelation of secret lives.

WINNIE-THE-POOH
Alan Alexander Milne
1926
Short Story
Children's, Series

A. A. Milne fashioned the loveable, slow-witted Winnie-the-Pooh after his son's toy teddy bear, whose adventures with Christopher Robin, (named after Milne's son) and their other toy animal friends, teach the importance of enjoying simple things and thinking creatively. These stories have been translated into more than fifty languages, with numerous adaptations for radio, cinema, and television productions. Pooh Bear has become a worldwide icon for the innocence and simplicity of childhood.

These small adventure stories center on the pudgy bear and his child friend, Christopher Robin, as they explore the Hundred Acre Wood with their other stuffed toy friends: Eeyore, the depressed and morose donkey with a penchant for losing his tail; the wise Owl whose wisdom is sometimes questionable; timid Piglet, who tries to put on a brave face; and Tigger, a hyperactive and rambunctious toy tiger, who drops in at inopportune moments. Winnie-the-Pooh's adventures range from trying to trick bees into thinking he is a cloud so he can steal honey, to getting stuck in Rabbit's den because he ate too much. Pooh's quizzical nature at first seems silly, but soon the reader realizes Pooh Bear's many questions are reasonable.

Winnie-the-Pooh is a book that helps both children and adults learn to look at things with a new, creative perspective. Through these short stories, readers see that Winnie-the-Pooh views the world with happiness and empathy. Friendships are of the greatest importance, even over his constant craving for honey and jam. The bear is rarely discouraged, and solves problems by thinking a little oddly. Each chapter is a complete story in itself, offering simple lessons for children, and important reminders for adults.

THE WINTER'S TALE
William Shakespeare
1611
Drama
Comedy, Romantic

Like Shakespeare's other romances this play hinges on near-miraculous restorations, reconciliations, and resurrections, following tragic disruptions and misunderstandings, much like a fairy tale.

One Winter's Tale, Theof Shakespeare's last plays, this work has the wisdom of age. The play's first half is wintry, with harsh, violent actions bringing about suffering, loss, and death. The second half, sixteen years later, offers a rural springtime festival and culminates in a moving, unsuspected bestowal of grace.

Like Shakespeare's earlier tragic hero Othello, Leontes becomes insanely jealous of a chaste wife, but Leontes' jealousy is far more sudden and unsubstantiated, so that Shakespeare can focus on its results: Leontes' loss of wife, children, and friends. Unlike Othello, Leontes lives on, in penitence.

The first half, nevertheless, ends in hope, for the baby daughter he had sought to abandon is taken in by an old shepherd. Sixteen years later, she is being courted by a disguised prince, son of Polixenes, whom Leontes had accused of adultery with his wife. Polixenes' rash outrage at discovering that his son's beloved is a commoner echoes Leontes' earlier foolishness. Thanks to two faithful courtiers, however, all is made right by the end. Leontes, Polixenes, and their children are reunited, and even Leontes' wife Hermione, presumed dead, is restored to him in the magical final scene.

This is one of the most beautiful endings in Shakespeare and shows a move beyond his earlier bleak, despairing tragedies, *Hamlet, Othello*, and *King Lear*, into a true spirit of rebirth. Perhaps not coincidentally, the three principal women in this play are among Shakespeare's most sublime creations.

THE WOMAN IN THE DUNES
Kōbō Abe
1962
Novel
Existential, Allegorical

The novel's allegorical, existential atmosphere is immediately established by its focus on a teacher and amateur ento-mologist, Niki Jumpei, who goes on a vacation to a remote Japanese sea coast village.

The teacher is caught by villagers, who preserve their territory from the encroaching sand dunes by maintaining a line of houses whose occupants shovel them free of sand every night in Sisyphean labors. Since he cannot climb out of the sand pit formed by their digging, he is forced to stay in one such dugout with its occupant, a young widow. His changing reactions to this entrapment form the body of the novel.

Kafkaesque in its straightforward exploration of a single, symbolic human situation, pitiless in its objective tone and concentration on realistic, meticulously rendered detail, the novel grips the reader, who is forced to consider the hero's situation as emblematic of everyone's.

Is all our work as meaningless as the protagonist's, shoveling away the sands which will inevitably return tomorrow? Are all our relationships as cruel, as dominated by force or the harsh requirements of our physical needs? Are we all insect specimens, trapped by walls we cannot scale? Are we all anonymous animals, foolishly suffering under the illusion that our actions and discoveries can make a difference in life?

As the hero undergoes changes in his attitude toward his imprisonment, the novel seems to suggest some value in the human relationship between the hero and the woman (never named). Meanwhile, the cruelty and selfishness of the villagers and, indeed, of the hero (who at first dominates the widow with force as the villagers dominate him), the nemesis provided by the indifferent sand, the poverty and meaninglessness of human relationships in this universe acquire mythic force.

This novel, made into a prizewinning film, reflects Abe's continuing interest (reflected in other novels, short stories, and plays) in the problem of finding one's identity in our modern, urbanized, alienating society.

THE WOMAN WARRIOR:
MEMOIRS OF A GIRLHOOD AMONG GHOSTS
Maxine Hong-Kingston
1976
Nonfiction
Autobiography

A pastiche of memories and imaginings about a first-generation Chinese immigrant family—their former life in China, and the challenges of integrating into an utterly alien culture that is occupied by seemingly absurd "ghosts."

The first chapter of *The Woman Warrior* was originally published as the 1975 short story, "No Name Woman," about a Chinese aunt (Hong-Kingston's father's sister) who became pregnant while her husband worked in America. She was castigated, and villagers ransacked her family's home. Upon giving birth in a pigsty, she killed herself and her newborn daughter, by jumping into the family well. It was forbidden to ever speak of her; for her family, she never existed. This story parallels, in contrast, that of Hong-Kingston's mother's sister, Moon Orchid, whose story comprises the fourth chapter, "The Western Palace." Hong-Kingston's mother, Brave Orchid, convinces her sister, Moon Orchid, to immigrate and reclaim the Chinese husband who abandoned her and their daughter thirty years earlier, when he left for

America and never returned. He is a physician, and has an American family who know nothing about his Chinese wife or daughter. When Brave Orchid finally confronts the husband on behalf of Moon Orchid, the two are flatly rejected, and the aunt, Moon Orchid, has no place to go. She eventually retreats into insanity.

At first, the second chapter, "White Tigers," seems to be unrelated to the autobiographical nature of the story. The author takes liberty in retelling the Chinese story of Fa Mu Lan, who grew up to become a great warrior, saving her aged father by taking his place in battle. In truth, the magical realism in this chapter provides a mythological base that reflects both the "magical" and foreign (to Western readers) thinking of the mother, Brave Orchid. It also contrasts with the powerlessness Hong-Kingston felt as child, growing up in the household of such an intractable, domineering mother.

One of the most captivating elements in the narrative is the juxtaposition of "Western" and "Chinese" thought processes. For a western reader, Brave Orchid's logic seems crazy. At the end of the novel she admits that the Chinese "like to say the opposite." If a child is beautiful, parents are obligated to call her ugly. Within a few short examples, the author evokes the deep pathos of a western mind trying to comprehend the mother's Chinese logic.

WOMEN IN LOVE
D. H. Lawrence
1920
Novel
Historical

A narrative of the friendships, loves, and often violent quarrels among two men and two women, the novel chronicles the social milieu of early 20th century British intellectuals and artists against the backdrop of the spiritual malaise engendered by World War I.

Continuing the saga of the last generation of Brangwens in a sequel to *The Rainbow*, this novel narrates the tragic involvement among four characters, Rupert Birkin, Ursula Brangwen, Gudrun Brangwen, and Gerald Critch. Gerald's seething passion for Gudrun culminates in his own suicide as he wanders into the Alpine snow where he will freeze to death. Rupert's love for Ursula, equally violent and potentially destructive at times, achieves an uneasy equilibrium that is upset by the death of his close friend Gerald, whom Rupert has loved as much as he has Ursula.

The novel opens with the wedding of Gerald's younger sister and with the boredom experienced by the Brangwen sisters, who are bound to tedious work in the small northern England town of their birth. Rupert's involvement with a willful, domineering aristocratic woman ceases as he becomes increasingly attached to Ursula. In turn, Gerald pursues and captures the mercurial artist Gudrun, and the four decide to vacation together in the Alps. Gerald's untimely end is occasioned by Gudrun's cruel rejection of his affection after the departure of Ursula and Rupert.

In part a roman a clef of Lawrence's relations with Frieda von Richtofen and their friends Katherine Mansfield and Middleton Murry, the novel is also an allegorical representation of the social crisis of Britain in the years immediately following the Great War. Less obviously salacious than *Lady Chatterley's Lover*, the novel is a more sober and philosophical assessment of the decline of Britain's ruling classes.

THE WONDERFUL WIZARD OF OZ
L. Frank Baum
1900
Novel
Children's, Fantasy

Dorothy is a young girl living on the dreary Kansas prairie with her dull Aunt Em, Uncle Henry, and dog, Toto, when her home is picked up by a cyclone and lands in the magical, whimsical land of Oz. Once there, she and her new friends journey to receive the things they most desire from the Wonderful for Wizard of Oz. Dorothy's greatest wish is to return home.

When she and Toto have landed, Dorothy is greeted by a crowd of Munchkins and the Good Witch of the North, who are thrilled that her house's landing has crushed the Wicked Witch of the East. They give Dorothy the dead witch's silver shoes. When Dorothy asks how to get to Kansas, they say only the Wizard of Oz in the Emerald City may know, and they send her down a yellow-paved road to find him.

Dorothy meets three individuals who have their own wishes for Oz to fulfill: the Scarecrow wants a brain; the Tin Woodsman wants a heart; and the Cowardly Lion wants courage. Each helps Dorothy by using the exact attributes they think they lack.

After many obstacles, they arrive in the Emerald City, and are given green goggles to "protect" their eyes from the city's glory, which actually just tints everything green. When Dorothy asks to return to Kansas, Oz tells her she and her companions must kill the Wicked Witch of the West.

The witch sees them coming, and sends out forces to attack them. The Scarecrow and the Tin Woodsman are left for dead, and Dorothy and the Lion are captured as servants. After weeks of servitude, Dorothy panics and pours a bucket of water on the witch, accidentally killing her. Dorothy becomes the commander of the Winged Monkeys by seizing the witch's Golden Cap. She saves her friends, and they all return to the Emerald City, demanding their wishes from the Wizard.

The Wizard is actually a ventriloquist from Omaha who landed in Oz much as Dorothy has. He was revered as a Wizard, and never confessed. He gives Dorothy's companions petty symbols to increase their confidence, but has nothing for Dorothy. They build a hot air balloon to return Dorothy and the Wizard to Kansas, but it flies off before Dorothy can jump in.

Finally, Dorothy finds Glinda, the Good Witch of the South, who uses the Golden Cap to restore Oz: the Scarecrow rules the Emerald City; the Tin Woodsman, rules the West; the Lion, rules the forest; and the Winged Monkeys are set free. Glinda reveals that Dorothy has had the power to send herself home all along, and when Dorothy clicks her heels three times, she returns to her home in Kansas.

A WRINKLE IN TIME
Madeleine L'Engle
1962
Novel
Children's, Fantasy

After a nighttime visit from a mysterious, strange woman, teenaged Meg Murry, her little brother Charles Wallace, and their new friend Calvin are whisked away in a journey through space and time to rescue Meg's father, who went missing on a government mission investigating the fifth dimension. This classic is accessible to readers of all ages with an exciting science fiction/fantasy plot that also explores issues of religion and morality.

Meg Murry wishes she were brilliant, like her scientist parents and her precocious, intuitive brother, Charles Wallace, but she would settle for pretty. Her loving father has gone missing on a government mission, leaving the family bereft. But when a strange woman named Mrs. Whatsit swoops in on a "dark and stormy night" and tells Mrs. Murry that "there is such a thing as a tesseract"—the theoretical concept Meg's parents had been studying—everything changes.

Mrs. Whatsit returns with Mrs. Who (who only speaks in quotations) and Mrs. Which, and whisks away Meg, Charles Wallace, and their new friend Calvin, who connects with Charles. The "women" turn out to be billions of years old Messengers of God, and were once stars. (This confluence of Judeo-Christian God and science is prominent in the novel.)

Mr. Murry has gone missing while fighting IT, a shadow that accounts for all Evil. He is stuck on Camazotz, a planet under IT's grasp, and the children must save him. They travel through the universe by tessering, or using the fifth dimension, meaning "you can travel through space [and time] without having to go the long way around." The Happy Medium tells them that IT is why there is evil on Earth, and people from Jesus to Shakespeare have been sent there to fight IT.

The three "women" send the children to Camazotz, an eerie dystopia. When the children meet IT, Charles realizes he must be possessed by IT's spirit in order to save their father, thus turning Charles evil. Meg finds Mr. Murry and frees him from prison. Meg, Calvin, and Mr. Murry tesser off of Camazotz, leaving Charles Wallace behind because they do not want to sever his mind. The tessering paralyzes Meg and she is healed by Aunt Beast, a tentacled, comforting creature.

Meg realizes she is the only one who can save Charles because she knows him best. The "women" say her weapon is the one thing IT does not have: love. Meg uses love to save Charles and the family safely returns to Earth.

WUTHERING HEIGHTS
Emily Brontë
1847
Novel
Gothic, Romance

Readers have thrilled to the intensity of characterization in this moody tale. Catherine Earnshaw and Heathcliff are larger than life, demonic souls whose turbulence is mirrored in the windswept Yorkshire moors that provide the novel's setting.

The novel, which features an unusually intricate plot, traces the effects that unbridled hate and love have on two families. Ellen Dean, who serves both families, tells Mr. Lockwood, the new tenant at Thrushcross Grange, the bizarre stories of the house's family, the Lintons, and of the Earnshaws of Wuthering Heights. Her narrative weaves the four parts of the novel, all dealing with the fate of the two families, into the core story of Catherine and Heathcliff. The two lovers manipulate various members of both families simply to inspire and torment each other in life and death.

Heathcliff dominates the novel. Ruthless and tyrannical, he represents a new kind of man, free of all restraints and dedicated totally to the satisfaction of his deepest desires no matter what the cost to others or himself. He meets his match in Catherine, who is also his inspiration. Her visionary dreams and bold identification with the powers of storm and wind at Wuthering Heights are precisely what make Heathcliff worship her.

When Catherine betrays Heathcliff by marrying Edgar Linton, Heathcliff feels she has betrayed the freedom they shared as children on the moor. He exacts a terrible revenge. However, he is no mere Gothic villain. Somehow, the reader sympathizes with this powerful figure who is possessed by his beloved.

The interchangeability of their souls—Catherine makes the astonishing statement, "I am Heathcliff"—calls attention to Emily Bronte's powerful projection of her own surcharged identity. Unlike her talented sister Charlotte, who wrote several novels, Emily wrote one great book, but into it she poured a vastness of contradictory emotions.

Y

YENTL THE YESHIVA BOY
Isaac Bashevis Singer
1962
Short Story

A young woman, rebelling against the limitations placed upon her gender by society, disguises herself as a man in order to complete formally studies that she had begun informally at home with her now-deceased father.

Yentl, the daughter of a rabbi, so excels at studies of the holy texts that clearly she is more man than woman. When her father dies, Yentl cuts off her braids, dons her father's clothes, and leaves her village, in flight from the fate of all young married women: domestic drudgery. Yentl takes a new name, Anshel, to complete the male disguise.

In Bechev she studies at the Yeshiva, a boy's school. She grows close to Avigdor, another student, who confides the reason he is still single: The betrothed's family rejected him. Anshel boards with Hadass, the lost love of Avigdor, and her family, where she learns that Avigdor was rejected because his brother committed suicide in a fit of melancholy.

Anshel loves Avigdor for his male like-mindedness. He is her ideal companion, and she is his. She increases the confusion in her life by reasoning that a marriage of Hadass to herself will exact vengeance for Avigdor's rejection by Hadass' family and bring Avigdor by association closer to Anshel. Anshel marries Hadass, sustaining the illusion over months while the stress of deceiving so many people becomes unbearable. Meanwhile, Avigdor marries Peshe, a materialistic shopkeeper abandoned by her husband.

Singer swiftly concludes the story without resolving the conflicts or revealing Anshel's true identity, except to a surprised Avigdor. The conflict between law and unpredictable nature provides the tension. Life will not be legislated, even by a Jewish society whose ancient legal code has apparently covered all situations. We see it operating in the consciences of the main characters but not controlling their action, a fact that Singer relishes. Even natural boundaries and enclosures, such as Yentl's physical sexuality, prove ineffective against human desire.

The story provides a drama of longing, but light drama, told for the fun of such confusion more than for its meaning. Singer's telling moves swiftly and lightly, unburdened by lengthy description or comment. The story has a meaning, but it works as the meanings in fairy tales. If you want to find it you must look for it. The real reason the story exists, as any child knows, is for the telling and hearing, the pictures and the people.

YOU CAN'T GO HOME AGAIN
Thomas Wolfe
1940
Novel
Autobiographical

George Webber, an American writer, is torn between his desire for fame and success and his devotion to truth and the cause of freedom. In this, his last novel, Wolfe continues his attempt to express the American experience in all its variety of people and places and to delineate the American character and soul.

George Webber returns to Libya Hill, a small town in the South, to find it is no longer the peaceful place of his youth. The town is caught up in frenzied real estate speculation that precedes the stock market crash of 1929. Then publication of his first novel angers Libya Hill's citizens; they write him abusive, threatening letters.

Back in New York, Webber ends a love affair with a stage designer and moves to Brooklyn, determined to live among ordinary people and devote himself to his next book.

When the book is finished, Webber travels to Europe. In London he meets Lloyd McHarg, an American writer who is all Webber yearns to be. Webber is disillusioned when he discovers that McHarg is an alcoholic, unfulfilled by his fame and success.

In Germany, where both his first and second books have been well received, Webber tastes fame and success, but he is troubled by the fear and hate which the Nazi regime has aroused since coming to power, and by the tyranny the Nazis have imposed on the country. Webber had lived happily in Germany before his first book was published. Now he realizes, just as he had when he returned to Libya Hill, that he cannot be at home in Germany, either.

Returning to America, Webber breaks with his editor. His view of his role as a writer and his editor's view are irreconcilable. In a long letter to his editor, Webber reviews his whole life and announces his intention to arouse the conscience of America against selfishness and greed. Webber has faith in America's greatness and goodness but believes that the "true discovery of America ... of our own democracy is still before us."

Highly autobiographical, as in his earlier novels, Wolfe merges his own story with America's story. His search for fame and success parallels the country's speculative binge during the 1920's. His alienated and restless search for someone and something to believe in parallels the country's self-estrangement and search for renewed belief in itself during the dark depression years leading to World War II.

Z

ZORBA THE GREEK
Nikos Kazantzakis
1946
Novel

Nikos Kazantzakis' novel is a first-person account of the adventures of a sensitive young man who takes up with a lusty Greek entrepreneur in a series of business ventures and love affairs. The book will entertain the general reader and provide the more serious student of philosophy with much food for thought.

Zorba the Greek is the story of a unique friendship between two men of markedly different life-styles. The narrator is a reserved, sensitive ascetic who is suffering from the trauma of a broken friendship. Zorba is everything the narrator is not. A man of the world, fond of drinking, dancing, womanizing, Zorba joins with the narrator in a lignite mining operation that he believes will make both their fortunes. While "the Boss," as Zorba calls the narrator, provides the capital and supervises from a distance, Zorba takes charge of operations and works with the hired hands. When the venture fails, the narrator is crushed, but Zorba bounces back quickly and resurrects the narrator's optimism. The same thing happens when their second business venture, a foresting operation, fails. From these failures, however, the narrator rises a stronger man, able to accept life's disappointments.

The real story in this novel is the education of the narrator in the hands of his worldly-wise friend. Zorba teaches him that the pleasures of this world are not in themselves evil. Though he plays to excess, Zorba is nevertheless too largehearted and concerned about others to be seen as a kind of devil. Zorba's tutoring is best exemplified in their love affairs. Both fall in love, Zorba with an old prostitute, the narrator with a comely widow. Both women die, the latter at the hands of an irate mob; Zorba is able to accept his beloved's death stoically and helps the narrator overcome his grief at the death of the widow. When the two are finally forced to part ways, the narrator is able to accept this, too, as inevitable. Instead of wallowing in grief, he instead decides to write an account of his life with Zorba, preserving for posterity the memory of that experience.

Zorba The Greek is Kazantzakis' most graphic illustration of the contract between asscetism and sensual fulfillment, a common concern in many of his works. The novel suggests that neither extreme is healthy, and that sensual fulfillment has its place in human nature and should not be rejected totally.

AUTHOR INDEX

LITERARY GENRE INDEX

LIST OF CATEGORIES

DRAMA

An Enemy of the People, 94
Ghosts, 122
The Glass Menagerie, 124
Peter Pan, 246
The Three Sisters, 318

African American
A Raisin in the Sun, 264

Baroque
The Cid, 59

Classical
Andromache (Euripedes), 11
Antigone, 16
The Bacchae, 25
Electra, 93
Lysistrata, 187
Oedipus at Colonus, 224
Oedipus Tyrannus, 225
The Oresteia, 234

Comedy
The Alchemist, 6
All's Well That Ends Well, 9
As You Like It, 20
The Beggar's Opera, 30
The Birds, 34
The Comedy of Errors, 62
The Country Wife, 67
The Importance of Being Earnest, 150
Lady Windermere's Fan, 167
Major Barbara, 191
Man and Superman, 192
Measure for Measure, 197
The Merchant of Venice, 198
A Midsummer Night's Dream, 201
The Misanthrope, 202

Much Ado About Nothing, 208
The Playboy of the Western World, 251
Private Lives, 260
Rosencrantz and Guildenstern Are Dead, 278
The Seagull, 285
She Stoops to Conquer, 290
Six Characters in Search of an Author, 296
The Taming of the Shrew, 311
Tartuffe, 312
Twelfth Night, 326
Under Milk Wood, 331
The Way of the World, 345
The Winter's Tale, 349

Existential
No Exit, 218

Gothic
Phantom of the Opera, 248

Greek
The Oresteia, 234
Prometheus Bound, 260
The Trojan Women, 325

Historical
The Crucible, 69
Cyrano de Bergerac, 71
Henry IV, Part I, 138
Henry IV, Part II, 138
Henry the Fifth, 139
Julius Caesar, 158
Murder in the Cathedral, 209
Richard the Second, 271
Richard The Third, 272
Saint Joan, 280

Lyric
Prometheus Unbound, 261

NONFICTION

African American
The Fire Next Time, 113

Autobiography
All God's Children Need Traveling Shoes, 7
Angela's Ashes, 12
Biographia Literaria, 33
Black Boy, 34
Confessions, 63
The Confessions, 64
The Education of Henry Adams, 92
I Know Why The Caged Bird Sings, 147
Narrative of the Life of Frederick Douglass, 214
Out of Africa, 236
Two Years Before the Mast, 327
*The Woman Warrior: Memoirs of a Girlhood Among
    Ghosts*, 350

Biography
The Diary of a Young Girl, 82
The Life of Samuel Johnson, LL.D., 174
The Lives of the Noble Romans, 179
The Lives of the Poets, 179

Civil Rights Manifesto
The Fire Next Time, 113

Collection
In the American Grain, 153

Diary/Journal
Boswell's London Journal: 1762 1763, 39

Epistemology
Critique of Pure Reason, 68
Summa Theologica, 307

Existential
The Outsider, 237

Feminist
A Vindication of the Rights of Woman, 336

Historical
Bury My Heart at Wounded Knee, 45
The Histories, 140
In the American Grain, 153
Let Us Now Praise Famous Men, 172
The Lives of the Noble Romans, 179
Narrative of the Life of Frederick Douglass, 214

Natural History
The Descent of Man, 80
On The Origin Of The Species, 230

Nature
Silent Spring, 294
Walden, 338

Philosophical
The Consolation of Philosophy, 65
Critique of Pure Reason, 68
The Dialogues of Plato, 81
The Essays, 97
Ethica Nicomachea, 100
Ethics, 100
Fear and Trembling, 111
On Liberty, 228
The Outsider, 237
Poetics, 252
Pragmatism, 255
The Praise of Folly, 255
The Rebel, 266
Representative Men, 269
Republic, 270
Rights of Man, 272
The Sickness unto Death, 291
Tao Te Jing, 312
A Vindication of the Rights of Woman, 336

Political
Areopagitica, 18
Civil Disobedience, 59
On Liberty, 228
The Prince, 258
Ten Days That Shook the World, 314

Psychological
On Death And Dying, 229

NOVEL / NOVELLA

POETRY

SACRED TEXT

SHORT STORY

PUBLICATION YEAR INDEX

2000s